PERCUSSIONISTS

PERCUSSIONISTS

A Biographical Dictionary

Stephen L. Barnhart

John Gillespie, Advisory Editor

GREENWOOD PRESS
Westport, Connecticut • London

Library of Congress Cataloging-in-Publication Data

Barnhart, Stephen L., 1950–
   Percussionists : a biographical dictionary / Stephen L. Barnhart.
     p. cm.
   Includes bibliographical references (p.   ), discographies, filmographies, and index.
   ISBN 0–313–29627–8 (alk. paper)
   1. Percussionists—Biography. I. Title.
ML399.B38   2000
786.8′092′2—dc21
 [B]   99–046021

British Library Cataloguing in Publication Data is available.

Library of Congress Catalog Card Number: 99–046021
ISBN: 0–313–29627–8

First published in 2000

Greenwood Press, 88 Post Road West, Westport, CT 06881
An imprint of Greenwood Publishing Group, Inc.
www.greenwood.com

Printed in the United States of America

The paper used in this book complies with the
Permanent Paper Standard issued by the National
Information Standards Organization (Z39.48–1984).

10 9 8 7 6 5 4 3 2 1

Copyright Acknowledgments

Every reasonable effort has been made to trace the owners of copyright materials in this book, but
in some instances this has proven impossible. The editor and publisher will be glad to receive information leading to more complete acknowledgments in subsequent printings of the book and in the
meantime extend their apologies for any omissions.

Dovie   Cordelia
Harold   Sadie

My earliest and most important influences

CONTENTS

Photographs follow page 220.

PREFACE

It seems a time-honored tradition that humans compile "fin du siècle" publications, each desperately trying to capture a picture of the preceding era before it is lost in the feverish embrace of the future and modern society's obsessive infatuation with all that is new. This text grew, first, from a frustrating need to centralize information about the lives of those within our percussion family and, second, from my genealogical curiosity for tapping into the bond that resonates through all percussionists across the millenia. Though still a part of the musical whole, we are set apart. We have enhanced the pulse of life since the realization of sound, supplying rhythms for human and spiritual communication; we have entertained the rich and the poor, setting the pace for their dances of life and death; and we have marched their armies to victory and defeat. The universal language of percussion transcends ethnic, economic, and sociopolitical boundaries, vicariously uniting listener with peformer in a multiple-sensory experience.

A dictionary that paints thumbnail sketches of human endeavors should be viewed, not as definitive, but as a flexible, dynamic entity willing to change in the face of new discoveries. A reference book of this nature is never finished. Five years have elapsed since starting this project; consequently, maintaining current information on living subjects while researching those who have passed on has been almost impossible. Because there are so few extant biographies on individual percussionists and since some of the details presented here are rather sparse, it is my hope that some scholars will adopt a person who intrigues them and accept the challenge of attempting singular, in-depth studies. My sincere apologies for any personalities that the reader may consider to have been overlooked. With a few notable exceptions, the personnel covered in this text share common threads (1) of performing primarily as a soloist or ensemble musician for most of their careers, and/or (2) of making a lasting contribution to the manufacture of percussion instruments, and/or (3) of having been born by around 1950 or earlier. The latter date was selected arbitrarily as an external parameter to keep the length of the book within reasonable limits. I have tried to avoid any opinions concerning the level or quality of these performers' abilities and have tried to report only ascertainable facts as best as I could determine. Personnel generally not included are those legendary educators whose primary lifelong career thrusts have been teaching. Perhaps a future, separate book should be dedicated solely to all the pedagogues who have given musical birth to so many of the lives contained herein. An attempt has been made to reflect most musical styles that include percussion and to cover most instrumental categories that fall under the broad heading of percussion.

Since images of drumset artists are, for the most part, well documented and readily available in jazz and popular media, the photographs supplied within represent rarer views of orchestral, theatrical, and recording percussionists who were famous within their musical spheres but largely unknown to the general public. Original photographers have been credited where known, and of course, my deepest thanks to the lending agencies whose names and permission notices appear with their respective pictures.

Individual bibliographies display articles by or about the person and include, where appropriate, compositions, arrangements, and method books. In order to save space, the General Bibliography (GEN. BIB.) following the main body of text includes broader reference works that have been cited in brief form and smaller script below a performer's material (see Abbreviations). An asterisk preceding an individual's name denotes a separate, full entry listed alphabetically by last name. Discographies and videographies reflect only samples of an artist's work as soloist and/or collaborative musician and should not be misconstrued as complete. Where available, the record label, catalog number, title and/or lead artist, and approximate date of recording or release are notated. LPs that are no longer in print may have been reissued in compact disc format; if so, both original and reissue dates with old and new catalog numbers and/or labels may appear. (With the demise of the LP and the advent of CD reissues, and since recording labels and their catalog numbers frequently change owners who then assign new numbers that creates a rather convoluted state of affairs for seeking out older recordings, I highly recommend consulting a reputable record retailer and/or the most current record catalogs when pursuing purchases prompted by any of the discographies in this text.)

My research process entailed combing through myriads of journals, reference works, newspapers, personal correspondence, photographs, and mailing questionnaires to addresses supplied either by the Percussive Arts Society or by living subjects. Responses to the questionnaires varied from overwhelming inundations to skeletal outlines or silence. Public institutions consulted included Coe Library (University of Wyoming), Willis Library (University of North Texas), Imig Music Library (University of Colorado), the Library of Congress (via Internet), and the Percussive Arts Society Museum and Archives (Lawton, Oklahoma).

Desiring to give something back to the larger percussion community in appreciation for all the pleasure that listening to and performing on these unique instruments has given me, I offer this small contribution to an art that has sustained me for years, and to which I responded—according to my parents—even before my first conscious thoughts. Inside these pages you will find many of my personal heroes, perhaps a few of your own—and you may discover some new ones. Here, then, are glimpses of a few lives who have taken the basic human attraction for rhythm to artistic levels.

ACKNOWLEDGMENTS

This project began with a personal recommendation from the author and clarinetist Ann McCutchan, who mentioned me to the editorial staff at Greenwood Press for whom I "auditioned" in 1994. The initial scope of the targeted Greenwood editorial series was to examine concert artists whose careers involved *solo* performance. However, given the nature of percussion and its traditional supportive role as accompaniment and tonal color (until the last three decades or so), I was hard pressed to find enough solo performers to sustain an entire book. At that point, it was decided that the material could be packaged in a free-standing biographical dictionary. Since then I have benefited from the patient, expert advice of editors John Gillespie, Alicia Merrit, Pamela St. Clair, David Palmer, Krystyna Budd, and Heather Malloy. I also owe a special debt of gratitude to Steve Beck, Shawn Brown, Cheryl Copes, Russ Girsberger, Randy Eyles, Cathy Flynn, Teresa Peterson, PAS® historian James Strain, and all the staff at the Percussive Arts Society (PAS®) Headquarters and Museum in Lawton, Oklahoma. A Basic Research Grant from the University of Wyoming College of Arts and Sciences enabled me to travel to Lawton for firsthand research in the PAS® archives. For their lifelong inspiration, I am grateful to my percussion teachers T. G. Campbell, Paul Mazzacano, Kalman Cherry, Ron Fink, Robert Schietroma, Tom Maguire, and George Boberg, and to my music research teachers Cecil Adkins, Dan Politoske, and Ed Williams. Deep appreciation goes also to the living contributors who responded to my questionnaire for entrusting me with the details of their or their relatives' professional lives, and to all the talented percussionists around the world with whom I've had the great fortune and pleasure to come into contact. This has been a fantastic journey of learning!

ABBREVIATIONS

AFM   American Federation of Musicians

ASCAPBD   *ASCAP Biographical Dictionary*, 4th ed. New York: Jaques
              Cattell Press/R. R. Bowker Co., 1980.

BDA-AAM   Southern, Eileen. *Biographical Dictionary of Afro-American
              and African Musicians*. Westport, CT: Greenwood
              Press, 1982.

BET-CP   Larrick, Geary. *Biographical Essays on Twentieth-Century
              Percussionists*. Lewiston, New York: Edwin Mellen
              Press, 1992.

DB   *Down Beat*

DM   Korall, Burt. *Drummin' Men*. New York: Schirmer Books,
              1990.

52nd St.   Hunt, Joe. *52nd Street Beat*. New Albany, IN: Aebersold
              Music, Inc., 1994.

GJD   Spagnardi, Ronald. *The Great Jazz Drummers*. Cedar Grove,
              New Jersey: Modern Drummer Publications, 1992.

IAJE   International Association of Jazz Educators

IM   *International Musician*

KB   Avgerinos, Gerassimos. *Künstler-Biographien: Die Miglieder im Berliner Philharmonischen Orchester von 1882–1972*. Gerassimos Avgerinos, 1972.

LD   *Ludwig Drummer*

LDT   Cook, Rob, compiler. *Leedy Drum Topics*. Anaheim Hills, CA: Cedarcreek Publishing, 1993.

MD   *Modern Drummer*

MP   *Modern Percussionist*

NG   Sadie, Stanley, ed. *The New Grove Dictionary of Music and Musicians*. London: Macmillan Press, 1980.

NGA   Hitchcock, H. Wiley, and Stanley Sadie, eds. *The New Grove Dictionary of American Music*. 4 vols. London: Macmillan, 1986.

NGJ   Kernfeld, Barry, ed. *The New Grove Dictionary of Jazz*, vols. 1–2. New York: Grove Dictionaries of Music, Inc., 1988.

PASIC®   Percussive Arts Society International Convention

PN   *Percussive Notes*

WWAMC   Borland, Carol, ed. *Who's Who in American Music: Classical*. New York: Jaques Cattell Press/R. R. Bowker Co., 1983.

XAR   Cahn, William L. *The Xylophone in Acoustic Recordings (1877–1929)*. Bloomfield, NY: William L. Cahn Publishing, 1996.

XYLO   Strain, James Allen. *The Xylophone, ca. 1878–1930: Its Published Literature, Development as a Concert Instrument, and Use in Musical Organizations*. DMA dissertation, University of Rochester, Eastman School of Music, 1995.

PERCUSSIONISTS

A

ABE, KEIKO [KEIKO ABE KIMURA] (b. 18 Apr 1937, Tokyo, Japan). An internationally acclaimed marimba virtuoso and composer, Keiko Abe received both a bachelor's (1960) and a master's (1961) degree from Tokyo–Gakugei University, where she studied xylophone with Kikuo Hamadate and Eiichi Asabuki (b. 22 Dec 1909), and percussion with Yukio Imamura and Yusuke Oyake. Her early associations with marimba ensembles included the Tokyo Marimba Group (1961) and the Xebec Marimba Trio, and she freelanced in studios and orchestras for 10 years. In 1968 Abe received the first of six prizes at the Fine Arts Festival (Tokyo) for her groundbreaking marimba recitals and recordings. Performances followed as leader of the Tokyo Quintet (marimba, flute, clarinet, percussion, bass; est. 1973), and as soloist with the Kroumata Ensemble, American Symphony, Japan Shinsei Symphony, NHK Symphony (Tokyo), Japan Philharmonic, and Yomiuri Nippon Symphony. In addition to premiering Miyoshi: *Concerto for Marimba and String Ensemble* (Concertgebouw Orchestra, 1984), Ptaszynska: *Marimba Concerto* (1986), and Sarmientos: *Marimba Concertino* (1989), she played Carnegie Hall (1981), appeared on Austrian and German television, and performed at the International Percussion Festival in Strasbourg, France (1983).

A visiting professor at Utrechts Conservatorium during the mid–1980s, Abe has taught at Toho–Gakuen School of Music since 1975 and at Soai University since the late 1970s. She has served as a contributing editor to *Percussive Notes* and as a member of the Percussive Arts Society board of directors; she was inducted into their Hall of Fame in 1993. Her performances, clinics, masterclasses (at over 70 universities worldwide since 1977), and compositions have been influential in elevating the technical demands and musical appreciation for the marimba in both East and West.

SELECTED DISCOGRAPHY

BIS CD–462: *Kroumata and Keiko Abe—Rin–Sai*, 1989.
Candide/Vox CE 31051: *Contemporary Music from Japan*, vol. 1—*Works for Marimba*, 1977.
CBS/Sony AG165: *Nocturne, The Tokyo Quintet*.
Columbia JX–9–11: *Keiko Abe—The Art of Marimba*, 1969.
Columbia OQ–7466: *Keiko Abe Presents Solo Marimba Selections*, 1981.
Denon 30CO–1727: *Keiko Abe—Solo Marimba Selections*, 1987.
Denon 30CO–1728: *Keiko Abe—Marimba Selections II*, 1987.
Denon 30CO–1729: *Keiko Abe—Marimba Selections III*, 1987.
Denon 33C0–1118: *Keiko Abe—Marimba Fantasy*, 1986.
Denon 33C37–7393: *Imagination* (with Walter Van Hauwe), 1985.
Denon 35C37–7279: *Keiko Abe Reveals the Essence of the Marimba*, 1984.
Denon 38C37–7280: *The World of the Tokyo Quintet*, 1984.
Denon CC–3446: *Lullaby of Itsuki* (with Walter Van Hauwe), 1989.
Denon CO–3678: *Iannis Xenakis—Pleiades/Ishii—Concertante* (Les Percussions de Strasbourg), 1989.
Denon CO–4219: *Keiko Abe and the World's Leading Percussionists—Marimba Spiritual*, 1989.
FMCA–7010: *Keiko Abe and Dave Samuels—Live in Concert*, 1993.
FME FECA–7033: *Keiko Abe—Marimba Encore*, 1994.
FME FECA–7039: *Fantastic Marimba*, 1994.
Fontec FOCD–3222: *Akira Ifukube—Works for Orchestra*, 1987.
Forte Music FMCA 7043: *Conversations* (Michigan Chamber Players), 1995.
PNCD 075: *Ptaszynska—Concerto for Marimba*, 1991.
RYE 7931: *Go Between* (New Percussion Group–Amsterdam), 1987.
Terpsichore 1982 517: *Ifukube—Lauda Concertata*, 1983.
Wergo WER 60177–50: *Keiko Abe—Marimba Fantasy*, 1990.

SELECTED VIDEOGRAPHY

FME FMVA–3042: *Nara–Yamatoji–No–Bi* (*Marimba Fantasy*), 1994.

SELECTED BIBLIOGRAPHY

Abe, Keiko. "The History and Future of the Marimba in Japan." *PN* XXII, 2 (January 1984): 41–43.
Abe, Keiko. "Percussion Education at Japanese Universities." *PN* XXIX, 2 (December 1990): 31.
Helmig, Martina. "Virtuose Schlagwerkerin." Berlin, Germany: *Berliner Morgenpost* (October 1988).
Lang, Morris. "A Talk with Marimba Virtuoso Keiko Abe, Pt. II." *PN* XXI, 5 (July 1983): 20–22.
Sabins, Jany. "Keiko Abe: Expanding the Marimba." *MP* II, 4 (September 1986): 14.
Via, David. "Interview with Keiko Abe." *PN* XXIX, 6 (August 1991): 11–13.
Weiss, Lauren Vogel. "Keiko Abe." *PN* XXXII, 3 (June 1994): 8–9.
GEN. BIB.: Larrick, *BET–CP*.

ABEL, ALAN D. (b. 1928, Hobart, Indiana). Inducted into the Percussive Arts Society Hall of Fame in 1998, Alan Abel started percussion lessons at the age of 7 and studied with Clarence Carlson at the *Roy Knapp School, *Haskell Harr, and *William Street at the Eastman School (1947–51), where he earned a performance degree and played part time with the Rochester Philharmonic. After two and one–half years in the U.S. Air Force Band (Sampson AFB, Geneva, NY), he secured a position as percussionist with the Oklahoma City Symphony (1953–59), then moved to the Philadelphia Orchestra (1959–1997; assistant principal, 1972). He taught at the University of Oklahoma, Oklahoma City University, Glassboro State College, Temple University (1972–), and Settlement Music School. Through his company, Alan Abel Productions, he developed and markets a unique triangle design and suspended bass drum stand. A master of snare drum and cymbal technique, he compiled two orchestral excerpt books for percussion and timpani (G. Schirmer, 1970). Abel served on the Percussive Arts Society board of directors (1987–94) and continues to play part time with the Philadelphia Orchestra.

SELECTED BIBLIOGRAPHY

Moore, James L. "Alan Abel: Percussionist." *PN* XVI, 2 (Winter 1978): 28–30.
O'Mahoney, Terry. "Alan Abel." *PN* XXXVI, 6 (December 1998): 6–8 (includes photos of the Philadelphia Orchestra percussion sections, 1959–1997).

ACUÑA, ALEX (b. Alejandro Neciosup Acuña, 12 Dec 1944, Pativilca, Peru). Initially studying piano and trumpet with his father, Alex Acuña was a self–taught drummer who played professionally locally by the age of 10 and, by 17, drummed for record and television productions in Lima. Between 1965 and 1975, he studied classical percussion at the Puerto Rico Conservatory of Music (where he played under Pablo Casals' direction), worked in recording studios there, and then came to the United States at 18 with the Perez Prado Band, working in Las Vegas and Los Angeles. Drumset artist and auxilliary percussionist for Weather Report (1975–77), he has also performed with Lee Ritenour ("Friendship" group), Ernie Watts and Abraham Laboriel, Sergio Mendes, Elvis Presley, and Diana Ross. His recording collaborators include the Crusaders, Manhattan Transfer, U2, Blondie, Paul McCartney, Clare Fischer (1978–79), Al Jarreau, Wayne Shorter, Andrae Crouch, Maynard Ferguson, Larry Carlton, Ella Fitzgerald (1980), Chick Corea (1984), Joni Mitchell (1985), and his own groups, Koinonia (1980) and Alex and the Unknowns. For his many movie score participations (e.g., *An Officer and A Gentleman* and *Batman and Robin*), he was a three–time recipient of the Los Angeles National Association of Recording Arts and Sciences' "Most Valuable Player" Award in the percussion category.

SELECTED DISCOGRAPHY

Candid CCD 79507: *Pasos Gigantes* (Luis Bonilla), 1991.
CBS/Columbia CK 34099: *Black Market* (Weather Report), 1976.
Columbia PC34418: *Heavy Weather* (Weather Report), 1976.
Escapade 63651–2: *My People* (Joe Zawinul), 1996.
GRP Records GRD–9522: *Harlequin* (Dave Grusin), 1985.
JVC–JD–3322: *Alex Acuña and the Unknowns*, 1990.
Royal Music CD: *Tia Dia—Nightlight*, 1993.
Tonga TNGCD 8304: *Tolú—Rumbero's Poetry*, 1998.
Warner/Reprise 9 26183–2: *Blue Pacific* (Michael Franks), 1990.

SELECTED VIDEOGRAPHY

DCI/Warner Bros./CPP Media: *Alex Acuña—Drums + Percussion*, 1991.
Music Source International MS 1093: *Acuña—South American, Caribbean, African, and American Jazz*, 1993.
Video Artists International: *Time Groove* (Louis Bellson, Steve Gadd, et al.), 1990.

SELECTED BIBLIOGRAPHY

McFall, Michael. "World Picture." *Rhythm* I, 12 (April 1989): 36–44.
Schroeter, John. "Alex Acuña: Putting It All Together." *Stick It* I, 1 (January 1998): 28–31.
GEN. BIB.: Kernfeld, *NGJ*, by Catherine Collins.

ADAMS, TIMOTHY K., JR. Earning bachelor's and master's degrees from the Cleveland Institute, Timothy Adams studied with *Paul Yancich, *Cloyd Duff, and *Richard Weiner, held positions in the Florida Philharmonic, Greater Miami Opera Orchestra, Indianapolis Symphony (1991–), and Eastern Philharmonic, and is now principal timpanist with the Pittsburgh Symphony. He has appeared and recorded with the Cleveland Orchestra, been a featured soloist with the Atlanta, Florida, and Indianapolis Symphonies, and taught at West Virginia and Butler Universities. Currently he serves on the faculties of the Brevard Music Center and Carnegie–Mellon University, where he heads percussion studies. In February 1999 Adams demonstrated timpani technique on the children's television show *Mr. Rogers' Neighborhood*.
PASIC® program biographies, 1998.

ADATO, JOSEPH "JOE." Starting percussion at the age of 8 and playing professionally by his teens, Joe Adato studied with *Morris Goldenberg at the Juilliard School (bachelor's) and later earned a master's degree at Columbia University. A faculty member of Akron University, Baldwin–Wallace College (OH), and Cleveland State, he performed on the *Ted Mack Amateur Hour* and with the National Orchestra Society, New York City Ballet, New York Philharmonic, Radio City Music Hall, Symphony of the Air, and Cleveland Symphony (1962–   ).

SELECTED DISCOGRAPHY

Advent USR 5004/Crystal S533: *Bubalo—Five Pieces for Brass Quintet and Percussion*, 1982.

SELECTED BIBLIOGRAPHY

Adato, Joseph, and George Judy. *The Percussionist's Dictionary.* Melville, NY: Belwin–Mills, 1984.

ADLER, HENRY (b. 1915, New York, New York).   Performer, teacher, publisher, manufacturer, retailer, and wholesaler who taught *Louie Bellson, *Sonny Igoe, *Roy Burns, *Alexander Lepak, *Alvin Stoller, and others, Henry Adler played with Wingy Manone, *Red Norvo, and Charlie Barnet and appeared at Randall's Island Jazz Concert in 1938.   He was inducted into the Percussive Arts Society Hall of Fame in 1988, received *Modern Drummer* magazine's Editors' Achievement Award in 1995, and authored graded method books that were reissued with editions by *Roy Burns and Sandy Feldstein and published by CPP/Belwin.

SELECTED VIDEOGRAPHY

CPP MEDIA VH0160: *Henry Adler: Hand Development Technique*, 1992.

SELECTED BIBLIOGRAPHY

Claghorn, Charles Eugene. *Biographical Dictionary of American Music.* West Nyack, NY: Parker Publishing Co., Inc., 1973.
Morales, Humberto, and Henry Adler. *Latin–American Rhythm Instruments and How to Play Them.* New York: H. Adler Publishing Corp., 1954.

ADZENYAH, ABRAHAM KOBENA (b. Gomoa Aboso, Ghana, West Africa).   Abraham Adzenyah is the former master drummer of the Ghana Dance Ensemble.   Since 1968 he has taught at Wesleyan University (CT).

SELECTED DISCOGRAPHY

Leonarda LPI 119: *On the Edge* (Julie Kabat), 1984.

SELECTED BIBLIOGRAPHY

Adzenyah, Abraham Kobena, and Dumisani Maraire, and Judith Cook Tucker. *Let Your Voice Be Heard!—Songs from Ghana and Zimbabwe.* Danbury, CT: World Music Press, 1986.
Adzenyah, Abraham. "The Role of Music in Ghana." *PN* XXXIII, 2 (April 1995): 34–38.
Hartigan, Royal, and Abraham Kobena Adzenyah. "The Role of the Drumset in Ghanaian Highlife and Its Relation to Traditional Drumming Styles of the Akan, Ga, and Ewe Peoples." *PN* XXXI, 4 (April 1993): 74–85.

AKINS, THOMAS (b. 22 Aug 1943, Allentown, Pennsylvania). A student of *Ed Wuebold, *Fred Begun, and *Fred Hinger, Thomas Akins earned bachelor's (1965) and master's (1967) degrees from the Cincinnati Conservatory and performed with the Indianapolis Symphony (from ca. 1966) as principal timpanist for 26 years. He commissioned and premiered *William Kraft's "Concerto for Timpani and Orchestra" in 1984, authored the "Timp Talks" column in early *Percussive Notes* (ca. 1965) and the timpani method, in *The Musical Timpanist* (out–of–print), and is music director of the Indy Pops Orchestra.

SELECTED DISCOGRAPHY

Crystal Records: *Sonic Boom*, 1977.
Harmonia Mundi HMU 907106: *William Kraft—Three Concerti*, 1993.

SELECTED BIBLIOGRAPHY

Akins, Thomas. "The Use of Percussion in the Wind Bands of Britain in the Eighteenth Century," *Percussionist* VI, 3 (March 1969): 90–94.

ALBRIGHT, FRED E. "FREDDY" (b. ca. 1898, Kokomo, Indiana; d. ca. 1976–78). Studying at age 12 with *U. G. Leedy and later with *Alfred Friese, Fred Albright began playing professionally around 1910 in New York. He performed with the CBS and NBC Orchestras, New York and "Voice of Firestone" Symphonies, and the B. A. Rolfe Orchestra (1929–1930s, including radio broadcasts and Lucky Strike commercials). A former faculty member of the Manhattan School, Albright also subbed in the New York Philharmonic and recorded in the RCA Victor and Columbia studios. [His identical twin, Ned E. (d. 1938, Cleveland?, OH), was also a percussionist who played in theater orchestras, served in the U.S. Army 67th Field Artillery Band during WWI, and taught at the Ohio Band Camp during the 1930s.]

SELECTED BIBLIOGRAPHY

Albright, Fred. *Contemporary Studies for the Snare Drum.* New York: Henry
    Adler, Inc., 1963.
Albright, Fred. *Rhythmic Analysis for the Snare Drum.* New York: Award Music,
    1978.
GEN. BIB.: Cook, *LDT,* p. 367 (photo).

ALEXANDER, ELMER "MOUSEY" (b. 29 Jun 1922, Gary, Indiana; d. 9
Oct 1988, Orlando, Florida). A jingle composer, drumset artist Mousey Alex-
ander toured, played, and/or recorded with the Sauter–Finnegan Orchestra in the
1950s, Georgie Auld (1960), Benny Goodman (1961/1966–67/1972), Paul
Anka (1966), Zoot Sims, Al Cohn, Lee Konitz, Sonny Stitt (1960s), Clark
Terry (1969–72), Billie Holiday, Doc Severinsen, and Sy Oliver (1973).

SELECTED DISCOGRAPHY

FD LP 130: *The Mouse Roars,* 1979.
London 44182–3: *On Stage with Benny Goodman and His Sextet,* 1972.
Milestone MSP–9038: *Spirits* (Lee Konitz), 1971.
Pablo OJCCD–683–2: *If I'm Lucky* (Zoot Sims), 1977.
Pablo PACD–2310–831: *Warm Tenor* (Zoot Sims), 1978.
RCA LM 1009: *The Sound of the Sauter–Finnegan Orchestra,* 1953.
Swingville 2017: *Buck and Buddy* (Buck Clayton), 1960.

SELECTED BIBLIOGRAPHY

Lewellen, R. "Mousey Alexander: Profile in Courage." *MD* XII (November 1988):
    46–47.
Obituary. *Cadence* XIV (December 1988): 93.
Obituary. *Variety* CCCXXXIII (2 Nov 1988): 86.
GEN. BIB.: Hunt, *52nd St.*; Kernfeld, *NGJ,* by Rick Mattingly.

ALEXIS, CLIFFORD (b. 1937, Port of Spain, Trinidad). Steel drum (aka
pan) builder, educator, and performing artist, Cliff Alexis matured in Diego Martin, Trinidad, and began playing pans at an early age in spite of the negative
social image of that activity at the time. By his early twenties he performed
with the National Steel Band of Trinidad and Tobago and toured the United
States (1964), Africa, and Europe. Freelancing in New York in 1965 led to a
stint as assistant to Liberace's personnel director and an appearance at Expo '67.
Alexis' pan group, the Trinidad Troubadors, subsequently toured America.
Moving in the early 1970s, he spent 13 years in Minneapolis–St. Paul teaching
in the public schools, where he was a two–time recipient of the "Outstanding
Black Musician" Award; since 1985 Alexis has taught pan building, tuning,
performing, and arranging at Northern Illinois University (NIU). With

co–director G. Allan O'Connor, he toured Taiwan, China, and Singapore with the NIU steel band in 1992. A frequent clinician at the Percussive Arts Society International Conventions, he was commissioned to compose and arrange music for the 100-plus member massed steel band concert at PASIC® 1992 in St. Louis.

SELECTED BIBLIOGRAPHY

Chappell, Robert. "An Interview with Clifford Alexis." *PN* XXV, 6 (September 1987): 51–53.
Holly, Rich. "Clifford Alexis and Liam Teague: The State of the Art of Pan." *PN* XXXIII, 1 (February 1995): 36–42.
PASIC® program biographies, 1994.

ALI, RASHIED (b. Robert Patterson, Jr., 1 Jul 1935, Philadelphia, Pennsylvania). A student of *Philly Joe Jones, avant–garde drumset artist Rashied Ali started drums at 11, studied at the Granoff School, served in the U.S. Army (ca. 1951–54), then played locally with Lee Morgan, the Heath Brothers, and McCoy Tyner before moving to New York (1963), where he performed with Pharoah Sanders, Don Cherry, Paul Bley, and John Coltrane. For Coltrane he played simultaneously with *Elvin Jones or *Jack DeJohnette before becoming the sole drummer (1965–67). Ali also worked with Jackie McLean (1968–69), Sun Ra, Albert Ayler, and Archie Shepp and opened a club in Manhattan, Ali's Alley (est. 1973). Moving to Europe in the late 1960s, he appeared and/or recorded with Sonny Rollins, Bud Powell, the Saheb Sarbib Quintet, the Afro Algonquin Trio, and the Funkyfreeboppers; he also led his own groups, recording on his own label, Survival Records (est. 1972). [His brother, Muhammad Ali (b. 1936, Philadelphia, PA), also plays drums and has appeared with some of Rashied's collaborators.]

SELECTED DISCOGRAPHY

Blue Note 84284: *Jackie McLean—'Bout Soul*, 1967.
GRP/Impulse 4–102: *Live in Japan* (John Coltrane), 1966.
GRP/Impulse ASD–9277/110: *Interstellar Space* (John Coltrane), 1967.
Impulse AS–9120: *Expression* (John Coltrane), 1967.
Impulse AS–9148: *Cosmic Music* (John Coltrane), 1966.
Impulse AS–9210: *Universal Consciousness* (Alice Coltrane—Turiyasangitananda), 1971.
MCA/Impulse 9124/29010: *Live at the Village Vanguard Again* (John Coltrane), 1966.
MCA/Impulse 33119: *Journey in Satchidananda* (Alice Coltrane), 1970.
MCA/Impulse AS–9110/39139: *Meditations* (John Coltrane), 1965.
Survival SR 101: *Duo Exchange* (Frank Lowe), 1973.
Timeless ALCR–123: *Blackbird* (Jaco Pastorius), 1984.

SELECTED BIBLIOGRAPHY

Milkowski, Bill. "Masters of the Free Universe." *MD* XVI, 12 (December 1992): 32–35.

GEN. BIB.: Hunt, *52nd St.*; Kernfeld, *NGJ*, by Michael Ullman; Spagnardi, *GJD.*

AMES, FRANK ANTHONY "TONY" (b. 12 Oct 1942, Wheeling, West Virginia). Tony Ames attended the Eastman School (bachelor's, 1964) and Carnegie–Mellon (master's, 1966), where he studied respectively with *William Street and *Stanley Leonard. He performed with the Rochester Philharmonic (1962–64), Pittsburgh Symphony (1964–66), Baltimore Symphony (1966–68), and National Symphony (since 1968) and composed, arranged, and produced *The Red Shoes*, an original musical for children. Producer and/or performer for *Music* (Public Broadcasting, 1977) and *The Advent of Polyphony*, a one–hour documentary on early music, Ames received the Gold Star Award at the Houston Film Festival in 1986.

SELECTED DISCOGRAPHY

London OS 26442: *Americana Festival Overture, New England Triptych* (National Symphony), 1975.
London: *Tchaikovsky—Symphony No. 4* (National Symphony), 1972.
Smithsonian N 022: *20th Century Consort,* vols. 1–2, 1981/82.
Information supplied by the subject, 1996.

ANDERSON, DALE (b. Chicago). A nephew of *Lou Chiha "Signor Friscoe," Hollywood percussionist Dale Anderson began snare drum at 3 and studied with *Roy Knapp and at Northwestern University. He served in the U.S. Air Force Drum and Bugle Corps (Bolling AFB, Washington, D.C.); then he returned to Chicago, where he performed on WGN–TV (ca. 1955–59). In 1959 Anderson relocated to Los Angeles, where, as a mallet specialist, he recorded for television and film (e.g., the *Dinah Shore, Andy Williams, Carol Burnett,* and *Steve Allen* shows, and *Doctor Zhivago* and *Indiana Jones and the Temple of Doom*).

SELECTED BIBLIOGRAPHY

Wilson, Patrick. "Dale Anderson: Mallets in Hollywood." *MP* I, 3 (June 1985): 15–17.

APPLEYARD, PETER (b. 26 Aug 1928, Cleethorpes, England). Vibist Peter Appleyard immigrated to Canada in 1951 and has since achieved success in North America and abroad, collaborating with Benny Goodman (1972–80),

Frank Sinatra, Mel Torme, Peanuts Hucko, Ella Fitzgerald, Count Basie, and Bucky Pizzarelli, among others. He appeared on CBC–TV (*Peter Appleyard Presents*, 1977–79) and on the *Today*, *Andy Williams*, and *Johnny Carson* shows in the United States. He has also recorded numerous albums.

SELECTED DISCOGRAPHY

Concord Jazz CCD–4475: *Barbados Cool*, 1991.
Concord Jazz CJ–436–C: *Barbados Heat*, 1990.
London 44182–3: *On Stage with Benny Goodman and His Sextet*, 1972.
Salisbury 001: *Peter Appleyard Presents*, 1977.

SELECTED BIBLIOGRAPHY

"Peter Appleyard, Genius on the Vibraphone." *IM* XC (February 1992): 9.
GEN. BIB.: Kernfeld, *NGJ*, by Mark Miller.

ARNOLD, HORACE EMMANUEL "HORACEE" (b. 25 Sep 1937, Wayland, Kentucky). While serving in the Coast Guard, Horacee Arnold studied piano at Los Angeles City College (1957) and appeared and/or recorded (including several solo albums) with Rahsaan Roland Kirk (1959 and later), Cecil McBee, Chick Corea, Sarah Vaughan, Charles Mingus, Carla Bley, Bud Powell, Kenny Dorham, Stan Getz, Archie Shepp, and others. He formed the ensemble Colloquium III with *Billy Hart and *Freddie Waits. Currently he teaches at the New School for Social Research (New York City) and William Patterson College (NJ). His many students include Will Calhoun (Living Color) and Bill Stewart (John Scofield).

SELECTED DISCOGRAPHY

Blue Note LA395–H2: *Chick Corea*, 1969.
Columbia KC 32150: *Tribe*, 1972.
Columbia KC 32869: *Tales of the Exonerated Flea*, 1974.
Denon 7538: *Live in Tokyo* (Archie Shepp), 1978.
Evidence ECD 22133: *Somalia* (Billy Harper), 1995.
Solid State 18055: *Is* (Chick Corea), 1969.
Soul Note 1001: *Billy Harper Quintet in Europe*, 1979.
Vortex 2005: *Until* (Robin Kenyattta), 1966–67.

SELECTED VIDEOGRAPHY

Yamaha: *The Drumset: A Musical Approach*, 1984.

SELECTED BIBLIOGRAPHY

Arnold, Horacee. "The Drummer inside the Music." *PN* XXXIII, 6 (December 1995): 15.
GEN. BIB.: Hunt, *52nd St.*; Kernfeld, *NGJ*, by Ed Hazell.

ARSENAULT, FRANK J. (b. 21 May 1919, Chelsea, Massachusetts; d. 26 Dec 1974, Chicago, Illinois). A 1975 inductee into the Percussive Arts Society Hall of Fame, Frank Arsenault was a three–time undefeated National Solo Snare Drum Champion who was named National Rudimental Champion at the New York World's Fair of 1939. He started drum lessons in New Haven, Connecticut, in 1929 and garnered two state championships in 1935 and 1936, winning the All–New England Championship (1937) and the Junior National Championship (1939). Arsenault served in the U.S. Army Band at Camp Kilmer, New Jersey, during WWII. After winning the Senior National Championship twice (1951/1952) and retiring from competition in 1952, he moved to Chicago and became instructor for the Chicago Cavaliers and Skokie Indians Drum & Bugle Corps around 1954, subsequently leading Skokie to first place in the National American Legion Drum Corps Contest. An influential teacher, he led his students to collect five Veterans of Foreign Wars National Drum Championships. For almost 20 years he toured the width and breadth of the United States as a clinician for the Ludwig Drum Company, logging 100,000 miles a year!

SELECTED DISCOGRAPHY

Ludwig Drum Co. 14–101: *The Twenty–six Standard American Drum Rudiments and Selected Solos*, 1982.

SELECTED BIBLIOGRAPHY

Hartsough, Jeff, and Derrick Logozzo. "Sixty Years of Drum Corps: An Interview with Elderick Arsenault." *PN* XXXVI, 1 (February 1998): 18–23.
"In Memoriam—Frank J. Arsenault, 1919–1974." *PN* XIII, 2 (Winter 1975): 12.
"Percussive Arts Society Hall of Fame 1975." *PN* XIV, 2 (Fall 1976): 24.
Tilles, Bob. "Frank Arsenault Discusses the Rudiments." *LD* IV, 2 (Fall 1964): 25.

ARTH, JOSEPH A. (b. 1840, Washington, D.C.; d. 22 Aug 1923, Washington, D.C.). A student of U.S. Marine Corps drummer "Daddy" McFarlan, Joseph Arth performed with the U.S. Marine Corps Band (1850–85), then free-lanced in Washington until serving with the U.S. Naval Academy Band (1893–1903). He had the distinction of playing for several presidential milestones, including Abraham Lincoln's inauguration, with the Ford's Theater orchestra on the night of Lincoln's assassination, and for the subsequent funeral. **GEN. BIB.:** Cook, *LDT,* p. 355.

ATWOOD, JAMES "JIM" (b. 24 May 1945, Colorado Springs, Colorado). Timpanist with the Louisiana Philharmonic (previously aka New Orleans Symphony), Jim Atwood studied with *Cloyd Duff and has played with the New Orleans Percussion Trio, the Mexico City Philharmonic, and the Colorado Music Festival; he has also toured and recorded with the Dukes of Dixieland. A

jingle writer and arranger for recording studios, he has served on the faculties of
Western Carolina (NC), Loyola, and Xavier Universities and hosted the 1992
Percussive Arts Society International Convention.
PASIC® program biographies, 1992.

AVGERINOS, GERASSIMOS (b. 11 Jan 1907, Luxor, Upper Egypt). After
seven years of violin lessons at the Gnuschke–Duprée Conservatory in Berlin,
Gerassimos Avgerinos, who was of Greek descent, began his musical career
around 1924 as a violinist in silent movie theater orchestras. There he became
interested in percussion, taught himself to play, and secured work as both a percussionist and a violinist, but eventually solely performed percussion. From
1927 to 1928 he attended the Berlin Hochschule für Musik, where he studied
total percussion with Franz Krüger. Avgerinos won the timpani chair with the
newly founded Landestheater Neustrelitz Orchestra (1928–31), which became a
resort ensemble during the summer. During the economic depression of the
1930s, music positions were hard to come by, so to survive he studied both
mechanical engineering and health care. Luckily, in 1936 he was engaged by
the Berlin Philharmonic as timpanist-percussionist, and after the departure of
August Lohse in 1948 he became principal timpanist until around 1970. A
faculty member of the Berlin Conservatory from 1942–50 through 1960–67,
Avgerinos was honored for his career by the city of Berlin (1963) and the Berlin
Philharmonic (1966). Following a 34–year tenure with the orchestra, he busied
himself writing percussion method books and articles for both German and
American music journals.

SELECTED BIBLIOGRAPHY

Avgerinos, Gerassimos. *Künstler–Biographien: Die Mitglieder im Berliner Phil-
harmonischen Orchester von 1882–1972.* Gerassimos Avgerinos, 1972.
Avgerinos, Gerassimos. *Lexikon der Pauke.* Frankfurt: Verlag das Musik-
Instrumente, 1964.

AYERS, ROY E., JR. (b. 10 Sep 1940, Los Angeles, California). A vibraphonist who was inspired by *Lionel Hampton and *Milt Jackson, Roy Ayers
studied piano with his mother at the age of 5. He attended Los Angeles City
College and played steel guitar in jazz groups until around 17 years of age, when
he bought his first set of vibes. In 1961 he turned professional and then worked
with Gerald Wilson, Phineas Newborn, Jack Wilson, Teddy Edwards, Curtis
Amy, Hampton Hawes, *Chico Hamilton, and led his own groups. Ayers
toured with Herbie Mann (1966–70), then formed the Roy Ayers Ubiquity,
which included sidemen such as *Bernard Purdie. Known for his fusion of rock,
jazz, and Latin styles, he has toured widely and recorded extensively.

SELECTED DISCOGRAPHY

Atlantic 1488: *Virgo Vibes*, 1967.
Blue Note 84251: *Jack Wilson—Something Personal*, 1966.
Polydor 6057: *Mystic Voyage*, 1976.
Polydor 6091: *Vibrations*, 1977.
Polydor 6246: *No Stranger to Love*, 1980.
United Artists 6325: *West Coast Vibes*, 1963.

SELECTED VIDEOGRAPHY

Music Video Distributors: *Roy Ayers—in London*, 1992.
Wadham Film/Music Video Distributors: *Jazz at Ronnie's*, 1991.
WPVI–TV (Philadelphia): *Music Makers—Show Number One*, 1980.
GEN. BIB.: Kernfeld, *NGJ*, by Gary Theroux; Southern, *BDA–AAM.*

B

BABELON, CLAUDE [ALSO BABLON] (fl. ca. 1700, France). Court timpanist (*Timbalier des plaisirs*) to Louis XIV of France, Claude Babelon composed two solo timpani marches that are contained in the Philidor Collection at Versailles, France.

SELECTED BIBLIOGRAPHY

Babelon, Claude. *Marche de timballes pour les garde du roi,* 1705.
Sandman, Susan. "Indications of Snare–Drum Technique in Philidor Collection MS 1163," *Galpin Society Journal* XXX (May 1977): 70–75.

BAILEY, COLIN (b. 9 Jul 1934, Swindon, England). Drumset artist Colin Bailey recorded in Australia with Bryce Rohde and Bill Benham (1960); he toured, performed, and/or recorded with Vince Guaraldi (1962–63), Clare Fischer (1962–64), Joe Pass (1963–64), Benny Goodman (Japan tour, 1964–65), George Shearing (1966–67), *Victor Feldman, *Terry Gibbs, Chet Baker, Red Garland (late 1970s–80s), and Richie Cole (mid–1980s). Bailey is the author of *Bass Drum Control* (Try Publishing/Hal Leonard, 1964/1992).

SELECTED DISCOGRAPHY

Blue Note LA645–G: *Barbara Carroll,* 1976.
Blue Note LT 1103: *Joy Spring* (Joe Pass), 1964.
Capitol ST2282: *Made in Japan* (Benny Goodman), 1964.
Concord 4083: *The Artful Dodger* (Victor Feldman), 1977.
Pablo 2310–961: *Nuages—Live at Yoshi's,* vol. 2 (Joe Pass), 1992.
Pacific Jazz TOCJ–5309: *For Django* (Joe Pass), 1964.

Pacific Jazz TOCJ–5767: *Catch Me* (Joe Pass), 1963. Telarc CD–83326: *My Song* (Joe Pass), 1993.
Verve V6–8835: *Jimmy Witherspoon and Ben Webster*, 1967.

SELECTED BIBLIOGRAPHY

Flans, Robyn. "Colin Bailey: Beyond *Bass Drum Control*." *MD* XIX (May 1995): 70–74.
"The Subtle Magnificence of Colin Bailey." *LD* VI, 2 (Fall 1966): 11.
GEN. BIB.: Hunt, *52nd St.*; Kernfeld, *NGJ.*

BAILEY, ELDEN CHANDLER "BUSTER" (b. 22 Apr 1922, Portland, Maine). "Buster" Bailey started drums at age 9 with Howard Shaw (a vaudeville artist who had studied with *Harry Bower), later studying clarinet, piano, and music theory; at 12 he first appeared as solo xylophonist in church; and as a teen he played with the Portland Symphony. A student at the New England Conservatory (1941–42), where he studied percussion with *Lawrence White of the Boston Symphony, Bailey served with the 154th Army Ground Forces Band during World War II (1943–46) and performed clarinet in the concert band, snare drum in the field band, and served as arranger, conductor, and pianist in the jazz band. Studying with *Saul Goodman and *Morris Goldenberg, he graduated from the Juilliard School (1946–49) and became a member of the New York Philharmonic percussion section for 42 years (1949–91). His varied performance experience runs the gamut from the Little Orchestra Society (original member), modern dance ensembles (e.g., José Limón), and circus bands (e.g., Ringling Brothers and Barnum and Bailey in the 1960s) to the Sauter–Finegan Jazz Orchestra (charter member, 1953). Bailey's notable premieres have included Michael Colgrass' "Déjà Vu," (New York Philharmonic, 1977), and he served on the faculties of Juilliard (1969–93), New York University, and the New York College of Music.

SELECTED DISCOGRAPHY

Angel CDC 0777–7–54728–20: *Under the Big Top—The Great American Main Street Band*, 1993.
CBS Records MK–42224: *Ludwig van Beethoven: Symphony No. 9.* (New York Philharmonic), 1969/1986.
CBS Records MYK–37218: *Dmitri Shostakovich: Fifth Symphony.* (New York Philharmonic), 1959/1981.
CBS–Odyssey MBK 38918: *"Stars and Stripes Forever"* (Andre Kostelanetz), 1989.
Columbia CML–5179: *Hovhaness—Suite for Violin, Piano, and Percussion*, 1957.
Columbia Jazz Masterpiece CD–40578: *Miles Davis: Sketches of Spain*, 1960/1986.
Columbia LP AL 41: *Strike Up the Band* (Morton Gould), 1959.
Columbia LP AL 57: *The Band Played On* (Morton Gould).

Columbia LP KH 32170: *Strike Up the Band—World's Best-Known Marches* (Andre Kostelanetz), 1986.
Columbia LP ML 2128: *Concerto for Two Pianos, Winds, and Percussion* (Paul Bowles), 1950.
Columbia LP ML 5241: *Facade* (William Walton) and *Music for a Farce* (Paul Bowles), 1958.
Columbia MS–6956: *Bartók—Concerto for Two Pianos, Percussion, and Orchestra* (New York Philharmonic), 1967.
Columbia Records Collectors Series JCS–8127: *Ellington Jazz Party* (Duke Ellington Orchestra), 1984.
Columbia Records XM–3353: *Footlifters: A Century of American Marches*, 1975.
CRI S–186: *Hovhaness—Koke No Niwa*, 1964.
MGM Records E–3454: *Cowell—Set of Five*, 1957.
RCA Records LSC–2569: *Sousa Forever* (Morton Gould), 1961.
RCA Victor Red Seal LP LM 2080/CD 09026–61255–2: *Gould—Brass and Percussion*, 1958/1993.
RCA Victor Red Seal LP LM 2308: *Gould—Doubling in Brass*, 1959.
RCA/Bluebird 6468–2–RB: *Directions in Music* (Sauter Finegan Orchestra), 1952/1988.
Urania URLP 7144: *Chavez—Toccata*, 1954

SELECTED BIBLIOGRAPHY

Bailey, Elden C. *Mental and Manual Calisthenics for the Modern Mallet Player.* New York: HenryAdler, 1963.
"Sauter–Finegan at Meadowbrook." *Metronome* (August 1953): 18.
"Sauter–Finegan: Hit the Road." *Metronome* (July 1953): 15.
Strain, James. "1996 PAS® Hall of Fame: 'Buster' Bailey." *PN* XXXIV, 6 (December 1996): 10–12.
GEN. BIB.: Larrick, *BET–CP.*

BALTER, MICHAEL HOWARD "MIKE" (b. 7 May 1952, Chicago, Illinois). A first–call percussionist-drummer in Chicago, Mike Balter studied with *Roy Knapp, *José Bethancourt, *Bob Tilles, *Louie Bellson, *Bobby Christian, Lou Singer, and *Al Payson and earned a bachelor's (1974) and a master's (1975) degree at DePaul University. He has taught at the Illinois Governor's State University, American Conservatory of Music, and DePaul and has performed for several national touring productions of Broadway hits including *Cats* and *A Chorus Line.* Backing such luminaries as Frank Sinatra, Bette Midler, Nancy Wilson, Pearl Bailey, Rosemary Clooney, Andy Williams, Johnny Mathis, and Patti LaBelle. Balter has played professionally since 1972 and is the founder-owner of Mike Balter Mallets manufacturing company.

SELECTED BIBLIOGRAPHY

Levinson, Joe. "The Two Sides of Mike Balter." *PN* XVI, 1 (Fall 1977): 28.

BARBARIN, ADOLPHE PAUL (b. 5 May 1899, New Orleans, Louisiana; d. 17 Feb 1969, New Orleans). Starting clarinet first, Paul Barbarin embraced the drumset at age 15 and played early on with the Silver Leaf Orchestra and the Young Olympia Band. By 1917 he was splitting his time between New Orleans with Luis Russell and Chicago with Freddie Keppard and King Oliver, among others. Between the 1920s and 1940s Barbarin toured with the Tennessee Ten and his own group (New Orleans, California, New York), and performed with Luis Russell (New York, 1928/1932/1935), Louis Armstrong (1935–38/1941), Henry "Red" Allen (1942–43), and Sidney Bechet (1943–44). A recording artist, Barbarin also appeared on television before suffering a fatal heart attack during a Mardis Gras parade as a member of the Onward Brass Band, with whom his father had also performed.

SELECTED DISCOGRAPHY

American Music AMCD–35/36:   *Paul Barbarin's Jazz Band from New Orleans—The Oxford Series,* vols. 15–16.
American Music AMCD–44: *John Reid Collection, 1940–44.*
American Music AMCD–71: *George Lewis with Red Allen.*
American Music AMCD–76: *Billie Pierce with Raymond Burke,* 1994.
American Music AMCD–78: *Johnny St. Cyr,* 1994.
American Music AMCD–88: *Percy Humphrey and His Sympathy Five,* 1996.
GHB–BCD–43: *Billie and DeDe Pierce and Paul Barbarin with Chris Barber's Jazz Band,* 1960.
GHB–BCD–141: *Sweet Emma Barrett and Her New Orleans Music,* 1994.
Masters of Jazz, Media 7: *Anthology of Jazz Drumming,* vols. 1–3, 1904–38.
Mosaic MD4–179: *The Atlantic New Orleans Jazz Sessions,* 1955/1998.

SELECTED VIDEOGRAPHY

DCI VH0248: *Legends of Jazz Drumming, Pt. 1, 1920–50,* 1996.
Film: *World by Night No. 2,* 1961.

SELECTED BIBLIOGRAPHY

"Closing Chord—Adolph Paul Barbarin [sic]." *IM* LXVII, 10 (April 1969): 22.
GEN. BIB.: Kernfeld, *NGJ*; Southern, *BDA–AAM.*

BAUDUC, RAYMOND "RAY" (b. 18 Jun 1909, New Orleans, Louisiana; d. 8 Jan 1988, Houston, Texas). Starting drums at around age 12, Ray Bauduc studied with his father (Jules, Sr.), his brother (Jules, Jr.), and New Orleans teacher–players Kid Peterson, Paul Dedroit, and Adrian Gosley. Influenced by *Baby Dodds, Emil Stein, Chinee Foster, and *Zutty Singleton, he played professionally by age 15, made his first record on the Pathe label with the Original Memphis Five (1926), and then relocated to New York (1926), where he worked with the Dorsey Brothers, Joe Venuti–Ed Land, and Freddie Rich

(1927), touring Europe with the latter. Wider recognition came with *Ben Pollack (1928–34) and Bob Crosby and the Bobcats (1935–42), with whom he recorded the legendary "Big Noise from Winnetka" and received an award from *Down Beat* magazine in 1940. His collaborators also included Benny Goodman, Tommy Dorsey, and Red Nichols; after serving in WWII with the U.S. Army (211th Coast Artillery), he was associated with Jimmy Dorsey (1948–50), Jack Teagarden, Nappy LeMare, and his own group, the Dixielanders. Bauduc invented a pedal–operated tom–tom (quasi timpani) and was one of the first drummers to employ two toms on the bass drum.

SELECTED DISCOGRAPHY

Black Lion 760171: *Sunset Swing,* 1945/1992.
Capitol T877: *Riverboat Dandies,* 1957.
Circle CCD–1: *Bob Crosby and His Orchestra,* 1938.
Coral CRL57089: *Bob Crosby, 1936–56.*
Masters of Jazz, Media 7: *Anthology of Jazz Drumming,* vols. 1–3, 1904–38.
MCA2–4083: *The Best of Bob Crosby,* 1975.
Sunbeam SB 229: *Bob Crosby and His Orchestra, 1938–40* (radio broadcasts), 1979.
Tempo MTT–2084: *Papa Laine's Children,* 1951.

SELECTED BIBLIOGRAPHY

Bauduc, Ray. *Dixieland Drumming.* Chicago: WFL Drum Co, 1937.
Schmidt, Paul William. *History of the Ludwig Drum Company.* Fullerton, CA: Centerstream Publishing, 1991.
GEN. BIB.: Kernfeld, *NGJ,* by T. Dennis Brown; Korall, *DM;* Spagnardi, *GJD.*

BECK, JOHN H. (b. 16 Feb 1933, Lewisburg, Pennsylvania). John Beck received both bachelor's (1955) and master's (1962) degrees from the Eastman School, where he studied with *William Street. From 1955 to 1959 he served as timpanist and marimba soloist with the U.S. Marine Band in Washington, D.C. Following his discharge, he taught at Eastman's Prep School, performed as timpanist with the Rochester Philharmonic (since 1962), and became the percussion professor at Eastman (since 1967). Beck has been a featured artist in Poland, in South America, at Memphis State University, at Syracuse University, with the Rochester Chamber and Philharmonic Orchestras, and with the Eastman Wind Ensemble. Elected president of the Percussive Arts Society (1987–90), he hosted its first international convention (1976), was inducted into its Hall of Fame (1999), and has been a contributing author to *Percussive Notes, NACWPI Journal, Grove Dictionary of American Music,* and *World Book Encyclopedia* and the editor of *Encyclopedia of Percussion* (Garland Press). His solo and ensemble compositions for percussion are generally considered standard repertoire, and he was honored in May 1998 by the Eastman School, his former students, and several music companies with a special tribute concert at Eastman, where a scholarship fund was established in his name.

SELECTED DISCOGRAPHY

Mark Records MES57577: *Reynolds—Concertare 1 for Brass Quintet and Percussion*, 1977.
Musical Heritage Society 3679: *Bartók—Sonata for Two Pianos and Percussion*, 1977.
Turnabout 34653: *Harrison—Concerto for Violin and Percussion Orchestra* (conductor, Eastman Percussion Ensemble), 1977.

SELECTED BIBLIOGRAPHY

Beck, John H., ed. *Encyclopedia of Percussion*. New York: Garland Publishing, 1995.
GEN. BIB.: Larrick, *BET–CP.*

BECKER, ROBERT "BOB" (b. 22 Jun 1947, Allentown, Pennsylvania). Perhaps the most eclectic and virtuosic percussionist of his generation whose performance ability reflects the global village, Bob Becker graduated from the Eastman School with both a bachelor's degree and a performer's certificate in 1969.   His teachers have included *William Street, *Warren Benson, Aldo Provenzano, *John Beck, Pandit Sharda Sahai, Prawotosaputro, Ramnad Raghavan, *Sumarsam, and *Abraham Adzenyah. After a tour of duty with the U.S. Marine Band in Washington, D.C., he received a master's degree from Eastman in 1971.   Between 1971 and 1975 Becker did postgraduate study in ethnomusicology at Wesleyan University (CT), where he explored the music cultures of North and South India, Africa, and Indonesia.

As a 1971 charter member of the percussion ensemble NEXUS, he has recorded extensively and been featured as soloist with the New York Philharmonic, Boston Symphony, and Cleveland Orchestra, among others.   The group was profiled on the *CBS Sunday Morning* television show (April 1992), was praised for the film score from *The Man Who Skied Down Everest* (an Academy Award–winning documentary), and was inducted into the Percussive Arts Society Hall of Fame (1999).   As a regular member of the ensemble "Steve Reich and Musicians," he appeared as soloist with the London Symphony and the Israel, Brooklyn, and New York Philharmonic Orchestras.   For many years Becker was percussionist with the Paul Winter Consort and has performed and recorded with Marion Brown, Gil Evans, *Steve Gadd, Paul Horn, and Chuck Mangione. He has served as percussionist and timpanist at the Marlboro Music Festival and has been spotlighted as tabla soloist in India, accompanying several major Hindustani musicians.

A composer for dance groups such as the Joffrey Ballet (NY), Becker is a founding member of Toronto's "Flaming Dono West African Dance and Drum

Ensemble" and was honored in 1991 with the National Arts Centre Award (Toronto) for best collaboration between composer and choreographer. The wide scope of his percussive activities also includes publishing, and he has served two years on the board of directors of the Percussive Arts Society and as percussion editor for the *Contemporary Music Revue* (UK).

SELECTED DISCOGRAPHY

CBC Musica Viva 2–1037: *Dance of the Octopus* (NEXUS et al.), 1989.

CBC SMCD 5154: *Music for Heaven and Earth* (NEXUS with Esprit Orchestra), 1995.

CP2 11: *Jo Kondo* (NEXUS performs "Under the Umbrella"), 1981.

Deutsche Grammophon 2740–106: *Drumming/Six Pianos/Music for Mallet Instruments/Voices, and Organ* (Steve Reich), 1974.

Black Sun CD 15002–2: *The Altitude of the Sun* (NEXUS and Paul Horn), 1989.

ECM 1–1129: *Music for Eighteen Musicians* (Steve Reich), 1978.

ECM 1–1168: *Octet/Music for Large Ensemble—Violin Phase* (Steve Reich), 1980.

ECM 1–1215: *Tehillim* (Steve Reich), 1982.

Epic KE 33561: *Paul Horn and NEXUS*, 1975.

InRespect IRJ 009302 H: *The Mother of the Book* (NEXUS et al.), 1994.

NEXUS 10251: *The Best of NEXUS* (1976–86), 1989.

NEXUS 10262: *NEXUS Now*, 1990.

NEXUS 10273: *NEXUS Plays the Novelty Music of George Hamilton Green*, 1990.

NEXUS 10284: *NEXUS Ragtime Concert*, 1992.

NEXUS 10295: *NEXUS—Origins*, 1992.

NEXUS 10306: *The Story of Percussion in the Orchestra* (NEXUS/Rochester Philharmonic), 1992.

NEXUS 10317: *Voices* (NEXUS and Rochester Philharmonic), 1994.

NEXUS 10328: *There Is a Time* (Becker), 1995.

NEXUS CD 10339: *The Solo Percussionist* (Music of William Cahn), 1997.

NEXUS CD 10410: *Toccata*, 1997.

NEXUS NE–01: *Music of NEXUS*, 1981.

NEXUS NE–02/03/04: *NEXUS and Earle Birney* (Albums 1–3), 1982.

NEXUS NE–05: *Changes* (NEXUS), 1982.

NEXUS Records: *Rune*, 1998.

Nonesuch 79101: *The Desert Music* (Steve Reich and Brooklyn Philharmonic), 1984.

Nonesuch 79170: *Drumming* (Steve Reich), 1987.

Nonesuch 79183–2: *Sextet/Six Marimbas*, (Steve Reich et al.), 1985.

Nonesuch 79220: *The Four Sections/Music for Mallet Instruments, Voices, and Organ* (London Symphony/Steve Reich), 1991.

Nonesuch 79327: *The Cave* (Steve Reich), 1994.

Nonesuch 79430: *City Life/Proverb/Nagoya Marimbas* (Steve Reich), 1996.

Papa Bear Records G01: *World Diary—Tony Levin* (NEXUS et al.), 1995.

Point Records 454 126–2: *Farewell to Philosophy* (Gavin Bryars), 1996.

RCA SX 2022: *Seiji Ozawa Conducts Toru Takemitsu* (Toronto Symphony), 1969.

Sony Classical SK 63044: *Takemitsu—From Me Flows What You Call Time* (Pacific Symphony), 1998.

SELECTED VIDEOGRAPHY

Necavenue A88V–3: *Supercussion* (Tokyo Music Joy Festival), 1988.

SELECTED BIBLIOGRAPHY

Becker, Bob, ed. "Contemporary Percussion—Performers' Perspectives." *Contemporary Music Review* VII, 1 (1992).
Bump, Michael. "A Conversation with NEXUS." *PN* XXXI, 5 (June 1993): 30–36.
Larrick, Geary. *Analytical and Biographical Writings in Percussion Music.* New York: Peter Lang Publishing, 1989.
Mattingly, Rick. "Nexus." *MP* I, 3 (June–August 1985): 8–13/36–41.
Stevens, Leigh Howard. "Bob Becker." *PN* XXXIV, 4 (August 1996): 8–10.
GEN. BIB.: Larrick, *BET–CP*; information provided by the subject, 1996.

BEDFORD, RONALD HILLIER "RONNIE" (b. 2 Jun 1931, Bridgeport, Connecticut). A member of New York City's musician's union (Local 802) from age 16, Ronnie Bedford studied in New York with *Fred Albright, Willie Rodriguez, *Terry Gibbs, and *Tiny Kahn and built a freelance career centered in New York from 1954 that covered almost four decades. From 1950 to 1951 he toured and made his first recording with Louis Prima and Keeley Smith, after which he served two years (1952–54) in the U.S. Second Army Bagpipe Band at Camp Pickett, Virginia. After touring (and learning to read music) with the Billy May orchestra from 1954 through 1956, he performed and recorded with the Sam Donahue big band (1956–57).

Those successes led to musical appearances on stage in the Broadway productions of *A Thurber Carnival* (jazz quartet, 1960) and Richard Rodgers' *No Strings* (big band, 1960–61), shows at the Copacabana and the Playboy Club, and various recording studio sessions that included such greats as Bobby Hackett (1964), Pee Wee Russell (1965), Lee Konitz (1966), Hank Jones (1976), and Arnett Cobb (1980). He worked with Eddie Condon in the early 1960s and the Rod Levitt Octet (1963–68), with which he made four albums highly acclaimed by *Down Beat* magazine. Bedford performed and recorded with Johnny Richards' orchestra for six years (1962–68) and toured internationally for two years (1974–75) with Benny Goodman. In 1977 and 1979–80 he was spotlighted with Buddy DeFranco at venues that included the Mexico City and JVC Jazz Festivals; he also served as house drummer at the Kool and Newport Jazz Festivals in 1980–85. After an initial collaboration with Benny Carter in 1977, in 1981 he taped the tenth anniversary show of *Jazz at the Smithsonian*, which was later nationally telecast on PBS and released on video format by the Sony Corporation. Bedford's two 1988 CD releases with Carter were also well received by jazz critics.

In 1986 he moved to Wyoming where he teaches at Northwest Community College and is a cofounder of the Yellowstone Jazz Festival. In 1993 he was honored for his contributions to jazz with the Governor's Award for the Arts in

Wyoming. Buddy DeFranco said of him: "He is one of the few drummers who plays for the soloist *and* the band, and whose solos are [as] 'melodic' as a horn."

SELECTED DISCOGRAPHY

Audiophile ACD–208: *Sweet and Swinging* (Chris Connor), 1978.
Audiophile ACD–236: *Warren Chiasson—Good Vibes for Kurt Weill*, 1978.
Audiophile ACD–291: *Hoagy's Children*, vol. 1, 1983.
Epic LN 20499: *Hello Louis* (Bobby Hackett), 1964.
Famous Door HL 144: *Roaring Back into NY, NY* (Bill Watrous), 1983.
Impulse 96: *Ask Me Now!* (Pee Wee Russell), 1966.
Music Masters 601964: *Over the Rainbow* (Benny Carter), 1988.
Pablo 2310–906: *Mr. Lucky* (Buddy DeFranco), 1984.
Pablo 52310 935: *My Kind of Trouble* (Benny Carter), 1988.
Progressive PCD–7004: *Arigato* (Hank Jones), 1976.
Progressive PCD–7014: *Like Someone in Love* (Buddy DeFranco), 1989.
Progressive PCD–7015/7017: *The Progressive Records All–Star Trumpet Spectacular*, 1979/1982.
Progressive PCD–7018/7019: *The Progressive All–Star Tenor Sax/Trombone Spectacular*, 1980/1982.
Progressive 7039: *Stepping on Cracks* (Walter Norris), 1983.
Progressive PCD–7043: *Invitation* (Don Friedman Trio).
Progressive 7052: *You've Changed* (Dick Meldonian Quartet).
Progressive 7055: *The Derek Smith Trio Plays Jerome Kern*, 1981.
Progressive UPS–2287–G: *The Great Encounter* (Buddy DeFranco/Tal Farlow), 1977.
RCA 6471–2–RB: *RCA Jazz Workshop* (Rod Levitt), 1964.
RCA Victor 3372: *Insight* (Rod Levitt), 1965.
Riverside 471/947: *Dynamic Sound Patterns* (Rod Levitt), 1964.
Roulette 25351: *Aquí Se Habla Español* (Johnny Richards), 1967.
Roulette 52114: *My Fair Lady—My Way* (Johnny Richards), 1969.

SELECTED VIDEOGRAPHY

Sony Video: *Benny Carter—Jazz at the Smithsonian*, 1981.

SELECTED BIBLIOGRAPHY

Berger, Monroe, and Edward Berger and James Patrick. *Benny Carter—A Life in American Music*. Metuchen, NJ: Scarecrow Press, 1982.
Bouchard, Fred. "Waxing On: Triology" (Record Review). *DB* L, 12 (December 1983).
"Pee Wee Russell: 'Ask Me Now' " (Record Review). *DB* (19 May 1966).
"Walter Norris: 'Stepping on Cracks.' " *The Victory Music Folk and Jazz Review* VIII, 4 (April 1983).
GEN. BIB.: Hunt, *52nd St.*; Kernfeld, *NGJ*.

BEGUN, FRED (b. 30 Aug 1928, Brooklyn, New York). Timpanist with the National Symphony (1951–99), Fred Begun moved to Washington, D.C., in his youth, studied with *Saul Goodman at the Juilliard School (1946–51), taught at the Peabody Conservatory and Catholic University, and performed at the Aspen Music Festival. He premiered Robert Parris' "Concerto for Five Kettledrums and Orchestra" and John Stephens' "Three Symphonic Etudes for Solo Timpani and Orchestra" (National Symphony, 1958/1999), Jorge Sarmientos' "Concerto for Five Timpani and Orchestra" (1965), and Blas Atehortua's "Concertante for Timpani and Chamber Orchestra" (1968).

SELECTED BIBLIOGRAPHY

Begun, Fred. "Drummers Can Be Good Neighbors, Too." *Instrumentalist* XIV (April 1960): 28–29.
Begun, Fred. *Twenty–one Etudes for Timpani.* Bethesda, MD: Benjamine Thomas Pub., 1975.
"Getting to Know You: Fred Begun." National Symphony Program Notes (2 January 1962): 16.
Howland, Hal. "Fred Begun: Timpani Virtuoso." *MD* IV, 2 (1980): 20–23.
"Meet Your First–Desk Players: Fred Begun." *IM* LVII (January 1959): 36.
"The Performers and Ensembles: PASIC®, 1986." *PN* XXIV, 5 (1986): 25.

BELLI, REMO D. (b. 22 Jun 1927, Mishawaka, Indiana). A 1986 inductee into the Percussive Arts Society Hall of Fame and a founding member of the Society, Remo Belli enlisted in the U.S. Navy in 1945, playing in a ship's band in Newport, Rhode Island, and for civilian engagements in the greater New England area. Upon discharge from the navy he moved to California, studied with *Murray Spivack, and from 1949 to 1959 played drumset professionally, accompanying Hollywood film and television personalities and performing in the University of Southern California Summer Symphony. As a percussion industry entrepreneur, he established Drum City, a Hollywood drum shop that catered to professionals, and Remo, Inc., which, with the help of chemist Samuel N. Muchnick adapted and bonded DuPont's Mylar polyester film with epoxy glue to produce and distribute the first plastic drum heads in 1957—an event that revolutionized drumming worldwide. Remo, Inc., also manufactures and markets the "roto–tom," invented by Chicago Symphony timpanist *Al Payson; and in 1982 the company introduced the novel "pretuned" drumhead concept. A long–time member of the board of directors of the Percussive Arts Society, Belli is also a member of the Music Educators National Conference Advisory Council.

SELECTED BIBLIOGRAPHY

"Advisory Council's Remo Belli Shares Success Story with Students," *Teaching Music* IV, 3 (December 1996): 20.

Belli, Remo. "Percussionist Is More Than Just a Drummer." *DB* XXIII, 14 (23 July 1956): 39.

Levine, D. "Inside Remo." *MD* IV, 2 (April/May 1980): 24–27.

Van Horn, Rick. "Remo Revisited." *MD* XIX, 7 (July 1995): 80–90.

BELLSON, LOUIS PAUL "LOUIE" (b. Luigi Paulino Alfredo Francesco Antonio Balassoni, 26 Jul 1924, Rock Falls, Illinois). After starting drums at age 4 and subsequent percussion studies with the legendary *Roy Knapp and timpanists *Saul Goodman and *Alfred Friese, Louie Bellson won the Slingerland/*Gene Krupa national drumming contest in 1941, surmounting a field of 4,000! He was studying at Augustana College (Illinois, 1942–   ) when military service in WWII interrupted his career until after 1946. Bellson appeared and recorded with a "who's who" list of the swing era: Ted Fio Rito (1941/1946), Benny Goodman [including the film *The Power Girl* (1942) with Peggy Lee], Tommy Dorsey (1947–50, including the Dorsey Brothers' TV show), Harry James, Count Basie, Duke Ellington (1951–53), and *Red Norvo, among others. In 1954 he toured Europe with Norman Granz's "Jazz at the Philharmonic" ensemble, which included Ella Fitzgerald, Oscar Peterson, Roy Eldridge, and Dizzy Gillespie. He eventually fronted his own band and began a composition career that included big band charts and extended works such as "Concerto for Percussion and Orchestra" and a ballet *The Marriage Vows.*

His early international fame rested in part on the unique inclusion of—and his ability to play—two bass drums on drumset that he began to employ in 1946. He credits the required foot coordination and independence to tap dance lessons in his youth. Stunning examples of his technique showcasing the possibilities of two bass drums can be heard on his recordings of "Skin Deep" (Duke Ellington Orchestra) and "Drumology" (Tommy Dorsey), which are actively sought by collectors. Always willing to share his experience with younger musicians, Bellson has done innumerable clinics and concerts with school groups throughout the United States, authored method books, and penned a column for *Down Beat* magazine, "The Musical Drummer" (1950–51). His inventions and innovations include the silent drum practice pad kit, metal drum sticks, and recessed spurs on the bass drum. He served as musical director for and was married in 1952 to the late singer Pearl Bailey. Recipient of an honorary doctorate from Northern Illinois University, Bellson was inducted into the Percussive Arts Society Hall of Fame (1978), *Modern Drummer* Reader's Poll Hall of Fame (1985), and International Association of Jazz Educators Hall of Fame (1989), and in 1994 he received an "American Jazz Masters" Fellowship from the National Endowment of the Arts. His 1980 album, *Note Smoking*, was a Grammy[®] Award nominee.

SELECTED DISCOGRAPHY

BIS CD–382: *Farberman: Concerto for Jazz Drummer and Orchestra*, 1986.

Capitol H 348: *Just Jazz All–Stars Featuring Louis Bellson*, 1959.

Capitol T 926: *Hi–Fi Drums*, 1957.
Chiaroscuro: *The Louis Bellson Quintet—Salute*, 1995.
Columbia 462987/462988: *Complete Ellington*, vols. 3 & 4 (Duke Ellington), 1951.
Columbia CL951: *A Drum Is a Woman* (Duke Ellington), 1956
Columbia ML–4639/CK40836: *Ellington Uptown*, 1952.
Concord CCD–4742–2: *Air Bellson*, 1997.
Concord Jazz CCD–4025: *Louie Bellson's 7—Live at the Concord Summer Festival*, 1976.
Concord 105: *Dynamite!*, 1979.
Concord 141: *Side Track*, 1979.
Concord CCD–4683: *Their Time Was the Greatest* (Each tune is a singular tribute to Chick Webb, Sid Catlett, Gene Krupa, Buddy Rich, Jo Jones, Max Roach, Steve Gadd, Dennis Chambers, Elvin Jones, Tony Williams, Art Blakey, and Shelly Manne), 1996.
Concord 4797–2: *George Gershwin 100* (Matt Catingub), 1998.
Concord 4800–2: *The Art of the Chart*, 1998.
Concord CCD–4817–2: *Louie Bellson*, 1998.
DRG 8471: *Louie in London*, 1970.
Famous Door HL–2000: *Zoot at Ease* (Zoot Sims), 1973.
Impulse S–9107: *Thunderbird*, 1963.
Mercer LP–1005: *Duke Ellington's Coronets*, 1951.
Mosaic MD 12–170: *Classical Capitol Jazz Sessions*, 1997.
MusicMasters Jazz 01612–65074–2: *Peaceful Thunder*, 1992.
Norgran EPN 70–3: *Louis Bellson Quintet*, 1954.
Norgran MGM–14: *The Exciting Louis Bellson*, 1953.
Official 3029: *Wardell Gray and the Big Bands*, 1952.
Pablo 2310–703: *Duke's Big 4*, 1973.
Pablo 2310–813: *Sunshine Rock*, 1977.
Pablo 2310–838: *Louie Bellson Jam*, 1978.
Pablo 2310–851: *The Best of Louie Bellson*, 1980.
Pablo 2310–880: *The London Gig*, 1982.
Pablo 2310–899: *Cool Cool Blue*, 1982.
Pablo/OJC 600: *For the Second Time* (Count Basie and Ray Brown), 1975.
Progressive PCD–7084: *Back to Bass–ics* (Milt Hinton Trio), 1989.
Project 3 PR 5029 QD: *Breakthrough! Louis Bellson and His Orchestra*, 1973.
Roulette 52099: *Basie in Sweden*, 1963.
Roulette 52087: *Big Band Jazz from the Summit*, 1962.
Telarc Jazz CD–83334: *Live from New York*, 1994.
Verve MGV8137: *Skin Deep*, 1985.
Verve MGV8150: *Used to Be Duke* (Johnny Hodges), 1954.
Verve MGV8256: *At the Flamingo*, 1959.
Vogue (F) LD–050: *Duke Ellington*, 1951.

SELECTED VIDEOGRAPHY

DCI VH005: *Louis Bellson—The Musical Drummer*, 1984.
DCI VH053: *Buddy Rich Memorial Scholarship Concert No. 1*, 1989.
Kultur Video: *Drum Course for Beginners*, 1990.

Music Video Distributors/Moonbeam Publications, Inc.: *Louis Bellson and His Big Band*, 1983.

Proscenium Entertainment: *Superdrumming*, 1991.

Video Artists International: *Time Groove* (Louis Bellson, Steve Gadd et al.), 1990.

VIEW Video/Moonbeam Publications, Inc.: *Cobham Meets Bellson*, 1983

SELECTED BIBLIOGRAPHY

Bailey, Pearl. *The Raw Pearl.* New York: Harcourt Brace Jovanovich, Ltd., 1968.

Bellson, Louie. *Louie Bellson Honors Twelve Super Drummers: Their Time Was the Greatest.* Miami, FL: Warner Bros, 1998 (with CD).

Black, David. "An Interview with Louie Bellson." *PN* XXV, 5 (Summer 1987): 35–38.

Buresh, Dorothy. "It Was Louie's Day." *Moline* (IL)*Daily Dispatch* (Wednesday, 10 November 1972).

Conversations with Jazz Musicians. Detroit: Gale Research Company/A Bruccoli Clark Book, 1977. S.v. "Louis Bellson" by Zane Knauss.

Cook, Rob, ed. *Franks for the Memories: A History of the Legendary Chicago Drum Shop and the Story of Maurie and Jan Lishon.* Alma, Michigan: Rebeats Publications, 1993.

Flans, Robyn. "In Session: Louie Bellson and Gregg Field." *MD* XXII, 3 (March 1998): 24–28.

Franckling, Ken. "Louis Bellson's Ducal Revival." *JazzTimes* XXIII, 9 (November 1993): 38–39.

"Louie Bellson Day—Moline, Illinois; May 9, 1972." *PN* XI, 1 (Fall 1972): 12.

"Louie Bellson, William 'Billy' Gladstone, Alfred Friese Inducted into PAS® Hall of Fame." *PN* XVII, 2 (Winter 1979): 27–28.

Mattingly, Rick. "They Keep Drumming, and Drumming, and... The Art of Percussive Longevity." *DB* LX, 11 (November 1993): 25–26.

GEN. BIB.: Hunt, *52nd St.*; Kernfeld, *NGJ*, by J. Bradford Robinson; Larrick, *BET–CP*; Spagnardi, *GJD*.

BENFORD, THOMAS P. "TOMMY" (b. 19 Apr 1905, Charleston, West Virginia; d. 24 Mar 1994). A pioneer drumset artist, Tommy Benford studied music at his orphanage, which sponsored a band trip to England in 1914. He toured with the Green River Minstrels (ca. 1920) and then moved to New York, where he played and/or recorded with Jelly Roll Morton (1928), Elmer Snowden, and Charlie Skeete. Joining Sy Devereaux for an extended European stay (ca. 1932–43), Benford made recordings with Coleman Hawkins (1937) and Joe Turner (1939). Returning to New York, he worked with Noble Sissle (1943), Bob Wilber (1948–49), Rex Stewart (1953), and Eddie South, Dick Wellstood, and others. He also toured with the "Jazz Train" revue, the "World of Jelly Roll Morton" (1972–74/1982), and the Harlem Blues and Jazz Band (1973–79/1981), among others.

SELECTED DISCOGRAPHY

Barron 401: *Sittin' on Top of the World* (Clyde Bernhardt), 1975.
Blue Note 48 & 509: *Alamo "Pigmeat" Markham*, 1945.
HMV K8511: "Out of Nowhere" (Coleman Hawkins), 1937.
Jazztet 1202: *Dixieland Free–for–all* (Rex Stewart), 1953.
Masters of Jazz, Media 7: *Anthology of Jazz Drumming,* vols. 1–2 (1904–35), 1997.
Riverside 2506: *The Stride Piano of Dick Wellstood,* 1954.
Smithsonian 006: *Music of Jelly Roll Morton* (Dick Hyman), 1978.
World Jazz 13: *Soprano Summit* (Bob Wilber), 1977.
GEN. BIB.: Kernfeld, *NGJ,* by Brian Peerless; Korall, *DM.*

BENSON, WARREN FRANK (b. 26 Jan 1924, Detroit, Michigan). Warren
Benson studied initially with Jerry Gerard, Selwyn Alvey at Cass Tech, and
Jack Ledingham (Detroit) and received bachelor's (1949) and master's (1951)
degrees in music theory from the University of Michigan while also serving as
percussion instructor. From 1946 to 1954, he was timpanist with the Detroit
Symphony, the Ford Sunday Evening Hour Orchestra, and the Brevard Festival
Orchestra. In 1952 Benson was awarded a Fulbright teaching position in
Greece, which led to posts at Mars Hill College (NC) (ensemble director,
1952–53), Ithaca College (percussion instructor, 1953–67), the Eastman School
(composition, since 1967), and Southern Methodist University (1986–88, as
visiting professor of composition). He has garnered composition awards from
the Ford Foundation, the New York State Council on the Arts, and the National
Endowment for the Arts and served guest residencies in Budapest, Norway, and
China. His works are published by Peters, Schirmer, Presser, Fisher, and
Boosey & Hawkes, among others.

SELECTED DISCOGRAPHY

Golden Crest 4016: *Warren Benson Presents Percussion* (Ithaca Percussion En-
     semble), 1960.
Golden Crest ATH–5085: *Symphony for Drums and Wind Orchestra* (as com-
     poser), 1972.
U.S. Air Force Band: *Dawn's Early Light* (as composer), 1989.

SELECTED BIBLIOGRAPHY

Udow, Michael. "An Interview with Warren Benson." *PN* XXVII, 2 (Winter 1989):
     42–50.
GEN. BIB.: *ASCAPBD*; Larrick, *BET–CP.*

BENZLER, ALBERT (b. 13 Nov 1867, Newark, New Jersey; d. 9 Jun 1953,
Newark, New Jersey). Xylophone and bell recording artist who flourished from

1906 to 1915, Albert Benzler first made Edison cylinders (1903–09), then became music director for the U.S. Phonograph Company (1909–13), where he recorded on bells, xylophone, and piano. Benzler may have recorded on discs for the Columbia Phonograph Company around 1911 under the pseudonym Albert Henry.

SELECTED DISCOGRAPHY

Edison Cylinder 8005: "I Have Grown So Used to You," ca. 1904–09.
Edison Cylinder 8412: "Down Where the Wurzberger Flows Medley," ca. 1904–09.
Edison Cylinder 8829: "Blue Bell" (xylophone and bells duet), ca. 1904–09.
U.S. Phonograph/Everlasting 223: "Peter Piper March," ca. 1910.
GEN. BIB.: Cahn, *XAR.*

BERGAMO, JOHN JOSEPH (b. 28 May 1940, Englewood, New Jersey). Percussionist, composer, conductor, and ethnic hand drumming specialist, John Bergamo received bachelor's (1961) and master's (1962) degrees from the Manhattan School, where he studied with *Paul Price. His subsequent percussion teachers have included *Max Roach (1959), *Fred Albright, Ustad Allah Rakha, *K.R.T. Wasitodiningrat, Alfred and Kobla Ladzekpo, Mahapurush Misra, Shankar Ghosh (Calcutta, 1992), Swapan Chaudhuri, T. H. Subashchandran, P. S. Venkatesan, T. H. Viniakram, T. Raganathan, and I. Nyoman Wenten at venues such as the Darmstadt Summer Institute (1962), Tanglewood (1963–65), Ali Akbar College, and the Lenox School of Jazz. A Rockefeller Foundation Grant enabled him to participate as a "creative associate" at SUNY–Buffalo for two years.

Bergamo has performed for and/or recorded with Frank Zappa, John McLaughlin, Herb Alpert, Shadowfax, Los Jaguares, Harry Nillson, Gunther Schuller, Lukas Foss, Charles Wuorinen, *Steve Gadd, *Glen Velez, Nexus, and his own group, Repercussion Unit (since 1976), among others. He is a published composer (Music for Percussion and Leisure Planet Music), and his teaching posts have included the Naropa (1986) and Ali Akbar Summer Institutes, the University of Washington, and since 1970 the California Institute of the Arts, where he is coordinator of the percussion program.

SELECTED DISCOGRAPHY

CMP CD–27: *On the Edge*, 1986.
CMP Records 31: *In Need Again* (Repercussion Unit), 1987.
CMP Records 34: *Bracha*, 1988.
Digital Drums (Cassette 009): *Tambo/Cloud Hands*, 1990.
Odyssey 32160155: *Music of Morton Feldman*, 1967.
Robey Records Rob.1: *Repercussion Unit*, 1978.

SELECTED VIDEOGRAPHY

Interworld Music VH076:   *The Art and Joy of Hand Drumming*, 1990.
Interworld Music VH0145: *Finding Your Way with Hand Drums*, 1991.
Talamala VHS009: *Hand Drumming with John Bergamo*, 1996.

SELECTED BIBLIOGRAPHY

Bergamo, John. "South Indian Drumming." *PN*, Research Edition (1985).
Bergamo, John. "The Tavil of South India." *Percussioner International* I, 2 (1986).
Bergamo, John (with Janet Bergamo). "Exploring Tambourine Technique." *PN* XXVIII, 3 (Spring 1990): 12–14.
Bergamo, John. "Transferring the Chops: Hand Drumming Techniques for Stick Drummers." *MD* XXI, 4 (April 1997): 128–134.
GEN. BIB.: Larrick, *BET–CP.*

BERGER, FRITZ ROBERT (b. ca. 1899, Basel, Switzerland; d. 1963, Basel, Switzerland). Expert field snare drummer in the "Basel" style, Fritz Berger held a doctorate degree in law and was made an honorary member of NARD (National Association of Rudimental Drummers) by *William Ludwig, Sr., in 1947. One of Berger's students, Alfons Grieder (b. 1939), is considered throughout Europe and the United States as the premier exponent of this drumming style. [The "father" of Swiss drumming was "Papa Otto," who died in 1925 at the age of 85. Issue 11 (ca. 1948) of the English drum pamphlet *STYX* includes his photo.]

SELECTED BIBLIOGRAPHY

Adams, Aubrey, and Craig Collison. "Interview with Alfons Grieder: Swiss Rudimental Drummer, Pt. 2." *PN* XXX, 6 (August 1992: 36–43.
Berger, Dr. F. R. *Instructor for Basel Drumming*. Basel, Switzerland: Basel Drum Editions, 1937/1964.
"Fritz Berger: The Wizard of the Swiss Rudiments." *LD* III, 2 (Fall 1963): 15.

BERGER, KARL HANS (b. 30 Mar 1935, Heidelberg, Germany). Vibraphonist Karl Berger began piano lessons at the age of 10, earning a Ph.D. in musicology and philosophy (1963, Heidelberg and Berlin). In 1965 he worked with Don Cherry in Paris, recording with him in New York (1966) and remaining there to play with *Horacee Arnold (1967–71). Director of the Creative Music Studio in Woodstock, New York, which he established in 1972 with Ornette Coleman, Berger appeared at the Kool Jazz Festival (1982), served as guest composer and conductor of the Westdeutscher Rundfunk Orchestra, recorded with Lee Konitz, *Babatunde Olatunji, and Dave Holland, among others, and has led his own groups.

SELECTED DISCOGRAPHY

Black Saint BSR 0092: *Transit*, 1987.
Blue Note 84247: *Don Cherry—Symphony for Improvisers*, 1966.
Calig 30607: *We Are You*, 1971.
Enja 2022: *With Silence*, 1972.
Enja 7029: *Crystal Fire*, 1993.
ESP 1041: *Karl Berger Quartet*, 1966.
Milestone 9026: *Tune In*, 1970.
MPS 68250: *Live at the Donaueschingen Music Festival*, 1979.
GEN. BIB.: Kernfeld, *NGJ*, by Barry Kernfeld. .

BERNS, PAUL S. Principal percussionist with the Indianapolis Symphony since 1969, Paul Berns served as faculty member at Butler University and as vice chair of the International Conference of Symphony and Opera Musicians (ICSOM). He hosted the 1981 Indianapolis Percussive Arts Society International Convention and led the Indianapolis Jazz-Rock Ensemble.

SELECTED BIBLIOGRAPHY

"New Board Members." *PN* XXIII, 2 (January 1985): 3.

BERTON, VIC (b. Victor Berton Cohen, 5 Jul 1896, Chicago, Illinois; d. 26 Dec 1951, Hollywood, California). Starting drums at age 6, Vic Berton was born into a family of vaudevillians, studied with *Ed Straight, Joe Russek, and *Joseph Zettleman, and at 7 played drums in the pit at Milwaukee's Alhambra Theater. He later performed with John Philip Sousa, the U.S. Navy Band (WWI), Chicago Symphony, and Art Kahn's Orchestra in Chicago; he then relocated to New York, where he worked with the New York Philharmonic and the Paul Ash Orchestra. Also a Broadway show drummer (e.g., Earl Carroll's *Vanities*, ca. 1926), Berton recorded with Bix Beiderbecke, Roger Wolf Kahn, Sam Lanin, Miff Mole, Don Vorhees, and Paul Whiteman, but his recordings with Red Nichols during the late 1920s are his best. These included the first examples of jazz (pedal) timpani, for example, "Delirium," "Allah's Holiday," and "Devil's Kitchen" (Columbia 3074D, 1935). Forming his own band in 1935, he also performed at the CBS, Twentieth-Century Fox, and Paramount studios, the RKO Music Hall, and the Roxy Theater, as well as in the Los Angeles Philharmonic. He is credited with patenting a forerunner of the hi–hat cymbal (1926).

SELECTED DISCOGRAPHY

Masters of Jazz, Media 7: *Anthology of Jazz Drumming*, vols. 1–2 (1904–35), 1997.

SELECTED BIBLIOGRAPHY

Brown, T. Dennis. "Vic Berton: The Greatest Drummer of All Time." Research paper
  presented at IAJE Conference, 1982. [Available from IAJE, *Jazz Research
  Papers,* vol. 2, compiled by Dr. Charles T. Brown and Dr. Larry Fisher.]
Korall, Burt. "From the Past: Vic Berton, the Unknown Star." *MD* XIX (May 1995):
  112–113.
GEN. BIB.: Cook, *LDT*, p. 140 (photo); Kernfeld, *NGJ*, by T. Dennis Brown.

BEST, DENZIL DACOSTA (b. 1917, Barbados; d. 25 May 1965, New York,
New York). Moving to New York in childhood, pianist, trumpeter, bassist, and
composer Denzil Best switched to drums (self–taught) in 1943 after contracting
tuberculosis. He played with Ben Webster (ca. 1943), Coleman Hawkins
(1944), Chubby Jackson (Scandinavian tour, 1947), Illinois Jacquet (ca. 1948),
George Shearing (1949–52, considered his best work), Artie Shaw (1954), Errol
Garner (1956–57), Nina Simone, and Eartha Kitt. Plagued with alcohol problems, he broke both legs in an auto accident in 1952 and developed calcium
deposits in both wrists in 1957.

SELECTED DISCOGRAPHY

Blue Note 89002: *Sheila Jordan—A Portrait of Sheila,* 1962.
Clef MGC140: *Teddy Wilson Trio,* 1953.
Progressive PCD–7001: *Ben Webster—The Horn,* 1944.
Savoy SJK 1117: *George Shearing—So Rare,* ca. 1949/1978.
Verve (E) VSP35/36: *George Shearing,* 1949–53.
Xanadu 120: *Bebop Revisited,* vol. 1 (Dexter Gordon, Fats Navarro, Chubby Jack-
  son), 1947/1975.

SELECTED BIBLIOGRAPHY

Korall, Burt. "From the Past: Denzil Best." *MD* XX, 1 (January 1996): 134–138.

BETHANCOURT, JOSÉ (b. Guatemala). The nephew of marimbist Jousis
Bethancourt, who was first famous in Guatemala and later New York, José
played with the Mexican Police Marimba Band before settling in Chicago. His
virtuosic marimba technique could be heard at the NBC studios in Chicago,
where he was a staff musician. He led his own orchestra, taught in Chicago, and
manufactured marimba mallets that were sold at one time by the *J. C. Deagan
Company.

SELECTED DISCOGRAPHY

Concert–Disc CS–33: *Beat Tropicale,* 1956.

SELECTED BIBLIOGRAPHY

Bethancourt, José. *Collection for Marimba or Vibraharp*. Chicago: Chart Music, 1940.

Cook, Rob, ed. *Franks for the Memories: A History of the Legendary Chicago Drum Shop and the Story of Maurie and Jan Lishon*. Alma, Michigan: Rebeats Publications, 1993 (photo, p.22).

Peters, Gordon. *The Drummer: Man*. Wilmette, Illinois: Kemper–Peters Publications, 1975.

GEN. BIB.: Cook, *LDT*.

BIBBY, DAVID. Principal percussionist of the BBC Welsh Symphony in Cardiff, Wales, David Bibby attended the Royal Manchester College of Music (aka Royal Northern College of Music) at 16 years of age. He served in a British army band and taught at one of the Royal Colleges of Music.

SELECTED BIBLIOGRAPHY

Bibby, David. "One Step Forward and Two Steps Back." *PN* XVII, 2 (Winter 1979): 12–13.

BILARDO, VINCENT J. "VINCE" (b. 22 Jul 1928, Cleveland, Ohio). At age 14, the youngest member of AFM Local No. 4 and a semifinalist in the *Gene Krupa Drum Contest at age 16, Vince Bilardo performed and/or recorded with the Wilson Humber, Russ Carlyle, and Clyde McCoy Orchestras from 1948 to 1951, then served in the 10th Infantry Division Band at Camp Funston (Ft. Riley, KS) from 1952 to 1954. He attended Case Western Reserve University (1955–59) and Cleveland Institute of Music (1957–59; bachelor's, 1959), having studied with *Cloyd Duff, *Charles Wilcoxon, and Jerry Borden. Bilardo worked with the St. Louis Symphonietta (1962) and the Cleveland Pops Orchestra (1960–62), and he served as principal percussionist with the Kansas City Philharmonic from 1959 to 1982, premiering Henry Cowell's "Concerto for Percussion" with the latter (ca. 1965).

SELECTED DISCOGRAPHY

Epic LC 3743: *On the Town* (Cleveland Pops), 1960.

Key LP–717: *Swingin' Close In* (Joe Howard), 1957.

SELECTED BIBLIOGRAPHY

Sanchez, Mary. "Years Nurtured Overland Park Man's Love, Respect for Music." *Overland Park* (KS) *Sun*, 1986.

Information supplied by the subject, 1996.

BLACKWELL, EDWARD JOSEPH "ED" (b. 10 Oct 1929, New Orleans, Louisiana; d. 7 Oct 1992). An African music scholar, drumset artist, and composer, Ed Blackwell was influenced by *Max Roach, *Baby Dodds, *Paul Barbarin, and *Zutty Singleton, but he played rhythm and blues early on before moving to Los Angeles (ca. 1951). He returned to New Orleans in 1956 and worked with the American Jazz Quintet (1957) and Ray Charles (1957). Relocating to New York (1960), Blackwell performed with Albert Heath, Eric Dolphy, Don Cherry, Booker Little, David Murray, Archie Shepp, John Coltrane, Randy Weston (1965–66), and Dewey Redman, but he was most famous for his collaborations with his former roommate, Ornette Coleman (CA, 1953; NY, 1960–65; Europe and elsewhere, 1969–72). During the 1970s–90s, he led his own group, Old and New Dreams, and served on the faculty of Wesleyan University (CT).

SELECTED DISCOGRAPHY

Affinity 774: *Mu (The Complete Session)* (Don Cherry), 1969.
Atlantic 1364–2: *Free Jazz* (Ornette Coleman), 1960.
Atlantic 90041–2: *The Avante–Garde* (John Coltrane & Don Cherry), 1960.
Atlantic 90978–2: *The Art of the Improvisers* (Ornette Coleman), 1988.
Atlantic SD 1378/90530–1: *Ornette!* (Ornette Coleman), 1961.
Atlantic SD–1353: *This Is Our Music* (Ornette Coleman), 1960.
Black Saint 120 113–1: *A Tribute to Blackwell* (Old and New Dreams), 1987.
Black Saint BSR 0092: *Transit* (Karl Berger/Dave Holland), 1987.
Black Saint BSR–0013: *Old & New Dreams*, 1979.
Black Saint CD 120093–2: *In Willisau*, 1992.
Blue Note 84226: *Don Cherry—Complete Communion*, 1965.
Blue Note 84247: *Don Cherry—Symphony for Improvisers*, 1966.
Blue Note 84311: *Don Cherry—Where Is Brooklyn?* 1966.
Blue Note 98363–2: *From the Soul* (Joe Lovano), 1992.
DIW–395: *Interpretations of Monk*, 1981/1994.
ECM 1154/829379–2: *Old and New Dreams*, 1979.
ECM 829 123–2: *Playing* (Old and New Dreams), 1988.
ECM 829199–2: *El Corazón* (Don Cherry), 1982.
Enja 7029: *Crystal Fire* (Karl Berger), 1993.
Enja 7089 2: *What It Is?* 1992.
Fantasy/OJC 133/247: *At the Five Spot,* vols. 1–2 (Eric Dolphy), 1991–92.
Fantasy/OJC 673–2: *Here & There* (Eric Dolphy), 1960/1991.
FR CD1037: *Fresh Sounds* (Lee Morgan).
Prestige/OJC–133–2: *Eric Dolphy at the Five Spot* (Eric Dolphy), 1961.
Verve V6–8387: *Jimmy Giuffre Quartet*, 1960.

SELECTED VIDEOGRAPHY

VAI Jazz Collection/Video Artists International: *Live at the Village Vanguard*, vols. 4 & 6 (Mal Waldron and David Murray), 1989.

SELECTED BIBLIOGRAPHY

Fish, Scott K. "Ed Blackwell: Singin' on the Set." *MD* V, 8 (1981): 91.
Milkowski, Bill. "Masters of the Free Universe." *MD* XVI, 12 (December 1992): 32–35.
Riley, Herlin, and Johnny Vidacovich. *New Orleans Jazz and Second Line Drumming.* Miami, FL: Warner Bros./Manhattan Music, 1995.
Schmalenberger, David. "Ed Blackwell's African Influences." *PN* XXXIV, 6 (December 1996): 21–24.
Wilmer, Valerie. "Ed Blackwell: Well–Tempered Drummer." *DB* XXXV, 20 (3 Oct 1968): 18–19.
GEN. BIB.: Hunt, *52nd* St.; Kernfeld, *NGJ*, by Michael Ullman; Spagnardi, *GJD.*

BLADES, JAMES (b. 9 Sep 1901, Peterborough, England; d. 19 May 1999, London, England). Graduating from formal percussion lessons with his uncle, George, James Blades began playing in 1919 for circus bands and the City Military Band; he then provided sound effects and orchestral percussion for silent movies. By 1928 he performed xylophone solos on radio and appeared on drumset and xylophone with several popular hotel dance bands (e.g., the Picadilly) during the 1930s. Prior to his notable long–lived collaborations with the composer Benjamin Britten (from 1935), he worked in early "talkies," recording soundtracks at Gaumont–British and Elstree Studios and with the London Film Symphony (1932). During WWII Blades played for the Entertainments National Service Association, subbed with the London Philharmonic, and secured a position with the London Symphony Orchestra. In 1947 he presented his first full–length BBC radio program, *The Orchestral Instruments of Percussion*, and also appeared in the film series *We Make Music*. Blades performed for King George VI and at the coronation of Queen Elizabeth II. He served on the faculties of the Royal Academy of Music in London and the University of Surrey. His scholarly work *Percussion Instruments and Their History* (Faber and Faber, 1984) remains the seminal study in the percussion field. He was awarded the Order of the British Empire (1972), and the Percussive Arts Society honored him in 1975 with induction into their Hall of Fame.

SELECTED DISCOGRAPHY

Argo ZRG–673: *Music of the Crusades*, 1971.
Decca 252–3: Benjamin Britten—*The War Requiem*, 1963.
Decca 274/6: Benjamin Britten—*Albert Herring*, 1964.
Discourses ABK–13: *Blades on Percussion*, 1973.
ECS–566/Peters International PLG 135: William Walton—*Façade*, 1980.

SELECTED BIBLIOGRAPHY

Blades, James. *Drum Roll —A Professional Adventure from the Circus to the Concert Hall* (autobiography). London: Faber and Faber, 1977.

Blades, James. "On Being Awarded the O.B.E." *PN* XI, 1 (Fall 1972): 10.

Blades, James. *Percussion Instruments and Their History.* London: Faber and Faber, 1984.

Blades, James, and Jeremy Montague. *Early Percussion Instruments.* London: Oxford University Press, 1976.

Goodwin, Simon. "James Blades: A Life of Percussion." *MP* I, 1 (December 1984–February 1985): 18–21.

"Honoring James Blades (95th Birthday Tribute)." *PN* XXXV, 1 (February 1997): 6–8.

Newman, Richard. "James Blades: A Musician for All Seasons." *PN* XVII, 2 (Winter 1979): 26.

Schoolfield, Rob. "A Visit with James Blades." *PN* XXX, 4 (April 1992): 46–53.

Shipway, Nigel. "James Blades Career Retrospective." *PN* XXX, 4 (April 1992): 42–45.

Shipway, Nigel. "The James Blades 90th Birthday Celebrations." *PN* XXX, 4 (April 1992): 54–55.

Skinner, Michael. "James Blades, OBE: 1901–1999." *PN* XXXVII, 4 (August 1999): 67–70.

GEN. BIB.: Larrick, *BET–CP.*

BLAINE, HAL (b. Harold Simon Belsky, 5 Feb 1929, Holyoke, Massachusetts). Studio legend Hal Blaine matured in Hartford, Connecticut, watching the famous big bands of the day at the local theater, and then moved to Los Angeles at age 14. He served in the U.S. Army (1946–48) in Korea, played shows with road bands (1948–49), attended the *Roy Knapp school, gigged in Chicago (1949–51), moved back to California (1951), and toured with various bands throughout the United States and Canada. Appearing with Tommy Sands on national television (e.g., *Ed Sullivan*, *Perry Como* shows), Blaine played for Patti Page in Las Vegas and started dubbing movie soundtracks (e.g., Elvis Presley's *Blue Hawaii*). He later played live and in the studio for television shows (e.g., *The Steve Allen Show* and *Happy Days*) and did stand–up comedy, dancing, singing, and bit parts in films.

Replacing the regular drummer for studio recordings, Blaine toured, performed, and/or recorded with the Beach Boys, the Mamas and the Papas, Elvis Presley, the Carpenters, John Lennon, Simon and Garfunkel, the Fifth Dimension, Jan and Dean, the Monkees, Frank and Nancy Sinatra, John Denver, and Barbra Steisand, among a host of others. He appeared on most of the Phil Spector–produced hits during the 1960s–70s, accumulating 350 "Top Ten" chart recordings including 41 No. 1 songs, seven "Records of the Year," over 300 gold records, and six Grammy® Awards (35,000 recorded tracks!). Among those Top Ten hits were "A Taste of Honey" (Herb Alpert and the Tijuana Brass), "Strangers in the Night" (Frank Sinatra), "Up, Up, and Away" and "Aquarius/Let the Sunshine In" (Fifth Dimension), "Mrs. Robinson," and "Bridge Over Troubled Water" (Simon and Garfunkel).

He developed the single–headed, gradated multi-tom concept for a drumset the Ludwig Drum Company dubbed the "Octaplus." After "semiretiring" in 1984, he established the Hal Blaine Drum Scholarship with corporate support and was honored by his hometown of Holyoke, Massachusetts, with "Hal Blaine Day" in 1991. A recording of Blaine's stand–up comedy and drumming was scheduled for release on the Acoustic Disk label recording (1998).

SELECTED DISCOGRAPHY

MCA/Varèse Sarabande VSD–5612: *Drums! Drums! À Go Go*, 1965.
Verve V6–8798: *Chet Baker*, 1970.

SELECTED BIBLIOGRAPHY

Blaine, Hal (with David Goggin). *Hal Blaine and the Wrecking Crew: The Story of the World's Most Recorded Musician.* Emeryville, CA: Mix Books, 1990.
Cianci, Bob. *Great Rock Drummers of the Sixties.* Milwaukee, WI: Hal Leonard Publishing, 1989.
Harrington, Richard. "Studio Drummer Blaine Is Hero Heard Often But Not Seen." *Denver Post* (Monday, 21 Jul 1997): 5G.

BLAKEY, ARTHUR "ART" (aka Buhaina Abdullah Ibn, b. 11 Oct 1919, Pittsburgh, Pennsylvania; d. 16 Oct 1990, New York, New York). Trained as a pianist and essentially self–taught as a drumset artist, Art Blakey performed with the Fletcher Henderson Orchestra (1939, 1943–44), Mary Lou Williams (1942), Billy Eckstine Orchestra (1944–47), and Buddy DeFranco's combo (1951–53). With pianist Horace Silver, he initiated the long–lived combo Jazz Messengers in 1955 and took over as leader from 1956 until 1990. That group became a launching pad for young jazz talent, including Donald Byrd, Lee Morgan, Freddie Hubbard, Wynton Marsalis, Wayne Shorter, Branford Marsalis, Joanne Brackeen, Cedar Walton, Kenny Dorham, and Keith Jarrett, among others. Blakey recorded with Miles Davis, Thelonius Monk, Charlie Parker, Dizzy Gillespie, Sonny Rollins, and John Coltrane, among others. He was inducted into *Modern Drummer* magazine's Reader's Poll Hall of Fame in 1991, and was awarded an "American Jazz Masters" Fellowship from the National Endowment for the Arts in 1988.

SELECTED DISCOGRAPHY

A&M 75021 5329 4: *One for All*, 1990.
Atlantic LP1278/Rhino R2 75598: *Jazz Messengers with Thelonius Monk*, 1958/1999.
Blue Note 1565: *Thelonius Monk: Who Knows?* 1947.
Blue Note 4004 and 4005: *Holiday for Skins*, 1958.
Blue Note 4054: *Meet You at the Jazz Corner of the World*, ca. 1959.
Blue Note 5037–9/CD B21Y–46519/20: *A Night at Birdland*, vols. 1–2, 1954.
Blue Note 54899: *Art Blakey—Jazz Profile*, 1997.
Blue Note 56586: *Orgy in Rhythm*, vols. 1–2, 1957.

Blue Note 59352: *Herbie Nichols—The Complete Blue Note Recordings*, 1955–56.
Blue Note 84029/B21Y–46400: *Big Beat*, 1960
Blue Note 84097: *The African Beat*, 1962.
Blue Note 84156: *The Freedom Rider*, 1961.
Blue Note B21K 46149: *One Night with Blue Note*, vol. 3, 1985.
Blue Note B21K 46338: *Somethin' Else* (Cannonball Adderley), 1958.
Blue Note B21Y 46140: *Horace Silver and the Jazz Messengers*, 1954.
Blue Note B21Y 84436: *First Blue Note Jazz Messengers New Sounds*, 1947.
Blue Note B21Y–46516: *Moanin'*, 1958.
Blue Note B21Y–46521/22: *At the Cafe Bohemia,* vols. 1–2, 1955.
Blue Note B21Y–46523: *Mosaic*, 1961.
Blue Note B21Y–46858: *Ritual*, 1957.
Blue Note BLP1558: *Sonny Rollins*, 1957.
Blue Note BLP4104/CDP 7 84104 2: *Buhaina's Delight*, 1961/1992.
Blue Note BLP5006: *James Moody and His Bop Men*, 1948.
Blue Note CDP 7 84170 2: *Free for All*, 1964.
Blue Note CDP 7–95636–2: *The Best of Thelonius Monk*, 1991.
Blue Note S–1554: *Orgy in Rhythm*, 1957.
Catalyst 7902: *Jazz Messengers '70*, 1970.
CDP 7243 8 34195 2 4: *Clifford Brown—The Complete Blue Note and Pacific Jazz
        Recordings (1953–54)*, 1996.
Columbia CK 47118: *Jazz Messenger*, 1956.
Columbia CL 1002: *Drum Suite* (percussion ensemble), 1957.
Columbia CL 1040: *Hard Bop*, 1957.
Evidence ECD 22001–2: *Art Blakey and the Jazz Messengers Live at Sweet Basil*,
        1992.
Mercury 6877 001–6877–010: *Jazz* (Lionel Hampton), 1966.
Mercury–Emarcy MG 36071: *Giants of Jazz,* vol. 8—*The Jazz Greats, Drum Role*,
        1959.
Milestone 47001: *Cannonball Adderley and Eight Giants*, 1973.
Mosaic MD6 141: *The Complete Blue Note Recordings of Arts Blakey's 1960 Jazz
        Messengers*, 1960–61.
Mosaic MR4–101: *Thelonius Monk Sextet*, 1947.
OJC 030/Riverside SMJ–6128: *Blues for Tomorrow* (Sonny Rollins et al.),
        1957/1976.
Pacific Jazz CP32–5372: *New Bottle, Old Wine* (Gil Evans), 1958.
Prestige–24054: *Dig* (Miles Davis), 1975.
Prestige–24077: *Tune Up* (Miles Davis), 1953/1977.
Prestige OJC CD–008–2: *The Brothers* (Zoot Sims), 1952.
Riverside 1128/OJCCD–032–2: *Things Are Getting Better* (Cannonball Adderley),
        1988.
Riverside 9438/OJC–038: *Art Blakey and the Jazz Messengers—Caravan*, 1962.
Riverside OJCCD–064–2: *The Unique Thelonius Monk*, 1956.
Roulette CDP 724382864127: *Gretsch Drum Night at Birdland*, 1960.
Soul Note CD 121155–2: *I Get a Kick Out of Bu*, 1992.
Timeless 155: *Album of the Year*, 1981.
Verve/Polygram 840 033–4: *Jazz Club—Drums*, 1951–77.
Verve CD J28J 25112: *Buddy DeFranco Quartet*, 1953.
Verve MGV8086: *Illinois Jacquet Quintet*, 1951.

Verve MGV8185: *Bud Powell Trio*, 1955.
Vik LX1115: *Night in Tunisia*.

SELECTED VIDEOGRAPHY

DCI VH0249: *Legends of Jazz Drumming, Pt. 2, 1950–70*, 1996.
Kultur Video: *Jazz at the Smithsonian—Art Blakey and the Jazz Messengers*, 1982.
Music Video Distributors: *Art Blakey and the Jazz Messengers—Japan, 1961*.
Music Video Distributors: *Art Blakey and the Jazz Messengers—The Jazz Life*, 1982.
Rhapsody Films: *Art Blakey—The Jazz Messenger*, 1989.
Rhapsody Films: *Jazz Is Our Religion*, 1972.
Wadham Film/Music Video Distributors: *Jazz at Ronnie's*, 1991.

SELECTED BIBLIOGRAPHY

"Art Blakey and the Jazz Messengers." *Swing Journal* XXXIII, 2 (1979).
DeMichael, Don. "Message Received—Art Blakey." *DB* XXVIII, 10 (11 May 1961): 15–16.
Frost, H. "Art Blakey in St. Louis." *Metronome* LXIII, 2 (1947).
Hentoff, Nat. "Blakey Beats Drum for 'That Good Old Feeling!' " *DB* XX, 19 (16 Dec 1953): 17.
Humphrey, T. "The Art of Blakey Considered." *Jazz Beat* III, 7 (1966).
Primack, Bret. "Art Blakey: A Drum Thunder Suite." *JazzTimes* XXIV, 9 (November 1994): 22–30.
Shultz, Thomas. "A History of Jazz Drumming." *Percussionist* XVI, 3 (Spring/Summer 1979): 125–126.
Stern, Chip. "Art Blakey" *MD* VIII (September 1984): 8–13.
Tynan, John. "Art Blakey: The Message Still Carries." *DB* XXIX, 13 (21 Jun 1962): 20.
Tynan, John. "The Jazz Message." *DB* XXIV, 21 (1957).
GEN. BIB.: Hunt, *52nd St.*; Kernfeld, *NGJ*, by Lewis Porter; Larrick, *BET–CP*; Spagnardi, *GJD*.

BLANCHARD, PORTER (fl. ca. 1778, Concord, New Hampshire). Porter Blanchard was perhaps the oldest drum manufacturer in the United States. Contemporaries who may have performed on his instruments were noncommissioned officers of the American Army "Life Guard" (ca. 4 Jun 1776): Corelies Wilson (PA), Diah Manning (CT), and John Fenton (NJ). Blanchard's business was succeeded around 1800 by Eli Brown & Son of Windsor, Connecticut. [The oldest-known bass drum in the United States may have been played as early as 1652 and was located in Hartford, CT, ca. 1942.]

SELECTED BIBLIOGRAPHY

Bessette, Charles. "Techniques of Modern Drumming." *IM* XLI, 2 (August 1942): 25; XLI, 4 (October 1942): 18; XLI, 5 (November 1942): 24.

BLOWERS, JOHN "JOHNNY" (b. 21 Apr 1911, Spartanburg, South Carolina). Johnny Blowers grew up in a small southern town, moved to New York in 1937, and broke onto the jazz scene in 1938 with Bobby Hackett and Bunny Berigan (for whom he replaced *Dave Tough). He appeared and/or recorded with Bing Crosby, Frank Sinatra, Ella Fitzgerald, Billie Holiday (1944), Yank Lawson (1944–45), Eddie Condon (1944–47), and Louis Armstrong (1945–50). A freelance artist in the New York recording studios during the 1940s–60s, Blowers toured Europe in 1981 and played with the Harlem Jazz and Blues Band in New York (1980s).

SELECTED DISCOGRAPHY

Audiophile ACD–175: *Barbara Lea—Do It Again!* 1983.
Decca 18652: *Jodie Man* (Louis Armstrong), 1945.
Jazzology JCD–42: *Wild Bill Davison and His All–Star Stompers—This Is Jazz!* 1994.
Jazzology JCD–1013–1016: *Eddie Condon—The Town Hall Concerts,* vols. 7–8.
Mosaic MR6–110: *Sidney Bechet—Blue Note Jazzmen,* 1953.

SELECTED BIBLIOGRAPHY

Deffaa, C. "Portraits." *MD* IX, 7 (July 1985): 38–40.
Vaché, Warren. *Back Beats and Rim Shots—The Johnny Blowers Story.* Lanham, MD: Scarecrow Press, 1996 (includes an extensive discography).
GEN. BIB.: Kernfeld, *NGJ*; Korall, *DM.*

BLUME, HUGO OTTO EMIL (b. 12 Feb 1855, Berlin, Germany; d. 17 Jun 1925, Berlin, Germany). A member of the Berlin Musicians' Union, Hugo Blume was a charter member of, and timpanist, percussionist, and flautist with, the Berlin Philharmonic Orchestra for 43 years.
GEN. BIB.: Avgerinos, *KB.*

BOLÁN, MANUEL (b. ca. 1810, Buena Vista, Chiapas, Mexico; d. 1863, Jiquipilas, Chiapas, Mexico). Pioneer marimbist and composer Manuel Bolán established regional fame by performing throughout Chiapas and Guatemala on the three–octave, single–keyboard (diatonic) marimba with two other players. Bolán's collaborators included marimbists José Martínez and Juan Zárate; and one of his disciples, Benjamin Roque, was among the first to experiment (unsuccessfully) with augmenting the Chiapan marimba in 1885, attaching a second *diatonic* keyboard in another tonal center; however, the entire instrument remained nonchromatic.

SELECTED BIBLIOGRAPHY

Kaptain, Larry. *The Wood That Sings: The Marimba in Chiapas, Mexico.* Everett, PA: Honey Rock Publications, 1992.

BOOKSPAN, MICHAEL LLOYD "MICKEY" (b. 7 Sep 1929, Brooklyn, New York). Starting drum lessons at age 10, Mickey Bookspan studied with show drummer Sam Gershak, former vaudevillian *Jimmy Lent (xylophone and drums, ca. ages 11–12), and performed with a local VFW drum corps as a teen, playing drumset professionally by age 16. Also a student of *Fred Albright (age 13–17), he performed as xylophone soloist in USO troop shows (1943–46) during high school in the New York–New Jersey region. Bookspan served one and one–half years in the 657th Army Air Force Band at Kelly Field (San Antonio, TX) and won the *Arthur Godfrey Talent Show* in 1948. Upon discharge from the service, he attended the Juilliard School (bachelor's, 1953), where he studied with *Morris Goldenberg and *Saul Goodman. During the Juilliard years, he performed with the New York City Ballet Orchestra, and Little Orchestra Society (1951–53), the Goldman Band (1953–55) and did studio, TV, and soundtrack recording.

Bookspan joined the Philadelphia Orchestra in 1953 as percussionist and assistant timpanist, becoming principal percussionist and associate timpanist in 1972. He was honored by the orchestra in 1981 with the C. Hartman Kuhn Award for his contributions and, with Philadelphia, toured the Soviet Union, Japan, China, Europe, and South America. Bookspan commissioned and premiered Robert Suderburg's "Concerto for Solo Percussionist and Orchestra." He has performed as soloist with the Philadelphia, Hong Kong, Winston–Salem (NC), Trenton (NJ), and Grand Teton Festival Orchestras and has also appeared at the Marlboro, Casals, and Aspen Festivals. He is past president of the Philadelphia Musicians for Nuclear Arms Control, and in 1969 he organized Philadelphia Drummers for Peace. Currently he serves on the faculty of the Curtis Institute of Music and Philadelphia's University of the Arts.

SELECTED DISCOGRAPHY

Moss Music Group D–MMG 115/MCD 100007: *The All–Star Percussion Ensemble*, 1983.

SELECTED BIBLIOGRAPHY

Bookspan, Michael. "Selecting Orchestral Cymbals." *PN* XXV, 1 (Fall 1986): 41–42.
Owen Charles. "An Interview with Michael Bookspan." *PN* XXII, 4 (April 1984): 38–39.
GEN. BIB.: Borland, *WWAMC.* Information supplied by the subject, 1996.

BORACCHI, CARLO ANTONIO (fl. ca. 1842, Milan, Italy). Timpanist of the Royal Opera Orchestra at La Scala in Milan, Carlo Boracchi wrote a timpani method book (*Manuale del Timpanista*, Milan, 1842) and within it described a mechanical tuning device that he had invented but never mass produced. His successor, Pietro Pieranzovini, was reportedly Giuseppi Verdi's favorite timpanist at La Scala. [Pieranzovini also authored a timpani method book, *Metodo, Teorico–pratico per timpani* (Ricordi, 1900/1957), and composed a concerto for two timpani and string quartet, which was edited by Luigi Torrebruno and published by Ricordi.]

SELECTED BIBLIOGRAPHY

Beck, John H., ed. *Encyclopedia of Percussion*. New York: Garland Publishing, 1995. S.v. "The Kettledrum" by Edmund A. Bowles.
Ludwig, William F. *Ludwig Timpani Instructor*. Chicago: Ludwig Drum Co., 1957.

BORODKIN, SAMUEL "SAMMY." Sammy Borodkin studied with Henry Denecke, Sr., and played with the training group American Orchestral Association (later aka National Orchestral Association), the New York Symphony, the N.B.C. Symphony under Toscanini, the Symphony of the Air, and the New York Philharmonic, from which he retired in 1949. During the 1941 season his section colleagues in the Philharmonic included Sidney Rich, *Saul Goodman, and Ruben "Ruby" Katz.

SELECTED BIBLIOGRAPHY

Phillips, Harvey. "Musical Stories—Sam Borodkin." *Instrumentalist* XLVI (March 1992): 4.

BORRAZ, CORAZÓN DE JESÚS (b. 1877, Venustiano Carranza, Chiapas, Mexico; d. 1960). Corazón de Jesús Borraz is credited with having invented the five–octave, chromatic marimba (*marimba grande*) around 1896 in Chiapas, allowing the addition of European classical music to marimba repertoire (see also *Hurtado, Sebastián). This instrument generally employed five players, whereas the smaller *requinta*, which overlapped tonally and extended the musical range of the *grande*, was developed by Francisco Santiago Borraz in 1916 and utilized three players.

SELECTED BIBLIOGRAPHY

Kaptain, Larry. *The Wood That Sings: The Marimba in Chiapas, Mexico*. Everett, PA: Honey Rock Publications, 1992.

BOTTERILL, CHARLES "CHARLIE." Studying snare drum with *Sanford Moeller and timpani with *Karl Glassman, Charlie Botterill played on cruise ships (ca. 1925–32), freelanced in film recording, and performed drums and timpani in Montovani's orchestra for all European, Canadian, South African, Oriental, and U.S. tours, including recordings, and television and radio concerts from 1945 to 1975. He served as sales manager for the Premier Drum Company (1932–36) and journalist and associate editor for the English drum pamphlet *STYX* incorporating *Modern Drummer* (1940s). Transcriber of *Lionel Hampton's vibraphone solos, Botterill was instrumental in introducing England to the Americans' National Association of Rudimental Drummers (NARD), as well as to the Swiss' "Basel" rudimental snare technique. He was the first English member of the Percussive Arts Society.

SELECTED BIBLIOGRAPHY

Botterill, Charlie. "Memories of Drummers." *PN* XVII, 2 (Winter 1979): 31.
"Letters to the Editor." *Percussionist* I, 4 (April 1964): 19–20.

BOWER, HARRY A. (b. ca. 1867; d. ca. January 1949, Hollywood, California). Drum manufacturer, columnist for *The Dominant*, author of *The Bower Imperial Method* and *The Bower System* (in three volumes: Drums, Timpani, Bells/Xylophone), Harry Bower played in the Tremont Theater Orchestra (timpani), performed with the Boston Symphony (cymbals, 1904–07), and with his pianist wife toured vaudeville. He patented a bass drum pedal "pull" device made of chain (without foot plate, 1897), a clamp for attaching snare drums to chairs (1897), a timpani-tuning system (1904), and a pedal with a semifoot plate (1907). Veteran Boston drum manufacturer Frank E. Dodge purchased many of these patents (ca. 1907). Composer of the xylophone solos "Electric Polka" (Church, ca. 1898) and "Quartette Polka" (Fischer, ca. 1911), he relocated to Hollywood, California, around 1926.

SELECTED BIBLIOGRAPHY

Bower, Harry. *The Harry A. Bower System (in Three Parts) for the Drums, Bells, Xylophone, Timpani.* Boston, MA: Harry A. Bower, 1911.
Bower, Harry. *The Imperial Method of Drumming.* New York: John Church Co., 1898.
Bower, Harry. "The Xylophone." *The Dominant* (1914).
Stone, George L. "Technique of Percussion." *IM* XLVII, 8 (February 1949): 19.
Stone, George L. "Technique of Percussion." *IM* L, 6 (December 1951): 23.
GEN. BIB.: Strain, *XYLO.*

BRAND, LEO, SR. (b. ca. 1870; d. ca. January 1940, Cincinnati?, Ohio). The son of Michael Brand, who founded and conducted the Cincinnati Grand Orchestra and was assistant conductor of its successor, the Cincinnati Symphony, timpanist Leo Brand performed with Cincinnati from its inception in 1895 and was considered an expert performer on "musical glasses."
GEN. BIB.: Cook, *LDT,* p. 13 (photo).

BRATMAN, CARROLL C. (b. 27 Jun 1906, Baltimore, Maryland; d. 15 Jul 1984). A 1984 inductee into the Percussive Arts Society Hall of Fame, Carroll Bratman began playing in 1921 with the *Baltimore Evening Sun* Newsboys' Band. He studied with Adolph Riehl and Harry Soistmann and attended Peabody Conservatory on scholarship in 1924. By 1925 he was performing with the Baltimore Symphony, then took a position with the National Symphony from 1930 to 1941. A veteran of radio shows, dance bands, and recordings, he performed in the NBC and CBS staff orchestras. Carroll Musical Instruments Company (Carroll Sound, Inc.), which Bratman formed in 1945 to serve the instrument rental needs of New York–area percussionists became a clearinghouse for drummers nationwide.

SELECTED DISCOGRAPHY

Urania URLP 7144: *Chavez—Toccata*, 1954.

SELECTED BIBLIOGRAPHY

Smith, Dick. "An Interview with Carroll Bratman." *PN* XXII, 2 (January 1984): 33–35.
Smith, Dick. "Carroll Bratman Donates Historical Musical Instruments." *PN* XXII, 2 (January 1984): 33–35.

BRAUN, GEORGE A. Timpanist with Victor Herbert's Orchestra (18 seasons) and the New York Metropolitan Grand Opera Orchestra (from 1921, first five as percussionist), George Braun performed for New York's Chatauqua concert series and in the New York Philharmonic for 12 years (from ca. 1917). His percussion colleagues in the Philharmonic (ca. 1917) included *Alfred Friese, T. Wahle, and G. Wolf; and in the Opera Orchestra (ca. 1929), Paul Schulze, Alvin Broemel, and Robert Kiesow.

SELECTED BIBLIOGRAPHY

The Philharmonic Society of New York and Its Seventy–fifth Anniversary. New York: The Society, 1917.
GEN. BIB.: Cook, *LDT*, p. 11, 13, 215 (photo).

BREUER, HARRY (b. 24 Oct 1901, Brooklyn, New York; d. 22 Jun 1989, Brightwaters, New York). When Harry Breuer was 13, an illness prevented his practicing the violin, so he took up the xylophone, an instrument his father had given him, subsequently studying with xylophonist *Charles Daab. Billed as the "Boy Wonder" of the xylophone in 1919 at the New York Academy of Music, he won a job at the Strand Theater in Brooklyn, Warner Brothers' Brooklyn studios, and went on to solo with many of the large movie theater orchestras of the 1920s. In 1920, he founded the White Way Trio and made his first re-cording, "Ida, Sweet as Apple Cider." His big break came in a radio broadcast from the Roxy Theater [where he replaced *James Jerome Ross (Rosenberg)], which led to appearances on various radio shows, including *Lucky Strike Hit Parade* (1927–29), *Let's Dance, American Album of Familiar Music*, and the *RKO Hour.* He played at CBS and WOR Mutual, but his 30–year association with the NBC staff orchestra yielded performances with the *Howdy Doody* and *Shari Lewis* children's shows, the *Jack Parr Show*, and the *Tonight Show* with both Steve Allen and Johnny Carson. When the network disbanded the staff orchestra in the 1960s, he continued to record on a freelance basis and joined Carroll Bratman's Musical Instrument Service as a consultant. He performed with Paul Whiteman and Benny Goodman and was consulted by George Gershwin when the latter was composing his "American in Paris."

With *Billy Dorn and *Joe Green, he performed on marimba accompanied by strings, saxes, and rhythm in the Flotilla and Yerkes Jazzarimba Orchestras. In 1933 the *J. C. Deagan Company built an unusual instrument for Breuer that was a combination marimba, xylophone, and vibraphone. His "Chokin' the Bell" (1932) was possibly the first published vibraphone solo with note–dampening instructions. Although most remain out of print, some of his xylophone solos were reissued during the 1950s and 1980s, and he was elected to the Percussive Arts Society Hall of Fame in 1980.

SELECTED DISCOGRAPHY

Audio Fidelity AFLP 1825: *Mallet Magic: Harry Breuer and His Quintet*, 1957.
Audio Fidelity AFLP 1882: *Mallet Mischief*, 1958.
Audio Fidelity AFSD 5912: The Happy Sound of Ragtime, 1950s.
Brunswick B15731–32: "Wildflower" and "Chicken Reel" (marimba/vibraphone), ca. 1935.
Emerson 10753: "Down Where the West Begins" and "Hoodoo, Who Do You Love?" (Harry Breuer Trio), 1924.
Lang Percussion 011: *Five New Ragtime Solos*, 1981.
Melotone 12072 E: "Roxyette," ca. 1931.
Tabby Sound Ltd: *Mallets in Wonderland*, 1987.
Verve V6–8508: *Oliver Nelson*, 1963.
Verve V6–8652: *Jimmy Smith*, 1966.
Vocalion 15723: "Flapperette," ca. 1928.

SELECTED BIBLIOGRAPHY

Breuer, Harry. *Five New Ragtime Solos*. New York: Lang Percussion Co., 1981.
Bush, Jeffrey E. "Interview with Harry Breuer." *PN* XVIII, 3 (Spring/Summer 1980): 50–53.
Eyler, David P. "Development of the Marimba Ensemble in North America during the 1930s." *PN* XXXIV, 1 (February 1996): 66–71.
Eyles, Randall. "Novelty Xylophone Recollections: An Interview with Harry Breuer." *PN* XXXV, 6 (December 1997): 59–61.

Kastner, Kathleen. "The Xylophone in the United States between 1880 and 1930, Part I: The Artists." *Percussive Arts Society: Illinois Chapter Newsletter* (Winter 1986): 1–2.
Larsen, Don. "The Harry Breuer Memorial Tribute Concert." *PN* XXIX, 4 (April 1991): 55–56.
GEN. BIB.: Cahn, *XAR*.

BROWN, GEORGE NORTHCUTT (b. Louisville, Kentucky). Studying with *Cloyd Duff, James Rago, *Fred Begun, and John Baldwin, George Brown attended the University of Louisville School of Music (1977–80) and by age 23 had performed in all 50 states. He has served as principal timpanist with the U.S. Coast Guard Band (1974), U.S. Armed Forces "Bicentennial Band" (1975–77), Colorado Springs (CO) Symphony (1980–87), Mexico City Philharmonic (1985), and Utah Symphony (since 1987). His premiere recordings include works by George Crumb, Donald Erb, *William Kraft, Peter Maxwell Davies, Jacob Druckman, and George Antheil, among others. He teaches on the University of Utah faculty and publishes instructional timpani essays on the World Wide Web.

SELECTED DISCOGRAPHY

Argo 430 834–2: *Mormon Tabernacle Choir—Songs from America's Heartland*, 1991.
Elektra/Nonesuch 79229–2: *William Kraft*, 1989.
London/Decca 425–431–2: *Songs of Inspiration* (Kiri Te Kanawa/Utah Symphony), 1989.
London/Decca 436–284–4: *Simple Gifts* (Frederica Von Stade/Utah Symphony), 1992.
Time/Warner Interactive CD: *Peter and the Wolf*, 1994.
Information supplied by the subject, 1996.

BROWN, RICHARD S. (b. 10 Sep 1947, Philadelphia, Pennsylvania). Percussionist Richard Brown earned a bachelor's degree from Temple University and a master's degree from Catholic Universisty (1972), and he has performed with the U.S. Army Band (Washington, D.C., 1969–72), Chamber Symphony of Philadelphia, New York Philharmonic, Metropolitan Opera, and Grand Teton Music Festival Orchestras. A faculty member of Rice University's Shepherd School of Music and the University of St. Thomas, he was formerly with the Da Camera of Houston, the Houston Grand Opera, Houston Ballet, and Houston Symphony, which featured him as soloist on Donald Erb's "Concerto for Solo Percussionist and Orchestra" in 1977.
GEN. BIB.: Borland, *WWAMC*; PASIC® program biographies, 1992.

BROWN, TEDDY (b. Abraham Himmelbrand, New York?, New York; d. 30 Apr 1946). Xylophonist, bandleader, and comedian-actor invited to relocate to England by the Prince of Wales after the latter heard him in New York, Teddy Brown became popular in Britain (1920s) and Canada (1920s–30s). His reported 500–pound stature necessitated his sleeping in a specially designed armchair to prevent heart problems. A multitalented musician who played several instruments, he had performed with the New York Philharmonic and, during WWII, organized shows for the troops in his capacity as president of the American Overseas Artists, a service later superseded by the USO (United Services Organization).

SELECTED BIBLIOGRAPHY

"Teddy Brown." *IM* XLIV, 11 (May 1946): 26.
GEN. BIB.: Cahn, *XAR*.

BRUCE, GEORGE B. (fl. 1860s). U.S. Army drum instructor on Governor's and Bedloe's Islands (New York), George Bruce, together with the organizer of the Virginia Minstrels (1843), fifer Daniel "Dan" Decatur Emmett, wrote *The Drummers' and Fifers' Guide* in 1862. [Emmett: b. 29 Oct 1815, Mount Vernon, Ohio; d. 28 Jun 1904, Mount Vernon, Ohio; composed the folk songs "Old Dan Tucker" and "Blue Tail Fly" (1846) and the Southern Civil War anthem "Dixie" (1859).] A rudimental style drum manual, it was similar to the earlier "Ashworth's Rudimental School." [Charles Stewart Ashworth, b. 1777, was the conductor of the U.S. Marine Band (1804–16) who penned *Rules to Be Observed by Young Drummers* (1812). In 1869, the U.S. government officially adopted the *Strube Drum and Fife Instructor*, written by Gardner A. Strube and Duryeas Zouaves, which was based on a previous text, *Upton's Tactics*. Another historical text in this genre is Elias Howe's *United States Army Regulation Drum and Fife Instructor*, ca. 1868. Howe (1820–1895) was also proprietor of a Boston music store that closed its doors ca. 1930.]
GEN. BIB.: Cook, *LDT*, p. 312.

BRUFORD, WILLIAM SCOTT "BILL" (b. 17 May 1949, Seven Oaks, Kent, UK). Influenced early on by jazz, drumset artist Bill Bruford was essentially an amateur who took a few lessons with Lou Pocock of the Royal Philharmonic; after attending Leeds University briefly in 1968, he became a founding member of the British "art–rock" movement during the 1970s, touring internationally as drummer for the groups King Crimson and Yes (1968–74). Subsequent bands with whom Bruford worked included Gong, National Health, Genesis, U.K., and his own compositional vehicle Bruford (1977–80).

In the reincarnation of King Crimson (1980–84), he revolutionized drumset performance by incorporating electronic drums with his acoustic setup, blending both in linear percussive "melodies." Bruford continued this creative approach in the electroacoustic jazz ensemble Earthworks (1986–94, with Django Bates and Iain Ballamy), and its first recording was named "third best jazz album of 1987" by the newspaper *USA Today*.

A career freelancer, Bruford was elected to *Modern Drummer* magazine's Reader's Poll Hall of Fame in 1990, continues to tour and record with both Earthworks and King Crimson, and is producing a computer CD–ROM that will provide insight to his technique. As a composer, he is credited with some 160 solos or co–compositions, which are available from BMG Music and Fuji Pacific Music. Among his many collaborators for recording and/or touring are Akira Inoue, Kazumi Watanabe, the New Percussion Group of Amsterdam, David Torn, Jamaaladeen Tacuma, and Al DiMiola.

SELECTED DISCOGRAPHY

Atlantic 82665: *The Yes Album* (Yes), 1971.
Atlantic 82680: *Yes*, 1969.
Atlantic 82699–2/83010–2: *Burning for Buddy* (Buddy Rich Orchestra), 1994/1997.
Caroline 007777 8676829: *The Essential King Crimson—Frame by Frame*, 1991.
Caroline 007777 8677529: *Larks Tongues in Aspic* (King Crimson), 1973.
Caroline 007777 8712527: *Earthworks*, 1987.
Caroline 007777 8712626: *Feels Good to Me*, 1977.
Caroline 007777 8775928: *The Bruford Tapes*, 1979.
CBS 38944: *Scenario* (Al DiMeola), 1983.
Charisma GE 2001: *Seconds Out* (Genesis), 1977.
Charisma GE 2002: *Three Sides Live* (Genesis), 1982.
Discipline DGM 9604: *Thrak Attack* (King Crimson), 1996.
Discipline Global Mobile Records DGM9705: *If Summer Had Its Ghosts*, 1997.
ESD: *Missing Pieces* (National Health), 1997.
Papa Bear G01: *World Diary* (Tony Levin), 1995.
Polydor Japan H33P 20249: *Spice of Life Too* (Kazumi Watanabe), 1988.
RCA Victor 09026 61938–2: *The Symphonic Music of Yes*, 1993.

SELECTED VIDEOGRAPHY

Axis Video/Warner Brothers VH 0016: *Bruford and the Beat*, 1982.
Caroline VJMC002: *An Evening of Yes Music Plus Fragile*, 1990.
DCI VH0270: *The Making of Burning for Buddy*, pt. 1, 1996.
Laser Disc Group HM088–3184: *Spice of Life Live* (Kazumi Watanabe), 1987.
Six West SW 5706: *In the Big Dream*, 1990.
Warner Music Vision 853650250–3: *Yes Years*, 1992.

SELECTED BIBLIOGRAPHY

"Ask a Pro." *MD* XIX, 9 (September 1995): 14.
Bruford, Bill. *When in Doubt, Roll!* Cedar Grove, NJ: Modern Drummer Pub., 1988.
Bruford, William S. "A Commentary." *PN* XXIX, 5 (June 1991): 74–75.

Goodwin, S. "Bill Bruford." *MD* XIII (February 1989): 18–23.

Griffith, Mark. "Artist on Track: Bill Bruford." *MD* XXIII, 1 (January 1999): 154–157.

Lange, A., and C. Doherty. "Bill Bruford: A Drummer's Discipline." *DB* LI (February 1984): 16–19.

Micallef, Ken. "Bill Bruford: Electric Renegade." *JazzTimes* XXI, 8 (November 1991): 24–25.

Miller, William F. "King Crimson's Bill Bruford and Pat Mastelotto...A Perfect Pair." *MD* XIX, 11 (September 1995): 42–57.

Rule, Greg. "Bill Bruford: A Decade of Electronic Mastery." *Drums and Drumming* III, 2 (February 1992): 60–62.

Shore, M. "Bill Bruford." *MD* III, 1 (1979): 9–11.

Information supplied by the subject, 1996.

BUDA, FRED (b. 25 Mar 1935, Boston, Massachusetts). A drumset specialist in the percussion section of the Boston Pops Orchestra since 1968, Fred Buda has become a familiar face to television audiences who tune in to the "Pops" broadcasts. A 1953 graduate of the U.S. Naval School of Music, he later attended Boston University, earning bachelor's and master's degrees in music. Among his teachers were *Charles Smith, *Sonny Igoe, and *George Lawrence Stone. His varied musical employment has included the U. S. Navy Band (Washington, D.C., and Italy), Herb Pomeroy Jazz Orchestra, Boston Opera Orchestra, Boston Philharmonia, Ice Capades, and staff percussionist for the WGBH television station. Buda has taught on the faculties of Berklee College of Music, the New England Conservatory, and the University of Lowell.

SELECTED DISCOGRAPHY

Phillips 6514–328: *Aisle Seat—Great Film Music* (Boston Pops with John Williams), 1982.

Time–Life Records STLS–7001: *American Classics—Great Moments of Music* (Boston Pops with Arthur Fiedler), 1980.

SELECTED BIBLIOGRAPHY

Buda, Fred. "The Drumset Player with the Orchestra." *PN* XXXI, 7 (October 1993): 22.
GEN. BIB.: Larrick, *BET–CP*.

BUNKER, LAWRENCE BENJAMIN "LARRY" (b. 4 Nov 1928, Long Beach, California). Hollywood studio percussionist, drumset artist, vibist, and pianist Larry Bunker has performed with Jim Hall, Dizzy Gillespie, Chet Baker, Gerry Mulligan, Art Pepper, Shorty Rogers, Bill Evans (1963–65), Hampton Hawes, Warne Marsh, Sonny Criss, his own quartet (1963), Judy Garland (1964), and Stan Getz (1965), among others. His combined television, film, and record studio career credits are innumerable.

SELECTED DISCOGRAPHY

Blue Note B21Y46847: *Konitz Meets Mulligan*, 1953.
Blue Note B21Y–98935: *The Birth of the Cool*, vol. 2, 1953.
Blue Note BLP5059/5060: *Leonard Feather Presents—Best of the West*, 1954.
Blue Note LA532–H2: *Gerry Mulligan*, 1953.
Blue Note LA635–G: *Carmen McRae—Can't Hide Love*, 1976.
Blue Note LT–1053: *Joe Pass—Catch Me*, 1963.
Cambria CD–1071: *The Music of William Kraft*, 1993.
Candide CE–31072: *Cadence III for Violin and Two Percussionists*, 1973.
Capitol ST11242: *Threshold* (Pat Williams), 1973.
Pacific Jazz 6K18P9260: *Cool Baker*, vol. 2 (Chet Baker), 1953.
Pacific Jazz 77: *Extension* (Clare Fischer), 1963.
Prestige PRLP7067: *Quartet* (Hampton Hawes), 1959.
RCA LPM 2880: *Something's Coming* (Gary Burton), 1963.
RCA LSP3642: *The Time Machine* (Gary Burton), 1966.
Riverside 9487: *At Shelly's Manne–Hole* (Bill Evans), 1963.
Savoy SV–0115: *Surf Ride* (Art Pepper), 1952.
Sheffield Lab 5: *Discovered Again!* (Dave Grusin), 1976.
Time 2140: *Taste of Drums*, 1969.
Verve 68613/POCJ–1908: *Trio '65* (Bill Evans), 1965.
Verve (J) OOMJ3480/89: *Billie Holiday*, 1955.
Verve MGV2043: *Anita O'Day*, 1956.
Verve MGV2069: *Woody Herman*, 1957.
Verve V6–8803: *Bill Evans Trio*, 1964.

SELECTED VIDEOGRAPHY

Rhapsody Films: *Zoot Sims Quartet*, 1987.
GEN. BIB.: Hunt, *52nd St.*; Kernfeld, *NGJ*, by J. Kent Williams

BURNS, ROY (b. Emporia, Kansas). Starting drums at age 8, Roy Burns studied with Jack Miller in Kansas City, *Jim Chapin, and *Henry Adler and freelanced in New Orleans before moving to New York. He played with Woody Herman starting in 1957, spent three years with Benny Goodman, and worked with *Lionel Hampton, Charles Mingus, Ben Webster, Charlie Shavers, Buck Clayton, and the Joe Bushkin Trio. A veteran of the recording studio, his television performance credits include the NBC Orchestra and the *Merv Griffin*, *Steve Allen*, and *Tonight* shows. Burns is an active clinician, has written a plethora of drum magazine articles, and is part owner of the drum company Aquarian Accessories (est. 1980). He received *Modern Drummer* magazine's Editors' Achievement Award in 1998.

SELECTED DISCOGRAPHY

Atco 33108: *Destry Rides Again* (Roland Hanna), 1959.
FPM 1001: *Big, Bad, and Beautiful*, 1970.

Mosaic MD5–173: *The Complete Verve Recordings—Teddy Wilson Trio*, 1952/1997.
Roulette R–52095: *Skin Burns*, 1961.

SELECTED BIBLIOGRAPHY

Allan, B. "On the Clinic Trail with Roy Burns." *MD* I, 2 (1977): 4–5.
Burns, Roy, and Joey Farris. *One Surface Learning*. Miami, FL: Warner Bros., 1996.
Burns, Roy, and Saul Feldstein. *Snare Drum Music*. New York: Alfred Publishing, 1977.
Burns, Roy, and Saul Feldstein. *Drum Set Music*. New York: Alfred Publishing, 1977.
Iero, Cheech. "My First Gig." *MD* XX, 12 (October 1997): 148–151.
Van Horn, Rick. "Aquarian Accessories." *MD* XXI, 10 (December 1996): 130–136.

BURTON, GARY (b. 23 Jan 1943, Anderson, Indiana). After early marimba lessons and local "gigs" at the age of 8, jazz vibraphone artist Gary Burton made his recording debut with guitarists Hank Garland and Chet Atkins in Nashville in 1960, studied piano at the Berklee College of Music from 1960 to 1962 (honorary doctorate, 1989), toured South America in 1962, and by 1963 had traversed the Far East with the George Shearing Quintet. After two years in the Stan Getz Quartet (1964–66), he formed his own groups and earned a *Down Beat* magazine award as "Jazzman of the Year" in 1968. His independent four–mallet technique opened musical doors for the popularization of the vibraphone with a new generation unfamiliar with the pioneering work of *Lionel Hampton, *Milt Jackson, and *Red Norvo. Burton's many musical collaborations and recordings include *Dick Schory's Percussion Pops Orchestra (an 18–piece orchestra fronted by three percussionists), Pat Metheny, Keith Jarrett, Chick Corea, and Makato Ozone. His sound is generally characterized by a straight tone, eschewing the use of the motor–driven mechanical vibrato supplied on most vibraphones. He is a prolific recording (50+ compact discs) and touring artist and has been associated with the Berklee School since 1971 as faculty, 1985 as dean of curriculum, and 1996 as executive vice president. Burton was voted into the Percussive Arts Society Hall of Fame in 1988 and has received three Grammy® Awards.

SELECTED DISCOGRAPHY

Atlantic SD–1577: *Gary Burton and Keith Jarrett*, 1971.
Atlantic SD–1598: *Alone at Last*, 1971.
Bluebird 6280–1–RB–B: *Gary Burton—Artist's Choice*, 1963/1988.
Columbia 67929: *Afterglow* (movie soundtrack), 1997.
Concord CCD–4749–2: *Gary Burton & Friends—Departure*, 1997.
Concord 4773–2: *Daydream* (Karrin Allyson), 1997.
Concord 4793–2: *Astor Piazzolla Reunion—A Tango Excursion*, 1998.
Concord 4803–2: *Like Minds*, 1998.

ECM 1–1140: *Duet* (with Chick Corea), 1979.
ECM 1–1182/1024 ST: *Crystal Silence*, 1973.
ECM 1030–ST: *The New Quartet*, 1973.
ECM 1040–ST: *Seven Songs for Quartet and Chamber Orchestra*, 1974.
ECM 1055: *Hotel Hello*, 1975.
ECM–1–1137: *Eberhard Weber—Fluid Rustle*, 1979.
ECM 1051ST: *Ring—the Gary Burton Quintet with Eberhard Weber*, 1974.
GRP GR–9598: *Reunion*, 1990.
GRP GRD–9685: *Gary Burton and Friends—Six Pack*, 1992.
GRP GRD–9738: *Gary Burton and Rebecca Parris—It's Another Day*, 1994.
RCA–ACL–1–0200: *Norwegian Wood*, 1973.
RCA LSP 3835: *Duster*, 1966.
RCA Victor LSP 2725: *3 in Jazz*, 1963.
RCA Victor LPM 3360: *The Groovy Sound of Music*, 1965.
RCA Victor LPM 2420: *New Vibe Man in Town*, 1962.
RCA Victor LSP–2665: *Who Is Gary Burton?* 1963.
RCA Victor LSP–3642: *The Time Machine*, 1966.
RCA Victor LSP–2880: *Something's Coming!* 1963.
RCA LSP 3901: *Lofty Fake Anagram* (Gary Burton), 1967.
RCA LSP 3985: *Gary Burton Quartet in Concert*, 1968.
Verve V6–8600: *Stan Getz*, 1964.
Verve V6–8623: *Stan Getz*, 1964.

SELECTED BIBLIOGRAPHY

Burton, Gary. "Evolution of Mallet Techniques, 1973." *Percussionist* X, 3 (Spring 1973): 74.
Burton, Gary. *Four–Mallet Studies*. Glenview, IL: Creative Music, 1968.
Burton, Gary. *Introduction to Jazz Vibes*. Glenview, IL: Creative Music, 1965.
Burton, Gary. *Six Unaccompanied Solos for Vibe*. Glenview, IL: Creative Music, 1966.
DeMichael, Don. "Gary Burton: Portrait of the Artist as a Young Vibraharpist." *DB* XXXII, 16 (29 Jul 1965): 20–22.
Eyles, Randall. "A Conversation with Gary Burton, Pts. 1–2." *PN* XXV, 2/4 (Spring/Winter 1987): 8–9/63–64.
Howland, Harold. "Gary Burton: The Enfant Terrible at Forty, Pt. 2." *PN* XXI, 5 (July 1983): 62–64.
Larrick, Geary. *Analytical and Biographical Writings in Percussion Music*. New York: Peter Lang Publishing, 1989.
Mattingly, Rick. "Gary Burton." *MP* I, 1 (December 1984–February 1985): 6–11.
Morgenstern, Dan. "Gary Burton: Upward Bound." *DB* XXXV, 16 (8 Aug 1968): 14–15.
Schroeter, John. "Gary Burton: Vibraphonic." *Stick It* I, 1 (January 1998): 37–43.
Wanamaker, Jay. "Gary Burton: A Profile of a Man and His Music, Pt. II." *PN* XVIII, 1 (Fall 1979): 36–37.
GEN. BIB.: Larrick, *BET–CP*.

C

CAHN, WILLIAM L. "BILL" (b. 11 Nov 1946, Philadelphia, Pennsylvania). Principal percussionist of the Rochester (NY) Philharmonic (1968–95), Bill Cahn received both the performer's certificate and a bachelor's degree from the Eastman School in 1968. His teachers and major influences have included *William Street, *John Beck, *Alan Abel, and *Fred Hinger. Cahn is known as a performer, composer, discographer, and publisher of percussion music. His association with the eclectic percussion ensemble NEXUS (Percussive Arts Society Hall of Fame, 1999) has given him a vehicle for which to produce various unusual projects such as accompanying silent movies on stage with "real–time" percussion ensemble arrangements. His wife Ruth McLean Cahn is herself a distinguished percussionist and teacher who has performed with the Rochester Philharmonic for 28 years. She is also president of Project UNIQUE, which brings the arts to inner–city children.

SELECTED DISCOGRAPHY

A&M LP–SP–4698: *Common Ground* (Paul Winter Consort), 1978.
Bainbridge BT–6241 et al.: *Rochester Philharmonic Orchestra.*
Black Sun CD 15002–2: *The Altitude of the Sun* (NEXUS and Paul Horn), 1989.
CBC Musica Viva 2–1037: *Dance of the Octopus* (NEXUS et al.), 1989.
CBC SMCD 5154: *Music for Heaven and Earth* (NEXUS with Esprit Orchestra), 1995.
Cum Laude D–VCS 9067: *A Midsummer Night's Dream* (Rochester Philharmonic and Pops), 1984.
Epic LP KE 33561: *Paul Horn and NEXUS*, 1975.
Living Music Records LP–LMR–1: *Callings* (Paul Winter Consort), 1980.
NEXUS CD 10251: *The Best of NEXUS* (1976–86), 1989.
NEXUS CD 10262: *NEXUS Now*, 1990.

NEXUS CD 10273: *NEXUS Plays the Novelty Music of George Hamilton Green*,
    1990.
NEXUS CD 10284: *NEXUS Ragtime Concert*, 1992.
NEXUS CD 10295: *NEXUS—Origins*, 1992.
NEXUS CD 10306: *The Story of Percussion in the Orchestra* (NEXUS and Roch-
    ester Philharmonic), 1992.
NEXUS CD 10317: *Voices* (NEXUS and Rochester Philharmonic), 1994.
NEXUS CD 10339: *The Solo Percussionist* (Music of William Cahn), 1997.
NEXUS CD 10410: *Toccata*, 1997.
Papa Bear Records CD G01: *World Diary—Tony Levin* (NEXUS et al.), 1995.
Point Records 454 126–2: *Farewell to Philosophy* (Gavin Bryars), 1996.
Pro–Arte CDD 220: *Christmas at the Pops* (Rochester Philharmonic and Pops),
    1985.
Pro–Arte CDD 264: *Syncopated Clock* (Rochester Philharmonic and Pops), 1986.
Pro–Arte CDD 350: *Pop Go the Beatles* (Rochester Philharmonic and Pops), 1987.
Pro–Arte CDS 576: *Classic Connections* (Rochester Philharmonic and Pops), 1991.
Pro–Arte CDS 577: *Romancing the Film* (Rochester Philharmonic and Pops), 1992.
Sony Classical SK 63044: *Takemitsu—From Me Flows What You Call Time* (Pa-
    cific Symphony), 1998.

SELECTED VIDEOGRAPHY

Necavenue A88V–3: *Supercussion* (Tokyo Music Joy Festival), 1988.

SELECTED BIBLIOGRAPHY

Beck, John. "Bill Cahn." *PN* XXXIV, 4 (August 1996): 10–12.
Bump, Michael. "A Conversation with NEXUS." *PN* XXXI, 5 (June 1993): 50–51.
Cahn, Willam L. "Rochester's Classic Percussion: A Short History of the Percus-
    sion Section of the Rochester Philharmonic Orchestra." *PN* XXX, 5 (June
    1992): 64–74.
Cahn, William. *Performing Live with MIDI: A Percussionist's (and Anyone Else's)
    Guide to the Fundamentals*. Everett, PA: Honeyrock Publishing, 1993.
Cahn, William. *The Xylophone in Acoustic Recordings (1877–1929)*. Bloomfield,
    NY: William L. Cahn Publishing, 1996.
Cahn, William. "The Xylophone in Acoustic Recordings (1877–1929)." *Percus-
    sionist* XVI, 3 (Spring/Summer 1979): 106–132.
Larrick, Geary. *Analytical and Biographical Writings in Percussion Music*. New
    York: Peter Lang Publishing, 1989.
Mattingly, Rick. "Nexus." *MP* I, 3 (June–August 1985): 8–13/36–41.
GEN. BIB.: Larrick, *BET–CP*.

CALZARETTA, CHARLES "CHUCK." A vibraphone soloist with the Art
Van Damme Quintette, Chuck Calzaretta performed for radio and television as an
NBC artist and recorded for the Columbia and Capitol labels (ca. 1940s–50s).

CANDIDO (b. Candido Camero de Guerra, 22 Apr 1921, El Cerro District, Havana, Cuba). Starting on bass and guitar at 14 but later switching to bongos (ca. 1946) and congas, self–taught Latin percussionist Candido played in clubs and on CMQ radio (Havana) before settling first in Miami and then New York (1952). His first Latin jazz recording was with an Afro–Cuban band led by Machito, followed by record dates and performances with the Billy Taylor Trio (1953–54). Candido toured the United States (1964), with *Lionel Hampton (1977), and with the Stan Kenton Orchestra (1954). He recorded and/or appeared with Coleman Hawkins, Woody Herman, George Shearing, Errol Garner (1954), Dizzy Gillespie (1952/1954), Duke Ellington, Charlie Parker (Carnegie Hall), and *Tito Puente, among many others. He was a featured artist with the Brooklyn Philharmonic in 1996.

SELECTED DISCOGRAPHY

ABC Paramount 125: *Candido, Featuring Al Cohn*, 1965.
ABC Paramount 178: *Candido—Calypso Dance Party*, 1957.
ABC Paramount 180: *Candido—The Volcanic*, 1957.
ABC Paramount 236: *Candido—In Indigo*, 1958.
ABC Paramount 286: *Candido—Latin Fire*, 1959.
ABC Paramount 453: *Candido—Comparsa*, 1963.
Blue Note 84333: *Bobby Hutcherson—Now!* 1969.
Blue Note 84342: *Green Is Beautiful* (Grant Green), 1970.
Blue Note 84357: *Candido—The Beautiful*, 1970.
Blue Note 84361: *Coalition* (Elvin Jones), 1970.
Blue Note LA506–H2: *The Prime Element* (Elvin Jones), 1969.
Jazz World JWD 102.303: *Dexterity* (Dexter Gordon), 1994.
Milan 7313835770–2: *Bending towards the Light...A Jazz Nativity*, 1995.
Polydor 5063: *Candido—Drum Fever*, 1973.
Prestige/OJCCD–1728–2: *Bennie Green Blows His Horn*, 1955/1988.
Roulette R 52078: *Candido—Conga Soul*, 1962.
Solid State 18066: *Candido—Thousand Finger Man*, 1970.
Verve MGV2024: *Chico O'Farrill and His Orchestra*, 1951.
Verve MGV2030: *Woody Herman and the Woodchoppers*, 1953.
Verve MGV8191/MGV8394: *Dizzy Gillespie and His Orchestra*, 1954/1960.
GEN. BIB.: Kernfeld, *NGJ*, by Catherine Collins. Information supplied by the subject, 1996.

CAPP, FRANK "FRANKIE" (b. Frank Cappuccio, 20 Aug 1931, Worcester, Massachusetts). Drumset artist Frank Capp moved to Los Angeles (1953) after having performed with Neal Hefti and Stan Kenton (1951). His performance and/or recording collaborators have included Stan Getz, Peggy Lee (1953–54), Billy May, Ella Fitzgerald (1955–56), Red Mitchell, Harry James, Art Pepper, André Previn (1957–64), Benny Goodman (1958), Ernestine Anderson, *Terry Gibbs (1960), Joe Williams, and Barney Kessell (1965). He worked in television and film studios (Warner Brothers) during the 1960s–70s and established the Capp–Pierce Juggernaut orchestra in 1975.

SELECTED DISCOGRAPHY

Concord 183: *Juggernaut Strikes Again*, 1981.
Concord 27: *Hello Rev.* (Bill Berry), 1976.
Concord CCD–4469: *The Frank Capp Trio Presents Ricky Woodard*, 1991.
Contemporary 7575: *Like Previn!* 1960.
Emerald 2401: *On Fire* (Barney Kessel), 1965.
JMI–7501–2: *The Tenor Trio* (Ernie Watts).
Verve MGVS6145: *Terry Gibbs Quintet*, 1960.
GEN. BIB.: Kernfeld, *NGJ*, by Rick Mattingly.

CAREY, DAVID AARON (b. 14 Feb 1926, Pittsburgh, Pennsylvania). David Carey studied at the University of Pittsburgh (1950–52) and with *Walter Rosenberger (1980). Percussionist on several Frank Sinatra tours, he has played for Dick Cavett on CBS–TV; performed in the NBC recording studios, for Broadway productions, Composer's Orchestra, Westchester Symphony, Hudson Valley Symphony, and Long Island Symphony; recorded television commercials and movie sountracks; and even appeared on camera in Woody Allen's *Radio Days*. Composer of the "Suite for Xylophone and Orchestra" (Galaxy Music, 1975), among other works for percussion, he has fronted various jazz combos.

SELECTED DISCOGRAPHY

Blue Note LA606–G: *Just a Matter of Time* (Marlena Shaw), 1976.
Pablo 2313–141: *Things Are Getting Better All the Time* (J. J. Johnson), 1983/1994.

SELECTED BIBLIOGRAPHY

Carey, Dave. "A Hard Question." *PN* XVI, 2 (Winter 1978): 12.
Information supplied by the subject, 1996.

CAREY, GEORGE J. (b. 1895, Boston, Massachusetts; d. 28 Jan 1958, Cincinnati, Ohio). George Carey grew up in Rochester, New York, studied with *George Braun and Harry Waterhouse, and started playing professionally around 1906. He was percussionist and xylophonist with the Royal Hussar Band of Chicago until he was shipped to France during WWI with the U.S. Marines, eventually serving as assistant director and solo timpanist of the 11th Regiment Marine Band. During the summers of 1920–26 [Bierley states 1923–25], Carey performed as timpanist and featured solo xylophonist in the United States and abroad with John Philip Sousa's Band. The winter months found him in the percussion sections of Frank Simon's ARMCO, Edwin Franko Goldman, or Frank Innes Bands, the Victor Herbert Orchestra (1924–   ), or the Metropolitan Opera (ca. 1920–25) or playing for vaudeville on the Keith circuit. Principal percussionist and groundbreaking xylophone and marimba soloist with the Cincinnati Symphony (1925–58), Carey actually passed away during a performance with Cincinnati. He could be heard on NBC radio broadcasts and was the composer of several xylophone solos, none of which was ever published.

SELECTED BIBLIOGRAPHY

Bierley, Paul E. *The Works of John Philip Sousa.* Columbus, OH: Integrity Press, 1984.
"Closing Chord: George J. Carey." *IM* LVI, 9 (March 1958): 32.
Strain, James. "Xylophone Pioneer: George J. Carey." *PN* XXXIII, 4 (August 1995): 86–87.
GEN. BIB.: Cook, *LDT*, p. 10, 16, 437b; Strain, *XYLO.*

CARLYSS, GERALD "GERRY" (b. 12 Sep 1941, Chicago, Illinois). Former member of the New York Philharmonic (1963–65), Gerry Carlyss studied with Robert Lentz (Pasadena), *Félix Passerone (Paris Conservatory), *Morris Lang, and *Morris Goldenberg, earning a master's degree from the Juilliard School (1965), where he was under the tutelage of *Saul Goodman. He served as principal timpanist with the Cincinnati Symphony (1965–67) and Philadelphia Orchestra (1967–88), has performed with the Boston and St. Louis Symphonies, the Metropolitan Opera, and the New York City Opera and Ballet and has chaired percussion departments at the Curtis Institute and Indiana University.

SELECTED DISCOGRAPHY

CRI CD 781: *Druckman—Windows for Orchestra* et al., 1963/1998.

SELECTED BIBLIOGRAPHY

Kupferberg, Herbert. *Those Fabulous Philadelphians.* New York: Charles Scribner's Sons, 1969.
Wacker, Jonathan. "Gerald Carlyss: On Developing an Orchestra Timpanist." *PN* XXXV, 3 (June 1997): 61–65.

CARRINGTON, TERRI LYNE (b. 4 Aug 1965, Medford, Massachusetts). Born into a musical family, Terri Lyne Carrington tried saxophone at 5, but she settled on drums at 7 and by 11 studied at the Berklee College of Music with *Alan Dawson. "Sitting in" with first–rate jazzers who included Clark Terry, Dizzy Gillespie, and Joe Williams, she established a reputation that led to an early guest spot on the *To Tell the Truth* television show. Her debut album, "TLC and Friends," featured pianist Kenny Barron and her father, saxophonist Sonny Carrington. In 1983 she was honored by the International Association of

Jazz Educators' "Young Talent Program" and moved to New York, where she collaborated with Stan Getz, David Sanborn, Pharoah Sanders, Wayne Shorter, James Moody, Dianne Reeves, and others. Relocating to Los Angeles in 1989, Carrington was staff drummer with the *Arsenio Hall Show*, played with Al Jarreau (ca. 1991–94), Herbie Hancock, Joe Sample, and others, and appeared in the films *Beat Street*, *Without You I'm Nothing*, and *Harley Davidson and the Marlboro Man*. A 1989 Grammy® Award nominee ("Best Jazz Instrumental"), she performed at the 1997 JVC Jazz Festival, has served as a clinician at schools throughout the United States, and produced the Dianne Reeves compact disc *That Day* on the Blue Note label. Carrington's career was profiled in 1989 on the CBS–TV program *Sunday Morning*.

SELECTED DISCOGRAPHY

32 Jazz 32055: *Chapters 1 & 2* (Mulgrew Miller), 1998.
Atlantic Jazz 82764–2: *Live at Cicada* (Nino Tempo), 1995.
Blue Note CDP 7243 8 56458 2 2: *Doky Brothers 2*, 1997.
Blue Note CDP 7243 8 56973 2 6: *That Day* (Dianne Reeves), 1997.
Impulse 190: *PanaMonk* (Danilo Perez), 1996.
Polygram 837 697–4: *Real Life Story* (Grammy® Award nominee), 1989.

SELECTED BIBLIOGRAPHY

Coffin, Jim. "Terri Lyne Carrington: Coordination and Technique—That's It!" *PN* XXXV, 5 (October 1997): 12.
Flans, Robyn. "Female Drummers Round Table." *MD* XX, 3 (March 1996): 64–78.
Flans, Robyn. "TLC: Terri Lyne Carrington." *MD* XIII, 9 (September 1989): 18–23.
Handy, D. Antoinette. *Black Women in American Bands and Orchestras*, 2nd ed. Lanham, MD: Scarecrow Press, Inc., 1998.
Panken, Ted. "JVC Jazz Festival Celebrates 25th Anniversary." *Jazz Educators Journal* XXX, 1 (July 1997): 48–55.
PASIC® program biographies, 1994, 1997.

CASTKA, JOSEPH "JOE" (d. 19 Aug 1984). Principal percussionist at the Roxy Theater (1925–32) and Radio City Music Hall (1932–50), Joseph Castka also performed with the New York Philharmonic, Metropolitan Opera Orchestra, Symphony of the Air, Bolshoi Ballet, and NBC Symphony under Toscanini. Radio shows on which he played include the *General Motors Motorama*, *Firestone Hour*, and *Bell Telephone Hour*.

SELECTED DISCOGRAPHY

Capitol P–8507: *Bartók—Music for Strings, Percussion, and Celeste* (includes Alvin Broemel, percussion), 1960.

SELECTED BIBLIOGRAPHY

Baldwin, Dr. John, ed. "In Memoriam: Joseph Castka." *PN* XXIII, 2 (January 1985): 13.

CATLETT, SIDNEY "BIG SID" (b. 17 Jan 1910, Evansville, Indiana; d. 25 Mar 1951, Chicago, Illinois). A pianist who switched to drums in school band, Sid Catlett was influenced by *Zutty Singleton and started his drumset career at age 16 in Chicago playing his first professional engagements with Darnell Howard in 1928. Catlett's first recording with Sammy Stewart in Chicago (1928) and subsequent move to New York led to jobs with Stewart (1929–30), Elmer Snowden (1931–32), Benny Carter (1932–33), Rex Stewart (1933), Jeter–Pillars Band (1935), Fletcher Henderson (1936), Don Redman (1936–38), Louis Armstrong (sporadically, 1938–42/All–Stars, 1947–49), Sidney Bechet (1940–41), Benny Goodman (1941–42), Teddy Wilson (1942–44), Dizzy Gillespie (1944–'45), Duke Ellington, Don Byas, Ben Webster, Charlie Parker, Count Basie, Lester Young, Eddie Condon (1949, NBC–TV Orchestra and recordings on the Atlantic label), Bob Wilber (1950), McKinney's Cotton Pickers, Sam Wooding, and others. A true showman who won *Esquire* magazine's Gold Award in the drum category in 1944 and 1945, he was versatile in any jazz style with both large and small groups, leading his own quartets (1946–47) and his own big band (1946). A denizen of the night, the friendly, gregarious Catlett left Armstrong's All–Stars in 1949 because of ill health, stopped recording in 1950, and freelanced in Chicago, New York, and Boston until he succumbed to kidney trouble and heart failure.

SELECTED DISCOGRAPHY

A Touch of Magic 6: *Miss Brown to You* (Billie Holiday), 1937–49.
ABC/Impulse ASH 9272B/Jazz Odyssey JO 008: *The Drums*, 1989.
Columbia C3T 57596: *A Study in Frustration* (Fletcher Henderson), 1994.
Columbia KG 31617: *Teddy Wilson and His All–Stars*, 1973.
Commodore/Teldec 8.24293zP: *Chu Berry—A Giant of the Tenor Sax*, 1938/1986.
Decca/MCA2–4057: *Satchmo at Symphony Hall* (Louis Armstrong and His All–Stars), 1947/1980.
Dets: *Duke Ellington*, vols. 26–27.
EmArcy 26010: *Lester Leaps Again* (Lester Young), 1943.
Epic SN 6042: *Swing Street* (Max Kaminsky), 1934.
Epic/Columbia CJT 40834: *Benny Goodman*, vol. 2—*Clarinet À La King*, 1987.
FDC 1001/1010: *Metropolitan Opera House Jam Session* (Lionel Hampton), 1944/1979/1986.
London LL1387: *Spike Hughes Orchestra*, 1933.
Mercury 830 920–2: *Complete Lester Young*, 1943.
Mosaic MD 12–170: *Classical Capitol Jazz Sessions*, 1997.
Mosaic MR1–108: *The Port of Harlem Jazzmen*, 1939.
Mosaic MR1–115: *Jimmy Hamilton and the Duke's Men*, 1945.
Mosaic MR4–107: *John Hardee's Swingtet*, 1946.

Mosaic MR6–109: *Blue Note Jazzmen* (Edmond Hall, James P. Johnson, Sidney De Paris), 1943–44.

Mosaic MR6–110: *Sidney Bechet—Blue Note Quartet*, 1940.

Musicraft MVSCD–53: *Shaw 'Nuff* (Dizzy Gillespie), 1945/1992.

Musidisc 550212: *Metropolitan Opera House Jam Session* (Lionel Hampton), 1944/1991.

Prestige PR 7643: *Benny Carter*, 1933.

Prestige P–24030: *In the Beginning* (Dizzy Gillespie), 1973.

Savoy SV–0152: *Groovin' High* (Dizzy Gillespie), 1945.

Signature AK–40950: *The Big Three: Coleman Hawkins, Ben Webster, Lester Young*, 1946.

Verve MGV8132: *Carnegie Hall Concert* (Hank Jones), 1947.

SELECTED VIDEOGRAPHY

DCI VH0248: *Legends of Jazz Drumming, Pt. 1, 1920–50*, 1996.

Soundies Corp./Afro–Am Distributing: *Louis Armstrong and His Orchestra, 1942–65* (1986).

Warner Brothers Film: *Jammin' the Blues*, 1944.

SELECTED BIBLIOGRAPHY

Hoefer, George. "Big Sid." *DB* XXXIII, 6 (24 Mar 1966): 26–29.

Hutton, James Michael. "Sidney 'Big Sid' Catlett: The Development of Modern Jazz Drumming Style." *PN* XXX, 1 (October 1991): 14–17.

Shultz, Thomas. "A History of Jazz Drumming." *Percussionist* XVI, 3 (Spring/Summer 1979): 120–121.

Stewart, Rex. "My Man, Big Sid: Recollections of a Great Drummer." *DB* XXXIII, 23 (17 Nov 1966): 20–22.

Ulanov, Barry. "Sidney Catlett, 1910–1951." *Metronome* (June 1951): 8.

GEN. BIB.: Hunt, *52nd St.*; Kernfeld, *NGJ*, by J. Bradford Robinson; Korall, *DM*; Southern, *BDA–AAM*; Spagnardi, *GJD*.

CHAMBERS, JOSEPH ARTHUR "JOE" (b. 25 Jun 1942, Stoneacre, Virginia). Launching his career in Washington, D.C., drumset artist, vibist, and composer Joe Chambers relocated to New York, where, during the 1960s he performed and/or recorded with legendary jazz greats such as *Bobby Hutcherson, Eric Dolphy, Donald Byrd, Freddie Hubbard, Duke Pearson, Andrew Hill, Sam Rivers, Chick Corea, Wayne Shorter, Miroslav Vitous, Jimmy Giuffre, and Joe Henderson. The decades of the 1970s–80s brought collaborations with Chet Baker, Joe Zawinul, Tommy Flanagan, Sonny Rollins, Reggie Workman, Charles Mingus, Art Farmer, and others. His compositions have been recorded by several groups, including Max Roach's M'Boom Re: Percussion, of which he was an original member (1970).

SELECTED DISCOGRAPHY

Atlantic 8803: *Me, Myself an Eye* (Charles Mingus), 1978.
Bay 8018: *New York Concerto*, 1981.
Blue Note 84231: *Happenings* (Bobby Hutcherson), 1966.
Blue Note 96685: *Mirrors*, 1999.
Columbia IC36247: *M'Boom Re: Percussion* (Max Roach), 1979.
Denon CCD 79517: *Phantom of the City*, 1992.
Finite 1976–2: *New World*, 1975.
Muse 5035: *The Almoravid*, 1971/1973.
Red Records 174: *Hands of Fire* (Ray Mantilla), 1984.
GEN. BIB.: Kernfeld, *NGJ*, by Rick Mattingly.

CHAPIN, JAMES "JIM" (b. 1919). Referred to as "the most renowned non-famous drummer in the world" and inducted into the Percussive Arts Society Hall of Fame in 1995, Jim Chapin attended college in 1936, started drums in spring 1937, and was playing gigs by summer 1938. He performed in Larry Bennet's group with Flip Phillips in New York (1942–43) before he was drafted into the army during WWII. Following his military service, Chapin toured with Glen Gray and his Casa Loma Orchestra, played in Atlanta, and worked at New York's Roseland and Acadia ballrooms with groups that included *Red Norvo, Tommy Dorsey, Tony Pastor, and Woody Herman. He credits his teacher, *Sanford Moeller, for initially bringing to his attention the concepts of limb independence and coordination that he applies in his legendary "rite of passage" drumset method book *Advanced Techniques for the Modern Drummer*. Compiled in the early 1940s, it has gone through numerous reprints since 1948 and was followed by a sequel, *Independence: The Open End*, in 1971.

A tribute to Chapin's percussive prowess: *Gene Krupa, who earlier had rejected Chapin's inquiry for lessons in 1936, appealed to Chapin for weekly lessons which he gave him during 1968–69. Among those with whom he has recorded are Simon and Garfunkel, and his son, the late singer Harry Chapin. He has served as artist–in–residence at the University of Maine, taught at the Hartnett National Studios and the Brooklyn Conservatory of Modern Music, and was recipient of the "Drum Master" Award in New York in 1997.

SELECTED DISCOGRAPHY

Classic Jazz CJ 6: *The Jim Chapin Sextet*, 1950s.
Classic Jazz CJ 7: *Skin Tight* (same as MMO 5002 but Chapin plays drum parts), 1977.
HQ Percussion Products HQCD 101: *Jim Chapin: Songs, Solos, Stories*, 1995.
Music Minus One 125: *Fun with Drum Sticks*, 1977.
Music Minus One 5001: *Theory and Practice of Modern Jazz Drumming*, 1970s.
Music Minus One 5002: *For Drummers Only!* 1990s.
Music Minus One 5003: *Wipe Out*, 1970/1990s.
Music Minus One 5004: *Sit In [Drummer Delights]*, 1974/1990s.

SELECTED VIDEOGRAPHY

DCI VH0123: *Jim Chapin—Speed, Power, Control, Endurance*, 1992.

SELECTED BIBLIOGRAPHY

Chapin, Jim. *Advanced Techniques for the Modern Drummer*. New York: Jim
   Chapin, 1948.
Chapin, Jim. *Independence: The Open End*. New York: Jim Chapin, 1971.
Lipincott, Proctor [sic]. "Jim Chapin, Drummer." *PN* XVIII, 1 (Fall 1979): 51 [edited
   and reprinted from *New York Times* (Sunday, 1 Apr 1979)].
Mattingly, Rick. "Jim Chapin." *PN* XXXIII, 6 (December 1995): 6–7.
Mattingly, Rick. "Jim Chapin: 75 Years of Independence." *MD* XVIII (September
   1994): 26–29.

CHARLES, TEDDY (b. Theodore Charles Cohen, 13 Apr 1928, Chicopee
Falls, Massachusetts). A self–taught jazz vibist who attended the Juilliard
School (1946), Teddy Charles was known as an arranger-composer who worked
with Benny Goodman, Artie Shaw, George Shearing, and Charles Mingus' Jazz
Composers' Workshop (1954–55). From 1946 he played professionally in
various bands, in 1952 led his own trio, which played on the *Voice of America*
radio program, and in the 1960s wrote experimental works that were forerunners
of "free jazz" and formed the Polaris record label (1965).

SELECTED DISCOGRAPHY

Atlantic 1229: *The Teddy Charles Tentet*, 1956.
Atlantic 1274: *A Word from Bird*, 1956.
Blue Note 40034: *Charles Mingus—Town Hall Concert*, 1962.
Prestige 132: *Teddy Charles and His Trio*, 1951.
Prestige 164: *New Directions*, 1953.

SELECTED BIBLIOGRAPHY

"Musicians in the News." *IM* (June 1952): 30.
GEN. BIB.: Kernfeld, *NGJ*, by Max Harrison.

CHENOWETH, VIDA S. (b. 18 Oct 1928, Enid, Oklahoma). A 1994 inductee into the Percussive Arts Society Hall of Fame, Dr. Vida Chenoweth initially
studied piano and clarinet, starting marimba at age 12 as the result of a finger
infection. She early on championed the acceptance of the marimba into serious
music circles, stimulating interest in new works written solely for the instrument—more than 20 of which have been written for and/or dedicated to her.
After attending William Woods College (Jameson Conservatory of Music in
Fulton, MO; 1947–49) and studying French at the L'Alliance Française (Paris)

in 1950, she received a double bachelor's degree in music literature and criticism and in performance from Northwestern University (1951). At the latter Chenoweth studied marimba with *Clair Omar Musser and performed with Musser's Marimba Orchestra at the Chicago National Association of Music Merchants (NAMM) convention in 1951. She earned a master's degree in music theory and percussion in 1954 from the American Conservatory in Chicago and toured that same year as composer, percussionist, and marimbist with a dance troupe from the University of Wisconsin at Madison.

As a concert artist, Chenoweth won the 30–state marimba contest sponsored by the *Chicago Tribune* in 1948, performing as guest soloist before an audience of 80,000 at the Chicagoland Music Festival, which was held at Chicago's Soldier Field (1948). She later presented the first concert of works written exclusively for the marimba (Chicago, 1953), appearing as soloist with major orchestras and on the *Arthur Godfrey* and other television shows. She debuted at New York's Town Hall in 1956, and her critically acclaimed Carnegie Hall premiere of Robert Kurka's "Concerto for Marimba" (11 Nov 1959), which she had commissioned, legitimized both the marimba and her career. Among her approximately 1,000 recitals involving every continent throughout the globe was a command performance for the president of Guatemala in 1960 and a European performance tour in 1962 (Vienna, Antwerp, Brussels, and Paris).

Chenoweth studied Spanish at the Instituto Guatemalteco Americano and received a U.S. State Department (Fulbright) grant to study Guatemalan marimbas (1957). Later pursuits included Greek and biblical literature at the Asbury Theological Seminary (1962–63), and in 1974 she was awarded the Ph.D. in ethnomusicology by the University of Auckland (New Zealand). Surviving a gas explosion that threatened the loss of the fingers on her right hand, she gave a "penultimate" concert with the Tulsa Philharmonic (OK) in 1964, continuing to perform occasional concerts. Chenoweth then chose linguistics as her life's work, ultimately translating the *New Testament* of the *Bible* into the Usarufa language of Papua, New Guinea, through the auspices of the Wycliffe Bible Translators, Inc., program. An international consultant in ethnomusicology and professor emerita, she served on the faculty of Wheaton College (IL) for 14 years, teaching analysis of unwritten music systems.

Chenoweth chose Lincoln Center in 1980 as the venue for her final public recital and was inducted into the Oklahoma Heritage Association Hall of Fame in 1985. An early contributing editor to the journal *Percussionist*, she wrote compositions published by Honey Rock and CPP Belwin.

SELECTED DISCOGRAPHY

CMP–VC1: *Creston—Concertino for Marimba and Orchestra; Sarmientos—Concertino for Marimba and Orchestra*, 1987.

Epic LC 3818/CBS Epic P–17808: *Vida Chenoweth—Classic Marimbist*, 1962 (reissued by The Contemporary Music Project in 1985).

SELECTED BIBLIOGRAPHY

Bergdall, Calvin. "Marimbist Swaps Careers." *Wichita Eagle* (12 Dec 1964).

Chenoweth, Vida. "Four–Mallet Technique" and "Mallet Position with Two Mallets." *Percussionist* I, 2 (1963).

Chenoweth, Vida. "The Marimba: A Challenge to Composers." *IM* (November 1959): 20–21.

Chenoweth, Vida. "The Marimba Comes into Its Own." *Music Journal* (May 1957).

Chenoweth, Vida. *The Marimbas of Guatemala*, 2nd ed. Hong Kong: Christian Communications, 1978.

Chenoweth, Vida. "Pioneering the Marimba." *PN* III, 2 (December 1964).

Hufford, Holly. "Backstage with Vida Chenoweth." *PN* XIX, 3 (Spring/Summer 1981): 70–74.

Kammerer, Raphael. "Marimba." *Musical America* (March 1961).

Stevens, Leigh Howard. "An Interview with Vida Chenoweth." *PN* XV, 3 (1977).

Vela, David. *Information on the Marimba*, translated by Vida Chenoweth. Auckland, New Zealand: Institute Press, 1972/1993.

Weir, Martin. "Catching up with Vida Chenoweth." *PN* XXXII, 3 (June 1994): 53–55.

GEN. BIB.: Larrick, *BET–CP*. Information supplied by the subject, 1996.

CHERRY, KALMAN (b. 9 Apr 1937, Philadelphia, Pennsylvania). A student of *Fred Hinger, timpanist Kalman Cherry earned a bachelor's degree from the Curtis Institute of Music (1958), performed at the Marlboro and Bethlehem Bach Festivals, and has been principal timpanist with the Dallas Symphony since 1959. He has also served as a column editor for *Percussive Notes* journal and taught as an adjunct professor at Southern Methodist University and the University of North Texas.

GEN. BIB.: Borland, *WWAMC*.

CHIHA, LOU "SIGNOR FRISCOE" (b. 10 Jul 1891, Chicago, Illinois). Drummer and xylophonist for opera and vaudeville (Orpheum Circuit, 1910s–20s), Signor Friscoe is credited as the first performer to use four hammers simultaneously (dubbed a "stunt" in 1916). In 1921 he stated that he did not like to play jazz, but preferred interpreting classical works with four hammers. A recording artist for the Edison Phonograph Company, he was featured with his Guatemalan marimba ensemble in 1924.

SELECTED DISCOGRAPHY

Edison 50342: "Silver Threads among the Gold," ca. 1914 (four–mallet xylophone).

Edison 50872: "A Perfect Day," 1922 (four–mallet xylophone).

Edison 51809: "Andantino," "I'll Take You Home Again Kathleen," ca. 1927 (vibraphone).

SELECTED BIBLIOGRAPHY

Kastner, Kathleen. "The Xylophone in the United States between 1880 and 1930, Part I: The Artists." *Percussive Arts Society: Illinois Chapter Newsletter* (Winter 1986): 1–2.
GEN. BIB.: Cook, *LDT*, p. 19; Cahn, *XAR*.

CHRISTIAN, SYLVESTER "BOBBY" (b. 20 Oct 1911, Chicago, Illinois; d. 31 Dec 1991, Oak Park, Illinois). Dubbed "Mr. Percussion" for his technical and stylistic expertise on all percussion instruments, and for his ability to create "substitute" percussive sounds from existing instruments, Bobby Christian was an arranger, composer, conductor, clincian, and performer who studied with *Roy Knapp for 20 years. He started snare drum lessons at age 6, and by 10 had embraced timpani and marimba. As a teen he played with the Louis Panico Band, Paul Riker Band, and the Sophie Tucker Band, joining the Paul White-man Orchestra as percussionist and arranger in 1938. Christian toured with the Percy Faith Orchestra, performed in the Far East with Arturo Toscanini's "Symphony of the Air," and recorded in the Hollywood studios of Warner Brothers, MGM, Universal, and Republic. He worked with the WGN, ABC, NBC, and CBS radio and television orchestras in Chicago (1960s) and New York, and performed part time with the Chicago Symphony (1960s). As an arranger and performer with *Dick Schory's Percussion Pops Orchestra (1960s), he played Khachaturian's "Sabre Dance," according to fellow percussionist *Duane Thamm, "sitting down, two mallets [in the right hand] on the xylo-phone, left hand playing two timpani, bass drum with the right foot, and bells in front of the xylophone. He brought the house down!" His television appear-ances included *Tales of Tomorrow*, the *Meredith Wilson Show*, and the *Dave Garraway Show*, where he played excerpts from Rimsky–Korsakov's "The Flight of the Bumblebee" on timpani. Aside from his myriad "jingle" recording sessions, he also performed live with such artists as Diana Ross, Perry Como, and the Ray Noble Orchestra and recorded with Sy Zentner, Al Hirt, Aretha Franklin, and a host of others. Christian served as president of Malcolm Music Publishers and Mallet Manufacturing, taught on the faculty of DePaul University (1977–   ) and was elected to the Percussive Arts Society Hall of Fame in 1989.

SELECTED DISCOGRAPHY

Ovation Records OV 14–06: *Bobby Christian—Vibrations* ["Vibe–rations"], 1970.

SELECTED VIDEOGRAPHY

WIBC Publishing c/o Malcolm Publishers, Oak Park, IL: *Tricks of the Trade*, 1989.

SELECTED BIBLIOGRAPHY

"Bobby Christian: Music Personified." *LD* VII, 2 (Fall 1967): 5–6.

Christian, Bobby, and Al Payson. *In the Studio.* Park Ridge, IL: Payson Percus-
    sion Products, 1980.
"In Memoriam: Bobby Christian, 1911–1991." *PN* XXX, 4 (April 1992): 3.

CIRONE, ANTHONY J. "TONY" (b. 8 Nov 1941, Jersey City, New Jersey).
After completing the bachelor's (1964) and master's (1965) degrees at the Juilliard School, where he studied with *Saul Goodman, Tony Cirone won a percussion position with the San Francisco Symphony and has remained there
since 1965. An educator at Stanford and at San Jose State University (1965–),
he studied with Vincent Persichetti and has composed several etude books for
percussion and works for percussion ensemble that have become standard repertoire.

SELECTED DISCOGRAPHY

Sonic Arts LS–11: *76 Pieces of Explosive Percussion,* 1976.

SELECTED VIDEOGRAPHY

Yamaha EV–30I/II: *Concert Percussion: A Performer's Guide,* vols. 1–2, 1989.

SELECTED BIBLIOGRAPHY

Cirone, Anthony J. *Orchestral Techniques of the Standard Percussion Instru-
    ments.* Miami: Belwin–Mills.
Cirone, Anthony J. *Portraits in Rhythm.* Miami: Belwin–Mills, 1966.
Cirone, Anthony J., and Joe Sinai. *The Logic of It All.* Menloe Park, CA: Cirone
    Publications, 1977.
Wacker, Jon. "Interpretation of Orchestral Percussion Parts: The Professsional
    Viewpoint—Anthony Cirone." *PN* XXXIV, 6 (December 1996): 54–58.
GEN. BIB.: Borland, *WWAMC*; Larrick, *BET–CP.*

CLARK, FORREST. Percussionist and timpanist with the Los Angeles Philharmonic (ca. 1969), Forrest Clark studied with *Murray Spivack, and recorded
as timpanist for Bruno Walter and Igor Stravinsky in Hollywood. He was a featured soloist with Leopold Stokowski and served on the faculties of Los Angeles
State College and the Music Academy of the West in Santa Barbara.

SELECTED DISCOGRAPHY

Cambria CD–1071: *The Music of William Kraft,* 1993.

SELECTED BIBLIOGRAPHY

Clark, Forrest. "Pros and Cons of Matched Grip Snare Drumming." *Percussionist* VI,
    3 (March 1969): 83–85.

Clark, Forrest. "Accurate Timpani Tuning." *MP* I, 1 (December 1984–February 1985): 30.

CLARK, OWEN (b. 16 Jul 1938, Winnipeg, Manitoba, Canada). Freelancing for TV, radio, and studio recordings in the Winnipeg area since 1975, Owen Clark received a bachelor's degree (1971) and performer's certificate from McGill University. He earned a master's degree from Moorhead State University (Minnesota) in 1973 and has served on the faculty of the University of Manitoba since 1977. Appearing with the Ice Capades, CBC Montreal Opera Orchestra, Winnepeg Symphony, and Les Grande Ballets Canadienne, he is known as a teacher, composer, and leading exponent of electronic music in Canada.
GEN. BIB.: Larrick, *BET–CP.*

CLARKE, KENNETH SPEARMAN "KENNY" "KLOOK" (aka Liaquat Ali Salaam, b. 9 Jan 1914, Pittsburgh, Pennsylvania; d. 26 Jan 1985, Montreuil–sous–Bois, France). A composer, pianist, and trombonist, drumset artist Kenny Clarke also played the mallet keyboards, and at the start of his career he appeared with Roy Eldridge (1935), the Jeter–Pillars Orchestra, and Edgar Hayes (European tour/recording, 1937); he made his first recording as leader (Kenny Clarke Kvintett) in Stockholm (1938). His subsequent recording and/or performance collaborators in the 1940s included Count Basie, Mildred Bailey, the *Chick Webb Band (led by Ella Fitzgerald), Sidney Bechet (1940–41), Benny Carter, Red Allen (1942–46), Claude Hopkins, and Billie Holiday and Lester Young. Leading the house band at Minton's Playhouse in New York (1941–43), Clarke, along with Charlie Parker, Thelonious Monk, and Dizzy Gillespie, was one of the founding fathers of the bebop jazz style, liberating the bass drum from playing "four–on–the–floor" (string bass domain) and maintaining the pulse with the ride cymbal. (In the late 1930s he lost jobs with Louis Armstrong and Teddy Hill because of his experimentation with the new style.) He served in the U.S. Army in Normandy, France, during WWII; upon his discharge (1946), he relocated to New York, married singer Carmen McRae, led his own group (Kenny Clarke and His 52nd Street Boys), and recorded with Dizzy Gillespie's big band. From 1948 to 1956, he performed and recorded as staff drummer for Savoy Records (1954–56) with an array of jazz artists including Hank Mobley, Tadd Dameron, Miles Davis, Hank Jones, and Cannonball Adderley. The original drummer with the Modern Jazz Quartet (1952–55), Clarke relocated to Paris, France, where he established a drumming school with Dante Augostini and performed from 1956 until 1985. He was awarded an "American Jazz Masters" Fellowship from the National Endowment for the Arts in 1983, and Michael Haggerty compiled a discography for and produced a tribute to Clarke called "A Flower for Kenny," aired on WHRB-Boston (12 May 1985).

SELECTED DISCOGRAPHY

ABC/Impulse ASH 9272B/Jazz Odyssey JO 008: *The Drums*, 1989.
ABC Paramount ABC101: *Blues and Other Shades of Green* (Urbie Green), 1955.
Atlantic 1217: *Lee Konitz with Warne Marsh*, 1955.
Atlantic 1401: *Jazz Is Universal* (Boland–Clarke Big Band), 1962.
Atlantic 1404: *Francy Boland Big Band*, 1963.
Blue Note 84092: *The Golden Eight* (Kenny Clarke/Francy Boland & Co.), 1961.
Blue Note BLP5043: *Frank Foster Quintet*, 1950s.
Blue Note BLP5053: *Julius Watkins Sextet*, 1954.
Blue Note BLP5057: *The Eminent Jay Jay Johnson*, 1954.
Blue Note BT85108: *Charlie Parker at Storyville*, 1953.
Blue Note CDP–7–46394–2: *Our Man in Paris* (Dexter Gordon), 1963.
Blue Note CDP–7–81501–2: *Miles Davis All Stars*, vol. 1, 1952.
Blue Note LA490–H2: *Milt Jackson Quintet*, 1952.
Fontana MGF–27532: *Back to Back*, 1960s.
Jazz Life 2673212: *Bud Powell in Europe*, 1988.
Mosaic MD6–174: *The Complete Atlantic Recordings of Lennie Tristano, Lee Konitz, and Warne Marsh*, 1997.
OJC 014: *All–Star Sessions* (Gene Ammons et al.).
Philips 83605–2: *Ascenser Pour L'Echafaud* (Miles Davis), 1957.
Prestige 7109: *Bag's Groove* (Miles Davis), 1954.
Prestige 7150: *Miles Davis and the Modern Jazz Giants*, 1954.
Prestige OJC CD–057–2: *Django* (Modern Jazz Quartet), 1953.
Prestige OJC CD–125–2: *MJQ* (Modern Jazz Quartet), 1952/1984.
Prestige OJCCD 213–2: *Walkin''* (Miles Davis), 1954.
Riverside RLP 12–201/OJC 024: *Thelonius Monk Plays Duke Ellington*, 1982.
Savoy MG–12006: *Kenny Clarke*, vol. 1, ca. 1955–56.
Savoy MG–12007: *Kenny Clarke/Ernie Wilkins Septet*, 1955.
Savoy/Denon MG–12017: *Bohemia after Dark*, 1955/1993.
Savoy MG–12023: *The Trio*, ca. 1955–56.
Savoy MG–12026: *Howard McGhee and Milt Jackson*, 1950s.
Savoy MG–12056: *Urso–Brookmeyer Quintet*, 1950s.
Savoy MG–12065: *Klook's Clique*, 1956.
Savoy MG–12072: *North, South, East...Wess* (Frank Foster/Frank Wess), 1991.
Status 8258: *Early Art* (Art Farmer), 1954.
Swing LP 8411: *Kenny Clarke in Paris*, 1957.
Verve 845 148–2: *Jazz Club Mainstream: Drums*, 1951/1991.
Verve MGV8010: *Charlie Parker Quintet*, 1951.
Verve MGV8301: *Bud Powell Trio*, 1955.
Verve MGV8378: *Lester Young*, 1959.
Verve (G) 2304034: *Stan Getz and the Kenny Clarke–Francy Boland Big Band*, 1971.
Vogue 651 600135: *Charlie Christian with Dizzy*, 1941.
Vox PLS 1/DL 180: *Spotlight on Percussion*, 1955.

SELECTED VIDEOGRAPHY

DCI VH0248: *Legends of Jazz Drumming, Pt. 1, 1920–50*, 1996.

SELECTED BIBLIOGRAPHY

Hennessey, Mike. *Klook: The Story of Kenny Clarke*. Pittsburgh, PA: University
of Pittsburgh Press, 1994.
Hoefer, George. "Klook." *DB* XXX, 8 (28 Mar 1963): 22–23.
Korall, Burt. "View from the Seine." *DB* XXX, 31 (5 Dec 1963): 16–17.
Shultz, Thomas. "A History of Jazz Drumming." *Percussionist* XVI, 3
(Spring/Summer 1979): 123–124.
GEN. BIB.: Hunt, *52nd St.*; Kernfeld, *NGJ*, by Olly Wilson; Spagnardi, *GJD*.

COATES, WILLIAM ELMER "EL COTA" (aka Lawrence Coates, b. ca.
1886, Wheeling, West Virginia). Xylophone artist and vaudevillian who flourished from 1906 to 1915, "El Cota" made disc recordings for the Columbia
Phonograph Company that demonstrate his technical prowess.

SELECTED DISCOGRAPHY

Columbia A1118: "Black and White Rag," 1911.
Columbia A1149: "Red Pepper Rag," 1912.
GEN. BIB.: Cahn, *XAR*.

COBB, WILBUR JAMES "JIMMY" (b. 20 Jan 1929, Washington, D.C.).
Starting drums at age 16 with Jack Denett of the National Symphony, drumset
artist Jimmy Cobb was essentially self–taught and appeared early on with Buck
Hill, Charlie Rouse, and Billie Holiday before joining Earl Bostic (1950–51).
He recorded first with Bostic and then worked several years with Dinah Washington, Cannonball Adderly, Stan Getz, Dizzy Gillespie, and Hank Mobley; but
he is most noted for his work with Miles Davis (1958–63) and John Coltrane.
In the 1960s Cobb played in a trio with Paul Chambers and Wynton Kelly that
later became a quartet when Wes Montgomery was added. Touring internation-
ally for nine years with Sarah Vaughan (1971–80) and J. J. Johnson (Japan,
1964), he has recorded with his group, Cobb's Mob, Nancy Wilson, Kenny
Barron, Hank Jones, Nat Adderley, Eddie Gomez, Kai Winding, Sonny Stitt,
Dave Holland, and Warren Bernhardt, among others, and has taught at the New
School in New York.

SELECTED DISCOGRAPHY

Atlantic 1354: *Coltrane Jazz* (John Coltrane), 1959–60.
Atlantic CD 1311–2: *Giant Steps* (John Coltrane), 1960.
Blue Note 84032: *Out of the Blue* (Sonny Red), 1960.
Columbia C2S–820: *Miles Davis in Person at the Blackhawk*, 1961.
Columbia CK 40647: *Porgy and Bess* (Miles Davis), 1958.
Columbia CL1355/CK–40579: *Kind of Blue* (Miles Davis), 1959.
Columbia CS8456/PC–8456: *Someday My Prince Will Come* (Miles Davis), 1961.

Columbia Jazz Masterpiece LP 7464–40578–11/CD–40578: *Miles Davis: Sketches of Spain*, 1960/1986.
Contemporary/OJCCD–169–2: *Gettin' Together* (Art Pepper), 1960/1986.
EmArcy 36146: *Jump for Joy* (Cannonball Adderley), 1958.
Evidence 22208: *Dedication* (Eddie Gomez), 1998.
Fable 54264–2: *Jimmy Cobb's Mob*, 1998.
Landmark LCD 1306–2: *Takes Charge* (Cannonball Adderley), 1959.
LCD 1528/32 Jazz 32082: *Talkin' About You* (Nat Adderley), 1998.
OJC 032: *Things Are Getting Better* (Cannonball Adderley), 1958/1988
Polygram 826 986–2: *Cannonball's Sharpshooters* (Cannonball Adderley), 1958.
Polygram 834 588–2: *Cannonball and Coltrane*, 1965.
Riverside OJCCD–106–2: *Full House* (Wes Montgomery), 1962.
Sony 32DP 515/Columbia CS8612: *Carnegie Hall Concert* (Miles Davis), 1961.
Sony 67397: *Miles Davis and Gil Evans—The Complete Columbia Studio Recordings*, 1996.
Verve 314 523 657–2: *Four* (Joe Henderson/Wynton Kelly), 1995.
Verve 38633/829 578–2: *Smokin' at the Half Note* (Wynton Kelly/Wes Montgomery), 1965.

SELECTED VIDEOGRAPHY

A*Vision Entertainment 50240–3: *JazzMasters Vintage Collection*, vols. 1–2 (1958–1961), 1990.
Medar: *Dizzy Gillespie: "A Night in Tunisia,"* 1990.

SELECTED BIBLIOGRAPHY

Mattingly, Rick. "Jimmy Cobb: Seasoned Sideman." *MD* III, 4 (1979): 28–30.
Primack, Bret. "Jimmy Cobb: Connections." *JazzTimes* XXVIII, 9 (November 1998): 44–47.
GEN. BIB.: Hunt, *52nd St.*; Kernfeld, *NGJ*, by J. Bradford Robinson; Spagnardi, *GJD*.

COBHAM, WILLIAM EMANUEL, JR., "BILLY" (b. 15 May 1944, Republic of Panama). The son of a professional jazz pianist, "fusion" drumset artist Billy Cobham immigrated to New York at the age of 3, and by 8 he was playing in his father's group. After performing in the Boy Scout Drum Corps (1956–58), he attended New York's High School of Music and Art and played with the Jazz Samaritans in his teens. During service in the U.S. Army Band (1965–68), Cobham worked with Billy Taylor (1967) and, after discharge, played with the New York Jazz Sextet, Horace Silver, his own jazz–rock band, Dreams (1969–70), Miles Davis (1971), the Mahavishnu Orchestra (1972–73), and McCoy Tyner. Appearing in the films *Jack Johnson* (1970) and *Salsa* (1976), he performed on the soundtrack for *The Last Temptation of Christ*, worked as an educator with Billy Taylor's Jazzmobile projects and Chris White's Rhythm Associates, and toured the United States and abroad in 1974. During the 1980s–90s, he led his group, Glass Menagerie, was honored with a Grammy® Award nomination for his album *Power Play* (1986), and was inducted into *Modern Drummer* magazine's Reader's Poll Hall of Fame (1987). Besides his own albums, he has appeared on over eighty-five as a guest artist and produced more than 20 for other artists. His website address is www.billycobham.com.

SELECTED DISCOGRAPHY

Atlantic 7268: *Spectrum*, 1973.
Atlantic 18121: *Total Eclipse*, 1974.
Atlantic 18194: *George Duke/Billy Cobham Band Live on Tour in Europe*, 1976.
Blue Note 84277: *Serenade to a Soul Sister* (Horace Silver), 1968.
Blue Note 84309: *You Gotta Have a Little Love* (Horace Silver), 1969.
CBS CK–31067: *Inner Mounting Flame* (Mahavishnu Orchestra), 1971.
Columbia C30225: *Dreams*, 1970.
Columbia CGT–30954: *Live Evil* (Miles Davis), 1970.
Columbia KC30455: *A Tribute to Jack Johnson* (Miles Davis), 1970.
CTI 79482: *Live from Bahia* (Larry Coryell), 1992.
ECD 22098–2: *The Traveler Evidence*, 1994.
Elektra 60123: *Observations &*, 1982.
Galaxy GXY–5102: *Richard Davis—Fancy Free*, 1977.
INAK 813: *Stratus*, 1981.
Milestone OJCCD–699: *Fly with the Wind* (McCoy Tyner), 1976.
Sony SRCS 5713–4: *Big Fun* (Miles Davis), 1969.
Verve V6–8749: *George Benson*, 1968.

SELECTED VIDEOGRAPHY

DCI VH0109: *Billy Cobham—Drums by Design*, 1991.
VIEW Video: *Bobby and the Midnites*, 1991.
VIEW Video/Moonbeam Publications, Inc.: *Cobham Meets Bellson*, 1983
VIEW Video: *Gil Evans and His Orchestra*, 1987.
VIEW Video: *Herbie Hancock Trio—Hurricane*, 1984.
Warner Bros./DCI VH0270: *The Making of Burning for Buddy*, pt. 2, 1996.

SELECTED BIBLIOGRAPHY

Alterman, Lorraine. "Who's Afraid of Jazz–Rock?" *New York Times* (26 May 1974).
Cobham, Billy. *Directions in Percussion*. Miami, FL: Warner/Chappell Music Ltd., 1996 (with CD).
Holly, Rich, and James Lambert. "Interview with Bill Cobham." *PN* XXX, 6 (August 1992): 10–13.
Miller, William F. "Billy Cobham: Alive and Kicking." *MD* XXII, 11 (November 1998): 56–72.
GEN. BIB.: Hunt, *52nd St.*; Kernfeld, *NGJ*, by J. Bradford Robinson; Southern, *BDA–AAM*.

COLAIUTA, VINNIE (b. ca. 1956, Pittsburgh, Pennsylvania). Inducted into *Modern Drummer* magazine's Reader's Poll Hall of Fame (1996), Vinnie Colaiuta studied with Gary Chaffee and *Alan Dawson while attending the Berklee School (1974–   ), then relocated to Los Angeles (1978), where he has become a studio mainstay, recording and/or performing with Frank Zappa, Los Lobotomies, the Commodores, Sting (including the Grammy® Award–winning album *Ten Summoner's Tales*, 1993), Tom Scott, Joni Mitchell, Eric Marienthal, Allan Holdsworth, David Sanborn, Jeff Beal, and Gino Vanelli, among others.

SELECTED DISCOGRAPHY

A&M 31 454 0070 4: *Ten Summoner's Tales* (Sting), 1993.
CBS 66368: *Shut Up and Play Yer Guitar* (Frank Zappa), 1981.
Creatchy SFB 1002: *Los Lobotomys*, 1989.
Enigma/Intima Records 7 73328–4: *Secrets* (Allan Holdsworth), 1989.
GRP GRC–9571: *Flashpoint* (Tom Scott), 1988.
GRP GRD 9553: *Portrait* (Lee Ritenour), 1987.
GRP GRD–9618: *Welcome to the St. James' Club* (The Rippingtons), 1990.
Imago 72787–23002–2: *Thanks 2 Frank* (Warren Cuccurullo), 1997.
Nova 9025–4: *Other Places* (Brandon Fields), 1990.
Stretch/GRP STD–1110: *Vinnie Colaiuta*, 1994.
Warner Bros. 1–25647: *Talk to Your Daughter* (Robben Ford), 1988.
Warner Bros/Reprise 9 26183–2: *Blue Pacific* (Michael Franks), 1990.
Whirlybird 9855: *Wigged Out* (Randy Waldman Trio), 1998.
Zappa Records SRZ–1–1603: *Joe's Garage* (Frank Zappa), 1979.
Zebra ZD 44005–2: *Tribute to Jeff Porcaro* (Dave Garfield), 1997.

SELECTED BIBLIOGRAPHY

Flans, Robyn. "Vinnie Colaiuta." *MD* XVII (October 1993): 20–24.
Mattingly, Rick. "Vinnie Colaiuta." *PN* XXXIII, 1 (February 1995): 8–15.
Micaleff, Ken. "Vinnie Colaiuta: Simple Complexity." *JazzTimes* XXIV, 9 (November 1994): 68–69.
Rule, Greg. "Vinnie Colaiuta: The Reluctant Hero." *Drums and Drumming* III, 1 (January 1991): 24–35.
"Something's a Bit Odd (Meters)." *MD* XVII (October 1993): 25.
PASIC® program biographies, 1985, 1994.

COLE, WILLIAM RANDOLPH "COZY" (b. 17 Oct 1906, East Orange, New Jersey; d. 29 Jan 1981, Columbus, Ohio). Born into a musical family and inspired by drummer *Sonny Greer, "Cozy" Cole worked as an equipment setup "roadie" for the latter prior to Greer's association with Duke Ellington. He embraced drums at age 5 and later studied with Harlem pit drummer Charlie Brooks at Wilberforce College (Ohio) for two years, and in New York with *Billy Gladstone (snare), *Fred Albright (mallets), and *Saul Goodman (timpani, Juilliard School, 1940s). In his youth he worked as a dancer to support his family, and citing *Jo Jones, *Chick Webb, and *Gene Krupa as role models, he was professionally engaged as a drummer by 1928. Cole performed with

Jelly Roll Morton (1930), Blanche Calloway (Cab's sister, 1931–33), Benny
Carter (1933–34), "Stuff" Smith (1936–38), and with Cab Calloway (1939–42),
who featured him as soloist on several recordings, including "Crescendo in
Drums" and "Ratamacue" (1939) and "Paradiddle Joe" (1940).

He played theaters with Benny Goodman, and, during 1942–53 was the first
black drummer on the CBS staff orchestra, appearing in the pit and on stage for
the opera *Carmen Jones* and on stage for *Seven Lively Arts* (1944). Performing
and recording with Frank Sinatra, Dizzy Gillespie and Charlie Parker (1945),
Coleman Hawkins, *Lionel Hampton, Roy Eldridge, and others, Cole toured
with Louis Armstrong's All–Stars (1949–53), Jack Teagarden and Earl Hines
(1957), and the Jonah Jones Quintet (1968); he led his own groups to Africa
(1962–63) under U.S. State Department sponsorship. He appeared in the films
Make Mine Music (1945), *The Strip* (1951), and *The Glenn Miller Story* (1953)
and earned a gold record for his version of "Topsy, Part 1" in the 1950s.

One of the first drumset players to employ independent coordination between
his hands and feet before the advent of the "bop" style of drumming, Cole operated a drum school with *Gene Krupa in New York (1952–60) and counted
*Philly Joe Jones among his stellar apprentices. At the time of his death, he
was a lecturer and a student seeking a music degree at Capital University in
Ohio.

SELECTED DISCOGRAPHY

Bluebird AXM6 5536: *The Complete Lionel Hampton* (1937–41), 1976.
Circle CCD–47: *Maxine Sullivan/John Kirby and His Orchestra*, 1940–41.
Coral CRL 57423: *Drum Beat for Dancing Feet*, 1963.
French CBS 62950: *16 Cab Calloway Classics*, ca. 1939–41.
Jazzology JCD–1011–1012: *Eddie Condon—The Town Hall Concerts*, vol. 6.
Masters of Jazz, Media 7: *Anthology of Jazz Drumming*, vols. 1–3, 1904–38.
Mercury–Emarcy MG 36071: *Giants of Jazz*, vol. 8—*The Jazz Greats, Drum Role*,
    1959.
RCA Victor LPV 546: *Mr. Jelly Lord* (Jelly Roll Morton), 1926–30/1967.
Savoy SJK 1117: *George Shearing—So Rare*, ca. 1949/1978.
Savoy SV–0112: *Blue Lester* (Lester Young), 1944.
Savoy SV–0152: *Groovin' High* (Dizzy Gillespie), 1945.
Savoy SV–0160: *Great Britain's* (George Shearing), 1947.
Verve MGV8233: *Red Allen, Jack Teagarden, and Kid Ory at Newport*, 1957.
Verve MGV8302: *Billie Holiday*, 1955.

SELECTED VIDEOGRAPHY

Rhapsody Films: *After Hours* (Coleman Hawkins and Roy Eldridge), 1986.

SELECTED BIBLIOGRAPHY

Krupa, Gene, and Cozy Cole. "Exploding a Drum Myth." *DB* XXII, 25 (14 Dec
    1955): 28.

Morgenstern, Dan. "Keep It Swingin'—Cozy Cole." *DB* XXXVI, 6 (20 Mar 1969): 22–23.
Shultz, Thomas. "A History of Jazz Drumming." *Percussionist* XVI, 3 (Spring/Summer 1979): 118.
GEN. BIB.: Hunt, *52nd St.*; Kernfeld, *NGJ*, by John Chilton; Korall, *DM*; Spagnardi, *GJD*.

COLGRASS, MICHAEL CHARLES (b. 22 Apr 1932, Chicago, Illinois). Voted into the Percussive Arts Society Hall of Fame in 1987, Michael Colgrass earned a bachelor's degree in 1956 from the University of Illinois. He studied percussion with *Paul Price and composition with Darius Milhaud, Lukas Foss, and Wallingford Rieger, among others. A freelance artist with the New York Philharmonic and Broadway musicals, Colgrass moved to Toronto, Canada, in 1974 to pursue a composition career. Many of his contributions to percussion literature have become standard repertoire, and his many accolades include the Pulitzer Prize (*Déjà Vu*, 1978), Rockefeller and Ford Foundation grants, Guggenheim Fellowships, and numerous commissions.

SELECTED DISCOGRAPHY

ADP–075S: "Fantasy–Variations" (*Percussion at Fredonia*), 1974.
Granadilla 1010: *New People*, 1969.
MGM E–3714: *Variations for Four Drums and Viola*, 1959.
New World NW318–2: *Works by Colgrass and Druckman* (St. Louis Symphony), 1983.
Nonesuch 71291: "Fantasy–Variations" (New Jersey Percussion Ensemble), 1960.
Orion 7276: *Percussion Music* (Paul Price Percussion Ensemble), 1953.
Turnabout 34704: *Concertmasters*, 1975.

SELECTED BIBLIOGRAPHY

Colgrass, Michael. "Small Essay on My Early Percussion Music." *PN* XXXIV, 4 (August 1996): 70–72.
GEN. BIB.: Larrick, *BET–CP*; Sadie, *NG*, by Kurt Stone.

CONNER, JOHN CHELLIS "JACK" (b. Oct 1913, Kahoka, Missouri). Starting both piano and percussion at age 6, mallet specialist Jack Conner was engaged professionally in a radio orchestra by 12, then later performed in a jazz trio that presented a 15-minute radio show on KWK (Mutual Network) in St. Louis, where he served as staff musician. He toured Europe with *Clair Omar Musser's International Marimba Symphony Orchestra in 1935, attended the U.S. Naval School of Music, played in the U.S. Navy Band, and served with the USO in the European theater during WWII.

Principal percussionist with the St. Louis Symphony (1948–49), he commissioned Darius Milhaud's "Concerto for Marimba and Vibraphone" and premiered it with them on 14 February 1949 to a standing ovation and eight curtain calls.

Later rave Milhaud performances included the Nippon Philharmonic (Japan, 1961) and the Rome Radio Symphony at the International Festival of Music in Venice, Italy. Conner also appeared with the Municipal Opera Orchestra (St. Louis) and on both NBC and CBS radio and television networks (e.g., *Mike Douglas*, *Ed Sullivan*, *Merv Griffin*, and *Lawrence Welk* shows). Making a critically acclaimed debut in New York's Town Hall, he was featured with the *Don Ho Show* in Hawaii and Las Vegas, toured South America with the Xavier Cugat Orchestra, was music director for both Roger Williams and Anita Bryant, and soloed with the Honolulu Symphony in a performance tour of the islands, for which he was honored by the state of Hawaii in the 1970s.

SELECTED BIBLIOGRAPHY

Bircher, John C., Jr. "Backgrounds in Percussion: John Chellis Conner." *PN* XV, 2 (Winter 1977): 21.
Eyler, David P. "Interview with Jack Connor [sic], William F. Ludwig, Jr., and Herschel Stark, Members of the International Marimba Symphony Orchestra of 1935." *PN* XXXI, 7 (October 1993): 66–76.
Fink, Ron. "An Interview with Jack Connor [sic], Marimba Virtuoso." *PN* XVI, 2 (Winter 1978): 26–27.
"More on the Milhaud Marimba/Vibe Concerto." *PN* XIV, 3 (Spring/Summer 1976): 9.
Information supplied by Garrett Conner, 1997.

CONTE, LUIS (b. ca. 1953, Santiago de Cuba, Cuba). Born into a family of doctors and lawyers, Luis Conte arrived in the United States in 1970 and quickly became a first–call studio musician. He has recorded for television (*Northern Exposure*) and movies [*Rainman*, *Bugsy*, *Coming to America*, *The Mambo Kings*, and *Truth or Dare* (on–screen appearance)] and has performed with the Supremes, Pat Metheny, Natalie Cole, Toto, Madonna, Kenny Loggins, Orlando Lopez Orchestra, Celia Cruz, Seal, Manhattan Transfer, Arturo Sandoval, Diana Ross, Doc Severinson, the Yellowjackets, and others. Conte previously served on the faculty of the Dick Grove School of Music.

SELECTED DISCOGRAPHY

Denon CJ–2237: *La Concina Caliente* (Luis Conte), 1987.
Denon CJ 74100: *Black Forest* (Luis Conte), 1989.
Nova 8139: *Common Ground* (Jude Swift), 1991.
Pablo 2310–807/OJC–632: *Ecué Ritmos Cubanos* (Louis Bellson), 1978.
Warner Bros/Reprise 9 26183–2: *Blue Pacific* (Michael Franks), 1990.
Zebra ZD 44005–2: *Tribute to Jeff Porcaro* (Dave Garfield), 1997.

SELECTED VIDEOGRAPHY

LP Music Group: *Luis Conte Live and in the Studio*, 1993.

SELECTED BIBLIOGRAPHY

McFall, Michael. "World Picture." *Rhythm* I, 12 (April 1989): 36–44.
PASIC® program biographies, 1995/1998.

CONTI, JOSEPH JOHN (b. 18 Jul 1947, Providence, Rhode Island). A student of *Vic Firth, Joseph Conti earned a bachelor's degree from the New England Conservatory (1970), performed at the Berkshire Music Festival, and was percussionist with the Milwaukee Symphony (1972–   ).
GEN. BIB.: Borland, *WWAMC.*

COPELAND, KEITH LAMONT (b. 18 Apr 1946, New York, New York). Drumset artist Keith Copeland, whose teachers include Gene Morvay, Walter Perkins, *Fred Buda, and *Alan Dawson, started percussion at age 10, acquired his musicians' union card by age 15, and enlisted in the U.S. Air Force in 1963, working abroad in cryptography and telecommunications. Leaving the military in 1967, he enrolled at the Berklee College of Music, where he studied percussion (1968–70) and composition (1973). Copeland has played with the Maggi Scott Trio (1975–78), the Heath Brothers (1978–79), Billy Taylor (1980–84), George Russell, Bill Evans, Jo Ann Brackeen, Harry "Sweets" Edison, Slide Hampton, Johnny Griffin, Frank Foster, Hank Jones (intermittently from 1986, recording six albums with him), and others. A member of Stevie Wonder's road band for one year, touring Europe and the United States, he has also worked with the National Jazz Ensemble, the Collective of Black Artists Repertory Orchestra, the Four Tops, Marvin Gaye, Billy Eckstine, Cab Calloway, and Eartha Kitt. With over 50 recordings to his credit as a sideman, Copeland has appeared on numerous television shows in the United States and Europe, with prominent symphony orchestras, and at most major jazz festivals.

A clinician at the Eastman School Summer Jazz Workshop (1979–93), the Banff Centre for the Arts Jazz Workshop (Canada) (1991–94), and the University of Ulster (Northern Ireland, 1992–   ), Copeland has taught at the Berklee College (1975–78), the Drummers Collective (1984–85), Rutgers University (1985–92), Queens College (1990–92), Long Island University (1982–92), and the New School (1987–92). He is currently professor of jazz drumset at the Hochschulen für Musik at both Köln (1992–   ) and Mannheim–Heidelberg (1993–   ), Germany.

SELECTED DISCOGRAPHY

Audiophile APCD–245: *Jackie Paris—Nobody Else But Me*, 1988.
Bee Hive BH7012: *Once in Every Life* (Johnny Hartman) (Grammy® Award nominee), 1980.
Blue Note BT 851003: *The African Game* (George Russell), 1983.
Cadence Jazz CJR 1016: *Nightwork* (Rory Stuart), 1983.

Columbia JC 35816: *In Motion* (The Heath Brothers), 1979.
Concord Jazz CJ–145: *Where've You Been?* (Billy Taylor), 1980.
Galaxy GX7 5117: *Return of the Griffin* (Johnny Griffin), 1978.
Interplay/Discovery DS–861: *The Bassist* (Sam Jones), 1979.
JazzMania JCD–6010: *Keith Copeland—On Target*, 1993.
Soul Note SN 1009: *Electronic Sonata for Souls Loved by Nature 1980* (George Russell), 1980.
Steeplechase SCCD 31395: *The Irish Connection*, 1996.

SELECTED BIBLIOGRAPHY

Copeland, Keith. *Creative Coordination for the Performing Drummer.* New York: Carl Fischer, 1986.
Fish, Scott K. "Keith Copeland: In the Tradition." *MD* VIII (May 1984): 28–31.
GEN. BIB.: Hunt, *52nd St..* Information supplied by the subject, 1996.

COSTA, EDWIN JAMES "EDDIE" (b. 14 Aug 1930, Atlas, Pennsylvania; d. 28 Jul 1962, New York, New York). Self–taught jazz vibist Eddie Costa initially studied piano and got his first break at the age of 18 with jazz violinist Joe Venuti. Following military service in the U.S. Army in Japan and Korea (where he continued to perform), he collaborated with Kai Winding, Tal Farlow, Sal Salvador (1954–57), and Woody Herman (1958–59); he also led his own trio and was honored as a pianist and vibist in 1957 by *Down Beat* magazine.

SELECTED DISCOGRAPHY

Coral 57230: *Guys and Dolls Like Vibes*, 1958.
Jubilee 1025: *Eddie Costa with the Vinnie Burke Trio*, 1956.
Mode 118: *Eddie Costa Quintet*, 1957.
Verve MGVS6016: *Harry Edison and Buck Clayton*, 1958.
Verve V6–8455: *Bob Brookmeyer*, 1961.
Verve V6–8548: *Kenny Hopkins and His Orchestra*, 1963.
GEN. BIB.: Kernfeld, *NGJ*, by Andrew Jaffe.

COTTLER, IRV (b. 1920, New York; d. 1989). Drumset artist Irv Cottler flourished in the Hollywood recording studios during the 1950s–60s and played with the Tommy Dorsey, Les Brown, and Claude Thornhill Orchestras. Author of a drumset chart reading book, he performed for the *Dinah Shore Show*, recorded for Billy May, and held a long–standing post as Frank Sinatra's drummer.

SELECTED DISCOGRAPHY

Calliope 3023: *Sessions Live* (Jimmy Rowles), 1955.
Capitol T 926: *Hi–Fi Drums*, 1957.
Contempo./OJC CD–317–2: *To Swing or Not to Swing* (Barney Kessel), 1961.
Reprise 9–6016: *Frank Rosolino*, 1956.

Somerset P–13900 (Miller International Co.): *Around the World in Percussion*, 1960.
Verve MGVS6128: *Paul Smith*, 1960.
Verve V6–8616: *Count Basie and His Orchestra*, 1965.
GEN. BIB.: Hunt, *52nd St.*

CRAMER, GERHARD (fl. ca. 1812, Munich, Germany). Royal Court Timpanist in Munich, Germany, around 1812, Gerhard Cramer invented a handle-and-gear mechanism to turn all timpani tuning screws at once, thereby enabling rapid pitch changes. After being sold, these drums resurfaced in the court orchestra at Darmstadt, but they have since disappeared.

SELECTED BIBLIOGRAPHY

Beck, John H., ed. *Encyclopedia of Percussion*. New York: Garland Publishing, 1995. S.v. "The Kettledrum" by Edmund A. Bowles.
Ludwig, William F. *Ludwig Timpani Instructor*. Chicago: Ludwig Drum Co., 1957.

CRAWFORD, JAMES STRICKLAND "JIMMY" "CRAW" (b. 14 Jan 1910, Memphis, Tennessee; d. 28 Jan 1980, New York, New York). One of the most reliable, consistent, and gentlemanly drummers, Jimmy Crawford made his early fame in the Jimmy Lunceford Band (1928–42). Lunceford was a teacher in Memphis who discovered Crawford when he was a student and gave him "on–the–job training." In 1942 he served in a U.S. Army Band with Sy Oliver and Buck Clayton and later worked with Ben Webster, Edmond Hall, Harry James, Stan Kenton, and Fletcher Henderson. Crawford became a pit drummer for Broadway shows in 1950 and played *Alive and Kicking* (with Jackie Gleason), *Pal Joey* (1952), *Jamaica* (1957), *Bye Bye Birdie* (1960), and *How to Succeed in Business without Really Trying* (1961), among others. Before his retirement in 1972, his many recording collaborators included Ella Fitzgerald, Dizzy Gillespie, Frank Sinatra, Bing Crosby, Count Basie, Benny Goodman, and Quincy Jones.

SELECTED DISCOGRAPHY

Circle CCD–11: *Jimmie Lunceford and His Orchestra*, 1940.
Columbia Hall of Fame Series CL–634/2715: *Lunceford Special*, 1959.
Decca/Jazz Heritage Series: *Rhythm Is Our Business/Harlem Shout/For Dancers Only/Blues in the Night* (Jimmie Lunceford), vols. 1–4, 1934–42.
Jazztone J–1285: *The Big Reunion* (Fletcher Henderson All–Stars), 1957.
Masters of Jazz, Media 7: *Anthology of Jazz Drumming*, vols. 1–3, 1904–38.
Palm Club 19: *Louis Armstrong with Edmond Hall*, 1947.
Savoy 15028: *Jazz at the Savoy Cafe, Boston* (Edmond Hall), 1949.
Verve MGV8085: *Illinois Jacquet and His Orchestra*, 1952.
Verve MGV8178: *Dizzy Gillespie Orchestra*, 1954.

GEN. BIB.: Cook, *LDT*, p. 356 (photo); Kernfeld, *NGJ*, by T. Dennis Brown; Korall, *DM*; Spagnardi, *GJD*.

CULP, PAULA N. (b. 9 Apr 1941, Ft. Smith, Arkansas). A member of the Minnesota Orchestra since 1968, Paula Culp attended the Mozarteum in Salzburg (1961–62) and received a bachelor's degree (Oberlin College, 1963) and a master's degree with performer's certificate (Indiana University, 1965). Her teachers have included Paul Hirsch (Salzburg), *Cloyd Duff (Oberlin), and *George Gaber (Indiana). Culp's previous performance experience includes two years as timpanist for the Metropolitan Opera National Company (1965–67) and one year as principal percussionist with the Indianapolis Symphony (1967–68). She has served on the faculties of DePauw University (1964–65) and the University of Minnesota (1969–   ).

SELECTED DISCOGRAPHY

Pro Arte DDD CDM–813: *World's Greatest Overtures* (Minnesota Orchestra), 1987.
GEN. BIB.: Borland, *WWAMC*; Larrick, *BET–CP*.

CYRILLE, ANDREW CHARLES (b. 10 Nov 1939, Brooklyn, New York). A student of *Philly Joe Jones and Lennie McBrowne, composer and drumset artist Andrew Cyrille attended the Juilliard School (1958–   ) and performed with Cedar Walton, Roland Hanna, Duke Jordan, and Jimmy Giuffre, but he established his reputation more widely with pianist, Cecil Taylor (1964–75). Forming his own quartet in the 1970s, he has served on the faculty of Antioch College and also played and/or recorded with, among others, Grachan Moncur, Freddie Hubbard, Junior Mance, *Walt Dickerson, Stanley Turrentine, Mary Lou Williams (1960), Coleman Hawkins (1962), and his percussion trio, Dialogue of the Drums, which included *Rashied Ali and Milford Graves. With the latter, Cyrille established the IPS recording label around 1974.

SELECTED DISCOGRAPHY

Affinity AFFD 74: *Student Studies* (Cecil Taylor), 1982.
Affinity AFFD 75: *What About?* 1969.
Black Saint 0025: *Metamusicians Stomp*, 1978.
Blue Note 84237: *Unit Stuctures* (Cecil Taylor), 1966.
Blue Note 84260: *Conquistador* (Cecil Taylor), 1966.
DIW/Columbia–858: *My Friend Louis*, 1992.
Evidence ECD 22185–2: *Ode to the Living Tree*, 1997.
Hat Art 6044: *Performance [Quartet]* (Anthony Braxton), 1979.
Hat Art 6052: *Eight [+3] Tristano Compositions* (Anthony Braxton), 1989.
IPS 001: *Dialogue of the Drums*, 1969/1974.
IPS 009: *The Loop*, 1977.

Prestige 34003: *The Great Concert* (Cecil Taylor), 1977.
Soul Note 121062–2: *The Navigator*, 1983.
Soul Note CD 121078–2: *Pieces of Time*, 1983.
Soul Note 121262–2: *X Man*, 1995.

SELECTED VIDEOGRAPHY

Alchemy Pictures: *Andrew Cyrille—Jazz Methodology in Drum Music*, 1992.

SELECTED BIBLIOGRAPHY

Milkowski, Bill. "Masters of the Free Universe." *MD* XVI, 12 (December 1992): 32–35.
GEN. BIB.: Kernfeld, *NGJ*, by Michael Ullman; Spagnardi, *GJD*.

D

DAAB, CHARLES "CHARLIE" (d. ca. February 1936, New York?, New York). Xylophonist for the Edison Record Company from 1910 to 1916, Charles Daab performed with the John Philip Sousa and Arthur Pryor Bands, Walter Damrosch's New York Orchestra, and the Metropolitan Opera Orchestra.

SELECTED DISCOGRAPHY

Edison 50332: "Dancing with Ma Honey" and "Twinkle Waltz," 1916.
Edison Blue Amberol 1514: *The Mocking Bird—Fantasia*, 1912. [Also recorded by William H. Reitz on Victor: 16969–A, 1911/1925.]
Edison Blue Amberol 2052: *Irish and Scotch Melodies–Fantasia*, 1913.
San Francisco M 33006: *1900 in Hi–Fi/Famous Cylinder Recordings*, 1957.

SELECTED BIBLIOGRAPHY

"Death Roll: AFM Local 802 (New York)." *IM* XXXIII, 9 (March 1936): 2.
Kastner, Kathleen. "The Xylophone in the United States between 1880 and 1930, Part I: The Artists." *Percussive Arts Society: Illinois Chapter Newsletter* (Winter 1986): 1–2.
GEN. BIB.: Cahn, *XAR*; Cook, *LDT*, p. 13.

DAEHLIN, VERA MCNARY. A student of *Clair Omar Musser, Herb Johnson, and William Drew, Vera Daehlin attended Northwestern University, securing a landmark position with the Kansas City Philharmonic at the age of 18 as the first female percussionist in a major American orchestra. Relocating to California, she performed with the Los Angeles Percussion Ensemble and the Glendale, Burbank, and Conejo Symphonies. Touring the United States and abroad for 18 years with pianist Roger Williams, she gave five presidential performances, has made television appearances conducting the Southern California Marimba and Percussion Orchestra, and has served on the faculties of University of Missouri at Kansas City (1943–48), University of Kansas (1944–50), California Lutheran University, Pepperdine University, and several California public schools. Daehlin continues to appear on cruise ships and other venues in the duo Marimba Mamas.

SELECTED BIBLIOGRAPHY

Stark, Herschel. "The Marimba Mamas." *Percussion News* (November 1999): 1–2.
PASIC* program biographies, 1991.

DAHLGREN, MARVIN (b. 8 Sep 1924, Minneapolis, Minnesota). Equally adept at both classical and jazz genres, Marv Dahlgren has performed with the Minneapolis Symphony since 1951, serving as principal percussionist and assistant timpanist. He received a bachelor's degree from McPhail College of Music in 1950 and studied with *Henry Denecke, Jr., timpanist with the Minneapolis Symphony (1941–52). Previously, he performed with the Minneapolis Pops Orchestra (1954–59) and served as staff percussionist at the Guthrie Theater (1959–67). Dahlgren has recorded extensively in the Minneapolis area and taught at McPhail College, the University of Minnesota, Saint Olaf College, Mankato State, and in his own retail drum shop (1946–79).

SELECTED DISCOGRAPHY

Pro Arte DDD CDM–813: *Strauss—Die Fledermaus Overture* (Minnesota Orchestra), 1987.
St. Paul 96583–4: *Gutchë—Bongo Divertimento*, 1969.
Turnabout Vox TV–S 34433: *Donald Erb—Concerto for Solo Percussionist* (Dallas Symphony), 1975.

SELECTED BIBLIOGRAPHY

Dahlgren, Marvin. *Drum Set Control.* Glenview, IL: Creative Music, 1971.
Dahlgren, Marvin, and Elliot Fine. *4–Way Coordination.* New York: Belwin–Mills, 1963.
GEN. BIB.: Larrick, *BET–CP.*

DASH, PATRICIA (b. 7 Aug 1961, Rochester, New York). A member of the Chicago Symphony since 1986, Pat Dash received a bachelor's degree from the Eastman School in 1983 and did graduate work at the Cincinnati Conservatory. Her teachers include *Doug Howard, Ruth Cahn, Richard Jensen, *Gordon Stout, William Platt, *Allen Otte, and *John Beck. She has performed with the Colorado Philharmonic (summers, 1982/1983), Rochester Philharmonic, Cincinnati Symphony, Cincinnati Pops, Summit Brass Ensemble, Philhar-

monic Orchestra of Florida (principal), Chicago Chamber Musicians, and Virtuosi de Landolfi. Dash's teaching appointments have included the American
Conservatory and Northwestern University.

SELECTED DISCOGRAPHY

NEXUS CD 10339: *The Solo Percussionist* (Music of William Cahn), 1997.
GEN. BIB.: Larrick, *BET–CP*.

DAVIS, RON (b. ca. 1945, New Jersey?; d. April 1996, New Jersey?).
Drummer for Joey Dee and the Starlighters while in high school, Ron Davis
later attended Berklee College of Music. Two of his albums with Chuck Mangione were nominated for Grammy® Awards, and he was a frequent guest drummer on the *Tonight Show* orchestra under Doc Severinsen, with whom he recorded two albums. His numerous collaborators have included Chet Baker,
Benny Goodman, Bill Watrous, Tony Bennett, Jack McDuff, Joe Farrell, Gerry
Mulligan, and Sarah Vaughan. While a member of Woody Herman's "Thundering Herd," he received a Grammy® Award for best big band album of 1972.

SELECTED DISCOGRAPHY

A&M/Horizon SP–719: *Gerry Niewood & Timepiece*, 1977.
Mercury 822 539–2: *Land of Make–Believe* (Chuck Mangione), 1985.
Mercury MCR4–1–631: *Quartet* (Chuck Mangione), 1972.
Mercury SRM–2–7501: *Together* (Chuck Mangione), 1971.
TelArc Jazz CD–83348: *Tonight I Need You So* (Jeanie Bryson), 1994.

SELECTED BIBLIOGRAPHY

Korall, Burt. "Obituary." *IM* XCV (September 1996): 20.
Read, John. "In Memoriam: Ron Davis." *MD* XX, 11 (November 1996): 111.

DAWSON, GEORGE ALAN (b. 14 Jul 1929, Marietta, Pennsylvania; d. 23
Feb 1996, Lexington/Boston, Massachusetts). Raised in Roxbury, Massachusetts, drumset educator and performer Alan Dawson started drums at age 12,
studied with Charles Alden, and played his first professional gig by age 14. He
served in the Ft. Dix (NJ) U.S. Army Band (1951–53), worked with Sabby
Lewis (1951), and toured Europe with *Lionel Hampton (1953). A "house
drummer" for many years in Boston (1957–70), Dawson performed with the
Dave Brubeck Quartet (1968–75) and the Boston Percussion Trio, appeared at
the Berlin Jazz Festival (1965), and toured with the "Two Generations of
Brubeck" family group. His other collaborators on stage and studio included
Hank Jones, Gerry Mulligan, Sonny Rollins, Oscar Peterson, Bill Evans, Dex-
ter Gordon, Earl Hines, George Shearing, Phil Woods, Herb Pomeroy

(1959–60), Jaki Byard, and Richard Davis (Prestige label, 1963–68), among others.

Through his teaching post at the Berklee School of Music (1957–75), Dawson gave birth to a new generation of drumset stars, including *Tony Williams, *Harvey Mason, *Terri Lyne Carrington, *Steve Smith, *Joe LaBarbera, *Keith Copeland, *Jake Hanna, *Vinnie Colaiuta, Kenwood Dennard, Casey Scheuerell, and *John "J. R." Robinson. He received *Modern Drummer* magazine's Editors' Achievement Award in 1996.

SELECTED DISCOGRAPHY

Accurate Records AC–3924: *"The Ruby and the Pearl"* (Dominique Eade), 1991.
Blue Note BLP5049/5050: *Gigi Gryce Ensemble*, 1953.
Concord 4575: *The Music of Jerome Kern* (Adam Makowicz Trio), 1993.
Concord 4788–2: *Full Circle* (Howard Alden), 1998.
Muse 5037: *Musique du bois* (Phil Woods), 1974.
Muse MCD–5334: *Tune Up* (Sonny Stitt), 1972.
Prestige 7295: *The Freedom Book* (Booker Ervin), 1963.
Prestige 7732: *Tal Farlow Returns*, 1969.
Prestige OJC CD–359–2: *Clifford Brown Big Band in Paris*, 1953.
Prestige OJC CD–770–2: *The Panther* (Dexter Gordon), 1970.
Prestige OJC CD–780–2: *The Blues Book* (Booker Ervin), 1964.
Prestige OJC 655: *A Portrait of Sonny Criss*, 1967.

SELECTED BIBLIOGRAPHY

Anderson, Dean. "1996 PAS® Hall of Fame: Alan Dawson." *PN* XXXIV, 6 (December 1996): 13–14.
Anderson, Dean. "Remembering George 'Alan' Dawson, 1929–1996." *Percussion News* (July 1996): 9.
Dawson, Alan. *A Manual for the Modern Dummer*. Boston: Berklee Press, 1964.
Morgenstern, Dan. "The Poll Winner as Teacher: Alan Dawson." *DB* XXXIII, 19 (22 Sep 1966): 27–29.
Scott, Arvin. "A Conversation with Alan Dawson on Creative Drumming." *PN* XXXIV, 6 (December 1996): 26–27.
Van Horn, Rick. "In Memoriam: Alan Dawson." *MD* XX, 7 (July 1996): 122–123.
GEN. BIB.: Hunt, *52nd St.*; Kernfeld, *NGJ*, by Bill Bennett; Spagnardi, *GJD*.

DEAGAN, JOHN CALHOUN (b. 6 Nov 1853, Hector, New York; d. 28 Apr 1934, Hermosa Beach, California). Born to Irish immigrant parents, J. C. Deagan attended public schools in Youngstown, Ohio, and Raines College. He enlisted in the U.S. Navy in 1871, was stationed aboard the USS *Brooklyn*, and while anchored in England, took music classes at the University of London, where he heard lectures by Hermann von Helmholtz, the noted authority on sound. Reportedly a virtuoso clarinetist, Deagan played in American orchestras after his discharge. Offended by the tone of the imported German orchestra bells, he sought to improve them; he was so successful that he founded the J. C. Deagan Musical Bells Company—a one–man operation—on the side in St. Louis, Missouri (ca. 1880). Following performance opportunities in San Francisco in 1891, he called his flowering cottage industry J. C. Deagan and Company (1895). After Deagan moved to Chicago (1897), the business was incorporated as J. C. Deagan Musical Bells, Inc. (1913); it was renamed J. C. Deagan, Inc., in 1916.

Relying upon Helmhotz's acoustic research, Deagan is credited with establishing A–440 as a musical benchmark for the various metallic or wooden "tuned" percussion he manufactured. The American Federation of Musicians (AFM) adopted this standard in 1910, and the U.S. government followed suit for all its military music groups in 1922. Touting 600 instruments and their variations by 1910, his vast array of improvements and innovations included orchestra bells (aka "glockenspiels," some employing resonators), xylophones (1886), marimbas, cathedral chimes (1886), "shaker" chimes (metallic copies of the Indonesian bamboo *angklung*), tuned sleigh bells (1893), electric tubular church bells/carillons (1916, played manually or automatically by perforated paper rolls controlled with a clock mechanism), clock chimes, tuning forks, vibraphone bars of aluminum alloy (1927), and an electric tower carillon ("Celesta–Chime," 1937). Melvin L. "Deacon" Jones, sales manager for the Deagan Company, compiled the *National School of Vibracussion* (1917, Chicago), a home study course for all mallet instruments that could be bought in weekly installments or was supplied free with instrument purchase.

Deagan was a charter member of the AFM, on the board of curators for Chicago's Field Museum, and, fascinated with light and sound, astronomy, physics, geology, and chemistry, was the namesake of the J. C. Deagan Astronomical Society of Riverside, California. His grandson, John C. "Jack" Deagan (b. 22 Mar 1910, Chicago, Illinois; d. 16 Oct 1973, Long Grove, Illinois), son of Jefferson Claude (1886–1924) and Ella Deagan, became president of the company in 1954, succeeding his mother, who had served in that capacity from 1932 to 1954. Deagan, Inc., was sold to the American Gauge and Machine Company (1967), and Jack retired in 1969. The C. G. Conn Company purchased Deagan in 1978, only to sell it, with the Slingerland Drum division of Conn, to the Sanlar Corporation (Sandra and Larry Rasp) in 1984, after which Deagan was purchased by the Yamaha Corporation who still produce the Deagan chimes and orchestra bells. In 1999 John Calhoun Deagan was inducted into the Percussive Arts Society's Hall of Fame.

SELECTED BIBLIOGRAPHY

The National Cyclopedia of American Biography, vol. 43. New York: James T. White & Co., 1961. S.v. "Deagan, John Calhoun" (photo).
"Pictorial History of the Marimba." *Etude* (August 1939): 494.
GEN. BIB.: Hitchcock and Sadie, *NGA,* by Edmund A. Bowles; Strain, *XYLO.*

DEEMS, BARRETT (b. 1 Mar 1914, Springfield, Illinois; d. 1998). In his midteens drumset artist Barrett Deems led his own groups and played with Paul Ash, then landed in New York, where he was first engaged by Joe Venuti (1937–45). He worked with *Red Norvo (1948), Charlie Barnet (1951), Francis "Muggsy" Spanier (1951–54), Louis Armstrong's All–Stars (worldwide tours, 1953–61), Jack Teagarden (1960–64), the Dukes of Dixlieland (1964), Benny Carter, Buck Clayton, and Teddy Wilson, among others. Deems made a musical screen appearance in the film *High Society* (1956) with Armstrong and Bing Crosby. From 1966 to 1970 he settled in Chicago, performing with "The World's Greatest Jazz Band" and recording with Art Hodes. A veteran of international jazz festivals, Deems toured Europe with Benny Goodman (1976), toured South America with Wild Bill Davison, and shared the stage with Jimmy McPartland and Milt Hinton at the 1986 Newport Jazz Festival.

SELECTED DISCOGRAPHY

Columbia C2 36426: *Louis Armstrong—Chicago Concert*, 1956.
Columbia CL1077: *Satchmo the Great* (Louis Armstrong), 1955–56.
Columbia CS8994: *World's Fair* (Dukes of Dixieland), 1964.
Decca 74807: *Sunrise, Sunset* (Dukes of Dixieland), 1966.
Decca 8741: *Louis Armstrong and the Good Book*, 1958.
Delmark DD–492: *Deemus*, 1978/1997.
Verve MGV8231–2: *Jazz at the Hollywood Bowl* (Ella Fitzgerald and Louis Armstrong), 1956.

SELECTED VIDEOGRAPHY

Video: *The Wonderful World of Louis Armstrong*, 1986.

SELECTED BIBLIOGRAPHY

Whyatt, Bert. CD from *Muggsy Spanier: The Lonesome Road*. New Orleans: Jazzology Press, 1996.
GEN. BIB.: Kernfeld, *NGJ*, by Jeff Potter; Spagnardi, *GJD*.

DEJOHNETTE, JACK (b. 9 Aug 1942, Chicago, Illinois). A veteran drumset artist of the avant–garde jazz and blues genres, Jack DeJohnette was actually a pianist (started playing professionally at 14) and bassist before becoming a drummer at 16, appearing early on with Roscoe Mitchell and Richard Abrams. In 1966 he relocated to New York, where he worked with Charles Lloyd, Jackie McLean, Abbey Lincoln, and Betty Carter. A composer who graduated from the American Conservatory of Music, he participated in the Association for the Advancement of Creative Musicians and has performed with and/or recorded over 50 albums with numerous jazz greats, including Keith Jarrett, Thelonius Monk, Chick Corea, Sonny Rollins, Pat Metheny, Stan Getz, Miles Davis (three years), John Coltrane, Bill Evans, Herbie Hancock (including 1997 tour),

Freddie Hubbard, and his own groups, Compost, Special Edition, and New Directions. Some of these collaborations have led to Grammy® Award citations. DeJohnette was recipient of the "Drum Master" Award in New York City; Berklee College (Boston) granted him an honorary doctorate degree; and *Down Beat* magazine's Reader's Poll has named him "Best Drummer" for several years.

SELECTED DISCOGRAPHY

Atlantic 1473: *Forest Flower* (Charles Lloyd), 1967.
Blue Note B4 0777 7 99089 4 3: *Music for the Fifth World*, 1992.
Blue Note CDP 7243 8 30494 2 4: *Jack DeJohnette—Extra Special Edition*, 1994.
Blue Note B1–92894: *Time on My Hands* (John Scofield), 1990.
Blue Note 55817: *Andalucia* (Kevin Hays), 1997.
Blue Note 56810: *Renee Rosnes—As We Are Now*, 1997.
Blue Note 7243 8 30491: *Imagine* (Gonzalo Rubalcaba), 1993–94.
Blue Note 84332: *Super Nova* (Wayne Shorter), 1969.
Blue Note 84345: *Demon's Dance* (Jackie McLean), 1967.
Blue Note 84416: *Natural Illusions* (Bobby Hutcherson), 1972.
Blue Note 89544: *Paulistana* (Eliane Elias), 1993.
Blue Note 93089: *Eliane Elias Plays Jobim*, 1990.
Blue Note 96146: *Fantasia* (Eliane Elias), 1992.
Blue Note BT 85107: *Twilight Time* (Bennie Wallace), 1985.
Blue Note BTDK 85117: *One Night with Blue Note Preserved*, 1985.
Blue Note LA395–H2: *Chick Corea*, 1969.
Blue Note LA457–H2: *Jacknife/High Frequency* (Jackie McLean), 1965–66.
Chiaroscuro CR 2021: *Chick Corea*, 1980.
Columbia 30038 or Sony 50 DP 714: *Miles Davis Live at the Fillmore*, 1970/1996.
Columbia CGT–30954: *Live–Evil* (Miles Davis), 1971.
Columbia KC31906: *On the Corner* (Miles Davis), 1972.
Columbia J2C 40577: *Bitches Brew* (Miles Davis), 1969.
Concord 4775–2: *Unspoken* (Chris Potter), 1997.
Denon CY–2180: *Cross Currents* (Eliane Elias), 1988.
ECM 78118–21180: *80/81* (Pat Metheny), 1980/1994.
ECM 78118–21558: *Dancing with Nature Spirits*, 1996.
ECM 1105: *Gateway 2* (John Abercrombie) 1978.
ECM: *Jack DeJohnette's Special Edition—Tin Can Alley*, 1981.
ECM 835 008–2: *Keith Jarrett Trio—Still Live*, 1988.
ECM 1637: *Oneness*, 1997.
ECM–1069: *Gnu High* (Kenny Wheeler), 1976/1994.
ECM–1102: *Deer Wan* (Kenny Wheeler), 1978/1989.
ECM–1121: *Batik* (Ralph Towner), 1978.
ECM–M5E 1152/827 694–2: *Special Edition*, 1979.
ECM–1157/829 158–2: *New Directions in Europe*, 1979.
ECM–1255/811966–2: *Standards,* vol. 1 (Keith Jarrett), 1987.
ECM–1262: *Double, Double You* (Kenny Wheeler), 1984.
ECM–1562: *Gateway—Homecoming* (John Abercrombie/Dave Holland), 1995.
ECM–1575–80: *Keith Jarrett—The Complete Blue Note Recordings*, 1996.
Geffen 24096: *Song X* (Pat Metheny/Ornette Coleman), 1986.

Geffen GEFD–24521: *Fictionary* (Lyle Mays), 1993.
GRP/Impulse IMPD–191: *Michael Brecker—Tales from the Hudson*, 1996.
GRP GRD–9685: *Gary Burton and Friends—Six Pack*, 1992.
King 6473: *Tribute to Coltrane* (David Liebman), 1987.
MCA MCAC 42313: *Parallel Realities*, 1990.
MCA/Impulse MCA 5980: *Michael Brecker*, 1987.
Milestone M–47058: *Foresight* (Joe Henderson), 1980.
Milestone 4421: *Bill Evans—The Secret Sessions*, 1966–75.
Milestone: *Silver City* (Sonny Rollins), 1997.
Milestone 9108: *Reel Life* (Sonny Rollins), 1982.
Milestone 55003: *Supertrios* (McCoy Tyner), 1977.
Milestone M–9079: *McCoy Tyner—Inner Voices*, 1977.
Milestone MSP 9017: *Tetragon* (Joe Henderson), 1967.
Owl 051: *Trio + One* (David Liebman), 1989.
Verve 314 523 600–4: *Betty Carter—Feed the Fire*, 1994.
Verve 314 529 584: *Herbie Hancock—The New Standard*, 1996.
Verve V6–8762: *At the Montreux Jazz Festival* (Bill Evans), 1968.
Verve 314 539 046–2: *Porgy and Bess* (Joe Henderson), 1997.
Warner Bros. P–7501A: *The Infinite Search* (Miroslav Vitous), 1969.
Westwind 2067: *First Visit* (David Liebman), 1971.

SELECTED VIDEOGRAPHY

DCI VH0249: *Legends of Jazz Drumming, Pt. 2, 1950–70*, 1996.
Homespun Video: *Jack DeJohnette—Musical Expression on the Drumset*, 1992.
Homespun Video: *Talking Drummers* (with Don Alias), 1997.
Public Media Home Vision: *Standards I/II* (Keith Jarrett), 1985–87.

SELECTED BIBLIOGRAPHY

Beuttler, Bill. "Jack DeJohnette Interview." *DB* (September 1987): 16–19.
Griffith, Mark. "Artist on Track: Jack DeJohnette." *MD* XIX, 1 (January 1995): 124–125.
Mattingly, Rick. "Jack DeJohnette: Track by Track." *MD* XIX, 6 (June 1995): 42–62.
Perry, Charles. "Jack DeJohnette Interview." *PN* XVIII, 2 (Winter 1980): 27–29.
Primack, Bret. "Jack DeJohnette: World Vision." *JazzTimes* XXII, 9 (November 1992): 28–32.
GEN. BIB.: Hunt, *52nd St.*; Kernfeld, *NGJ*, by Lewis Porter; Larrick, *BET–CP*; Spagnardi, *GJD*; PASIC[R] program biographies, 1994.

DELANCEY, CHARLES (b. 5 Jul 1929, Gordon, Nebraska).   Earning a bachelor's (1953) and a master's (1958) degree from the University of California at Los Angeles, percussionist and composer Charles DeLancey studied with Lukas Foss, served in the 64th U.S. Army Band (Tokyo) for 15 months, and was a member of the Los Angeles Philharmonic.

SELECTED DISCOGRAPHY

Cambria CD–1071: *The Music of William Kraft*, 1993.
Sony Classical SMK 63164: *Lukas Foss—Time Cycle*, 1958/1997.

DELLA PORTA, ALBERT (b. 1903, England?; d. 1965). Albert Della Porta founded the Premier Drum Company, Ltd., in 1922, manufacturing drums in London with his younger brother, Fred. WWII Nazi bombardments prompted a move to Leicester in 1941. The company remained solvent under Della Porta's three sons until 1983, when shortfalls forced it into receivership; it was purchased by Premier management, who subsequently sold it in 1987 (under the title Premier Percussion Limited) to the Yamaha Corporation. Taking advantage of Yamaha's corporate problems in 1993, former director Tony Doughty purchased Premier, only to resell it in 1995 to a British firm, the Verity Group. A unique feature of the company is that each instrument is completely manufactured in–house.

SELECTED BIBLIOGRAPHY

Saccone, Teri. "Inside Premier." *MD* XX, 4 (April 1996): 84–93.

DENECKE, HENRY, JR. (b. 4 Aug 1911, New York, New York). The grandson and son of drummers (his grandfather started the Bass Drum Club of New York to install bass drums in all the music halls to avoid carrying them across town), Henry Denecke, Jr., studied at Columbia University and with his father who performed for 38 years in New York's Jewish Theater and for Fritz Scheel in Philadelphia before the Philadelphia Orchestra was established. Denecke, Sr. [d. ca. Mar 1943, New York?, New York], a frustrated violinist, taught percussion to 75–100 students a week (15-minute lessons) and enlisted his son (also initially a violinist-violist who was allergic to rosin!) to check their snare rudiments before they went in for the main lesson. Denecke, Jr., continued to play both strings and percussion in junior high school. After studying timpani with his father, he performed at 14 as timpanist for the YMHA and YMCA Orchestras and with the American Orchestral Association (later aka National Orchestral Association), a preprofessional training group. He was moved to stagehand when it was discovered that he was under 16, but he eventually became section leader. True professional work and union membership came with the New York Opera Comique, where he stayed for five years.

Denecke served as timpanist and tour xylophonist for the original production of George Gershwin's *Porgy and Bess*. Replacing a student of his father's, Harry Miller, as timpanist in the Cleveland Orchestra (1936–37), he played timpani with the Pittsburgh Symphony (1938–39) and performed in *The Devil and Daniel Webster* in New York (1939). As a freelancer in New York between his orchestra positions, he worked for the *Firestone Hour* radio show, performed with the NBC Orchestra, and played the American premiere of Béla Bartók's "Sonata for Two Pianos and Percussion" (New York, 1940) with timpanist *Saul Goodman, featuring Bartók and Bartók's wife, Ditta, on pianos.

Timpanist for the Minneapolis Symphony (now aka Minnesota Orchestra) from 1941 to 1952, during which time he began a conducting career (ca. 1950) by founding the Northwest Sinfonietta and the Minneapolis Civic Orchestra, Denecke was full–time conductor of the Cedar Rapids Symphony from 1953 to 1970 and then returned to New York and freelanced in the Metropolitan Opera Orchestra. In 1995 he was living in Wisconsin with his wife, Julia, a veteran flautist with the Minneapolis Symphony and Phil Spitalny's All–Girl Orchestra.

SELECTED BIBLIOGRAPHY

Kogan, Peter. "Henry Denecke, Jr." *PN* XXXIII, 3 (June 1995): 56–64.

DENOV, SAM (b. 11 Dec 1923, Chicago, Illinois). After studying with *Roy Knapp (1938–41) under a Chicago Board of Education Scholarship, Sam Denov graduated from the U.S. Navy School of Music (1943) and served as a bandsman in the navy's Fourth Fleet until 1946. Holding percussion positions in the Chicago Civic Training Orchestra, San Antonio Symphony (1947–50), and Pittsburgh Symphony (1950–52), he finally settled in the Chicago Symphony (1954–85, as percussionist, cymbalist, and assistant timpanist), where he received 24 Grammy® Awards (1971–82). Since then, he has appeared as a substitute with the Minnesota, Seattle, and San Diego Symphonies. Inventor of an automatic timpani-tuning device, Denov attended Roosevelt University (1971–73, Chicago) receiving a bachelor's degree in general studies. He serves as president of the Chicago Symphony Orchestra Alumni Association and can be heard with the Chicago Symphony (1954–85) on RCA, Mercury, Columbia, Angel, London, and Deutsche Grammophon recording labels.

SELECTED VIDEOGRAPHY

Yamaha EV–30I/II and Warner Bros. Publications VHO 136–7: *Concert Percussion: A Performer's Guide*, vols. 1–2, 1989.

SELECTED BIBLIOGRAPHY

Denov, Sam. "A New Tuning Device for Timpani." *PN* XVI, 1 (Fall 1977): 10.
Denov, Sam. "Cymbalists and the Laws of Physics." *PN* XXXIV, 4 (August 1996): 62–64.
Denov, Sam. *The Art of Playing the Cymbals*. New York: Henry Adler/Belwin–Mills/Warner Bros., 1963.
Furlong, William Barry. *Season with Solti: A Year in the Life of the Chicago Symphony*. New York: Macmillan Publishing, 1974.
Siwe, Tom. "An Interview with Sam Denov." *PN* XXIV, 2 (January 1986): 22–28.
GEN. BIB.: Borland, *WWAMC*; Larrick, *BET–CP*. Information provided by the subject, 1996.

DEPONTE, NEIL BONAVENTURE (b. 3 May 1953, New York, New York). Since 1977 Neil DePonte has held the principal percussion chair with the Oregon Symphony and in 1980 was appointed musical director and conductor of the West Coast Chamber Orchestra (Portland, Oregon). He received a bachelor's degree and performer's certificate from SUNY at Fredonia (1974) and a master's degree and performer's certificate from the Eastman School (1976). DePonte's percussion teachers have included *Fred Hinger, *John Beck, and Ted Frazeur. A multifaceted percussionist, conductor, and composer whose works have become standard percussion repertoire, he has also written newspaper articles and music reviews. His teaching posts have included Lewis and Clark College (started 1977), University of Massachusetts (1976–77), and the Interlochen National Music Camp (1976–79).

SELECTED DISCOGRAPHY

Delos DE 3070: *Bravura* (Oregon Symphony, snare and mallet percussion), 1987/1994.
Delos DE 3081: *Tchaikovsky: 1812 Overture* (Oregon Symphony, snare and tambourine), 1989.
Music for Percussion IRC ADP–075 S: *Percussion at Fredonia*, 1974.

SELECTED BIBLIOGRAPHY

DePonte, Neil. "*No. 9 Zyklus:* How and Why?" *Percussionist* XII, 4 (Summer 1975): 136–149.
GEN. BIB.: Borland, *WWAMC*; Larrick, *BET–CP*.

DETRY, CHARLES (fl. 1870, Paris). Charles DeTry was considered a virtuoso on a *quasi* xylophone instrument dubbed the *Tryphone*. It is not known if the bars were configured in double–row or four–row, or whether it was chromatic or diatonic.

SELECTED BIBLIOGRAPHY

Peters, Gordon. *The Drummer: Man.* Wilmette, IL: Kemper–Peters Publications, 1975.

DICKERSON, WALT (b. 1931, Philadelphia, Pennsylvania). A graduate of Morgan State College (Baltimore, MD, 1953), vibist Walt Dickerson served in the U.S. Army (1953–55), moved from Philadelphia to New York in 1961, and then worked with *Andrew Cyrille and Andrew Hill in California before his notable association with Sun Ra (1965). Following a 10–year hiatus from performing, he resurfaced in Europe with Sun Ra and others around 1975.

SELECTED DISCOGRAPHY

MGM 4358: *Impressions of a Patch of Blue* (Sun Ra), 1965.
New Jazz 8283: *To My Queen*, 1963.
Steeplechase 1126: *Visions* (Sun Ra), 1978.

SELECTED BIBLIOGRAPHY

Beck, John H., ed. *Encyclopedia of Percussion*. New York: Garland Publishing,
        1995. S.v. "The Vibraphone, Vibraharp, and Vibes," by Hal Trommer.
De Michael, Don. "Impressions of Walt Dickerson." *DB* XXIX, 20 (25 Oct 1962):
        19.
GEN. BIB.: Kernfeld, *NGJ*, by Roger T. Dean.

DODDS, WARREN "BABY" (b. 24 Dec 1898, New Orleans, Louisiana; d. 14
Feb 1959, Chicago, Illinois). The most famous of the early New Orleans drumset artists, Baby Dodds studied with Dave Perkins, Walter Brundy, Louis
Cotrelle, and others and played with Papa Celestin and Bunk Johnson, on riverboats with Fate Marable (1918–21), and with King Oliver's Creole Jazz Band
(starting 1921) in San Francisco (1922) and Chicago (first recording, 1923). For
20 years he freelanced in Chicago, recording and working with his brother, clarinetist Johnny Dodds, Louis Armstrong's Hot Seven (1927), Freddie Keppard,
and Jelly Roll Morton. He served as house drummer at the Three Deuces in
New York (1936–39); and when the public's taste returned to Dixieland around
1940, Dodds was in demand again with Sidney Bechet, Jimmie Noone, and
Bunk Johnson (1944), playing on radio (1946–47) and touring Europe in 1948
with Mezz Mezzrow. His health declined steadily (suffered strokes, 1949–50),
but he relocated and continued performing in Chicago (1952) until he was forced
to retire in 1957.

  His technique of changing drum, rim, and cymbal tone colors to accompany
contrasting musical phrases and his pioneering attention to drum head tuning
were imitated by successful drummers of the next generation, including *Gene
Krupa and *Dave Tough, who learned from Dodds in Chicago. He supposedly
was the first to play drum "fills" between musical phrases, which led Krupa to
remark that Dodds was the first great soloist.

SELECTED DISCOGRAPHY

ABC/Impulse ASH 9272B/Jazz Odyssey JO 008: *The Drums*, 1989.
American Music AMCD–1: *Bunk Johnson—King of the Blues*, 1944/1989.
American Music AMCD–2: *George Lewis with Kid Shots*. 1944/1990.
American Music AMCD–3: *Bunk Johnson, 1944*.
American Music AMCD–4: *George Lewis—Trios and Bands*, 1945/1991.
American Music AMCD–5: *Wooden Joe Nicholas*, 1992.
American Music AMCD–6: *Bunk's Brass Band and Dance Band*, 1992.
American Music AMCD–8: *Bunk Johnson, 1944, Second Masters*.

American Music AMCD–12: *Bunk Johnson, 1944/45.*
American Music AMCD–18: *Natty Dominique's Creole Dance Band.*
American Music AMCD–17: *Baby Dodds* (Re–release of documentary recordings, 1944–45), 1993.
American Music AMCD–45: *Bunk and Mutt in New York, 1947.*
American Music AMCD–72: *Mutt Carey and Lee Collins.*
American Music AMCD–75: *Original Zenith Brass Band* et al.
American Music 101: *"In Gloryland"* (Bunk Johnson), 1945.
Bluebird 2293–2–RB: *Johnny Dodds—Blue Clarinet Stomp,* 1927–29.
Bluebird 2361–2–RB: *The Centennial Jelly Roll Morton—His Complete Victor Recordings,* 1927.
Bluebird 2402–2–RB: *Sidney Bechet—The Victor Sessions, Master Takes, 1932–43.*
Blue Note 518: *"Careless Love,"* 1945.
Columbia CK 44253/44422: *Louis Armstrong—The Hot Fives and Sevens,* vols. 2–3, 1927.
Folkways FJ 2290: *Baby Dodds—Talking and Playing Drum Solos* (Footnotes to Jazz, vol. 1), 1951.
Gennett 5134: *"I'm Going to Wear You off My Mind"* (King Oliver), 1923.
GHB 50: *The Baby Dodds Trio,* 1971.
Jazzology J–15: *Tony Parenti's Ragtimers and Ragpickers,* 1947.
Jazzology J–33: *Muggsy Spanier and His All–Stars,* 1947.
Jazzology J–113: *Art Hodes—The Trios,* 1953.
Jazzology JCD–35: *The Genius of Sidney Bechet,* 1995.
Jazzology JCD–42: *Wild Bill Davison and His All–Star Stompers—This Is Jazz!* 1994.
Jazzology JCD–82: *Art Hodes—The Jazz Record Story,* 1980.
Jazzology JCD–301/302: *World's Greatest Jazz Concert No. 1/No. 2,* 1993.
Masters of Jazz, Media 7: *Anthology of Jazz Drumming,* vols. 1–2 (1904–35), 1997.
MCA/Decca MCAD–42326: *Johnny Dodds—South-Side Chicago Jazz,* 1990.
MCA/Decca MCAD–42328: *Louis Armstrong of New Orleans,* 1927.
Mosaic MR5–114: *Baby Dodds' Jazz Four,* 1945.
Okeh 8474: *"Wild Man Blues"* (Louis Armstrong), 1927.
Savoy SJL 2251: *Giants of Traditional Jazz,* 1947.
The Smithsonian Collection R001: *King Oliver's Jazz Band,* 1923.
Victor 20772: *"Billy Goat Stomp"* (Jelly Roll Morton), 1927.
Victor 38004: *"Weary City"* (Johnny Dodds), 1928.

SELECTED VIDEOGRAPHY

DCI VH0248: *Legends of Jazz Drumming, Pt. 1, 1920–50,* 1996.

SELECTED BIBLIOGRAPHY

Dodds, Warren "Baby." *The Baby Dodds Story, as Told to Larry Gara,* rev. ed. Baton Rouge: Louisana State University Press, 1992.
King, Bruce. "The Gigantic Baby Dodds." *Jazz Review* III, 7 (August 1960): 14.
Riley, Herlin, and Johnny Vidacovich. *New Orleans Jazz and Second Line Drumming.* Miami, FL: Warner Bros./Manhattan Music, 1995.

Russell, Bill. *New Orleans Style*. New Orleans: Jazzology Press, 1994.

Shultz, Thomas. "A History of Jazz Drumming." *Percussionist* XVI, 3 (Spring/Summer 1979): 112.

Wettling, George. "A Tribute to Baby Dodds." *DB* XXIX, 7 (29 Mar 1962): 21.

Whyatt, Bert. CD from *Muggsy Spanier: The Lonesome Road*. New Orleans: Jazzology Press, 1996.

GEN. BIB.: Hitchcock and Sadie, *NGA*, by J. Bradford Robinson; Spagnardi, *GJD*.

DOLBY, PAUL MORRISON (b. 1913, Columbus, Ohio; d. 17 May 1995, San Antonio, Texas). Starting percussion in public school, Paul Dolby attended Capital School of Music, Asbury College (1933–35, KY), and Ohio State University (1935/1937), then moved to New York (1938–40), where he studied with *Alfred Friese, *Fred Albright, and *Saul Goodman. After serving in the 258th Field Artillery Band, 212th Ground Force Band, and the U.S. Army Band–Washington, D.C. (1941–45, where he was a featured xylophone soloist on Major Bowes and Ted Hussing radio programs), Dolby enlisted in the U.S. Air Force Band–Washington, D.C. (1946–67), touring Europe, the Far East, and South America. He earned a bachelor's degree from the University of Maryland in 1954, joined the Denver Symphony as percussionist (1967–80), and then retired to El Paso, Texas, where he played with the El Paso Symphony (1981–   ).

Percussive Arts Society Hall of Fame nominee biographies.

DORN, WILLIAM "BILLY" (b. 23 Feb 1893, Newark, New Jersey; d. ca. 1970, New Jersey?). Billy Dorn began percussion at age 11 and played the first movie houses in Newark. A teacher who composed several solos and arranged for mallet ensembles, he owned a music store and played with Arthur Pryor's Band, the Green Brothers Orchestras, *Joe Green's Novelty Marimba Band, and the Yerkes Jazzarimba Orchestra. He was in demand as a recording artist in most of the New York studios and worked as xylophonist in the New York Philharmonic, the NBC Symphony under Toscanini, and the Symphony of the Air, retiring in 1968 to Belmar, New Jersey.

SELECTED DISCOGRAPHY

Edison 50362: "Marriage Bells" (bells and xylophone duet with Dorn on xylophone), 1916.

SELECTED BIBLIOGRAPHY

Dorn, Billy. *A Simple and Practical Method for Xylophone, Marimba, and Bells*. New York: Belwin–Mills, Inc., 1953.

Dorn, Billy. *Advanced Reading and Technical Studies*. New York: Belwin–Mills, Inc., 1962.

Dorn, Billy. *Instant Scales and Chords*. New York: Henry Adler, Inc., 1966.

Dorn, Billy. *Series of Solos.* New York: Henry Adler, Inc., 1958.

Dorn, Billy. "Trippin' and Skiddin' for Xylophone, Marimba, or Vibes." New York: Henry Adler, 1958.

Eyler, David P. "Development of the Marimba Ensemble in North America during the 1930s." *PN* XXXIV, 1 (February 1996): 66–71.

Stone, George L. "Technique of Percussion." *IM* (July 1951): 21.

The ASCAP Biographical Dictionary of Composers, Authors, and Publishers. New York: ASCAP/Lynn Farnol Group, 1966. S.v. "Dorn, William," p. 182.

GEN. BIB.: Cook, *LDT*, p. 165 (photo).

DRUCKMAN, DANIEL (b. New York, New York). The son of well–known composer Jacob Druckman, Daniel Druckman studied at the Berkshire Music Center at Tanglewood and earned a bachelor's and a master's degree from the Juilliard School (1980). A recording artist for radio, television, and film, he has appeared as soloist and chamber-orchestral percussionist in the United States, Europe, and Japan with such organizations as the Los Angeles Philharmonic, American Composers Orchestra, New York Philharmonic, and San Francisco Symphony. Studio labels on which he has recorded include Columbia, Angel, Teldec, DGG, CRI, Nonesuch, Bridge, and New World.

Druckman has premiered numerous works by contemporary composers, performing at music festivals in Santa Fe, Ravinia, Saratoga, Caramoor, and Tanglewood and holds positions in the New York Philharmonic, Speculum Musicae, and New York New Music Ensemble. He has appeared with the Saint Paul Chamber Orchestra, Chamber Music Society of Lincoln Center, Da Capo Chamber Players, Group for Contemporary Music, Steve Reich and Musicians, and the Philip Glass Ensemble. An original cast member of Peter Brook's production of *Carmen* at Lincoln Center, Druckman is coordinator of percussion studies and director of the percussion ensemble at the Juilliard School and has taught masterclasses at Columbia University, the California Institute of the Arts, and the University of Colorado, among others.

SELECTED DISCOGRAPHY

Grenadilla GSC–1066: *Ivey—Prospero*, 1984.
Information supplied by the subject, 1996.

DRUSCHETZKY, GEORG "JIRI" (b. 7 Apr 1745, Jemniky, Western Bohemia; d. 6 Sep 1819, Pest). Druschetzky was known both as an oboist and as a virtuoso timpanist who studied early on in Dresden but gained a reputation as a composer of various musical genres that included 27 symphonies and unusual works featuring timpani as a solo instrument. Since pedal timpani had not been invented, these pieces required multiple sets of drums tuned to all the necessary pitches. After 13 years of service in the Austrian army, he attained the rank of

Kapellmeister in 1775. Upon leaving the army, and through his engagement to a member of the social elite of Linz, Druschetzky was appointed regional timpanist (Landschaftspauker) in 1777. He accepted a position in 1787 with a 24–piece orchestra in Pressburg (Bratislava) until his final appointment in 1807 as composer to Archduke Joseph Anton Johann at Pest.

SELECTED DISCOGRAPHY

CRDC 4149: *Jonathan Haas—Virtuoso Timpanist,* 1988.

SELECTED BIBLIOGRAPHY

Altenburg, Johann. *Trumpeter's and Kettledrummer's Art (1795).* Translated by Ed Tarr. Nashville: Brass Press, 1974.
Brook, Barry S., ed. *The Symphony.* Vol. B 14, "Druschetzky," by Harrison Powley. New York: Garland, 1985.
GEN. BIB.: Sadie, *NG,* by Alexander Weinmann.

DUFF, CLOYD E. (b. 26 Sep 1915, Marietta, Ohio). A 1938 graduate of the Curtis Institute (attended 1935–39) and a 1977 inductee into the Percussive Arts Society Hall of Fame, Cloyd Duff acquired a drumset at age 6 and by high school had studied xylophone and timpani and had won the Ohio State Snare Drumming Championship. Supporting himself in college by playing in commercial dance bands and for vaudeville acts, he studied with *Oscar Schwar, performed summers with the Robin Hood Dell Orchestra (the Philadelphia Orchestra's summer home, where he later returned) and joined the Indianapolis Symphony (1939–42). Duff toured abroad under Stokowski with the All–American Youth Orchestra (summers, 1940–41) before winning the timpani chair with the Cleveland Orchestra (1942–81), where his colleagues included *Emil Sholle, Frank Sholle, Harry Miller, and later *Robert Matson and *Richard Weiner. While in Ohio he taught at the Oberlin Conservatory, the Cleveland Institute, Case Western Reserve, and Baldwin–Wallace College. Duff has served as artist–in–residence at Colorado State University and on the faculty of the Aspen Music School. His unusual setup for timpani is based on Germanic performance technique (i.e., largest or lowest–pitched drum on the right–hand side of the player), and he manufactures his own signature timpani mallets. His Cleveland Orchestra recordings and re–releases (1942–81) were made on Columbia, DGG, Odyssey, Victor, Angel, Epic, CBS–Sony, Decca, Telarc, and London recording labels.

SELECTED DISCOGRAPHY

Cleveland Institute of Music STV 20039: *Bartók—Sonata for Two Pianos and Percussion,* 1950s.
Columbia MS7291: *Great Orchestra Highlights from the "Ring of the Nibelungs"* (Cleveland Orchestra), 1985.

Columbia Y32223: *Mussorgsky—Pictures at an Exhibition* (Cleveland Orchestra), 1960/1969.

SELECTED VIDEOGRAPHY

Tap Products: *The Art of Timpani—Tucking Calfskin Timpani Heads*, 1995.
Yamaha EV–30I/II: *Concert Percussion: A Performer's Guide*, vols. 1–2, 1989.

SELECTED BIBLIOGRAPHY

"Cloyd Duff: A Biography." *PN* XVI, 2 (Winter 1978): 23.
Duff, Cloyd. "The Timpanist: Musician or Technician?" *PN* XXV, 5 (Summer 1987): 65–67 [reprinted from *Percussionist* V, 4 (May 1968)].
Faulkmann, Roger. "An Exclusive Interview with Cloyd Duff." *PN* XX, 3 (June 1982): 24–30.
Simco, Andrew. "An Interview with Cloyd Duff." *PN* XXXI, 3 (February 1993): 55–60.
Smith, Dick. "Cloyd Duff, Timpanist." *PN* XVI, 1 (Fall 1977): 32–33.
GEN. BIB.: Larrick, *BET–CP.*

DUPIN, FRANÇOIS (25 Sep 1931, Marcq–en–Baroeul, France; d. 17 Jul 1994, Paris, France). François Dupin entered the National Conservatory in Paris at the age of 16 and by 1961 received honors in percussion, percussion chamber music, and music composition. His teachers included *Félix Passerone and Darius Milhaud, among others, and he held the timpani chair with the Strasbourg Orchestra and taught at the Conservatories of Le Mans and Lyon. From 1961 to 1967, Dupin was keyboard specialist with the French Radio Philharmonic until the Paris Orchestra enlisted him as principal percussionist and assistant timpanist. He penned several percussion compositions and was the author of numerous percussion etude books.

SELECTED DISCOGRAPHY

EMI CO64–12836: *Marim' Bach*, 1975.
EMI CO69–11326: *Percussions de l'Orchestre de Paris*, 1970.

SELECTED BIBLIOGRAPHY

Dupin, François. *Courtes Pieces*, vols. 1–7 (Snare, timpani, drumset). Paris: Leduc (Theodore Presser, U.S. agent), 1972.
Dupin, François. "Dupin's Directory of French Percussionists." *PN* XXXII, 2 (April 1994): 29–31.
Dupin, François. *Les baguettes de timbales.* Paris: Leduc, 1978.
Dupin, François. *Lexique de la percussion.* Paris: Richard–Masse, 1971.
Dupin, François. *Vingt–huit miniatures* [Twenty–eight miniatures for snare drum]. Paris: Leduc (Theodore Presser, U.S. agent), 1973.

Olmstead, Gary. "An Interview with François Dupin." *PN* XXII, 5 (July 1984): 34–38.
Rosen, Michael. "In Memoriam: François Dupin." *PN* XXXIII, 1 (February 1995): 56–57.
GEN. BIB.: Larrick, *BET–CP*.

E

EDDY, VAL (b. Chester William "Chet" Smith, 11 May 1912, Cuyahoga Falls, Ohio). Val Eddy started playing drums in 1925 and xylophone in 1927, studying with R. C. Light of Akron, Ohio. Matriculating at Ohio State University (1935–37), he broadcast 15–minute radio programs on xylophone three times a week (WOSU, 1937) and toured with a floor show–theater act in Pittsburgh, Philadelphia, Boston, and New York during 1938–42 as "Val Eddy and His Symphony in Wood." Assigned to the U.S. Naval School of Music (1942–43), he was spotlighted with military bands on NBC radio and served as both a musician and a radio operator in the Pacific theater during WWII on the battleship USS *California*. After the war Eddy served in the U.S. Naval Academy Band until his discharge in 1948. He won the *Arthur Godfrey Talent Scout Program* (1952), was a featured soloist on the show in the 1950s, and made guest appearances on television shows in New York and Montreal (e.g., Horace Heidt's *Hit Parade* and *Live like a Millionaire*). Graduating from the New York University School of Commerce in 1954, he became a real estate broker in Spring Valley, California (1954–74); after retiring he performed miniconcerts at Kiwanis International Conventions (1980/1984).

SELECTED BIBLIOGRAPHY

Eddy, Val. *Xylophone Solos*. Spring Valley, CA: C. S. Records, 1995.
"Val and Venus Eddy Contribute $10,000.00 to PAS® Endowment." *PN* XXV, 5 (Summer 1987): 4.

ENGELMAN, JOHN ROBIN (b. 21 Mar 1937, Baltimore, Maryland). Percussionist, educator, composer, recording artist, and conductor, Robin Engelman received a bachelor's degree in music performance (1961) from Ithaca College (NY), where he studied with *Warren Benson. He has served as principal percussionist with the Pittsburgh Wind Symphony (1960), North Carolina Symphony (1962), and Louisville Symphony (1962–64), percussionist in the Milwaukee Symphony (1964–66), and principal percussionist in the Rochester Philharmonic (1966–68), Toronto Symphony (1968–72), and Canadian Opera Company (1986–93). Thanks to Seiji Ozawa, Engelman met composer Toru Takemitsu, who invited him to perform in Japan for Expo '70; he performed for Ozawa with the San Francisco Symphony on a 1973 European tour.

In 1971 he became a charter member of the long–lived world percussion ensemble NEXUS (Percussive Arts Society Hall of Fame, 1999), and in 1976 he made the first of five Japanese tours under Takemitsu's sponsorship, presenting more than 50 notable performances of Takemitsu's "From Me Flows What You Call Time" (e.g., the 100th anniversary of Carnegie Hall). Celebrating its twenty-fifth anniversary in 1996, NEXUS has appeared at music festivals throughout Indonesia, Japan, Europe, Canada, England, New Zealand, and the United States. Engelman received the Toronto Arts Award as part of NEXUS in 1989.

He has taught at the Eastman School (Preparatory Department, 1966–68), Ithaca College (1966–68), York University (1972–75), and the University of Toronto, where he established the percussion ensemble (1976) and conducted the Contemporary Music Ensemble (1984–91). Engelman also conducted New Music Concerts in Toronto and on CBC radio (1969–89) and has composed and self–published several solo and chamber works for percussion, including *Lullaby* (1996) for steel pan and four percussionists.

SELECTED DISCOGRAPHY

Black Sun CD 15002–2: *The Altitude of the Sun* (NEXUS and Paul Horn), 1989.
CBC Musica Viva 2–1037: *Dance of the Octopus* (NEXUS et al.), 1990.
CBC SM 148: *The Lyric Arts Trio of Canada with Percussion*, 1970.
CBC SMCD 5154: *Music for Heaven and Earth* (NEXUS with Esprit Orchestra), 1995.
CBS Masterworks 35842: *Rossini–Respighi–La Boutique Fantasque* (Toronto Symphony), 1981.
CBS Masterworks 42019: *Salome* (Toronto Symphony), 1985.
Centrediscs CMC–CD 4492: *Prouesse—Rivka Golani*, 1992.
CP2 11: *Jo Kondo* (NEXUS performs "Under the Umbrella"), 1981.
Epic KE 33561: *Paul Horn and NEXUS*, 1975.
Golden Crest CR4016: *Warren Benson Presents Percussion* (Ithaca Percussion Ensemble), 1958.
InRespect IRJ 009302 H: *The Mother of the Book* (NEXUS et al.), 1994.
New Music Concerts NMC–001: *New Music 90*, 1992.
NEXUS 10251: *The Best of NEXUS* (1976–86), 1989.
NEXUS 10262: *NEXUS Now*, 1989.
NEXUS 10273: *NEXUS Plays the Novelty Music of George Hamilton Green*, 1989.
NEXUS 10284: *NEXUS Ragtime Concert*, 1992.
NEXUS 10295: *NEXUS—Origins*, 1992.

NEXUS 10306: *The Story of Percussion in the Orchestra* (NEXUS/Rochester Philharmonic), 1992.
NEXUS 10317: *Voices* (NEXUS and Rochester Philharmonic), 1994.
NEXUS 10339: *The Solo Percussionist* (Music of William Cahn), 1997.
NEXUS 10410: *Toccata*, 1997
NEXUS NE–01: *Music of NEXUS*, 1981.
NEXUS NE–02/03/04: *NEXUS and Earle Birney* (Albums 1–3), 1982.
NEXUS NE–05: *Changes* (NEXUS), 1981.
Papa Bear Records G01: *World Diary—Tony Levin* (NEXUS et al.), 1995.
Point Records 454 126–2: *Farewell to Philosophy* (Gavin Bryars), 1996.
RCA SX 2022: *Seiji Ozawa Conducts Toru Takemitsu* (Toronto Symphony), 1969.
Sony Classical SK 63044: *Takemitsu—From Me Flows What You Call Time* (Pacific Symphony), 1998.
Vivarte Sony SK 46 696: *Deutsche Tanze* (Mozart), 1991.

SELECTED VIDEOGRAPHY

Necavenue A88V–3: *Supercussion* (Tokyo Music Joy Festival), 1988.

SELECTED BIBLIOGRAPHY

Bump, Michael. "A Conversation with NEXUS." *PN* XXXI, 5 (June 1993): 30–36.
Ford, Mark. "NEXUS Now." *PN* XXIX, 3 (February 1991): 64.
Mather, Bruce. "Robin Engelman." *PN* XXXIV, 4 (August 1996): 14–15.
Mattingly, Rick. "Nexus." *MP* I, 3 (June–August 1985): 8–13/36–41.
Topping, Graham. "NEXUS Makes the Connection." *BBC Music Magazine* IV, 3 (November 1995).
Information supplied by the subject, 1996.

EPSTEIN, FRANK BENJAMIN (b. 7 May 1942, Amsterdam, Holland). Frank Epstein immigrated to the United States in 1952, settling initially in Hollywood, California. Studying with Robert Sonner, *Earl Hatch, *Murray Spivack, *William Kraft, and *Vic Firth, he attended the Berkshire Music Center, and earned a bachelor's degree from the University of Southern California (1965) and master's degree from the New England Conservatory (1969). Epstein performed with the Los Angeles Philharmonic (1963–65) and San Antonio Symphony (1965–67), has been percussionist and cymbal specialist with the Boston Symphony since 1968, and has recorded with the Los Angeles, Boston, and Boston Pops Orchestras. A faculty member of the Tanglewood Music Center, Oberlin Percussion Institute, and New England Conservatory (1971–), where he founded the percussion ensemble and serves as chair of the brass and percussion department (1992–). He established the Collage New Music Ensemble in Boston (1972) and was its music director through 1991. The latter has spawned over 200 new works and 17 recordings of twentieth–century works, garnering for Epstein a Presidential Commendation from the New England Conservatory. Consultant to the Zildjian Cymbal Company on new product development and appearing often as a clinician, he has also published a practical performance percussion part to Igor Stravinsky's "L'Histoire du Soldat" and markets his own symphonic castanets and Cymbelt® bass drum cymbal attachment.

SELECTED DISCOGRAPHY

Albany TROY 054: *Irwin Bazelon—Collage New Music*, 1992.
CRI CD 580: *Fred Lerdahl—Collage New Music*, 1990.
CRI CD 605: *Peter Child—Collage New Music*, 1991.
CRI SD 517: *Joan Tower—Collage New Music*, 1990.
CRI SD–486: *Collage*, 1982.
CRI SD–507: *Gunther Schuller—Collage New Music*, 1983.
Delos 3124: *Henri Lazerof—Collage New Music*, 1992.
GM 2008D: *Collage*, 1982/1986.
GM 2032CD: *Griffin Music Ensemble—Collage New Music*, 1988/1992.
Inner City Records IC 1015/Centaur CRC 2326: *Professor Jive* (Clark Terry & Collage New Music), 1976/1997.
Nonesuch 979129–2: *John Harbison—Collage New Music*, 1986.

SELECTED BIBLIOGRAPHY

Englander, Michael. "An Interview with Frank Epstein: Percussionist of the Boston Symphony." *PN* XXIV, 4 (April 1986): 21–26.
GEN. BIB.: Borland, *WWAMC*; PASIC® program biographies, 1994.

ERLICH, W. F. (b. Mainz, Germany). W. F. Erlich studied with timpanist Walter Pelzner of the Hanover (Germany) Symphony, immigrated to the United States in 1927, and held the timpani chair with the St. Louis Symphony (1927–41+).
GEN. BIB.: Cook, *LDT*, p. 453 (photo).

ERSKINE, PETER CLARK (b. 5 Jun 1954, Somers Point, New Jersey). Studying with *Alan Dawson and *Billy Dorn, drumset artist and composer Peter Erskine began drums at age 4, attended the Interlochen Arts Academy High School (1968–71), Stan Kenton Stage Band Camps, and Indiana University (1971–72/1975–76), where he studied with *George Gaber. His long, impressive vita includes positions with Stan Kenton (1972–75), Maynard Ferguson (ca. 1976–77), Weather Report (1978–82, recorded five albums, including the Grammy® Award–winning "8:30"), Steps Ahead (ca. 1982, with Mike Brecker, *Mike Mainieri, and Eddie Gomez), Chick Corea, Boz Scaggs, Joe Henderson, Freddie Hubbard, Pat Metheny, Ralph Towner, Rickie Lee Jones, Sadao Watanabe, Hubert Laws, Vanessa Williams, Al DiMeola, Miroslav Vitous, Jan Garbarek, Joni Mitchell, and *Gary Burton, Eliane Elias, and with the groups, Steely Dan, Bass Desires, John Abercrombie Trio, Kenny Wheeler Quintet/Big Band, Bob Mintzer Big Band, and Erskine's own combo.

He has recorded over 200 albums—10 under his own name—and was the featured soloist with the Ensemble Modern at Queen Elizabeth Hall (London, 1996) in the world premiere of Mark–Anthony Turnage's "Blood on the Floor."

As a composer, he has written scores for several Shakespeare productions including *Hamlet, Romeo and Juliet, King Richard II, A Midsummer Night's Dream* (honored by the Los Angeles Drama Critics Circle as "Best Original Musical Score of 1987"), and the American Conservatory Theatre's production of *Twelfth Night*, which received the Bay Area Drama Critics' Circle award for "Best Dramatic Score of 1989." Recently he has written a dance piece, "History of the Drum—Transitions in Rhythm," for the Kokuma Dance Company of Birmingham, England, and is currently scoring music for two Japanese animated feature films and a Home Box Office (HBO) television animation project. A four–time winner of *Modern Drummer* magazine's Reader's Poll "Mainstream Jazz Drummer" category, Erskine received an honorary doctorate degree from the Berklee College of Music in 1992. He has created his own recording label, Fuzzy Music, and his discography is available on the Internet.

SELECTED DISCOGRAPHY

ACT 9215–2: *Sketches* (Vince Mendoza), 1994.
Blue Note 89544: *Paulistana* (Eliane Elias), 1993.
Blue Note 91411: *So Far, So Close* (Eliane Elias), 1989.
Blue Note 96146: *Fantasia* (Eliane Elias), 1992.
Blue Note BT 85101: *Magic Touch* (Stanley Jordan), 1984.
CBS/Columbia CK 34457: *Conquistador* (Maynard Ferguson), 1977/1988.
CBS/Columbia CD 64627: *Weather Report* (Weather Report), 1981/1996.
CBS PC2–36030: *8:30* (Weather Report), 1979.
Columbia JC 36793: *Night Passage* (Weather Report), 1980.
Concord 4749: *Departure* (Gary Burton), 1997.
Contemporary 14001: *Cables' Vision* (George Cables), 1980.
Creative World STD 1070: *7.5 on the Richter Scale* (Stan Kenton), 1973/1991.
Denon CJ–72582: *Motion Poet*, 1988.
Denon CY–2180: *Cross Currents* (Eliane Elias), 1988.
DMP 451: *Incredible Journey* (Bob Mintzer), 1985.
DMP 456: *Camouflage* (Bob Mintzer), 1986.
DMP 479: *Art of the Big Band* (Bob Mintzer), 1991.
DMP CD–495: *Departure* (Bob Mintzer), 1993.
ECM 1299: *Bass Desires* (Marc Johnson), 1986.
ECM 1415/1416: *Music for Large and Small Ensembles* (Kenny Wheeler), 1990.
ECM 1502: *November* (John Abercrombie et al.), 1993.
ECM 78118–21532–2: *Time Being*, 1993.
ECM 1594: *As It Is*, 1996.
ECM 1497 314 517 353–2: *You Never Know*, 1992.
Elektra 60168: *Steps Ahead* (Steps Ahead), 1983.
Elektra/Musician 9 60351 2: *Modern Times* (Steps Ahead), 1984.
Fuzzy Music: *From Kenton to Now*, 1995.
Geffen/Warner Bros. 9 47249–2: *Street Dreams* (Lyle Mays), 1988.

GRP GR–9598: *Reunion* (Gary Burton), 1990.
GRP GRD–9701: *Dream Come True* (Arturo Sandoval), 1992.
GRP GRC–9617: *Sketchbook* (John Patitucci), 1990.
GRP GRD–9738: *Gary Burton and Rebecca Parris—It's Another Day*, 1994.
Interworld Music CD–917: *History of the Drum*, 1995.
Manhattan CDP–7–96545–2: *Instructions Inside* (Vince Mendoza), 1991.
Manhattan Records 95476: *A Long Story* (Eliane Elias), 1991.
Novus 63140–2: *Sweet Soul*, 1992.
NYC 6015–2: *An American Diary* (Mike Mainieri), 1995.
Pony Canyon: *Photogenic Memory* (Randy Roos), 1990.
Telarc 83433: *The Infinite Desire* (Al DiMeola), 1998.
Warner Bros. 9 45290–2: *Jaco Pastorius—the Birthday Concert*, 1981/1995.
Warner Bros. BSK 3586/NYC 6002–2: *Wanderlust* (Mike Mainieri), 1981/1992.
Warner/Reprise 9 26183–2: *Blue Pacific* (Michael Franks), 1990.
Zebra ZD 44005–2: *Tribute to Jeff Porcaro* (Dave Garfield), 1997.

SELECTED VIDEOGRAPHY

DCI/CPP Media: *Timekeeping II: Afro–Caribbean, Brazilian, and Funk*, 1990.
DCI VH047: *Peter Erskine—Everything Is Timekeeping*, 1989.
Hal Leonard: *Peter Erskine Trio—Live at JazzBaltica*, 1993.
Pioneer L.D. PS–86–009: *Live at the Village Vanguard*, vol. 3 (John Abercrombie and Michael Brecker), 1985.

SELECTED BIBLIOGRAPHY

Erskine, Peter. "Learning the Music for a Gig." *PN* XXXIII, 6 (December 1995): 17–21.
Erskine, Peter. *Drum Concepts and Techniques*. Milwaukee, WI: 21st C./Hal Leonard, 1987.
Erskine, Peter. *The Drum Perspective*. Milwaukee, WI: 21st C./Hal Leonard, 1997.
Erskine, Peter. *My Book*. New York: Side Zone Music, 1996.
Hipskind, Tom. "Peter Erskine: Time and Being." *Jazz Educators Journal* XXX, 3 (November 1997): 30–39.
Micallef, Ken. "Peter Erskine: Making Movies." *JazzTimes* XXII, 9 (November 1992): 35.
GEN. BIB.: Spagnardi, *GJD.*

ERVIN–PERSHING, KAREN (b. Karen Willene Jackson, 4 Aug 1943, Bakersfield, California). Initially a pianist and cellist, Karen Ervin–Pershing started percussion in high school, earned a bachelor's degree from the University of Southern California and a master's degree from the University of Arizona; she has had an active freelance career in the Los Angeles area. Her teachers included *William Kraft, *Earl Hatch, and *Mitchell Peters, and she was a two–time prize winner in the Concours Internationale d'Execution Musicale in Geneva, Switzerland (1972), and the Competition for Contemporary Percussion (France, 1974). She has taught at California State University at Northridge since 1976 and commissioned and premiered Kraft's "Soliloquy: Encounters I" (1975), as well as numerous other works for solo percussion. A featured performer and clinician at Percussive Arts Society International Conventions, Ervin–Pershing has appeared with the Los Angeles Percussion Ensemble and the Tintinnabulum Percussion Quartet (founded ca. 1978). Her arrangements of well–known classics by Scarlatti, Debussy (1990), and Kreutzer (*Etudes for the Advanced Mallet Player*, 1996) are published by Studio 4 and Alfred Publishing. She has been a contributing editor for *Wind Player* magazine and, in 1996, became owner and president of Studio 4 Music.

SELECTED DISCOGRAPHY

Crystal Records CD124: *Percussion by William Kraft*, 1993.
Crystal Records CD850: *Lou Harrison*, 1972/1992.
Crystal Records S–164: *Music for Winds and Percussion*, 1973.
Studio 4 Productions S4P–R101: *Karen Ervin—A Marimba Recital*, 1977.
Studio 4 Productions S4P–R102: *Gordon Stout II*, 1981.
WIM Records WIMR–5: *Karen Ervin, Percussionist*, 1972.

SELECTED BIBLIOGRAPHY

Black, Dave. "Doing It Her Way: Karen Ervin Pershing." *MP* II, 1 (December 1985): 22–25.
Peterscak, Jim. "I Love to Play...P.A.S. Interview with Karen Ervin, Solo Percussionist." *PN* XV, 2 (Winter 1977): 23–24.
GEN. BIB.: Larrick, *BET–CP*. Information supplied by the subject, 1997.

ESPINO, EUGENE SANTIAGO (b. 26 Sep 1939, Oakland, California). A member of the Cincinnati Symphony and Cincinnati Pops since 1967, principal timpanist Eugene Espino studied with *Saul Goodman (Juilliard School, 1961–66) and *Roland Kohloff and graduated from the University of California at Berkeley (1961). Prior to his association with Cincinnati, he performed with the St. Louis Symphony for one year.
PASIC® program biographies, 1999. Information supplied by the subject, 1999.

EYLES, RANDALL "RANDY" (b. 17 Apr 1951, LaPorte, Indiana). Randy Eyles earned a bachelor's degree from the University of Illinois (1973) and both master's (1976) and doctorate (DMA, 1989) degrees from Catholic University. His teachers include Tom Siwe, Terry Applebaum, *Fred Begun, and *Anthony Orlando. He served with the U.S. Air Force Concert Band, Symphony Orchestra, and Chamber Players (1973–1996) and was appointed principal percussionist (1986) and concert band superintendent (1991).

As a marimba soloist, he has been featured on recordings and numerous concert tours of the United States, Japan, People's Republic of China, Belgium, England, France, and Germany. Before joining the U.S. Air Force, Eyles taught at the National Music Camp (Interlochen Arts Camp), was a member of the faculty of Catholic University (1977–96), served as a board member and percussionist with Washington, D.C.'s Contemporary Music Forum, and became executive director of the Percussive Arts Society in 1996. His numerous works for percussion are published by Meredith Music Publications, Inc.

SELECTED DISCOGRAPHY

U.S. Air Force Band: *Spotlight: Outstanding Solo Performances*, 1980.
U.S Air Force Band BOL–8908T: *Niel DePonte—Concertino for Marimba*, 1990.

SELECTED BIBLIOGRAPHY

Eyles, Randy. *Ragtime and Novelty Xylophone Performance Practices.* DMA dissertation, Catholic University, 1989.
Eyles, Randy. "Ragtime Music and Novelty Music." *PN* XXVIII, 3 (Spring 1990): 71–73.
Information supplied by the subject, 1997.

F

FAETKENHEUER, WILLIAM [ALSO FAETKENHAUER] (d. ca. February 1941, Minneapolis, Minnesota). William Faetkenheuer was the original timpanist with the Minneapolis Symphony (1903–41). His colleagues in that orchestra around 1935 included Samuel W. Segal (snare) and Carl P. Rudolph (bass drum).

SELECTED BIBLIOGRAPHY

Kogan, Peter. "Henry Denecke, Jr." *PN* XXXIII, 3 (June 1995): 56–64.

FARBERMAN, HAROLD (b. 2 Nov 1929, New York, New York). Performer, arranger, and conductor, Harold Farberman attended the Juilliard School, was featured on drumset at Radio City Music Hall (1949), and at 20 years of age was the youngest member of the Boston Symphony where he stayed for twelve years as snare drummer and assistant timpanist. He left the symphony in 1963 to concentrate on composition and conducting, earning a master's degree in composition from the New England Conservatory. Farberman conducted the Oakland (CA), New Philharmonia, Swedish and Danish Radio Orchestras, and the BBC and London Symphonies, among others.

SELECTED DISCOGRAPHY

Boston B207/CRM–805: *Evolution* (conductor, Boston Percussion Group), 1962.
Grammafon AB–BIS–CD–382: *Farberman—Concerto for Jazz Drummer* (composer-conductor), 1986.
Moss Music Group D–MMG 115: *The All–Star Percussion Ensemble* (arranger-conductor), 1983.
GEN. BIB.: Sadie, *NG*, by Jeffrey Levine.

FARNLUND, EMIL LOWE (b. 2 Jan 1898, Hooper, Utah; d. 2 Jan 1994, Encinitas, California). Studying with Squire Coop in Utah, Emil Farnlund played drums at age 8 with his father's dance band, played timpani with the Salt Lake Symphony during his teens, and left home at 16 to perform on the vaudeville circuit, arriving in Hollywood (1924), where he drummed for Gus Arnheim and Paul Whiteman. He worked in silent movie pit orchestras and was a marimba soloist in cabarets, dance bands (e.g., Pat West, Rube Wolf), and combos throughout Utah, Oregon, and California, as well as for the "Fanchon and Marco" vaudeville act at the Paramount Theater (L.A.). Road shows he played included *No, No, Nanette*, *Lady Be Good*, and *Tip Toes*, and he was a featured vibraphone and xylophone soloist on KFWB (Warner Brothers). In the late 1920s Farnlund was the second musician contracted to record for the "talkies" at film studios including RKO, Universal, MGM, and Paramount where he remained until 1958. In the early 1930s he worked on radio and later recorded music for Walt Disney's animated film *Fantasia* and the *Mousketeers* television show. He also played on movie soundtracks featuring Bob Hope and Bing Crosby (*The Road to...* film series), Judy Garland, John Wayne, Fred Astaire, and others.

As a pioneer percussion educator, he founded the Rhythmusic Foundation, which offered instruments, lessons, and method books for $10 per student to schools in Los Angeles, Hollywood, and Glendale. In 1936 Farnlund also established a teaching studio in Hollywood and published method books for drums, marimba, and piano. With the opening of the Crenshaw Studio Marimba Center in 1940, he started children's marimba groups, including the Happy Woodchoppers (ages 9–13) which won an all–expense paid trip to Carnegie Hall in 1946 and the National Amateur Music Championship sponsored by *Look* magazine. His younger group, the Marimba Merry Makers (ca. ages 3–6, aka Four Tones and Star Tones as they reached their teens), premiered their own 30–minute television show (*Star Tones*) on 7 June 1956 from KCOP's Music Hall Theater. In 1941 he opened a North Hollywood branch of the Crenshaw Marimba Center with *Earl Hatch, who had studied marimba with Farnlund. Their students played for radio broadcasts, movies, and a mass marimba ensemble (75–100 members), which Farnlund and Hatch conducted on 2 September 1948 (plus two more seasons) for a half–time performance at a charity football game between the Rams and the Redskins that took place in the Los Angeles Coliseum and was sponsored by the *Los Angeles Times*.

Farnlund retired from studio playing in 1958 but continued to form young marimba ensembles in the Anaheim, Arcadia, and Monrovia (CA) areas. In 1970 he moved north to the Santa Cruz area, where he worked in the Montessori and public schools, but failing eyesight forced him to cease teaching in 1986.

SELECTED BIBLIOGRAPHY

Cirone, Anthony J. "Emil Farnlund: A Pioneer in the Percussive Arts." *PN* XXIII, 4 (April 1985): 24–25.

Farnlund, Emil. *Howell and Aretta System of Modern Marimba Study.* Howell and Aretta Pub., ca. 1950s.
Farnlund, Emil. *Merry Maker Drum–ette Book,* ca. 1946.
Farnlund, Emil. *Marimba Method,* vols. 1–2, 1944.
Farnlund, Emil. *Musical Zoo* (piano book). Chicago, Rubank, 1937.
Farnlund, Emil. *Rhythm First on the Demi–Drum,* 1965.
GEN. BIB.: Cook, *LDT,* p. 183. Information supplied by Helen Farnlund, 1996.

FATOOL, NICHOLAS "NICK" (b. 2 Jan 1915, Millbury, Massachusetts). A highly active drumset artist who played early on with Joe Haymes (1937) and Don Bestor (1938), Nick Fatool performed, toured, and/or recorded with Buddy Hackett in New York (1939), Benny Goodman in Cleveland (1939), *Lionel Hampton (1940), Artie Shaw (1940–41), Claude Thornhill, Les Brown (1942), and Alvino Rey (1942–43). A move to Los Angeles into the recording studios brought collaborations with, among others, Erroll Garner (1946), Louis Armstrong (1949–51), Harry James (1940s–50s), Tommy Dorsey (1951), Dukes of Dixieland (1964), Pete Fountain (1962–65), and Bob Crosby (1949–51), with whom he also toured the Orient (1964) and Europe (1981). Fatool can be heard on the soundtracks for the semibiographical movies *Pete Kelly's Blues* (1955) and *The Five Pennies* (1959).

SELECTED DISCOGRAPHY

Atlantic LP–1225: *Tribute to Benny Goodman* (Jess Stacy), 1987.
Audiophile APCD–240: *Yank Lawson's Jazz Band—Something Old, Something New, Something Borrowed, Something Blue,* 1988.
Black Lion 760171: *Sunset Swing,* 1945 (reissue).
Capitol T678: *Big Band Dixieland* (Ray Anthony), 1955.
Capitol W1022: *Sounds of the Great Bands* (Glen Gray), 1958.
Coral 757453: *Pete's Place* (Pete Fountain), 1964.
Jazzology J–158: *Nick Fatool's Jazz Band—Spring of '87,* 1987.
Jazzology JCD–217: *Pete Fountain at Piper's Opera House,* 1992.
Jazzology JCD–277: *Bud Freeman—California Session,* 1997.
Jazzology JCD–300: *The World's Greatest Jazz Band of Yank Lawson and Bob Haggart,* 1997.
RCA APLI–1744: *Clarinet Gumbo* (Barney Bigard), 1973.
RCA Victor VPS 6062/AXK2 5533: *This Is Artie Shaw,* vol. 2, 1977.
Verve MGV4013: *Benny Goodman Sextet,* 1939.
GEN. BIB.: Kernfeld, *NGJ,* by T. Dennis Brown.

FEDDERSEN, JOHN (b. 6 Oct 1944, Evanston, Illinois). John Feddersen studied at Ithaca College with *Warren Benson, the Manhattan School with *Paul Price, and Indiana University with *George Gaber and has performed in the U.S. Navy Band, in the North Carolina Symphony (principal timpanist), and at the Eastern Music Festival (NC).
Information supplied by the subject, 1996.

FELDMAN, VICTOR STANLEY "VIC" (b. 7 Apr 1934, London, England; d. 12 May 1987, Los Angeles, California). Although Victor Feldman played drums professionally at the age of 6, making high–profile appearances with Glenn Miller, on the BBC, and in Switzerland (1949) and Paris (1952), by 1954 he chose to specialize on vibraphone and piano. He immigrated to New York in 1955, intially touring with Woody Herman (1956–57), and then performed and/or recorded with Buddy DeFranco, Howard Rumsey (CA, 1957–59), Cannonball Adderley (1960–61), Peggy Lee, Benny Goodman (Russian tour, 1962), Miles Davis, Frank Sinatra, and June Christy (London, 1965). Settling in Los Angeles, Feldman was a first–call Hollywood studio percussionist and film score composer.

SELECTED DISCOGRAPHY

AVA Records A/As–19: *World's First Album of Soviet Jazz* (Victor Feldman All–Stars), 1963.
Blue Note 84328: *Jack Wilson*, 1968.
Blue Note LA426–G: *Dom Minasi—I Have the Feeling I've Been Here Before*, 1975.
Blue Note LA584–G: *Alphonse Mouzon—The Man Incognito*, 1975.
Blue Note LA635–G: *Carmen McRae—Can't Hide Love*, 1976.
Blue Note LA645–G: *Barbara Carroll*, 1976.
Cohearent Sound CSR–1001: *In My Pocket*, 1978.
Columbia CK–48827/PC–8851: *Seven Steps to Heaven* (Miles Davis), 1963.
Concord 38: *Artful Dodger*, 1977.
Contemporary 7577–80: *Shelly Manne and His Men at the Black Hawk*, 1959.
Contemporary C3549: *The Arrival of Victor Feldman*, 1958.
Landmark 1304/Riverside 9355: *The Poll–Winners* (Cannonball Adderley), 1960.
Landmark 1305–2: *At the Lighthouse* (Cannonball Adderley), 1960/1986.
Milestone 9275: *Cannonball Adderley Greatest Hits—The Riverside Years*, 1958–62.
Riverside/OJC 306: *Quintet Plus* (Cannonball Adderley), 1987.
Pablo 2310–957–2: *Art n' Zoot* (as pianist), 1981.
Pablo 5303: *The Cannonball Adderley Quintet—Paris, 1960*.
Pacific Jazz PJ 10121: *Victor Feldman Plays Everything in Sight.*
Palo Alto 8056: *To Chopin with Love*, 1983.
Riverside 9366: *Merry Olde Soul*, 1960–61.
TBA 208: *High Visibility*, 1985.
Tempo TAP8: *Victor Feldman in London*, 1956.
Verve MGV8253: *Bert Dahlander*, 1957.
Verve MGVS6063: *Mel Torme*, 1959.
Verve MGVS6141: *Frank Marocco Quintet*, 1960.
Verve MGVS6166: *Buddy DeFranco*, 1958.
Verve V/V6–8540: *Jazz at the Philharmonic in Europe*, 1960.
VJ 2506: *Blues Bag* (Buddy DeFranco), 1964.

SELECTED BIBLIOGRAPHY

Feldman, Victor. *All Alone by the Vibraphone.* Sherman Oaks, CA: Gwyn Pub., 1971.

Feldman, Victor. *Mallets in Wonderland.* Delevan, NY: Kendor Music, 1984 (with recording).

Tynan, John. "Victor Feldman: A Long Way from Piccadilly." *DB* XXX, 13 (6 Jun 1963): 13–15.

GEN. BIB.: Kernfeld, *NGJ*, by Steve Larson.

FERRERAS, SALVADOR "SAL" (b. 20 May 1954, San Juan, Puerto Rico). Passing through San Juan, Caracas, Chicago, and Detroit, Sal Ferreras earned a bachelor's degree from the University of Windsor (Ontario, Canada, 1978) and did graduate work at Wayne State University (Detroit, MI, 1978–80). He was percussionist with the Warren Symphony (1978–80), timpanist with the Windsor (1976–80) and Victoria Symphonies (1980–82), and part-time musician with the Vancouver Symphony (1982–present) and Vancouver Opera Orchestra (since 1987). Serving as artistic director for the Vancouver Folk Music Festival (1994–95) and International Talent and Commonwealth Drum Festival in Victoria (1994), he was nominated for a Juno Award ("World Beat" category) for his solo recording *Invisible Minority.*

Ferreras performs with Viveza, DrumHeat, the CBC Vancouver Orchestra, and the Vancouver New Music Ensemble. Frequently featured on Canadian radio as performer, host, and commentator, he has played or recorded with Chicago, Robbie Robertson, Raffi, and K. D. Lang, among others, and composes film scores and percussion works. A Canadian Arts Council grant recipient, he has toured in Canada, the Northwest Territories, the United States, Japan, China, Brazil, and Taiwan. Selected Classical Musician of the Year (1987) by the Canadian Academy of Recording Arts and Sciences (CARAS), he has taught at the University of Victoria, University of British Columbia, Simon Frasier University, and Vancouver Community College. Ferreras has also held positions as music director of the Vancouver International Writer's Festival and Literary Cabaret, director of the Simon Frasier University's World Percussion Intensive, artistic director of the Commonwealth Performers Midsummers Night Gala for H.R.H. Queen Elizabeth II, and coordinator for the Banff Centre's Afrocubanismo '96 Festival.

SELECTED DISCOGRAPHY

Aural Traditions ARCD 121: *Invisible Minority,* 1992.

Miramar Records 1001: *To Drive in L.A.,* 1987.

Skylark 9300: *Encuentros,* 1993.

Information supplied by the subject, 1996.

FINK, SIEGFRIED HELMUT (b. 8 Feb 1928, Zerbst/Anhalt, Germany). Having studied percussion formally with Hans Wrede and later Alfred Wagner at the Franz Liszt Hochschule, Siegfried Fink served as principal percussionist for the Magdeburg Opera Orchestra (1951–58) and timpanist in the Lubeck Opera Orchestra (1958–65). He performed in the Ensemble für Neue Musik on Radio Hannover (1959–72) and has appeared as a soloist throughout the world. Fink's teaching positions have included the Telemann Conservatory, Musikhochschule Hannover, and since 1965 the Würzburg Hochschule für Musik. A prolific composer and author, his percussion works and method books are widely performed and employed. He was awarded the "Bundesverdienstkreuz" by the Federal Republic of Germany—its highest civilian honor—and a "Doctor honoris cause" by the Bulgarian State Academy of Music for his lifelong contributions to percussion.

SELECTED DISCOGRAPHY

Cantate CAN 658 225: *Neue geistliche Musik* (Penderecki) (Percussion Ensemble Siegfried Fink), 1969.
Thorofon CTH–2003: *Drums* (Würzburg Percussion Ensemble, conductor), 1986.
Thorofon CTH 2063: *Impulse—20th Century Works* (Würzburg Percussion Quartet), 1989.
Thorofon CTH–2085: *Art of Percussion*, 1990.
Wergo SM 1049/50: *Sound Sculptures* (Würzburg Percussion Quartet), 1985.

SELECTED BIBLIOGRAPHY

Fink, Siegfried. *Orchesterstudien für Pauken* (vol. 1, Dvorak Symphonies). Hamburg: Musikverlag N. Simrock, 1989.
Fink, Siegfried. "PASIC® Banquet Address." *PN* XVIII, 2 (Winter 1980): 18–19.
Fink, Siegfried. "Percussion in the Teaching of Music." *Percussionist* XIII, 1 (Fall 1975): 2–11.
GEN. BIB.: Larrick, *BET–CP.*

FINKEL, IAN (b. 13 Aug 1948, Brooklyn, New York). Virtuoso xylophone soloist and showman, Ian Finkel studied with *Walter Rosenberger and Norman Grossman and, as a freelance artist whose talent runs the gamut from jazz to classical, has performed with the New York Philharmonic, Metropolitan Opera Orchestra, and on television and radio, and has done extensive recording studio work. Often accompanied by his pianist–brother, Elliot, he has amassed over 2,500 appearances as a soloist and has toured Japan, Korea, Canada, Mexico, and every major American city. Finkel has performed on Broadway and in nightclubs. He has given clinics and masterclasses at the Manhattan and Juilliard Schools, Peabody Conservatory, Brooklyn College, and Aspen Festival, and elsewhere. As an arranger and orchestrator, he has written for performances by *Tito Puente, Michael Feinstein, Ginger Rogers, Teri Garr, the *Tonight Show* band, the *Martin Mull Show*, and *Nick At Nite T.V. Land*.

SELECTED DISCOGRAPHY

Sunset 7 84002–2: *Johnny H. and the Prisoners of Swing*, 1994.

SELECTED VIDEOGRAPHY

Rosewood Productions: *Ian Finkel Live from New York*, 1996.

SELECTED BIBLIOGRAPHY

Finkel, Ian. *Solos for the Vibraphone Player*. New York: G. Schirmer, 1973.
Information supplied by the subject, 1996.

FIRTH, EVERETT JOSEPH "VIC" (b. 2 Jun 1930, Winchester, Massachusetts). Growing up in Sanford, Maine, and initially studying cornet, trombone, piano, and clarinet, Vic Firth played drumset and vibes and was leader of a big band by the time he was 16. His teachers included Salvy Cavicchio, Robert Ramsdell, *Lawrence White, *George Lawrence Stone, *Charles Smith, and *Saul Goodman. He earned a bachelor's degree with honors (1952) from the New England Conservatory, where he studied with former Boston Symphony timpanist *Roman Szulc and where he has taught since 1950. At 21, the youngest principal of the orchestra, Firth replaced Szulc as solo timpanist with Boston in 1952 and has performed and recorded with the Boston Pops Orchestra and Boston Symphony Chamber Players and taught at the Berkshire Music Center since 1956. The drum stick and mallet manufacturing company that bears his name as president and CEO was his "cottage industry," now recognized as a leader in the field. His percussion compositions and etude books have become standard repertoire, and in 1995 the Percussive Arts Society inducted him into their Hall of Fame. He can be heard with the Boston Pops Orchestra and Boston Symphony on Philips, RCA Victor, Polydor, Columbia, Cambridge, DGG, and Mercury recording labels.

SELECTED DISCOGRAPHY

Moss Music Group D–MMG 115: *The All–Star Percussion Ensemble*, 1983.
RCA Victor LSC 2567: *Poulenc—Concerto for Organ, Strings, and Timpani* (Boston Symphony), 1961.
RCA Victor LSC 6184: *Colgrass—Variations for Four Drums and Viola* (Boston Symphony Chamber Players), 1968.
RCA Victor LSC 6189: *Dahl—Duettino Concertante* (Boston Symphony Chamber Players), 1969.

SELECTED VIDEOGRAPHY

Video Artists International: *Time Groove* (Louis Bellson, Steve Gadd, et al.), 1990.

SELECTED BIBLIOGRAPHY

Firth, Vic. *Percussion Symposium.* New York: Carl Fischer, 1966.
Firth, Vic. "Reflections of a Timpanist." *Percussionist* XVII, 2 (Winter 1980): 106–109.
Firth, Vic. "Sound." *MP* I, 1 (December 1984–February 1985): 48–50.
Iero, Cheech. "My First Gig." *MD* XX, 12 (December 1996): 148–151.
Strain, James A. "Vic Firth." *PN* XXXIII, 6 (December 1995): 8–9.
GEN. BIB.: Larrick, *BET–CP.*

FISHER, CHARLES E. An arranger of solos for the Dixie Music House (est. 1902) in Chicago, Charles Fisher performed in Seattle theaters, was xylophone soloist with Duss' Band, edited the "Chicago Notes" column in *Jacobs' Band and Orchestra Journal*, and authored a mail–order xylophone method book, *The Fisher Correspondence School of Music* (ca. 1920).
GEN. BIB.: Strain, *XYLO.*

FLORES, CHARLES WALTER "CHUCK" (b. 5 Jan 1935, Orange, California). A student of *Shelly Manne (1953), drumset artist Chuck Flores played, toured, and/or recorded with Shorty Rogers (1953), Woody Herman (Europe, 1954–55), Al Cohn (1955), Art Pepper (1956–58), Conte Candoli (1957), Bud Shank (1956–59/1963), and Carmen McRae (1971). He led his own groups during the 1970s–80s.

SELECTED DISCOGRAPHY

Blue Note CDP 7 46868–2: *Modern Art* (Art Pepper), 1956–57.
Concord 49: *Drum Flower*, 1977.
Jam Session 100: *Superstars of Jazz*, 1953.
Verve MGV8014: *Woody Herman and His Orchestra*, 1954.
VSOP 47 CD: *Mucho Calor* (Art Pepper), 1958.
World Pacific WP1215: *Bud Shank Quartet*, 1956.
Zeta 729: *West Coast Jazz* (Art Pepper), 1957.

SELECTED BIBLIOGRAPHY

Deffaa, Chip. "The Drummers of Woody Herman." *MD* XI, 1 (1987): 26.
GEN. BIB.: Hunt, *52nd St.*; Kernfeld, *NGJ.*

FOSTER, ALOISIUS "AL" (b. 18 Jan 1944, Richmond, Virginia). Starting his drumset career as a teenager in New York, Al Foster collaborated with Earl May, Larry Willis, Horace Silver, Cannonball Adderley, and Blue Mitchell. He performed with Miles Davis sporadically for 13 years and has recorded and/or appeared with Pat Metheny, McCoy Tyner, Carmen McRae, Michael and Randy

Brecker, Sonny Rollins, Freddie Hubbard, *Bobby Hutcherson, Herbie Hancock, and others.

SELECTED DISCOGRAPHY

A&M/Horizon SP–721: *David Liebman—Light'n Up, Please!* 1977.
Artists House–8: *Pendulum* (Dave Liebman), 1979.
Black Hawk 522–2: *Life's Magic* (Steve Kuhn), 1986.
Blue Note 37718: *Joe Lovano—Celebrating Sinatra*, 1997.
Blue Note 7243 8 34634 2 8: *Ancestors* (Renee Rosnes), 1996.
Blue Note 84178: *Blue Mitchell—The Thing to Do*, 1964.
Blue Note 84214: *Down With It* (Blue Mitchell), 1965.
Blue Note 84272: *Blue Mitchell—Heads Up!* 1967.
Blue Note BLJ–46993: *Charnett Moffett—Net Man*, 1987.
Blue Note BLJ–46994: *Eliane Elias—Illusions*, 1986.
Blue Note BT 85102: *McCoy Tyner and Jackie McLean—It's About Time*, 1985.
Blue Note CDP 7 46426–2: *Joe Henderson—The State of the Tenor: Live at the Village Vanguard*, 1985.
Blue Note LA406–G: *Horace Silver—Silver 'n Brass*, 1975.
Blue Note LA581–G: *Horace Silver—Silver 'n Wood*, 1976.
Blue Note LA701–G: *Horace Silver—Silver 'n Voices*, 1976.
Blue Note LA853–H: *Horace Silver—Silver 'n Percussion*, 1977.
Blue Note LWB–1033: *Horace Silver—Silver 'n Strings Play the Music of the Spheres*, 1979.
Chesky: *New York Reunion* (McCoy Tyner Quartet), 1991.
Columbia PG33236: *Get Up With It* (Miles Davis), 1974/1996.
Contemporary CCD–14052–2: *Reflections* (Frank Morgan Allstars), 1989.
Denon 71569: *Illusions* (Eliane Elias), 1987.
IC–2080/SteepleChase SCCD–31080: *Biting the Apple* (Dexter Gordon), 1986.
Landmark Records LLP–1513: *In the Vanguard* (Bobby Hutcherson), 1987.
Milestone 2MCD–2501–2: *Silver City* (Sonny Rollins), 1996.
Palo Alto 8061: *Quest* (David Liebman), 1982.
Progressive PCD–7059: *The Magnificent Tommy Flanagan*, 1990.
Sony CSCS 5131: *We Want Miles* (Miles Davis), 1981.
Sony SRCS 6513–4: *Miles! Miles! Miles!* (Miles Davis), 1981.
Timeless T1–313: *In, Out, and Around* (Mike Nock), 1979.
Verve 314 557 199–2: *I Remember Miles* (Shirley Horn), 1998.
Verve 314 529 223: *7th Ave. Stroll* (Mark Whitfield), 1995.
Xanadu 151792: *Duke Jordan with Cecil Payne*, 1973.
GEN. BIB.: Hunt, *52nd St.*; Spagnardi, *GJD.*

FOURNIER, VERNEL ANTHONY (b. 30 Jul 1928, New Orleans, Louisiana). A student of Sidney Montigue, drumset artist Vernel Fournier started on snare drum at the age of 10, set at 13, and performed Dixieland in New Orleans while in high school. He attended Alabama State Teachers College briefly (finishing a degree in Chicago later in life) before working with King Kolax; he then settled in Chicago from around 1948 until 1980, when he relocated to New

York. Fournier played with Teddy Wilson (1949–53), George Shearing (1962–64), and the Ahmad Jamal Trio (1957–62/1965–66); and his many collaborators on stage and in the recording studio include Ben Webster, Gene Ammons, Lester Young, Red Rodney, Nancy Wilson (1965–66), Billy Eckstein, J. J. Johnson, Sonny Stitt, *Gary Burton, Clifford Jordan (1980s), Joe Williams, and Bud Freeman. He recorded in Switzerland in 1991 with his own trio and taught at the Mannes College of Music (NY).

SELECTED DISCOGRAPHY

Argo LP 667: *At the Pershing,* vol. 2 (Ahmad Jamal), 1958.
Capitol ST–2447: *Rare Form* (George Shearing), 1966.
Capitol T–1874: *Touch Me Softly* (George Shearing), 1963.
Criss Cross 1025: *Royal Ballads* (Clifford Jordan), 1987.
MCA/Chess CHD 9108/Argo LP 628: *But Not For Me—Live at the Pershing* (Ahmad Jamal), 1958.
Milestone 9197: *Down Through the Years* (Clifford Jordan), 1987.
Pair Records PCD–2–1244: *Ahmad Jamal at His Very Best*, 1989.
Soul Note SN 1084: *Repetition* (Clifford Jordan), 1984.
TCB: *Vernel Fournier Trio*, 1991.

SELECTED VIDEOGRAPHY

A*Vision Entertainment 50240–3: *Jazzmasters Vintage Collection*, vols. 1–2 (1958–1961), 1990.

SELECTED BIBLIOGRAPHY

Fournier, Vernel. *Drum Techniques.* Milwaukee, WI: Hal Leonard, 1997.
Mattingly, Rick. "Vernel Fournier: New Orleans Bebop." *MD* XXII, 3 (March 1998): 92–99.
GEN. BIB.: Hunt, *52nd St.*; Kernfeld, *NGJ*; Korall, *DM.*

FRANCIS, DAVID ALBERT "PANAMA" (b. 21 Dec 1918, Miami, Florida). Drumset artist Panama Francis began his career in Florida in the 1930s before moving to New York, where his collaborators included Roy Eldridge (1939), Lucky Millinder (1940), and Cab Calloway (1947–52). A studio drummer in the 1950s, he played both coasts, recording with Ray Charles, *Lionel Hampton, Buddy Holly, and Mahalia Jackson, among others. Appearing on camera in the Billie Holiday story (*Lady Sings the Blues*, 1972), Francis worked with the Benny Goodman Quartet in 1982 and coordinated a European tour, recordings, and eventual New York performances with his own group, the Savoy Sultans.

SELECTED DISCOGRAPHY

Black and Blue: *Getting in the Groove*, 1979.
Coral CRL 57423: *Drum Beat for Dancing Feet*, 1963.
Epic BN 629: *Exploding Drums!* 1962.
Epic 3839: *The Battle of Jericho*, 1962.
Smithsonian 21: *The Music of Fats Waller and James P. Johnson*, 1979.
GEN. BIB.: Kernfeld, *NGJ*, by T. Dennis Brown.

FRIEDMAN, DAVID (b. 10 Mar 1944, New York, New York). Jazz vibist and marimbist, David Friedman received a master's degree from the Juilliard School and has studied with *Gary Burton and *Saul Goodman. Essentially a classical marimbist who started studying jazz at 22, he is much sought–after in the United States and Europe for both stage and studio. Among his collaborators have been George Benson, Jackie and Roy Kral, Horace Silver, Wayne Shorter, *Horacee Arnold, Harvie Swartz, Marc Johnson, *Peter Erskine, and Hubert Laws. Friedman's appearances and recordings with the mallet duo Double Image (with keyboard artist *David Samuels), are often imitated by percussionists aspiring to the group's high level of improvisatory expertise. He was voted "Talent Deserving Wider Recognition" (No. 1 vibist) by critics in *Down Beat* magazine two years in row. Friedman has taught at the Manhattan School and the Institute for Advanced Musical Studies in Montreux, Switzerland.

SELECTED DISCOGRAPHY

Blue Note 84363: *Wayne Shorter—Odyssey of Iska*, 1970.
Blue Note LA054–F: *Horace Silver—In Pursuit of the 27th Man*, 1972.
DMP CD–491: *Junkyard* (David Charles), 1992.
DMP CD–503: *Double Image—Open Hand*, 1994.
Enja 2096: *Double Image*, 1977.
Enja 3089: *Of the Wind's Eye* (Hubert Laws), 1981.
Enja 5017: *Shades of Change*, 1986.
Enja 2068: *Futures Passed*, 1976.
Intuition 2130: *Jerry Ganelli—Another Place*, 1995.
Marimba Productions MP–002: *Dialogues* (Double Image), 1985.
Traumton Records 2406: *David Friedman—Air Sculpture*, 1994.

SELECTED BIBLIOGRAPHY

Friedman, David. *Vibraphone Technique: Dampening and Pedaling.* Boston: Berklee Publications, 1973.
Mattingly, Rick. "David Friedman." *MP* II, 1 (December 1988): 8.
Schupp, Roger B. "Reunion: An Interview with David Samuels and David Friedman." *PN* XXXII, 2 (April 1994): 37–41.
GEN. BIB.: Kernfeld, *NGJ*, by Gary Theroux; Larrick, *BET–CP*.

FRIESE, ALFRED P. (b. 7 Nov 1876, Germany). Called the "Dean of American Timpanists," Alfred Friese graduated with an artist's diploma from the Leipzig Royal Conservatory as a violist and performed in the viola section with the Leipzig Gewandhaus Orchestra. He studied with Hermann Schmidt, principal timpanist of the Gewandhaus Orchestra, and secured a timpani job with Hans Winderstein's Orchestra. In 1902 he was invited to come to America to perform in a group that would later become the Philadelphia Orchestra. [Herbert Kupferberg, *Those Fabulous Philadelphians* (NY: Charles Scribner's Sons, 1969), states: A. Friese played Battery from 1901 to 1905.] Friese then served as timpanist in the Pittsburgh Symphony; in 1909 Gustav Mahler chose him for the timpanist's chair with the New York Philharmonic. In 1926 he retired from that orchestra [legend has it that he damaged his right hand from a still explosion].

Having performed for Scheel, Reiner, Toscanini, Mahler, Fiedler, Ormandy, Stravinsky, Stokowski, Beecham, and Richard Strauss (who in 1922 dubbed Friese "the ablest kettledrummer in the world"), he established the Friese School of Timpani and Percussion on 10 May 1926. It advertised lessons for "drummers of both sexes." His tenure as chair of the percussion department at the Manhattan School began around 1949, and he was named to the Percussive Arts Society Hall of Fame in 1978.

SELECTED DISCOGRAPHY

Benjamin Sachs Artist Recordings (New York): *Timpani Studies* (pedagogical demonstration by Friese; three discs including orchestral timpani excerpts), 1950.

SELECTED BIBLIOGRAPHY

Clark, Alfred E. "$46,000 is stolen from musician, 83." *New York Times* (Sunday, 25 Oct 1959): 38.
Friese, Alfred, and Alexander Lepak. *The Friese–Lepak Timpani Method.* Rockville Centre, NY: Belwin, Inc., 1966.
Kogan, Peter. "Henry Denecke, Jr." *PN* XXXIII, 3 (June 1995): 58.
"Louie Bellson, William 'Billy' Gladstone, Alfred Friese Inducted into PAS® Hall of Fame." *PN* XVII, 2 (Winter 1979): 27–28.

G

GABER, GEORGE (b. 24 Feb 1916, New York, New York). Inducted into the Percussive Arts Society Hall of Fame in 1995, George Gaber started on piano and violin, but received his first snare drum at 7 and was taking lessons by 13. He attended the Juilliard School (1934–38), the New School (1942–45), Queens College (1954–55), and the Manhattan School (1954–55). Studying with *David Gusikoff (snare), *Karl Glassman (timpani), and *Joseph Castka (keyboards), Gaber played with dance bands, Latin groups, the All–American Youth Orchestra under Stokowski (South American tour, 1940), then played with the Pittsburgh Orchestra as timpanist under Fritz Reiner (1939–43). In New York he performed for the NBC, ABC, and CBS Orchestras, freelanced in RCA, MGM, Capitol, Decca, Vox, Mercury, Laurel, Urania, Boston, Golden Crest, and Columbia recording studios, and did recordings and films for Menotti, Ellington, Foss, Whiteman, and Villa–Lobos. He toured with the Ballet Russe de Monte Carlo Orchestra (1937–39), and played for the New York World's Fair Band and on Broadway (e.g., *Tropical Holiday*). Gaber premiered several works for Stravinsky, Hindemith, Milhaud, and Bartók, and he performed with the Los Angeles, Jerusalem, Baltimore, Minnesota, New York, and Israeli Philharmonic Orchestras under Bernstein, Mehta, and others.

A reknowned pedagogue, Gaber served on the faculties of the Manhattan School, Carnegie–Mellon University, and Hofstra University, but he held his longest tenure at Indiana University (1960–86), where he premiered 136 new works for percussion ensemble, served as chair of the percussion department, and was honored as a "Distinguished Professor of Music" in 1983. Gaber has appeared as either performer, conductor, or clinician in Canada, Chile, China, Israel, Turkey, Brazil, Mexico, Costa Rica, Japan, Haiti, Fiji, Hong Kong, Australia, Italy, Iran (as UNESCO representative for their Festival of the Arts/"Percussion of the World" program in 1969), and elsewhere. Articles by or about him appear in the *Instrumentalist, Japan Review, Reiner Society, Harvard*

Dictionary (Apel), *Ludwig Drummer*, and *Percussive Notes*, and he has been interviewed on BBC radio.

SELECTED BIBLIOGRAPHY

Gaber, George. "The Percussion Ensemble: A Light–Hearted Historical Overview." *MP* I, 1 (December 1984–February 1985): 32–33.
Kite, Rebecca. "George Gaber." *PN* XXXIII, 6 (December 1995): 10–11.
Kite, Rebecca. "George Gaber's Melodic Timpani Techniques." *PN* XXXIII, 2 (April 1995): 46–49.
Smith, Dr. D. Richard. "George Gaber: Master Percussionist/Professor of Music." *PN* XVII, 3 (Spring/Summer 1979): 29–31.
GEN. BIB.: Cook, *LDT*, p. 455 (photo); Information supplied by the subject, 1996.

GADD, STEPHEN K. "STEVE" (b. 4 Sep 1945, Rochester, New York). Studio recording artist Steve Gadd, whose relaxed, rudimental-linear approach to the drumset was extremely influential on the younger generation of drummers during the late 1970s–80s, was introduced to drums at age 3 by his uncle. Performer and arranger for the Rochester Crusaders Drum and Bugle Corps, Gadd studied with *William and Stanley Street and *John Beck; he attended the Manhattan School (two years) and the Eastman School, where he performed with the Rochester Philharmonic. His first professional recording was made in 1967 with Gap Mangione (GRC 9001: *Diana in the Autumn Wind*), and after a tour of duty with the U.S. Army Field Band (Ft. Meade, MD), Gadd started working with the group Stuff (1976), which included drummer Chris Parker. Recording jingles and leading his own combo, the Gadd Gang, he has toured, performed, and/or recorded with the ensemble Steps; with artists Roland Hanna, Eric Clapton, Paul McCartney, Aretha Franklin, Stevie Wonder, Carol King, Gap (1971–72) and Chuck Mangione, Chick Corea (1975–81), Phoebe Snow, Al Jarreau, Carly Simon, Nancy Wilson, Steely Dan, Tom Scott, Quincy Jones, Al DiMeola, James Brown, Paul Simon (Rhythms of the Saints Tour, 1991), and Bob James; and with the Manhattan Jazz Quintet and the studio collaborative Steely Dan, among a host of others. He was inducted into *Modern Drummer* magazine's Reader's Poll Hall of Fame in 1984.

SELECTED DISCOGRAPHY

A&M SP–4612: *Main Squeeze* (Chuck Mangione), 1976.
Atlantic 82699–2/83010–2: *Burning for Buddy* (Buddy Rich Orchestra), 1994/1997.
Blue Note BLJ–46994: *Eliane Elias—Illusions*, 1986.
Blue Note LA667–G: *Earl Klugh—Living Inside Your Love*, 1976.
Blue Note LA736–H: *Noel Pointer—Phantazia*, 1977.
Blue Note LA737–H: *Earl Klugh—Finger Paintings*, 1977.
CBS CK 40864: *The Gadd Gang*, 1986.
Columbia PCA 33540: *Still Crazy After All These Years* (Paul Simon), 1975.

Columbia FC38373: *Tour de force—Live* (Al DiMeola), 1982.
Columbia JC36581: *What It Is* (David Liebman).
Creed Taylor CTI 8014: *George Benson—Take Five*, 1979.
CTI ZK–40807: *Concierto* (Jim Hall), 1975.
Denon 71569: *Illusions* (Eliane Elias), 1987.
Epic PET36974: *Journey to Love* (Stanley Clarke), 1975.
Kudu 24: *Feels So Good* (Grover Washington, Jr.), 1975.
MCA MCAD–37214: *Aja* (Steely Dan), 1977.
Mercury SRM 1–650: *Alive* (Chuck Mangione), 1972.
NYC 6021: *White Elephant* (Mike Mainieri & Friends), 1969–71.
Polydor 6062: *The Leprechaun* (Chick Corea), 1976.
Polydor 825657–2: *My Spanish Heart* (Chick Corea), 1976.
Polydor PD 16160: *Friends* (Chick Corea), 1978.
ProJazz CDJ 604: *Gaddabout*, 1984.
Reprise 45422–2: *Tenderness* (Al Jarreau), 1994.
Warner Bros. 9552/Stretch STD–1103: *Three Quartets* (Chick Corea), 1981.
Warner Bros. HS–3472: *One Trick Pony* (Paul Simon), 1980.
Warner Bros. 2K5 3277: *Livin' Inside Your Love* (George Benson), 1979.
Warner Bros. 3432–2: *Pirates* (Rickie Lee Jones), 1981/1985.
Warner Bros. BSK 2968: *Stuff*, 1976.
Zebra ZD 44005–2: *Tribute to Jeff Porcaro* (Dave Garfield), 1997.

SELECTED VIDEOGRAPHY

CPP Media: *Steve Gadd Live at PAS*®, 1995.
DCI: *A History of R&B/Funk Drumming* by Yogi Horton, 1983.
DCI: *Steve Gadd and Giovanni Hidalgo*, 1997.
DCI: *The Buddy Rich Memorial Scholarship Concert* No. 2, 1989.
MCA Home Video: *Dave Grusin and the NY–LA Dream Band*, 1987.
VAJ GAD01: *The Gadd Gang—Live on Digital Video*, 1988.
Video Artists International: *Time Groove* (Louis Bellson, Steve Gadd, et al.), 1990.
Warner Bros./DCI VH0270: *The Making of Burning for Buddy*, pt. 1, 1996.
Yamaha EV–1/DCI VH004: *Steve Gadd—Up Close*, 1983.
Yamaha EV–7/DCI VH012: *Steve Gadd—In Session*, 1985.

SELECTED BIBLIOGRAPHY

Griffith, Mark. "Steve Gadd." *MD* XIX, 11 (November 1995): 116–118.
Larkin, Colin, ed. *The Guiness Encyclopedia of Popular Music*. New York: Stockton Press, 1995.
Mattingly, Rick. "Gadd." *MD* VII, 7 (July 1983): 9–13.
Mattingly, Rick. "Steve Gadd: Track by Track." *MD* XX, 4 (April 1996): 36–58.
Pitt, Daryl. "Gadd about Town." *DB* XLIX, 7 (July 1982): 14–17.
Santelli, R. "Steve Gadd." *MD* X, 1 (January 1986): 18–19.
Sekelsky, Michael J. *The Drum Set Language of Steve Gadd*. DMA lecture–recital, University of Kansas, 1989.
Tomkins, L. "Drummer of the Decade: Steve Gadd." *Crescendo International* XIX, 7 (February 1981): 20–21.
GEN. BIB.: Kernfeld, *NGJ*, by Chuck Braman; Larrick, *BET–CP*; Spagnardi, *GJD*.

GARDNER, CARLTON EDWARD (b. 1885). Carlton E. Gardner attended Harvard University, appeared with concert bands and operas, and played on vaudeville as a xylophone soloist. A 13–year veteran of the Boston Theater Orchestra, he served as drummer and timpanist with the Boston Symphony Orchestra (1915–20), as president of the Boston Musicians' Union (AFM, Local 9, 1923–24), and as supervisor of bands and orchestras for the Boston Public Schools. He also penned percussion method books and edited "The Drummer" column for *Metronome* magazine.

SELECTED BIBLIOGRAPHY

Gardner, Carlton E. *The Gardner Modern Method for the Instruments of Percussion (in Three Parts).* New York: Carl Fischer, 1919.
GEN. BIB.: Cook, Rob, *LDT*, p. 169; Strain, *XYLO*.

GARIBALDI, DAVID (b. San Francisco Bay area, California). Initially successful with the funk group Tower of Power (1970–80), drumset artist Dave Garibaldi served in the U.S. Air Force 724th Band (McChord AFB, Tacoma, WA) and has played with Boz Scaggs, the Carpenters, Natalie Cole, the *Buddy Rich Orchestra, Jermaine Jackson, Larry Carlton, Gino Vanelli, *Mickey Hart's Mystery Box, and the Yellowjackets, among others. He began studio, television, and film soundtrack work in Los Angeles (1977) and in 1991 formed the Afro–Cuban percussion trio, Talking Drums. Journalist and winner of *Modern Drummer* magazine's Reader's Poll Hall of Fame (1980–85), Garibaldi has taught for the Dick Grove School of Music and California State University at Northridge.

SELECTED DISCOGRAPHY

Atlantic 83010–2: *Burning for Buddy: A Tribute to the Music of Buddy Rich,* vol. 2, 1997.
Paulsa Records C7187: *Wishful Thinking,* 1985.
Rykodisc RCD 10396: *Supralingua* (Mickey Hart), 1998.
Warner Bros. BS 2749: *Back to Oakland* (Tower of Power), 1974.

SELECTED VIDEOGRAPHY

DCI VH0188: *Dave Garibaldi—Tower of Groove,* pt. 2, 1994.
DCI/CPP Media: *Talking Drums,* 1994.
Warner Brothers: *Funky Drummers,* 1996.

SELECTED BIBLIOGRAPHY

"David Garibaldi: Talking Drums." *Yamaha Drum Lines* VIII, 1, 1994.
Doerschuk, Andy. "No Mystery: The Percussion Tour of the Year." *DRUM!* V, 7 (November–December 1996): 36–45.

Garibaldi, David. *Future Sounds*. Van Nuys, CA: Alfred, 1990.
Garibaldi, David. *The Funky Beat*. Miami, FL: Manhattan Music/Warner Bros., 1996.

GAUGER, THOMAS LEE (b. 20 Dec 1935, Wheaton, Illinois). Earning a bachelor's degree from the University of Illinois in 1959, Tom Gauger studied with Jack McKenzie and *Paul Price, then performed and recorded with the inconoclastic composer *Harry Partch. He was appointed as principal percussionist of the Saskatoon Summer Music Festival, spent four years as principal with the Oklahoma City Symphony (1959–63), and since 1963 has performed with the Boston Symphony and Boston Pops Orchestras. As a jazz artist Gauger played drum set on tour with Ray Eberly and is one of the founders of "The WUZ," a jazz ensemble comprised of both Boston Symphony and Boston area jazz musicians. He performs with the contemporary music group Collage, and several of his compositions for percussion ensemble (e.g., *Gainsborough* and *Portico*) are considered standard repertoire. Manufacturer of a signature line of percussion sticks and mallets since 1969, Gauger has taught at the Tanglewood Institute, Boston University (since 1965), Oklahoma University, and Oklahoma City University.

SELECTED DISCOGRAPHY

Philips 6514–328: *Aisle Seat—Great Film Music* (Boston Pops), 1982.
Philips 9500–140: *Sibelius—Symphony No. 1 and Finlandia* (Boston Symphony), 1976.
Time–Life Records STLS–7001: *American Classics—Great Moments of Music* (Boston Pops), 1980.

SELECTED BIBLIOGRAPHY

Gauger, Thomas. *Celebration*. Gauger, 1995.
Gauger, Thomas. *Gainsborough*. San Antonio: Southern Music, 1974.
Gauger, Thomas. *Past Midnight*. Gauger, 1991.
Gauger, Thomas. *Portico*. Gauger, 1983.
GEN. BIB.: Larrick, *BET–CP*.

GERLACH, MALCOLM M. "HEINE." Principal percussionist of the Pittsburgh Symphony in the 1930s, Malcolm Gerlach was also a National Rudimental Snare Drum Champion (1930–31) who served in WWI.

SELECTED BIBLIOGRAPHY

Byrne, Frank, and John Beck, eds. "Charlie Owen: The Marine Band Years." *PN* XXV, 4 (Spring 1987): 45–50.
GEN. BIB.: Cook, *LDT*, p. 272 (photo).

GIBBS, TERRY (b. Julius Gubenko, 13 Oct 1924, Brooklyn, New York). Initially a drummer, Terry Gibbs practiced on his brother's xylophone, studied with *Fred Albright, won the *Major Bowes Amateur Hour* in 1936, and became a road musician (drummer and xylophonist) before he had reached his teens. Considered the first great "bop" vibist, he worked with *Buddy Rich in the 1940s, Woody Herman (mid-1940s), Tommy Dorsey (1947), and Chubby Jackson Sextet (1947) and was one of the "Big Four" vibists with *Milt Jackson, *Lionel Hampton, and *Red Norvo. He served in the Eighth Service Command Band (Dallas, Texas, 1943–46) during WWII and won both *Down Beat* and *Metronome* polls in 1950. Gibbs later played with Benny Goodman, co–led a group with Buddy DeFranco, and moved to Los Angeles (1957), where he became musical director, composer, and conductor for Ella Fitzgerald and for the *Operation Entertainment, Regis Philbin* (1964), and *Steve Allen* (1965) shows. He appeared in *A Man and His Music* with Steve Allen at the Roxy Club in Los Angeles in 1977 to rave reviews and has written over 300 compositions and recorded more than 35 albums.

In 1959 and 1996 he formed the Terry Gibbs Dream Band in Los Angeles, releasing a multivolume live album of the original group in 1986. *Down Beat* magazine's Critics' Poll named it "Best Band in the World" in 1959, and its stellar personnel included *Mel Lewis and *Frank Capp on drums. Among his many collaborators have been Bud Powell, Dizzy Gillespie, Charlie Parker, and Miles Davis. [Gibbs gave *Cal Tjader his initial vibe lessons when Tjader was drumming for Dave Brubeck in the 1940s.]

SELECTED DISCOGRAPHY

Calliope Records CAL 3010: *Sessions, Live* (1958, Terry Gibbs, Pete Jolly, and Red
      Norvo), 1976.
Contemporary 7647/52/54/56/57: *Dream Band,* vols. 1–5 (Terry Gibbs Big Band),
      1986.
EmArcy 36064: *Vibes on Velvet,* 1955.
EmArcy 36103: *Swingin' with Terry Gibbs,* 1956.
EmArcy Mercury MG 36075: *Mallets Aplenty—Terry Gibbs,* 1957.
Impulse 58: *Take It from Me,* 1964.
Mercury 60112: *Launching a New Band,* 1959.
Palo Alto 8011: *Jazz Party—First Time Together* (with Buddy DeFranco), 1981.
Prestige/OJC 654: *Early Stan* (Stan Getz and Jimmy Raney), 1962.
Roost LP2260: *El Latino!—Terry Gibbs,* 1964.
Verve 62151: *The Exciting Big Band of Terry Gibbs,* 1961.
Verve MGVS6140: *Terry Gibbs and His Big Band,* 1960.
Verve MGVS6145: *Terry Gibbs Quintet,* 1960.
Verve V6–2151: *Terry Gibbs Big Band,* 1961.
Verve V6–8496: *Terry Gibbs Quartet,* 1962.

SELECTED BIBLIOGRAPHY

Gibbs, Terry. *The Terry Gibbs Method: Vibes, Xylophone, and Marimba.* Pacific, MO: Mel Bay Pub., 1986.

"Meet Terry Gibbs." *DB* XXV, 23 (13 Nov 1958): 18.

Moore, Dan. "Terry Gibbs, Still Swinging." *PN* XXXIII, 4 (August 1995): 45–49.

Tracey, Jack. "Please Note: Terry Gibbs Is No Girk." *DB* XVII, 5 (10 Mar 1950): 18.

GEN. BIB.: Kernfeld, *NGJ*, by Gary Theroux; PASIC® program biographies, 1997.

GLADSTONE, WILLIAM DAVID "BILLY" (b. David Goldstein, 15 Dec 1892, Rumania; d. Oct 1961, New York, New York). Dubbed the "Paderewski of Percussion," Billy Gladstone came to the United States at the age of 11 with an aunt, and, when an immigration official mistook Goldstein for Gladstone, he changed his name to Gladstone. [Gladstone's English father, Charles, was supervisor of the Rumanian Government Orchestra.] He started playing professionally in 1909 and performed at New York's Rialto, Capitol (e.g., *Major Bowes Family Hour*), and Roxy Theaters, for early MGM sound motion pictures, Radio City Music Hall (1932–early 1950s), and with the national touring company of *My Fair Lady* (1957–61). [His colleagues at the Capitol Theater (ca. 1931) included Ray Becraft, Bill Bitner, and Richard Becher (timpanist).] A tireless inventor, Gladstone patented a double–action bass drum pedal in 1924, created his own sticks, the hand sock–cymbal ("slap–hand" cymbals), practice pads, a vibraphone dampening device (1927), bass drum spurs, a snare drum stand, and meticulously detailed snare drums (50 total) that are considered collector's items today. The Fred Gretsch Drum Company manufactured his snare models from 1937 to the 1940s until Gladstone asked the company to cease because it wasn't reproducing them properly. Among his other inventions are the illuminated tongue depressor, orange juice extractor, and electrically lighted orchestra baton. Also a pianist who adapted finger technique to drumming, Gladstone was a 1978 inductee into the Percussive Arts Society Hall of Fame. *Buddy Rich once remarked: "Billy Gladstone is the greatest drummer in the world."

SELECTED BIBLIOGRAPHY

Cangany, Harry. "Billy Gladstone Snare Drum." *MD* XXI, 4 (April 1997): 104.

Cangany, Harry. *The Great American Drums and the Companies That Made Them, 1920–1969.* Cedar Grove, NJ: Modern Drummer Publications, Inc., 1996.

Falzerano, Chet. "Billy Gladstone 'No Break' Vibe Mallets." *PN* XXXV, 1 (February 1997): 82–83.

"Gladstone Invents Gadgets while Drumming." *The Metronome* (September 1937): 83.

"Louie Bellson, William 'Billy' Gladstone, Alfred Friese Inducted into PAS® Hall of Fame." *PN* XVII, 2 (Winter 1979): 27–28.

New York Times Obituary Index, vols. 1–2 (1858–1978). New York: New York Times Co., 1980.

Reed, Ted. "A Tribute to Billy Gladstone." *MD* (October 1981).
GEN. BIB.: Cook, *LDT*, p. 25, 214.

GLASSMAN, KARL [b. 1883, Breslau, Poland (Germany); d. 11 Oct 1975, Clearwater, Florida]. Initially a violinist who studied with Jake Wolf [a student of Henry Denecke, Sr.], Karl Glassman matured in Indianapolis, Indiana, moved to New York at the age of 18, and eventually became timpanist with the New York Symphony Orchestra for 14 years. He appeared with Victor Herbert's Orchestra, the Russian Symphony, the Sousa Opera Company, Webber & Fields Musical Comedy, George White's Scandals, Ziegfeld Follies, the Metropolitan Opera Orchestra, and the NBC Orchestra (1937–54). (His colleagues in the NBC percussion section included Harry Stillman, Harry Edison, and Dave Grupp.) As a pedagogue, he offered timpani lessons via correspondence (*The Art of Timpani Playing*) and around 1926 established the New York School of Drums and Timpani (later aka New York School of Drumming), where he taught with Milton Schlesinger (xylophone and vibraphone) and Alvin Broemel (timpani and drums). In Paterson, New Jersey (ca. 1926), Glassman directed and performed an unusual dance and vocal program at the Fabian Theater that featured six pairs of timpani played in both classical and jazz styles by a group of timpanists that included himself, Edward H. Montray (Pittsburgh Symphony, d. ca. June 1941), Leo Ruffman (Vienna Symphony), Joseph Sears (New York Philharmonic), and Irving Friedel (Russian Symphony). He retired to Clearwater, Florida, where he performed with the Clearwater Symphony and Community Band, as well as Tampa's Egypt Temple Shrine Band.

SELECTED BIBLIOGRAPHY

"Closing Chord—Karl Glassman." *IM* LXXIV, 6 (December 1975): 15.
GEN. BIB.: Cook, *LDT*, p. 149.

GLENNIE, EVELYN ELIZABETH ANN (b. 19 Jul 1965, Aberdeen, Scotland, UK). Initially studying piano and clarinet in a family that supported her musical efforts, Evelyn Glennie suffered gradual and, ultimately, profound hearing loss between the ages of 8 and 12. Destined to adapt and succeed, she began percussion studies at age 12, attended Ellon Academy in Aberdeenshire, toured with the National Youth Orchestra of Scotland, then entered the Royal Academy of Music in London in 1982, winning its highest award: the coveted Queen's Commendation Prize. Glennie captured the Gold Medal in the Shell/London Symphony Music Scholarship competition in 1984 and studied with *Keiko Abe in Japan in 1986—the same year as her critically acclaimed solo debut at Wigmore Hall in London. She gave the BBC Promenade ("The Proms") Concerts' first–ever percussion recital in 1989, was voted "Scots Woman of the Decade" in 1990, and won the Royal Philharmonic Society's "Charles Heidsieck Soloist of the Year" Award in 1991. A recipient of honorary doctorate degrees from Aberdeen (1991), Warwick (1993), Bristol (1995), Loughborough (1995), and Portsmouth (1995) Universities, Glennie was elected a Fellow of the Royal College (1991) and Royal Academy (1992) of Music, made an Honorary Fellow of the Welsh College of Music and Drama (1995), and bestowed the Officer of the British Empire (OBE) Award in 1993.

Her worldwide performance venues include North and South America, India, Indonesia, the Far East, the Middle East, Britain, Europe, Australia, and New Zealand, and she has appeared as soloist with the London Sinfonietta and Baltimore, Boston, Cleveland, Detroit, National (U.S.), New York, Philadelphia, St. Louis, Toronto, London, and Scottish National Symphonies. Contracted exclusively with the RCA/BMG recording company, Glennie received a Grammy® Award in 1988 for her recording of Bartók's "Sonata for Two Pianos and Percussion" and a Classic CD Award in 1994 for *Veni, Veni, Emmanuel.*

In 1993 she founded the "Evelyn Glennie Award for Percussion Composition," which is open to all UK composers; and in tribute to her artistry, several works have been written for her (e.g., Richard Rodney Bennett's *Concerto for Solo Percussion and Chamber Orchestra*). Glennie is also a film and television composer whose compositions are published by Faber Music and have been aired on British television's *The Music Show, See Hear, Everyman's "The Body Collectors of Bangkok,"* and *Survival.*

A popular guest on British electronic media, she has appeared and performed on the BBC-TV's *Soundbites* and *Great Journeys II* series and has been profiled in documentaries at home and abroad [e.g., *A Will to Win* (1987, BBC-TV) and *The Glennie Determination* (1988, Yorkshire TV)]. The *Evelyn Glennie Newsletter* provides her fans a calendar of upcoming performances and information for ordering her recordings and videos.

SELECTED DISCOGRAPHY

CBS Masterworks M 42625: *Bartók—Sonata for Two Pianos and Percussion,* 1989.
RCA/BMG 09026–61277–2: *Rebounds,* 1992.
RCA/BMG 60242–2: *Rhythm Song,* 1990.
RCA/BMG 60557–2: *Light in Darkness,* 1991.
RCA/BMG 60870: *Dancin',* 1991.
RCA/BMG Catalyst 09026 68195–2: *Drumming,* 1996.
RCA/BMG Catalyst 09026–61916–2: *Veni, Veni Emmanuel,* 1993.
RCA/BMG Catalyst 9026–68193–2: *Wind in the Bamboo Grove,* 1996.
Teldec/BBC CD 4509–97868–2: *Last Night of the Proms—100th Season,* 1994.

SELECTED VIDEOGRAPHY

Decca Video 0171121–3: *Evelyn Glennie in Rio,* 1991.
Teldec/BBC Video 4509–97869–3: *Last Night of the Proms—100th Season,* 1994.

SELECTED BIBLIOGRAPHY

Blower, Gill. "A Passion for Percussion." *Home and Country* (UK) (November 1994): 14–15.

Buchalter, Gail. "I Hear the Notes in My Head." *Parade Magazine* (12 Feb 1994): 19–21.

Cowley, Deborah. "Sound Sensations from Evelyn Glennie." *Reader's Digest* (UK) (June 1992): 47–51.

Glennie, Evelyn. *Good Vibrations* (autobiography). London: Arrow, 1991; Japan: Simul Press, 1992.

Glennie, Evelyn. "Percussion in the U.K." *PN* XXX, 4 (April 1992): 13–14.

International Who's Who, 1995–96. London: European Publications, Ltd., 1996.

Malcangi, Greg. "Drummer, Percussionist or Musician?" *PN* XXXIV, 4 (August 1996): 60–61.

Oestreich, James R. "Thumps and Thwacks to a Spiritual Ecstasy." *New York Times* (Saturday, 9 Mar 1996).

Rockwell, John. "A Percussionist Gives Pluck New Meaning." *New York Times* (Sunday, 3 Oct 1993).

Stewart, Andrew. "On the Beat." *Classical Music* (UK) (27 Apr 1996): 14–15.

PASIC® program biographies, 1994. Information supplied by the subject, 1996.

GOLDENBERG, MORRIS "MOE" (b. 28 Jul 1911, Holyoke, Massachusetts; d. 17 Aug 1969, New York, New York). A 1974 inductee into the Percussive Arts Society Hall of Fame, Morris Goldenberg was the first percussion major to graduate (1932) from the Institute of Musical Arts (aka Juilliard School of Music) in New York. In 1938 he served as staff percussionist at WOR radio and subsequently played with the Russian Opera Company, toured with Ballet Russe, the NBC Symphony under Toscanini, the Wallenstein Symphonette, and the New York Orchestra, among others. His work is documented in recordings, film scores, and television commercials. As an educator, Goldenberg taught at the Juilliard (1941–69) and Manhattan Schools of Music and Carroll Sound (NY). He served as percussion coach to the National Orchestral Association (NY, 1944–69), and his students are employed by professional symphonies throughout the world. A Mason, Goldenberg joined with his wife in helping the physically challenged.

SELECTED DISCOGRAPHY

Columbia Masterworks ML 4956: *The Music of George Antheil and Henry Brant*, 1955.

SELECTED BIBLIOGRAPHY

Goldenberg, Morris. *Classical Symphonies for Timpani.* New York: Chappell, 1963.

Goldenberg, Morris. *Modern School for Snare Drum.* New York: Chappell, 1955.

Goldenberg, Morris. *Modern School for Xylophone, Marimba, and Vibraphone.* New York: Chappell, 1950.

Goldenberg, Morris. *Romantic Symphonies for Timpani.* New York: Chappell, 1964.

"Percussive Arts Society Hall of Fame, 1974." *PN* XII, 3 (Spring 1974): 23.

GOODALL, GREGORY S. (b. 1954, California). Earning a bachelor's and a master's degree from the University of California at Los Angeles (UCLA), Greg Goodall studied with *Murray Spivack, *Charles DeLancey, *Mitchell Peters, and *William Kraft. A freelance percussionist, he has worked with the Santa Barbara Symphony (timpanist), Roger Wagner Chorale, Joffrey Ballet, Los Angeles Opera (timpanist), Hollywood Bowl Orchestra (percussionist), and Los Angeles Philharmonic; he has also recorded for television (*Hart to Hart, Matlock, Beauty and the Beast*), for films (*Star Trek II, Star Trek III, Jurassic Park, Titanic*), and in studios (Bernstein's "Symphonic Dances" from *West Side Story* with the Los Angeles Philharmonic). Goodall has taught at California State University at Long Beach and Northridge and at the University of California at Santa Barbara (UCSB).

SELECTED BIBLIOGRAPHY

Glassock, Lynn. "Conversing with Gregory Goodall." *PN* XXV, 5 (Summer 1987): 39–41.

PASIC® program biographies, 1985. Information supplied by the subject, 2000.

GOODMAN, SAUL (b. 18 Jul 1906, Brooklyn, New York; d. 26 Jan 1996, Palm Beach, Florida). A 1972 inductee into the Percussive Arts Society Hall of Fame, Saul Goodman began drums at age 4 and as a teen was planning a career in medicine when he heard a New York Philharmonic concert featuring Tchaikovsky. He asked the timpanist, *Alfred Friese, for lessons and began playing in vaudeville, burlesque shows, and silent movie theaters. When Friese retired because of a physical ailment, Goodman, then a 19–year–old pre–med student at New York University, succeeded him as timpanist with the New York Philharmonic. Starting 14 Oct 1926, he performed 6,168 concerts with them over 46 years—longer than anyone else in the orchestra's history. For 41 years Goodman taught at the Juilliard School, where he initiated a percussion ensemble in 1944 and was visiting professor at the Conservatoire du Musique in Montreal, Canada. A composer and inventor, he created his own replaceable–ball timpani mallet line, a patented timpani-tuning device, a suspended–shell snare drum based on the Dresden timpani suspended–shell design, and a freestanding hand-crank timpano (patented 1952), which is tuned by means of sprockets and a bicycle chain. Goodman's many appearances include the first radio broadcast of a timpani concerto, a lecture–demonstration on the television show *Omnibus*, and the world premiere of Béla Bartók's "Sonata for Two Pianos and Percussion" featuring Bartók and Bartók's wife in 1940. He began an autobiography, *View from the Rear* (1982); his timpani method book remains a popular didactic text; and many of his compositions are considered standard repertoire.

SELECTED DISCOGRAPHY

Angel 35269/Capital HBR 21003: *Saul Goodman—Bell, Drum, and Cymbal*, 1969.
Columbia CL 8333: *Mallets, Melody, and Mayhem: The Exciting World of Saul Goodman* (Saul Goodman Percussion Ensemble), 1961.
Columbia MS–6956: *Bartók—Concerto for Two Pianos, Percussion, and Orchestra* (New York Philharmonic), 1967.
CRI S–263: *Lewis—Toccata for Solo Violin and Percussion*, 1971.
Vox DL 180: *Spotlight on Percussion*, 1955.

SELECTED BIBLIOGRAPHY

Derrickson, Max. "Focus on Performance: Timpani Clinic—A Transcript of a Masterclass with Saul Goodman." *PN* XXVII, 4 (Summer 1989): 38–44.
Goodman, Saul. *Modern Method for Timpani*. New York: Mills Music, 1948.
Goodman, Saul. "Timpani Talk." *Percussionist* XVII, 2 (Winter 1980): 103–105.
Jasionowski, Paul. "An Interview with Saul Goodman about the Bartók Sonata." *PN* XXXII, 2 (April 1994): 53–59.
Lambert, James. "Saul Goodman's Percussion Experiences in Japan." *PN* XXIX, 5 (June 1991): 53–55.
Mattingly, Rick. "Saul Goodman: Master Tympanist." *MD* V, 9 (December 1981–January 1982): 26–27.
Mattingly, Rick. "Saul Goodman: 1907–1996." *PN* XXXIV, 3 (June 1996): 6–11.

GOODWIN, WILLIAM RICHARD "BILL" (b. 8 Jan 1942, Los Angeles, California). Self-taught drumset artist and record producer (100+ albums) who studied piano and tenor sax, Bill Goodwin was influenced by *Stan Levey. He first worked with Charles Lloyd, then collaborated with various musicians, including Michel Legrand, Bud Shank (1961–63), June Christy, Frank Rosolino (1962), Art Pepper and Howard Rumsey (1964), Paul Horn (1965–66), Joe Williams, Gábor Szabó (1967), George Shearing (1968), Mose Allison (1968–75), Tony Bennett, *Gary Burton (1969–71), Toshiko Akiyoshi (1971), Stan Getz (1972), Gerry Mulligan (1973–74), Chuck Israels (1973–78), Al Cohn/Zoot Sims (1974), the Manhattan Transfer, Tom Waits (1975), and Phil Woods (1974–   ).

SELECTED DISCOGRAPHY

Adelphi 50120/Mobile Fidelity 775: *The Phil Woods Quartet—"More" Live*, 1978.
Antilles 1006: *Birds of a Feather* (Phil Woods), 1982.
Antilles 1013: *At the Vanguard* (Phil Woods), 1982.
Asylum 7E2008: *Nighthawks at the Diner* (Tom Waits), 1975.
Atlantic 1577/Rhino R271594: *Gary Burton and Keith Jarrett*, 1970.
Atlantic 1597: *Paris Encounter* (Gary Burton and Stephane Grappelli), 1969.

Atlantic SD 1511: *I've Been Doin' Some Thinking* (Mose Allison), 1968.
Black Hawk BKH–50401: *Heaven* (Phil Woods), 1984.
Churiasco 140/152: *National Jazz Ensemble* (Chuck Israels), 1975.
Concord CCD–4739: *Mile High Jazz—Live in Denver* (Phil Woods), 1996.
Mainstream 396: *Windows* (Jack Wilkins). 1973.
Milan 7313835770–2: *Bending towards the Light...A Jazz Nativity*, 1995.
Omni 1029: *Solar Energy*, 1979–80.
Omni 1050: *Network*, 1982.
RCA BGL1–1391: *The New Phil Woods Album*, 1975.
RCA–BGL2–2202: *Phil Woods Six—"Live" from the Showboat*, 1976.
Red 177: *Integrity* (Phil Woods), 1993.
Red 123236: *David Liebman Plays the Music of Cole Porter*, 1991.
Red RR 123260–2: *Bésame Mucho* (David Liebman), 1994.
Venus: *Chasing the Bird* (Phil Woods), 1998.

SELECTED VIDEOGRAPHY

Rhapsody Films: *Phil Woods Quartet*, 1979/1995.
GEN. BIB.: Hunt, *52nd St.*; Kernfeld, *NGJ*, by Jeff Potter.

GOTTLIEB, DANIEL RICHARD "DANNY" (b. 18 Apr 1953, New York, New York). Starting on cello in the fourth grade, drumset artist Danny Gottlieb studied with *Joe Morello, *Mel Lewis, and *Fred Wickstrom, earning a bachelor's degree from the University of Miami. He performed with *Gary Burton (1976), was an original member of the Pat Metheny Group (1977–83), and appears on over 350 albums, including five Grammy® Award winners. He has played and/or recorded with Nguyen Le, Herbie Hancock, Nnenah Freelon, Randy Brecker, Stan Getz, Sting, Manhattan Transfer, John McLaughlin (1984), Al DiMeola (1985), and others. Gottlieb has produced nine albums with his own group, Elements (1983), co–led by Mark Egan, with whom he also composed the soundtrack to the movie *Blown Away* (1985). His latest projects involve real–time computer–generated graphics while performing live on both acoustic and electronic percussion.

SELECTED DISCOGRAPHY

Audiophile ACD–158: *Jackie Paris*, 1981.
Big World BW2005: *Brooklyn Blues*, 1992.
Blue Note BLJ–48016: *Bireli Lagrene—Inferno*, 1987.
Blue Note BT 85111: *Bill Evans—The Alternative Man*, 1985.
ECM 827 134–4: *American Garage* (Pat Metheny), 1979.
ECM 1114: *Pat Metheny Group* (Pat Metheny), 1978.
ECM 23791–4: *Travels* (Pat Metheny), 1983.
ECM 1097: *Watercolors* (Pat Metheny), 1977.
ECM 1216: *Offramp* (Pat Metheny), 1981.
Jazzline JL 1137: *No JAMF's Allowed* (Contempo Trio), 1994.

Manhattan 53011: *Soaring through a Dream* (Al DiMeola), 1985.
Warner Bros. 25190: *Mahavishnu* (John McLaughlin), 1984.

SELECTED VIDEOGRAPHY

Homespun Video: *Danny Gottlieb—The Complete All–Around Drummer*, pts. 1–2, 1994.

SELECTED BIBLIOGRAPHY

Floyd, Dr. John M. "An Interview with Danny Gottlieb at PASIC® '83 in Knoxville, Tennessee." *PN* XXII, 5 (July 1984): 25–29.
Seidel, Mitchell. "Danny Gottlieb and Joe Morello: Skinship." *JazzTimes* XXI, 8 (November 1991): 22–23.
GEN. BIB.: Kernfeld, *NGJ*, by Patrick T. Will.

GOTTLIEB, GORDON STUART (b. 23 Oct 1948, Brooklyn, New York). Earning a bachelor's (1970) and a master's degree (1971) from the Juilliard School, where he has taught since 1991, Gordon Gottlieb studied with James Wimer, *Saul Goodman, and *Elden Bailey and has performed with the New York, London, and Royal Philharmonic Orchestras. He has made several recordings with the New York Philharmonic featuring the works of Shostakovich, Holst, Rimsky–Korsakov, Respighi, Varèse, Mahler, Gershwin, Schoenberg, and others, and has appeared at the Casals, Madeira Bach, and Mostly Mozart Festivals, and with the Contemporary Chamber Ensemble, Speculum Musicae, Chamber Music Society of Lincoln Center, Group for Contemporary Music, Juilliard Ensemble, and major opera, ballet, and Broadway companies. His numerous collaborators for performance and/or recordings include Keith Jarrett, Debbie Harry, Lena Horne, Sarah Vaughan, Bette Midler, George Benson, Lena Horne, Patti La Belle, and Tony Bennett, among many others.

As a composer Gottlieb penned *The River Speaks* (Gorgot Music, 1989), *Ritual Dance* (Gorgot Music, 1994), *Fanfare* (Living Music, 1994), and several jingles (since 1994). He has conducted in Carnegie Hall, Santa Fe, and Switzerland with both instrumental and operatic chamber ensembles, and his extensive studio and television background includes work for over 40 record labels and performances on over 100 films (e.g., *Fame*, *The Wiz*, *A Chorus Line*, *Lethal Weapon 3*, *The Cotton Club*, *Malcolm X*, and *Beauty and the Beast*). As a journalist he has published articles on recording technique, critical music review, and world music and is one of the few Americans to perform in the Rio de Janeiro "Carnaval" parade—three times!

An adjunct professor at the Yale School (1987–), Gottlieb teaches at the Juilliard School (1991–) and has been honored by the National Academy of Recording Arts and Sciences (NARAS) as a "Most Valuable Player." A corecipient of a grant from the Massachusetts Council on the Arts to combine electroacoustic percussion and visual arts, he was also awarded a Martha Baird Rockefeller grant (1980).

SELECTED DISCOGRAPHY

Angel CDC 72435 54893 2 3: *Sketches of Coltrane* (Byron Olson), 1994.
Angel CDQ0777 7 54915 2 4: *Romulus Hunt* (Carly Simon), 1993.
Arista ARCD–8582: *My Romance* (Carly Simon), 1990.
Auvidis AV 4831: *Jay and Gordon Gottlieb—Piano and Percussion*, 1984.
Capitol CDP7 91737 2: *Bulletproof Heart* (Grace Jones), 1989.
Delos DE 3151: *Bartók—Sonata for Two Pianos and Percussion* (Chamber Music
    Society of Lincoln Center), 1993.
DMP CD–468: *Heat of the Moment* (Warren Bernhardt), 1989.
Elektra/Nonesuch 9 71269–2: *Music of Edgard Varèse* (Contemporary Chamber
    Ensemble), 1972.
Epic E2K59000: *History* (Michael Jackson), 1995.
Island 314–524 096–2: *A Secret Life* (Marianne Faithfull), 1994.
Living Music LD 0024: *Solstice Live!* (Paul Winter), 1994.
Living Music LD 0028: *Prayer for the Wild Things* (Paul Winter), 1994.
Living Music LMUS 0032: *Pete* (Pete Seeger), 1996.
Music Masters 01612–67086–2: *Les Noces* (Stravinsky), 1992.
Music Masters 01612–67152–2: *L'Histoire du Soldat* (Stravinsky), 1995.
New World NW 357–2: *An Idyll for the Misbegotten* (Crumb), 1987.
New World Records 209: *Bassoon Variations* et al. (Wuorinen), 1976.
O.O. Discs 8: *Electricity* (Rolnick), 1983.
Premiere PRCD 1010: *Siegmeister—Sextet for Brass and Percussion* (American
    Brass Quintet), 1991.

SELECTED BIBLIOGRAPHY

Gottlieb, Gordon. "The Percussion of Carnaval." *MP* I, 1 (December 1984–February
    1985): 12–17.
Gottlieb, Gordon. "World Influences: Africa and South India." *MP* (December
    1985).
Information supplied by the subject, 1996.

GOULDEN, HOWARD N. (b. 1888, Bridgeport, Connecticut; d. 2 Nov 1957, Bridgeport, Connecticut). An assistant bandmaster for the U.S. Navy Band (Groton, Connecticut) in WWI, Howard Goulden began drumming at age 15 and served as timpanist with the Arthur Pryor and Bachman Million Dollar Bands, and as drummer and xylophone soloist for the John Philip Sousa Band (1920–1931). He was heard with the Raymond Paige Orchestra in 1939 on CBS radio, the Don Vorhees Orchestra on the *Telephone Hour* for 19 years, and the World's Fair Band (1939–40) and also operated a drum shop in Bridgeport. [*Fred Hinger used, and in 1984 still owned, the four–and–one–half octave Leedy xylophone that Goulden played with the Sousa Band in the 1920s.]

SELECTED BIBLIOGRAPHY

Bierley, Paul E. *The Works of John Philip Sousa*. Columbus, OH: Integrity Press, 1984.
GEN. BIB.: Cook, *LDT*, p. 10; Strain, *XYLO*.

GREEN, GEORGE HAMILTON, JR. (b. 23 May 1893, Omaha, Nebraska; d. 11 Sep 1970, Woodstock, New York). George Hamilton Green's grandfather, Joseph Green (I), violinist and violin maker in New York City, moved to Omaha, Nebraska, to become conductor and baritone horn soloist of the Seventh Ward Cornet Band. Joseph's son, George, Sr. (d. ca. Jan 1929), became conductor, arranger, and cornet soloist with the same band in 1889.

G. H. Green, Jr., piano prodigy at the age of 4, played his first xylophone solo ("American Patrol") on a self–made instrument with his father's band in 1905. Between 1911 and 1913 he attended Creighton College (Omaha) and at 17 started drum lessons. Green appeared in vaudeville shows by age 19 and started a solo recording career with the Edison Company in February 1917. Included on hundreds of records and various labels during the "Golden Age" of the xylophone [the "acoustic era" of recording: ca. 1877–1925], his repertoire boasted 300 standard overtures, violin concerti, and piano arrangements. Articles featuring Green appeared in the *Metronome* and the *International Musician* magazines. Students demanding lessons increased in proportion to his popularity, so with an older brother, *Joseph ("Joe" II), Green coauthored a mail–order instruction course of 50 lessons at $1 each.

Among the ensembles with which he recorded are Patrick Conway's Band, American Republic Band, American Marimbaphone Band, All–Star Trio, Earl Fuller's Rector House Orchestra, Fred Van Eps Quartet, Imperial Marimba Band, Happy Six, Yerkes Jazzarimba Orchestra, and Green Brothers Novelty Band (fl. 1919–39). The latter two included his brother, *Joe, who was also a xylophone soloist, composer, and percussionist, and in 1928 a younger brother, Lewis, who played banjo, guitar, and percussion. The combined Green brothers also recorded music for the first three Walt Disney cartoons.

In 1925 electronic recording allowed improved reproduction quality of "sustaining" instruments such as the piano, so xylophonists evolved from center stage soloists to studio musicians for radio broadcasts. Although George worked for many years in radio, it is rumored that he had difficulty with this transition and, allegedly, in the middle of a 1946 broadcast walked out of the studio and never returned. (Other possible contributing factors included the death of his brother and business manager, Joe (1939), the loss of many of his students to military service in WWII, and the cancellation of his Sunday morning radio show, *Cloister Bells*, which was preempted by war news broadcasts.) In his second career, which he had nurtured for years, Green became a well–known commercial illustrator, water–colorist, and magazine cartoonist. Some of his work can be seen in older editions of *Collier's*, the *Saturday Evening Post*, *Argosy*, *Look*, and *Life*. His son, Gerald Hamilton Green, followed in his footsteps as a professional cartoonist. George H. Green was a 1983 inductee into the Percussive Arts Society Hall of Fame.

SELECTED DISCOGRAPHY

Columbia Phonograph Co. Catalog 265–D E, matrix 140179 & 140180: "Cross Corners" and "Ragtime Robin," ca. 1925.

Columbia Phonograph Co. Catalog 977–D E: "Jovial Jasper."

Conservatory Collectors' Series Album 7101M: *The Xylophone Genius of George Hamilton Green* (Conservatory Recording, Inc., 400 W. Madison St., Chicago, IL 60606).

Edison 51550–R: "A Little Love, a Little Kiss" (vibraphone), ca. 1924.

Emerson Phonograph Co. Catalog 10122, matrix 4711–3: "Chromatic Fox Trot" (The Imperial Three) (10" record), ca. 1920.

Emerson Phonograph Co. Catalog 10169, matrix 4882: "Triplets," (George Hamilton Green's Novelty Orchestra), 1920.

Emerson Phonograph Co. Catalog 7473/9138: "Log Cabin Blues" (Emerson Military Band) (7"/9" record), 1919.

Pathe Freres Phonograph Co. Catalog 22276: "Chromatic Fox Trot," ca. 1920.

Thomas A. Edison, Inc., Catalog 50625, matrix 6983: "Triplets" (Judas Society Orchestra) (10" vertical cut), ca. 1920.

Thomas A. Edison, Inc., Blue Amberol Cylinder and Diamond Disc, Catalog 3968: "Triplets," 1919.

Thomas A. Edison, Inc. Catalog 51527, matrix 10254 & 10253: "Chromatic Fox Trot" and "Log Cabin Blues" (10" vertical cut), ca. 1925.

Victor 52410: "I Wanna Be Loved by You" and "I Can't Give You Anything but Love" (Green Brothers Marimba Band/George and Joe on xylophone), ca. 1928.

Victor Talking Machine Co., Victor Orthophonic (electronic process), Catalog 19944E: "Triplets" and "Rainbow Ripples," ca. 1926.

Xylophonia Music: *Masters of the Xylophone—George Hamilton Green and Joe Green* (recordings from 1916 to 1928), 1994.

SELECTED BIBLIOGRAPHY

Bridwell, Barry, and Scott Lyons. "A Salute to George Hamilton Green, Xylophone Genius." *PN* XXV, 5 (Summer 1987): 54–56.

Bush, Jeffrey E. "Interview with Harry Breuer." *PN* XVIII, 3 (Spring/Summer 1980): 50–53.

Cahn, William. "The Xylophone in Acoustic Recordings (1877–1929)." *Percussionist* XVI, 3 (Spring/Summer 1979): 106–132.

Eyles, Randy, and Garwood Whaley, eds. *Xylophone Rags of George Hamilton Green.* Ft. Lauderdale, FL: Meredith Music Publications, 1984.

"George Hamilton Green, Xylophonist of Chicago." *United Musician* I, 7, series 7. New York (July 1915).

Green, George H. *Instruction Course for Xylophone: A Complete Course of Fifty Lessons,* edited by Randy Eyles and Garwood Whaley. Ft. Lauderdale, FL: Meredith Music Publications, 1984.

Harvey, David. "A George Green Centennial Tribute." *PN* XXXI, 5 (June 1993): 40–42.

McCutchen, Thomas W. *An Examination of Selected Ragtime Solos by Zez Confrey, George Hamilton Green, Charles Johnson, and Red Norvo as Transcribed for Xylophone Solo with Marimba Ensemble Accompaniment.* DMA lecture–recital, North Texas State University, 1979.

"Omaha Boy Is Pronounced the Greatest Xylophonist in World." *Omaha Sunday Bee* (14 Nov 1915).

GEN. BIB.: Cahn, *XAR*; Cook, *LDT*, p. 158 (cartoons).

GREEN, JOSEPH PETER (b. 9 Feb 1892, Omaha, Nebraska; d. 16 Oct 1939, New York, New York). Starting on piano and drums, Joe Green matured in his father's "George Green Band" and began playing professionally as a theater and hotel orchestra drummer, freelancing in Omaha, Chicago (where he studied with *Joseph Zettleman for three years), New York (1916, with Bohumir Kryl's Band), Minneapolis, and Kansas City. In 1917 he moved to New York, having mastered the xylophone, and was a featured soloist for summer tours with John Philip Sousa's Band (1917–20). During the winter he and his brothers, *George and Lewis, collaborated on numerous musical projects that Joe managed under Joe Green Music Enterprises. These varied groups were alternately named the Green Bros. Xylophone Soloists, Green Bros. Novelty Marimba-Phone Band, and Joe Green's Novelty Marimba Band, among others. First recorded in 1918, Joe and George were in demand at all the major labels, and their combined record output numbered in the thousands by 1922. Joe performed in the Yerkes Jazzarimba Orchestra, was employed as staff drummer for the Victor Company in the early 1920s, broadcast shows over radio on the CBS and NBC networks (e.g., *Cloister Bells*), and coauthored mail–order xylophone methods with his brother George. Among his popular compositions still available is the 1925 favorite "Xylophonia."

SELECTED DISCOGRAPHY

Decca: "Lady of Madrid"/"My Toreador" (Played on a Leedy "Octarimba" with organ accompaniment), 1938.

Xylophonia Music: *Masters of the Xylophone—George Hamilton Green and Joe Green* (recordings from 1916 to 1928), 1994.

SELECTED BIBLIOGRAPHY

Strain, James Allen. "Joe Green: The Most Famous of the Green Brothers?" *PN* XXXIV, 5 (October 1996): 84–85.

GEN. BIB.: Cahn, *XAR*; Cook, *LDT*, p. 14, 20, 45+ (several photos); Strain, *XYLO*.

GREER, WILLIAM ALEXANDER "SONNY" (b. 13 Dec 1903, Long Branch, New Jersey; d. 23 Mar 1982, New York, New York). Singer, entertainer, and showman who took a few lessons with Frank Wolf, Sonny Greer started drums in high school but was essentially self–taught and influenced by vaudeville drummers Eugene "Peggy" Holland and J. Rosmond Johnson. He played locally with Wilbur Gardner, Harry Yerek, and Mabel Ross and in a hotel pit orchestra in Asbury Park, New Jersey, before moving to Washington, D.C., where he performed with Marie Lucas at the Howard Theater. He was associated with Duke Ellington in Washington, D.C. (1920), and with Ellington's orchestra (1923–1951), including the Cotton Club years in New York. His large drum setup sported timpani, chimes, gongs, vibraphone, and so on, but Greer rarely took solos. Later working with Johnny Hodges (1951), Henry "Red" Allen (1952–53), Tyree Glenn (1959), J. C. Higginbotham (1960s), and Brooks Kerr (1974), he recorded under his own name, fronted some of his own groups, appeared in films [e.g., *Check and Double Check* (1930), *Cabin in the Sky* (1942), *The Night They Raided Minsky's* (1968)], and also played on Broadway (Ziegfeld's *Show Girl*).

SELECTED DISCOGRAPHY

Camden CAL–459: Duke Ellington at the Cotton Club, 1958.
Circle CCD–101–105: *Duke Ellington and His Orchestra*, vols.1–5, 1943–45.
Columbia C3L–27/39: *The Ellington Era, 1927–40*, vols. 1–2.
Jazzology JCD–1001–1002: *Eddie Condon—The Town Hall Concerts,* vol. 1.
Masters of Jazz, Media 7: *Anthology of Jazz Drumming,* vols. 1–2 (1904–35), 1997.
RCA 51364: *Duke Ellington—In a Mellowtone*, 1940–42.
RCA Victor LPV–517: *Jumpin' Punkins* (Duke Ellington), 1965.
RCA Victor LPV–541: *Johnny Come Lately* (Duke Ellington), 1967.
Smithsonian R 018: *Duke Ellington* (1938–40), 1976.
Verve MGV8139/8136: *Johnny Hodges and His Orchestra*, 1951/1955.
Victor V–38036–A: "High Life," ca. 1930.

SELECTED BIBLIOGRAPHY

"From the Past: Sonny Greer." *MD* XIX, 4 (April 1995): 118–119.
GEN. BIB.: Cook, *LDT*; Kernfeld, *NGJ*, by John Chilton; Korall, *DM*; Southern, *BDA–AAM*; Spagnardi, *GJD*.

GRETSCH, FRIEDRICH F. (d. 1895, Germany). Immigrating to the United States in 1872, Friedrich Gretsch established the Fred F. Gretsch Manufacturing Company in Brooklyn, New York (1883). Importing instruments from Europe, Gretsch produced his own banjos, accordions, drums, string instruments, and phonograph needles. Upon Friedrich's death, his sons, Fred (later known as "Sr.") and Walter Gretsch [b. ca. 1882, Brooklyn, New York; d. ca. June 1940, Brooklyn, New York] became president and secretary–treasurer respectively. [The parallel firm of Gretsch and Brenner, Inc. (headed by Walter Gretsch), opened in Manhattan around 1915 and imported high-quality instruments to complement the Brooklyn entry–level products. Walter was also president of three retail outlets that operated under the name New York Band Instrument Company.] Gretsch opened a satellite office in Chicago (1928), but manufacturing remained in Brooklyn. After WWII Fred "Sr.'s" son, Fred, Jr., assumed leadership of the company until selling it in 1967 to the Baldwin Piano Company, which moved the factory to Arkansas. In 1983 the fourth–generation Gretsch, Fred III, repurchased the company and set up operations in South Carolina.

SELECTED BIBLIOGRAPHY

Cangany, Harry. *The Great American Drums and the Companies That Made Them, 1920–1969*. Cedar Grove, NJ: Modern Drummer Publications, Inc., 1996.
Cook, Rob. *Complete History of the Leedy Drum Company*. Fullerton, CA: Centerstream Publishing, 1993 (p. 171).
Falzerano, Chet. *Gretsch Drums: The Legacy Of That Great Gretsch Sound*. Fullerton, CA: Centerstream Publishing, 1996.
Schmidt, Paul William. *History of the Ludwig Drum Company*. Fullerton, CA: Centerstream Publishing, 1991 (p. 59).
"Trade Talk: Walter Gretsch." *IM* XXXVIII, 1 (July 1940): 17.
GEN. BIB.: Hitchcock and Sadie, *NGA*, by Edmund A. Bowles.

GROVER, NEIL W. (b. 7 Jul 1955, Queens, New York). Studying with Ronnie Benedict, *Joseph Castka, Robert McCormick, and *Vic Firth, Neil Grover attended Florida State University (1973–74) and earned a bachelor's degree from the New England Conservatory (1977). He has performed and/or recorded with the Boston Symphony (DGG and Philips labels) and Boston Pops Orchestra (Sony and Philips labels) since 1977, the Boston Ballet (as percussionist and assistant timpanist), the Philip Glass Ensemble, Empire Brass, Royal Ballet of England, Boston Musica Viva, American Ballet Theater, and Bolshoi Ballet. A cymbal, tambourine, and triangle specialist, Grover recorded a special percussion segment for the movie *Indiana Jones and the Temple of Doom*, and appeared in the movie *Blown Away* and on a music video with the rock group, Aerosmith. He has toured the United States and/or recorded with the "Music from Marlboro" chamber music series, with the Boston Symphony Chamber Players, and as mallet soloist with the Broadway production of *Pirates of Penzance*. A featured clinician at various state percussion festivals, on college campuses, for Percussive Arts Society International Conventions, and at the First International Percussion Festival in Puerto Rico, Grover has also appeared as soloist for the Fromm Festivals at Tanglewood and Harvard, Berkshire Music Center, and Marlboro Festival. Founder and president of Grover Pro Percussion, Inc., he has taught at the Boston Conservatory and the University of Massachusetts and has served on the board of directors for the Percussive Arts Society.

SELECTED BIBLIOGRAPHY

"Artist Profile: Neil Grover." *Drum Tracks* VI, 4 (1989).
Grover, Neil W. "Creative Tambourine Technique." *PN* XXX, 6 (August 1992): 18–21.
"Neil Grover and Grover Pro Percussion." *Musical Merchandise Review* (February 1994).
Information supplied by the subject, 1996.

GUALDA, SYLVIO. Timpanist for the Paris Opera, Sylvio Gualda attended the Paris Conservatory, premiered Karlheinz Stockhausen's "Zyklus," and is considered the first French percussion soloist, having performed works by Boulez, Constant, and Jolivet. He serves on the faculty of the Conservatory in Versailles.

SELECTED DISCOGRAPHY

Adda 581224: *Xenakis—Oophaa*, 1991.
Angel CDC–47446: *Bartók—Concerto/Sonata for Two Pianos and Percussion.*

SELECTED BIBLIOGRAPHY

Dupin, François. "Dupin's Directory of French Percussionists." *PN* XXXII, 2 (April 1994): 29–31.
Rosen, Michael. "Focus on Performance: An Interview with Sylvio Gualda Concerning *Psappha* (Iannis Zenakis)." *PN* XXVII, 4 (Summer 1989): 32–36.

GUBIN, SOL (b. 11 Jul 1928, Atlantic City, New Jersey; d. 15 May 1996, Los Angeles, California). Starting in the mid–1940s, Sol Gubin performed with the Hal McIntyre, Tex Beneke, and Charlie Barnett Orchestras and was a first–call drummer in New York (1954–70). His numerous collaborators in the studio and on stage included Melissa Manchester, Patti Page, Johnny Mathis, Frank Sinatra, Benny Goodman, Count Basie, Barbra Streisand, Tony Bennett, Lena Horne, Zoot Sims, Stan Kenton (percussion on *Cuban Fire Suite*), Al Cohn, Julie Andrews, and Leonard Bernstein. As a staff drummer for two television networks, he played live for the *Perry Como Show* and *Steve Lawrence Show*, George Burns and Bob Hope television specials, and the Academy, Emmy, and Tony Awards shows. Resettling in California in 1970, he landed gigs with the *Carol Burnett Show*, *Barney Miller*, and *M*A*S*H*, as well as musicals (*Annie*) and movie soundtracks.

SELECTED DISCOGRAPHY

Brunswick BL54114: *Swinging Friends*, 1963.
Fresh Sounds 2003: *Big Band Sound* (Elliot Lawrence), 1958.

Philips 32 JD 159: *Legrand Jazz* (Michel LeGrand), 1962.
Verve V6–8603: *Gary McFarland*, 1964.
Verve V6–8620: *Kai Winding*, 1965.
Verve V6–8642: *Wes Montgomery*, 1965.

SELECTED BIBLIOGRAPHY

Van Horn, Rick. "In Memoriam: Sol Gubin." *MD* XX, 11 (November 1996): 111.
GEN. BIB.: Hunt, *52nd St.*

GUERIN, JOHN PAYNE (b. 31 Oct 1939, Hawaii). A self–taught drumset artist who matured in San Diego, producer-arranger-composer John Guerin appeared and/or recorded with Buddy DeFranco (1960–61), George Shearing (1965–66), *Victor Feldman, the Byrds, Roger Kellaway, Frank Zappa, Dianne Schuur, Thelonius Monk, Joe Farrell (1978), *Milt Jackson (1981), Oliver Nelson, Bobby McFerrin (1982), Ray Brown, and Tom Scott, with whom he established the L.A. Express. Through the latter Guerin collaborated with Joni Mitchell on several projects, including song–writing (e.g., "The Hissing of Summer Lawns"). His numerous television and movie studio credits include *Hawaii Five–O*, *Streets of San Francisco*, and *Bird*.

SELECTED DISCOGRAPHY

Asylum 1001: *Court and Spark* (Joni Mitchell), 1974.
Asylum 1051: *The Hissing of Summer Lawns* (Joni Mitchell), 1975.
Bizarre–Rep. 6365: *Hot Rats* (Frank Zappa), 1969.
Blue Note 84324: *Blue Mitchell—Bantu Village*, 1969.
Blue Note LA462–G: *Carmen McRae—I Am Music*, 1975.
Blue Note LA632–H2: *Jean–Luc Ponty—Live at Donte's*, 1969.
Columbia CBS 4671822: *Monk's Blues* (Thelonius Monk), 1968.
Concord CJ 19: *Brown's Bag* (Ray Brown), 1975.
Ode 77021: *Tom Scott and the L.A. Express*, 1973.
Pablo 2310.867: *Big Mouth* (Milt Jackson), 1981.
Warner/Reprise 9 26183–2: *Blue Pacific* (Michael Franks), 1990.
Warner/Reprise 2230–2: *The Art of Tea* (Michael Franks), 1975/1989.
Warner 3004–2: *Sleeping Gypsy* (Michael Franks), 1977.
Zebra ZD 44005–2: *Tribute to Jeff Porcaro* (Dave Garfield), 1997.

SELECTED BIBLIOGRAPHY

Flans, Robyn. "John Guerin: LA Studio Guru." *MD* XXIII, 1 (January 1999): 84–94.
GEN. BIB.: Hunt, *52nd St.*; Kernfeld, *NGJ*, by Bill Milkowski.

GURTU, TRILOK (b. 30 Oct 1951, Bombay, India). Born into a musical family that led him to embrace tabla at the age of 5, Trilok Gurtu is a self–taught drumset artist who employs a unique eclectic drumming technique combining Indian and Western instruments and rhythms. He studied tablas with Ahmed Jan Thirakwa and by his teens played professionally for Indian film music studios. He relocated to Europe (1973), lived in New York (1976), settled in Germany (1977), and has performed and/or recorded with his own group Crazy Saints, Oregon (1984–   ), Jan Garbarek, John McLaughlin, *Airto Moreira, Lee Konitz, Nana Vasconcelos, Joe Zawinul, Don Cherry, Pat Metheny, and John Abercrombie, Charlie Mariano, and many others. Gurtu was named "Best Percussionist" several times by the readers of *Down Beat* magazine.

SELECTED DISCOGRAPHY

CMP CD 80: *Bad Habits Die Hard* (Crazy Saints), 1995.
CMP CD 66: *Crazy Saints*, 1993.
Silva Screen Records STD 5015: *The Trilok Gurtu Collection*, 1997.

SELECTED BIBLIOGRAPHY

Larkin, Colin, ed. *The Guiness Encyclopedia of Popular Music.* New York: Stockton Press, 1995.
Shoemaker, Bill. "Rhythm of the Saints." *JazzTimes* XXIII, 9 (November 1993): 56–57.
PASIC® program biographies, 1992, 1997.

GUSIKOFF, DAVID. Eminent snare drummer and teacher during the early mid-twentieth century in New York, David Gusikoff started playing around 1911, eventually appearing at the Capitol (seven years) and Roxy Theaters, Radio City Music Hall, with the Edwin Franko Goldman Band, the Cleveland Symphony, the Russian Symphony, and the NBC Orchestra. He served overseas in WWI and performed in the Broadway production of *South Pacific* in 1949. Legendary drummer and teacher *Ted Reed once remarked, "Dave had rubber wrists, like *Billy Gladstone's."

SELECTED BIBLIOGRAPHY

Stone, George Lawrence. "Technique of Percussion." *IM* (July 1949): 19.
GEN. BIB.: Cook, *LDT*, p. 204.

GUSIKOV, MICHAEL JOSEF [GUZIKOW, MICHAL JÓZEF] [b. 2 Sep 1806, Szklow, Poland (aka Belorussia); d. 21 Oct 1837, Aix–la–Chapelle (aka Aachen, Germany)]. A Polish-Jewish xylophone soloist whose pale countenance was framed by a long beard, Michael Josef Gusikov was born into a musical family and single-handedly popularized the crude strohfiedel ("straw–fiddle," xylophone) in Europe. He initially played flute, studying and touring with his father, also a flutist and violinist. With a violinist brother, the trio appeared before Emperor Nikolai I in Moscow and elsewhere until Gusikov contracted early stages of tuberculosis in 1831 and was forced to take up the primitive xylophone as his principal instrument. To ensure its acceptance in more musically critical circles, he made improvements in this folk instrument by extending the range and altering the shape of the bars for better tone. The bars were bound with ribbon upon straw and laid horizontally to the performer on a table that served as a resonator. Utilizing spoon–shaped mallets held between the index and middle fingers, his physical performance technique resembled that of the cimbalom.

In 1834 Gusikov began a tour to rave reviews in Kiev, through Odessa, Krakow, and Vienna (1835), where he performed for Emperor Franz II and garnered the patronage of Prince von Metternich. Continuing through Prague, Leipzig, Berlin, and Frankfurt, he played for King Leopold I of Belgium before arriving in Paris in 1836. Despite his popular success in Paris, his health deteriorated and he decided to return to Poland, but he died at Aix–la–Chapelle a few days after giving one last concert.

His technical prowess won the attention of Meyerbeer, Chopin, Liszt, and particularly Mendelssohn, who after hearing him in Leipzig stated: "A real phenomenon who...delights me more on his odd instrument than many do on their pianos. I must own that the skill of the man beats everything that I could have imagined, for with his wooden sticks resting on straw, his hammers of wood, he produces all that is possible." Unable to read music, Gusikov featured his own works and arrangements of well–known pieces, including his rendition of Paganini's "La Campanella" (third movement of his Concerto in B Minor, Op. 7), which frequently elicited a standing ovation.

SELECTED BIBLIOGRAPHY

Beckford, John Stephen. "Michal Józef Guzikow: Nineteenth–Century Xylophonist, Part I." *PN* XXXIII, 3 (June 1995): 74–76.
Beckford, John Stephen. "Michal Józef Guzikow: Nineteenth–Century Xylophonist, Part II." *PN* XXXIII, 4 (August 1995): 73–75.
Peters, Gordon. *The Drummer: Man.* Wilmette, IL: Kemper–Peters Publications, 1975.
GEN. BIB.: Sadie, *NG*, by Irena Poniatowska.

H

HAAS, JONATHAN LEE "JOHNNY H." (b. 9 Jun 1954, Chicago, Illinois). Principal timpanist with the Charlotte Symphony (NC, 1979–80), New York Chamber Symphony since 1980, and principal percussionist and coprincipal timpanist with the American Symphony since 1978, Jonathan Haas received a bachelor's degree from Washington University (St. Louis, 1976), where he studied with *Rich O'Donnell, and a master's degree from the Juilliard School (1979) under the tutelage of *Saul Goodman. Presenting the first timpani recital in the history of Carnegie Hall in 1980, he debuted as timpani soloist in 1984 with the New York Chamber Symphony and in 1987 with the Bournemouth (England) Sinfonietta. His solo and chamber timpani repertoire includes baroque, jazz, rock, and contemporary music, and he has performed adjunct timpani and percussion with the New York Philharmonic (1979–86), St. Louis Symphony (1975–92), Canadian Brass, American Brass Quintet, the Orpheus Chamber (since 1984), American Composers Orchestras (since 1984), New York Pops Orchestra (principal timpanist and percussionist since 1982), Mostly Mozart Festival (timpanist since 1988), and Waterloo Festival (timpanist since 1987). Haas is a featured soloist on the Grammy® Award–nominated *Gerald McBoing Boing* (Gail Kubik, composer, New World Records), has played on tour in the Emerson, Lake, and Palmer Orchestra (1978), performed with the Paul Taylor Dance Company, and appeared on the Distinguished Artist Recital Series and Chamber Music Series at New York's 92nd St. "Y."

Founder of his own recording company (Sunset Records), a percussion instrument rental company (Kettles and Company), and a musician-contracting company (Gemini Music Productions, Ltd.), he has resurrected and recorded rare forgotten eighteenth-century *melodic* timpani solo material and works from the first half of the twentieth century that contained jazz timpani parts composed by Duke Ellington. A charter member of the music education–focused percussion quartet Drumfire, Haas has served on the faculties of the Hartt School (CT,

1991), the Aspen (CO) Music Festival (since 1984, where he once studied with
*Charles Owen and *Barry Jekowsky), and the Peabody Conservatory (since
1982). He has been honored with the Martha Baird Rockefeller Foundation and
American Music Center Commission awards.

SELECTED DISCOGRAPHY

Bridge BCD 9023: *Jan DeGaetani in Concert,* vol. 1, 1988.
CRD 3449: *Jonathan Haas—Virtuoso Timpanist* (Bournemouth Sinfonietta), 1988.
Leonarda LPI 114: *New Music from England* (Capricorn Players), 1982.
Music Masters 0612-67067-2: *Peter and the Wolf/Gerald McBoing Boing* (Little
    Orchestra Society), 1991.
Newport Classic Premier NPD 85552: *Chambers—Symphony of the Universe,* 1993.
New World NW 326-2: *Crumb—A Haunted Landscape* (New York Philharmonic),
    1985.
New World 80422-2: *The Music of Barbara Kolb,* 1989/1992.
O.O. Discs 26: *Off-Hour Wait State,* 1996.
Polygram 314 513 575-4: *Zappa's Universe* (Orchestra of Our Time), 1993.
Pro Arte CDD 448: *Richard Strauss—Le Bourgeois Gentilhomme* (New York
    Chamber Symphony), 1989.
Sefel SEFD 5026: *Skitch Henderson and the New York Pops—Live at Carnegie Hall,*
    1983.
Sunset 7-84002-2: *Johnny H. and the Prisoners of Swing,* 1993.

SELECTED BIBLIOGRAPHY

Baldwin, John, ed. "Chapter News and Membership News." *PN* XXX, 3 (February
    1992): 78–79.
Keiger, Dale. "Bangin' Around with Johnny H." *Johns Hopkins Magazine* (Febru-
    ary 1995).
Nelson, Judy. "Teaching Percussion with Bach and Zappa—An Interview with
    Jonathan Haas." *Instrumentalist* L, 4 (November 1995): 18–22 (includes
    short discography).
Powley, Harrison, and Jonathan Haas. "In Search of Multiple Timpani Repertoire."
    PN XXIII, 5 (July 1985): 52–54.
GEN. BIB.: Borland, *WWAMC.* Information supplied by the subject, 1996.

HADDAD, JAMEY (b. 1952, Cleveland, Ohio). A Fulbright fellow and two-
time National Endowment for the Arts grant recipient, drumset and hand-drum
artist Jamey Haddad started on doumbek (didibuki), taking drumset lessons by
age 5. He attended Berklee College (Boston), studied Indian drumming with
Ramnad Raghavan and Karaikudi R. Mani, and has performed and/or toured
with Randy Brecker, David Liebman, *Airto Moreira, Carly Simon, Ralph
Towner, the Paul Winter Consort, Oregon, Eliane Elias, Joe Lovano, and others. Haddad serves on the faculties of the New School (Mannes College of Music) and Berklee College and has appeared in Spain, Canada, and Australia. He

has performed on over 75 recordings, and his most recent book-video is entitled *Global Standard Time*.

SELECTED DISCOGRAPHY

Concord CCD-4574: *Taken to Heart* (Tom Lellis), 1993.
Owl OWL0788304852: *Miles Away* (David Liebman), 1995.
Owl 71: *Turn It Around* (David Liebman).
Soul Note 121295-2: *Songs for My Daughter* (David Liebman), 1995.

SELECTED BIBLIOGRAPHY

Haddad, Jamey. "Plugging into the Indian Music Scene." *PN* XXVIII, 3 (Spring 1990): 48–52.
Moore, Ted. "A Lesson with Jamey Haddad." *Sticks and Mallets* I, 1 (November/December 1997): 66–67.
Thompson, Woody. "A Profile of Jamey Haddad." *PN* XXXI, 6 (August 1993): 74–78.

HAMILTON, FORESTSTORN "CHICO" (b. 21 Sep 1921, Los Angeles, California). Initially starting on clarinet, Chico Hamilton cites *Sonny Greer and a gig at age 16 with the Duke Ellington Orchestra as his earliest drumset influences. He went on to perform in the 1940s with Ernie Royale, Charles Mingus, Illinois Jacquet, *Lionel Hampton, and Lester Young, among others. While in the U.S. Army (1942–46), Hamilton studied drums with *Jo Jones; after his discharge he played with James Mundy, Count Basie, Nat King Cole, Ella Fitzgerald, Tony Bennett, Billie Holiday, Billy Eckstine, Lena Horne (sporadically, 1948–55), Charlie Barnet, and Gerry Mulligan (with whom he organized a quartet in 1952). A master of brushes, he fronted his own groups (from 1955, including Euphoria) with such stellar musicians as Ron Carter, Eric Dolphy, Buddy Collette, Jim Hall, and Charles Lloyd, among others, including an unusual quintet that featured cello and flute in 1956.

A staff musician at Paramount Studios, Hamilton appeared on movie soundtracks with groups or as soloist in films including *Road to Bali* (1952) and *Sweet Smell of Success* (1957). He also wrote scores for television, radio, and film, [e.g., *Confessor* (1968), *Coonskin/Bustin' Out* (1975), *Repulsion* (1965)]. Organizing his own production company, Chico Hamilton Productions, he moved to New York in 1966, and during the mid-1970s he produced special television shows and began appearing in nightclubs, jazz festivals, and recording sessions.

SELECTED DISCOGRAPHY

Blue Note B21Y-98935: *The Birth of the Cool*, vol. 2, 1953.
Blue Note LA456-H2: *Lester Young*, 1945.
Blue Note LA520-G: *Peregrinations*, 1975.

Blue Note LA622-G: *Chico Hamilton and the Players*, 1976.
Blue Note LT-1101: *Gerry Mulligan*, 1952.
Impulse AS-29: *Passin' Thru*, 1962/1972.
Impulse A-59/GRP GRD-127: *Man from Two Worlds*, 1964/1993.
Mosaic 175: *The Complete Pacific Jazz Recordings of the Chico Hamilton Quintet*,
        1954–59.
Pacific Jazz TOCJ-5411: *The Gerry Mulligan Quartet*, 1952.
Pacific Jazz CDP-746860: *California Concerts* (Gerry Mulligan), 1954.
Pacific Jazz PJ-1209: *Spectacular*, 1955.
Soul Note CD 121241-2: *Arroyo*, 1992.
Soul Note 121 246-2: *Trio!* 1993.
Verve (J) OOMJ3480/89: *Billie Holiday*, 1954.
Verve MGV8184: *Tal Farlow*, 1954.
Warner Bros. 1271/Discovery DSCD-831: *Gongs East*, 1958/1989.
Warner Bros. S1344: *Chico Hamilton Quintet*, 1959.
World Pacific 1209: *Quintet*, 1955.
World Pacific 1220: *Trio*, 1953–55.

SELECTED BIBLIOGRAPHY

Gold, Don. "Cross Section: Chico Hamilton." *DB* XXV, 11 (29 May 1958): 13.
Morgenstern, Dan. "The Flexible Chico Hamilton." *DB* XXXIV, 12 (15 Jun 1967):
        18–19.
Tynan, John. "Chico Hamilton Builds Group on New Lines." *DB* XXIII, 6 (21 Mar
        1956): 12.
Tynan, John. "Chico's Changed." *DB* XXX, 8 (28 Mar 1963): 18–19.
GEN. BIB.: Hunt, *52nd St.*; Spagnardi, *GJD*.

HAMILTON, JEFF (b. 1953, Richmond, Indiana). Starting on piano at age 5, snare drum at 8, and drumset at 13, Jeff Hamilton studied locally with John McMahan before attending Ball State University (IN), where he studied timpani and keyboards with Dr. Erwin C. Mueller. Transferring to Indiana University, he worked two years with *George Gaber and David Baker; later he studied privately with *John von Ohlen. His major professional associations began with the New Tommy Dorsey Orchestra (1974), *Lionel Hampton Big Band (1975), Monty Alexander Trio (1975), and Woody Herman Band (1977), with whom he recorded three albums. In 1978 he filled *Shelly Manne's spot with the LA 4, recording six records with them—some of which featured his own compositions and arrangements. Between 1983 and 1987, Hamilton worked with Ella Fitzgerald, Count Basie, Rosemary Clooney, and again with Monty Alexander. He has recorded over 100 albums and appeared with artists such as Barbra Streisand, Frank Sinatra, Mel Tormé, George Shearing, Nina Simone, *Milt Jackson, Herb Ellis, Barney Kessel, Scott Hamilton, Keely Smith, Mark Murphy, and Toshiko Akioshi. Appearing on Natalie Cole's TV Special "Unforgettable" from the *Great Performances* series for PBS, Hamilton has performed with the Ray Brown Trio (1978–95), Oscar Peterson (for five years), the Clayton Brothers Quartet, and the Clayton-Hamilton Jazz Orchestra. Also a pedagogue, he has toured Europe and played on West Deutsche Rundfunk (radio) in Köln, Germany.

SELECTED DISCOGRAPHY

Arbors 19182: *Something Tells Me* (John Sheridan), 1997.
Capri 74024: *The Jiggs Up* (Jiggs Whigham).
Capri 74028-4: *Heart and Soul* (Clayton-Hamilton Jazz Orchestra), 1991.
Capri 74037-2: *The Music* (Clayton Brothers), 1992.
Century CR-1090: *Together—Flip and Woody* (Woody Herman), 1978.
Century CR-1110: *Chick, Donald, Walter, Woodrow* (Woody Herman), 1978.
Concord 4716: *Rickey Woodard—The Silver Strut*, 1996.
Concord CCD-214: *Big City* (Ernestine Anderson), 1983.
Concord CCD-4084: *Chamber Jazz* (Laurindo Almeida), 1990.
Concord CCD-4226: *My Buddy* (Woody Herman/Rosemary Clooney), 1983/1985.
Concord CCD-4231-2: *Reunion in Europe* (Monty Alexander), 1984/1997.
Concord CCD-4520: *Three Dimensional* (Ray Brown), 1992.
Elektra 61496-2: *Take A Look* (Natalie Cole), 1993.
GHB/BCD-171/172: *The Magnolia Jazz Band and Art Hodes*, 1984.
GHB/BCD-331: *Jacques Gauthé and His Creole Rice Jazz Band of New Orleans*, 1996.
JVC-6004-2: *Bill Holman Band*, 1988/1995.
Lake Street LSR 52002 CD: *Absolutely!* (Clayton-Hamilton Jazz Orchestra), 1994.
Mons MR 874-777: *Jeff Hamilton Trio Live!* 1996.
Qwest/Warner Bros. 9 47286: *Explosive!* (Clayton-Hamilton/Milt Jackson), 1999.
Telarc CD-83340: *Bassface* (Ray Brown), 1993.

SELECTED BIBLIOGRAPHY

Flans, Robyn. "Jeff Hamilton: Definitely *His* Time." *MD* XX, 1 (January 1996): 13.
Korall, Burt. "Jeff Hamilton: A Passion for Jazz." *MD* XXI, 9 (September 1997): 66–82.
Silsbee, Kirk. "Jeff Hamilton: Renaissance Drummer." *JazzTimes* XXI, 8 (November 1991): 28.
PASIC® program biographies, 1997.

HAMPTON, LIONEL LEO "HAMP" (b. 20 Apr 1908, Louisville, Kentucky). Voted into the Percussive Arts Society Hall of Fame in 1984, Lionel Hampton started on drumset, timpani, and marimba. A member of the *Chicago Defender* Newsboys Band, he was ultimately responsible for popularizing the vibraphone in the jazz genre. He grew up in Birmingham, Alabama, moved to Chicago around 1916, and studied snare drum with one of the nuns at the Holy Rosary Academy in Kenosha, Wisconsin. His later teachers included Jimmy Bertrand (xylophone) and Clifford Jones (drums).

After making his drumset debut in 1923 with Louis Armstrong's backup band (Les Hite) in Culver City, California, he moved to Los Angeles in 1927 and worked with the Spikes Brothers, Paul Howard's Quality Serenaders (with whom he first recorded on drums, 1929), and the Louis Armstrong/Les Hite Band (1930–34), making what is regarded as the first recorded vibraphone solo, "Memories of You," with Armstrong in 1930. [Legend has it that Armstrong saw a set of vibes in the room and asked Hampton if he knew how to play them; Hampton immediately played Armstrong's trumpet solo from "Big Butter and Egg Man" as an audition!] His future wife purchased a set of vibes for him, and Hampton quit the Les Hite Band when Hite demanded more drums and less vibraphone. In 1934 he studied music at the University of Southern California and fronted his own bands, but later he joined Benny Goodman following an impromptu jam session with Goodman, Teddy Wilson, and *Gene Krupa when Hampton was appearing in San Pedro, California. The next day Goodman invited Hampton to record "Vibraphone Blues," "Moonglow," "Exactly like You," and "Dinah." He worked with Goodman from 1936 to 1940 and was a pioneer in breaking the "onstage" musical racial barrier.

Hampton formed his first big band in 1940, toured throughout the world in the 1950s, and introduced new talent to American audiences including Betty Carter, Dinah Washington, and Joe Williams. It is also believed that he was the first to incorporate electric organ and electric bass in a jazz group. Because of financial problems he dissolved the big band in the 1960s and established a touring sextet in 1965. His long career included several film appearances, for example, *A Song Is Born* (1948), *The Benny Goodman Story* (1955), and *Rooftops of New York* (1960).

Receiving honorary doctorate degrees from Allen, Xavier, Pepperdine (1975), and Daniel Hale Universities, he performed at the White House in 1978 and is the namesake of the annual Lionel Hampton Jazz Festival at the Lionel Hampton School of Music at the University of Idaho. His sociopolitical activity included founding the Lionel Hampton Community Development Corporation, and he was honored with the George Frideric Handel Medallion from the City of New York (1966), the New York Governor's Award for Fifty Years of Music (1978), and the Papal Medal from Pope Paul VI. The 1942 recording of his composition "Flying Home" remains his signature piece, which is characterized by a tonal preference based on the use of fast vibrato supplied by the vibraphone's attached motor. Hampton was inducted into the International Association of Jazz Educators Hall of Fame and was awarded an "American Jazz Masters" Fellowship from the National Endowment for the Arts in 1988.

SELECTED DISCOGRAPHY

51 West Q-16074: *Good Vibes*, 1979.
Affinity AFS 1000: *Leapin' with Lionel*, 1944–49/1986.
Affinity AFS 1017: *In the Bag*, 1942–63/1985.
ASV CD AJA 5090: *I'm in the Mood for Swing*, 1992.
Atlantic 7 81644-1: *Sentimental Journey*, 1986.
Audio Fidelity AFLP 1849: *Lionel Hampton*, 1958.
Audio Fidelity AFSD 5849: *Lionel*, 1958.

Black and Blue 59.237 2/59.238 2: *Lionel Hampton Story,* vols. 1 (1930–38) and 2 (1938–39), 1991.
Bluebird/RCA 07863-66157-2: *Reunion At Newport,* 1967.
Bluebird AXM6 5536: *The Complete Lionel Hampton (1937–41),* 1976.
Blue Note BLP5046: *Lionel Hampton and His Paris All Stars,* 1953.
Brunswick LA 8551: *Moonglow,* 1959.
Chiaroscuro CR 2021: *Chick Corea,* 1980.
Classics 624: *Lionel Hampton and His Orchestra (1940–41),* 1991.
Clef MG C-611: *The Lionel Hampton Quartet,* 1953.
Clef MG C-667: *The Lionel Hampton Quartet/Quintet,* 1954.
Clef MG C-681: *Gene Krupa, Lionel Hampton, Teddy Wilson,* 1955.
Clef MG C-709: *The Hampton-Tatum-Rich Trio,* 1955.
Clef MG C-727: *Airmail Special,* 1953–54.
Clef MG C-735: *Flying Home,* 1954.
Columbia CK 46996: *Louis Armstrong,* vol. 6 (Hampton, drums), 1925–30.
Columbia CL-1304/CS 8110: *Golden Vibes,* 1959.
Columbia CL-1486: *Silver Vibes,* 1960.
Columbia CL-1661: *Soft Vibes, Soaring Strings,* 1961.
Columbia CL-1791: *Selections from "All American,"* 1962.
Columbia Masterworks ML 4358: *Benny Goodman Carnegie Hall Jazz Concert,* vol. 1, 1950.
Concord Jazz CJ-134: *Swingin' for Hamp,* 1980.
Contemporary C3502: *Lionel Hampton,* 1954.
Decca 18394: *Flying Home,* 1942.
Decca 24429/GRP GRD 626: *Midnight Sun,* 1946–47.
Decca DL-4194: *Gene Norman Presents the Original Stardust,* 1959.
Decca DL-74296: *Hamp's Golden Favorites,* 1962.
Decca DL-79244: *Lionel Hampton,* vol. 1 (1942–45); *Steppin' Out,* 1969.
Decca DL-8088: *Lionel Hampton—Carnegie Hall Concert,* 1945.
Decca DL-9055: *Gene Norman Presents Just Jazz,* 1953.
Denon 33C38-7973: *Hamp's Blues,* 1986.
EmArcy MG 2 6038: *Crazy Hamp,* 1959.
Epic LA 16027: *Many Splendored Vibes,* 1962.
EPM Musique ZET 737: *Classics—Lionel Hampton,* 1937–39/1990.
FDC 1001/1010: *Metropolitan Opera House Jam Session,* 1944/1979/1986.
Flapper PAST CD 9789: *Lionel Hampton and His Orchestra,* 1992.
Glad-Hamp GH-1005: *Lionel Hampton and His International Orchestra on Tour,* 1994.
Glad-Hamp GH-1006: *Hamp in Japan—Live,* 1994.
Groove Merchant GM 4400: *Hampton—the Works!* 1975.
Harmony KH 32165: *Good Vibes,* 1973.
Impulse GRD-140: *You Better Know It!* 1964.
International Association of Jazz Record Collectors IAJRC 31: *European Concert 1953,* 1988.
Jass Records Jass Eight: *Santa Claus Blues,* 1925–55/1986.
Jazz Archives 158252: *Lionel Hampton,* 1994.
Jazz Club 2M056-64824: *Blackout 1977.*
Jazz Man JAZ-5011: *Sweet Georgia Brown,* 1981.
Jazz World JWD 102.303: *Dexterity* (Dexter Gordon), 1994.

Joyce LP-1055:   *One Night Stand with Lionel Hampton, Culver City*, 1944/1947/1989.

Joyce LP-5008: *Lionel Hampton's Jubilee*, 1944/1970s.

Laurie Records LES 6004: *Grease*, 1979.

Lester Recording LRC, Ltd. CDC 9063: *Lionel Hampton—Flying Home*, 1992.

Masters of Jazz, Media 7: *Anthology of Jazz Drumming*, vols. 1–3, 1904–38.

MCA MCAD-42349: *Lionel Hampton—Flying Home*, 1942–45/1990.

MCA Records MCA-27094: *Best of the Big Bands*, 1984.

Mercury 6877 001-6877-010: *Jazz*, 1966.

Mercury-Emarcy MG 36071: *Giants of Jazz*, vol. 8—*The Jazz Greats, Drum Role*, 1959.

Milan 7313835770–2: *Bending towards the Light...A Jazz Nativity*, 1995.

Musica Jazz 2MJP-1035: *Lionel Hampton*, 1937–53/1985.

Musical Heritage Society MHS 7153T: *The Tatum Group Masterpieces* (Art Tatum), 1955/1976.

Musidisc 550212: *Metropolitan Opera House Jam Session, 1944/1991*.

Norgran 1080: *Lionel Hampton's Jazz Giants*, 1955.

Pathâe 1727301: *Lionel Hampton & Son Orchestre*, 1956/1983.

RCA 2698: *Together Again* (Benny Goodman), 1996.

RCA 68764: *Benny Goodman—The Complete RCA Victor Small Group Recordings*, 1935–39.

RCA Victor LPM 1422: *Jazz Flamenco*, ca. 1957.

RCA Victor LPT 18: *Lionel Hampton*, 1959.

Rosetta RR 1313: *Wise Woman Blues* (Dinah Washington), 1943–63/1984.

Sutra SU2 1006:   *Lionel Hampton 50th Anniversary Concert—Live at Carnegie Hall*, 1981.

Swing House SWH 45: *Jiving the Blues*, 1954/1984 (Hampton, vibes and drums).

Telarc CD-83308: *Lionel Hampton and the Golden Men of Jazz*, 1991.

Telarc CD-83313:   *Just Jazz—Live at the Blue Note (Lionel Hampton and the Golden Men of Jazz)*, 1992.

Time-Life Music STBB-24: *Lionel Hampton*, 1942–49/1986.

Timeless CDSJP 120: *Live at the Muzeval*, 1978.

Timeless SJP 163: *Outrageous*, 1982.

Timeless SJP 175: *Made in Japan*, 1983.

Versatile NED-1127: *Jazzmaster*, 1977.

Versatile NED-1128: *The New Look*, 1977.

Versatile NED-1131: *Moods*, 1977.

Verve (F) 813091-1: *Lionel Hampton Quartet*, 1954.

Verve MGV-8105: *King of the Vibes*, 1953–54.

Verve MGV8128: *Hamp and Getz*, 1955.

Verve MGV-8215: *The Genius of Lionel Hampton*, 1955.

Verve MGV-8223: *Lionel Hampton '58*, 1958.

Victor 25658: *Drum Stomp*, 1937.

Victor 26114: *Down Home Jump*, 1938.

Who's Who In Jazz WWLP 21004: *Lionel Hampton Presents Earl "Fatha" Hines*, 1977.

Who's Who In Jazz WWLP 21007: *Lionel Hampton Presents Gerry Mulligan*, 1977.

Who's Who In Jazz WWLP 21010: *Lionel Hampton Presents Jazz All-Stars,* vol. 1, 1977.
Who's Who In Jazz WWLP 21011: *Lionel Hampton Presents Dexter Gordon,* 1977.
Who's Who In Jazz WWLP 21016: *Chick & Lionel at Midem,* 1980.
World R-757: *Ted Heath, Xavier Cugat, and Lionel Hampton Orchestras,* 1959.

SELECTED VIDEOGRAPHY

Digit Recordings/Facets Multimedia, Inc.: *Lionel Hampton,* 1983.
Swingtime Video 101/108/118: *Meet the Bandleaders,* 1984/1985.
Video Artists International/Evart Enterprises, Inc./CFTO-TV, Toronto, Canada: *Lionel Hampton—One Night Stand* (video/16mm film documentary), 1971.

SELECTED BIBLIOGRAPHY

Campbell, Mary. "Even at 75, the Beat Goes on for Lionel Hampton." *Champaign-Urbana News-Gazette* (Sunday, 15 May 1988).
Coss, Bill. "Lionel Hampton: Bothered and Bewildered." *DB* XXIX, 10 (10 May 1962): 19–21.
Hampton, Lionel, and Jean-Claude Forestier. *The New Lionel Hampton Vibraphone Method.* Zurich: Musik Hug, 1981.
Hampton, Lionel, and James Haskins. *Hamp: An Autobiography.* New York: Warner Books, 1989; and Penguin USA, 1993 (discography by Vincent H. Pelote).
Jones, C. "The Illustrious Past and Present of Lionel Hampton." *Crescendo International* XVI, 7 (1978): 10.
Korall, Burt. "Lionel Hampton: 1986." *IM* (July 1986).
Mattingly, Rick. "They Keep Drumming, and Drumming, and...The Art of Percussive Longevity." *DB* LX, 11 (November 1993): 25–26.
Noonan, John P. "Hampton Tinkered with Xylophone—And a Vibe Artist Was Born." *DB* V, 11 (November 1938): 25.
"PAS® Hall of Fame Welcomes Hampton." *PN* XXIII, 4 (April 1985): 4.
Tuttle, Gene. "Lionel Hampton in Action." *DB* XXVI, 7 (2 Apr 1959): 14–15.
GEN. BIB.: Kernfeld, *NGJ,* by J. Bradford Robinson; Larrick, *BET-CP*; Southern, *BDA-AAM.*

HANNA, JOHN "JAKE" (b. 4 Apr 1931, Roxbury, Massachusetts). A student of Stanley Spector, drumset artist Jake Hanna matured in Dorchester, Massachusetts, served in a U.S. Air Force band, and played with Toshiko Akiyoshi (1957), Maynard Ferguson (1958), Marian McPartland (1959–61), and Woody Herman (periodically, 1957/1962–64). He served as staff drummer for the *Merv Griffin Show* (1964–75) and has toured, performed, and/or recorded with *Red Norvo, Carl Fontana, Supersax, Harry James, Herb Ellis, and Duke Ellington, among others.

SELECTED DISCOGRAPHY

Audiophile ACD-248: *The Jane Jarvis L.A. Quartet.*

Audiophile ACD-252: *You're the Cats!* (Barbara Lea and Lawson-Haggart Jazz Band), 1989.

Audiophile ACD-260: *Barbara Lea and the Lawson-Haggart Jazz Band—Sweet and Slow.*

Audiophile ACD-276: *Polly Podewell with the Ross Tomkins Trio—Don't You Know I Care?* 1995.

Concord 11: *Live at Concord,* 1975.

Concord 22: *Kansas City Express,* 1976.

Concord 35: *Jake Takes Manhattan,* 1976.

Concord 47: *Everything's Coming Up Rosie* (Rosemary Clooney), 1977.

Concord 54: *Live from Concord to London* (Ernestine Anderson), 1990.

Concord 91: *Horn of Plenty* (Snooky Young), 1979.

Concord 155: *Nonpareil* (Al Cohn), 1981.

Concord 464: *13 Strings* (Howard Alden), 1991.

Concord 4713: *Keepin' Time* (George Van Eps and Howard Alden), 1996.

Concord 4788-2: *Full Circle* (Howard Alden), 1998.

Concord CCD 4101: *Portrait of Marian MacPartland,* 1979.

Jazzology JCD-183: *The Legendary Lawson-Haggart Jazz Band—Jazz at Its Best.*

Jazzology JCD-193: *The Legendary Lawson-Haggart Jazz Band—Singin' The Blues.*

Jazzology JCD-203: *The Legendary Lawson-Haggart Jazz Band—With a Southern Accent.*

Pablo 2310908: *Kansas City Seven* (Count Basie), 1980.

Philips 200092: *Herman 1963* (Woody Herman).

Verve MGV8236: *Toshiko Akiyoshi,* 1957.

SELECTED BIBLIOGRAPHY

McPartland, Marian. "Just Swinging: Jake Hanna." *DB* XXX, 27 (10 Oct 1963): 16–17.

GEN. BIB.: Kernfeld, *NGJ*, by J. Kent Williams.

HANSEN, HANS (b. 25 Oct 1907, Görlitz, Germany). After 10 years of violin lessons at the Görlitz Conservatory and basic percussion lessons from his father, a music contractor, Hans Hansen began total percussion lessons with Franz Krüger at the Berlin Hochschule für Musik. During summer vacations he performed at resorts and by fall 1929 had secured a position as principal timpanist with the Königsberg Radio Symphony. From 1931 to 1939, he held a similar position with the Berlin Radio Symphony before serving in the military (1939–42), during which time he was also employed by the newly founded St. Florian Bruckner Orchestra in Linz, Austria. After the war he returned to Linz in 1945 and, with the surviving members of the Bruckner Orchestra combined with those of a resort orchestra, toured Austria, giving concerts for the American troops. Late in 1945 Hansen joined the Stuttgart Orchestra and, by 1946, took back his old position as principal timpanist with the Berlin Radio Symphony. Here he became a "West Berliner" in 1961 and entered the Berlin Philharmonic as principal percussionist and substitute timpanist that same year. Licensed as a music teacher in Berlin in 1935, he taught at the Berlin Conservatory, composed popular songs that were broadcast on radio (*Berliner Lieder*), and was director of the organization Composers in the Field, during the war.

GEN. BIB.: Avgerinos, *KB*.

HARBISON, KENNETH C. (b. 2 Nov 1949, Huntington, West Virginia). A graduate of the Eastman School (bachelor's degree and performer's certificate, 1971) and Catholic University (master's degree, 1974), Ken Harbison studied respectively with *John Beck and *Tony Ames. He served as percussionist with the U.S. Army Band in Washington, D.C. ("Pershing's Own," 1971–75) and has held the assistant principal percussion chair with the National Symphony since 1976.

Information supplied by the subject, 1997.

HARR, HASKELL WARREN (b. 27 Jun 1894, Baraboo, Wisconsin; d. 24 Sep 1986, Glendora, California). A musical jack-of-all-trades whose career spanned 65 years and covered circus bands to vaudeville, Haskell Harr entered high school at age 12, performing on cornet in silent movie pit orchestras by 13, and later on saxophone with Al Sweet's Royal Huzar Band at Wisconsin fairs. In 1911 he became a drummer and xylophone soloist with the Goldman Brothers Band, and by the 1920s he was receiving rave reviews for his xylophone and marimba work as leader of the Haskell Novelty Trio, which featured one player on sax, flute, and clarinet, and the other on organ and piano. An excellent sight-reader, he would play—and transpose when needed—violin, flute, oboe, cornet, and treble-clef baritone parts, since xylophone parts were rarely available. Relocating to Chicago in 1922, Harr studied with *Roy Knapp, who arranged many of his xylophone selections, and he later took lessons with *George Hamilton Green (1927). From 1922 to 1928, Harr performed either solo xylophone or with his trio on WGN, WJJD, WMAQ, WEBH, and WLS radio stations in Chicago, sometimes broadcasting remotely (occasionally without a rehearsal!) from a recital hall or hotel ballroom. He played drums with a dance band (1923) on the *Christopher Columbus*, a "whaleback" steamer that made daily trips between Milwaukee and Chicago, and later for Sally Rand's infamous exotic fan dance act at the Chicago World's Fair of 1933.

Harr directed the 122nd Field Artillery Band of the Illinois National Guard and, during WWII, was a senior warrant officer with the 33rd Field Artillery Band at Camp Forrest, Tennessee (1941–42), where he composed the "Camp Forrest March." After studying at DePaul University and receiving a bachelor's degree from Vandercook College in 1952 (and later, an honorary doctorate), he directed bands in grade school and high school; he was also associated with Vandercook, achieving the rank of associate professor. Harr retired from teaching in 1961 and became educational director for Slingerland Drum Company, where he left a legacy of percussion method books that are still utilized today.   (His two snare method books have sold more than a million copies combined.)

In 1966 he participated in the memorial 55-piece Bachman's Million Dollar Band in Chicago, which consisted of all-star circus musicians directed by Merle Evans and sponsored by the Conn Company.   In his later years Harr presented a slide show on circuses complete with musical accompaniment.   Inducted as a charter member into the Percussive Arts Society Hall of Fame in 1972, Harr received a Medal of Honor from the National Band and Orchestra Association.

SELECTED DISCOGRAPHY

M. M. Cole Publishing (Chicago):   Harr Drum Record No. 1 (contains organ accompaniments to exercises in Book 1), 1968.
M. M. Cole Publishing (Chicago)/Slingerland 1185:   Harr Drum Record No. 2:   *The 26 Rudiments Played and Explained by Haskell W. Harr*, 1969.

SELECTED BIBLIOGRAPHY

Harr, Haskell W.   *Drum Method,* Bks. 1–2. Chicago: M. M. Cole, 1968/1969.
Harr, Haskell W.   *Haskell W. Harr's Simplified Drum Solos with Piano Accompaniment.* Chicago: M. M. Cole, 1949.
Harr, Haskell W.   *Marimba & Xylophone Method.* Chicago: M. M. Cole, 1975.
Harr, Haskell W.   *Marimba & Xylophone Solos.* Chicago: M. M. Cole, 1940.
Harr, Haskell W.   *Timpani Method.* Chicago: M. M. Cole, 1950.
Olive, William D.   "Haskell Harr: Tribute to a Friend." *PN* XXV, 1 (Fall 1986): 27–29.

HARRIS, WILLIAM GODVIN "BEAVER" (b. 20 Apr 1936, Pittsburgh, Pennsylvania).   A student of *Stanley Leonard, *Kenny Clarke, and Dante Augustini, Beaver Harris started drumset at age 20, served in the U.S. Army in the late 1950s, returned to Pittsburgh, where he played with Horace Silver, Benny Golson, and Slide Hampton, and then moved to New York in 1962.   A versatile drumset artist whose collaborators cross diverse musical settings, he has played with Al Cohn, Freddie Hubbard, Chet Baker, Lee Konitz, Joe Henderson, Charlie Rouse, Eddie Gomez, Sonny Rollins (1965), Jim Hall, Thelonius Monk (1970), Larry Coryell, Cecil Taylor (three years in the 1970s), Gato Barbieri (1969–70), Steve Lacy, and Albert Ayler, among others.   Harris appeared with Archie Shepp in Europe (1967) and in 1968 formed, fronted, and composed for the "360 Degree Music Experience" with Grachan Moncur, Ron Carter, and others, touring Japan in 1973.

SELECTED DISCOGRAPHY

360 Degree Music 2001: *From Ragtime to No Time* (360 Degree), 1975.
BS 0006-7: *In: Sanity* (360 Degree), 1976.
BS 0008: *Trickles* (Steve Lacy), 1976.

Cad. 1003: *Negcaumongus* (360 Degree), 1979
FD 10117: *The Third World* (Gato Barbieri), 1969.
Impulse 9139: *Three for Shepp* (Marion Brown), 1966.
Impulse 9155: *Albert Ayler Live in Greenwich Village*, 1966–67.
JCOA 1007: *Numatik Swing Band* (Roswell Rudd), 1973.
Saba 15148: *Archie Shepp Live at the Donaueschingen Music Festival*, 1967.
Shemp 2701: *A Well Kept Secret* (360 Degree), 1980.
Uniteledis 22975YX2: *U-jaama (unité)* (Archie Shepp), 1975.

SELECTED BIBLIOGRAPHY

Claghorn, Charles Eugene. *Biographical Dictionary of Jazz.* Englewood Cliffs, NJ: Prentice-Hall, Inc., 1982.
GEN. BIB.: Kernfeld, *NGJ*, by Ed Hazell; Spagnardi, *GJD.*

HARRISON, LOU (b. 14 May 1917, Portland, Oregon). Inducted into the Percussive Arts Society Hall of Fame in 1985, composer Lou Harrison attended San Francisco State College (1934–35) and studied with Henry Cowell and Arnold Schoenberg. Influential for the burgeoning interest in "world music–world percussion" during the twentieth century, he employed just intonation and quasi-gamelan instruments in his compositions. Recipient of numerous grants, fellowships, and awards, Harrison taught at several U.S. universities, including San Jose State and Mills College, where he was awarded an honorary doctorate.

SELECTED DISCOGRAPHY

Crystal Records CD850: *Lou Harrison*, 1992.

SELECTED BIBLIOGRAPHY

Baker, Don Russell. *The Percussion Ensemble Music of Lou Harrison: 1939–42.* Dissertation, University of Illinois, Champaign-Urbana, 1985.
Fierz, Stephen D. "Lou Harrison and Harry Partch: A Brief Comparison." *PN* XXXV, 2 (April 1997): 74–75.
Siwe, Tom. "Lou Harrison at the University of Illinois." *PN* XVIII, 2 (Winter 1980): 30–33.
Von Gunden, Heidi. *The Music of Lou Harrison.* Lanham, MD: Scarecrow Press, 1995.

HART, MICKEY (b. Brooklyn, New York). Percussionist and drummer of the long-lived rock group Grateful Dead (1968–1970/1975–), Mickey Hart was born into a drumming family and has been, to some extent through his performances, recordings, publications, and productions, a major influence in popularizing ethnic hand drumming with the general public in the last two decades of the twentieth century. A member of the Folkways recording company's board of directors, he studied with Alla Rakha Khan, made his solo debut on the recording "Rolling Thunder" (1972), and performed on the soundtrack of the movie *Apocalypse Now*.

SELECTED DISCOGRAPHY

Ellipsis Arts CD3405: *The Big Bang—Global Percussion Masters*, 1994/1997.
Rykodisc RCD RAC 10396: *Supralingua*, 1998.
Rykodisc RCD RAC 10338: *Mickey Hart's Mystery Box*, 1996.
Rykodisc RCD 10101: *Diga* (Diga Rhythm Band), 1976.
Rykodisc RCD 10108: *Däfos* (Airto Moreira/Flora Purim), 1989.
Rykodisc RCD 10109: *The Apocalypse Now Sessions* (Rhythm Devils), 1990.
Rykodisc RCD 10124: *At the Edge of Magic*, 1990.
Rykodisc RCD 10206: *Planet Drum*, 1997 (Grammy® Award winner).
Rykodisc RCD 20112: *Music to Be Born By*, 1989.

SELECTED BIBLIOGRAPHY

Doerschuk, Andy. "No Mystery: The Percussion Tour of the Year." *DRUM!* V, 7
      (November–December 1996): 36–45.
Edgar, Jacob. "Mickey Hart: Return to Planet Drum." *RhythmMusic* (October
      1998): 32–36.
Hart, Mickey, and Fredric Lieberman. *Planet Drum*. New York: HarperCollins,
      1991.
Hart, Mickey, and Jay Stevens. *Drumming at the Edge of Magic*. New York:
      HarperCollins, 1990.
Larkin, Colin, ed. *The Guiness Encyclopedia of Popular Music*. New York:
      Stockton Press, 1995.

HART, WILLIAM W. "BILLY" (aka Jabali, b. 29 Nov 1940, Washington, D.C.). Influenced by *Art Blakey, *Shadow Wilson, *Philly Joe Jones, and *Sid Catlett, Billy Hart is essentially a self-taught drumset artist who has appeared and/or recorded since the 1960s with Tom Harrell, McCoy Tyner, Marian McPartland, Eddie Harris, Joe Lovano, Jimmy Smith (1964), Wes Montgomery, Pharoah Sanders, Branford Marsalis, Herbie Hancock (1970–73), Miles Davis (1972), Stan Getz (1974–1980s), Jimmy Rowles (1976), Niels-Henning Ørsted Pedersen (1977–79), Shirley Horn (1977–81), Lee Konitz and Clark Terry (1979), and Chico Freeman (1980–82). *Down Beat* magazine's "Drummer of the Year Deserving Wider Recognition," he formed Colloquium III, a New York percussion workshop collaboration, with *Horacee Arnold and *Freddie Waits. Since 1992 he has served as artist-in-residence at Western Michigan University where teaches drumset and has recorded with the Western Jazz Quartet. With almost 500 recordings to his credit, Hart has led his own groups and toured internationally.

SELECTED DISCOGRAPHY

A&M Horizon 725: *Enhance*, 1977.

Arabesque AJ0105: *Amethyst*, 1993.

Arkadia Jazz 71043: *The Elements: Water* (David Liebman), 1999.

Atlantic 16031: *Live at Montreux* (Mingus Dynasty), 1980.

Blue Note 57729: *Bob Dorough—On My Way Home*, 1997.

Blue Note 84363: *Wayne Shorter—Odyssey of Iska*, 1970.

Blue Note BT 85109: *James Newton—The African Flower*, 1985.

Blue Note LA223-G: *McCoy Tyner—Asante*, 1970.

Brownstone BRCD 9802: *Mean What You Say* (Cecil Bridgewater), 1998.

CMP 57: *Of One Mind* (Quest), 1990.

Columbia 467138: *The Master* (Stan Getz), 1975.

Columbia KC31906: *On the Corner* (Miles Davis), 1972.

Concord CCD-4168: *Pure Getz* (Stan Getz), 1982.

Denon: *Second Look* (Joe Lovano), 1996.

Gramavision 8304: *Luella* (James Newton), 1983.

Metro M (S) 521: *Jimmy Smith Trio*, 1963.

Milestone 9248: *Jazz* (George Mraz), 1996.

Muse MCD 5075: *Exit* (Pat Martino). 1976/1988.

Muse 5303: *Comin' Home* (Larry Coryell), 1984.

Nonesuch 79438-2: *Bug Music* (Don Byron), 1997.

Pathfinder 8839: *Natural Selection* (Quest), 1994.

Progressive PCD-7035: *The Man I Love* (Derek Smith Quartet), 1979.

Progressive PCD-7036: *Hot Knepper and Pepper* (Don Friedman), 1980.

Progressive PCD-7037: *Arnett Cobb Is Back*, 1991.

Regent 6055: *Jazz...It's Magic* (Curtis Fuller and Tommy Flanagan), 1957.

SteepleChase 1073-4: *Live at Montmartre* (Stan Getz), 1977.

SteepleChase 1095: *This Is Buck Hill*, 1978.

Storyville 4121: *Midpoint* (Quest), 1988.

Storyville 4132: *Quest II*, 1987.

Warner Brothers SW 1898: *Mwandishi* (Herbie Hancock), 1970.

SELECTED VIDEOGRAPHY

Kultur Video: *Art Farmer*, 1982.

New Line Home Video: *Jazz in America*, 1981.

SELECTED BIBLIOGRAPHY

Claghorn, Charles Eugene. *Biographical Dictionary of Jazz*. Englewood Cliffs, NJ: Prentice-Hall, Inc., 1982.

Gribetz, Sid. "Billy Hart: Straight from the Hart." *JazzTimes* XXII, 9 (November 1992): 33–34.

Hart, Billy. *Jazz Drumming*. Rotenburg, Germany: Advance Music, 1988.

Primack, B. "Drummers Coloquium III: Multiple Percussionists." *DB* XLVI, 17 (1979): 25.

GEN. BIB.: Hunt, *52nd St.*; Kernfeld, *NGJ*, by J. Kent Williams; Spagnardi, *GJD*.

HARTENBERGER, JOHN RUSSELL (b. 21 Jul 1944, Watonga, Oklahoma). Russell Hartenberger studied with *Fred Hinger and *Alan Abel, is a graduate of the Curtis Institute (bachelor's, 1966) and Catholic University (master's, 1969), and holds the Ph.D. (1974) in world music from Wesleyan University (Middletown, CT). At Wesleyan he studied mrdangam with Ramnad Raghavan, tabla with Sharda Sahai, Javanese gamelan with Prawotosaputro, and West African drumming with *Abraham Adzenyah. Professor of percussion at the University of Toronto (1974–present), he performs with the Steve Reich Ensemble (1971–present) and has been a member of the Oklahoma City (1960–62) and New Haven (1970–74/principal percussion, 1971–74) Symphonies. Hartenberger performed with the Paul Winter Consort (1972–74), played at the Marlboro Music Festival, and is a founding member of NEXUS (1971–present). Xylophone soloist with the U.S. Air Force Band (1966–70), he also served as principal percussionist and timpanist with the Canadian Opera Company (1988–92) and Philadelphia Lyric Opera Orchestra (1963–66). Interviewed on *CBS Sunday Morning* with NEXUS (1992), he has performed with New York, Philadelphia, Boston, Cleveland, London, Israel, Cologne Radio, and Toronto Symphonies and has toured throughout North and South America, Europe, Australia, China, Korea, and Japan. In 1999 Hartenberger was inducted into the Percussive Arts Society Hall of Fame as a member of NEXUS.

SELECTED DISCOGRAPHY

Black Sun CD 15002-2: *The Altitude of the Sun* (NEXUS and Paul Horn), 1989.
CBC Musica Viva 2-1037: *Dance of the Octopus* (NEXUS et al.), 1989.
CBC SMCD 5154: *Music for Heaven and Earth* (NEXUS/Esprit Orchestra), 1995.
CBS MK 44545: *The Mozart Album* (Canadian Brass), 1990.
CP2 11: *Jo Kondo* (NEXUS performs "Under the Umbrella"), 1981.
Deutsche Grammophon DDG-3-2740-106: *Drumming/Six Pianos/Music for Mallet Instruments/Organ and Voices* (Steve Reich), 1977.
ECM 1-1129: *Music for Eighteen Musicians* (Steve Reich), 1978.
ECM 1-1168: *Music for Large Ensemble* (Steve Reich), 1980.
ECM 1-1215: *Tehillim* (Steve Reich), 1982.
Epic KE 33561: *Paul Horn and NEXUS*, 1975.
InRespect IRJ 009302 H: *The Mother of the Book* (NEXUS et al.), 1994.
Marquis Classics ERAD 145: *Stravinsky—L'Histoire du Soldat*, 1992.
Melbourne SMLP 4040: *The York Winds*, 1981.
NEXUS 10251: *The Best of NEXUS* (1976–86), 1989.
NEXUS 10262: *NEXUS Now*, 1990.
NEXUS 10273: *NEXUS Plays the Novelty Music of George Hamilton Green*, 1990.
NEXUS 10284: *NEXUS Ragtime Concert*, 1992.
NEXUS 10295: *NEXUS—Origins*, 1992.
NEXUS 10306: *The Story of Percussion in the Orchestra* (NEXUS and Rochester Philharmonic), 1992.
NEXUS 10317: *Voices* (NEXUS and Rochester Philharmonic), 1994.
NEXUS 10328: *There Is a Time* (Becker), 1995.
NEXUS 10339: *The Solo Percussionist* (Music of William Cahn), 1997.

NEXUS 10410: *Toccata*, 1997
NEXUS NE-01: *Music of NEXUS*, 1981.
NEXUS NE-02/03/04: *NEXUS and Earle Birney* (Albums 1–3), 1982.
NEXUS NE-05: *Changes* (NEXUS), 1982.
Nonesuch 9-79101-1: *The Desert Music* (Steve Reich and Brooklyn Philharmonic), 1985.
Nonesuch 9-79138-1: *Sextet/Six Marimbas*, (Steve Reich et al.), 1986.
Nonesuch 9-79170-1: *Drumming* (Steve Reich), 1987.
Nonesuch 9-79220-2: *The Four Sections/Music for Mallet Instruments, Voices, and Organ* (London Symphony/Steve Reich), 1990.
Nonesuch 79327-2: *The Cave* (Steve Reich), 1995.
Nonesuch 79430: *City Life/Proverb/Nagoya Marimbas* (Steve Reich), 1996.
Papa Bear Records G01: *World Diary—Tony Levin* (NEXUS et al.), 1995.
Point Records 454 126-2: *Farewell to Philosophy* (Gavin Bryars), 1996.
Sony Classical SK 63044: *Takemitsu—From Me Flows What You Call Time* (Pacific Symphony), 1998.

SELECTED VIDEOGRAPHY

Necavenue A88V-3: *Supercussion* (Tokyo Music Joy Festival), 1988.
Rhombus Media: *World Drums* (Vancouver Expo), 1986.

SELECTED BIBLIOGRAPHY

"America's High School Soloist Hall of Fame: Russell Hartenberger." *School Musician* XXXIII, 4 (December 1961): 13 (includes photo).
Bump, Michael. "A Conversation with NEXUS." *PN* XXXI, 5 (June 1993): 30–36.
Kvistad, Garry. "Russell Hartenberger." *PN* XXXIV, 4 (August 1996): 16–18.
Mattingly, Rick. "Nexus." *MP* I, 3 (June–August 1985): 8–13/36–41.
Information supplied by the subject, 1996.

HATCH, EARL WALLACE GRANT (b. 24 Aug 1906, Greeley, Colorado; d. 5 Nov 1996, North Hollywood, California). A snare drummer in the town band at age 8 and a trap drummer for silent movies by 10, Earl Hatch bought his first large marimba with war savings stamps (WWI), which he had purchased with his music earnings. He played his first marimba solo with a pit theater orchestra at around 12, and by 15 he had gone on the road as pianist with a small jazz band. Learning accordion technique while on the road, Hatch played celeste, vibes, and marimba in Jimmy Joy's Brunswick Recording Orchestra from the University of Texas. He performed for vaudeville, toured hotel ballrooms nationwide for the Music Corporation of America (MCA), and broadcast on early radio (he debuted in Sioux City, IA) by playing into a microphone made of an upright desk telephone.

Hatch left Joy's band to be musical director on radio in Dallas and Ft. Worth, Texas (KRLD and KTAT); after unsuccessfully trying to organize his own band, he moved to California around 1933. Working in Ocean Park, he played in a piano duo for two years on the radio show *Al Pearce and His Gang*. Hired as a drummer for the Raymond Paige Orchestra, he could be heard on *Hollywood Hotel* for about four years, working on all major radio networks and finally snagging a staff job at KECA. He was co-musical director at KMPC for a short time before performing and recording on vibes with the Merry Macs Singing Group (Decca Records) for a few years, landing in the music and sound effects department of Walt Disney Studios (ca. 1940–41). There he worked on the animated classics *Fantasia*, *Bambi*, *Pinnochio*, *Dumbo*, and several Mickey Mouse, Goofy, and Pluto cartoons, even scoring music and effects for one Donald Duck short. Hatch also participated in training films for the military during WWII.

Offered a position with Paramount Pictures' music department, he worked on soundtracks for *Lady in the Dark*, *The Californian*, *Out of This World* (in which he created a comedy drum sequence), *The Story of Dr. Wassel*, *The Uninvited*, *Dixie*, and several movies with Bing Crosby and Bob Hope, including a couple of the famous *Road to...* series. During his last year at Paramount he became interested in children's marimba groups which *Emil Farnlund had started, and he and Farnlund, with whom he had worked at Hollywood's Paramount Theater, established the first marimba school in the United States. One of their marimba bands, the Happy Woodchoppers, competed in a *Look* magazine–sponsored Carnegie Hall contest; after its success, the group was dubbed the "All America Junior Marimba Orchestra." One of his older-age groups, the Marimbatones, produced hit radio recordings (e.g., "The Down Home Rag" and "Soliloquy" on Kem Records, ca. 1950).

Leaving Paramount, Hatch worked at Twentieth-Century Fox and Universal Studios and freelanced as a first-call, noncontract player. He taught, wrote, and published (over 600 titles) at his own marimba school, Marimbas Unlimited, which had endured more than 38 years when he moved operations to his home. During this period he recorded soundtracks for *Dr. Zhivago*, *Sound of Music*, *Sayonara*, *The King and I*, and several Disney productions. Named an honorary member of the Japanese Xylophone Association and recipient of an honorary doctorate (1988), Hatch taught at the Los Angeles Conservatory of Music and Art and later briefly at the University of Southern California and California State University at Northridge.

SELECTED BIBLIOGRAPHY

Ervin Pershing, Karen. "Earl Hatch: Mallet Master." *MP* II, 2 (March 1986): 22–25.
Hatch, Earl. *My Marimba and I*. North Hollywood, CA: Hatch Publications, 1973.
Hatch, Earl. *Challenge I*. North Hollywood, CA: Hatch Publications, 1970.
Information supplied by Carol C. Hatch, 1996.

HAYES, LOUIS SEDELL (b. 31 May 1937, Detroit, Michigan). Citing the influence of *Max Roach, *Kenny Clarke, and others, Louis Hayes initially studied drumset with his cousin, played in Detroit clubs during his teens, then appeared in New York at Birdland by 19. He gained national prominence with

Yusef Lateef (1955), Horace Silver (1956–59), Cannonball Adderly (1959–65), and Oscar Peterson (sporadically, 1965–71) and has performed and/or recorded with Freddie Hubbard, John Coltrane, Joe Farrell, Kenny Drew, Lee Morgan, Phineas Newborn, J. J. Johnson, Joe Henderson, Junior Cook, Sonny Stitt, McCoy Tyner, and Cedar Walton. He toured Europe and led his own bands during the 1970s–90s under the names Louis Hayes Sextet (1972), Louis Hayes–Junior Cook Quintet (1975), and Woody Shaw–Louis Hayes Quintet, which included Dexter Gordon (1976).

SELECTED DISCOGRAPHY

Blue Note B21Y 81539: *Six Pieces of Silver* (Horace Silver), 1956.
Blue Note B21Y 84008: *Finger Poppin'* (Horace Silver), 1959.
Columbia CS8537: *A Touch of Satin* (J. J. Johnson), 1960–61.
Columbia PG34650: *Homecoming* (Dexter Gordon), 1976.
Gryphon 787: *Variety Is the Spice*, 1979.
Impulse IMPD-238: *Horace Silver—A Prescription for the Blues*, 1997.
Landmark 1304: *The Poll-Winners* (Cannonball Adderley), 1986.
Landmark 1305-2/Riverside 9344: *The Cannonball Adderley Quintet at the Lighthouse*, 1960.
Landmark LCD 1301-2: *Them Dirty Blues* (Cannonball Adderley), 1985.
Landmark LCD 1307-2: *Cannonball in Europe*, 1987.
Limelight 86039: *Blues Etude* (Oscar Peterson), 1965–66.
MPS 15267: *The Hub of Hubbard* (Freddie Hubbard), 1969.
Muse MR 5139: *Live at the Berliner Jazztage* (Woody Shaw), 1979.
Muse 5010/5022: *A Night at Boomer's* (Cedar Walton), 1973.
Muse 5125: *The Real Thing*, 1977.
Night Records 9159: *Radio Nights* (Cannonball Adderley), 1991.
Pablo 5303: *The Cannonball Adderley Quintet—Paris, 1960.*
Prestige 7107: *New Trombone* (Curtis Fuller), 1957.
Prestige 8202/OJC 062: *Prestige All-Stars* (Pepper Adams), 1983.
Prestige PS 7378: *The Last Trane* (John Coltrane), 1989.
Reservoir 113: *Conjuration* (Pepper Adams), 1990.
Riverside/OJC 306: *Quintet Plus* (Cannonball Adderley), 1987.
Riverside/OJC CD-035-2: *Cannonball in San Francisco* (Cannonball Adderley), 1959.
Riverside/OJC CD-208-2: *Barry Harris at the Jazz Workshop*, 1960.
Riverside RLP404/OJC 142: *In New York* (Cannonball Adderley), 1985.
Timeless 102: *Ichi-ban*, 1976.
Timeless 197: *Vim n' Vigor*, 1983.
Verve MGV8217: *Yusef Lateef*, 1957.
Verve V6-8406: *Johnny Hodges*, 1961.
VJ 3010: *Louis Hayes*, 1960.

SELECTED BIBLIOGRAPHY

Micallef, Ken. "Louis Hayes: Conviction." *MD* XXII, 1 (January 1998): 80–94.
GEN. BIB.: Hunt, *52nd St.*; Kernfeld, *NGJ*, by J. Kent Williams; Spagnardi, *GJD*.

HAYNES, ROY OWEN (b. 13 Mar 1925, Roxbury, Massachusetts). Drumset artist Roy Haynes started drums as a child and played locally in the Boston area (1944) before moving to New York (1945) where he worked with Luis Russell (1945–47), Miles Davis and Bud Powell (1949), Lester Young (1947–49), Kai Winding, Charlie Parker (1949–52), Stan Getz (occasionally, 1950–65), Ella Fitzgerald, Billie Holiday, Sarah Vaughan (1953–58), and Thelonius Monk (1958). Since 1960 Haynes has recorded and/or appeared with Eric Dolphy, John Coltrane (subbing for *Elvin Jones, 1963–65), Andrew Hill, Lee Konitz, Oliver Nelson, Chick Corea (Trio Music, 1981), *Gary Burton (1960s–70s), Phineas Newborn, Art Pepper and Hank Jones (1978), McCoy Tyner, Dizzy Gillespie (Newport and Monterey Jazz Festivals, 1979), Pat Metheny, and others. Fronting his own groups including the Hip Ensemble (1970s), he has toured the United States, Europe, and Japan (with Duke Jordan, 1976), appeared on television and radio, was awarded the "American Jazz Masters" Fellowship by the National Endowment of the Arts (1995) and the 1994 Jazzpar Prize from the Danish Jazz Center, and was inducted into the Percussive Arts Society Hall of Fame in 1998.

SELECTED DISCOGRAPHY

Atlantic 80108: *Sweet Return* (Freddie Hubbard), 1983.
Blue Note 84160: *Smokestack* (Andrew Hill), 1963.
Blue Note 84165: *Destination ...Out!* (Jackie McLean), 1963.
Blue Note 84179: *It's Time* (Jackie McLean), 1964.
Blue Note BT85108: *Charlie Parker at Storyville*, 1953.
Blue Note CDP 7 90055 2: *Now He Sings, Now He Sobs* (Chick Corea), 1968.
Blue Note LA456-H2: *Lester Young*, 1947.
Blue Note LA598-H2: *Randy Weston*, 1959.
Candid CD 9007: *The Straight Horn of Steve Lacy*, 1960.
Charlie Parker PLP409: *Just You, Just Me* (Lester Young), 1949.
Concord 4803-2: *Like Minds* (Gary Burton), 1998.
Contemporary OJC CD-166-2: *Portrait of Art Farmer*, 1958.
Dreyfus DRY-CD 36598: *Praise*, 1998.
Dreyfus CD-DRY-36556: *When It's Haynes It Roars*, 1992.
Dreyfus FDM 36569-2: *Te Vou!* 1994.
ECM 1111: *Times Square* (Gary Burton), 1978.
ECM 1232-3: *Trio Music* (Chick Corea), 1981.
Electra Musician 71009: *Inner Fires* (Bud Powell), 1953.
EmArcy 36058: *In the Land of Hi-Fi* (Sarah Vaughan), 1955.
Evidence 22140: *Great Jazz Trio—Flowers for Lady Day*, 1996.
Evidence ECD 22092: *Homecoming*, 1994.
Evidence ECD 22171: *Roy Haynes—True or False*, 1997.
Fresh Sounds CD1017: *Birdland '53* (Bud Powell).
Galaxy 5116: *Vistalite*, 1977.
Geffen M5G 24293: *Question and Answer* (Pat Metheny), 1990.
GRP STD-1112: *Live in Montreux* (Chick Corea/Joe Henderson), 1994.
Impulse 180/23: *Out of the Afternoon*, 1962.
Impulse 9161: *Selflessness* (John Coltrane), 1963.

Impulse GRP CD GRD-128: *Coltrane at Newport '63.*
Impulse/MCA-29063: *The Blues and the Abstract Truth* (Oliver Nelson), 1972.
Mainstream 313: *Hip Ensemble*, 1970.
Mainstream 351: *Senyah*, 1972.
Mercury-Emarcy MG 36071: *Giants of Jazz,* vol. 8—*The Jazz Greats, Drum Role,* 1959.
Mosaic MR5-116: *Bud Powell's Modernists*, 1949.
New Jazz 8210: *We Three*, 1958.
New Jazz 8236: *Outward Bound* (Eric Dolphy), 1960.
New Jazz NJLP-8210: *Just Us.*
New Jazz NJLP-8286: *Cracklin'*, 1963.
New Jazz OJC CD-400: *Far Cry* (Eric Dolphy), 1960.
New Jazz NJLP 8287: *Cymbalism*, 1963.
Riverside RLP 279/1190: *Misterioso/Monk Live at the Five Spot* (Thelonius Monk), 1958.
Riverside/OJCCD-092-2: *The Sound of Sonny* (Sonny Rollins), 1957.
Riverside 262/OJCCD-103-2: *Thelonius in Action* (Thelonius Monk), 1958.
Stretch 9017: *Chick Corea and Friends—Remembering Bud Powell*, 1997.
Verve 314 526 373-2: *Alone Together—The Best of the Mercury Years* (Clifford Brown), 1995.
Verve MGV8008: *Charlie Parker's Jazzers*, 1951.
Verve MGVS6131: *Lee Konitz*, 1959.
Verve V6-8412: *Focus* (Stan Getz), 1961.
Verve V6-8430: *Sonny Rollins and the Big Brass*, 1958.
Verve V6-8693: *Reaching Forth* (McCoy Tyner).

SELECTED VIDEOGRAPHY

DCI VH0249: *Legends of Jazz Drumming, Pt. 2, 1950-70*, 1996.
Kultur Video: *Celebrating Bird—The Triumph of Charlie Parker*, 1987.

SELECTED BIBLIOGRAPHY

"Cross Section: Roy Haynes." *DB* XXVI, 5 (5 Mar 1959): 15.
DeMichael, Don. "The Varied Peripteries of Drummer Roy Haynes, or, They Call Him 'Snap Crackle.' " *DB* XXXIII, 25 (15 Dec 1966): 18–19.
"The Fantastick Roy Haynes." *LD* VI, 1 (Spring 1966): 13.
Jenkins, Willard. "Chick Corea/Roy Haynes: Synchronized Times." *JazzTimes* XXVIII, 9 (November 1998): 28–33.
Jones, Leroi. "A Day with Roy Haynes." *DB* XXIX, 7 (29 Mar 1962): 18–20.
Mattingly, Rick. "Roy Haynes." *PN* XXXVI, 6 (December 1998): 10–11.
Micallef, Ken. "Roy Haynes and Lewis Nash: Two Generations of Hip." *MD* XXI, 1 (January 1997): 44–66.
Remonko, Guy. "An Interview with Roy Haynes." *PN* XXVI, 1 (Fall 1987): 12–14.
GEN. BIB.: Hunt, *52nd St.*; Kernfeld, *NGJ*, by Barry Kernfeld; Southern, *BDA-AAM*; Spagnardi, *GJD*.

HEARD, JAMES CHARLES "J. C." (b. 8 Oct 1917, Dayton, Ohio). Drumset artist, tap dancer, and singer, J. C. Heard was a self-taught drummer who was playing locally in Detroit by age 13, joining Teddy Wilson's New York big band (and later, his sextet) in 1939. He worked with Benny Goodman, Benny Carter, Count Basie, and others, and did radio broadcasts from the Savoy Ballroom with Cab Calloway (1942–45), Woody Herman, and Coleman Hawkins. Heard appeared in the movies *Boogie Woogie's Dream* and *Stormy Weather* (1940s) and toured Japan, Europe, and the United States with the "Jazz at the Philharmonic" series (1950s). Credited on over 1,000 recordings, he performed and/or recorded with Erroll Garner (1948), Charlie Parker, Billie Holiday, Sidney Bechet, Ray Charles, Sarah Vaughan, Dizzy Gillespie, Nat King Cole, Howard McGhee, Roy Eldridge, Lester Young, *Red Norvo, and many others. His own quartet appeared from New York to Los Angeles; he danced, drummed, and sang across Australia and Japan (1953–57); and *Esquire* magazine named him "Drummer of the Year" in 1946.

SELECTED DISCOGRAPHY

BB 33167: *God Bless My Solo* (Illinois Jacquet), 1978.
Clef EPC159: *Nick Esposito Sextet*, 1952.
Jazztone J-1235: *The Chase* (Dexter Gordon), 1956.
Mosaic MR3-121: *Ike Quebec Quartet*, 1960.
Mosaic MR4-107: *Ike Quebec Swing Seven*, 1945.
RCA 2177 2-RB: *The Bebop Revolution* (Dizzy Gillespie), 1946.
Spotlite 127: *Red Norvo's Famous Jam*, 1945.
Spotlite 148: *Jazz off the Air, Vol. IV (Cab Calloway and His Orchestra, 1943-46)*.
Spotlite 150D: *Every Bit of It* (Charlie Parker), 1945.
Sunbeam 204: *Coleman Hawkins at the Savoy*, 1940.
Verve 10 837141-2: *The Complete "Jazz at the Philharmonic: Bird"* (Charlie Parker), 1952.
Verve MGV2011: *Teddy Wilson Trio*, 1953.
Verve MGV8084: *Illinois Jacquet Quintet*, 1951.
Verve MGV8160: *Benny Carter Quintet*, 1952.
Verve MGV8179: *Johnny Hodges and His Orchestra*, 1952.
Verve MGV8181: *Lester Swings Again* (Lester Young), 1950–52.
Verve MGV8214: *Dizzy Gillespie and Stuff Smith*, 1957.
Verve V6-8616: *Count Basie and His Orchestra*, 1965.
Verve VE2-2502: *Lester Young with the Oscar Peterson Trio*, 1952.
Verve VE2-2503: *Billie Holiday and Her Orchestra*, 1952.
GEN. BIB.: Hunt, *52nd St.*; Kernfeld, *NGJ*, by Peter Vacher; Spagnardi, *GJD*.

HEATH, ALBERT "TOOTIE" (aka Kuumba, b. 31 May 1935, Philadelphia, Pennsylvania). Brother to Percy and Jimmy, drumset artist Tootie Heath began his professional career in New York at the age of 19 and played with Cedar Walton, J. J. Johnson (1958–60), the Jazztet, Kenny Dorham, George Russell, Clifford Jordan, the Modern Jazz Quartet, Reggie Workman, and the Heath

Brothers. A California Arts Council grant recipient, he presents drumming clinics and workshops for schools and penal institutions.

SELECTED DISCOGRAPHY

Blue Note 84181: *Trompeta Toccata* (Kenny Dorham), 1964.
Blue Note 84321: *The Prisoner* (Herbie Hancock), 1969.
Concord 4772-2: *As We Were Saying* (Heath Brothers), 1997.
Concord 4846-2: *The Heath Brothers—Jazz Family*, 1998.
Jazzland JLP 52: *Starting Time* (Clifford Jordan), 1961.
Original Jazz Classics OJC: *In Person* (Bobby Timmons), 1961.
Prestige OJC CD-020-2: *Coltrane*, 1957.
Riverside OJC CD-036-2: *The Incredible Jazz Guitar of Wes Montgomery*, 1960.
Riverside OJC CD-1799: *Really Big!* (Jimmy Heath), 1992.
Riverside OJC CD-766-2: *Spellbound* (Clifford Jordan), 1960.
Verve V6-8580: *Ray Brown and Milt Jackson*, 1964.

SELECTED BIBLIOGRAPHY

Wittet, T. Bruce. "Albert 'Tootie' Heath: Drum Brother." *MD* XXII, 6 (June 1998): 72–88.
GEN. BIB.: Hunt, *52nd St.*; Southern, *BDA-AAM*.

HELMECKE, AUGUST, JR., "GUS" (b. ca. 1872, New York, New York; d. 26 Feb 1954, Long Island, New York). Bass drummer for John Philip Sousa (ca. 1912–32), Gus Helmecke launched his career with the Innes Band at the Chicago World's Fair and World's Columbian Exposition in 1893; he was reportedly the highest-paid bass drummer in the world by 1925. Retired at 82, he played bass drum in Dr. Edwin Franko Goldman's concert band for some 37 years, appearing with the Metropolitan Opera and the New York Philharmonic during the band's off-season. [Auguste Helmecke, Sr., member of AFM Local 310 (New York), d. ca. October 1919.]

SELECTED BIBLIOGRAPHY

Bierley, Paul E. *The Works of John Philip Sousa*. Columbus, OH: Integrity Press, 1984.
Helmecke, August. "How Sousa Played His Marches." *Etude* LXVIII, 8 (August 1950): 23 (includes photo of Helmecke with Goldman).
New York Times Obituary Index, vols, 1–2 (1858–1978). New York: New York Times Co., 1980.
Stone, George Lawrence. "Technique of Percussion." *IM* XLVII, 7 (January 1949): 19.
GEN. BIB.: Cook, *LDT*, p. 10 (photo).

HENTSCHEL, FRIEDRICH (fl. 1853–80, Berlin, Germany). Timpanist for the Royal Berlin Opera, Friedrich Hentschel improved the Einbigler-Pfundt timpani design [see Pfundt, Ernst] with the help of engineer Carl Hoffmann. Carl Pittrich later substituted a pedal (patented, Dresden, 1881) for the lever on Hentschel's [Pfundt-Hoffman type] drum; hence, the "Dresden" pedal timpani were born. Otto Lange, timpanist of the court orchestra in Dresden at that time, was the first to employ them.

SELECTED BIBLIOGRAPHY

Beck, John H., ed. *Encyclopedia of Percussion.* New York: Garland Publishing, 1995. S.v. "The Kettledrum" by Edmund A. Bowles.
Benvenga, Nancy. "August Knocke's Timpani." *Percussionist* XVI, 1 (Fall 1978): 33–34.

HERMAN, BENJAMIN "BEN." Turning "pro" at 17, Ben Herman earned a bachelor's and a master's degree from the Juilliard School, where he studied with *Saul Goodman, *Elden "Buster" Bailey, and *Morris Goldenberg. He has played with the New York Metropolitan and City Opera Orchestras, the Santa Fe Chamber Music Festival, Lincoln Center Chamber Music Society, New York City Ballet, American Ballet Theater, Joffrey Ballet, American Symphony, American Composers Orchestra, the Orpheus Chamber Orchestra, among others. A frequent substitute timpanist with the New York Philharmonic, Herman is a veteran of Broadway shows, commercials and film soundtracks, and has taught and/or performed at the Aspen Music Festival (1974–   ), the Festival of Two Worlds (Spoleto, Italy), Bach Festival (Madeira Island), and the Canary Islands' Winter Festival.

SELECTED DISCOGRAPHY

New World NW-357-2: *Crumb—An Idyll for the Misbegotten,* 1987.
Aspen Music Festival biographies, 1996-99.

HERMAN, SAMUEL HERBERT "SAMMY" (b. 7 May 1903, Bronxwood Park, New York; d. 1995). Inducted into the Percussive Arts Society Hall of Fame in 1994 and a 70-year member of the American Federation of Musicians, Sammy Herman started piano lessons at the age of 8 and took drum lessons from his uncle. By 22 he was praised in *Metronome* magazine as one of the most virtuosic improvising xylophonists in America. He appeared with the Dorsey Brothers, Earl Carroll's Vanities, George Gershwin, the *Hit of the Week* Orchestra, Frank Sinatra, Bing Crosby, the Paul Specht Orchestra (1923–24), Benny Goodman, Al Jolson, and Phil Spitalny. Touring with the Victor Eight Artists, Herman performed for NBC radio and television (1928–66) on shows such as *Hit Parade, Manhattan Merry-Go-Round, Concentration, Old Gold*

Hour (Paul Whiteman), and *Waltz Time* (Abe Lyman). Arranger of Zez Confrey's "Kitten on the Keys," he played a duo act with Frank Banta (*The Herman and Banta Show*, 1927–29) and with *Harry Breuer in the Lucky Strike and B. A. Rulfe Orchestras on NBC.

SELECTED DISCOGRAPHY

Victor 20558: "Al Fresco," ca. 1925.

SELECTED BIBLIOGRAPHY

Eyler, David P. "Development of the Marimba Ensemble in North America during the 1930s." *PN* XXXIV, 1 (February 1996): 66–71.
Kastner, Kathleen. "The Xylophone in the United States between 1880 and 1930, Part I: The Artists." *Percussive Arts Society: Illinois Chapter Newsletter* (Winter 1986): 1–2.
Kimble, Dana and James A. Strain. "Sammy Herman." *PN* XXXII, 6 (December 1994): 10–11.
GEN. BIB.: Cahn, *XAR*; Strain, *XYLO.*

HIGGINS, BILLY (b. 11 Oct 1936, Los Angeles, California). Citing the influence of *Kenny Clarke, *Roy Haynes, and *Ed Blackwell, Billy Higgins initially played rhythm and blues for Bo Diddley and others in Los Angeles, and then switched to jazz with the Jazz Messiahs and Dexter Gordon. He worked with the Ornette Coleman Quartet in New York (1959 and occasionally thereafter) and Thelonius Monk in San Francisco (1960); he also made a film appearance in the Dexter Gordon vehicle *Round Midnight*. One of the most frequently recorded drummers (500+ albums), Higgins led his own quartet and collaborated with numerous artists, including Hank Mobley, Herbie Hancock, Cedar Walton (European and Far East tours), Art Pepper, Sonny Rollins (three years), Joe Henderson, J. J. Johnson, Clifford Jordan, Lee Morgan, Pat Metheny, Donald Byrd, *Milt Jackson, John Coltrane, Jackie McLean, and the Timeless All-Stars. Recipient of the Phineas Newborn Award for Excellence (1998), Higgins founded the recording and performance venue World Stage Cultural Center in Los Angeles (late 1970s–present), and the National Endowment of the Arts honored him with an "American Jazz Masters" Fellowship in 1997.

SELECTED DISCOGRAPHY

Atlantic 1317-2: *The Shape of Jazz to Come* (Ornette Coleman), 1959.
Atlantic 1364-2: *Free Jazz* (Ornette Coleman), 1960.
Atlantic CD 81341-4: *Change of the Century* (Ornette Coleman), 1959.
Bluebird: *On the Outside* (Sonny Rollins), 1963.
Blue Note 7243 8 33579 2 5: *The Procastinator* (Lee Morgan), 1967.
Blue Note 7243 8 37643 2 7: *Takin' Off* (Herbie Hancock), 1962.
Blue Note 84157: *The Sidewinder* (Lee Morgan), 1963.

Blue Note B21Y 46094: *Go!* (Dexter Gordon), 1962.
Blue Note BST 84204: *Gettin' Around* (Dexter Gordon), 1987.
Columbia 67929: *Afterglow* (movie soundtrack), 1997.
Concord CJ 192: *The Arioso Touch* (James Williams), 1982.
Contemporary 14009: *Solo/Quartet* (Bobby Hutcherson), 1982.
Criss Cross 1015: *Roots* (Slide Hampton), 1991.
Delos D/CD 4006: *Essence* (Timeless All-Stars), 1986.
DMP CD-480: *The Essence*, 1991.
East Wind-8042: *Art Farmer Quintet Live at Boomers*, 1976.
ECM 817 795-2: *Rejoicing* (Pat Metheny), 1984.
Inner City IC-6004: *The Summer Knows* (Art Farmer), 1978.
Inner City IC-6014: *To Duke with Love* (Art Farmer), 1979.
Landmark LLP-1508: *Color Schemes* (with Airto Moreira), 1986.
Muse MCD 6008: *The Maestro* (Cedar Walton), 1989.
Pablo 2310-957-2: *Art n' Zoot*, 1981.
Prestige/OJC 6002: *Cedar Walton Plays Cedar Walton*, 1988.
Red 193: *The Trio* (Cedar Walton), 1986.
Riverside OJC CD-305-2: *Monk at the Blackhawk* (Thelonius Monk), 1960.
Steeplechase SCCD-31060/Inner City IC-2060: *Bouncin' with Dex* (Dexter Gordon),
    1975/1990.
Steeplechase SCCD-31085/Timeless 158: *First Set* (Cedar Walton), 1977/1985.
Theresa TR129CD: *Among Friends* (Cedar Walton), 1990.
Timeless 101: *Eastern Rebellion I* (Cedar Walton), 1989.
Timeless 240: *Up Front* (Cedar Walton).
Triloka 182-2: *Live at the Studio Grill* (Freddie Redd), 1991.
Verve 314 529 142-2: *Star Seeding* (Bheki Mseleku), 1996.
Verve 314 529 237-2: *Saga* (Randy Weston), 1996.

SELECTED VIDEOGRAPHY

A*VisionVideo/Warner Vision: *Sara Vaughan and Friends—A Jazz Session*, 1991.
VIEW Video: *Ron Carter and Art Farmer—Live at Sweet Basil*, 1991.

SELECTED BIBLIOGRAPHY

"1997 NEA Jazz Masters." *Jazz Educators Journal* XXIX, 4 (January 1997): 19.
Davis, Steve. *Drummers: Masters of Time*. New Albany, IN: Aebersold Music,
    Inc., 1986.
Kiely, Bill. "Billy Higgins: The Master Is Back!" *MD* XXI, 7 (July 1997): 18.
Milkowski, Bill. "Billy Higgins: Transcendent Soul." *JazzTimes* XXVIII, 9 (No-
    vember 1998): 28–33.
Wilmer, Valerie. "Billy Higgins: Drum Love." *DB* XXXV, 6 (21 Mar 1968): 27.
GEN. BIB.: Hunt, *52nd St.*; Spagnardi, *GJD*.

HILL, WILLIAM RANDALL "BILL" (b. 31 Jan 1954, Burlington, North
Carolina). Bill Hill earned a bachelor's degree and performer's certificate from
Indiana University (1977) and a master's degree from the Cleveland Institute
(1980), studying respectively with *George Gaber and *Cloyd Duff. He has

served as principal timpanist and percussionist with the Omaha Symphony (1978–80), Honolulu Symphony, and Denver (aka Colorado) Symphony. His CD recording *Rhythms of Innocence* (1997) includes his Colorado Symphony colleagues. An award-winning composer, Hill has premiered several of his own works with the Colorado Symphony.

GEN. BIB.: Borland, *WWAMC.*

HINGER, FRED DAN (b. 9 Feb 1920, Cleveland, Ohio). A student of *William Street, *Benjamin Podemski, and Ned Albright, Fred Hinger received a bachelor's degree and performer's certificate from the Eastman School, where he also performed with the Rochester Philharmonic (1939–41). While serving as percussionist and xylophone soloist with the U.S. Navy Band, Washington, D.C. (1942–48), he auditioned for, and was offered a position in, the Pittsburgh Symphony, but he could not obtain a discharge. When he did leave the service, he returned to Cleveland and enrolled as a graduate student at Case Western Reserve for a brief time. Hinger joined the Philadelphia Orchestra in 1948 as principal percussionist and assistant timpanist, replacing *Benjamin Podemski until 1951, when he became full-time timpanist (1951–67) upon Podemski's return. In reaction to labor union unrest, he secured a position as principal timpanist with the Metropolitan Opera Orchestra from 1967 to 1983. He taught on the faculties of the Curtis Institute, Yale (from 1972), the Manhattan School (from 1967; chair of the percussion department, 1982), and the University of Alabama (Huntsville) and presented clinics in the United States and abroad, including Europe and Israel. His Hinger Touch-Tone Corporation manufactured high-quality timpani, snare drums, timpani mallets, and snare drum sticks. He was inducted into the Percussive Arts Society Hall of Fame in 1986.

SELECTED DISCOGRAPHY

CBS Records MYK-37217: *Orff—Carmina Burana* (Philadelphia Orchestra), 1960/1981.
Columbia M2L-263: *George Frederick Handel—Messiah* (Philadelphia Orchestra), 1959.
Columbia ML 5798: *Poulenc—Concerto for Organ, Strings, and Timpani* (Philadelphia Orchestra).
Columbia ML-5596: *Finlandia* (Philadelphia Orchestra).
Columbia ML-5617: *The Blue Danube—A Johann Strauss Festival* (Philadelphia Orchestra).
Columbia ML-5641: *Invitation to the Dance* (Philadelphia Orchestra).

SELECTED BIBLIOGRAPHY

Hinger, Fred D. *Solos for the Virtuoso Timpanist.* Hackensack, NJ: Jerona Music Corporation, 1981.
Hinger, Fred D. *Techniques for the Virtuoso Timpanist.* Hackensack, NJ: Jerona Music Corporation, 1981.

Hinger, Fred D. *The Timpani Player's Orchestral Repertoire,* vols. 1–5. Hackensack, NJ: Jerona Music Corporation. 1982.
Hinger, Fred D. "My Career: A Short Synopsis." *PN* XXII, 2 (January 1984): 69–70.
Mattingly, Rick. "Fred Hinger: Individuality." *MP* II, 2 (March 1986): 18.
Smith, Dr. D. Richard. "Fred Hinger." *PN* XV, 2 (Winter 1977): 18–19.
Werdesheim, Gary. "An Interview with Fred Hinger." *PN* XXII, 4 (April 1984): 69–72.
GEN. BIB.: Borland, *WWAMC*; Larrick, *BET-CP.*

HIRAOKA, YOICHI (b. Hyogo Prefecture, Japan). Xylophone and marimba artist Yoichi Hiraoka began keyboard percussion at an early age, graduated from Keio University in Tokyo and made his first U.S. performance tour in 1930. He contracted with NBC radio, which broadcast his popular marimba concerts in New York. Composer Alan Hovhaness wrote "Fantasy on Japanese Wood Prints" for him, which he premiered with the Chicago Symphony in 1965. A veteran of more than 4,000 programs, Hiraoka resided in New York and Los Angeles and appeared as soloist with the New York Philharmonic (1966/1972), and the Manila, Nippon, and Tokyo Symphonies, among others.

SELECTED DISCOGRAPHY

Columbia CL 2581/CS-9381: *Hovhaness—Fantasy on Japanese Woodprints*, 1967.

SELECTED BIBLIOGRAPHY

Hiraoka, Yoichi. "The Modern Marimba and Its Relation to the Xylophone." *Etude* (September 1938): 569–570 (photo features four mallets).
Hiraoka, Yoichi. "Hiraoka, His Way to Prominence." *Newsweek* (2 Jan 1937).
"Meet Xylophone Soloist Yoichi Hiraoka." *PN* XII, 1 (Fall 1973): 13.

HIRSCH, GODFREY M. (b. ca. 1907, New Orleans, Louisiana). Pianist, drummer, and vibist who played with Pete Fountain (1960s), Al Hirt, and the Dave Roberts Trio, among others, Godfrey Hirsch took piano lessons at age 14–16, then switched to drums and marimba in 1923. He studied architecture at Tulane University in 1926, playing percussion in the college bands, and then secured his first professional job around 1928, performing as the sole percussionist for the 40-member Saenger Theater orchestra in New Orleans by 1930. He worked in radio from 1933 to 1937 at WSMB, WDSU, and WWL in New Orleans, then relocated to Hollywood as Louis Prima's first drummer in 1937. Replacing *Adrian Rollini in the Richard Himber Orchestra (1938–43), Hirsch served in the Admiral's Band at the Brooklyn Navy Yard (1943–45), was on staff at CBS in New Orleans (WWL, 1945–60), and won the Horace Heidt "Youth Opportunity Contest" in 1949 with Al Hirt.

SELECTED BIBLIOGRAPHY

Claghorn, Charles Eugene. *Biographical Dictionary of American Music.* West Nyack, NY: Parker Publishing Co., Inc., 1973.

Tilles, Bob. "The Background of a Professional Mallet Player—An Interview with Godfrey Hirsch." *PN* VII, 2 (1969): 12.

GEN. BIB.: Cook, *LDT*, p. 405 (photo).

HOCHRAINER, RICHARD (b. 26 Sep 1904, Vienna, Austria; d. 3 May 1986, Vienna, Austria). A 1979 inductee into the Percussive Arts Society Hall of Fame, Richard Hochrainer attended the Vienna Academy of Music, where he was a student of *Hans Schnellar, the timpanist of the Vienna Philharmonic. From 1929 to 1939, he was timpanist and percussionist with orchestras in Austria, Switzerland, France, and Germany, finally settling as timpanist with the Vienna Philharmonic and the Vienna State Opera Orchestra (1939–70). Besides publishing several method books that incorporated his onomatopoeic approach to teaching tone production, he redesigned the Viennese timpani and snare drum (including mallets and sticks). In 1960 he was appointed to the faculty of the Vienna Academy of Music.

SELECTED BIBLIOGRAPHY

Hochrainer, Richard. "The Beat." *Percussionist* XVI, 2 (Winter 1979): 56–65.

Hochrainer, Richard. "Beethoven's Use of Timpani." *Percussionist* XIV, 3 (Summer 1977): 66–71.

Hochrainer, Richard. "Der Orchesterstimmer." *Das Orchester* XVIII (September 1970): 410–412.

Hochrainer, Richard. "Die Cassa." *Das Orchester* XXV (September 1977): 599–601.

Hochrainer, Richard. "Drum Talk from Vienna—Embellishments." *Percussionist* XII, 4 (Summer 1975): 160–162.

Hochrainer, Richard. *Etuden für Kleine Trommel.* Vienna: Doblinger, 1962.

Hochrainer, Richard. *Etuden für Timpani*, vols. 1–3. Vienna: Doblinger, 1958/1967/1983.

Hochrainer, Richard. "A Full Sounding Cymbalbeat." *Percussionist* VII, 3 (March 1970): 93–95.

Hochrainer, Richard. "The Viennese Timpani and Percussion School." *Percussionist* XVII, 2 (Winter 1980): 88–102.

"PAS® Hall of Fame, 1979." *PN* XVIII, 2 (Winter 1980): 20.

Powley, Dr. Harrison. "Richard Hochrainer—Seventieth Birthday Tribute." *PN* XIII, 1 (Fall 1974): 25.

HOLLAND, JAMES (b. 1933). James Holland started percussion at age 13 and while attending Trinity College studied with Peter Allen, timpanist of the London Philharmonic, Max Abrams (drumset), and Charles Donaldson, principal percussionist of the London Symphony. He performed with the Royal Air

Force Central Band (three years) and the London Philharmonic (1956–62), then served as principal percussionist with the London Symphony (1962–71) and the London Sinfonietta, retiring from the BBC Symphony (1971–ca. 1997). A veteran performer on film soundtracks and producer of a forthcoming percussion video, Holland can be heard on the Mercury recording label with the London Symphony. His colleagues in the BBC Symphony at one time included Janos Kesztei, timpani [Eric Pritchard was timpanist before Kesztei], Gary Kettel, Terry Emery, David Johnson (former principal percussion with the Philharmonia), and Kevin Nutty (also formerly of the Philharmonia).

SELECTED DISCOGRAPHY

EMI XY-2231: *Bartók—Sonata for Two Pianos and Percussion*, 1968.
Largo 5126: *Friedrich Cerha—Eine Art Chansons*, 1993.

SELECTED BIBLIOGRAPHY

Holland, James. *Percussion*. New York: Schirmer Books, 1978.
Simco, Andrew P. "An Interview with James Holland." *PN* XXXV, 2 (April 1997): 68–71.

HOLMES, RICHARD "RICK." A graduate of the Juilliard School, where he was *Saul Goodman's assistant on the faculty, Rick Holmes initially studied piano, attending the Eastman School on a vocal scholarship, as well as, the San Francisco Conservatory as a conducting major and percussionist. His percussion instructors include Goodman, Peggy Cunningham, *Morris Goldenberg, and *Elden "Buster" Bailey. He is principal timpanist of the St. Louis Symphony (1969–   ) and a member of the St. Louis Symphony Percussion Quartet and has performed with the Los Angeles Philharmonic, New York Philharmonic, Metropolitan Opera, and Boston Symphony, as well as at the Aspen Festival, where he taught conducting, percussion, and chamber music. Holmes also conducted the New York City Youth Symphony and teaches at the St. Louis Conservatory of Music.

SELECTED DISCOGRAPHY

New World NW318-2: *Works by Colgrass and Druckman* (St. Louis Symphony), 1983.
PASIC® program biographies, 1987.

HOUGHTON, STEPHEN ROSS "STEVE" (b. 29 Mar 1954, Racine, Wisconsin). Initially a drumset specialist whose father was a high school band director in Kenosha, Wisconsin, Steve Houghton has emerged as a broad-based percussion soloist with at least 10 commissioned concerti, which he has performed with orchestras throughout the United States. He studied with James Latimer at the University of Wisconsin at Madison (1973) and Ron Fink at the University of North Texas (1974–75), where he performed with the Grammy® Award–nominated "One O'Clock" Lab Band); he has also appeared, recorded, and/or toured with Woody Herman, Freddie Hubbard, Toshiko Akiyoshi, Lyle Mays, *Gary Burton, Carl Fontana, Barry Manilow, Rosemary Clooney, Joe Henderson, Maureen McGovern, Melissa Manchester, Arturo Sandoval, and others. Active as a studio recording artist in Los Angeles for movies (e.g., *Return of Jafar*), television (e.g., *Northern Exposure*, *Coach*), and commercials (e.g., Apple Computers, Toyota, and ESPN), he has authored several method books and appeared in instructional videos. Houghton is a faculty member of the Percussion Institute of Technology (PIT) in Hollywood and the Henry Mancini Institute in Los Angeles; he also serves in leadership positions for both the International Association of Jazz Educators and the Percussive Arts Society.

SELECTED VIDEOGRAPHY

CPP Media: *Drummers Guide to Reading Drum Charts*. 1993.
CPP Media: *The Contemporary Rhythm Section—Complete*, 1997.

SELECTED DISCOGRAPHY

Fantasy F-9635: *Classics* (Freddie Hubbard), 1984.
Pablo 2310-884: *The Best of Freddie Hubbard*, 1983.
SHPERC: *Windsong*, 1998.
Signature-Mesa Bluemoon R2 79195: *Signature Series Presents...Steve Houghton*, 1994.
Warner Bros./CPP Media EL96163CD: *Remembrances*, 1996.

SELECTED BIBLIOGRAPHY

Houghton, Steve. *The Drumset Soloist*. Miami, FL: Warner Bros., 1996 (with CD).
Houghton, Steve. *A Guide for the Modern Jazz Rhythm Section*. Oskaloosa, IA: C. L. Barnhouse, 1982.
Houghton, Steve. *Studio and Big Band Drumming*. Oskaloosa, IA: C. L. Barnhouse, 1986.
Houghton, Steve, and George Nishigomi. *21st Century Percussion Solo Recital Series, Levels 1–3*. Miami, FL: CPP Belwin, 1995 (with CDs).
Houghton, Steve, and George Nishigomi. *The Contemporary Rhythm Section*. Miami, FL: Warner Bros/CPP-Belwin, 1997 (text and video).
Houghton, Steve, and Tom Warrington. *Essential Styles for the Drummer and Bassist, Books I–II*. Alfred Pub. Co., 1990/1992.
Houghton, Steve, and Tom Warrington. *Master Tracks*. Van Nuys, CA: Alfred Pub. Co., 1996 (play-along series with CD).
Houghton, Steve, and Tom Warrington. *The Ultimate Drumset Reading Anthology*. Van Nuys, CA: Alfred Pub. Co. (with CD).
Information supplied by the subject, 1999.

HOWARD, DANA DOUGLAS "DOUG" (b. 21 Apr 1948, Greeneville, Tennessee). Principal percussionist and assistant timpanist (1982) with the Dallas Symphony since 1975, Doug Howard received a bachelor's degree in 1970 from the University of Tennessee (Knoxville). During his tenure with the U.S. Air Force Band in Washington, D.C. (1970–74), he received the master's degree from Catholic University (1973). After his discharge he performed one season with the Louisville Orchestra (Kentucky) during 1974–75. His principal teachers have included *Tony Ames, Michael Combs, *Alan Abel, *Charles Owen, and *Cloyd Duff. He has a long-standing association with the Aspen Music Festival (1982–), having served as faculty member and as timpanist-percussionist of the Orchestra and Chamber Symphony. With appearances and clinics both in the United States and abroad, Howard has also taught on the faculty of Southern Methodist University (1977–). He can be heard on Dallas Symphony recordings since 1975 on RCA, Pro Arte, Telarc, and Angel-EMI record labels, and with the Louisville Orchestra from the 1974–75 season on First Edition Records.

SELECTED BIBLIOGRAPHY

Vogel, Lauren. "Doug Howard." *MP* III, 2 (March 1987): 8.
GEN. BIB.: Borland, *WWAMC*; Larrick, *BET-CP*.

HUDLER, ANTON (fl. ca. 1820–50, Vienna, Austria). A timpanist with the Vienna Orchestra (ca. 1820s), Anton Hudler may have developed a mechanical timpani tuning mechanism. His son, timpanist Georg Hudler, also claimed in 1831 to have done the same. No examples of these drums are known to exist.

SELECTED BIBLIOGRAPHY

Beck, John H., ed. *Encyclopedia of Percussion*. New York: Garland Publishing, 1995. S.v. "The Kettledrum" by Edmund A. Bowles.
Ludwig, William F. *Ludwig Timpani Instructor*. Chicago: Ludwig Drum Co., 1957.

HUMPHREY, PAUL NELSON (b. 10 Oct 1935, Detroit, Michigan). Studying piano first, drumset artist Paul Humphrey served in the U.S. Navy Band (1955–57), eventually performing and/or recording with Lee Konitz and Gene Ammons (1962), Les MacCann (1963–65/1974–76), Wes Montgomery, Monty Alexander (1965), Harry James (1966), Harry "Sweets" Edison (1967), Jean-Luc Ponty (1969), and Eddie Harris (1975–77). He worked in television (*Lawrence Welk Show*) during the 1970s–80s, toured with Jimmy Rowles, Gerald Wilson, and Buddy Collette, and recorded with his own sextet (1981–83).

SELECTED DISCOGRAPHY

A & M SP 3034: *Roger Kellaway 'Cello Quartet*, 1971.
Blue Note 84300: *Collision in Black* (Blue Mitchell), 1968.
Blue Note 84301: *Elegant Soul* (Gene Harris and The Three Sounds), 1968.
Blue Note 84324: *Bantu Village* (Blue Mitchell), 1969.
Blue Note 84378: *Gene Harris and the Three Sounds*, 1971.
Blue Note (J) K23P-6726 and W-5510: *Monty Alexander*, 1964–65.
Blue Note LA171-G2: *Les McCann*, 1965.

SELECTED BIBLIOGRAPHY

Humphrey, Paul. *Drumset Principles*. Van Nuys, CA: Alfred Publishing, 1982.
Humphrey, Paul. *No. 1 Soul Drums*. Sherman Oaks, CA: Gwyn Pub., 1970.
GEN. BIB.: Kernfeld, *NGJ*, by Barry Kernfeld.

HUMPHREY, RALPH S. (b. 11 May 1944, Berkeley, California). Earning a bachelor's degree from San Jose State University (1967) and master's degree from California State University at Northridge (1969), Ralph Humphrey has performed and/or recorded with Don Ellis (1969–73), Frank Zappa (1973–74), Seals and Crofts (1976), Carmen McRae, Al Jarreau, John Klemmer, Wayne Shorter, Tony Bennett, Manhattan Transfer, Joe Williams, Toshiko Akiyoshi-Lew Tabackin, Clare Fischer, Free Flight (1982), and others. His film and television sountrack work includes *Star Trek—The Next Generation, Cheers, The Simpsons, MacGyver, The French Connection, Kansas City Bomber*, and *Working Girl*, among others. Cofounder and department chair of percussion curriculum at the Percussion Institute of Technology (PIT), he now serves in a similar capacity at the Los Angeles Music Academy (LAMA, 1996–), has authored didactic works for drumset, and been a contributing journalist to *Percussive Notes, Modern Drummer, Drums and Drumming*, and *Musician*.

SELECTED DISCOGRAPHY

Columbia G30927: *Tears of Joy* (Don Ellis), 1971.
Warner Brothers DSK 2288: *The Mothers/Overnight Sensation* (Frank Zappa), 1973.
Zebra ZD 44005-2: *Tribute to Jeff Porcaro* (Dave Garfield), 1997.

SELECTED BIBLIOGRAPHY

Ellis, Don. *The New Rhythm Book*. North Hollywood, CA: Ellis Music Enterprises, 1972.
Flans, Robyn. "Joe Porcaro and Ralph Humphrey: Partners in Education." *MD* XXI, 8 (August 1997): 134–140.
Humphrey, Ralph. *Even in the Odds*. Oskaloosa, IA: C. L. Barnhouse, 1980.
GEN. BIB.: Kernfeld, *NGJ*, by Barry Kernfeld; PASIC® program biographies, 1991, 1995, 1997.

HUMPHRIES, LEX P., III (b. 22 Aug 1936, Rockaway, New Jersey; d. 11 Jul 1994). Drumset artist Lex Humphries appeared and/or recorded with Lester Young and Chet Baker (1956), Lee Morgan, Bud Powell, Dizzy Gillespie (1958), Benny Golson and Art Farmer's Jazztet (1959–60), Junior Mance and John Coltrane (1959), Duke Pearson and Donald Byrd (1959–60), Doug Watkins and Paul Chambers (1960), Wes Montgomery (1961), McCoy Tyner (1963), Chris Connor (1959/1962), Yusef Lateef (1960–63), and Sun Ra (1965).

SELECTED DISCOGRAPHY

Argo 664: *Meet the Jazztet*, 1960.
Blue Note 84026: *Fuego* (Dizzy Gillespie), 1959.
BYG 529340-41: *The Solar Myth Approach* (Sun Ra), 1970–71.
Impulse 39: *Nights of Ballads and Blues* (McCoy Tyner), 1963.
Moodsville 22: *Eastern Sounds* (Yusef Lateef), 1961.
Verve MGVS6057: *Junior Nance Trio*, 1959.
Verve MGVS6068: *The Ebullient Mr. Gillespie*, 1959.
GEN. BIB.: Kernfeld, *NGJ*, by Rick Mattingly.

HURTADO, CELSO BENITEZ (b. 6 Apr 1891, Guatemala; d. 3 Feb 1968, San Francisco). Classical marimba artist Celso Hurtado toured Guatemala with his father, Sebastián, and brothers, Vicente, Arnulfo (d. 1913), Jesús, and Mariano until 1908 when the sons all sailed to New Orleans for a six-month U.S. tour which, for various reasons, turned into five years. They appeared coast-to-coast with Arnulfo as leader on the American Music Hall circuit and by 1910 were performing in Europe when they had to return to Guatemala because of Arnulfo's eventually fatal illness.

Reborn with new personnel as the Hurtado Brothers' Royal Marimba Band of Guatemala under the leadership of Celso, they were appointed official Guatemalan representatives to the Panama-Pacific International Exposition in San Francisco (1915), where their success led to recording contracts with the Columbia label and a stint on the Orpheum vaudeville circuit. Between 1915 and 1917, they made approximately 38 recordings for the Columbia, Victor, and Brunswick companies and appeared in New York's Ziegfeld Follies with W. C. Fields and Will Rogers (1916). After more nationwide concert tours and extended hotel engagements (1918–25), the group centralized in New York as the popularity of the "talkies" took its toll. (At this point, Jesús left the group but returned later in the 1930s.) Celso kept the group active throughout the 1930s, performing on over 20 radio sations in 1934 as "Celso Hurtado and His Marimba Typica Band." The ensemble settled in San Francisco around 1940, disbanding around that time, and all the brothers became U.S. citizens.

In the 1920s Celso gave solo concerts at Aeolian Hall and Town Hall (New York), and later in Carnegie Hall to critical acclaim (1946)—the first marimbist to do so. A member of AFM Local 6 in San Francisco, he was a guest artist on the *Maxwell House Hour*, *Nelson Eddy Show*, and the *Standard of California*

Symphony Hour. Celso refined the chromatic marimba by adding a volume control/vibrato device accessed by a foot pedal—an improvement not adopted by marimba manufacturers.

SELECTED DISCOGRAPHY

Columbia Recording Company: "Pique Dame Overture" and "Poet and Peasant Overture" (Hurtado Brothers' Royal Marimba Band of Guatemala), 1915.
Victor Talking Machine Company: "Love's Power Waltz" and "Stars and Stripes Forever" (Hurtado Brothers' Royal Marimba Band of Guatemala), 1916.
Victor 18093: "El Choclo," 1917.

SELECTED BIBLIOGRAPHY

"Closing Chord: Celso Hurtado." *IM* LXVII, 2 (August 1968): 23.
The Edwin L. Gerhardt Marimba-Xylophone Collected Materials. Percussive Arts Society Museum Archives, Lawton, Oklahoma.
Eyler, David P. "The Hurtado Brothers' Royal Marimba Band of Guatemala." *PN* XXXI, 3 (February 1993): 48–54.
Rust, Brian A. L., and Allen G. Debus. *The Complete Entertainment Discography from 1897–1942,* 2nd ed. New York: Da Capo Press, 1989.
GEN. BIB.: Cahn, *XAR.*

HURTADO, SEBASTIÁN (b. Almolongo, Quezaltenango, Guatemala; d. 1912). Sebastián Hurtado toured Mexico as a marimba artist as early as 1894 and by 1896 had established a marimba ensemble with his sons, Vicente, Arnulfo, Celso, Jesús, and Mariano, which toured Guatemala. They eventually added Western European classical music to their popular native repertoire. After much experimentation, Sebastián changed the one-row diatonic marimba in 1894 to a double-row chromatic, but the upper row was placed *in line* with the lower row instead of offset as in piano configuration. He also replaced the original gourd resonators with tapered wooden resonators. This new chromatic marimba made its concert debut in 1899 for the birthday celebration of the president of Guatemala, who honored Sebastián for his musical achievements (1901).

SELECTED BIBLIOGRAPHY

"Backgrounds in Percussion." *PN* XVII, 3 (Spring/Summer 1979): 70.
Eyler, David P. "The Hurtado Brothers' Royal Marimba Band of Guatemala." *PN* XXXI, 3 (February 1993): 48–54.
Peters, Gordon. *The Drummer: Man.* Wilmette, IL: Kemper-Peters Publications, 1975.

HUTCHERSON, ROBERT "BOBBY" (b. 27 Jan 1941, Los Angeles, California). Vibraphonist Bobby Hutcherson (aka "Mr. Good Vibes") was inspired by *Milt Jackson and started with a foundation in piano before studying mallets with *Dave Pike and Terry Trotter, embracing vibraphone at age 15. His early West Coast collaborations included work with Curtis Amy, the Al Grey–Billy Mitchell group (1960–61), and Charles Lloyd. Moving to New York around 1961, Hutcherson performed with top-flight musicians including Jackie McLean, Charles Tolliver, *Tony Williams, Grachan Moncur, Gerald Wilson, McCoy Tyner, Herbie Hancock, Eric Dolphy, Archie Shepp, Hank Mobley, and Andrew Hill. Hutcherson added the marimba to his musical arsenal in 1965 and, with Harold Land, co-led a quintet (1967–71) that featured, among others, Joe Sample, Chick Corea, Reggie Johnson, Don Bailey, and *Billy Higgins. After relocating to California (1969) and San Francisco during the 1970s, he toured extensively during the 1980s, recorded with the Timeless All-Stars, and has appeared as a clinician at the Percussive Arts Society International Convention.

SELECTED DISCOGRAPHY

Atlantic Jazz 82591-2: *Acoustic Masters II*, 1994.
Blue Note 7243 8 33579 2 5: *The Procastinator* (Lee Morgan), 1967.
Blue Note 84198: *Dialogue*, 1965.
Blue Note 84213: *Components*, 1966.
Blue Note 84244: *Stick Up!* 1966.
Blue Note 84333: *Now!* 1969.
Blue Note 84416: *Natural Illusions*, 1972.
Blue Note B21K 46289/BT-85119: *Foreign Intrigue*, 1985.
Blue Note BST 84153: *Evolution* (Grachan Moncur III), 1985.
Blue Note BST 84204: *Gettin' Around* (Dexter Gordon), 1987.
Blue Note BST 84291: *Total Eclipse*, 1985.
Blue Note BST 84307: *Time for Tyner* (McCoy Tyner), 1986.
Blue Note CDP 7 46821 2: *One Step Beyond*, 1987.
Blue Note CDP 7 84154 2: *Idle Moments* (Grant Green), 1988.
Blue Note CDP 7 84180 2/BCT 84180: *Life Time*, 1987.
Blue Note CDP 7 92051 2: *Eternal Spirit* (Andrew Hill), 1989.
Blue Note LA-551: *Montara*, 1975.
Blue Note LA-615: *Waiting*, 1976.
Blue Note LA-789: *Knucklebean*, 1977.
Blue Note/Capitol CDP 7-46530-2: *Happenings* (Herbie Hancock), 1966/1987.
Blue Note/Capitol Series CDP 7 84227 2: *Joe Henderson—Mode for Joe*, 1988.
Celluloid CELCD 5015: *Iron Man* (Eric Dolphy), 1986.
Columbia FC36402: *Un Poco Loco*, 1980.
Columbia FC37093: *The Best of Bobby Hutcherson*, 1981.
Columbia JC 35550: *Highway One*, 1978.
Columbia JC 35814: *Conception: The Gift of Love*, 1979.
Columbia KC2 37100: *One Night Stand*, 1981.
Concord Jazz CJ-251: *Full Circle* (Bruce Forman), 1984.
Concord Jazz CJ-332: *There Are Times* (Bruce Forman), 1987.
Contemporary 14001: *Cables' Vision* (George Cables), 1980.
Contemporary 14009: *Solo/Quartet*, 1982.
Contemporary CCD-14044-2: *Red Hot and Blues* (Barney Kessel), 1988.

Contemporary CCD-14052-2: *Reflections* (Frank Morgan Allstars), 1989.
Delos D/CD 4006: *Essence* (Timeless All-Stars), 1986.
Elektra Musician 60299-1: *Night Music* (Woody Shaw), 1983.
Fantasy F-9635: *Classics* (Freddie Hubbard), 1984.
Landmark LCD-1517-2: *Cruisin' the 'Bird*, 1988.
Landmark LCD-1522-2: *Ambos Mundos*, 1989.
Landmark LCD-1529-2: *Mirage*, 1991.
Landmark LLP-1508: *Color Schemes*, 1986.
Landmark Records LLP-1513: *In the Vanguard*, 1987.
Landmark Records LLP-501: *Good Bait*, 1985.
Quartet Records: Q-1004: *Sasha Bossa*, 1988.
Theresa TR119: *John Hicks*, 1984.
Theresa TR129CD: *Among Friends* (Cedar Walton), 1990.
Timeless Records CDSJP 210: *Four Seasons*, 1985.
United Artists/Blue Note BN-LA369-G: *Linger Lane*, 1975.

SELECTED BIBLIOGRAPHY

"Bobby Hutcherson Discography." *Swing Journal* XXVIII, 13 (1974): 244.
Bourne, Michael. "Bobby Hutcherson: A Natural Player." *DB* XLI, 5 (1974): 18.
Miller, William F. "Bobby Hutcherson." *MP* I, 3 (June 1985): 69.
Tolleson, Robin. "Bobby Hutcherson: Street Vibes." *MP* I, 2 (March 1985): 12.
GEN. BIB.: Kernfeld, *NGJ*, by Lee Jeske; Larrick, *BET-CP*; Southern, *BDA-AAM*.

HYAMS, MARJORIE "MARGIE" (b. 1923, New York, New York). Vibist Margie Hyams played with Woody Herman (1944–45), led her own trio (1945–48), appeared in George Shearing's first quintet (1949–50), then married and retired in June 1950.

SELECTED DISCOGRAPHY

Verve (E) VSP35/36: *George Shearing*, 1949–50.
Verve MGV8132: *Charlie Ventura*, 1947.

SELECTED BIBLIOGRAPHY

Claghorn, Charles Eugene. *Biographical Dictionary of Jazz*. Englewood Cliffs, NJ: Prentice-Hall, Inc., 1982.

I

IGOE, OWEN JOSEPH "SONNY" (b. 8 Oct 1923, Jersey City, New Jersey). Drumset artist Sonny Igoe played with Benny Goodman (1948–49), Woody Herman (1950–52), Charlie Ventura (1953–55), Chuck Wayne, and worked in New York recording studios. Active as a pedagogue since the 1960s, he recorded with Dick Meldonian (1982–83).

SELECTED DISCOGRAPHY

ABC Paramount 109: *The Four Most Guitars* (Chuck Wayne), 1956.
Cool 'N Blue CD 116: *Light Gray* (Wardell Gray), 1948.
Discovery DSCD-944: *Early Autumn* (Woody Herman), 1952.
Progressive Records PRO 7058: *The Jersey Swing Concerts* (Dick Meldonian), 1982.
MGM 1010: *New Golden Wedding* (Woody Herman), 1951.
Verve MGV8143: *Charlie Ventura Quartet*, 1954.
GEN. BIB.: Hunt, *52nd St.*; Kernfeld, *NGJ*, by Chip Deffaa.

J

JACKSON, DUFF CLARK "DUFFY" (b. 3 Jul 1953, Freeport, Long Island, New York). A student of *Don Lamond and *Roy Burns, drumset artist Duffy Jackson matured in Florida, playing in his father's (Chubby Jackson) groups, and by 14 he performed with Flip Phillips. He appeared in Hollywood with the *Milt Jackson–Ray Brown Quintet (1971), in Japan with Benny Carter (1973), on television with Sammy Davis, Jr. (1974–75), toured with Lena Horne, and has collaborated with *Terry Gibbs, Urbie Green, Woody Herman, Kai Winding, *Lionel Hampton, and Count Basie (early 1980s), among others.

SELECTED DISCOGRAPHY

Audiophile AP-178: *Old Shoes* (Millie Vernon), 1983.
Stash ST-208: *The Incredible Ira Sullivan Plays...*, 1980.

SELECTED BIBLIOGRAPHY

Feather, Leonard and Ira Gitler. *The Encyclopedia of Jazz in the Seventies.* New York: Horizon Press, 1976.

JACKSON, MILTON "MILT" "BAGS" (b. 1 Jan 1923, Detroit, Michigan; d. 9 Oct 1999, New York, New York, but resided in Teaneck, New Jersey). After a solid musical foundation in guitar at age 7 and piano at 11, vibraphonist Milt Jackson played violin, timpani, xylophone, drums, and sang in choir. In 1941 *Lionel Hampton inspired him in a concert at the Michigan State Fair, so he took lessons on a school-purchased vibraphone and eventually studied at Michigan State University. After early professional associations with the Clarence Ringo and George E. Lee bands, an introduction to Dizzy Gillespie led to an offer with the Earl Hines big band. Unfortunately, Jackson was drafted into the military in 1942 and picked up the mallets again in 1944 with his own group, "The Four Sharps," in Detroit.   Around this time he was dubbed "Bags" by a bass player for the bags under his eyes created by late-night gigs. At the age of 22, he was coaxed away by Dizzy Gillespie and worked with him in New York (1945–47/1950–52), playing vibes and piano.   By 1950 he had performed with Jimmy and Percy Heath, Howard McGhee, Woody Herman (1949–50), Charlie Parker, Tadd Dameron, and Thelonius Monk, among others. During his second stint with Gillespie, he launched a quartet with pianist John Lewis, bassist Ray Brown, and drummer *Kenny Clarke that gave the other members of the band a rest.   Horace Silver subbed for Lewis and Percy Heath for Brown when this foursome played at the first Newport Jazz Festival.   When Lewis, Jackson, Heath, and Clarke recorded together in 1952, the Modern Jazz Quartet was born (Lewis became leader in 1954).   Although Jackson often performed and recorded outside the group, it became one of the longest-lived jazz chamber ensembles in music history.   *Connie Kay replaced Clarke in 1955 as a permanent member of the rhythm section.   Though the group's style could be subheaded "cool" jazz, its fusion of classical form and jazz gave rise to the term *third-stream* music.   They performed with symphony orchestras and string quartets, on TV in Europe and the United States, and were featured in the films *Sait-on jamais* (1971), *Little Murders* (1971), and *Monterey Jazz* (1973), and a tv documentary, *The Modern Jazz Quartet* (1964).   The inevitable dissolution of the quartet opened new doors to Jackson in 1974 as a soloist and collaborative artist, though the Modern Jazz Quartet occasionally staged reunion concert tours (e.g., Japan, 1981).   Utilizing essentially two-mallet technique, his sound is characterized by the use of slow-medium vibrato supplied by the motor attached to the vibraphone.   Voted into *Down Beat* magazine's Hall of Fame (1980), he received an honorary doctorate from Berklee College of Music and an "American Jazz Masters" Fellowship from the National Endowment of the Arts (1997).

SELECTED DISCOGRAPHY

Atlantic 30XD-1012: *Modern Jazz Quartet with Sonny Rollins*, 1958.
Atlantic 1231: *Fontessa* (Modern Jazz Quartet), 1956.
Atlantic SD 1269-2: *Plenty, Plenty Soul*, 1957.
Atlantic 1279: *Soul Brothers*, 1957.
Atlantic 1342: *The Ballad Artistry of Milt Jackson*, 1961.
Atlantic SD 1368-2: *Bags and Trane*, 1959.
Atlantic 1385-6: *European Concert*, 1960.
Atlantic 1468: *Blues at Carnegie Hall*, 1966.
Atlantic QD 1652: *The Modern Jazz Quartet—Blues on Bach*, 1974.
Atlantic SD-1486: *MJQ Live at the Lighthouse*, 1967.
Blue Note 1592: *What's New?* 1952.
Blue Note CDP 7 81509 2: *Milt Jackson*, 1989.
Blue Note LA490-H2: *Milt Jackson Quintet*, 1952.
Blue Note LA590-H2: *Hank Mobley and His All Stars*, 1957–58.
CBS ZK 44174: *Olinga*, 1988.
Dee Gee 3702: *Bluesology*, 1951.

East-West 7 90991-1: *Bebop*, 1988.
GRP/Impulse! GRD-130: *Statements*, 1993.
Jazztone J-1235: *The Chase* (Dexter Gordon), 1956.
Milestone 47001: *Cannonball Adderley and Eight Giants*, 1973.
Milestone 47006: *Big Band Bags*, 1973.
Milestone 9275: *Cannonball Adderley Greatest Hits—The Riverside Years*, 1958–62.
Milestone M-47013: *Wes Montgomery and Friends*, 1973.
Mosaic MR4-101: *Thelonius Monk Quartet*, 1948.
Musica Jazz MJCD 1105: *Milt Jackson*, 1995.
Musical Heritage Society MHS 7514A: *Ain't but a Few of Us Left*, 1987.
Pablo 2308-235: *Memories of Thelonius Sphere Monk*, 1982.
Pablo 2310-916: *Brother Jim*, 1985.
Pablo 2310-867: *Big Mouth*, 1981.
Pablo 2310-897: *Jackson, Johnson, Brown, & Co.*, 1983.
Pablo Live OJCCD-375-2: *Milt Jackson/Ray Brown Jam—Montreux '77*, 1989.
Pablo 2308-210/OJCCD-380-2: *The Pablo All-Stars Jam—Montreux '77*, 1989.
Pablo/OJC 498: *Quadrant* (Joe Pass), 1977.
Pablo 2310-909/OJC 601: *It Don't Mean a Thing If You Can't Tap Your Foot to It*, 1976/1984.
Pickwick Records QJ-25391: *Milt Jackson*, 1979.
Prestige 7003/OJC-001: *Milt Jackson Quartet*, 1955/1987.
Prestige 7005/24005/OJC-002: *The Modern Jazz Quartet—Concorde*, 1979.
Prestige 7029/OJC-011: *Sonny Rollins with the Modern Jazz Quartet*, 1951/1988.
Prestige 7034/OJC-012: *Miles Davis/Milt Jackson—Quintet/Sextet*, 1959.
Prestige 7057/OJC-057: *Modern Jazz Quartet—Django*, 1953/1987.
Prestige 7109: *Bag's Groove* (Miles Davis), 1954.
Prestige 7150: *Miles Davis and the Modern Jazz Giants*, 1954.
Prestige OJC-125: *MJQ*, 1954/1984.
Prestige P-24048: *Milt Jackson—Opus de Funk*, 1975.
Qwest 46607: *Milt Jackson—Sa Va Bella (For Lady Legends)*, 1997.
Qwest/Warner Bros. 9 47286: *Explosive!* (Clayton-Hamilton Jazz Orchestra), 1999.
Rhino Atlantic Jazz R2 71984: *John Coltrane—The Heavyweight Champion; The Complete Atlantic Recordings*, 1995.
Riverside OJCCD-234-2: *Bags Meets Wes* (Wes Montgomery), 1987.
Riverside OJCCD-260-2: *Milt Jackson Sextet—Invitation*, 1979.
Riverside OJCCD-309-2: *Milt Jackson Quintet "Live" at the Village Gate*, 1979.
Riverside 1128/OJCCD-032-2: *Things Are Getting Better* (Cannonball Adderley), 1988.
Riverside OJCCD-366-2: *Big Bags*, 1989.
Savoy MG 12006: *Kenny Clarke*, vol. 1, 1955.
Savoy MG 12061: *Meet Milt Jackson*, 1992.
Savoy Jazz SV-0167: *Howard McGhee and Milt Jackson*, 1992.
Savoy Jazz SV-0175: *Jackson's Ville*, 1992.
Savoy SJL 2204: *Second Nature*, 1976.
Verve 314537896: *Ella* (Dee Dee Bridgewater), 1997.
Verve MGVS6069: *The Modern Jazz Quartet at the Opera House*, 1957.
Verve V/V6-8580: *Much in Common* (Ray Brown), 1964.
Verve V6-8429: *Very Tall* (Oscar Peterson/Milt Jackson/Ray Brown), 1961.

Verve V6-8580: *Ray Brown and Milt Jackson*, 1964.
Verve V6-8761: *Milt Jackson and the Hip String Quartet*, 1968.
Vogue VG 655: *Milt Jackson, J. J. Johnson, Henri Renaud All-Stars*, 1990.

SELECTED VIDEOGRAPHY

VIEW Video: *Forty Years of M.J.Q.*, 1995.
WCBS-New York/Camera Three: *The Modern Jazz Quartet*, 1973.
WCBS-New York/Camera Three: *Modern Jazz Quartet and the Juilliard String Quartet*, 1974.

SELECTED BIBLIOGRAPHY

"1997 NEA Jazz Masters." *Jazz Educators Journal* XXIX, 4 (January 1997): 19. [Available from IAJE, *Jazz Research Papers,* vol. 11, compiled by Dr. Charles T. Brown and Dr. Larry Fisher.]
"Bags: 'The Consummate Foil' Moves out on His Own." *PN* XIII, 1 (Fall 1974): 26.
Blum, J. "Milt Jackson: Vibes Original." *JazzTimes* (July 1984): 13.
DeMichael, Don. "Jackson of the MJQ." *DB* XXVIII, 14 (6 Jul 1961): 18–21.
Hentoff, Nat. "The Modern Jazz Quartet." *High Fidelity* V, 3 (1955): 36.
Mattingly, Rick. "1996 PAS® Hall of Fame: Milt Jackson." *PN* XXXIV, 6 (December 1996): 15–16.
Rehbein, S. "An Examination of Milt Jackson's Improvisational Style." Research paper presented at IAJE Conference, 1991.
Samuel, Dave. "Milt Jackson." *MP* III, 4 (September 1987): 1.
Smith, Arnold Jay. "The Modern Jazz Quartet Turns 40." *JazzTimes* XXI, 8 (November 1991): 30.
GEN. BIB.: Kernfeld, *NGJ*, by Thomas Owen; Larrick, *BET-CP*; Southern, *BDA-AAM.*

JACKSON, RONALD SHANNON (b. 1940, Texas).   Avant-garde drumset artist Ronald Shannon Jackson established the group Decoding Society later in his career, but he initially worked in blues bands before arriving in New York, where he played for Albert Ayler, Charles Mingus, Junior Cook, Cecil Taylor, Betty Carter, and Ornette Coleman, among others.

SELECTED DISCOGRAPHY

Blue Note BT 85136: *America, Do You Remember the Love?* (James Blood Ulmer), 1986.

SELECTED BIBLIOGRAPHY

Stern, C. "Ronald Shannon Jackson's Rhythms of Life." *MD* VIII (March 1984): 14–17.
GEN. BIB.: Spagnardi, *GJD.*

JAHN, FRANZ. A member of the Berlin Musician's Union, Franz Jahn was a founding member of the Berlin Philharmonic who served as timpanist and percussionist from around 1882 to 1896.
GEN. BIB.: Avgerinos, *KB.*

JEANNE, RUTH STUBER (b. near Chicago). Ruth Stuber Jeanne began drums at age 4, studied piano and composition, and majored in violin at Northwestern University (graduated 1932), specializing in marimba. Taking lessons with marimbist *Clair Omar Musser in Evanston, Illinois, she participated in the 100-piece Marimba Band at the Chicago World's Fair of 1933, then relocated with her family to Alabama, where she taught at her father's private music school. After serving two years on the faculty of a Montgomery (AL) women's college, she left for New York in search of better pay and more musical opportunities. There she studied xylophone (ca. 1937) with *George Hamilton Green, timpani with *George Braun, led her own trio (marimba, cello, and piano), and played timpani for Frédérique Petrides, female conductor of the 30-member, all-girl, Orchestrette Classique. It was Petrides who commissioned Paul Creston to compose a marimba solo for Ruth, which the Orchestrette premiered on April 29, 1940, in Carnegie Hall. *Concertino*, op. 21, written between February and March of 1940, was dedicated to Ruth and has become the most-often performed selection of its type in percussion history. She later played for John Cage at New York's Museum of Modern Art, taught at the Ohio Marimba Camp, and taught, organized, and arranged for the Granville (OH) Marimba Ensemble.

SELECTED BIBLIOGRAPHY

Groh, Jan Bell. *Evening the Score: Women in Music and the Legacy of Frédérique Petrides.* Fayetteville, AR: University of Arkansas Press, 1991.
Hixcon, Shirley. "From Whence Came Paul Creston's 'Concertino for Marimba and Orchestra,'Opus 21?" *PN* XIV, 1 (Fall 1975): 22–23.
Smith, Sarah. "The Birth of the Creston Marimba Concerto: An Interview with Ruth Jeanne." *PN* XXXIV, 2 (April 1996): 62–65.
"Young Woman with a Drum." *Philadelphia Inquirer* (31 Aug 1940), *Everybody's Weekly* (magazine section).

JEKOWSKY, BARRY. Former principal timpanist with the San Francisco Symphony (from age 22) who became associate conductor of the National Symphony (1994), Barry Jekowsky took piano lessons at 5, later adding trumpet and violin. He attended Aspen and Tanglewood and earned a bachelor's and a master's degree from the Juilliard School, where he studied with *Elden "Buster" Bailey and *Saul Goodman. A 1985 recipient of the Leopold Stokowski Conducting Prize with the American Symphony, he has conducted the Oregon Symphony, London Philharmonic, and Oklahoma Symphony, has performed at both Aspen and Tanglewood Festivals, and is founder and director of the California Symphony. Jekowsky appeared as percussionist and timpanist with the New York Philharmonic, Metropolitan Opera, New York City Opera, and American Ballet Theater; he performed the New York premiere of Donald Erb's "Concerto for Solo Percussion." On the faculty of the San Francisco Conservatory and Aspen Music Festival, he was featured on CBS-TV's *48 Hours*, served on the music panel of the National Endowment for the Arts, and can be heard as timpanist with San Francisco on Philips, CBS, Decca, and Deutsche Grammophone record labels.

SELECTED DISCOGRAPHY

Opus One 18: *Carmine Pepe—Octets*, 1974.
PASIC® program biographies, 1985/1991.

JEPSON, TIMOTHY JAMES (b. 25 Jul 1960, Onawa, Iowa). Principal timpanist with the Kansas City Symphony since 1983, Tim Jepson earned a bachelor's degree from Morningside College (1982, Sioux City, IA) and studied with *Sal Rabbio, Earl Yowell, and Courtland "Skip" Swenson (the latter at the University of South Dakota). He has performed and/or recorded with the Sioux City Symphony (1978–83), Missouri Symphony Society, Kansas City Lyric Opera, State Ballet of Missouri, and the Kansas City Brass and at the Arkansas (1986–90), Sunflower (KS, 1987–), and Western Slope Music Festivals (CO, 1999). Since 1997 he has served as adjunct faculty at Washburn University (KS).
Information supplied by the subject, 1999.

JOHNSON, GUS, JR. (b. 15 Nov 1913, Tyler, Texas). Jay "Hootie" McShann's drummer in Kansas City (1938–43, featuring Charlie Parker; 1972/1977), Gus Johnson was also a singer and bass player who performed with *Jo Jones (1935), Loyd Hunter, and Ernest Redd (1937). Working in Chicago and New York after WWII, he collaborated with Eddie "Cleanhead" Vinson, Oscar Pettiford, Earl Hines (1947), Cootie Williams, Count Basie (1948/1950/1979), Buck Clayton, Lena Horne, Zoot Sims (1956), Ella Fitzgerald (for nine years), Al Cohn (1961), Gerry Mulligan (1962), Woody Herman (1962), Stan Getz, Eddie "Lockjaw" Davis (1974), Yank Lawson, and the World's Greatest Jazz Band (Bob Haggart).

SELECTED DISCOGRAPHY

ABC Paramount 227: *Oscar Pettiford Orchestra*, 1957.
Audiophile ACD-203: *Close as Pages in a Book* (Maxine Sullivan and Bob Wilber), 1969.
Audiophile ACD-220: *The Music of Hoagy Carmichael*, 1993.
Clef 626/647: *Dance Session* (Count Basie), 1952–54.

Impulse 89: *Inspired Abandon* (Les Brown), 1965.

Jazzology J-165: *The Compleat Bud Freeman*, 1970.

Jazzology JCD-300: *The World's Greatest Jazz Band of Yank Lawson and Bob Haggart*, 1997.

Jazztet 1268: *The Big Challenge* (Rex Stewart and Cootie Williams), 1957.

RCA Victor LPM 1279: *The Drum Suite* (with Osie Johnson, Teddy Sommer, Don Lamond), 1956.

Sony Col. 468411-2: *Gerry Mulligan—Arranger*, 1957.

Stash CD 542: *Early Bird* (Jay McShann), 1940.

Swingville 2030: *Buck and Buddy Blow the Blues* (Buck Clayton), 1961.

Verve MGV4052: *Ella in Hollywood* (Ella Fitzgerald), 1961.

Verve MGV8027: *Billie Holiday and Her Orchestra*, 1952.

Verve MGV8070: *The Count* (Count Basie), 1952.

Verve V6-4065: *Ella Fitzgerald*, 1964.

Verve V6-8466: *The Gerry Mulligan Quartet*, 1962.

Verve V6-8525: *Kai Winding*, 1963.

World Jazz 3: *World's Greatest Jazz Band of Yank Lawson and Bob Haggart in Concert at Massey Hall*, 1972.

GEN. BIB.: Hunt, *52nd St.*; Kernfeld, *NGJ*, by Chris Sheridan.

JOHNSON, JAMES OSIE (b. 11 Jan 1923, Washington, D.C.; d. 10 Feb 1966). Drumset artist, singer, and composer-arranger, Osie Johnson started his professional career in 1941, playing in Boston with Sabby Lewis (1942–43). During WWII he served in a U.S. Navy band (1944–45), and after his discharge he played with Earl "Fatha" Hines (1951–53) and Tony Scott. He toured Europe with Illinois Jacquet (1954) and performed with Dorothy Donegan (1954), then was active in New York's recording and television studios (1940s–60s) with Johnny Hodges (1954/1962–64), Milt Hinton, Clark Terry, Gil Evans, Al Cohn, Jimmy Raney (1956/1964), Coleman Hawkins (intermittently, 1955–65), Zoot Sims, Dinah Washington (1956, including song arrangements), Bobby Brookmeyer, Carmen McRae, Wes Montgomery (1963), Ben Webster (1964), and Sonny Stitt (ca. 1963–65).

SELECTED DISCOGRAPHY

Bethlehem 66: *The Happy Osie Johnson*, 1957.

Blue Note (J) GXF-3057: *Kenny Burrell*, 1963.

Columbia CL-1486: *Silver Vibes* (Lionel Hampton), 1960.

Impulse 32XD-612: *Into the Hot* (Gil Evans), 1961.

Impulse 55: *Tell It the Way It Is* (Paul Gonsalves), 1963.

Impulse A-78: *You Better Know It!* 1964.

Moodsville 7: *At Ease with Coleman Hawkins*, 1960.

MGM E-3764: *Billie Holiday*, 1959.

Pacific Jazz WP 1239: *Street Swingers* (Bobby Brookmeyer), 1957.

Period 1108: *Osie's Oasis*, 1955.

Period 1112: *Johnson's Whacks*, 1955.

Philips 32 JD 159: *LeGrand Jazz* (Michel LeGrand), 1958.

Prestige 7052/OJCCD-1728-2: *Bennie Green Blows His Horn*, 1955/1988.
RCA LPM 1369: *A Bit of the Blues*, 1956.
RCA 6471-2-RB: *RCA Victor Jazz Workshop* (George Russell), 1956.
RCA Victor LPM 1279: *The Drum Suite* (with Gus Johnson, Teddy Sommer, Don
      Lamond), 1956.
Verve MGV8065: *Illinois Jacquet and His Orchestra*, 1954.
Verve MGV8130: *Ben Webster with Strings*, 1955.
Verve MGV8172: *Billy Bauer*, 1956.
Verve MGV8180: *Johnny Hodges and His Orchestra*, 1954.
Verve MGV8218: *Bud Powell Trio*, 1956.
Verve MGV8238: *Gigi Gryce–Donald Byrd Jazz Laboratory*, 1957.
Verve MGV8290: *Ray Brown*, 1958.
Verve V6-8443: *Gary McFarland*, 1961.
Verve V6-8444: *Ray Brown and His All-Star Big Band*, 1962.
Verve V6-8508: *Oliver Nelson*, 1963.
Verve V6-8836: *Clark Terry and Bob Brookmeyer*, 1961.
Verve 314 526 373-2: *Alone Together—The Best of the Mercury Years* (Clifford
      Brown), 1995.

SELECTED VIDEOGRAPHY

A*Vision Entertainment 50240-3: *Jazzmasters Vintage Collection*, vols. 1–2
      (1958–1961), 1990.

SELECTED BIBLIOGRAPHY

"Osie Johnson Dies." *DB* XXXIII, 6 (24 Mar 1966): 14.
GEN. BIB.: Hunt, *52nd St.*; Kernfeld, *NGJ*, by Jeff Potter.

JOHNSON, ORVILLE WARREN (b. 4 Feb 1948. St. Paul, Minnesota).
Assistant principal percussionist with the San Antonio Symphony since 1971,
Warren Johnson attended the University of Minnesota (1967) and San Antonio
(TX) College (1981), and he studied with Conway C. Villars of the St. Paul
Opera (1958–64), Elliot Fine of the Minnesota Orchestra (1967), and *Lawrence
White of the Boston Symphony and New England Conservatory (1968).   A
charter member of the San Antonio Brass, he has performed as percussionist
and/or soloist with the Minneapolis Civic (1962–73), St. Paul Chamber, Min-
neapolis Pops (1967–73), Manhattan Pops (1968), St. Paul Civic (1962–66),
and Minnesota Orchestras, as well as, the Florida Symphony (principal,
1966–71), St. Paul Opera (1968–74), and Les Grande Ballet Canadian (1967).
As a composer and pedagogue, he has several compositions published by
Southern Music Company, and he served on the faculty of San Antonio College
(1972–89), where he founded and directed the San Antonio College Colonial
Fife and Drum Corps.

SELECTED BIBLIOGRAPHY

Johnson, Warren. "Techniques of Orchestral Cymbal Playing." *PN* XII, 4 (1974). Information supplied by the subject, 1998.

JOHNSON, WALTER (b. 18 Feb 1904, New York, New York; d. 26 Apr 1977, New York, New York). A drumset artist whose innovative hi-hat cymbal technique helped usher in 1930s swing drumming style, Walter Johnson began his career in 1924 with Freddy Johnson; he then performed and/or recorded with Fletcher Henderson (1929–34), Lucky Millinder (1938–39), Claude Hopkins (1939), and Tab Smith (1944–54), among others.

SELECTED DISCOGRAPHY

Masters of Jazz, Media 7: *Anthology of Jazz Drumming,* vols. 1–2 (1904–35), 1997.
GEN. BIB.: Kernfeld, *NGJ,* by T. Dennis Brown.

JOHNSTON, BEVERLY JEAN (b. 4 Jun 1957, Lachine, Quebec, Canada). Percussionist Beverly Johnston earned a bachelor's degree (1980) as the first female graduate in percussion from the University of Toronto, where she studied with *Russell Hartenberger. Also a student of Lanny Levine (Vanier College, 1974–76), she was featured at the Percussive Arts Society International Convention (1988), with the Manitoba and Canadian Chamber Ensembles, and at Expo '90 (Osaka, Japan). She has commissioned several works and premiered Maki Ishii's *Afro-Concerto* (Esprit Orchestra, 1993) and Michael Colgrass' *Te Tuma Te Papa* (Guelph Spring Festival, 1994). A charter member of the Toronto Percussion Ensemble (1980), Johnston has performed with the National Ballet of Canada (1979–), the New Music Concerts, the Canadian Opera Company Orchestra (1986–), and the ensemble Array (1983).

SELECTED DISCOGRAPHY

Artifact ART-002: *Beating,* 1988.
CBC Musica Viva MVCD-1033: *Marimbach,* 1987.
Centredisques CMC-2786: *Impact,* 1986.
Centredisques CMC-CD-3288: *The Everlasting Voices* (Toronto Percussion Ensemble), 1988.
RCI 569: *Hand—Soliloquy/Gougeon—Prophétie,* 1984.

SELECTED BIBLIOGRAPHY

Kallmann, Helmut, and Gilles Potvin, eds. *Encyclopedia of Music in Canada,* 2nd ed. Toronto: University of Toronto Press, 1992.

JONAK, ANTON (b. Austria). Timpanist with the Aachen (Germany) Orchestra, Anton Jonak was employed by the Berlin Opera Orchestra in 1940 upon Herbert von Karajan's recommendation. Following his brief enlistment in the German military in 1945, Jonak filled the timpani position temporarily after the death of Kurt Ulrich before moving to Vienna in 1946. He performed there with the Viennese Folk Opera.
GEN. BIB.: Avgerinos, *KB.*

JONES [KAUFMAN], ELAYNE (b. 30 Jan 1928, New York, New York). A 1949 graduate of the Juilliard School, where she studied with *Saul Goodman and *Morris Goldenberg, timpanist Elayne Jones studied piano with her mother from age 6, then later attended both New York's Music and Art High School and Boston's Tanglewood Summer Institute (1949). Her performance associations include several Broadway productions (*Greenwillow*, 1960; *Carnival*, 1961; *On A Clear Day You Can See Forever*, 1965; and *Purlie*, 1970), the National Orchestra Association, New York City Ballet (1949–52) and Opera (1949–61) Orchestras, American Symphony Orchestra (1962–72), Brooklyn Philharmonic (1969–71), Westchester (NY) Philharmonic (1969–72), San Francisco Symphony and Opera Orchestra (1972–74), New York Philharmonic, and the Metropolitan Opera Orchestra, among many others. A founding member (1965) and later president of New York's Symphony of the New World, she has appeared several times in televised music programs in California. A veteran of more than 300 lecture-demonstrations on percussion, she has held teaching posts at the Metropolitan Music School (NY), Bronx Community College, Westchester Conservatory, and San Francisco Conservatory. Jones was the subject of the 1965 public television program *A Day in the Life of a Musician* and received the "Distinguished Service Award" from the National Association of Negro Musicians (1993).

SELECTED BIBLIOGRAPHY

Field, Sidney. "Only Human: Drums Are Her Beat." *New York Daily News* (Wednesday, 1 Dec 1965).
Handy, D. Antoinette. *Black Women in American Bands and Orchestras*, 2nd ed. Lanham, MD: Scarecrow Press, Inc., 1998.
Harvey, Duston. "People in Percussion—Elayne Jones: Tympanist." *PN* XII, 1 (Fall 1973): 17.
Zakariasen, Bill. "Frisco Rumblings." *New York Daily News* (9 Sep 1975).
GEN. BIB.: Larrick, *BET-CP*; Southern, *BDA-AAM.*

JONES, ELVIN RAY (b. 9 Sep 1927, Pontiac, Michigan). A 1991 inductee into the Percussive Arts Society Hall of Fame and brother of Hank and Thad, Elvin Jones was raised in a musical family; after serving in the U.S. Army Band (1946–49), he returned to the Michigan jazz scene, working (1949–1950s) with

Billy Mitchell, Donald Byrd, Thad Jones, Pepper Adams, Kenny Burrell, and Barry Harris. A move to New York City in 1956 paired him on recording dates and/or performances with Bud Powell, Harry "Sweets" Edison, J. J. Johnson, Miles Davis, Tyree Glenn, Donald Byrd, Sonny Rollins, and others. Jones' interaction within the John Coltrane Quartet (1960–65) established his reputation and the drumset's validity worldwide as an equal musical voice—not just accompaniment. Touring the United States, Europe, the Orient, and South America (sponsored by the U.S. State Department, 1973/1975), he leads his own group, Jazz Machine (1978–present) and has appeared on television and in films, including *Zachariah* (Playhouse/Fox Video 8023, 1970). Jones was voted into *Modern Drummer* magazine's Reader's Poll Hall of Fame in 1995.

SELECTED DISCOGRAPHY

Atlantic: *African Exchange Student* (Kenny Garrett), 1990.
Atlantic 1361-2: *My Favorite Things* (John Coltrane), 1960.
Atlantic 1373: *Olé* (John Coltrane), 1989.
Atlantic 1382-2: *Coltrane Plays the Blues*, 1960.
Atlantic 1419-2: *Coltrane's Sound*, 1960.
Atlantic 1428: *Together!* (Philly Joe Jones), 1964.
Blue Note 84369: *Genesis*, 1971.
Blue Note 7243 8 32094/TOCJ-4085: *Ready for Freddie* (Freddie Hubbard), 1961.
Blue Note B21Y 84173: *Night Dreamer* (Wayne Shorter), 1964.
Blue Note B21Y-46512: *The Real McCoy* (McCoy Tyner), 1967.
Blue Note B21Y-46517/46518: *A Night at the Village Vanguard,* vols. 1–2 (Sonny Rollins), 1957.
Blue Note B21Y-84189: *Inner Urge* (McCoy Tyner), 1964.
Blue Note B21Y46509: *Speak No Evil* (Wayne Shorter), 1964.
Blue Note BN-LA015-62/CDP7 84447/8: *Live at the Lighthouse*, 1972.
Blue Note BST 84221: *Unity* (Larry Young), 1965.
Blue Note CDP 7243 8 28981 2 2: *Judgement* (Andrew Hill), 1964.
Blue Note CDP 724383358021: *Solid* (Grant Green), 1964.
Blue Note CJ28-5105: *JuJu* (Wayne Shorter), 1964.
Blue Note CP32-5212/CDP 724382915621: *In 'n Out* (Joe Henderson), 1964.
Blue Note LA 110-F: *Mr. Jones*, 1972.
Blue Note LA-506 H2: *The Prime Element*, 1973.
Blue Note LP 1546: *Magnificent* (Thad Jones), 1957.
Blue Note 84305: *The Ultimate*, 1968.
Columbia CK 52975: *Stan Getz—The Peacocks*, 1977/1994.
Columbia CL-1486: *Silver Vibes* (Lionel Hampton), 1960.
DIW 305 CD: *Overseas* (Tommy Flanagan), 1957.
Enja-7095: *Going Home* (Jazz Machine), 1993.
Everest FS 270: *The Jones Boys—Quincy, Thad, Jimmy, Jo, Eddie, Elvin,* 1957/1973.
FSRCD 143: *Live at Cafe Bohemia* (J. J. Johnson), 1957.
Impulse A 9160: *Heavy Sounds*, 1974/1990.
Impulse A 9121/MCAD33120: *East Broadway Rundown* (Sonny Rollins), 1965.
Impulse A-5O/MCA-29015: *Coltrane "Live" at Birdland*, 1963/1997.

Impulse A-42: *Impressions* (John Coltrane), 1961.
Impulse IMPD-250: *Illumination!* 1963/1998.
Impulse MCAD-5660: *A Love Supreme* (John Coltrane), 1964/1995.
MCA-24157: *The Early Trios* (McCoy Tyner), 1978.
MCA-29012/Impulse-GRP GRD-156: *Ballads* (John Coltrane), 1961/1995.
MCA-29016/Impulse IMPD-200: *Crescent* (John Coltrane), 1964/1996.
MCA-29018/Impulse IMPD-214: *John Coltrane Quartet Plays*, 1965/1997.
MCAD 39136: *Live at the Village Vanguard* (John Coltrane), 1961.
Mosaic MD6-137: *The Complete Blue Note Recordings of Larry Young*, 1964/1991.
OJC CD-043-2: *Blue Moods* (Miles Davis), 1955.
Palo Alto PA-8039: *Brother John*, 1982/1984.
Palo Alto PA 8016: *Earth Jones*, 1982.
Prestige OJC CD-398-2: *Farmer's Market* (Art Farmer), 1956.
Rhino Atlantic Jazz R2 71984: *John Coltrane—The Heavyweight Champion; The Complete Atlantic Recordings*, 1995.
Riverside 409/OJC 259: *Elvin*, 1961.
Riverside/OJC CD 031-2: *10 to 4 at the 5 Spot* (Pepper Adams), 1958.
Roulette CDP 724382864127: *Gretsch Drum Night at Birdland*, 1960.
Savoy CD SV-0188: *Swing Not Spring* (Thad Jones and Billy Mitchell), 1948.
Sony 32 DP 594/SRCS 7130: *Dial J. J. 5* (J. J. Johnson), 1957.
Sony 67397: *Miles Davis and Gil Evans—The Complete Columbia Studio Recordings*, 1996.
Telarc Jazz 83385: *Passion Dance* (Roseanna Vitro), 1996.
Verve 845 148-2: *Jazz Club—Drums*, 1958/1991.
Verve 833802-2: *Stan Getz and Bill Evans*, 1964.
Verve 314 527 467-2: *After the Rain* (John McLaughlin), 1996.
Verve V6-8399: *Lee Konitz*, 1961.
Verve V6-8555: *Gil Evans*, 1964.

SELECTED VIDEOGRAPHY

BMG Music Video 80067: *The World According to John Coltrane*, 1993.
DCI VH0249: *Legends of Jazz Drumming, Pt. 2, 1950–70*, 1996.
Rhapsody Films 9014/25411: *Different Drummer—Elvin Jones*, 1979.
Video Artists International 69035: *The Coltrane Legacy* (John Coltrane), 1985.
View Video Jazz Series 1346: *Elvin Jones Jazz Machine*, 1991.

SELECTED BIBLIOGRAPHY

Bravos, Anthony G. "An Interview with Elvin Jones." *PN* XXI, 2 (January 1983): 40–45.
DeMichael, Don. "The Sixth Man." *DB* XXX (28 Mar 1963): 16–17.
Griffith, Mark. "Elvin Jones, Part One: 1948–1964." *MD* XX, 10 (October 1996): 144–149.
Griffith, Mark. "Elvin Jones, Part Two: Coltrane and Beyond." *MD* XX, 11 (November 1996): 128–132.
Hart, Howard. "Elvin Jones: A Different Drummer." *DB* XXXVI, 6 (20 Mar 1969): 20–21.

Hennessey, Mike. "The Emancipation of Elvin Jones." *DB* XXXIII, 6 (24 Mar 1966): 23–25.

Kettle, Rupert. "RE: Elvin Jones." *DB* XXXIII, 16 (11 Aug 1966): 17–19.

Mahoney, Mark. "Great Rhythm Sections in Jazz." *MD* XXII, 12 (December 1998): 158–161.

Shultz, Thomas. "A History of Jazz Drumming." *Percussionist* XVI, 3 (Spring/Summer 1979): 126.

GEN. BIB.: Hunt, *52nd St.*; Kernfeld, *NGJ*, by Olly Wilson; Southern, *BDA-AAM*; Spagnardi, *GJD.*

JONES, HAROLD (b. 27 Feb 1940, Richmond, Indiana). Active in Chicago and Los Angeles, Harold Jones was Count Basie's drummer (1967–72), worked with Benny Carter, and accompanied Sarah Vaughn for 12 years during the 1980s. A Los Angeles recording studio drummer in the 1990s, he is now based in San Francisco and backs Natalie Cole.

SELECTED DISCOGRAPHY

Argo LP 766: *Playin' for Keeps* (Bunky Green), 1966.
Blue Note LA251-G: *Live at Montreux* (Marlena Shaw), 1973.
Discovery DS 892: *Summer Strut* (Andy Simpkins), 1983.
Dot 25902: *Straight Ahead* (Count Basie), 1968.
PL 2308216: *Benny Carter—Alive and Well in Japan*, 1977.
GEN. BIB.: Hunt, *52nd St.*

JONES, JONATHAN DAVID SAMUEL "JO" "PAPA JO" (b. 7 Oct 1911, Chicago, Illinois; d. 3 Sep 1985, New York, New York). A 1990 inductee into the Percussive Arts Society Hall of Fame, Jo Jones grew up in Alabama, where he sang and danced, played trumpet, sax, piano, vibraphone, and timpani, and was reputedly a good boxer and checker player. He suffered serious full-body burns as a child, convalescing for over a year. His aunt bought him a snare drum after they had heard the Ringling Brothers Circus band, and by age 11 Jones was touring with carnivals and shows as a singer-dancer-drummer-entertainer. He never studied drums formally but cited the influence of Wilson Driver, a theater drummer in Birmingham, and *Walter Johnson of the Fletcher Henderson Orchestra. The popularity of radio, recordings, and "talkies" spelled the demise of the traveling minstrel, so he embraced dance bands and played piano and vibraphone, finally settling on drums because they offered better re-muneration.

From the late 1920s to 1934, Jones played with Ted Adams, Harold Brown's Brownskin Syncopators, Walter Page, Lloyd Hunter's Serenaders (with whom he made his recording debut in Omaha, 1931), and the Bennie Moten Ensemble, using Omaha as his base of operations. He performed briefly with Count Basie (1934), Tommy Douglas (with whom he played piano and vibes), and other bands in Minneapolis and St. Louis, before joining Basie again in Kansas City

(1936–48, excluding an occasional hiatus with others, e.g., the Jeter-Pillars Orchestra, 1936), where he was an integral part of the "All-American Rhythm Section" with Basie, Freddie Green, and Walter Page. *Shadow Wilson replaced Jones in Basie's band when Jones was an infantryman in the U.S. Army at Ft. McClellan, Alabama (September 1944–February 1946).

After his discharge he played with Illinois Jacquet (1948–50), Lester Young (1950), Joe Bushkin (1952–53), Ella Fitzgerald and Oscar Peterson (Euopean tour, 1957), and traveled internationally with "Jazz at the Philharmonic" (1947/1951). Leading his own groups in New York (1957–60), Jones played and recorded with a variety of musicians during the 1960s–70s, including Teddy Wilson, Benny Carter, Claude Hopkins, Milt Buckner, and Benny Goodman. He appeared on television and film [e.g., *The Unsuspected* (1947) and *Born to Swing* (1973)] and was awarded an "American Jazz Masters" Fellowship from the National Endowment for the Arts in 1985. Jones employed a smaller bass drum, dispelled with the previously popular accessory percussion instruments, was a master of brush technique, and elevated the role of the hi-hat to one of rhythmic prominence rather than simple, metronomic "back-beats."

SELECTED DISCOGRAPHY

Blue Note 56586: *Orgy in Rhythm*, vols. 1–2 (Art Blakey), 1957.
Classics Records 503/504/513/533/563/623: *The Chronological Count Basie*, 1936–41.
Columbia P3M 5869: *Billie Holiday, The Golden Years*, 1962.
Columbia CK 40608/40835/44150: *The Essential Count Basie*, vols. 1–3, 1987–88.
Columbia PC 11891: *Smithsonian Collection of Classic Jazz* ("Doggin' Around").
Columbia/Contemporary Master Series C2 34849: *The Lester Young Story*, vols. 1–5, 1980.
Denon MJ 7047: *Our Man Papa Jo*, 1983.
Everest 1099: *Vamp 'Til Ready*, 1960.
Everest FS 270: *The Jones Boys—Quincy, Thad, Jimmy, Jo, Eddie, Elvin*, 1957/1973.
Everest FSR-CD-40: *Jo Jones Trio*, 1958.
French CBS: *The Complete Count Basie*, vols. 1–10/11–20, 1936–41/1941–51.
Fresh Sound Records FSR CD-40: *The Jo Jones Trio*, 1959.
Fresh Sound Records FSR CD-88/Jazztone J-1201: *Timeless Jazz* (Coleman Hawkins), 1959.
Fresh Sound Records FSR CD-144: *Jo Jones Sextet*, 1960.
Fresh Sound Records FSR CD-204/Everest 1110: *Percussion and Bass* (with Milt Hinton), 1960.
GRP 3 611: *The Complete Decca Recordings* (Count Basie), 1937–39.
Jazz Odyssey 008: *The Drums*, 1973 (out-of-print).
Jazz Odyssey JO-006: *The Lion and the Tiger* (Willie "The Lion" Smith), 1974.
Masters of Jazz, Media 7: *Anthology of Jazz Drumming*, vols. 1–3, 1904–38.
Mercury 830 920 2: *The Complete Lester Young on Keynote*, 1944.
Mosaic MR6-109: *Vic Dickenson Quartet*, 1952.
Pablo 2310-799: *The Main Man*, 1976.

Pablo PACD 2405 429: *The Tatum Group Masterpieces,* vol. 6 (Art Tatum), 1956.
Prestige OJC CD-014-2: *All-Star Sessions with Sonny Stitt* (Gene Ammons), 1950.
Riverside OJCCD 0272: *The Hawk Flies High* (Coleman Hawkins), 1957.
Roost LP 2204: *Sonny Stitt Plays Quincy Jones,* 1955.
Signature AK-40950: *The Big Three: Coleman Hawkins, Ben Webster, Lester Young,* 1943.
Vanguard VSD 103/104: *The Essential Buck Clayton,* 1977.
Vanguard CD 101/2-2: *The Essential Jo Jones* [aka The Jo Jones Special] [both out-of-print], 1977
Verve MG V-8272: *The Impeccable Teddy Wilson,* 1969.
Verve 2V6S-8822: *Johnny Hodges and His Orchestra,* 1959.
Verve 823 637-2: *Back To Back—Duke Ellington & Johnny Hodges Play the Blues,* 1959.
Verve 825 672-2: *Lester Young Meets the Jazz Giants,* 1956.
Verve 831 270-2: *Prez and Teddy* (Lester Young and Teddy Wilson), 1956.
Verve 840 815-2: *Count Basie at Newport,* 1957.
Verve MGV1006: *Meade Lux Lewis Trio,* 1955.
Verve MGV2026: *Ben Webster Quartet,* 1954.
Verve MGV2069: *Woody Herman,* 1957.
Verve MGV2073: *Teddy Wilson Trio,* 1956.
Verve MGV2081: *Blossom Dearie,* 1957.
Verve MGV8075: *Flip Phillips Quintet,* 1951.
Verve MGV8089: *Roy Eldridge Quintet,* 1953.
Verve MGV8146: *Jazz Giants* (Lester Young), 1956.
Verve MGVS6022: *Ella Fitzgerald/Billie Holiday at Newport,* 1957.
Verve VE2-2516: *Lester Young Quartet,* 1951.
Zeta EPM ZET 704: *Sonny Rollins/Thad Jones,* 1956.

SELECTED VIDEOGRAPHY

A*Vision Entertainment 50240-3: *Jazzmasters Vintage Collection,* vols. 1–2 (1958–1961), 1990.
DCI VH0248: *Legends of Jazz Drumming, Pt. 1, 1920–50,* 1996.
Kino International/Rhapsody Films: *Born to Swing—the Count Basie Alumni,* 1989.
Music Video Distributors: *Count Basie and Friends Plus Louis Jordan,* 1986.
Rhapsody Films: *Jazz Is Our Religion,* 1972.
Warner Brothers Film: *Jammin' the Blues,* 1944.

SELECTED BIBLIOGRAPHY

Hentoff, Nat. "Jazz Always Has to Evolve, Says Jo Jones." *DB* XVIII, 21 (19 Oct 1951).
Mahoney, Mark. "Great Rhythm Sections in Jazz." *MD* XXII, 12 (December 1998): 158–161.
Morgenstern, Dan. "Jo Jones: Taking Care of Business." *DB* XXXII, 7 (25 Mar 1965): 15.
Shultz, Thomas. "A History of Jazz Drumming." *Percussionist* XVI, 3 (Spring/Summer 1979): 121–122.

Stern, C. "Papa Jo." *MD* VIII (January 1984): 8–13.
GEN. BIB.: Hunt, *52nd St.*; Korall, *DM*; Southern, *BDA-AAM*; Spagnardi, *GJD*.

JONES, JOSEPH RUDOLPH "PHILLY JOE" (b. 15 Jul 1923, Philadelphia, Pennsylvania; d. 30 Aug 1985, Philadelphia, Pennsylvania). Drumset artist Philly Joe Jones studied piano with his mother, played drums locally while in high school, and then served in the U.S. Army (1941), returning to Philadelphia to drive a streetcar. While there he appeared with John Coltrane, Fats Navarro, Ben Webster, the Heath Brothers, and Dizzy Gillespie; he then moved to New York in 1947 and 1952 (with a three-year hiatus in Washington, D.C., 1949–52). In New York he worked with Charlie Parker (1947), Tadd Dameron (1953), Tony Scott, and Bill Evans (1958/1967/1976). Jones studied with Cozy Cole for three years, subbed for *Buddy Rich at the Apollo Theater (1951, for the dance and entertainment acts while Buddy played the swing tunes), and made his fame with Miles Davis (1952/1955–58). At one time a staff drummer for Prestige Records, he recorded with his own groups (1958).

During 1967–72 Jones performed in England and Europe and taught in France with *Kenny Clarke. He was an active performer for television, radio, and film scores and also worked with "Slide" Hampton, the Clarke-Boland Orchestra, and the Franz Black Orchestra. Forming a quintet in Philadelphia (1972), he led the jazz-rock group Le Gran Prix in 1975.

SELECTED DISCOGRAPHY

Atlantic 1340: *Philly Joe's Beat*, 1960.
Atlantic 1428: *Together!* (Elvin Jones), 1964.
Blue Note B21Y-84149: *No Room for Squares* (Hank Mobley), 1963.
Blue Note BLP 1577: *Blue Train* (John Coltrane), 1957.
Blue Note BLP 4001/BST-84001: *Newk's Time* (Sonny Rollins), 1957.
Blue Note BLP 4051: *Jackie's Bag*, 1958.
Blue Note CDP 7243 8 28978 2 8: *Whistle Stop* (Kenny Dorham), 1961.
Columbia CK 40610: *'Round about Midnight* (Miles Davis), 1956.
Columbia CK 40647: *Porgy and Bess* (Miles Davis), 1958.
Columbia CK 40837: *Milestones* (Miles Davis), 1958.
Columbia Legacy CK 64936: *Meet Betty Carter and Ray Bryant*, 1955/1996.
Columbia PC-32470: *Jazz at the Plaza* (Miles Davis), 1973.
Contemporary OJC CD 338-2: *Art Pepper Meets the Rhythm Section*, 1957.
Epic SN 6031: *Lester Young Memorial Album*, 1959.
Landmark Records LLP-501: *Good Bait* (Bobby Hutcherson), 1985.
Milestone 4421: *Bill Evans—The Secret Sessions*, 1966–75.
Milestone 47001: *Cannonball Adderley and Eight Giants*, 1973.
Milestone M 47048: *Blues on Down* (Benny Golson), 1978.
Milestone M-47013: *Wes Montgomery and Friends*, 1973.
New Jazz 8290/Prestige: *Steeplechase* (Jackie McLean), 1969.
OJC CD-068-2: *Everybody Digs Bill Evans*, 1958.
OJC CD-143-2: *The Magic Touch* (Tadd Dameron), 1962.

Prestige OJC CD 124-2: *Tenor Madness* (Sonny Rollins), 1956.
Prestige PR 24001: *Miles Davis*, 1972.
Prestige 7094: *Cookin'* (Miles Davis), 1984.
Prestige 7129: *Relaxin'* (Miles Davis), 1956/1985.
Prestige 7166: *Workin'* (Miles Davis), 1956/1987.
Prestige 7200: *Steamin'* (Miles Davis), 1956/1989.
Riverside: *Homecoming* (Elmo Hope Sextet), 1961.
Riverside OJC CD 179-2: *Drums around the World*, 1959.
Riverside OJC CD 230-2: *Blues for Dracula*, 1958.
Riverside RLP 12-224: *Kenny Drew Trio*, 1956/1985.
Riverside RLP 1120 (OJC 303): *Chet Baker—It Could Happen to You*, 1958.
Roulette CDP 724382864127: *Gretsch Drum Night at Birdland*, 1960.
Sony 67397: *Miles Davis and Gil Evans—The Complete Columbia Studio Recordings*, 1996.
Timeless Records CDSJP 210: *Four Seasons* (Bobby Hutcherson), 1985.
Verve VE2-2545: *Bill Evans Trio*, 1967.

SELECTED VIDEOGRAPHY

DCI VH0249: *Legends of Jazz Drumming, Pt. 2, 1950–70*, 1996.

SELECTED BIBLIOGRAPHY

Davis, Sandy. "Philly Joe Jones: Straight Ahead and Rarin' To Go." *DB* XLIII (9 Sep 1976): 18–21.
Gleason, Ralph J. "The Forming of Philly Joe." *DB* XXVII, 5 (3 Mar 1960): 28–29.
Griffith, Mark. "Artist on Track: Philly Joe Jones." *MD* XIX, 7 (July 1995): 136–141.
Jones, Philly Joe. *Brush Artistry*. London: Premier Drum Co., 1975.
Mahoney, Mark. "Great Rhythm Sections in Jazz." *MD* XXII, 12 (December 1998): 158–161.
"Philly Joe Jones: Dracula Returns." *DB* XXVI, 5 (5 Mar 1959): 22.
Shultz, Thomas. "A History of Jazz Drumming." *Percussionist* XVI, 3 (Spring/Summer 1979): 126.
Stone, R. "The Final Appearances of Philly Joe Jones in Washington, D.C., 1985." Research paper presented at IAJE Conference, 1986. [Available from IAJE, *Jazz Research Papers*, vol. 6, compiled by Dr. Charles T. Brown and Dr. Larry Fisher.]
GEN. BIB.: Hunt, *52nd St.*; Spagnardi, *GJD*.

JONES, LINDLEY ARMSTRONG "SPIKE" (b. 14 Dec 1911, Calipatria/Long Beach, California; d. 1 May 1965, Los Angeles, California). Musical parodist and satirist, bandleader and drummer, Spike Jones started drums at age 11, studying with O. F. Rominger, who performed with Herbert L. Clarke's Long Beach Municipal Band. He played in local groups, by 1937 becoming a Hollywood studio drummer working with the Victor Young Concert Orchestra. In the late 1930s and early 1940s he began "burlesqueing" songs with horns, cowbells, doorbells, live goats bleating in key, and so on, which gave birth to the group Spike Jones and His City Slickers (est. 1942). Their smash hit "Der Fuehrer's Face" was heard on a Walt Disney satirical cartoon, and in 1947 he toured with his band in a "Musical Depreciation Revue." A master of sound effects who was called the "King of Corn," Jones made legendary recordings from the late 1940s and early 1950s, including "Chloe," "You Always Hurt the One You Love," "Cocktails for Two," "The Glow-Worm," and "All I Want for Christmas Is My Two Front Teeth." Between the 1950s and 1960s he appeared on television and in films, and he also made Dixieland jazz recordings.

SELECTED DISCOGRAPHY

Mind's Eye: *Spike Jones—Unforgettable Songs You'd Like to Forget* (complete radio shows), 1986.
Verve V6-8564: *Spike Jones*, 1956.
Verve MGV2065: *Freddy Morgan with Spike Jones Orchestra*, 1957.
Verve MGV2066: *The Polka Dots with Spike Jones Orchestra*, 1957.
Verve MGV4005: *Spike Jones*, 1957.

SELECTED VIDEOGRAPHY

Paramount Home Video: *The Best of Spike Jones* (1952–57), 1988.
Paramount Home Video: *Spike Jones—A Musical Wreck-We-Um*, 1957.
Storyville Films/Music Video Distributors: *The Spike Jones Story*, 1988.

SELECTED BIBLIOGRAPHY

"Closing Chord—Spike Jones." *IM* LXIII, 12 (June 1965): 29.
Mirtle, Jack, compiler. *Thank You Music Lovers: A Bio-Discography of Spike Jones and His City Slickers, 1941–65.* Westport, CT: Greenwood Press, 1986.
Young, J. R. *Spike Jones off the Record—The Man Who Murdered Music.* Beverly Hills, CA: Past Times Publishing, 1994 [rev. ed. of *Spike Jones and His City Slickers* (Beverly Hills, CA: Disharmony Books, 1984), includes discography and videography].
GEN. BIB.: Cook, *LDT*, p. 177 (photo); Hitchcock and Sadie, *NGA*, by Deane L. Root.

K

KAHN, NORMAN "TINY" (b. ca. 1923, New York, New York; d. 19 Aug 1953). Nicknamed "Big Veal Catlett" after *Sid Catlett, drumset artist Tiny Kahn started drums at age 15, played vibraphone, and was also a composer-arranger. He flourished in New York City, where he performed and/or recorded on CBS radio and with Red Rodney (1947), Lester Young and Boyd Raeburn (1948), Charlie Barnet and Chubby Jackson (1949), Stan Getz (1951), among others.

SELECTED DISCOGRAPHY

Blue Note LA456-H2: *Lester Young*, 1947.
Capitol B21Y 96052/Roost 407/411/420: *Jazz at Storyville* (Stan Getz), 1951.
Columbia CK 40972: *The Bebop Era* (Chubby Jackson), 1949.
Mercury 830 922-2: *Early Bebop* (Red Rodney), 1947.
Savoy SV-0187: *Cohn's Tones* (Al Cohn), 1950.
Verve MGV8152: *The Bill Harris Herd*, 1952.

SELECTED BIBLIOGRAPHY

Harris, Pat. "Drummers Should Be Musicians, Too: Tiny Kahn." *DB* XVII, 7 (7 Apr 1950): 3.
GEN. BIB.: Hunt, *52nd St.*; Spagnardi, *GJD.*

KAPTAIN, LAURENCE D. "LARRY" (b. 1 Sep 1952, Elgin, Illinois). Marimbist, percussionist, and cimbalom artist, Larry Kaptain studied initially with *James Lane, *Duane Thamm, George McNabney, and G. Allan O'Connor. He received the bachelor's degree (1974) from Ball State University, master's degree (1975) from the University of Miami, and the doctor of musical arts degree (1987) from the University of Michigan. His other teachers include Erwin C. Mueller, *Fred Wickstrom, *Michael Udow, *Charles Owen, and *Vida Chenoweth. He appeared with the Colorado Philharmonic Repertoire Orchestra and Fort Wayne Philharmonic and was featured with the New York, Montreal, San Antonio, Boston, Rochester, St. Louis, Minnesota, Milwaukee, Philadelphia, Kansas City, and Chicago Symphonies, and the Detroit Contemporary Chamber Players and at the Aspen and Tanglewood Festivals. Kaptain recorded with the Orpheus Chamber Ensemble and has served on the faculties of the University of Missouri at Kansas City (UMKC) Conservatory of Music and Stephen F. Austin University (TX), and as a visiting professor at the University of Michigan, Oberlin Conservatory, and University of Wisconsin at Madison. In 1994 he was cited for excellence in teaching at UMKC and was named a Trustee Faculty Fellow in 1996.

A former Fulbright Scholar in Chiapas, Mexico, Kaptain has been the only foreigner ever invited to judge (three times) at the annual state marimba competition there. In 1996 he received a grant from the joint U.S.–Mexico Fund for Culture to construct a "virtual museum" of the Mexican marimba on the Internet's World Wide Web. Marimba Yajalón, his ensemble-in-residence (est. 1988) at UMKC, performs Central American music on authentic instruments (four players on a single 5.5-octave marimba). They have toured and participated in International Festivals of the Marimba (1991–95) in Mexico and premiered James Mobberley's *Concerto for Chiapan Marimba and Symphony Orchestra* with the Kansas City Symphony (1997).

Kaptain was featured as solo percussionist on George Burt's score to the Robert Altman film *Secret Honor* (1984); he also recorded for the documentary film *Dancing Hands* (1983), which was scored by *Michael Udow. In addition to publishing several of his own arrangements of Guatemalan and Mexican marimba selections, he is a contributing author to the forthcoming texts *Musical Life in Latin America: A Historical Handbook* (Greenwood Press) and *Composers in Latin America: A Biographical Dictionary* (Greenwood Press).

SELECTED DISCOGRAPHY

Deutsche Grammophon: *Stravinsky—Ragtime* (Orpheus Chamber Ensemble), 1997.

Deutsche Grammophon: *Stockhausen—Samstag aus Licht* (La Scala Opera) (solo percussion, Act III), 1989.

Heart of Wood Project HWP 001: *HAUPANGO* (Marimba Yajalón), 1991.

Heart of Wood Project HWP 002CD: *¡Chiapas!* (Marimba Yajalón), 1994.

Heart of Wood Project HWP 003CD: *Echoes of Chiapas* (Marimba Yajalón), 1997.

London/Decca 443 444-2: Suite from *Kodaly—Hary Janos* (Chicago Symphony) (solo cimbalom), 1994.

Teldec 4509-94548-2: *Stravinsky—Renard, Ragtime* (St. Paul Chamber Orchestra), 1996.

SELECTED BIBLIOGRAPHY

Beck, John, ed. *The Encylopedia of Percussion.* New York: Garland Publications, 1994. S.v. "The Marimba in Mexico and Related Areas," by Larry Kaptain.

Chamorro, Arturo. *The Percussion Instruments of Mexico,* translated by Laurence Kaptain. Everett, PA: Honeyrock, in progress.

Gipson, Richard. "An Interview with Laurence Kaptain." *PN* XXIII, 2 (January 1985): 20–21.

Kaptain, Larry. "Heart of Wood Song." *Mexico Journal* III, 25 (1989): 25–26.

Kaptain, Larry. "Interview with Zeferino Nandayapa." *PN* XXVIII, 2 (Winter 1990): 48–50.

Kaptain, Larry. *The Wood That Sings: The Marimba in Chiapas, Mexico.* Everett, PA: Honey Rock Publications, 1992. [His Spanish translation of this text is published in Mexico.]

Kaptain, Laurence. "The Hungarian Cimbalom." *PN* XXVIII, 5 (August 1990): 8–14.

Kaptain, Laurence D. "Chiapas and Its Unusual Marimba Tradition." *PN* XXVI, 5 (September 1988): 28–31.

KASICA, JOHN (b. Clifton, New Jersey). A graduate of the Juilliard School (bachelor's), where he studied with *Saul Goodman and *Elden "Buster" Bailey, John Kasica has accrued more than 75 solo appearances with major U.S. orchestras. He has performed as mallet specialist and percussionist with the St. Louis Symphony (since 1971) and Pops Orchestra, St. Louis Symphony Percussion Quartet, the New York Philharmonic, Metropolitan Opera, Da Camera (Houston), New York City Opera and Ballet, Erick Hawkins Modern Dance Company, Summit Brass, Musica Aeterna (New York), Suzuki and Friends (Indianapolis), Juilliard Ensemble, Young Audiences Percussion Quartet, and Chamber Music of St. Louis and at the Aspen, Spoleto (Italy), and Kerkrade (Netherlands) Music Festivals.

A former faculty member of the University of Missouri at St. Louis, St. Louis Community College, and Webster College, Kasica teaches at the St. Louis Conservatory of Music. After his solo debut with the St. Louis Symphony (Tircuit: *Percussion Concerto*), he premiered Tilo Medic's *Marimba Concerto* (North Carolina Symphony, 1983) and Minoru Miki's *Marimba Concerto* (St. Louis Symphony, 1986). Kasica toured the Far East with the St. Louis Symphony and in 1990 gave solo debuts at Carnegie Hall and the Kennedy Center.

SELECTED DISCOGRAPHY

New World NW318-2: *Works by Colgrass and Druckman* (St. Louis Symphony), 1983.

GEN. BIB.: Borland, *WWAMC.* Information supplied by the subject, 1996.

KASTNER, JEAN-GEORGES (b. 9 Mar 1810, Strasbourg, France; d. 19 Dec 1867, Paris, France). Jean-Georges Kastner was a timpanist, composer, and author of a timpani method book.

SELECTED BIBLIOGRAPHY

Hall, Charles. *A Nineteenth-Century Musical·Chronicle.* Westport, CT: Greenwood Press, 1989.
Kastner, Jean Georges. *Methode complète et raisonné de timbales.* Paris: Schlesinger, ca. 1845.
Powley, Harrison. "Some Observations on Jean Georges Kastner's *Methode complete et raisonnee de timbales* (ca. 1845)." *Percussionist* XVII, 2 (Winter 1980): 63–74.

KAY, CONNIE (b. Conrad Henry Kirnon, 27 Apr 1927, Tuckahoe, New York; d. 30 Nov 1994). Connie Kay studied piano and was a self-taught drummer who played early on with Miles Davis (1944–45), Cat Anderson (1945), Lester Young (1949/1952), Coleman Hawkins, Charlie Parker, and Stan Getz but would gain fame from his association with the Modern Jazz Quartet (MJQ)(1955–74/1981–94). Known for his sensitive additions of auxilliary percussion instruments to the MJQ's unique blend of classical and jazz styles, he played four years with Benny Goodman during the MJQ hiatus; he also recorded with Sonny Rollins, Randy Weston, Tommy Flanagan, Cannonball Adderley, *Red Norvo, and Herbie Hancock, among others.

SELECTED DISCOGRAPHY

Atlantic 30XD-1012: *Modern Jazz Quartet with Sonny Rollins,* 1958.
Atlantic 1231: *Fontessa* (Modern Jazz Quartet), 1956.
Atlantic 1269-2: *Plenty, Plenty Soul* (Milt Jackson), 1957.
Atlantic QD 1652: *The Modern Jazz Quartet—Blues on Bach,* 1974.
Atlantic SD 1368-2: *Bags and Trane* (Milt Jackson), 1959.
Audiophile AP-196: *Warren Vaché—First Time Out,* 1976.
Blue Note LA590-H2: *Milt Jackson,* 1958.
DCC Compact GZS 1090/OJC 105: *Know What I Mean?* (Cannonball Adderley), 1961/1995.
Prestige OJC CD-002-2: *Concorde* (Modern Jazz Quartet), 1955.
Progressive PCD-7026: *The Grand Appearance* (Scott Hamilton), 1990.
Riverside OJCCD-260-2: *Milt Jackson Sextet—Invitation,* 1979.
Verve 8311 272-2: *Stan Getz and J. J. Johnson,* 1957.
Verve MGV8161: *Lester Young Quintet,* 1953.
Verve MGV8131: *The Modern Jazz Society,* 1955.
Verve MGVS6028: *Coleman Hawkins and Roy Eldridge,* 1957.

SELECTED VIDEOGRAPHY

WCBS-New York/Camera Three: *The Modern Jazz Quartet,* 1973.

WCBS-New York/Camera Three: *Modern Jazz Quartet and the Juilliard String Quartet*, 1974.

SELECTED BIBLIOGRAPHY

Smith, Arnold Jay. "The Modern Jazz Quartet Turns 40." *JazzTimes* XXI, 8 (November 1991): 30.
Van Horn, Rick. "In Memoriam: Connie Kay." *MD* XIX, 4 (April 1995): 97.
Wilson, John S. "Connie Kay's Jazz World." *DB* XXVI, 5 (5 Mar 1959): 20–21.
GEN. BIB.: Hunt, *52nd St.*; Spagnardi, *GJD.*

KELTNER, JAMES "JIM." Los Angeles studio drumset artist Jim Keltner moved to California at the age of 13, studied briefly with *Forrest Clark, and has since collaborated with many of the greats of popular music, including Steely Dan, George Harrison, John Lennon, Neil Young, Bob Dylan, Eric Clapton, and his own group, Little Village, among many others.

SELECTED DISCOGRAPHY

A&M SP 3038: *The Class of 1971* (Jack Daughterty), 1971.
Mobile Fidelity UDCD 603: *Bring the Family* (John Hiatt), 1987.
Nonesuch 79479: *Gone, Just like a Train* (Bill Frisell), 1998.
Virgin 7243 8 41860 4 3: *Omnipop* (Sam Phillips), 1996.
Warner Bros./Reprise 4-26713: *Little Village* (Little Village), 1992.
Zebra ZD 44005-2: *Tribute to Jeff Porcaro* (Dave Garfield), 1997.

SELECTED BIBLIOGRAPHY

Flans, Robyn. "Jim Keltner: The Studio Legend Joins a Band." *MD* XV, 12 (December 1991): 20–25.

KIEFFER, WILLIAM D. "BILL" [ALSO KIEFER] (b. 1888, Lancaster, Pennsylvania). A theater percussionist who played for presidential inaugurations and funerals and appeared as xylophone soloist with the U.S. Marine Band (ca. 1915–35) in Washington, D.C., Bill Kieffer studied in Pennsylvania with Civil War drummers W. H. Potts and Dan Clemmens.

SELECTED DISCOGRAPHY

Victor 18817: *"The Yorktown Centennial March"* (U.S. Marine Band), ca. 1920s.
GEN. BIB.: Cook, *LDT*, p. 15, 40 (photo), 361; Strain, *XYLO.*

KLUGER, IRVING "IRV" (b. 9 Jul 1921, New York, New York). Bebop drumset artist and vibist Irv Kluger studied violin intially and later pursued percussion lessons at New York University, performing professionally at age 15. He worked with Georgie Auld (1942–43/1945), Boyd Raeburn (1945–47), Benny Goodman, Stan Kenton (1947–48), Artie Shaw (1949–50), Tex Beneke, and Woody Herman and played Broadway (1950–53), Hollywood, and Las Vegas.

SELECTED DISCOGRAPHY

Capitol WDX569: *The Kenton Era*, 1940–55.
RCA LPM1123: *Modern Brass*, 1955.
RCA LPM1320: *Jazz Goes Dancing* (Dave Pell), 1956.
Verve MGV2014: *Artie Shaw and His Gramercy Five*, 1954.
GEN. BIB.: Hitchcock and Sadie, *NGA*, by Jeff Potter; Korall, *DM.*

KNAPP, ROY CECIL (b. 26 Oct 1891, Waterloo, Iowa; d. 16 Jun 1979, Chicago, Illinois). Regarded as the "Dean of American Percussion Teachers" and inducted into the Percussive Arts Society Hall of Fame in 1972, Roy Knapp studied with his father, theater owner Jerry Knapp, with *William Faetkenheuer of the Minneapolis Symphony, and with Casey Kasolowsky of the Duluth Symphony. He worked as a theater drummer in Waterloo, Iowa, spent a year in New York, and then established himself in 1921 as a drummer, percussionist, and xylophone soloist in many of the large radio orchestras in Chicago. As a member of the staff orchestra at WLS from 1928 to 1960, he could be heard on shows such as the *National Barn Dance* and the *Don McNeil Breakfast Club*. Organizations for whom he played and recorded include the Minneapolis and Duluth Symphonies; WLS, NBC, and CBS broadcasting companies; and RCA and Wilding Recording Companies.

Knapp began his teaching career in 1921 at Chicago's Dixie Music House (est. 1902). After the store suffered fire damage (1937), he established the Roy C. Knapp School of Percussion at Kimball Hall (1938), which was fully accredited by 1946 to grant the bachelor's degree and the performer's certificate in voice, orchestral instruments, and piano. The school also offered percussion ensemble classes and lessons for elementary and secondary students. Legendary drummers who passed through Knapp's studio included *Gene Krupa, *Louie Bellson, *Dave Tough, *Warren "Baby" Dodds, and *Bobby Christian. Knapp retired from performing in 1960 and closed his school in 1966. From then until his death, he taught at Frank's Drum Shop, which was established in 1938 by Frank Gault, brother of George Gault, who was a partner in the original Dixie Music House. (Frank's was subsequently purchased by *Maurie Lishon in 1959.) Knapp's sons, Donald (Donald Roy, b. 26 Dec 1919, Minneapolis) and James were also drummers who taught at their dad's school. The original drumset from his WLS-Chicago days is on permanent display at the Percussive Arts Society International Headquarters Museum in Lawton, Oklahoma.

SELECTED BIBLIOGRAPHY

Cook, Rob, ed. *Franks for the Memories: A History of the Legendary Chicago Drum Shop and the Story of Maurie and Jan Lishon.* Alma, MI: Rebeats Publications, 1993.
Elias, Shelly. "Testimonial Day: A Grand Success!" *PN* XIII, 1 (Fall 1974).
"In Memoriam" *MD* III, 5 (October/November 1979): 64.
"In Memoriam: Roy Knapp, 1891–1979." *PN* XVIII, 1 (Fall 1979).
Knapp, Roy. "The Percussionist." *Percussionist* II, 3 (June 1965): 10–12.
Knapp, Roy C. *Fundamental Rudiments of Mallet Technique and Timpani Tuning.* Chicago: Roy C. Knapp Drum Center, 1939.
Knapp, Roy C. *The Fundamentals of Modern Drumming.* Chicago, 1939.
Knapp, Roy C. "Matched Grip vs. Conventional Grip." *PN* XVI, 1 (Fall 1977): 49.
"The Percussive Arts Society Hall of Fame." *PN* XI, 2 (Winter 1972): 7.
"Roy Knapp... The Grandaddy of Percussion with Young Ideas." *LD* VIII, 1 (1968): 18.

KNAUER, HEINRICH (fl. first half twentieth century, Germany). Timpanist Heinrich Knauer, along with a "Herr Stein," taught percussion at Dresden's Akademie für Theater und Musik ca. 1935.

SELECTED BIBLIOGRAPHY

Ludwig, William F. *Ludwig Timpani Instructor.* Chicago: Ludwig Drum Co., 1957 (photo, p. 4).

KNUTH, AXEL (b. 10 Oct 1934, Berlin, Germany). After studying percussion fundamentals privately, Axel Knuth studied with *Kurt Ladentine at the Berlin Conservatory (1955) before transferring to the Berlin Hochschule für Musik in 1960 where he completed his studies with Hans Lembens (1962). For a little over a year (1962–63), he served as percussionist and substitute timpanist in the Malmö (Sweden) Concert House, and from 1964 to 1971 he was a member of the Berlin Philharmonic. He often appeared as a percussion soloist with modern chamber music groups.
GEN. BIB.: Avgerinos, *KB.*

KODO (est. 1981). A Japanese traditional village taiko drumming group whose name means "children of the drum" and "heartbeat," Kodo was an offshoot of the ensemble Ondekoza (est. 1971), but members still train on the island of Sado, where the group sponsors an annual Earth Celebration. Each year Kodo accepts 10–12 applicants (18–25 years of age) for a two–year apprenticeship. Utilizing approximately 14 players who perform on the ancient o-daiko and miya-daika drums, Kodo has toured throughout the world, collaborating with such diverse ensembles and individuals as the Cirque du Soleil, the Tokyo and Berlin Symphonies, *Elvin Jones, *Babatunde Olatunji, and others. Recipient of a Gold Disc Award, Kodo was cited for excellence by the Cannes International Visual Music Festival, and the group's work can be heard on the soundtrack of the film *The Hunted*.

SELECTED DISCOGRAPHY

TriStar Music WK 35055: *Kodo Live at the Acropolis*, 1995.
TriStar Music WK 36852: *Ibuki*, 1997.
TriStar Music WK 57776: *Best of Kodo*, 1988/1993.

SELECTED VIDEOGRAPHY

Rhapsody Films: *Kodo—Heartbeat Drummers of Japan*, 1983.
Sony: *Kodo*, 1992.
Sony: *Kodo—Live at the Acropolis*, 1995.

SELECTED BIBLIOGRAPHY

Movshovitz, Howie. "Kodo Drummers Capture Pulse of Ancient Japanese Traditions." *Denver Post* (Saturday, 1 Feb 1997).
O'Mahoney, Terry. "Kodo: Japanese Taiko Masters." *PN* XXXVI, 1 (February 1998): 6–10.

KOGAN, PETER (b. 19 Apr 1945, Yonkers, New York). A student of *Saul Goodman, *Cloyd Duff, *George Gaber, *Elden "Buster" Bailey, and *Fred Hinger, Peter Kogan earned a master's degree from the Cleveland Institute (1972). Securing positions with the Cleveland Orchestra (1969–72), the Pittsburgh Symphony (principal percussionist and associate timpanist, 1972–77), and the Honolulu Symphony (timpani and drumset, 1984–86), he also freelanced in New York as a drumset artist and composer, becoming principal timpanist with the Minnesota Orchestra in 1986. Kogan presented the world premiere of David Schiff's *Speaking in Drums: Concerto for Timpani and String Orchestra* (1995) and serves as principal timpanist with the Santa Fe Opera (1999–).

SELECTED BIBLIOGRAPHY

Kogan, Peter. "Auditioning for the Minnesota Orchestra." *PN* XXXVII, 4 (August 1999): 20–21.
Information supplied by the subject, 1999.

KOHLOFF, ROLAND (b. 1935, Mamaroneck, New York). Earning a bachelor's degree and the performer's certificate from the Juilliard School (1956), where he studied with *Saul Goodman, Roland Kohloff played with the San Francisco Symphony and the San Francisco Opera Orchestra (1956–72), the Aspen Festival Orchestra, the Philadelphia Orchestra, and the Goldman Band.

He has taught on the faculties of San Francisco State, Aspen Music Festival, Waterloo Music Festival, and Juilliard School (1978–   ) and directed the San Francisco Percussion Ensemble. Succeeding Goodman on timpani with the New York Philharmonic (1972), Kohloff has soloed numerous times with the San Francisco and New York Orchestras and appeared on the television program *Omnibus* with the New York Philharmonic percussion section.

SELECTED DISCOGRAPHY

Moss Music Group D-MMG 115: *The All-Star Percussion Ensemble*, 1983.
GEN. BIB.: Borland, *WWAMC.*

KOPP, HOWARD. Xylophonist who recorded on snare, bells, and chimes for Columbia Records (1913–17), Howard Kopp played for Charles A. Prince's Orchestra, Broadway shows, the Victor Recording Orchestra, and the Goldman Band (1920s). [A Howard C. Kopp is listed in the *IM* obituaries as having died ca. May 1928, New York.]

SELECTED DISCOGRAPHY

Columbia A139: "St. Louis Tickle," 1905.
Columbia A854: "Temptation Rag" (Henry Lodge), 1909.
Columbia A1038: "High Society March" (Porter Steele), 1911.
Columbia A1560: "Twinkling Star Polka," 1914.
Columbia A1629: "Soup to Nuts" (Felix Arndt), 1914.
Columbia A1948: "Debutante Intermezzo," 1916.
Columbia A2327: "Beale Street" (W. C. Handy), 1917.
Columbia A2376: "One More Step," 1917.
Columbia A2524: "Going Up" (Louis Hirsch), 1918.
Masters of Jazz, Media 7: *Anthology of Jazz Drumming,* vols. 1–2 (1904–35), 1997.
Saydisc SDL 210: *Ragtime, Cakewalks, and Stomps* (1898–1917), 1960.
GEN. BIB.: Cahn, *XAR*; Cook, *LDT.*

KOSS, DONALD (b. Chicago, Illinois). After earning a bachelor's and a master's degree in mathematics from Northwestern University, Don Koss taught math in high school while playing summers with the Grant Park Symphony in Chicago. Essentially a self-taught timpanist who learned percussion in public schools, he played with the Oak Park, North Side, and Evanston Symphonies, served in the Fifth U.S. Army Band at Ft. Sheridan (IL), secured a position with the Chicago Civic Orchestra, and won the principal timpanist's chair in the Chicago Symphony (1963). For the latter, he also served as head of the player's committee in labor contract negotiations. His recordings of William Walton's *Façade* and Igor Stravinsky's *L'Histoire du Soldat* with Chicago Pro Musica earned him a Grammy® Award in 1985.

SELECTED DISCOGRAPHY

Reference Recordings RR-16CD and RR-17CD: *Works by Stravinsky, Rimsky-Korsakov, Walton, Strauss, Scriabin, and Nielsen.*

SELECTED BIBLIOGRAPHY

Furlong, William Barry. *Season with Solti: A Year in the Life of the Chicago Symphony.* New York: Macmillan Publishing, 1974.

KOZAK, EDWARD JOHN "EDDY" (b. 17 Nov 1925, Chicago, Illinois). Born into a musical family, Eddy Kozak studied drums from age 3 with his father, who played at the Palace Theater in Chicago. Later adding mallets, he was a child vaudeville star who performed percussion with the Chicago Chamber Orchestra at age 7 and wrote a concerto for marimba at 12. Kozak studied with *Roy Knapp at the Dixie Music House (aka Frank's Drum Shop) and earned performer's and teacher's certificates from the *Roy Knapp School of Percussion in Chicago, a bachelor's degree in piano from Centenary College (LA), and master's degrees in percussion and composition from Northwestern State University (LA). He spent 25 years on the road in theaters, in clubs, and on the RKO circuit, appearing as a marimba soloist for one year with the Xavier Cugat Orchestra and on the same bill with Frank Sinatra, Dick Van Dyke, Jackie Gleason, George Gobel, and Burl Ives. Featured as a marimba soloist in the U.S. Navy during WWII, he appeared on the *Ed Sullivan Show* and network radio as percussionist and marimba soloist, recorded for Columbia and Mitch Miller, was a business partner of *Clair Omar Musser, and served as principal percussionist with the Shreveport Symphony (1957–60).

His teaching positions have included Centenary College (1954–65), Northwestern State University (1966–69), and his own Kozak Music Studio in Shreveport, Louisiana (since 1953). A clinician for the Juilliard School, Oral Roberts University, Louisiana State University, and the University of North Texas, he invented the voice-operated computer program *Pro-Think MotorVator®* (produced by 10X Corporation and distributed by the Rand McNally Corporation) as an aid for coordination, concentration, and reaction time tested in music therapy classes. Musical director at the Marjorie Lyons, Centenary, and Shreveport Theaters, Kozak has written several biblical musicals and plays; he has also recorded as piano soloist, arranger, and composer on Red River Records.

Information supplied by the subject, 1996.

KRAFT, WILLIAM (b. 6 Sep 1923, Chicago, Illinois). Multitalented percussionist, conductor, and composer, William Kraft attended San Diego State College (1941–42), University of California at Los Angeles (1942), Cambridge University (1945), and Brooklyn College (1948) and studied at Columbia University and the Juilliard School, receiving both a bachelor's (1951) and a master's (1954) degree from Columbia. A veteran of the U.S. Air Force, he studied percussion and timpani, respectively, with *Morris Goldenberg and *Saul Goodman; composition with Henry Brant, Seth Bingham, Paul Henry Lang, Vladimir Ussachevsky, Henry Cowell, Jack Beeson, and Otto Luening; and conducting with Rudolph Thomas and Fritz Zweig. Kraft freelanced in the Metropolitan Opera Orchestra (1951–54), performed in the Dallas Symphony (1954–55), and served as percussionist (1955–62), principal timpanist (1962–81), assistant conductor (1969–72), and composer-in-residence (1981–85) during his 30-year tenure with the Los Angeles Philharmonic. His recordings with the latter and the Hollywood Bowl Orchestra can be heard on RCA, DG, Chesterfield, and London Decca labels (1956–81). As a percussion soloist, he recorded "L'Histoire du Soldat" under Igor Stravinsky's direction and performed the U.S. premieres of Karlheinz Stockhausen's "Zyklus" and Pierre Boulez's "Le Marteau sans Maître."

Kraft is the founder and director of the Los Angeles Percussion Ensemble and Chamber Players (since 1956) and the Los Angeles Philharmonic's New Music Group (1981–85). He is the recipient of two Guggenheim Fellowships (1967/1972), two Ford Foundation commissions, two Kennedy Center Friedheim awards, three National Endowment for the Arts grants (1975/1977/1979), Rockefeller Foundation grants in 1973 and 1996 for study in Italy, and an award from the American Academy and Institute of Arts and Letters (1984).

He composed and conducted music for the Hollywood films *The Psychic Killer* (1975), *Avalanche* (1976, starring Rock Hudson and Mia Farrow), a Ralph Bakshi animated film *Fire and Ice* (1980), and the television shows *Chisholm* (1977–79), *Ripley's Believe It or Not* (1982–83), and *Bill* (with Mickey Rooney). Kraft conducted film scores by Patrick Doyle for *Dead Again*, *Indochine*, and *Carlito's Way*; he also composed music for Samuel Beckett's radio play *Cascando*, which was distributed by National Public Radio. He has received commissions from United Air Lines, the Library of Congress, the U.S. Air Force Band, the Kronos Quartet, the St. Paul Chamber Orchestra, the Boston Pops, and others. Many of his works have been performed around the globe, and more than 40 of his works are available on recordings.

He served on the board of the National Academy of Recording Arts and Sciences (NARAS) and the music panel of the National Endowment for the Arts, chaired the American Society of Composers and Publishers (ASCAP) Board of Review, and is the chair of the composition department at the University of California at Santa Barbara. The Percussive Arts Society elected Kraft to their Hall of Fame in 1990.

SELECTED DISCOGRAPHY

Albany Records TROY 218: *Concerto for Percussion and Chamber Ensemble* (as composer; Dean Anderson performs), 1996.
Cambria CD-1071: *The Music of William Kraft* (as performer/composer), 1993.

Columbia Masterworks ML 5847: *Ginastera—Cantata para América Mágica; Chavez—Toccata* (Los Angeles Percussion Ensemble, director), 1959.
CRI CD 639: *Gallery '83* (includes "Des Imagistes"), 1983.
Crystal Records CD124: *Percussion by William Kraft* (composer), 1993.
Crystal Records CD667: *Thomas Stevens* (Encounters III, as composer), 1989.
Crystal Records CD740: *Voices of Change* (as composer), 1991.
Crystal Records CD850: *Lou Harrison* (Los Angeles Percussion Ensemble, conductor), 1992.
Crystal S-8211: *Nonet for Brass and Percussion* (Los Angeles Percussion Ensemble, composer and conductor), 1959/1971.
Delos DEL 254325 Q: *Des Imagistes* (as composer), 1978. (Karen Ervin and Mitchell Peters perform)
Delos DEL/F-25452: *Avalanche* (soundtrack composer), 1978.
Elektra/Nonesuch 79229-2: *William Kraft* (as composer), 1989.
Harmonia Mundi HMU 907106: *William Kraft—Three Concerti* (as composer), 1993.
London CS-6613: *Concerto for Four Percussion Soloists and Orchestra*, 1976.
Louisville S-653: *Concerto Grosso*, 1961.
Protone CSPR-163: *Encounters III—Duel for Trumpet and Percussion*, 1971.

SELECTED BIBLIOGRAPHY

Kraft, William. "J. Carewe's Edition of Stravinsky's 'l'Histoire du Soldat'—A Music Review." *Notes—Quarterly Journal of the Music Library Association* XLVI, 1 (September 1989): 12–16.
Kraft, William. "The Complete Percussionist." *LD* IV, 2 (Fall 1964): 18–19.
Pershing, Karen Ervin. "William Kraft." *MP* II, 4 (September 1986): 22.
Wilson, Patrick. "Kraft: The Composer as Orchestral Timpanist, an Interview." *PN* XXV, 1 (Fall 1986): 37–39.
GEN. BIB.: Hitchcock and Sadie, *NGA*, by David Cope; Larrick, *BET-CP*.

KRAUS, PHILIP "PHIL" (b. 24 Jul 1918, New York, New York). For many years one of New York City's leading studio percussionists, Phil Kraus graduated from the Juilliard School (1938), played on television and records (1948+), and was appointed personnel manager of the Houston Symphony around 1978. The first recipient of the National Association of Recording Arts and Sciences' "Most Valuable Studio Musician" Award, he also penned several method books and solos and taught privately.

SELECTED DISCOGRAPHY

Golden Crest CR 3004: *The Percussive Phil Kraus.*
Golden Crest CR-4004: *Conflict*, 1960.
Verve V6-5056: *Pat Williams*, 1968.
Verve V6-8508: *Oliver Nelson*, 1963.
Verve V6-8587: *Jimmy Smith*, 1964.

SELECTED BIBLIOGRAPHY

Kraus, Phil. *Mallet Methods*, vols. 1–3. New York: Henry Adler, Inc., 1958/1960.

KRETSCHMER, PAUL OTTO WILHELM (b. 3 Jul 1868, Berlin, Germany; d. 10 Feb 1936, Berlin, Germany). Paul Kretschmer was probably influenced early on by his father, who manufactured drum sticks and timpani mallets. After a musical education, he performed in a circus band, appearing in various cities, including Moscow, finally securing employment in the Hamburg Opera under Gustav Mahler's direction. He entered the Berlin Philharmonic in 1896, served on the pension fund supervisory board (1908–12), as secretary of the Widow's and Orphan's Fund (1925), and then as secretary of the board until his death. Still an active member after 40 years of service, he died from a cold that he had caught during a January concert tour.
GEN. BIB.: Avgerinos, *KB*.

KROUMATA (founded Stockholm, 1978). Percussion ensemble Kroumata's name comes from ancient Greek for "percussion," and the group is Sweden's only state-funded, permanent contemporary chamber ensemble. They have toured Europe, the United States (including Percussive Arts Society International Convention appearances), and Japan with Keiko Abe and have recorded new ballet music by Jan Sandström. Members include Anders Holdar, Ingvar Hallgren, Johan Silvmark, Leif Karlsson, Anders Loguin, and Roger Bergström.

SELECTED DISCOGRAPHY

Grammofon BIS CD-232: *The Kroumata Percussion Ensemble*, 1983.
Grammofon BIS CD-272: *Jolivet—Suite en Concert* et al., 1984.
Grammofon BIS CD-382: *Shchedrin—Carmen Suite*, 1987.
Grammofon BIS CD-462: *Kroumata and Keiko Abe—Rin-Sai*, 1989.
Grammofon BIS CD-482: *Iannis Xenakis—Pléiades*, 1981/1990.
Grammofon BIS CD 512: *Stonewave* (Kroumata with Manuela Wiesler), 1989/1991.
Grammofon BIS CD-734: *Carl Orff—Carmina Burana*, 1995.
Grammofon BIS CD 932: *Kroumata—Percussion Music*, 1998.
LCM CD 102: *Kroumata and Friends—Live in Stockholm*, 1987.

SELECTED BIBLIOGRAPHY

Weiss, Lauren Vogel. "Kroumata." *PN* XXXVII, 3 (June 1999): 6–12.
PASIC® program biographies, 1995.

KRUPA, EUGENE BURTRAM "GENE" (b. 15 Jan 1909, Chicago, Illinois; d. 16 Oct 1973, Yonkers, New York). The first drumset player ever to acquire worldwide notoriety, Gene Krupa started playing drums at age 12 with a young group called the Frivolians. He bowed to his mother's wishes and attended St. Joseph's College (Indiana, 1924–25) in possible preparation for the priesthood. Partially because of the influence of his music teacher there, he withdrew after a year and landed a job with the Wolverines (Bix Beiderbecke). His early association with the Austin High Gang brought him in contact with Benny Goodman, Eddie Condon, and Jimmy McPartland. During a 1927 recording session with the McKenzie-Condon Chicagoans for the Okeh label, his bass drum was the first ever to be recorded. Gigging in both New York and Chicago (ca. 1928–29), Krupa played for Red Nichols, was hired for the Broadway productions of George Gershwin's *Strike Up the Band* (opened January, 1930) and *Girl Crazy* (opened October, 1930), then worked with the Russ Columbo, Buddy Rogers, and Benny Goodman Bands (1934–38), including the latter's *Let's Dance* radio broadcasts. Krupa experimented with journalism in the 1930s, writing drum articles for *Metronome* magazine. From 1938 to 1943 and 1944 to 1951, traveling with Tommy Dorsey's Band during the interim, he fronted his own successful groups, which included Roy Eldridge, Charlie Ventura, Anita O'Day, and Gerry Mulligan. His career was threatened in 1942 by a misdemeanor marijuana conviction and jail time in San Francisco; but in 1944 the public voted him America's outstanding drummer. He toured with Norman Granz's "Jazz at the Philharmonic" (1951–57) and, in 1954, established a school of drumming in New York with Cozy Cole.

A very physical, animated drummer, Krupa was featured on television and in several films (e.g., *Some Like It Hot*, *The Glenn Miller Story*, and *The Benny Goodman Story*), and he was immortalized in the autobiographical movie *The Gene Krupa Story* (1959), which featured Sal Mineo in the title role. His drum "battles" with *Chick Webb, *Buddy Rich, and others are legendary. Numerous recordings spotlighted his drum solos, but none is as memorable as the 1937 performance of "Sing, Sing, Sing" with Benny Goodman at the Carnegie Hall concerts. After a heart attack in 1960, Krupa retired in 1967 with emphysema, only to return three years later as a member of the original Benny Goodman quartet, with whom he made his last public appearance. Called the "King of the Drums," he was inducted into both the Percussive Arts Society (1975) and the *Modern Drummer* Reader's Poll Halls of Fame (1979).

SELECTED DISCOGRAPHY

Bandstand Records BS7117: *Wire Brush Stomp*, 1938–41.
Bluebird AXK2-5567/RCA: *The Complete Benny Goodman*, vols. 1–5/8, 1980.
Chiaroscuro Records CR-110: *Jazz at the New School*, 1972.
Circle CCD-111: *Benny Goodman—The Complete 1934 Bill Dodge All-Star Recordings*, 1987.
CK 45445: *The Jazz Arranger*, vol. 2, 1946–63.
Clef MGC-668: *The Gene Krupa Quartet*, 1955.
Clef MGC-681: *Gene Krupa, Lionel Hampton, Teddy Wilson*, 1955.
Clef MGC-684: *Krupa and Rich*, 1955.
Columbia CK 53425: *Drum Boogie*, 1993.

Columbia C3L 32: *The Sound of Chicago*, vol. 2 (1923–40), 1964.
Columbia G2K 40244: *Live at Carnegie Hall* (Benny Goodman), 1938.
Columbia Masterworks ML 4358: *Benny Goodman Carnegie Hall Jazz Concert*, vol. 1, 1950.
Columbia C2L-29: *Drummin' Man/Gene Krupa*, (1938–49), 1963.
DBK Jazz 70015: *Gene Krupa in Concert*, 1971/1998.
Epic Encore Series EE 22027 (VSP S-4): *That Drummer's Band*, 1940–42.
Jazzology JCD-1003-1010: *Eddie Condon—The Town Hall Concerts*, vols. 2–5, 1944/1972.
Masters of Jazz, Media 7: *Anthology of Jazz Drumming*, vols. 1–3, 1904–38.
Metro S-518: *Gene Krupa Quartet*, 1958.
RCA 2698: *Together Again* (Benny Goodman, Lionel Hampton, Teddy Wilson), 1996.
Roulette S52098: *The Mighty Two* (Bellson and Krupa), 1978.
Verve 845 148-2: *Jazz Club Mainstream: Drums*, 1951/1991.
Verve 8292: *Gene Krupa Plays Gerry Mulligan Arrangements*, 1958.
Verve V6-8450: *Gene Krupa*, 1961.
Verve V/V6-8571: *Let Me Off Uptown*, 1958.
Verve 6-8584: *Great New Quartet*, 1964.
Verve MGV8190: *Sing, Sing, Sing*, 1954.
Verve MGV8310: *Big Noise from Winnetka*, 1959.
Verve MGV8369: *Jazz at the Philharmonic: Gene Krupa and Buddy Rich, the Drum Battle*, 1952.
Verve MGVS6105: *The Gene Krupa Story*, 1959.
Verve V-8414: *Percussion King*, 1961.
Verve V6-8471: *Burnin' Beat*, 1962 (Krupa and Rich).
Verve V/V6-8594: *The Best of Gene Krupa (Verve's Choice)*, 1958.

SELECTED VIDEOGRAPHY

DCI VH0129: *Gene Krupa*, 1993.
DCI VH0197: *Buddy Rich—Jazz Legend, Pt. 2, 1970–87*, (1994).
DCI VH0248: *Legends of Jazz Drumming, Pt. 1, 1920–50*, (1996).
Music Video Distributors: *Jazz Legends*, pt. 3, 1987.
Republic Pictures Home Video: *Jazz Ball*, 1956.
Vitaphone/Music Video Distributors: *Symphony of Swing* (1939–48), 1986.
Vintage Jazz Classics Video 2002: *Chicago and All That Jazz*, 1961.

SELECTED BIBLIOGRAPHY

Brown, Bernie. "Krupa on Drumming Today and Yesterday." *DB* XXXII, 25 (2 Dec 1965): 12.
Cerulli, Dom. "Gene Krupa: What's New?" *DB* XXV, 6 (20 Mar 1958): 17.
Crowther, Bruce. *Gene Krupa: His Life and Times*. New York: Universe Books, 1987.
Hester, Mary Lee. "The Exciting Gene Krupa." *The Mississippi Rag* XXX, 10 (Minneapolis, MN) (August 1986): 1–4.
Kettle, Rupert. "Krupa: A Musical Perspective." *MD* III, 5 (October/November 1979): 24–25.

Klauber, Bruce. "Krupa and the Small Groups: A Lesson in Individuality and Swing." *MD* III, 5 (October/November 1979): 20–21.

Klauber, Bruce. *World of Gene Krupa, That Legendary Drummin' Man.* Ventura, CA: Pathfinder Publishing, 1990.

Korall, Burt. "A Day with Gene Krupa." *DB* XXIX, 7 (29 Mar 1962): 16–17.

Korall, Burt. "That Ace Drummer Man." *JazzTimes* XXII, 9 (November 1992): 39–40.

Korf, Anthony. "Gene Krupa Remembered." *PN* XXII, 4 (April 1984): 31–35.

Krupa, Gene. *The Gene Krupa Drum Method.* New York: Robbins Music, 1938/1966 [reprinted by Warner Bros. Publications, 1995].

Krupa, Gene. *The Science of Drumming,* Books 1–2. New York: Robbins Music, 1946.

Larcombe, Karen. "Gene Krupa: 1909–1973." *MD* III, 5 (October/November 1979): 12–14.

Lind, Jack. "Gene Krupa Keeps Rolling." *DB* XXVI, 5 (5 Mar 1959): 16–17.

"Percussive Arts Society Hall of Fame, 1974." *PN* XII, 3 (Spring 1974): 21.

Shultz, Thomas. "A History of Jazz Drumming." *Percussionist* XVI, 3 (Spring/Summer 1979): 115–116.

Spagnardi, Ron. "Krupa in Solo." *MD* III, 5 (October/November 1979): 26–27.

GEN. BIB.: Kernfeld, *NGJ,* by Gunther Schuller; Korall, *DM;* Spagnardi, *GJD.*

KRUSE, PETER JOCHEN (b. 16 May 1939, Dresden, Germany). A student of Peter Sondermann at the Dresden Fachschule für Musik (1953–57), Peter Kruse performed as timpanist-percussionist with the Sonneberg-Thüringen Orchestra (1957–58), the Cottbus Theater Orchestra (1958–60), the Berlin City Symphony (percussion, 1960), and the Berlin Philharmonic (1960–62); he was then hired as substitute timpanist with the Bamberg Symphony (1962).
GEN. BIB.: Avgerinos, *KB.*

KUEHN, DONALD (b. 3 Mar 1947, Denver, Colorado). A student of *Walter J. Light during his formative years, Donald Kuehn later attended Boston University (1965–68), where he studied with *Tom Gauger and *Charles Smith from the Boston Symphony and, later, with *Cloyd Duff of the Cleveland Symphony. Kuehn secured a percussionist and assistant timpanist position with the Baltimore Symphony from 1968 until 1973, when he accepted a position as principal percussionist with the Toronto Symphony. He has taught on the faculties of the Peabody Conservatory and Susquehanna University (PA).
GEN. BIB.: Larrick, *BET-CP.*

KVISTAD, GARRY MICHAEL (b. 9 Nov 1949, Oak Park, Illinois). A graduate of the Interlochen Arts Academy, Garry Kvistad earned a bachelor's degree from Oberlin Conservatory and a master's degree from Northern Illinois University. He studied with *Al Payson, Jack McKenzie, *Michael Ranta, *Richard Kvistad, *Cloyd Duff, and *Richard Weiner, and he performed with

Lukas Foss's Contemporary Chamber Ensemble (1970s), Grant Park Symphony (timpanist, 1972), Blackearth Percussion Group (cofounder, 1972–79), Steve Reich and Musicians (1980–present), Giri Mekar Gamelan Orchestra (founder, 1986–present, the first Balinese gamelan in the Hudson Valley), and the Woodstock Beat (1992–present). A Tanglewood Fellow (summer, 1968), Kvistad taught at the Cincinnati Conservatory and Northern Illinois University, where he was honored with a Distinguished Alumnus Award.

Founder and president of Woodstock Percussion, Inc., since 1979, he established the *Anyone Can Whistle Catalogue* and retail store, received the "Entrepreneur of the Year" Award from Ernst & Young/*Inc.* magazine (1995), and served as a New York state delegate to the White House Conference on Small Business (1995). He has won the Parents' Choice and Oppenheim Toy Portfolio Awards. As an instrument builder, he is responsible for the development of Woodstock Chimes and serves on the board of directors of the Woodstock Guild of Craftsmen and the Catskill Center for Conservation and Development. Kvistad established a nonprofit organization, the Woodstock Chimes Fund, in 1986 to support food, shelter, music, and arts programs in the region.

SELECTED DISCOGRAPHY

ECM 1-1215: *Tehillim* (Steve Reich), 1982.
Nonesuch 79101: *The Desert Music* (Steve Reich and Brooklyn Philharmonic), 1984.
Nonesuch 79170: *Drumming* (Steve Reich), 1987.
Nonesuch 79183-2: *Sextet/Six Marimbas*, (Steve Reich), 1985.
Nonesuch 79327: *The Cave* (Steve Reich), 1994.
Opus One 20: *Blackearth Percussion Group* (Frederic Rzewski), 1973.
Opus One 22: *Blackearth Percussion Group*, 1974.
Opus One 31: *The Canons of Blackearth* (Blackearth Percussion Group), 1977.
The Relaxation Company: *Music for a Pipedream*, 1993.

SELECTED BIBLIOGRAPHY

Open Ears: Musical Adventures for a New Generation. Roslyn, NY: Ellipsis Kids, 1995 (contributing author).
Information supplied by the subject, 1996.

KVISTAD, RICHARD T. "RICK" (b. 10 Sep 1943, Chicago, Illinois). A graduate of Oberlin College (bachelor's, 1965) and the University of Illinois (master's, 1969), Richard Kvistad studied with Frank Rullo, *Cloyd Duff, Jack McKenzie, *Al Payson, *George Gaber, and from the Mozarteum Orchestra in Salzburg, Austria, Paul Hirsch. His professional career began as timpanist and/or percussionist with the American Wind Symphony (1965), Florida Symphony (Orlando, 1965–66), Grant Park Symphony (Chicago), Buffalo Philharmonic, and Chicago Lyric Opera Orchestra. Kvistad performed with the Pittsburgh Symphony as principal percussionist and associate principal timpanist from 1969 until 1972, when he became a charter member of the avant-garde percussion quartet Blackearth Percussion Group. [Blackearth still exists as a trio, The Percussion Group, in residence at the Cincinnati Conservatory.] Blackearth toured extensively, stimulated several new chamber works, and "stretched the musical envelope" for percussion ensembles.

Relocating to San Francisco in 1974, Kvistad freelanced with the San Francisco Symphony, Ballet Orchestra, and Opera Orchestra before settling into the principal percussionist-associate principal timpanist chair in the Opera Orchestra, which he has held since 1980. He embraced ethnic percussion in 1974 at the Center for World Music (Berkeley, CA), studying Indonesian gamelan and Indian hand drumming. Among his many appearances are the premiere of his own timpani concerto with the Sinfonia San Francisco, his performance as soloist with the Pittsburgh Symphony, a timpani demonstration for television's *Mr. Rogers' Neighborhood*, and performances with the Bolshoi, Kirov, and American Ballet companies, and the Dance Theater of Harlem. Kvistad has taught at Interlochen Arts Academy, San Francisco State (1981–84), Sonoma State (CA), Northern Illinois University, and Carnegie-Mellon and has recorded with the San Francisco percussion quartet, Xylo.

SELECTED DISCOGRAPHY

Clover Music: *People Who Hit Things*, 1992.
Deutsche Gramofone DGG 2530-788: *Gershwin—American in Paris* (San Francisco Symphony), 1981.
Direkt to Disk Records LS-11: *76 Pieces of Explosive Percussion* (Sonic Arts Symphonic Percussion Consortium), 1976.
MMG 201-X: *Paul Chihara—The Tempest* (San Francisco Performing Arts Orchestra), 1982.
Non Sequitur Records 1–3: *Compositions by Herbert Brün*, 1983.
Opus One 20: *Blackearth Percussion Group*, 1973.
Opus One 22: *Blackearth Percussion Group*, 1974.
Opus One 31: *The Canons of Blackearth* (Blackearth Percussion Group), 1977.
Polydor 24-5001: *Music of Salvatore Martirano*, 1970.

SELECTED BIBLIOGRAPHY

Kvistad, Richard. *Concerto for Timpani and Chamber Orchestra.* Belmont, CA: Xylo Pub., 1988.
Rossing, Thomas D., and Garry Kvistad. "Acoustics of Timpani: Preliminary Studies." *Percussionist* XIII, 3 (Spring 1976): 90–98.
GEN. BIB.: Larrick, *BET-CP*.

Photo 1. John Philip Sousa's percussion section, 1921. L-R: George J. Carey, Howard N. Goulden, August "Gus" Helmecke. Reprinted with permission from the Percussive Arts Society.

Photo 2. Haskell Harr Trio (Harr at xylophone), 1927. Reprinted with permission from the Percussive Arts Society.

Photo 3. James Blades, ca. 1930. Reprinted with permission from the Percussive Arts Society.

Photo 4. Roy Knapp in the WLS radio broadcast studio, ca. 1930s. Reprinted with permission from the Percussive Arts Society.

Photo 5. Saul Goodman, ca. 1930s, timpanist for the New York Philharmonic. Reprinted with permission from the Percussive Arts Society.

Photo 6. Harry Breuer in NBC recording studio, ca. 1940. Reprinted with permission from the Percussive Arts Society.

Photo 7. José Bethancourt, Bobby Christian, Roy Knapp, ca. 1940s. Reprinted with permission from the Percussive Arts Society.

Photo 8. Ben Udell [Yudelowitz], ca. 1949. Reprinted with permission from *International Musician*, the Official Journal of the American Federation of Musicians.

Photo 9. The Chicago Symphony percussion section, ca. 1949. L-R: Lionel Sayers, Thomas Glenecke, Allen Graham [Edward Metzenger, timpanist, not pictured]. Reprinted with permission from *International Musician*, the Official Journal of the American Federation of Musicians.

Photo 10. The Houston Symphony percussion section, ca. 1949. L-R: E. E. Stokes, Leo Mosler, Geraldine Ball, David Wuliger. Reprinted with permission from *International Musician*, the Official Journal of the American Federation of Musicians. [Photographer: Bob Bailey, Houston, TX].

Photo 11. L-R: Walter J. Light and Walter E. Light, son and father, ca. 1949. Two generations of timpanists with the Denver Symphony. Reprinted with permission from *International Musician*, the Official Journal of the American Federation of Musicians.

Photo 12. Cleveland Orchestra percussion section, ca. 1945–48. L-R: Cloyd Duff, Emil Sholle, Frank Sholle, Harry Miller. Reprinted with permission from *International Musician*, the Official Journal of the American Federation of Musicians.

Photo 13. Roman Szulc, ca. 1949, timpanist of the Boston Symphony. Reprinted with permission from *International Musician*, the Official Journal of the American Federation of Musicians. [Photographer: David Nilsson].

Photo 14. The Rochester Philharmonic percussion section, ca. 1949. L-R: Stanley Street, Hugh Robertson, Robert Swan, William Street. Reprinted with permission from *International Musician*, the Official Journal of the American Federation of Musicians.

Photo 15. The Philadelphia Orchestra percussion section, ca. 1949. L-R: Leonard Shulman, Fred D. Hinger, James Valerio, David Grupp. Reprinted with permission from *International Musician*, the Official Journal of the American Federation of Musicians.

Photo 16. Del Roper with his invention, "the monster," ca. 1946. Reprinted with permission from Del Roper.

Photo 17. Frank Simon's ARMCO Band percussion section, ca. 1950. L-R: George Carey, Fred Noak (timpani), Ferd Weiss (bass drum), unknown, James Rosenberg [Jim Ross] (snare drum). Reprinted with permission from the Percussive Arts Society.

Photo 18. L-R: Oliver Zinsmeister and Charles Owen, ca. 1936, percussionists with the U.S. Marine Band ("The President's Own"). Reprinted with permission from the Percussive Arts Society.

Photo 19. Vida Chenoweth, ca. 1960. Reprinted with permission from the Percussive Arts Society.

Photo 20. Fred Noak, 1949, timpanist for the Cincinnati Symphony and New York Metropolitan Opera Orchestra. Reprinted with permission from *International Musician*, the Official Journal of the American Federation of Musicians. [KLT Photos, Cincinnati, OH]

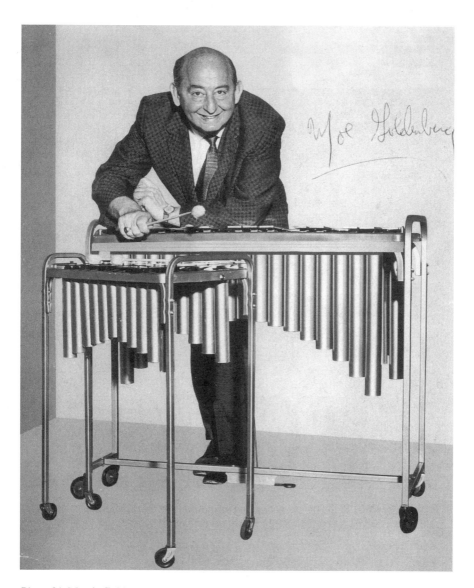

Photo 21. Morris Goldenberg, ca. 1960. Reprinted with permission from the Percussive Arts Society.

Photo 22. New York Philharmonic percussion section, ca. 1977. L-R: Elden "Buster" Bailey, Walter Rosenberger, Morris "Arnie" Lang, Roland Kohloff. Reprinted with permission from the Percussive Arts Society.

L

LABARBERA, JOE (b. 22 Feb 1948, Mount Morris, New York). Drumset artist who first performed professionally at the age of 6, Joe LaBarbera played saxophone in high school, but he studied drumset with *Alan Dawson at the Berklee College of Music. He has performed and/or recorded with Woody Herman, Gap Mangione, Chuck Mangione (1973–77), Jim Hall, *Gary Burton, Bobby Brookmeyer, Phil Woods, John Scofield, Bill Evans (1978–80), Art Pepper, Tony Bennett (1980–92), Art Farmer, the Kenny Wheeler Quintet, among others. LaBarbera serves on the faculty of the California Institute of the Arts.

SELECTED DISCOGRAPHY

Audiophile AP-158: *Jackie Paris*, 1981.
Audiophile ACD-211: *Carol Sings* (Carol Sloane), 1980.
Dreyfus Jazz FDM 36554: *Letter to Evan* (Bill Evans), 1980.
Elektra 28P2 2478: *The Paris Concert—Edition I* (Bill Evans), 1979.
Gryphon 628479DX: *Bob Brookmeyer Small Band*, 1978.
Jazz Lab, Vol. II: *Concert in Buenos Aries* (Bill Evans), 1979.
Mama MMF 1013: *Heavyweights* (Bobby Shew/Carl Fontana), 1996.
RCA 68929: *I Remember Bill*, 1997.
Warner Bros. HS 3411: *We Will Meet Again* (Bill Evans), 1979.
Warner Brothers 9 45925-2: *Turn out the Stars: The Final Village Vanguard Recordings* (Bill Evans), 1980.

SELECTED VIDEOGRAPHY

Music Video Distributors: *Bill Evans—Live at the Maintenance Shop*, 1979.
Rhapsody Films: *The Bill Evans Trio*, 1995.

SELECTED BIBLIOGRAPHY

Soph, Ed. "Interview with Joe LaBarbera." *PN* XXXII, 1 (February 1994): 10–13.
GEN. BIB.: Hunt, *52nd St.*; PASIC® program biographies, 1997.

LABORDUS, JAN (b. 14 Sep 1931, Amsterdam, Netherlands). Principal solo timpanist with the Concertgebouw Orchestra of Amsterdam (1953–91), Jan Labordus studied at the Amsterdam Conservatorium (1945–49) with Cor Smit.

SELECTED DISCOGRAPHY

Philips 416378-2: *Béla Bartók—Concerto for Two Pianos and Percussion*, 1985. Information supplied by the subject, 1996.

LADA, ANTON (b. 1893, New Orleans, Louisiana; d. ca. Sep 1944, Los Angeles, California). Drummer and xylophonist Anton Lada led both Lada's Louisiana Orchestra and Five Southern Jazzers, recording Dixieland with the Louisiana Five.

SELECTED DISCOGRAPHY

Columbia A2775: "I Ain't-en Got-en No Time to Have the Blues," 1919.
Emerson 1083: "Ringtail Blues" and "Blues My Naughty Sweetie Gives to Me," 1919.
Emerson 10567: "Alibi Blues," and "Early in the Morning Blues," 1922.
Emerson 10570: "When Will I Know," and "Jimbo Jambo," 1922.

SELECTED BIBLIOGRAPHY

Kastner, Kathleen. "The Xylophone in the United States between 1880 and 1930, Part I: The Artists." *Percussive Arts Society: Illinois Chapter Newsletter* (Winter 1986): 1–2.
GEN. BIB.: Cahn, *XAR*.

LADENTINE, KURT RICHARD PAUL (b. 8 Oct 1905, Berlin, Germany; d. 13 Jun 1960, Berlin, Germany). A piano accompanist for dance lessons in his youth, Kurt Ladentine studied percussion privately with Franz Krüger in Berlin from 1933 to 1935. He performed in Köln, Marienbad, Vienna, and Prague and was percussionist with the Broadcasting Orchestra of Germany (1935–46). Ladentine played with the Berlin Philharmonic (1946–60), taught timpani and percussion at the Berlin Conservatory (1947–60), and died while teaching a lesson.
GEN. BIB.: Avgerinos, *KB*.

LAMB, CHRISTOPHER S. (b. 28 Mar 1959, Sandusky, Ohio). A student of *Salvatore Rabbio, *Leigh Howard Stevens, *John Beck, and *Glen Velez, Christopher Lamb was raised in Flint, Michigan, and completed the requirements for a bachelor's degree from the Eastman School in 1981. His professional performance experience includes positions as percussionist and assistant timpanist with the Buffalo (NY) Philharmonic (1981–82), percussionist with the Metropolitan Opera Orchestra (1982–85), and since 1985 principal percussionist in the New York Philharmonic. At that time he was the youngest principal percussionist in any major American orchestra and during his first year was featured with Ravi Shankar and the orchestra on the legendary sitar player's "Concerto No. 1." In 1995 he premiered (and reprised in 1996 with the Nashville Symphony) Joseph Schwantner's "Concerto for Percussion and Orchestra," which was written for Lamb and was the first solo percussion concerto ever commissioned by the New York Philharmonic. He has taught at Mannes College of Music (NY) and served as chair of the percussion department at the Manhattan School since 1989. *Modern Drummer* magazine selected him as one of the top three classical percussionists in 1990, and his performances, including the percussion and piano chamber duo Lambchops, can be heard on the CRI, Teldec, CBS, and RCA recording labels, among others.

SELECTED DISCOGRAPHY

Deutsche Grammophon-4191701: *Aaron Copland—Symphony No. 3* (New York Philharmonic, xylophone/bells), 1985.
Deutsche Grammophon CD1 A: *Peter Tchaikovsky—Symphony No. 6 in B minor* (New York Philharmonic, bass drum), 1987/1991.
Deutsche Grammophon: *Antonin Dvorak—Carnival Overture* (New York Philharmonic, tambourine), 1989.
Deutsche Grammophon-4191691: *Richard Wagner—Die Meistersingers von Nurnberg* (New York Philharmonic, triangle), 1985.
New World NW 372-1: *Music of Zwillich* (marimba and vibraphone), 1989.
Vox MW CD-7100: *The Heroic Mr. Handel* (New York Trumpet Ensemble, snare drum), 1996.

SELECTED BIBLIOGRAPHY

Mattingly, Rick. "Chris Lamb: New York's Newest." *MP* I, 4 (September 1985): 18.
GEN. BIB.: Larrick, *BET-CP*; PASIC® program biographies, 1994.

LAMOND, DON (b. 18 Aug 1920, Oklahoma City, Oklahoma). Raised in Washington, D.C., big band drummer Don Lamond studied at the Peabody Institute with Horace Butterworth, then played with Sonny Dunham (1943), Boyd Raeburn (1944–45), Woody Herman (1945–49), the Newport All-Stars, the Sauter-Finnegan Jazz Orchestra, Chubby Jackson, Charlie Parker, Stan Getz, Benny Goodman, and Alvino Rey. After working as a recording artist in New

York and in television studios for the *Pat Boone, Steve Allen, Garry Moore,* and *Perry Como* shows, Lamond moved to Florida (1972), where he co-led a group at Disney World and recorded with his wife, singer Terry Lamond.

SELECTED DISCOGRAPHY

Audiophile ACD-170: *Lee Wiley—The Carnegie Hall Concert,* 1972.
Audiophile ACD-250: *Maxine Sullivan and Dick Hyman.*
Audiophile ACD-300: *Lee Wiley—Back Home Again,* 1994.
Capitol CDP798453: *Keeper of the Flame* (Woody Herman), 1949.
Circle CCD-148: *Don Lamond—Extraordinary!* 1996.
Clef MGC139: *Charlie Barnet and His Orchestra,* 1952.
Columbia CK44108: *The Thundering Herds* (Woody Herman), 1945.
Prestige OJC CD 711-2: *Gerry Mulligan/Chubby Jackson,* 1950.
RCA Victor LPM 1279: *The Drum Suite* (with Osie and Gus Johnson, Teddy Sommer), 1956.
Stash STCD567-8-9-10: *Complete Bird on Dial* (Charlie Parker), 1947.
Verve MGV2024: *Chico O'Farrill and His Orchestra,* 1951.
Verve MGV2049: *Anita O'Day with Ralph Burns'Orchestra,* 1952.
Verve MGV8003: *Charlie Parker and His Orchestra,* 1952.
Verve MGV8152: *The Bill Harris Herd,* 1952.
Verve V6-8692: *Johnny Smith,* 1967.

SELECTED BIBLIOGRAPHY

Cerulli, Dom. "Don Lamond: Studio Staffer." *DB* XXV, 6 (20 Mar 1958): 23.
GEN. BIB.: Hunt, *52nd St.*; Spagnardi, *GJD.*

LANE, JAMES LEE (b. ca. 1941, Wabash, Indiana; d. 17 Nov 1978). Percussionist with the Chicago Symphony (1967–78), James Lane earned a bachelor's degree from Ball State University (1964). He studied with Dr. Erwin Mueller and *Edward Metzenger, performed with the Indianapolis Symphony, where he served as principal percussionist for one season, and penned percussion articles for the *International Musician.*

SELECTED BIBLIOGRAPHY

"In Memoriam." *PN* XVII, 2 (Winter 1979): 19.
Payson, Al, and James Lane. *Concert Etudes for Snare Drum.* Park Ridge, IL: Payson Percussion.

LANG, MORRIS ARNOLD "ARNIE" (b. 2 Feb 1931, New York, New York). Percussionist and associate timpanist with the New York Philharmonic since 1955, Arnie Lang started lessons around age 10 with an amateur drummer who was a butcher by trade. Graduating from New York's Music and Art High School, he received a bachelor's degree from the Juilliard School in 1953, and his professional teachers included *Saul Goodman, *Morris Goldenberg, and *Billy Gladstone. Between 1950 and 1955, Lang worked at Radio City Music Hall and with the New York Opera Society, New York City Ballet (1953–55), and Little Orchestra Society. He has performed in the United States and abroad with Broadway productions, the Metropolitan Opera, and for the 1977 world premiere of Michael Colgrass' "Déjà Vu." His faculty positions have included the Manhattan School (1971–75), the New York College of Music, the Kingsborough Community College (Brooklyn, NY), and since 1973 chair of the percussion department at Brooklyn College Conservatory. With the Brooklyn College Percussion Ensemble, he toured Roumania and Hungary (1973/1977) and Korea (1995), and he personally presented clinics in Russia (1976), Hong Kong, Japan, and Korea. Lang hosted the 1979 Percussive Arts Society International Convention and has subsequently appeared as a clinician at several of those events. His business venture, Lang Percussion, Inc., faithfully reproduces *Billy Gladstone's legendary snare drums and drumsets and *Saul Goodman's timpani; it also publishes percussion music and literature.

SELECTED DISCOGRAPHY

CBS Records MK-42224: *Beethoven—Symphony No. 9*, 1969.
Columbia MS-6956: *Bartók—Concerto for Two Pianos, Percussion, and Orchestra* (New York Philharmonic), 1967.
CRI SD 327: *Bazelon—Propulsions*, 1974.
Moss Music Group D-MMG 115: *The All-Star Percussion Ensemble*, 1983.
Odyssey Y-34137: *Carter—Eight Pieces for Four Timpani*, 1975.
Urania URLP 7144: *Chavez—Toccata*, 1954.

SELECTED BIBLIOGRAPHY

Lang, Morris. "A Journey to the Source on 'L'Histoire du Soldat.' " *Percussionist* XII, 2 (Winter 1975): 50–54.
Lang, Morris. *Dictionary of Percussion Terms.* New York: Lang Percussion, 1977.
Rendón, Victor, and Ken Ross. "Lang Percussion." *MD* XX, 9 (September 1996): 124–126.
Smith, Dr. D. Richard. "Arnie Lang: Student, Professor, Writer, Inventor, Timpanist." *PN* XVI, 3 (Spring/Summer 1978): 24–26.
GEN. BIB.: Borland, *WWAMC*; Larrick, *BET-CP*.

LAROCA, PETE (b. Peter Sims, 7 Apr 1938, New York, New York). Drumset artist and composer who was influenced early by timpani and Latin styles while a student at Manhattan's High School of Music and Art, Pete LaRoca performed with Stan Getz, Slide Hampton, Art Farmer, Paul Bley, Sonny Rollins, Charles Lloyd, Jackie McLean, and John Coltrane and led his own groups. He took an extended hiatus from the music business in 1968 to drive a cab and practice law (graduated 1975) only to resurface in the late 1970s and early 1990s with his group, Swingtime.

SELECTED DISCOGRAPHY

Atlantic P-81038A: *Sing Me Softly of The Blues* (Art Farmer), 1965.
Blue Note 54876: *Pete (LaRoca) Sims—Swingtime*, 1997.
Blue Note 84013: *New Soil* (Jackie McLean), 1959.
Blue Note 84067: *Bluesnik* (Jackie McLean), 1961.
Blue Note 84140: *Page One* (Joe Henderson), 1963.
Blue Note 84144: *Little Johnny C* (Johnny Coles), 1963.
Blue Note 84152: *Our Thing* (Joe Henderson), 1963.
Blue Note 84207/84208: *Live at Club La Marchal/The Night of the Cookers* (Freddie Hubbard), 1965.
Blue Note B21Y 81542: *A Night at the Vanguard* (Sonny Rollins), 1957.
Blue Note CDP 7243 8 32091 2 5: *Basra*, 1965/1995.
Blue Note CDP 7 46545-2: *Blue Spirits* (Freddie Hubbard), 1965.
Blue Note J61016: *Sonny Clark Quintet*, 1957.
Douglas SD 782/32 Jazz: *Turkish Women at the Baths*, 1967.
Dragon DRLP 73: *In Stockholm* (Sonny Rollins), 1984.
Savoy SV-0140: *Footloose* (Paul Bley), 1962.

SELECTED BIBLIOGRAPHY

Gilter, Ira. "Pete LaRoca." *DB* XXXI, 8 (26 Mar 1964): 20–21.
Micaleff, Ken. "Pete LaRoca Sims: Dedication to Swing." *MD* XXII, 5 (May 1998): 60–74.
GEN. BIB.: Hunt, *52nd St.*

LAYFIELD, ARTHUR "ART" (b. 1891, Chicago, Illinois; d. 1 Mar 1974, Watsonville, California). Initially a pianist, Art Layfield studied percussion with *William F. Ludwig, Sr., (early 1910s), worked as a theater drummer, and then replaced Ludwig, Sr. in the Chicago Opera Orchestra (1916–21). Drummer for the Benson-Victor (1923), Roy Bargy, Ralph Williams, Isham Jones (London tour, 1925), and Paul Ash (featured drum and xylophone soloist, 1926) Orchestras, he studied xylophone with *Charles Fisher and timpani with *Joseph Zettleman of the Chicago Orchestra, occasionally subbing in that group. Considered the top freelance percussionist in Chicago, Layfield relocated to New York, where he became a member of the New York Philharmonic (1942–55) until severe arthritis forced him to retire.

SELECTED BIBLIOGRAPHY

"Closing Chord—Arthur Layfield." *IM* LXXIII, 4 (October 1974): 26
Noonan, John. "Art Layfield Is Alive and Well and Living in Watsonville, California." *PN* IX, 2 (Winter 1971): 8.
"Paul Ask and His Stage Band, ca. 1924." *PN* IX, 1 (Fall 1970): 23 (photo).

LEEDY, ULYSSES GRANT (b. 16 Nov 1867, Fostoria, Ohio; d. 7 Jan 1931, Indianapolis, Indiana). Drumming for tips near a railroad at the age of 7 on a Civil War drum, U. G. Leedy was in a drum corps by 14; by 18 he had studied other instruments (e.g., string bass), performing in the town band and orchestra. He was an accomplished drummer-xylophonist at 22 and worked with the Great Western Band. After playing on the road with circuses and minstrel shows, Leedy held a permanent position at the Empire Theater in Indianapolis, Indiana (1890–93). In 1892 he developed the first snare and bass drum thumb screw tension rods; by 1896 in Toledo, Ohio, had invented the first folding drum stand. With the help of his father, who was a cabinet maker, he also manufactured his first snare drum. Back in Indianapolis by 1897, Leedy secured a post with the English Opera House and with clarinet player Sam Cooley established the Leedy-Cooley Drum Company. This enterprise was renamed the Leedy Manufacturing Company, Inc., by 1900, when Cooley dissolved the partnership. Leedy offered a complete line of percussion instruments; and as his business and family grew, he ceased performing professionally but continued to teach privately.

Leedy's expert keyboard percussion tuner, Herman Winterhoff, is credited with developing mechanically produced vibrato from the steel marimba (marimbaphone, aka "vibratone," ca. 1916–early 1920s), which was marketed as the vibraharp/vibraphone by others who secured the patents first [see *Schluter, Henry]. Leedy also helped produce the largest concert bass drum in the world for Purdue University in 1921 [still in existence].

Conn purchased Leedy in 1929 and moved operations to Elkhart, Indiana. Before his death Leedy incorporated a new venture in 1930, General Products Company, which featured L & S (Leedy & Strupe) drums as well as nonmusical products. This failed, however, and was sold in 1939 to Indiana Music. In 1950 Conn merged Leedy and Ludwig & Ludwig (which it had previously purchased in 1929) into Leedy & Ludwig Drums. In 1955 Conn sold the Leedy name to the Slingerland Company, which sold Leedy products as their second line until 1958. Both the Slingerland and Leedy names were sold to Fred Gretsch, Jr., in 1986. [See also *Ludwig, William F., Sr., and *Gretsch, Friedrich.]

SELECTED BIBLIOGRAPHY

Cangany, Harry. *The Great American Drums and the Companies That Made Them, 1920–1969.* Cedar Grove, NJ: Modern Drummer Publications, Inc., 1996.
Cook, Rob. *Complete History of the Leedy Drum Company.* Fullerton, CA: Centerstream Publishing, 1993.
GEN. BIB.: Cook, *LDT.*

LEEMAN, CLIFFORD "CLIFF" (b. 10 Sep 1913, Portland, Maine; d. 26 Apr 1986, New York, New York). Drumset artist Cliff Leeman studied xylophone and drums in Portland and, stranded in 1934 with a novelty band in Kansas City, cited the influence of hearing Count Basie's drummer, *Jo Jones, as well as *Chick Webb, *Sid Catlett, and *Zutty Singleton. His big band collaborators included Artie Shaw (1936–39), Tommy Dorsey (1939), Charlie Barnet (1940–42/1949), and Woody Herman (1942–44). Smaller groups with whom Leeman performed and recorded included John Kirby (1944–45), Ben Webster, Don Byas (1944), Yank Lawson and Bob Haggart (1951–60/World's Greatest Jazz Band, 1976–77), Bob Crosby (1960), Wild Bill Davidson and Bobby Hackett (1962/European tour, 1976), Eddie Condon (Australia, Japan, and New Zealand tours, 1964), Kings of Jazz (European tour, 1974), *Red Norvo, Teddy Wilson, Joe Venuti, Bud Freeman, Zoot Sims (1974), the Dukes of Dixieland, Red Nichols, Jimmy Rushing, among others. A proponent of the "Chinese" cymbal for big band playing, he also recorded studio commercials later in his career and could be heard on radio (CBS's *Hit Parade*, 1950s) and television (e.g., the *Perry Como*, *Steve Allen*, and *Jack Benny* shows).

SELECTED DISCOGRAPHY

Bluebird AXM2-5517: *The Complete Artie Shaw*, vol. 1 (1938–39), 1976.
Bluebird AXM2-5581: *The Complete Charlie Barnet*, vols. 3–6 (1939–42), 1981.
Chiaroscuro 130: *Don Ewell*, 1974.
Chiaroscuro 154: *Eddie Condon in Japan*, 1964.
Circle CCD-65: *Charlie Barnet and His Orchestra*, 1941.
Circle CCD-112: *Charlie Barnet and His Orchestra*, 1942.
Decca DL5498: *I Got Rhythm* (Ralph Sutton), 1953.
Jazzology J-76: *Bobby, Vic, and Maxine at Manassas*, 1970.
Jazzology J-128: *"Wild Bill" Davison—Lady of the Evening*, 1985.
Jazzology JCD-112: *Cliff Leeman and His All Stars*.
Jazzology JCD-181: *Wild Bill Davison and His New Yorkers—S' Wonderful*, 1962.
Masters of Jazz, Media 7: *Anthology of Jazz Drumming*, vols. 1–3, 1904–38.
Storyville 8280: *The Ralph Sutton Quartet*, vol. 1, 1969/1998.

SELECTED BIBLIOGRAPHY

Obituary in *Bulletin du Hot Club de France*.
GEN. BIB.: Kernfeld, *NGJ*, by Johnny Simmen; Korall, *DM*; Spagnardi, *GJD*.

LENT, JAMES IRVING "JIMMY" (d. ca. Apr 1943, New York, New York). Drummer and manager of the New York Hippodrome Orchestra for many years, Jimmy Lent founded the Jimmy Lent Society Orchestra in New York in 1924 and served as recording secretary of the Percussion Club of New York City (ca. 1928). Lent's band feature, "Ragtime Drummer," was arranged for xylophone, marimbas, and snare drum by William Cahn in 1981/1993 (Keyboard Percussion Publications).

SELECTED DISCOGRAPHY

Folkways FS 3886: *Phono Cylinders*, vol. 1, 1904/1961 (Lent's "Ragtime Drummer").
Masters of Jazz, Media 7: *Anthology of Jazz Drumming*, vols. 1–2 (1904–35), 1997.
GEN. BIB.: Cook, *LDT*, p. 13, 23, 45, 183.

LEONARD, STANLEY SPRENGER (b. 26 Sep 1931, Philadelphia, Pennsylvania). As a teen Stanley Leonard played timpani for the local orchestra in Independence, Missouri, and took lessons from *Vera McNary (principal percussionist) and *Ben Udell (timpanist) of the Kansas City Philharmonic, with whom he began his professional career at 17. He attended the Interlochen Music Camp before college studies at Northwestern University and the Eastman School, where he worked respectively with *Edward Metzenger and *William Street. After receiving a bachelor's degree and performer's certificate from Eastman (1954), he served in the military (1955–56) as percussionist and assistant conductor of the 19th U.S. Army Band at Ft. Dix, New Jersey. Discharged in 1956, Leonard then held the principal timpanist position and was a featured soloist with the Pittsburgh Symphony (retired 1994) and the Pittsburgh Pops Orchestra (1965–69). A handbell enthusiast and prolific composer, he penned works for handbell choir; and many of his percussion solos, chamber works, ensembles, and timpani method books have become standard repertoire. Percussion editor for Ludwig Music Company, he taught at Carnegie-Mellon University (1958–78, organizing its first percussion ensemble in 1958) and has served on the music faculty at Duquesne University since 1983. Leonard can be heard with the Pittsburgh Symphony (1956–94) on MCA, Telarc, Sony, Mercury, Capitol, Everest, Columbia, Command, Angel, Philips recording labels.

SELECTED DISCOGRAPHY

Ludwig Music ATR 26203: *Canticle—Music of Stanley Leonard*, 1995.

SELECTED BIBLIOGRAPHY

Leonard, Stanley. *Pedal Technique for the Timpani.* Published by author, 1988.
Soroka, John. "Stanley Leonard: A Life in Percussion." *PN* XXXIII, 4 (August 1995): 58–61.
GEN. BIB.: Larrick, *BET-CP*.

LEPAK, ALEXANDER (b. 1920, Hartford, Connecticut). Percussionist, author, teacher, and composer, Alexander Lepak started percussion lessons at age 12 and, during WWII, served with the U.S. Marines in the South Pacific, where he conducted the Third Brigade Orchestra. After the war he moved to New York and studied timpani with *Alfred Friese and percussion with *Henry Adler, performing in Les Elgart's orchestra. Returning to Connecticut and earning a bachelor's degree (1950) from the Hartt School of Music (CT), Lepak chaired the percussion area, founded the Hartt Percussion Ensemble (1950), taught music theory (1947–93), and conducted the concert jazz band. He was named Alumnus of the Year (1981), received an award for excellence in teaching (ca. 1992), and also taught at Queen's University in Canada and at the *Henry Adler Studios (NY). Solo timpanist and principal percussionist with the Hartford Symphony since 1948, he has performed with the Hartford Ballet and the Connecticut Opera Association Orchestra. He can be heard with the Hartford Symphony on both Decca and Vanguard recording labels. During 1979–80 Lepak took sabbatical leave to perform in the New American Orchestra and record television and movie soundtracks (e.g., *Star Trek, Shogun, The Jerk*) and record albums (e.g., Frank Sinatra's *Trilogy*) in Hollywood. He founded Windsor Publications (1967) and retired as professor emeritus from Hartt in 1991.

SELECTED BIBLIOGRAPHY

Baldwin, John, ed. "Connecticut Chapter News." *PN* XXXI, 1 (October 1992): 87–88.

Friese, Alfred, and Alexander Lepak. *The Friese-Lepak Timpani Method.* Rockville Centre, NY: Belwin, Inc., 1966.

Lepak, Alexander. *Control of the Drum Set.* Windsor, CT: Windsor Music Publications, 1978.

Lepak, Alexander. *Fifty Contemporary Snare Drum Etudes.* Windsor, CT: Windsor Music Publications, 1977.

Lepak, Alexander. *Thirty-two Solos for Timpani.* Windsor, CT: Windsor Music Publications, 1975.

Strain, James. "Alexander Lepak: 1997 PAS® Hall of Fame." *PN* XXXV, 6 (December 1997): 6–7.

LESBINES, TELE (b. 29 Oct 1928, Middletown, Connecticut). Having studied with *Paul Price, *Fred Hinger, *Alexander Lepak, *Vic Firth, and *Saul Goodman, Tele Lesbines attended the University of Connecticut and the Hartt School, where he received a bachelor's degree. After serving as timpanist for the Hartford Symphony, he won the principal timpanist chair with the Milwaukee Symphony—a position he has held since 1969. Active as a recording artist in Wisconsin, Vermont, New York, Connecticut, and Massachusetts, Lesbines has performed with the Connecticut Opera, Bridgeport Symphony, New Britain Symphony, Milwaukee Chamber Orchestra, Springfield Symphony, and Brattleboro Music Festival. Currently he is a faculty member of the Wisconsin Conservatory of Music.

SELECTED DISCOGRAPHY

Pro Arte PCD-169: *Stravinsky, Foss, and Ives* (Milwaukee Symphony), 1984.

SELECTED BIBLIOGRAPHY

Joslyn, Jay. "Lesbines Striking as Quintet's Guest." *PN* XV, 1 (Fall 1976): 8 [reprinted from *Milwaukee Sentinel* (Thursday, 25 Mar 1976)].
GEN. BIB.: Larrick, *BET-CP*; PASIC® program biographies, 1997.

LES PERCUSSIONS DE STRASBOURG (founded January 1961). Considered the first professional percussion ensemble in history, Les Percussions de Strasbourg, a sextet, was founded by Jean Batigne, timpanist and faculty respectively for the Strasbourg Opera and Conservatory, and Georges Van Gucht, faculty member of the Toulon Conservatory who is former timpanist with Strasbourg Radio and former faculty at the Lyon Conservatory. Comprised originally of Batigne, van Gucht, Gabriel Bouchet, Jean Paul Finkeiner, Detlef Kieffer, and Claude Ricoll, Les Percussions de Strasbourg all trained under *Félix Passerone at the Conservatoire National de Paris. In 1973 the entire group joined the Strasbourg Philharmonic Orchestra as its percussion section; since then the ensemble has toured the United States and Europe, premiering more than 100 new works and receiving numerous Grand Prix du Disque awards for their recordings. Other members through the years have included Lucien Droeller, Bernard Balet, and Christian Hamouy.

SELECTED DISCOGRAPHY

Denon CO 73678: *Music of Xenakis and Ishii* (with Keiko Abe), 1989.
Harmonia Mundi HMC 905185: *Xenakis—Pleiades*, 1987/1996.
Limelight LS-86051: *The Percussions of Strasbourg*, 1968.
Philips 442 218-2: *Les Percussions de Strasbourg*, 1993.
Philips 836.922 DSY: *Les Percussions de Strasbourg*, 1969.
Pierre Vernay PV-787032: *Stravinsky—Les Noces*.

SELECTED BIBLIOGRAPHY

Dupin, François. "Dupin's Directory of French Percussionists." *PN* XXXII, 2 (April 1994): 29–31.
"The International Scene." *LD* (1976): 28–29.

LEVEY, STAN (b. 5 Apr 1925, Philadelphia, Pennsylvania). A left-handed drumset artist whose career flourished in New York and Los Angeles, Stan Levey started drums at age 7, was influenced by *Chick Webb and *Max Roach, and as a teenager played with Dizzy Gillespie, Charlie Parker, Ray Brown, *Milt Jackson, and Al Haig. His move to New York in 1944 led to a renewed association with Gillespie and Parker and collaborations with Erroll Garner, George Shearing, Coleman Hawkins, Thelonius Monk, Ben Webster, Charlie Ventura, Frank Rosolino, Conte Candoli, Dexter Gordon, Woody Herman (1945), Stan Kenton (1952-), and others. After performing with Howard

Rumsey for six years in California, then touring Europe with Ella Fitzgerald and Peggy Lee (1962–63) and Japan with Pat Boone (1964), Levey settled in as a studio drummer in Los Angeles and also worked with Nelson Riddle, Frank Sinatra, Oscar Peterson, Jimmy Guiffre, and Billy May. He retired there in 1972, owned a photography business, and produced, among other things, album cover photos.

SELECTED DISCOGRAPHY

Affinity 768 Bethlehem: *Stanley the Steamer*, 1954.
Blue Note 84328: *Song for My Daughter* (Jack Wilson), 1968.
Blue Note BLP5059/5060: *Leonard Feather Presents—Best of the West*, 1954.
Blue Note (F) BNP25114: *Tenors Head-On* (Bill Perkins), ca. 1952.
Capitol B21Y 92865: *New Concepts* (Stan Kenton), 1952.
Capitol T 926: *Hi-Fi Drums*, 1957.
Contemporary/OJC 636: *Music for Lighthousekeeping* (Howard Rumsey), 1956.
Savoy SV0-0188: *Swing Not Spring*, 1948/1992.
Verve 837 435-2: *For Musicians Only* (Dizzy Gillespie), 1956.
Verve MGV2079: *Oscar Peterson with Buddy Bregman's Orchestra*, 1957.
Verve MGV8011: *Tal Farlow*, 1955.
Verve MGV8252: *Herb Ellis*, 1957.
Verve MGV8294: *Stan Getz Quartet*, 1956.
Verve MGV8305: *Howard Roberts*, 1959.
Verve MGVS6045: *Herb Ellis and Jimmy Guiffre*, 1959.
Verve VE2-2536: *Ben Webster Quintet*, 1957.
Verve VE2-2537: *Stan Getz and Gerry Mulligan*, 1957.
Verve V6-4053: *Ella Fitzgerald*, 1961.
Verve V6-8837: *Sonny Stitt*, 1960.

SELECTED BIBLIOGRAPHY

"Cross Section: Stan Levey." *DB* XXVI, 3 (5 Feb 1959): 13.
GEN. BIB.: Hunt, *52nd St.*; Spagnardi, *GJD.*

LEWIS, MEL (b. Melvin Lewis Sokoloff, 10 May 1929, Buffalo, New York; d. 2 Feb 1990, New York, New York). The son of a drummer, Mel Lewis played euphonium in school, was a self-taught drummer, and started his professional career in 1944, performing with Ray Anthony (who shortened Lewis' name ca. 1949), Alvino Rey, Boyd Raeburn, Sonny Stitt, and Dizzy Gillespie, among others. He established his reputation with the Stan Kenton Orchestra (1954); in 1957 a move to Los Angeles brought connections with *Terry Gibbs and a group co-led with Bill Holman. Lewis toured the Soviet Union with Benny Goodman (1962), worked with Gerry Mulligan in New York (1963), and by 1965 had formed the legendary Thad Jones–Mel Lewis Big Band, which became the Mel Lewis Orchestra in 1978 when Jones departed. A vehicle for Jones' compositions, the Big Band/Orchestra toured, recorded, and was a weekly mainstay at New York's Village Vanguard Club for several years. Lewis was a posthumous recipient of *Modern Drummer* magazine's Editors' Achievement Award in 1996.

SELECTED DISCOGRAPHY

A&M/Horizon SP-701: *Thad Jones & Mel Lewis—Suite for Pops*, 1977.

A&M/Horizon SP-707: *Thad Jones & Mel Lewis—New Life*, 1975–76.

A&M/Horizon SP-716: *Mel Lewis and Friends*, 1977.

A&M SP 724: *Live in Munich*, 1976.

Audiophile ACD-218: *Marlene VerPlanck Sings Alec Wilder*, 1992.

Audiophile ACD-241: *Mr. Tram Associates—Getting Some Fun out of Life*, 1988.

Biograph 12059: *Greetings and Salutations*, 1978.

Blue Note 84298: *Always Something There* (Stanley Turrentine), 1968.

Blue Note 84346: *Consummation*, 1970.

Blue Note 89905: *Jazz Wave LTD. on Tour* (Thad Jones-Mel Lewis Orchestra), 1969.

Blue Note BN-LA392-H2: *Thad Jones/Mel Lewis*, 1966–69.

Blue Note (F) BNP25112: *Benny on the Coast* (Benny Carter), 1959.

Capitol: *Contemporary Concepts* (Stan Kenton), 1955.

Concord CJ 378: *The Howard Alden Trio*, 1989.

Contemporary 7647/52/54/56/57: *Dream Band,* vols. 1–5 (Terry Gibbs Big Band), 1986.

Contemporary/OJC CD-341-2: *Art Pepper + Eleven*, 1959.

Mosaic MD5-151: *The Complete Solid State Recordings of the Thad Jones/Mel Lewis Orchestra*, 1966–70.

MusicMasters: *Soft Lights and Hot Music*, 1988.

MusicMasters 5024-2-C: *The Definitive Thad Jones*, vol. 1, 1989.

OJC 464: *Mean What You Say* (Thad Jones), 1966.

Philadelphia International KZ 33152: *Potpourri*, 1974.

Red Baron JK 53752: *Mel Lewis and the Jazz Orchestra—Music of Bob Brook-meyer*, 1982.

Solid State 18003: *Thad Jones, Mel Lewis and the Jazz Orchestra*, 1966.

Solid State SD 18045: *The Worm* (Jimmy McGriff), 1968.

Solid State SS 18048: *Monday Night Recorded Live at the Village Vanguard*, 1969.

Telarc Digital DG 10044: *Mel Lewis and the Jazz Orchestra*.

Telarc CD-83301: *Naturally*, 1979.

Verve 838 933-2: *The Concert Jazz Band* (Gerry Mulligan), 1960.

Verve MGV8111: *Bob Brookmeyer Quartet*, 1955.

Verve MGV8247: *Herbie Mann*, 1957.

Verve MGVS6019: *Ella Fitzgerald with Marty Paich's Dek-Tette*, 1958.

Verve MGVS6051: *Buddy DeFranco*, 1958.

Verve MGVS6104: *Gerry Mulligan and Ben Webster*, 1959.

Verve MGVS6140: *Terry Gibbs and His Big Band*, 1960.

Verve MGVS6162: *Sonny Stitt*, 1959.

Verve MGVS6146: *Mel Torme*, 1960.

Verve UMV 2687: *Saxophone Supremacy* (Sonny Stitt), 1959.

Verve V6-8469: *Don Randi*, 1962.

Verve V6-8485: *Anita O'Day*, 1958.

Verve V6-8730: *Cal Tjader*, 1967.
VSOP 25: *Big Band in a Jazz Orbit* (Bill Holman), 1987.

SELECTED VIDEOGRAPHY

Kultur Video: *Jazz at the Smithsonian—Mel Lewis*, 1984.
Kultur Video: *Mel Lewis*, 1983.
Tel Ad/VIEW Video: *Mel Lewis and His Big Band*, 1983
VAI Jazz Collection/Music Video Distributors: *Live at the Village Vanguard*, vol. 5 (Lee Konitz et al.), 1989.

SELECTED BIBLIOGRAPHY

Breithaupt, Robert, ed. "In Memoriam: Mel Lewis Talks." *PN* XXVIII, 3 (Spring 1990): 66–70.
Lewis, Mel and Clem De Rosa. *It's Time for the Big Band Drummer*. Delevan, NY: Kendor, 1978.
Michael, Chris. "Mel Lewis: 'Stompin' at the Savoy.' " *PN* XXXII, 1 (February 1994): 14–17.
Morgenstern, Dan. "Mel Lewis: The Big Band Man." *DB* XXXIV, 6 (23 Mar 1967): 20–21.
Tynan, John. "The Peripatetic Mel Lewis." *DB* XXIX, 10 (10 May 1962): 24.
Tynan, John. "Time Is the Quality Mel Lewis Has." *DB* XXIV, 25 (12 Dec 1957): 22.
GEN. BIB.: Hunt, *52nd St.*; Spagnardi, *GJD.*

LEWIS, VICTOR (b. Omaha, Nebraska). Drumset artist and composer Victor Lewis first collaborated in the 1970s with Woody Shaw, David Sanborn, Oliver Lake, and in the 1980s with Stan Getz, Carla Bley, Dexter Gordon, and the Charles Mingus "Epitaph" Orchestra. He co-led the group Horizon with Bobby Watson in the early 1990s and has appeared with Cedar Walton (European tour), Art Farmer (NYC), J. J. Johnson (Port Townsend Jazz Fest), and the Smithsonian Jazz Masterworks Orchestra.

SELECTED DISCOGRAPHY

Astor Place 4001: *Cedar Walton—Composer*, 1996.
Audioquest AQ 1010: *Family Portrait*, 1992.
Blue Note 91984: *Nightingale* (George Adams).
Blue Note CDP 7 91915 2: *The Inventor* (Bobby Watson & Horizon), 1990.
Columbia CBS 467181: *Sophisticated Giant* (Dexter Gordon), 1977.
EmArcy 838 769: *Anniversary* (Stan Getz), 1987.
EmArcy 838 770: *Serenity* (Stan Getz), 1987.
Enja 9030: *Kevin Mahogany—You Got What It Takes*, 1995.
Jazzheads JH9495: *Manhattan Morning* (Lenny Hochman), 1996.
Red 123255: *Know It Today, Know It Tomorrow*, 1992.
Red 123532: *Setting the Standard* (David Liebman).
Soul Note 1049CD: *Live in the Time Spiral* (George Russell), 1982.
Spirit Song: *Blues for McCoy* (Dave Panichi), 1995.

Verve 314-527-382: *Abbey Lincoln—A Turtle's Dream*, 1995.
Verve 314533232: *Those Who Were* (Niels-Henning Ørsted Pedersen), 1997.

SELECTED VIDEOGRAPHY

A*Vision/Warner Vision: *Jazz Masters—Vintage Getz*, vols. 1–2 (Stan Getz), 1991.

SELECTED BIBLIOGRAPHY

Kiely, Bill. "Victor Lewis: Man in Motion." *MD* XXI, 2 (February 1997): 10.
Micallef, Ken. "Victor Lewis: Jazz Chameleon." *MD* XVI (June 1992): 28–31.
Micallef, Ken. "Victor Lewis' Relaxed Abandon." *JazzTimes* XXII, 9 (November 1992): 36.
GEN. BIB.: Hunt, *52nd St.*

LIGHT, WALTER JOSEPH (b. 30 Jul 1927; d. 1 Jun 1979, Denver, Colorado). Percussionist (1943) and timpanist (succeeding his father, ca. 1952) with the Denver Symphony, Walter Joseph Light played a strip club in his teens, and his percussive colleagues in the orchestra included Bill Werner and *Ted Small. The garage operation where Walter J. began making the Dresden-style Light Timpani, around 1949, eventually became the American Drum Company, which is owned and operated by Walter J.'s son, Marshall Light. [Not to be confused with the mallet manufacturer American Drum of Virginia.] Walter J.'s father, Walter Ellis Light (d. ca. 1952, Denver, CO), was timpanist with the Denver Symphony from around 1924 to 1952, and cut his percussive teeth with the Barnum & Bailey Circus and in vaudeville at the Rialto Theater in Denver.

SELECTED BIBLIOGRAPHY

"Percussion in Our Orchestras." *IM* (June 1949): 24–25 (photo).
Pfannenstiel, Karen. "Walter Light: The End of an Era." *PN* XVIII, 3 (Spring/Summer 1980): 76–77 [reprinted from *Denver Magazine* (September 1979)].
GEN. BIB.: Cook, *LDT*, p. 124, 187 (photo of Walter E. Light).

LISHON, MAURICE "MAURIE" (b. 7 Aug 1914, Chicago, Illinois). A former member of their board of directors who was inducted into the Percussive Arts Society Hall of Fame in 1989, Maurie Lishon started drums at age 5. He attended Crane Junior College and Northwestern School of Journalism for two years but studied percussion with *Roy Knapp, Lou Singer, Abe Zipperstein, *Bobby Christian, and Walter Dellers. Turning professional at 14, Lishon established himself in Chicago as staff drummer for WBBM radio (CBS) at age 19 and eventually played for NBC and ABC radio as well. During WWII he served with the official band of the Sixth Service Command (Ft. Sheridan, IL), which was named the best dance band in the Continental U.S. Army by Les

Brown, Benny Goodman, and Woody Herman. Upon discharge, he freelanced and filled the staff drummer position for the first television shows at Chicago stations (19 years with CBS) playing as many as 35 shows per week.

During his 45-year tenure as a performing artist, Lishon played virtually every club, theater, and recording-broadcasting studio in Chicago. Among the many notables with whom he worked were Boyd Raeburn, Victor Borge, George Gobel, Eddie Cantor, George Jessel, Sophie Tucker, Joe E. Lewis, Milton Berle, Vic Damone, Arthur Godfrey, Danny Thomas, and Jimmy Durante. He and his wife, Jan, were instrumental in initiating the career of singer Patti Page (aka Clara Ann Fowler), with whom he produced the first multitrack (overdub) recording.

Lishon purchased Frank's Drum Shop in 1959, which through his nurturing became a mecca for all percussionists, young and old, to exchange ideas and see and hear the latest equipment played by the greatest percussionists throughout the world. He was cited by the Chicago American Federation of Musicians Local 10-208 for his many contributions to the music industry, and he served as percussion editor of *Intermezzo*, the local union paper. Honored many times for his civic contributions, he received the Dal Segno "Man of the Year" award in 1975. After extensive heart surgery in 1974, he sold the store to his son, Marty, and relocated to Florida, where he played drums with the big band Second Time Around (est. 1980), which has made recordings and was featured on the CBS *Sunday Morning* television show in May 1988.

SELECTED BIBLIOGRAPHY

Cook, Rob, ed. *Franks for the Memories: A History of the Legendary Chicago Drum Shop and the Story of Maurie and Jan Lishon.* Alma, MI: Rebeats Publications, 1993.
Randolph, Marvin. "Musical Echoes: Drummer Maurie Lishon Hasn't Stopped Playing." *Palm Beach Post,* (5 May 1989): 18.

LIUZZI, DON (b. Weymouth, Massachusetts). Timpanist with the Philadelphia Orchestra (since 1989), with whom he made his solo debut in 1996, Don Liuzzi studied with *John Soroka, *Alan Abel, and *Charles Owen and earned a bachelor's degree from the University of Michigan and a master's degree from Temple University. He has performed with the Pittsburgh Symphony (1982–89), Colorado Philharmonic, Flint Symphony, Spoleto Festival, Michigan Opera, and Berkshire Music Center Orchestras and has conducted master classes throughout the United States, China, Mexico, Korea, and Spain. A member of the Curtis Institute faculty since 1994, Liuzzi also taught at Duquesne University, has recorded for the CRI label, appeared on Public Broadcasting's television show *Mr. Rogers' Neighborhood,* conducted the Three Rivers Young Peoples Orchestra, and played with Network for New Music.

SELECTED DISCOGRAPHY

CRI CD 681: *Tina Davidson—I Hear the Mermaids Singing*, 1996.
CRI CD 720: *Robert Maggio—Seven Mad Gods*, 1996.
Philadelphia Orchestra personnel biographies, 1996; PASIC® program biographies, 1997.

LOHSE, AUGUST KARL (b. 21 Mar 1887, Oberholsten/Westfalia, Germany; d. 16 Sep 1965, Bad Orb, Germany). After teaching himself percussion fundamentals, August Lohse played for a short time in the Hagen City Orchestra and then fulfilled his military service at a very young age in a music corps in Bremen. From 1907 to 1911, he performed with the Düsseldorf Opera, entering the Berlin Philharmonic as percussionist and timpanist in 1911. Following military service in WWI (1914–18), he returned to the Berlin Philharmonic and, by 1938, was named to the newly created position of principal timpanist. (Before this, all percussion personnel were expected to play both timpani and percussion.) Lohse was honored by the Berlin Philharmonic in 1941 for his musicianship, then retired around 1948. A self-taught, prominent connoisseur and collector of art—particularly the Dutch school—he lost his eyesight in later years, undergoing an operation that brought him only slight improvement.
GEN. BIB.: Avgerinos, *KB*.

LONDIN, LARRIE (b. Ralph Gallant, 1943; d. 24 Aug 1992, Nashville, Tennessee). One of the first white musicians contracted to Motown Records (VIP label), Larrie Londin performed with the Detroit-based "Headliners" in the mid-1960s and recorded with the Temptations, Supremes, and Marvin Gaye, as well as George Strait, Joe Cocker, Olivia Newton-John, Waylon Jennings, Randy Travis, B. B. King, Linda Ronstadt, Barbara Mandrell, Reba McEntire, and Dolly Parton, among many others. Touring with Elvis Presley (1977), Glen Campbell, Jerry Reed, and Chet Atkins, he was honored by the National Academy of Recording Arts and Sciences (NARAS) as "Most Valuable Player" (1978–80), as "Best Drummer" for 1984/1986 by the Academy of Country Music, and as "Country Drummer of the Year" in 1985/1986 by *Modern Drummer* magazine. He was inducted into the latter's Reader's Poll Hall of Fame in 1994. A tribute to his successful career, Sabian, Ltd., cymbal company established the Larrie Londin Memorial Scholarship Fund through the auspices of the Percussive Arts Society.

SELECTED VIDEOGRAPHY

DW Video/Drum Workshop, Inc.: *A Day with Larrie Londin*, 1991.

SELECTED BIBLIOGRAPHY

Donovan, Dan. "Larrie Londin." *PN* XXIII, 1 (October 1984): 26–27.

Flans, Robyn. "Larrie Londin Remembered." *MD* XVII (March 1993): 22–27.
"Obituary." *The Journal of Country Music* XV, 2 (1993): 55.
Wyant, D. "In Memory of Larrie." *MD* XVII (March 1993): 4.

LOWE, CHARLES P. "CHARLIE." Drummer and xylophone soloist for the Sousa Band (1882/1894, 1907), Charles Lowe recorded polkas, galops, waltzes, and pop songs for the Edison and Columbia Companies (1889?/1896–1906) and appeared for over 12 years with the Henry Savage musical show (ca. 1911–25). Legend has it that he was the first person to record a xylophone solo, though he was probably the second. [According to *William Cahn: A. T. Van Winkle probably made the first one on 26 Aug 1889 for North American Phonograph, a company formed by Thomas Edison which produced the first series of recordings employed in coin-operated machines.]

SELECTED DISCOGRAPHY

Columbia A207: "Washington Post March," 1902.
Edison 3003: "Carnival of Venice," ca. 1896–99.
Edison 3004: "Charleston Blues," ca. 1896–99.
GEN. BIB.: Cahn, *XAR*; Cook, *LDT*, p. 18, 345 (photo); Strain, *XYLO*.

LUCCHESI, MARGARET C. "PEGGY" (b. 12 Jun 1928, Oakland, California; d. 1985, Oakland, California). A student at the University of California at Berkeley (bachelor's, 1949), the Royal Academy of Music in London (LRAM, 1952—the first female to receive a degree in conducting), and San Francisco State College (master's, 1957), Peggy Lucchesi was percussionist with the San Francisco Symphony (1955–80), San Francisco Opera (part time, 1961/full time, 1980), and taught at the San Francisco Conservatory (1955–62/1972–) and University of California at Berkeley (1968–).

SELECTED BIBLIOGRAPHY

Baldwin, Dr. John, ed. "In Memoriam." *PN* XXIII, 5 (July 1985): 14.
GEN. BIB.: Borland, *WWAMC*.

LUDWIG, WILLIAM FREDERICK, JR. [II] (b. 1916, Chicago, Illinois). Inducted into the Percussive Arts Society Hall of Fame in 1993 for his decades of service to percussion instrument development and education, William F. Ludwig, Jr., performed with the Chicago Civic Orchestra and had aspirations of becoming a full-time orchestral timpanist, but he joined his father's firm, Wm. F. Ludwig Drum Company, in 1937 as sales and advertising manager. He served in the U.S. Navy in WWII, was elected president in 1966 of the Music Industry Council, served as president of the National Association of Band Instrument Manufacturers, and became the head of Ludwig Drum Company in

1971. After the Selmer Company purchased Ludwig in 1981 and moved operations to North Carolina, he maintained the Ludwig Industries Artist Relations
Department in Chicago with his son, William III, and continues to present lecture-demonstrations on percussion for schools and conventions.

SELECTED DISCOGRAPHY

Ludwig Drum Co. 14-100/WFL-301: *The 13 Essential Drum Rudiments*,
    1948/1960 (includes J. Burns Moore, Edward B. Straight, William F.
    Ludwig, Sr. and Jr.).

SELECTED VIDEOGRAPHY

Rebeats Publications/Cook's Music AA: *Introduction to Vintage Drums*, 1991.

SELECTED BIBLIOGRAPHY

Durrett, Ward. "An Interview with Mr. William Ludwig, Jr." *PN* XXIX, 3 (February
    1991): 7.
Ludwig, William F., Sr. *My Life at the Drums: Eighty Years a Drummer.* Chicago:
    Ludwig Industries, 1972.
Ludwig, William F., Jr. *Swing Drumming.* Chicago: W.F.L. Drum Co., 1942.
Rusch, J. J. "William F. Ludwig, Jr." *PN* XXXII, 3 (June 1994): 10–11.
Schmidt, Paul William. *History of the Ludwig Drum Company.* Fullerton, CA: Cen-
    terstream Publishing, 1991.
"Three Generations of the Drumming Ludwigs." *LD* IV, 2 (Fall 1964): 3–5.

LUDWIG, WILLIAM FREDERICK, SR. (b. 15 Jul 1879, Nenderoth, Germany; d. 8 Jul 1973, Chicago, Illinois). Immigrating with his family to Chicago at the age of 8, William Ludwig, Sr., was the son of professional trombonist Henry J. Ludwig, who insisted that he study violin with his grandfather
while simultaneously starting drum lessons (his real desire!). After giving up
violin, he tried piano. His drum instructor, John Catlin, required him to perfect
rudiments from the Bruce & Emmet book on a practice pad before playing them
on snare drum—a three-year process. An early drumset artist, he performed with
a plethora of musical organizations, including circus bands (Wood Brothers,
1895–96, with his father), dance bands, minstrel road shows, and concert bands
and orchestras (Salisbury's Concert Orchestra, 1899, and Arthur Pryor, 1913), as
well as at venues such as the Omaha Exposition (1898). Leaving the unpleasant
experiences of touring behind, he joined the Chicago musician's union and began playing theater, burlesque, and vaudeville jobs with a set of bells and a ma-
ple bar xylophone (mounted on straw, no spacers or resonators), which he purchased from one of his teachers, Joseph Schumacher, a Chicago theater drummer.
Ludwig later purchased a set of timpani and took lessons with *Joseph Zettleman, timpanist of the Theodore Thomas Symphony Orchestra (later aka Chicago Symphony). He performed on timpani with the Henry W. Savage English

Grand Opera (six seasons, starting in 1904), Ziegfield Follies (Chicago, 1908), Pittsburgh Symphony (1910–11), Chicago Grand Opera and Civic Opera (snare drum, 1911–14), and Chicago Symphony (bass drum, 1916–18). The Chicago Grand Opera percussion section included (ca. 1911) *Frederick Seitz on timpani, Ruben Katz on bass drum, and Aldo Bartolotti on cymbals and accessories.

With his brother-in-law, Robert C. Danly, a designer and machinist who patented the first "complete" snare throwoff device, Ludwig invented and manufactured the first "spring-balanced-action," pedal-tuned, collapsible timpani (Universal Model, 1919–21). Their previous unsuccessful prototypes had employed hydraulic tuning by means of a pressure pump and expandable tension ring (1911) and a cable-driven model (1917). They also improved and patented the first efficient bass drum pedal and designed and patented the horizontal-valve piston bugle and the first chromatic bell lyre. In 1909 Ludwig and his younger brother, Theobald R. (b. ca. 1889; d. 28 Oct 1918), who was also a drummer, established the Ludwig & Ludwig percussion manufacturing company and made rope-tensioned field snares for the U.S. military during WWI. Spawning a new movement of decorative drum exteriors, the Ludwigs created a gold-plated snare drum in 1917 for Vernon Castle of the famous Castle dance duo (with wife, Irene) as a gift for their drummer, Max H. Manne, who was leaving to manage the new Roxy Theater. As the company grew, William Ludwig retired in 1918 from professional performing but remained active instructing drum and bugle corps (e.g., Skokie, Illinois Indians), adjudicating, and performing in the Chicago Shrine Band for over 50 years.

Succumbing to the Great Depression, Ludwig & Ludwig and the Leedy Drum Company merged with the C. G. Conn Company and all operations were relocated to Elkhart, Indiana. For 25 years these two subsidiaries were consolidated as "Leedy and Ludwig." Ludwig, as a minority stockholder and without direct creative input, left Conn in 1936 and started the Wm F. Ludwig Drum Company in 1937 in Chicago. His first product was the legendary "Speed King" bass drum pedal (1937), and in 1939 he changed the name to W.F.L. Drum Company to avoid confusion with Conn's Leedy & Ludwig division. He served on the Musical Instrument Committee of the War Production Board during WWII, when metal restrictions caused him to cease timpani, bass drum pedal, and hi-hat stand production and to exclusively manufacture virtually complete wooden drums and wooden drum stands. Barely subsisting on government orders for drumsets in military dance bands, Ludwig worked for a while in Cleveland as management for a former band instrument company that produced radar parts. After WWII he returned to the factory in Chicago to recommence, only to be thwarted for three years by government restrictions during the Korean War. In 1955 he purchased the Ludwig machinery and all rights to Leedy & Ludwig from Conn, and soon the W.F.L. Drum moniker became Ludwig Drum Company. The Musser Marimba Company in LaGrange, Illinois, was acquired by Ludwig in 1966, but the Musser name was retained on all keyboard percussion products. Known as Ludwig Industries in the late 1960s, it became one of the largest drum companies in the world until it was absorbed by the Selmer Corporation (a North American Philips subsidiary) in 1981.

Ludwig was well known for his compositions, method books, and the periodical *Ludwig Drummer*, which focused on percussion education. He was a charter member of the National Association of Rudimental Drummers, serving as its first secretary in 1933, and was honored by the Percussive Arts Society in 1972 with induction into its Hall of Fame and with posthumous election to the American Music Conference Hall of Fame in 1978.

SELECTED DISCOGRAPHY

Ludwig Drum Co. 14-100/WFL-301: *The 13 Essential Drum Rudiments*, 1948/1960 (includes J. Burns Moore, Edward B. Straight, William F. Ludwig, Sr. and Jr.).
Mercury Golden Imports SRI-75048: *The Spirit of '76—Music for Fifes and Drums*, 1957.

SELECTED BIBLIOGRAPHY

Cangany, Harry. *The Great American Drums and the Companies That Made Them, 1920–1969.* Cedar Grove, NJ: Modern Drummer Publications, Inc., 1996.
"In Memoriam." *PN* XII, 1 (Fall 1973): 11.
Ludwig Drum and Bugle Manual. Chicago: Ludwig Drum Co., 1920/1956.
Ludwig Drummer. Chicago: Ludwig Drum Co. (published 1925–39/1954–1970s).
Ludwig, William F., Sr. "67 Years of Drum Pedals." *LD* I, 2 (Spring 1962): 5–7.
Ludwig, William F., Sr. *My Life at the Drums: Eighty Years a Drummer.* Chicago: Ludwig Industries, 1972.
Schmidt, Paul William. *History of the Ludwig Drum Company.* Fullerton, CA: Centerstream Publishing, 1991.
"The Percussive Arts Society Hall of Fame" *PN* XI, 2 (Winter 1972): 7 (photo).
GEN. BIB.: Larrick, *BET-CP*.

LUSBY, FRANK W. (b. ca. 1848–51, Washington, D.C.; d. December 1889, Washington, D.C.). John Philip Sousa's military music manual *Book of Instructions for the Field Trumpet and Drum* (1886) was authored in cooperation with his childhood friend, F. W. Lusby, who was drum instructor for the U.S. Marine Corps. Lusby enlisted in 1861 as a snare drummer and served for 28 years, appearing as xylophone soloist with the U.S. Marine Band under Sousa's baton. Before his discharge in 1889 because of illness, he played for all presidential inaugurations and funerals and was known as a composer of military tunes.

SELECTED BIBLIOGRAPHY

"National Association of Rudimental Drummers." *LD* VII, 2 (Fall 1967): 44.
Spalding, Dan C. "The Evolution of Drum Corps Drumming." *Percussionist* XVII, 3 (Spring/Summer 1980): 116–131.
GEN. BIB.: Cook, *LDT*, p. 355; Strain, *XYLO*.

LYLLOFF, BENT (b. 21 Dec 1930, Copenhagen, Denmark). Nicknamed the "Dean of Scandinavian Percussion," Bent Lylloff began studying drums at age 7, playing in a Boy Scout band. At 10 he took piano and mallet lessons and, after studying with Danish teachers, continued his work with Gilbert Webster in London, Robert Tourte in Paris, and *Morris Goldenberg and *Saul Goodman at the Juilliard School. Before 1961 Lyloff freelanced in various orchestras and jazz groups, and then from 1961 to 1989 he was principal percussionist and timpanist with the Royal Danish Orchestra. An avant-garde recording artist, clinician, and composer, he had several works written for him and appeared as soloist in Europe, the United States, Japan, and Australia. Lyloff conducted the Percussions Copenhague and Malmo Percussion Ensemble (founded 1973) and appeared with Frank Sinatra, Louis Armstrong, Dizzy Gillespie, Lena Horne, among others. Since 1989 he has been a professor at the Royal Danish Academy of Music in Copenhagen, founding the International Bent Lylloff Percussion Competition, which was inaugurated in Copenhagen in 1996.

SELECTED DISCOGRAPHY

AST (Astrée) AS 75: *Percussions Copenhague.*
Cambridge 2824: *Pieces* (Copenhagen Percussion Group).
Moss Music Group D-MMG 115: *The All-Star Percussion Ensemble*, 1983.
Information supplied by the subject, 1996.

M

MACCALLUM, FRANK KENNETH (b. 29 Jul 1913, El Paso, Texas; d. 6 Feb 1970, El Paso, Texas). Initially a pianist who became a self-taught marimbist, Frank MacCallum embraced the marimba after hearing recordings of the Blue and White Marimba Band, the Hurtado Brothers from Guatemala, and live concerts by the Mexican Orquesta Típica. Even though he worked as a chemist after attending El Paso College of Mines and Metallurgy in 1936 (aka Texas Western College and University of Texas at El Paso), he remained active as a concert marimba soloist. He served in the U.S. Army (1942–46) and built his own marimbas (from 1942), including bass marimbas. MacCallum contributed articles on the xylophone to the *Encyclopedia Americana* (1958), and on marimba, vibraphone, and xylophone for the fifth edition of *Grove Dictionary of Music and Musicians* (1961). Retiring in 1966, he redevoted his efforts to performing, composing, and arranging and produced several works, including an unpublished "Concerto for Two Marimbas and Orchestra" before his death.

SELECTED BIBLIOGRAPHY

The Edwin L. Gerhardt Marimba-Xylophone Collected Materials. Percussive Arts Society Museum Archives, Lawton, OK.

MacCallum, Frank. *The Book of the Marimba*. New York: Carlton Press, 1969.

MacCallum, Frank. "Marimba." *Hobbies Magazine* (August 1949).

MacCallum, Frank. "The Marimba's Bass Notes." *Percussionist* V, 2 (December 1967): 266–269 (photo in VI, 2: 12).

"MacCallum: Outstanding Texas Composer." *El Paso Times* (1 Nov 1942).

"In Memoriam." *PN* IX, 1 (Fall, 1970).

"Recital Program." *PN* V, 4 (1966).

Stevenson, Robert M. *Music in El Paso: 1919–1939* (from *Southwestern Studies*, Monograph 27). El Paso, TX: Texas Western Press, 1970.

MACDONALD, RALPH (b. 15 Mar 1944, Harlem, New York). Born into a family of drummers and essentially a self-taught conga drummer who apprenticed by listening to his father's calypso group, Ralph MacDonald performed and/or recorded as leader or as studio artist with Harry Belafonte (1961–71) and various other collaborators (1972–present), including Paul Simon, Rahsaan Roland Kirk, Tom Scott, Paul Desmond, Aretha Franklin, Bette Midler, Ron Carter, Roberta Flack (1970–75, including the hits "Killing Me Softly" and "Feel like Makin' Love"), Grover Washington, Jr., Idris Muhammad, Bob James, David Sanborn, the Brecker Brothers, and Steve Kahn.

SELECTED DISCOGRAPHY

Arista 4037: *The Brecker Brothers*, 1975.
Atlantic SD 7238: *Bette Midler—The Divine Miss M*, 1972.
Blue Note 84415: *Grant Green—The Final Comedown*, 1971.
Blue Note LA551-G: *Montara* (Bobby Hutcherson), 1975.
Blue Note LA667-G: *Earl Klugh—Living Inside Your Love*, 1976.
Blue Note LA736-H: *Noel Pointer—Phantazia*, 1977.
Blue Note LA737-H: *Earl Klugh—Finger Paintings*, 1977.
Marlin 2210: *The Path—Ralph MacDonald*, 1978.
Warner Brothers BS 3121: *Joe Farrell—La Catedral y el Toro*, 1977.
GEN. BIB.: Kernfeld, *NGJ*, by Catherine Collins; PASIC® program biographies, 1979.

MAINIERI, MICHAEL T., JR., "MIKE" (b. 4 Jul 1938, Bronx, New York). Born into a family of vaudevillians, musicians, and dancers, Mike Mainieri was initially influenced by *Lionel Hampton and started employing four mallets at the age of 12. By 14 he had won a Paul Whiteman talent contest and toured with the Whiteman Orchestra, broadcasting on radio and television. Mainieri played and arranged for *Buddy Rich's sextet (ca. 1956–62) and at 18 won the International Jazz Critics' Award. Playing amplified vibraphone in a visionary jazz-rock group eventually known as Jeremy and the Satyrs (led by flutist Jeremy Steig, 1962), he formed a 20-piece, experimental ensemble, White Elephant Orchestra (1969–72). The latter performed, recorded, and spawned smaller groups such as L'Image, Dreams, and the fusion group Steps (founded, 1979, and later renamed Steps Ahead), which became a gateway for younger artists who have since established separate artistic careers. Producer, arranger, and composer who has written film scores and jingles and participated on over 100 gold or platinum records, Mainieri was a pioneer in the fusion movement and has collaborated with Coleman Hawkins, Wes Montgomery (recordings, 1967–68), Billie Holiday, Dizzy Gillespie, Benny Goodman, Art Farmer, Joe Henderson, Larry Coryell, David Liebman, Jim Hall, Paul Simon, Janis Ian, Billy Joel, Bonnie Raitt, Dire Straits, Aerosmith, Linda Ronstadt, James Taylor, George Benson, among others. In 1992 he created his own recording label, NYC Records, which is dedicated to "exposing new ideas grounded in the jazz idiom" and "reshaping jazz in the '90s."

SELECTED DISCOGRAPHY

AN 3009: *Free Smiles* (Warren Bernhardt), 1978.

Argo LPS-706: *Blues on the Other Side*, 1962.

Arista/Novus AL 4133: *Loveplay*, 1977.

Blue Note 84358: *Who Knows What Tomorrow Gonna Bring* (Brother Jack McDuff), 1970.

Columbia 35539: *The Blue Man* (Steve Khan), 1978.

Elektra/Musician 60168: *Magnetic* (Steps Ahead), 1986.

Elektra/Musician 9 60351 2: *Modern Times* (Steps Ahead), 1984.

Nippon/Columbia YB-7010/11: *Step by Step* (Steps).

Nippon/Columbia YF-7044: *Paradox* (Steps).

Nippon/Columbia (NYC): *Smokin' at the Pit* (Steps).

NYC 6001: *Yin Yang* (Steps Ahead), 1992.

NYC 6002: *Wanderlust*, 1982.

NYC 6004: *Come Together: Guitar Tribute to the Beatles* (various artists), vols. 1–2, 1993–95.

NYC 6006: *Live in Tokyo* (Steps Ahead), 1986.

NYC 6012: *Vibe* (Steps Ahead), 1995.

NYC 6015: *An American Diary*, 1995.

NYC 6018: *Alone* (George Garzone), 1995.

NYC 6021: *White Elephant* (Mainieri & Friends), 1969-71.

NYC 6026-2: *An American Diary—The Dreamings*, 1997.

Private Music 01005-82120-2: *East Coast, West Coast* (Toots Thielemans), 1994.

Solid State SS-18029: *Insight*, 1968.

Verve-Forecast FTS-3049: *Tim Hardin*, 1968.

Verve V6-8425: *Blues Caravan* (Buddy Rich), 1961.

SELECTED VIDEOGRAPHY

Sony: *The Jazz Life* (Steps Ahead), 1983.

VIEW Video: *Gil Evans and His Orchestra*, 1987.

SELECTED BIBLIOGRAPHY

Birnbaum, Larry. "Mike Mainieri's Big Idea." *DB* LXII (December 1995): 42–45.

DeMichael, Don. "Mike Mainieri Unlimited." *DB* XXVII, 22 (27 Oct 1960): 22.

Mattingly, Rick. "Mike Mainieri: The Paths Less Traveled." *PN* XXXV, 4 (August 1997): 8–17.

Piltzecker, Ted. "The Pioneer of Pickups: An Interview with Vibraphonist, Mike Mainieri." *PN* XXX, 2 (December 1991): 55–56.

Sabins, J. "Mike Mainieri." *MP* II, 3 (June–August, 1986): 8–13.

Schietroma, Robert. "Mike Mainieri." *PN* XXII, 1 (October 1983): 56–58.

Seligman, Adam Ward. "Mike Mainieri's American Plan." *MD* XX, 12 (December 1996): 13.

GEN. BIB.: Kernfeld, *NGJ*, by Paul Rinzler.

MANNE, SHELDON "SHELLY" (b. 11 Jun 1920, New York, New York; d. 26 Sep 1984, Los Angeles, California). A drumset proponent of both the "Cool" and "West Coast" jazz styles, Shelly Manne was the son of drummer Max H. Manne, who played for the Vernon and Irene Castle dance duo (ca. 1917) and managed the new Roxy Theater. The younger Manne began on saxophone but switched to drums around age 18, studied with *Billy Gladstone, and started his career in 1939, playing on a European cruise ship, and working for Bobby Byrne (first recording, 1939), Joe Marsala, Les Brown, Benny Goodman, "Jazz at the Philharmonic" (1949), Woody Herman (1949), Charlie Ventura, and Stan Kenton (1946–48/1950–52). He performed with Coleman Hawkins on the legendary "The Man I Love" (1943), on Dizzy Gillespie's first bop efforts (1945); in between, he served in the U.S. Coast Guard during WWII (1942–45).

A move to Los Angeles in 1952 led him to Shorty Rogers, Howard Rumsey, and Hollywood, where he composed for television and movies (e.g., *Daktari*), performed, and made innumerable recordings in film and record studios. Manne replaced *Davey Tough on Joe Marsala's Band early in his career; he subsequently performed Tough's role in Red Nichols' 1958 biographical film *The Five Pennies* starring Danny Kaye. Winner of the 1947 *Down Beat* Reader's Poll and noted for his melodic, coloristic combo drumming style, he led his own band, Manne's Men, in the 1950s and played and recorded for Andre Previn's trio (from 1956), co-leading the "Poll Winners" group with Barney Kessel and Ray Brown (1957–60/1975). His many collaborators included Thelonius Monk, Charlie Parker, and Bill Evans.

Owner of one of the premier Hollywood venues for jazz, Shelly's Manne Hole (1960–74), he formed the L.A. Four quartet in 1974 and was honored in 1984—a few days before his death—by the Hollywood Arts Council and other agencies with a six-hour concert tribute ("Jazz Pilgrimage"/"Shelly Manne Day") during which he also performed. A three-time Grammy® Award nominee, Manne was cited as the "Most Valuable Player" by the National Academy of Recording Arts and Sciences (1980/1983). His widow, Florence ("Flip"), donated several of his instruments and memorabilia for display in 1996 to the Percussive Arts Society Museum in Lawton, Oklahoma.

SELECTED DISCOGRAPHY

Atlantic 1469: *Boss Sounds*, 1966.
Blue Note CDP 7 46848-2: *The Return of Art Pepper*, 1956.
Capitol 289: *Artistry in Percussion* (Stan Kenton), 1946.
Capitol 28008: *Shelly Manne*, 1950.
Capitol B21Y 98935: *The Birth of the Cool*, vol. 2 (Shorty Rogers), 1951.
Capitol ST 2610: *Sounds!* 1966.
CDP 7243 8 34195 2 4: *Clifford Brown—The Complete Blue Note and Pacific Jazz Recordings* (1953–54), 1996.
Concord 8: *The L.A. Four Scores*, 1974.
Contemporary C2503/OJC CD 152-2: *Shelly Manne and His Men*, vol. 1, 1953.

Contemporary C2518: *Shelly Manne—Russ Freeman*, 1954.
Contemporary 3527: *My Fair Lady* (Andre Previn), 1956.
Contemporary 3535: *The Poll Winners* (Kessel/Brown), 1957.
Contemporary 3543/OJC 637: *Pal Joey* (Andre Previn), 1957.
Contemporary 3577-80: *At the Black Hawk,* pts. 1–4, 1959.
Contemporary 7609: *My Son, the Jazz Drummer*, 1963.
Contemporary 7624: *Outside*, 1969.
Contemporary M 3593/4: *Shelly Manne and His Men at the Manne-Hole*, 1961.
Contemporary Records 2516: *The Three*, 1954.
Contemporary Records M 3584: *The Three and the Two*, 1954/1960.
Contemporary/OJCCD 337 2: *Way Out West* (Sonny Rollins), 1988.
DAG 8430/Sony/Red Baron JK 57759: *Kansas City Breaks* (John Lewis), 1994.
Galaxy 5101: *French Concert*, 1977.
Guild 1001: *Blue 'n Boogie* (Dizzy Gillespie), 1945.
Impulse 20: *2-3-4*, 1962.
Mainstream MRL 375: *"Mannekind"—Shelly Manne*, 1972.
Mercury-Emarcy MG 36071: *Giants of Jazz*, vol. 8—*The Jazz Greats, Drum Role*, 1959.
Mosiac MD6-174: *The Complete Atlantic Recordings of Lennie Tristano, Lee Konitz, and Warne Marsh*, 1997.
OJC 1711: *Claire Austin Sings*, 1956/1980.
Pacific Jazz B21Y 46850: *The Immortal Clifford Brown*, 1954.
Signature 9001: *"The Man I Love"* (Coleman Hawkins), 1943.
Verve/Polygram 840 033-4: *Jazz Club—Drums*, vol. 8, 1951–77.
Verve 837 757-2: *Empathy/A Simple Matter* (Bill Evans), 1962.
Verve MGV8124: *Barney Kessel Quartet*, 1952.
Verve MGV8128: *Hamp and Getz*, 1955.
Verve MGV8200: *Stan Getz Quartet*, 1955.
Verve V/V6-8491: *Mel Torme*, 1960.
Verve V6-8565: *Andre Previn*, 1959.
Verve V6-4071: *Ella Fitzgerald*, 1966.
Verve V6-8675: *Bill Evans Trio*, 1966.
Verve V6-8760: *Michel Legrand Trio*, 1968.

SELECTED VIDEOGRAPHY

DCI VH0249: *Legends of Jazz Drumming, Pt. 2, 1950–70*, 1996.
Green Line Video: *Trombone and Drums* (Frank Rosolino), 1991.
Rhapsody Films: *Shelly Manne Quartet*, 1986.
Shanachie Entertainment: *Jazz Scene U.S.A.*, 1962/1994.

SELECTED BIBLIOGRAPHY

Baldwin, Dr. John, ed. "In Memoriam: Shelly Manne/Joseph Sinai." *PN* XXIII, 4 (April 1985): 20.
Brand, Jack. *Sounds of the Different Drummer*. Rockford, IL: Percussion Express, 1997.
Cerulli, Dom. "Manne!" *DB* XXIII, 15 (25 Jul 1956): 14.
Feather, Leonard. "Shelly: The Whole Manne." *DB* XXXVII, 25 (1970): 16.

"From the PAS® Museum Collection: Shelly Manne Exhibit." *PN* XXXIV, 2 (April 1996): 88.

Gold, Don. "Cross Section: Shelly Manne." *DB* XXIV, 21 (17 Oct 1957).

Levine, D. "Shelly Manne." *MD* V, 7 (1981): 10.

Manne, Shelly. "Shelly Manne Offers His Concept of Jazz Drums." *DB* XXII, 25 (14 Dec 1955): 9.

"Shelly, The Modern Manne." *DB* XVI, 5 (5 Mar 1959): 18–19.

Shultz, Thomas. "A History of Jazz Drumming." *Percussionist* XVI, 3 (Spring/Summer 1979): 124–125.

Strain, James. "Shelly Manne: 1997 PAS® Hall of Fame." *PN* XXXV, 6 (December 1997): 8–9.

Traill, S. "The Shelly Manne Story." *Jazz Journal International* XXXII, 8 (1979): 21.

Tynan, John. "Portrait of a Jazz Success." *DB* XXIX, 14 (5 Jul 1962): 20–22.

GEN. BIB.: Hitchcock and Sadie, *NGA*, by Barry Kernfeld; Hunt, *52nd St.*; Spagnardi, *GJD*.

MANNETTE, ELLIOT "ELLIE" (b. Trinidad). Considered the principal innovator and craftsman of steel drums, Ellie Mannette first became involved with the steel drum evolution in 1937. He made his first pan in Trinidad from a 55-gallon oil drum in 1946, developed the single- and double-second pans, invented the triple-cello pans, extended the range of the bass pans, and has perfected and taught the art of pan tuning in the United States for over 30 years. Since 1991 he has been artist-in-residence at West Virginia University, where he established the University Tuning Project for training future pan builders. Mannette is a recipient of Trinidad's "Pegasus" and "Hummingbird" medals of honor, and some of his instruments grace the halls of museums, such as the Metropolitan, the Contemporary Art Gallery, and the Smithsonian.

SELECTED DISCOGRAPHY

RCA LPB-3007: *1962 Calypso Hits* (Shell Invaders Steel Orchestra), 1962.
United Artists UAS-6739: *Steel & Brass*, 1970.

SELECTED BIBLIOGRAPHY

George, Kaethe. "Interview with Ellie Mannette." *PN* XXVIII, 3 (Spring 1990): 34–38.

Mannette, Ellie. *Introductory Booklet for Starting Steel Band Programs.* Phoenix, AZ: Mannette Touch, 1991.

PASIC® program biographies, 1994.

MANZER, LAWRENCE "LARRY." Timpanist with the St. Paul Symphony (ca. 1911) and the Detroit Symphony (from its inception, ca. 1917, until ca. 1952), Lawrence Manzer was the first to use the prototype Ludwig & Ludwig hydraulically tuned timpani, which worked by means of water pressure inside a rubber tube at the rim underneath the head. [Ludwig abandoned this method when it was discovered that the rubber deteriorated after six months, allowing the water inside to explode!]

SELECTED BIBLIOGRAPHY

Ludwig, William F., Sr. *My Life at the Drums: Eighty Years a Drummer.* Chicago: Ludwig Industries, 1972.
Schmidt, Paul William. *History of the Ludwig Drum Company.* Fullerton, CA: Centerstream Publishing, 1991 (photo, p. 15).

MARCUS, ABRAHAM "ABE." Percussionist and personnel manager with the New York Metropolitan Opera Orchestra, Abe Marcus studied with *Morris Goldenberg and recorded Bartók's "Sonata for Two Pianos and Percussion" with *Saul Goodman.

SELECTED DISCOGRAPHY

Dial 1: *Bartók—Sonata for Two Pianos and Percussion,* 1950.
Moss Music Group D-MMG 115: *The All-Star Percussion Ensemble,* 1983.

MARKOVICH, MITCHEL K. (b. 19 Aug 1944, Chicago, Illinois). An undefeated National Association of Rudimental Drummers (NARD) champion in the 1960s who won numerous Illinois state drumming championships, Mitch Markovich studied with *Frank Arsenault, Larry LaVita, and Dick Brown. He attended the University of Indiana, the American Conservatory, and Fort Hays State University (KS), where he earned a bachelor's degree (1975). He served as instructor for the Chicago Cavaliers drum corps, taught at Fort Hays State, and was percussion director for the Argonne Rebels Drum and Bugle Corps of Great Bend, Kansas, during the 1970s.

SELECTED BIBLIOGRAPHY

Markovich, Mitchel K. "Matched Grip." *LD* (1976).
Markovich, Mitchel K. "New Concepts in Bass Drumming." *LD* V, 1 (Spring 1965): 32.
Markovich, Mitchel K. "Rock N'Roll—Now What?" *LD* VI, 1 (Spring 1966): 28.

MARSH, GEORGE W. (b. ca. 1900; d. ca. 1962). Drumset artist and percussionist who recorded in the early 1920s with the Eddie Elkins Orchestra and played with the Paul Whiteman Orchestra (ca. 1922–27), George Marsh appeared with Isham Jones (ca. 1927–31) and Ferde Grofe (ca. 1932). His brother, Lloyd, was also a professional drummer who toured worldwide.

SELECTED DISCOGRAPHY

Columbia ML 4812: *The Bix Beiderbecke Story*, vol. 2, 1927–28/1959.
Victor 19692: "Steppin' in Society," 1925.
GEN. BIB.: Cook, *LDT*, p. 29, 33.

MARSHALL, BERT "BERTIE." Singer-drummer who played in Paris at the Folies Bergère and Bricktop's during the 1920s, Bert Marshall recorded as vocalist with Django Reinhardt and Stéphane Grappelli in 1934.

MASON, HARVEY (b. 22 Feb 1947, Atlantic City, New Jersey). After attending Berklee College, Harvey Mason completed a bachelor's degree at the New England Conservatory. Following tours and record dates with pianists Errol Garner and George Shearing (1970–71), he relocated to Los Angeles, where he is in demand for television (e.g., the *Academy Awards* show), film (*Roger Rabbit*), and recording studios. Among the many artists with whom he has collaborated are Bob James, Duke Ellington, Quincy Jones (1973); Donald Byrd, Freddie Hubbard, and Gerry Mulligan (Carnegie Hall recording, 1974); Grover Washington, Jr., Herbie Hancock, Lee Ritenour (1977), George Benson, Ray Charles, James Brown, Seals and Croft, Carole King, and *Victor Feldman (1983).

SELECTED DISCOGRAPHY

Arista 4283: *Marching in the Streets*, 1981.
Atlantic 82904: *Ratamacue*, 1996 (Grammy® Award nominee).
Blue Note BT 85140: *Wonderland* (Stanley Turrentine), 1986.
Blue Note LA047-F: *Black Byrd* (Donald Byrd), 1972.
Blue Note LA140-G: *Street Lady* (Donald Byrd), 1973.
Blue Note LA142-G: *Blacks and Blues* (Bobbi Humphrey), 1973.
Blue Note LA260-G: *Saudade* (Moacir Santos), 1974.
Blue Note LA313-G: *Astral Signal* (Gene Harris), 1974.
Blue Note LA344-G: *Satin Doll* (Bobbi Humphrey), 1974.
Blue Note LA368-G: *Stepping into Tomorrow* (Donald Byrd), 1974.
Blue Note LA369-G: *Linger Lane* (Bobby Hutcherson), 1975.
Blue Note LA463-G: *Carnival of the Spirits* (Moacir Santos), 1975.
Blue Note LA635-G: *Can't Hide Love* (Carmen McRae), 1976.
Columbia KC-32731: *Headhunters* (Herbie Hancock), 1973.
GRP 9863: *Blues for Schuur* (Diane Schuur), 1998.
GRP Records GRD-9522: *Harlequin* (Dave Grusin), 1985.
Kudu 20: *Mister Magic* (Grover Washington, Jr.), 1974.
Warner Bros. 3111: *Breezin'* (George Benson), 1976.
Warner Bros. 9 46921-2: *Fourplay 4*, 1998.

SELECTED VIDEOGRAPHY

DCI: *A History of R&B/Funk Drumming* by Yogi Horton, 1983.
Video Artists International: *Time Groove* (Louis Bellson, Steve Gadd, et al.), 1990.

SELECTED BIBLIOGRAPHY

Flans, Robyn. "Harvey Mason: Drummer, Percussionist, Solo Artist, Session King—And Now, Band Member?" *MD* XVI (March 1992): 22–27.
Flans, Robyn. "Harvey Mason: Studio Chameleon." *MD* XXII, 10 (October 1998): 64–78.
GEN. BIB.: Larrick, *BET-CP*; Kernfeld, *NGJ*, by Jeff Potter.

MATSON, ROBERT L. "BOB" (b. 1924, Cleveland, Ohio). A graduate of the Juilliard School (artist's diploma, 1949), Bob Matson studied with *Charles Wilcoxon, *Morris Goldenberg, and *Saul Goodman, joined the St. Louis Symphony as percussionist (1949–52), and was assistant timpanist and percussionist with the Cleveland Orchestra for 30 years (ca. 1952–82). He headed the Cleveland Settlement School for 17 years, taught at Cleveland State University (started 1972), and edited Wilcoxon's *Drum Method* (1982).

MAXEY, LINDA WOODS (b. 15 Jan 1942, Toccoa, Georgia). Linda Maxey began piano at age 4, played marimba at 6, and by 11 had performed in Madison Square Garden (NY) for a Kiwanis International Convention. Earning a bachelor's degree from North Texas State University (1963) and a master's degree from the Eastman School (1967), she was the first marimbist on the Columbia Artists Management (NY) roster in 1981 and made her Carnegie Hall debut in 1990. Maxey was a featured soloist at Percussive Arts Society International Conventions in Philadelphia (1990) and San Antonio (1988), has performed solo recitals, been a cruise ship guest artist, appeared with orchestras, and given clinics, lectures, and masterclasses throughout the United States, Canada, and Europe. Following a successful 1996 Lithuanian tour, she received a Fulbright Scholar Award to teach marimba in Vilnius, Lithuania, at the Lithuanian Academy of Music (1999). The first marimbist to perform at the International Festival de Musica in Figuera de Foz, Portugal (1994), she was an adjudicator for the 1996 Music Teachers National Association (MTNA) percussion finals, and her arrangements and transcriptions are published by Southern Music Company.

SELECTED DISCOGRAPHY

Verdi LM 1293: *The Artistry of the Marimba—Linda Maxey*, 1994.

SELECTED BIBLIOGRAPHY

Maxey, Linda. "Note Grouping." *PN* XXX, 6 (August 1992): 54–56.

Maxey, Linda. "A Remembrance of Paul Creston." *PN* XXV, 4 (Spring 1987): 24–25.
Pederson, Stephen. "Marimbist's Performance Close to Perfection." *Chronicle Herald/Mail-Star* (Dartmouth, Nova Scotia) (Saturday, 6 Oct 1990).

MCCURDY, ROY WALTER, JR. (b. 28 Nov 1936, Rochester, New York). Drumset artist Roy McCurdy studied at the Eastman School at the age of 10, served in a U.S. Air Force band, then performed and/or recorded with Gap and Chuck Mangione (1960–61), the Jazztet (with Art Farmer and Benny Golson, 1961–62), Betty Carter (1962–63), Sonny Rollins (1963–64), Julian "Cannonball" Adderley (1965–75), Nancy Wilson, and Kenny Rankin, among others. Active in California television and recording studios, he appeared in performance tours in Europe (1962) and Japan (1963).

SELECTED DISCOGRAPHY

Capitol B21Y 93560/C2 7 93560 2: *Cannonball in Japan* (Cannonball Adderley), 1966.
Capitol TOCJ-5323: *Mercy, Mercy, Mercy* (Cannonball Adderley), 1966.
Concord 121: *Moon and Sand* (Kenny Burrell), 1979.
Elek. Mus. 960298: *In Performance at the Playboy Jazz Festival*, 1982.
Fantasy 9435: *Inside Straight* (Cannonball Adderley), 1973.
Little David 1013: *The Kenny Rankin Album*, 1977.
Mama Records: *Playing with Fire* (Bobby Shew), 1997.
Perea BP003: *Day by Day* (Barbara Paris), 1998.
RCA 2179-2-RB: *All the Things You Are* (Sonny Rollins), 1963.
RCA PL43268: *The Alternative Rollins* (Sonny Rollins), 1964.
RCA R25-5-1011/OJ-25241: *Now's the Time* (Sonny Rollins), 1964.
Timeless 180: *One More Mem'ry* (Benny Golson), 1981.
GEN. BIB.: Hunt, *52nd St.*; Kernfeld, *NGJ*, by Jeff Potter.

MCKINLEY, RAYMOND FREDERICK "RAY" (b. 18 Jun 1910, Fort Worth, Texas; d. 7 May 1995, Florida). Singer and drumset artist Ray McKinley began playing at age 4 and never took formal drum lessons, although he did study timpani with *Arthur Layfield in Chicago (ca. 1927) because *Vic Berton was experimenting with pedal timpani in Red Nichols' band. In 1926 he joined the Duncan-Marin Serenaders, played in Nashville (Smith-McDowell Orchestra, until 1928) and Pittsburgh (Tracy-Brown Band, 1928), then joined Milt Shaw and the Detroiters at New York's Roseland Ballroom in 1930. At the height of the Depression (1932), he played for Smith Ballew's group, which included Glenn Miller; he then joined the Dorsey Brothers Band (1934), featuring three trombones (Miller included), one trumpet, and singer Bing Crosby. This ensemble recorded over 100 tunes for the Decca label (1934–35). After the brothers parted on a sour note, he stayed with Jimmy Dorsey (who led the band until 1939), appearing on the *Kraft Music Hall* radio show from Los Angeles with Bing Crosby. When *Dave Tough relieved him in Dorsey's band, McKinley co-led a "boogie-woogie" band with Will Bradley (aka Wilbur Schwichten-burg). For the latter he experimented briefly with two bass drums (made by Slingerland) around 1940, before Louis Bellson perfected the art with his Gretsch versions. He then formed his own band in 1942, recorded for Capitol, and made a film called *Hit Parade of 1943* in which the Count Basie and Freddie Martin Bands also made appearances.

McKinley tried to enlist his band in the U.S. Marines as a unit, since every-one was being drafted or volunteering, but ultimately he joined Glenn Miller's Army Air Force Band in 1943 and was first posted at Yale University. They broadcast the *I Sustain the Wings* national radio show each Saturday from New York, went overseas a few weeks after D-Day in June 1944, and were stationed in England. After Miller's tragic plane disappearance, Sergeant McKinley as-sumed command, receiving the Bronze Star for his work with the band. He was discharged in 1945 and formed his own band again until 1951, using experimen-tal charts by arranger-composer Eddie Sauter. Working in radio and early tele-vision, he led studio bands for TV variety shows, played with the Sauter-Finnegan Jazz Orchestra, and fronted the Glenn Miller "ghost" Orchestra (1956–66/1973–78). McKinley remained a big band swing drummer who did not embrace bebop and was considered a rhythm section team player.

SELECTED DISCOGRAPHY

Bandstand BS-1: *Will Bradley and His Orchestra* (1939–41), 1965.
Circle CCD-88: *Will Bradley and His Orchestra, Featuring Ray McKinley*, 1941.
Decca DL5262: *Dixieland Jazz Battle*, vol. 2 (McKinley's band), 1950.
Decca DL 8631: *The Fabulous Dorseys Play Dixieland Jazz* (1934–35), 1959.
Dot DLP 3740: *Ray McKinley's Greatest Hits*, 1969.
Grand Award : *Hi-Fi Dixie* (McKinley sextet), 1955.
Grand Award 33-333: *The Swingin' 30s* (with Peanuts Hucko), 1955.
Joyce 1115/LP-1033: *One Night Stand with Ray McKinley*, 1946/1989.
RCA 09026-68320: *Glenn Miller—The Lost Recordings*, 1944.
RCA Victor LPM 6700: *Glenn Miller Army Air Force Band* (5-LP set), 1959.
Savoy Jazz SV-0203/Majestic: *Ray McKinley Orchestra—Borderline* (1946–47), 1993.
Soundcraft 1004: *Glenn Miller and His Army Air Force Orchestra*, 1944.

SELECTED BIBLIOGRAPHY

Van Horn, Rick. "In Memoriam: Ray McKinley." *MD* XIX, 9 (September 1995): 140 (photos).
GEN. BIB.: Korall, *DM*; Spagnardi, *GJD*.

METZENGER, EDWARD MARION "METZ" (b. 9 Apr 1902, Chicago, Illinois; d. 9 Apr 1987, Muncie, Indiana). Encouraged by his father to study stringed instruments, former principal percussionist (1930–32) and timpanist (1932–63) with the Chicago Symphony Edward Metzenger instead studied percussion with *Ed Straight, *Fred Seitz (Chicago Grand Opera), and Max Wintrich (Chicago Symphony), whose individual percussion and timpani positions Metzenger eventually filled. He performed for dance bands and vaudeville shows early on and owned over 100 types of mallets to please eccentric conductors, supplying *Haskell Harr with his mallets. A radio, television, and recording studio artist, Metzenger taught at Northwestern (1942–60) and Ball State Universities.

SELECTED DISCOGRAPHY

Mercury 434 378-2: *Bartók—Music for Strings, Percussion, and Celeste* (Chicago
        Symphony), 1951/1996.
Percussive Arts Society Hall of Fame nominee biographies.

MILES, CHARLES J. "BUTCH" (b. 4 Jul 1944, Ironton, Ohio). Drumset artist Butch Miles, who is equally at home in combo and big band jazz settings, attended West Virginia State College (1962–66), where he performed with the Charleston Symphony. His musical collaborations read like a "who's who" of the jazz world: Mel Torme (1971–74), Count Basie (1975–79), Dave Brubeck (1979–80), Tony Bennett (1980–81), Bob Wilber (1982–84), Gerry Mulligan (1982–1990s), and Lena Horne (1986–88). Miles is a three-time Grammy® Award recipient as a member of the Count Basie Orchestra and has been featured at the Stuttgart, Munich, Montreaux, Berlin, North Sea, Nice, Cologne, and Newport Jazz Festivals, among others. He appeared in a Royal Command Performance before the Queen of England in 1976 and has toured throughout the world.

Miles' visual media resume includes the *Merv Griffin Show*, *60 Minutes*, the *Tonight Show* with Johnny Carson, the *Mike Douglas Show*, the *Jerry Lewis Telethon*, and the *Dick Cavett Show*. With the Dave Brubeck Quartet and the Count Basie Orchestra, he appeared respectively in the documentary films *The Australian Jazz Fest* and *The Last of the Blue Devils* (bassist Walter Page's group). He recorded more than 70 albums and has also appeared with Billy Eckstein, Frank Sinatra, Woody Herman, Benny Goodman, Sammy Davis, Jr., and a host of other jazz legends.

SELECTED DISCOGRAPHY

Arbors 19145: *Nostalgia* (Bob Wilber), 1995.
Atlantic CS 18129: *Live at the Maisonette* (Mel Torme), 1975.
Audiophile ACD-201: *Dolly Dawn—Memories of You*, 1989.
Audiophile ACD-204: *Ronny Whyte—Soft Whyte*, 1985.
Audiophile APCD-138: *Marlene Verplanck Loves Johnny Mercer*, 1988.
CBS Records PC 37691: *The Glory of Alberta Hunter*, 1982.
Circle CLP-98: *Bob Wilber with the Bodeswell Strings—Reflections*, 1983.
Concord CCD-4103: *Back Home* (Dave Brubeck), 1979/1990.

Dreamstreet DR-101: *Blues Walk* (Warren Vaché), 1978.
Dreamstreet DR-102: *Butch and Bucky—Lady Be Good*, 1978.
Dreamstreet DR-106: *Live at the Dome* (Lou Stein), 1982.
Dreamstreet DR-107: *Steamin' Mainstream*, 1983.
Dreamstreet DR-110: *Christmas in Jazztime* (Glenn Zottola), 1986.
Famous Door HL 117: *Miles and Miles of Swing*, 1978.
Famous Door HL 124: *Butch's Encore*, 1979.
Famous Door HL 142: *Butch Miles Salutes Gene Krupa*, 1982.
Famous Door HL 135: *Butch Miles Swings Some Standards*, 1981.
GRP-D-9503: *Little Big Horn* (Gerry Mulligan), 1983.
Jazzology JCD-142: *Bob Wilber and the Bechet Legacy—Ode to Bechet*, 1986.
Jazzology JCD-214/Bodeswell BW105: *Bob Wilber and the Bechet Legacy—On the Road*, 1982.
Jazzology JCD-263: *Rick Hardeman "All-Star Rhythm,"* 1996.
Laserlight 17133: *Basie in Europe*, 1998.
Pablo PACD 2312-132-2: *A Classy Pair—Ella and Basie*, 1982.
Pablo/OJC-377: *Basie at Montreux*, 1977.
Pablo 2308-207: *Basie Big Band*, 1977.
Pablo KO8-246: *Basie in Japan*, 1985.
Pablo/OJCCD-740-2: *Milt Jackson + Count Basie + The Big Band*, vols. 1–2, 1978/1992.
Pablo/OJCCD-824-2: *I Told You So* (Count Basie), 1976/1994.
Pablo PACD-2310-797-2: *Prime Time* (Count Basie), 1977/1987.
Progressive PCD-7075: *Ronny Whyte Trio—Something Wonderful*, 1985.
Sackville 2044: *Sunday Session* (Ralph Sutton Trio), 1992.

SELECTED BIBLIOGRAPHY

Houliff, Murray. "An Interview with Butch Miles." *PN* XXI, 1 (October 1982): 50–54.
GEN. BIB.: Larrick, *BET-CP.*

MILLER, DONALD. Percussionist with the Cleveland Orchestra (1972–   ), Don Miller studied early on with Robert Bell and later earned a bachelor's degree from the Oberlin Conservatory, where he studied with *Michael Rosen and *Peter Kogan.   He has served as librarian for the Cleveland Orchestra since 1986, owns Belle Press and Henry Call Music Publishing Companies, is composer-arranger of several works, including "Five Short Pieces for Percussion Quintet" and "Four Marches for Snare Drum" (both from Ludwig Music), and has taught at the Saskatchewan Summer School of the Arts, Cleveland State, Cleveland Institute, and Kent State University.

SELECTED DISCOGRAPHY

Crystal Records S-533: *Works by Bubalo and Griffith*, 1982.

SELECTED BIBLIOGRAPHY

"The Percussion Section of the Cleveland Symphony Orchestra." World Percussion
     Network (wpn.org/library/biography/), adapted from a Cleveland Orchestra
     biography.

MILLS, THOMAS "TOMMY." Tommy Mills performed in John Philip
Sousa's Band as snare drummer and xylophone soloist (1900), cut an Edison
cylinder solo ("Four Little Black Berries") as a member of the U.S. Marine
Band (ca. 1912), and later was a recording artist and staff percussionist for the
CBS network.
GEN. BIB.: Strain, *XYLO.*

MOELLER, SANFORD AUGUSTE "GUS." A nonsmoker and teetotaler,
Gus Moeller performed in a coast-to-coast road show (ca. 1910s), at the Metropolitan Opera House, and with the Seventh Regiment Army Band at the Armory
on Park Avenue (NYC). He was a member of the Polar Bear Club [ice swim-
ming] in New York and once marched from New York to Boston (for an American Legion National Convention), sporting an eighteenth-century uniform and
playing a rope-tensioned drum to draw public attention to rudimental drumming
style. With information gleaned from retired Civil War drummers, Moeller's
rudimental snare method book reflected the well-known *Bruce and Emmett text
(1863). His multitude of students included *Gene Krupa and *Jim Chapin.

SELECTED BIBLIOGRAPHY

Hartsough, Jeff, and Derrick Logozzo. "George Carroll: Marching and Field Percus-
     sion Historian." *PN* XXXIV, 2 (April 1996): 30–36.
Moeller, Sanford A. *The Ludwig Instructor in the Art of Snare Drumming.* Chi-
     cago: Ludwig & Ludwig, 1921 (rev. 1929, 1939).

MOERSCH, WILLIAM NORMAN (b. 17 Apr 1954, Detroit, Michigan). A
student of *Charles Owen and a graduate of the University of Michigan with
both bachelor's (1975) and master's (1976) degrees, William Moersch has
commissioned more than 50 new works for marimba and premiered more than
100 works for percussion. Since moving to New York in 1976, he has appeared
as soloist throughout the United States (solo recital debut was 21 May 1984 in
Merkin Concert Hall, New York), Europe, Australia, and Japan. As a percussionist, he has performed with the Metropolitan Opera Orchestra, Orchestre de la
Suisse Romande, Royal Liverpool Philharmonic, New York Chamber Symphony, New Jersey Symphony, American Symphony, and American Composers
Orchestra. With radio, TV, and film appearances to his credit, he also created
and performed the mallet score to the Broadway production of *The Pirates of*

Penzance and can be heard on the soundtrack of *Michael Collins* (Warner Brothers, 1996). He is a founding member of the chamber groups Musical Elements, New York Quintet (flute, clarinet, marimba, double bass, and percussion), Piccolodeon (piccolo, harp, and percussion), and SingleTree (flute, tuba, and marimba). As an educator, he teaches at the University of Illinois and has served on the faculty of the Peabody Conservatory and the Mason Gross School of the Arts at Rutgers University, where he directed the first graduate and doctoral marimba degree programs in the United States. In 1986 Moersch was the first marimbist to receive a Solo Recitalist Fellowship from the National Endowment for the Arts, and he is the founder and artistic director of New Music Marimba, a nonprofit organization established to encourage and commission new music for marimba (e.g., Richard Rodney Bennett's *Concerto for Marimba and Chamber Orchestra*, Andrew Thomas's *Loving Mad Tom for Marimba and Orchestra*, and Libby Larsen's *Marimba Concerto: After Hampton*), which he has performed with the Louisiana Philharmonic and San Antonio Symphony, among others.

SELECTED DISCOGRAPHY

CRI CD 580: *Musical Elements—10th Anniversary Recording*, 1990.
Delos DE 3059: *TreeStone* (Stephen Albert), 1992.
Elektra/Asylum VE 601: *The Pirates of Penzance* (Gilbert & Sullivan), 1981.
Musical Heritage Society MHS 512419A: *Piccolodeon*, 1989.
Newport Classic NPD 85528/Sony Classical re-release: *The Modern Marimba*, 1991/1996.

SELECTED BIBLIOGRAPHY

Holly, Rich. "Marimba Clinic: William Moersch." *PN* XXII, 5 (July 1984): 21–22.
Holly, Rich. "Selected Reviews: *The Modern Marimba*." *PN* XXX, 6 (August 1992): 73.
Louisiana Philharmonic Orchestra Program Notes (1992–93): 31.
Moersch, William. *Master Technique Builders for Vibraphone and Marimba*, ed. Anthony Cirone. New York: Belwin-Mills, 1985.
Moersch, William. *New Music Marimba Repertoire Guide*, vol. 1. New York: New Music Marimba, 1990.
Porter, Andrew. "Musical Events: Chatter, Patter, and Rant." *New Yorker* (4 Jun 1984): 102.
Tircuit, Heuwell. "The Modern Marimba." *Fanfare* XV, 5 (May/June 1992): 315–16.
Via, David. "PASIC® '89: An Individual Entrepreneur—A Discussion with William Moersch." *PN* XXVII, 5 (September 1989): 28–32.

MOLENHOF, WILLIAM "BILL" (b. 2 Jan 1954, St. Louis, Missouri). A unique mallet keyboard artist whose dexterity allows him to simultaneously incorporate multiple mallet instruments into one performance (e.g., vibraphone, marimba, and electronically synthesized mallet instruments), Bill Molenhof studied with William Clark of the St. Louis Symphony (1967–71), *George Gaber at Indiana University (1971–73), and *Gary Burton at Berklee College (1973–74). His solo and chamber ensemble performance venues encompass the United States and Europe, and he has appeared with Pat Metheny, Arnie Lawrence, Jackie Cain/Roy Kral; on the NBC *Today Show* with Ruby Braff; and with stellar drumset artists including *Ed Thigpen, *Alan Dawson, and *Danny Gottlieb. An active composer of mallet solos, duets, and mixed combos that include mallet instruments, he has served on the faculties of Berklee College (1975–76), the Manhattan School (1979–81), Ithaca College (1987–89), Temple University (1989), and the Meistersinger Konservatorium in Nürnberg, Germany (1995).

SELECTED DISCOGRAPHY

Cexton Records 201: *All Pass By*, 1988.
Mark Records MJS 57596: *Beach Street Years*, 1981.

SELECTED BIBLIOGRAPHY

Molenhof, Bill. *Contemporary Marimba Solos.* Delevan, NY: Kendor, 1981.
Molenhof, Bill. *Music of the Day.* Delevan, NY: Kendor, 1977.
Molenhof, Bill. *New Works for New Times.* Delevan, NY: Kendor, 1981.
Molenhof, Bill. *Vibe Songs.* Miami, FL: Belwin-Mills, 1985.
GEN. BIB.: Larrick, *BET-CP*; PASIC® program biographies, 1994.

MOORE, J. BURNS (b. 17 Mar 1872, North Sydney, Cape Breton, Nova Scotia; d. 2 Nov 1951, Hamden, Connecticut). Called the "Dean of Drummers," Burns Moore composed the often-performed snare drum solo *Connecticut Half-Time* and was the first president of the National Association of Rudimental Drummers (NARD, 1933). He started drumming at age 10, came to the United States at age 16, and studied with Jack Lynehan [John E. Lynehan, New Haven, CT; played several years for the Ziegfield Follies] of the Governor's Footguard Band in New Haven, Connecticut, where his family had settled. Moore joined the New Haven Regimental Drum Corps and Governor's Footguard Band, played in dance bands and pit orchestras (35 years), and eventually supplanted Lynehan, serving as timpanist in the New Haven Symphony for more than 45 years. Moore was an undefeated Snare Drum Champion in the Connecticut Fifer's and Drummer's Association (1890–92), and judged several Veterans of Foreign Wars and American Legion National Drum Championships. Among his students were Carl Frolich, Vincent L. Mott, and the highly influential Earl Sturtze. [The original 13 charter members of NARD included Moore, *George L. Stone (Boston), *Bill Kieffer (U.S. Marine Band), Bill Hammond (Pittsburgh), *Malcolm "Heine" Gerlach (Pittsburgh), *Ed Straight (Chicago), *Roy Knapp (Chicago), Harry Thompson (Chicago), George Robertson (Chicago),

Bill Flowers (Chicago), Joe Hathaway (Chicago), *William F. Ludwig, Sr. (Chicago), and Billy Miller (Chicago).]

SELECTED DISCOGRAPHY

Ludwig Drum Co. 14-100/WFL-301: *The 13 Essential Drum Rudiments,* 1948/1960 (includes J. Burns Moore, Edward B. Straight, William F. Ludwig, Sr. and Jr.).
Mercury Golden Imports SRI-75048: *The Spirit of '76—Music for Fifes and Drums,* 1957.

SELECTED BIBLIOGRAPHY

McGrath, William A. "The Contribution of Senior Drum and Bugle Corps to Marching Percussion." *Percussionist* XVII, 3 (Spring/Summer 1980): 149–175.
Moore, J. Burns. *The Art of Drumming.* Chicago: Ludwig Drum Co., 1937; and Hamden, CT: J. Burns Moore Publisher, 1949.
Mott, Vincent L. "What's What and Who's Who in Drumming." *IM* XL, 2 (August 1941): 23.
Stone, George L. "Technique of Percussion." *IM* XLVIII, 4 (October 1949): 28–29.
Stone, George L. "Technique of Percussion." *IM* L, 7 (January 1952): 20.

MOREHEAD, DONALD KEITH (b. 9 Sep 1939, Wheeling, West Virginia). A student of *Stanley Leonard and *Fred Begun, Donald Morehead earned a bachelor's degree from West Virginia University (1965) and a master's degree from Catholic University (1968). Timpanist with the Florida Symphony (1959–62) and the Lake George Opera Company (NY, 1965), he later served as principal percussionist and assistant timpanist with the Indianapolis Symphony (1970–80/percussionist 1981–   ). As an educator, he taught at the U.S. Naval School Music (VA, 1966), Indiana Central University (1976–   ), and Indiana State University (1982).
GEN. BIB.: Borland, *WWAMC.*

MOREHOUSE, CHAUNCEY (b. 11 Mar 1902, Niagara Falls, New York; d. 3 Nov 1980, Philadelphia, Pennsylvania). The son of a silent movie pianist, drumset artist Chauncey Morehouse toured London in 1923, recording with violinist Paul Specht. He performed and/or recorded with Jean Goldkette (1925–27), Bix Beiderbecke (1927), *Adrian Rollini, Frankie Trumbauer, Red Nichols, Joe Venuti, Don Vorhees, and the Dorsey Brothers (1927–29). Later establishing a reputation as a studio musician for radio (e.g., the *Fred Allen Show*) and television, Morehouse occasionally employed an unusual circular auxiliary setup of 14 chromatically tuned snare drums (ca. 1932).

SELECTED DISCOGRAPHY

Brunswick 8122: "Plastered in Paris" and "Mazi-Pani," 1938.
Brunswick 8142: "Ku-li-a" and "Oriental Nocturne," 1938.
Circle CCD-71: *Bill Challis and His Orchestra*, 1936.
Okeh 40923: "At the Jazz Band Ball" and "Jazz Me Blues" (Bix Beiderbecke), 1927.
Victor 19947: "After I Say I'm Sorry" and "Dinah" (Jean Goldkette), 1926.
Victor 21560: "Harlem Twist" and "Five Pennies" (Red Nichols), 1928.
GEN. BIB.: Cook, *LDT* (several photos); Kernfeld, *NGJ*, by T. Dennis Brown.

MOREIRA, AIRTO GUIMORVA (b. 5 Aug 1941, Itaiópolis, Brazil). Percussionist Airto Moreira immigrated to the United States in 1968, settling first in Los Angeles and then New York (1970), collaborating with Miles Davis (1970s), Joe Zawinul (Weather Report), and Chick Corea (Return to Forever). A perennial winner of *Down Beat* magazine's Reader's and Critic's Polls in the percussion category since 1972, he has toured Europe, Russia, South America, the United States, and the Far East with the group Fourth World, which he established in 1990 with his wife, singer Flora Purim, guitarist José Neto, and woodwind and keyboard specialist Gary Meek.

SELECTED DISCOGRAPHY

Blue Note 84332: *Super Nova* (Wayne Shorter), 1969.
Blue Note 84344: *How Insensitive* (Duke Pearson), 1969.
Blue Note 84349: *Electric Byrd* (Donald Byrd), 1970.
B&W 041: *Killer Bees* (Airto Moreira and the Gods of Jazz), 1994.
B&W 046: *Gathering Forces II* (Darius Brubeck/Deepak Ram), 1994.
Buddah 5085: *Seeds on the Ground*, 1970.
Columbia KC30661: *Weather Report*, 1971.
Columbia KC32706: *Stan Getz Quartet*, 1972.
Columbia KG30038: *Miles Davis at the Fillmore*, 1970.
CTI 6020: *Free*, 1972.
CTI 6028: *Fingers*, 1973.
ECM 1022: *Return to Forever* (Chick Corea), 1973
Ellipsis Arts CD3405: *The Big Bang—Global Percussion Masters*, 1994/1997.
Landmark LLP-1508: *Color Schemes* (Bobby Hutcherson), 1986.
Milestone 9070: *Five Hundered Miles High at Montreux* (Flora Purim), 1974.
Milestone/OJC 649: *...Where Would I Be?* (Jim Hall), 1971.
Polydor PD 5525: *Light as a Feather* (Chick Corea/Return to Forever), 1972.
Rykodisc RCD: *Supralingua*, 1998.
Rykodisc 10108: *Däfos* (with Flora Purim and Mickey Hart), 1989.
Rykodisc 10207: *The Other Side of This*, 1992.
Warner Bros. 3279: *Touching You, Touching Me*, 1979.

SELECTED VIDEOGRAPHY

DCI VH0179: *Airto Moreira—Listen and Play*, 1993.

DCI VH0158: *Airto Moreira—Rhythms and Colors*, 1993.
DCI VH0182/CPP Media: *Airto Moreira—Brazilian Percussion*, 1993.
VIEW Video: *Airto and Flora Purim—Latin Jazz All-Stars, Live at the Queen Mary Festival*, 1988.

SELECTED BIBLIOGRAPHY

Mattingly, Rick. "Airto." *MD* XII (September 1988): 19–23.
Moreira, Airto. *The Spirit of Percussion*. Wayne, NJ: 21st Century Productions, 1988.
GEN. BIB.: Kernfeld, *NGJ*, by Michael Ullman.

MORELLO, JOSEPH ALBERT "JOE" (b. 17 Jul 1928, Springfield, Massachusetts). A violinist at age 5, Joe Morello embraced drums by 12 and played locally, studying with Joseph D. Sefchick, *George Lawrence Stone, and *Billy Gladstone. His first New York gigs (1952) were with Johnny Smith, Stan Kenton, and Marian McPartland (1953–56/1977), but he achieved widespread fame with the Dave Brubeck Quartet (1956–69). A technical wizard who recorded 75 albums with Brubeck (including several gold records and Grammy® Awards), Morello made 150 more albums, led his own groups, and had numerous other collaborators including Gil Melle (1953), Jimmy Raney, Phil Woods (1954), Hank Garland, Gil Evans, Charles Mingus, Oscar Pettiford, Charlie Parker, Tal Farlow, Sal Salvador (1956/1978), and Jackie Cain/Roy Kral (1955).

Morello authored numerous method books (e.g., *Rudimental Jazz, Off the Record*), and his compositions are published by Jean Ann Music (e.g., "Shimwah," "Calypso Joe," "The Way It Goes"). He has appeared on the covers of *Modern Drummer* and *Down Beat* magazines, winning the latter's poll awards for five years, the *Playboy* poll for seven years, and the *Melody Maker* poll for three years. Recipient of the Thomas Edison Award (1994) and a lifetime achievement award from the state of New Jersey, he was inducted into *Modern Drummer* magazine's Reader's Poll (1988) and the Percussive Arts Society Halls of Fame (1993). Morello taught *Gene Krupa briefly near the end of Krupa's life.

SELECTED DISCOGRAPHY

A&M Horizon 714: *The Dave Brubeck Quartet 25th Anniversary Reunion*, 1976.
Atlantic 83010-2: *Burning for Buddy: A Tribute to the Music of Buddy Rich*, vol. 2, 1997.
Blue Note BLP5020: *Gil Melle Quintet*, 1953.
Blue Note BLP5033: *Gil Melle Quintet*, 1953.
Blue Note BLP5042: *Tal Farlow Quartet*, 1954.
Blue Note CDP 746863: *The Return of Art Pepper*, 1957.
Capitol T785: *The Marian McPartland Trio*, 1956.
Columbia 16 10 0298: *Dave Brubeck's Greatest Hits*, 1997.

Columbia C2S826: *The Dave Brubect Quartet at Carnegie Hall*, 1963.
Columbia CL1059: *Dave Digs Disney* (Dave Brubeck), 1994.
Columbia CL1347: *Gone With The Wind* (Dave Brubeck), 1986.
Columbia CL1397: *Time Out* (Dave Brubeck), 1959.
DMP CD-497: *Going Places*, 1993.
DMP 506: *Morello Standard Time*, 1995.
New Jazz 1103: *Jimmy Raney Quintet*, 1954.
RCA LSP 2486: *It's About Time*, 1961.
RCA Victor LPM 2420: *New Vibe Man in Town* (Gary Burton), 1962/1994.
Savoy 15032: *Jazz at the Hickory House* (Marian McPartland), 1953.
Verve MGV8138: *The Tal Farlow Album*, 1954.

SELECTED VIDEOGRAPHY

DCI VH0249: *Legends of Jazz Drumming, Pt. 2, 1950–70*, 1996.
Homespun Video: *The Complete All-Around Drummer*, vol. 1, 1994.
Hot Licks VDB 179: Joe Morello Drum Method 1, *The Natural Approach to Technique*; and Drum Method 2, *Around the Kit*, 1993.
Warner Bros./DCI VH0270: *The Making of Burning for Buddy*, pt. 2, 1996.

SELECTED BIBLIOGRAPHY

Mattingly, Rick. "Joe Morello." *PN* XXXII, 3 (June 1994): 12–14.
McPartland, Marian. "The Fabulous Joe Morello." *DB* XXVII, 5 (3 Mar 1960): 24–27.
McPartland, Marian. "Joe Morello: With a Light Touch." *DB* XXXII, 7 (25 Mar 1965): 16–17.
Morello, Joe. "Developing Control of the Bass Drum." *LD* IV, 2 (Fall 1964): 12–13.
Morello, Joe. *Master Studies*. Cedar Grove, NJ: Modern Drummer Pub., Inc., 1983.
Morello, Joe. "New Directions in Rhythm." *LD* III, 2 (Fall 1963): 6.
Morello, Joe. "Wire Brush Technique." *LD* V, 2 (Fall 1965): 16.
Seidel, Mitchell. "Danny Gottlieb and Joe Morello: Skinship." *JazzTimes* XXI, 8 (November 1991): 22–23.
Tracey, Jack. "Joe Morello." *DB* XXII, 18 (7 Sep 1955): 13.
GEN. BIB.: Hunt, *52nd St.*; Kernfeld, *NGJ*, by Barry Kernfeld; Spagnardi, *GJD.*

MOSES, ROBERT LAURENCE "BOB" (aka Moses, Rahboat Ntumba, b. 28 Jan 1948, New York, New York). Drumming by age 10 and influenced by *Dannie Richmond and *Max Roach, vibist, drumset artist, author, and composer Bob Moses first played jazz-rock in the group Free Spirits, with Larry Coryell. He appeared with Rahsaan Roland Kirk (1967), *Gary Burton (1966–68), Open Sky with Dave Liebman (intermittently, late 1960s–1984), and *Jack DeJohnette's "two-drummer" combo Compost (1970s). His many collaborators have included Pat Metheny, Hal Galper, Steve Swallow, Steve Kuhn, Mike Gibbs, Sheila Jordan (1979–82), George Gruntz's Concert Jazz Band (1983), and Emily Remler (1983–84). Leading his own groups since the 1980s, Moses serves on the faculty of the New England Conservatory.

SELECTED DISCOGRAPHY

Accurate ACRE 5016: *Falling from Grace* (Plunge), 1996.
Bronze 2012: *The Only Chrome Waterfall Orchestra* (Mike Gibbs), 1975.
Brownstone BRCD 9801: *Pamela Hines Quintet*, 1998.
ECM 1073: *Bright Size Life* (Pat Metheny), 1975.
ECM 1160: *Home* (Steve Swallow), 1979.
ECM-1-1213: *Last Year's Waltz* (Steve Kuhn), 1981.
Gramavision 8307: *Visit with the Great Spirit*, 1983/1996.
Gramavision R2-79491: *When Elephants Dream of Music*, 1993.
Mozown 001: *Bittersweet in the Ozone*, 1975.
MPS 1514ST: *Guitar Workshop* (Jim Hall), 1967.
Owl 046: *Homage to John Coltrane* (David Liebman), 1987/1993.
PM PMR001: *Open Sky.* 1973.
PM PMR003: *Spirit in the Sky*, 1975.
RCA LSP 3901: *Lofty Fake Anagram* (Gary Burton), 1967.
RCA LSP 3985: *Gary Burton Quartet in Concert*, 1968.

SELECTED BIBLIOGRAPHY

Iero, Cheech. "Bob Moses: Beneath the Surface." *MD* III, 6 (1979): 18–20.
Micaleff, Ken. "Bob Moses' World Beat Wedding." *MD* XVIII (October 1994): 26–29.
Moses, Bob. *Drum Wisdom.* Cedar Grove, NJ: Modern Drummer Publications, 1984.
GEN. BIB.: Hunt, *52nd St.*; Kernfeld, NGJ, by Rick Mattingly; Spagnardi, *GJD*; PASIC® program biographies, 1994.

MOTIAN, STEPHEN PAUL (b. 25 Mar 1931, Philadelphia, Pennsylvania). Drumset artist, pianist, and composer, Paul Motian embraced drums at 13, studying with *Alfred Friese and *Fred Albright at the Manhattan School and privately with *Billy Gladstone. After serving in the Korean War (U.S. Army), his many collaborators included Gil Evans and George Russell (1950s), Paul and Carla Bley (1964), Keith Jarrett (1966), and Bill Evans (initially, 1959) and Scott La Faro on the legendary June 1961 Village Vanguard sessions. Recording under his own name, Motian has led groups (e.g., Electric Bebop Band) and worked with Lee Konitz, Arlo Guthrie, Bill Frisell, Art Farmer, Charles Lloyd, Charlie Haden, Zoot Sims, Stan Getz, Lennie Tristano, Joe Lovano, Thelonius Monk, Jazz Composers Orchestra, and Al Cohn, among others.

SELECTED DISCOGRAPHY

Atlantic ATL8808: *Somewhere Before* (Keith Jarrett), 1981.
Atlantic SD 1596: *The Mourning of a Star* (Keith Jarrett), 1971.
Blue Note CDP 795474: *Dream Keeper* (Charlie Haden), 1991.
Blue Note (F) BNP25105: *Jazz Alive! A Night at the Half Note* (Zoot Sims), 1959.
Blue Note LA459-2: *Andrew Hill*, 1970.

Contemporary CCD 14059: *Form* (Tom Harrell), 1990.
DIW 833: *Segments* (Geri Allen), 1989.
ECM 1283: *It Should've Happened a Long Time Ago*, 1984.
Improvising Artists 841: *Turning Point* (Paul Bley), 1964.
JMT 697 124 060-2: *Reincarnation of a Love Bird*, 1995.
JMT 834421-2: *Monk in Motian*, 1988.
JMT 834430/834440/849157: *On Broadway*, vos. 1–3, 1989–92.
JMT 834445: *Paul Motian/Bill Evans*.
JMT 849154: *Live in Tokyo*.
Mercury SR 60600: *Jazz Is a Kick* (Bob Brookmeyer), 1960.
Riverside OJC CD 140: *Sunday at the Village Vanguard* (Bill Evans), 1961/1987.
Riverside OJC CD 210: *Explorations* (Bill Evans), 1961.
Riverside OJC CD 315: *Portrait in Jazz* (Bill Evans), 1959.
Riverside OJC CD 037: *Waltz for Debby* (Bill Evans), 1992.
Riverside OJC CD 223: *New Jazz Conceptions—Bill Evans*, 1956.
Riverside OJC CD 428: *Moonbeams* (Bill Evans), 1962/1990.
Riverside OJC CD 473: *How My Heart Sings* (Bill Evans), 1962/1989.
Soul Note 121182: *Village Rhythm* (Joe Lovano), 1989.
Soul Note CD 121224-2: *One Time Out*, 1992.
Verve 314 521 659-2: *Lee Konitz Live at the 1/2 Note*, 1959.
Verve V6-8578: *Bill Evans Trio*, 1963.
Warner Bros. 46621: *Awareness* (Larry Goldings), 1998.

SELECTED VIDEOGRAPHY

Camera Three Productions, Inc.: *Bill Evans*, 1962.

SELECTED BIBLIOGRAPHY

Braman, Chuck. "Paul Motian: Method of a Master." *PN* XXXII, 2 (April 1994): 11–16.
Griffith, Mark. "Artist on Track: Paul Motian." *MD* XIX, 3 (March 1995): 104–105.
Micaleff, Ken. "Paul Motian: Nice Work If You Can Get It." *MD* XVIII (June 1994): 26–29.
GEN. BIB.: Hunt, *52nd St.*; Kernfeld, *NGJ*, by Chuck Braman; Spagnardi, *GJD*.

MOUZON, ALPHONSE (b. 21 Nov 1948, Charleston, South Carolina). Owner of the Tenacious recording label, Alphonse Mouzon flourished in New York during the 1970s; and although he is known as a fusion artist, his roots are in soul and rhythm and blues. He has performed with Larry Coryell in the group Eleventh House, with the original Weather Report group, and McCoy Tyner, Gil Evans, George Benson, and Herbie Hancock. His website is www.tenaciousrecords.com.

SELECTED DISCOGRAPHY

Blue Note 84363: *Odyssey of Iska* (Wayne Shorter), 1970.

Blue Note 84421: *Dig This* (Bobbi Humphrey), 1972.
Blue Note LA059-G: *The Essence of Mystery*, 1972.
Blue Note LA222-G: *Funky Snakefoot*, 1973.
Blue Note LA398-G: *Mind Transplant*, 1974.
Blue Note LA584-G: *Alphonse Mouzon—The Man Incognito*, 1975.
Blue Note LA633-G: *Caricatures* (Donald Byrd), 1976.
Blue Note LA663-J2: *Blue Note Live at the Roxy*, 1976.
Columbia CK 48824: *Weather Report* (Joe Zawinul et al.), 1971.
Enja ENJ-79611-2: *Blues in Orbit* (Gil Evans), 1971.
Milestone OJC CD-311: *Sahara* (McCoy Tyner), 1972.
Milestone OJC CD-618: *Song for the New World* (McCoy Tyner), 1973.
Tenacious 9201-2: *The Survivor*, 1993.
Tenacious 9202-2: *By All Means*, 1993.
Tenacious 9203-2: *Early Spring*, 1993.
Tenacious 9204-2: *Love Fantasy*, 1993.
Tenacious 9205-2: *Back to Jazz*, 1993.
Tenacious 9206-2: *On Top of the World*, 1994.
Tenacious 9211: *The Night Is Still Young*, 1997 (Mouzon performs trumpet, drums, keyboards, and bass).

SELECTED BIBLIOGRAPHY

Tolleson, Robin. "Alphonse Mouzon." *MD* XXI, 3 (March 1997): 11.
GEN. BIB.: Hunt, *52nd St.*

MÜLLER, FRED (b. 18 Jun 1942, Kassel, Germany). After studying at the Kassel Music Academy, percussionist Fred Müller played two years in Regensburg, seven years in Gelsenkirchen, and two years in Duisburg; then he joined the Berlin Philharmonic in 1971.
GEN. BIB.: Avgerinos, *KB.*

MURRAY, JAMES MARCELLUS ARTHUR "SUNNY" (b. 21 Sep 1937, Idabel, Oklahoma). Avant-garde drumset artist Sunny Murray matured in Philadelphia, began drumming at 9, and in 1956 relocated to New York, where his earliest collaborators included Jackie McLean, Henry "Red" Allen, and Willie "the Lion" Smith. Finding his own voice within "free jazz," he played with John Coltrane (1963), Albert Ayler (sporadically, 1965–67), Cecil Taylor (1980), Archie Shepp, and others, led his own eclectic groups from 1966 to the 1990s (including Grachan Moncur III, 1980s); eventually he moved to Europe.

SELECTED DISCOGRAPHY

BYG 529303: *Homage to Africa*, 1969.
BYG 529304: *Yasmina, a Black Woman* (Archie Shepp), 1969.
BYG 529332: *Never Give a Sucker an Even Break*, 1969.
ESP 1002: *Spiritual Unity* (Albert Ayler), 1964.

ESP 1010: *Bells* (Albert Ayler), 1965.
ESP 1032: *Sunny Murray Quintet*, 1966.
Fantasy 86014: *Live at the Cafe Montmartre* (Cecil Taylor), 1962.
Music Unlimited 7432: *Crossroads* (David Eyges), 1981.
Philly Jazz 1004: *Apple Cores*, 1978.

SELECTED VIDEOGRAPHY

Rhapsody Films: *Jazz Is Our Religion*, 1972.
GEN. BIB.: Hunt, *52nd St.*; Kernfeld, *NGJ*, by Michael Ullman.

MUSSER, CLAIR OMAR (b. 14 Oct 1901, Manheim, Pennsylvania).   Marimba virtuoso, composer, arranger, instrument designer, and conductor Clair Omar Musser first studied violin with his father; later he added the xylophone and piano. His initial exposure to xylophone came by way of an Edison cylinder recording of *Thomas Mills performing "Four Little Black Berries" with the U.S. Marine Band (ca. 1912). After hearing Abraham Himmelbrand [aka *Teddy Brown] perform using four mallets in Earl Fuller's Band in Lancaster, Pennsylvania, he sought out Himmelbrand's teacher, Philip Rosenweig (of dulcimer, cimbalom, and marimba fame) in Washington, D.C. Musser was a featured soloist with several orchestras, including the Chicago Symphony in the 1920s, with which he premiered the large "Marimba-Celeste," manufactured by the *J. C. Deagan Company based on his own design. This unwieldy instrument featured microphone pickups, multiple volume control foot pedals on the performer's side, and two "sousaphone bell" speakers in front for amplification. During the 1930s–40s, Musser toured throughout the United States, Canada, and Europe performing in theaters, for a Warner Brothers Vitaphone film, and with the Los Angeles Philharmonic.

Ever the innovative entrepreneur, he organized and conducted a 25-piece "all-girl" marimba orchestra that played for the opening of Paramount Pictures' Oriental Theater in Chicago (1929). Prompted by his father's recounting of the 19-piece Honduran marimba orchestra that had appeared at the San Francisco World's Fair of 1915, Musser proposed a 100-piece marimba orchestra (eighty 3.5-octave and twenty 4-octave marimbas) for Chicago's "Century of Progress Exposition" (1933). The Exposition group's success led to the organization of the International Marimba Symphony Orchestra, which consisted of 50 women and 50 men, beginners to professionals (ages 17–25), who played on 100 "King George" model marimbas designed by Musser and manufactured by the Deagan Company. He arranged music and conducted for this group in Carnegie Hall (1935), preparing them for a European tour culminating with the coronation of King George V of England in 1935. (The tour took place, but the coronation performance was cancelled.) Musser dedicated their European performances to the xylophone virtuoso *Michael Josef Gusikov, who had died almost 100 years earlier (1837). When the ensemble parted ways, performers was allowed to keep their instrument.

Selling the popularity of these homogeneous groups to the public, Musser organized a 50-piece marimba ensemble appearance in Tulsa, Oklahoma (1940), a 125-piece group at Phillips University in Enid, Oklahoma (1941), and a 150-piece ensemble at the Chicagoland Music Festival (1941). The *Chicago Tribune* sponsored a 200-piece marimba group at Soldier's Field for an audience of 111,000 (1949); that ensemble was eclipsed the following year by a 300-piece concert at the Chicago Fair (1950), featuring a 100-voice choir and several contra-bass marimbas. In 1951 the National Association of Music Merchants (NAMM) sponsored a 75-member group in Chicago that spotlighted 50 of the members performing Paganini's "Moto Perpetuo" in unison!

Musser became manager of the mallet instrument division of Deagan in 1930; in 1948 he left them to form his own marimba, xylophone, and vibraphone manufacturing company. After a brief association with the Lyons Musical Instrument Company and Kitching Company, his Musser Marimba Company in LaGrange, Illinois, was sold in 1966 to the Ludwig Drum Company, which retained his name on all their keyboard products.

As an arranger and composer, he set many popular works by Chopin, Brahms, Dvorak, among others, and wrote several didactic etudes, both accompanied and unaccompanied, for the marimba. Musser headed the marimba department at Northwestern University from 1942 to 1952 and was inducted into the Percussive Arts Society Hall of Fame in 1975. For his numerous contributions to the marimba, he was cited by the French government and received the Borez Award from the Brazilian government in 1934. In later years he invented and patented several successful devices for the study of astronomy and created the "Celestaphone" (1970s), a 30-tone mallet keyboard whose bars were fashioned from metals extracted from meteorites which Musser had collected from around the world.

SELECTED BIBLIOGRAPHY

"A 75th Birthday Salute to Clair Omar Musser." *PN* XV, 3 (Spring/Summer 1977): 38–39.

Eyler, David P. "The 'Century of Progress' Marimba Orchestra." *PN* XXIX, 3 (February 1991): 57.

Eyler, David P. "Clair Omar Musser and His Contributions to the Marimba." *PN* XXVIII, 2 (Winter 1990): 62–63.

Eyler, David P. "Largest Marimba Orchestra Ever Organized under Clair Omar Musser." *PN* XXIX, 6 (August 1991): 39–45.

Eyler, David P. "The Truth about the King George Marimba as Used in the International Marimba Symphony Orchestra." *PN* XXIX, 2 (December 1990): 47.

Gerhardt, Edwin L. "Clair Omar Musser: A Brief Biography." *PN* IV, 2 (December 1965): 7.

"Hear the New Marimba Play; Boy, It's Just One Mile Away." *Reading Times* (1920s?) Reading, PA (photo).

Holmgren, Marg. "Clair Omar Musser and the Marimba Symphony Orchestra." *PN* XVI, 3 (Spring/Summer 1978): 20–21 (cover photo).

Ingman, Dan S. "A Remarkable Instrument." *The Melody Maker* (London, England) (July 1931): 557 (photo).

Musser, Clair Omar. "Forty Centuries of Progress in Percussion." *The School Musician* (May 1933): 10–11.

Musser, Clair Omar. "The Marimba-Xylophone." *The Etude* (April 1932): 251.

Musser, Clair Omar. *Master Solo Arrangements (for Vibraphone)*. Chicago: Gamble Hinged Music, 1941.

Musser, Clair Omar. *Masterworks for the Marimba: Music of Chopin.* Chicago: Forster Music, 1940.

Musser, Clair Omar. *Modern Vibraharp Method for Beginners*: Park Ridge, IL: Neil Kjos Pub., 1939.

GEN. BIB.: Larrick, *BET-CP*.

N

NANDAYAPA (RALDA), ZEFERINO (b. 26 Aug 1931, Chiapa de Corzo, Chiapas, Mexico). In the absence of a piano, composer and virtuoso Zeferino Nandayapa practiced his music lessons on the marimba, learning technique from his father, Norberto Nandayapa, who was director of symphonic bands in Mexico City and, following the family tradition, a marimbist. The younger Nandayapa, a performer with the National Symphony of Mexico and the Philharmonic Orchestras of the University of Mexico and Mexico City, studied at the National Conservatory in Mexico City in the 1950s and toured the United States in 1957 with other Chiapan marimbists. Encouraged by the popularity of the instrument, he established Marimba Nandayapa in 1960, premiered the group in Carnegie Hall (1973), and included his four sons (Oscar, Norberto, Mario, and Javier) by 1977. The ensemble received the Highest Excellence Award from the Mexican Board of Education in 1980; with over 50 recordings of classical music, Mexican folk songs, and international favorites, the marimbists have appeared at the Royal Festival Hall in London with the Royal Philharmonic Orchestra, New York's Metropolitan Museum of Art, and the First International Folklore Festival in Austria.

SELECTED DISCOGRAPHY

Alfa Musical Internacional CDAMI-4: *Música Mexicana para el mundo*, 1992.
EMI CDPE-003: *Marimba Nandayapa*, 1991.
EMI CDPE-005: *Grandes Exitos*, 1992.
EMI/Angel SAM-35080: *Alvarez—El espíritu de la tierra* (Mexico City Philharmonic), 1985.
GAS-CD-1138: *Marimba Nandayapa en concierto*, 1994.

SELECTED BIBLIOGRAPHY

Kaptain, Larry. "Interview with Zeferino Nandayapa." *PN* XXVIII, 2 (Winter, 1990): 48–50.
PASIC® program biographies, 1995.

NARELL, ANDY (b. 18 Mar 1954, New York, New York). A graduate of the University of California at Berkeley (1973), percussionist, pianist, composer, steel pan virtuoso, and recording artist Andy Narell has led his own groups (the Andy Narell Group, 1978–) and performs with Paquito d'Rivera and *Dave Samuels in the Caribbean Jazz Project. He has recorded numerous film soundtracks including, *48 Hours*, *Ghostbusters*, and *Trading Places*, and has collaborated with the Pointer Sisters, Freddie Hubbard, Manhattan Transfer, Kronos Quartet, Toto, and Aretha Franklin, among others. Founder of Hip Pocket Records and an artist-in-residence at several American universities, Narell has been interviewed on CBS-TV's *Sunday Morning*, has written music for the *Jane Fonda Caribbean Workout* video and for television commercials (e.g., Apple Computers), and has been a featured performer and clinician at several Percussive Arts Society International Conventions as well as European, Canadian, Japanese, and U.S. music festivals.

SELECTED DISCOGRAPHY

Heads Up 3033: *The Caribbean Jazz Project,* 1995.
Heads Up HUCD 3047: *Behind the Bridge*, 1998.
Heads Up HUCD 3039: *Island Stories* (Caribbean Jazz Project), 1997.
Nova/BC 9107: *Intimate Notions* (Pocket Change), 1991.
Windham Hill Jazz 01934-10139-2: *Andy Narell—Down the Road*, 1992.
Windham Hill Jazz 019343-11172: *The Long Time Band*, 1995.
Windham Hill Jazz/Hip Pocket 103: *Light in Your Eyes*, 1983.
Windham Hill Jazz/Hip Pocket 105: *Slow Motion*, 1985.
Windham Hill Jazz WT-0120: *Little Secrets*, 1989.
Windham Hill Jazz WT-0107: *The Hammer*, 1987.
Windham Hill Records/Hip Pocket 101: *Stickman*, 1981.

SELECTED BIBLIOGRAPHY

Jette, Susan. "Conversation with Andy Narell." *PN* XXIX, 6 (August 1991): 14–17.
Underwood, L. "Andy Narell." *DB* XLVII, 6 (1980): 56.
GEN. BIB.: Kernfeld, *NGJ*, by Jeff Potter; PASIC® program biographies, 1985, 1991.

NEUMANN, EMIL (d. ca. 1941, Berlin, Germany). Principal timpanist of the Berlin Symphony in its first year (ca. 1909), Emil Neumann interned in Russia before the outbreak of WWI; in 1918 he returned to Germany, where he was

percussionist with the Berlin Philharmonic from 1936 to 1937, performing with the newly founded Berlin Folk Opera thereafter.
GEN. BIB.: Avgerinos, *KB.*

NOAK, FRED WILLIAM (b. 2 May 1898, Dresden, Germany; d. 11 Sep 1975, Fort Orange, Florida). Timpanist, composer, and painter Fred Noak started on violin and piano, studying at the Dresden Music Academy. Drafted into WWI as a medic (ca. 1915–18), he later took up timpani at the Academy; after graduation he played in Frankfurt and for the Karlsbad Orchestra, with whom he also made his debut as a composer. Noak performed with the Dresden Opera Orchestra, Vienna State Opera, and Vienna Philharmonic Orchestra. He also appeared at the Salzburg Festival and toured South America, moving to the United States in 1923 at the request of fellow Dresden student Fritz Reiner. With the latter he served as timpanist of the Cincinnati Symphony (1923–52) and New York Metropolitan Opera Orchestra (1952–62) until health concerns forced him into semiretirement in Cincinnati (ca. 1962) and Florida (ca. 1969). Noak held positions on the faculties of both the Cincinnati Conservatory and Stetson University.

SELECTED BIBLIOGRAPHY

"In Memoriam: Fred William Noak." *PN* XIV, 3 (Spring/Summer 1976): 11 [reprinted from *International Musician* (February 1976)].
Noak, Theresa. "Fred William Noak (1898–1975)." *PN* XXV, 2 (Winter 1987): 21.
GEN. BIB.: Cook, *LDT*, p. 295 (photo).

NOONAN, JOHN P. "JACK" (b. 28 Sep 1904, Lincoln, Illinois; d. 18 Jan 1984, Normal, Illinois). A charter member of the Percussive Arts Society Hall of Fame in 1972, John Noonan studied with Max Nickell (San Francisco Symphony), *Ed Straight, *Edward Metzenger, and *Roy Knapp. He played in vaudeville shows, in silent movie theaters, and with numerous bands and orchestras. He also served as educational director for the Ludwig & Ludwig Drum Company (1937–41). Noonan taught at Illinois Wesleyan University for 14 years (1940–54) and owned Noonan Music Store in Bloomington, Illinois (1943–61). An active clinician, he was an influential percussion educator and the orginal editor of the "Percussion Clinic" column in the *Instrumentalist* magazine.

SELECTED BIBLIOGRAPHY

Noonan, John. "Percussionists and Drummers." *Percussionist* II, 3 (June 1965): 1–3.
Noonan, John P. "Yesterday, Today, and Tomorrow." *LD* V, 2 (Fall 1965): 28.

NORVO, RED (b. Kenneth Norville, 31 Mar 1908, Beardstown, Illinois; d. 6 Apr 1999, Santa Monica, California). Inducted into the Percussive Arts Society Hall of Fame in 1992, jazz xylophonist and vibraphonist Red Norvo was born into a musical family, studied piano briefly, and began his career with a trio (violin, piano, and xylophone). After playing in a marimba band, the Collegians, in 1925, he toured on vaudeville, featuring marimba and tap dancing in his act. Norvo worked as a staff percussionist at NBC-Chicago, and his early collaborators included Victor Young on radio (1928–31, the *Maytag Program*), Paul Whiteman (1931–33), Paul Ash, Ferde Grofe, and Ben Bernie. His first recordings were made with the Dorsey Brothers (1931, vibes on "Mooncountry") and Whiteman (1932, "Rockin' Chair"). [The Dorsey recording may have been the first recording of a vibraphone that employed no motor or dampening pedal.] After establishing his reputation on the xylophone and marimba as a recording artist ["Hole in the Wall," "Knockin' on Wood," and "Dance of the Octopus" (requiring four-mallet technique), 1933], he led several small groups that featured arrangements by Eddie Sauter. He recorded with Artie Shaw, Bunny Berigan, Charlie Barnet, among others, and was honored in 1936 by *Metronome* magazine's Musicians' Hall of Fame. After fronting several short-lived ensembles, he survived the post–WWII years in small groups with the likes of Benny Goodman (1944, with Slam Stewart and Teddy Wilson), Woody Herman (1945, Norvo formed the "Woodchoppers" within this band), Charles Mingus, Red Mitchell, Tal Farlow, Shorty Rogers, and Jimmy Raney. His own groups (1949–53) included his wife, singer and pianist Mildred Bailey, which earned them the label "Mr. and Mrs. Swing." Exploiting the vibraphone full time in 1944, he could also be heard on recordings with Dizzy Gillespie and Charlie Parker. Following tours of Europe (1954/1959 with Benny Goodman) and Australia (1956), Norvo opened his own club in California and worked in Las Vegas in the 1960s, rejoining Goodman in 1961. He penned several mallet compositions and served as a staff percussionist at NBC-Chicago; his characteristic vibraphone tone usually featured no vibrato with an occasional use of mallets covered in lambskin for a "slap" tonal effect. His 1949 Columbia recording of "Congo Blues" with Teddy Wilson was honored as "Record of the Year."

SELECTED DISCOGRAPHY

Bluebird 6278-2-RB: *The Red Norvo Small Bands*.
Blue Note 37513: *Live in Australia, 1959* (Frank Sinatra with the Red Norvo Quintet), 1992.
Blue Note CDP 7 46848-2: *Art Pepper Quintet*, 1957.
Calliope CAL 3010: *Sessions, Live* (Terry Gibbs and Pete Jolly), 1958/1976.
Charlie Parker PLP408: *Once There Was Bird*, 1945.
Columbia CK 53424: *Featuring Mildred Bailey*, 1993.
Concord CJ-90: *Red and Ross* (Ross Tompkins), 1979.
Contemporary C3534: *Music to Listen to Red Norvo By*, 1957/1984.
Dot DLP3126: *Windjammer City Style*, 1958.
Epic JEE 22009: *Red Norvo and His All-Stars*, 1974.

Fantasy/OJC 641: *Red Norvo Trio* (Jimmy Raney and Red Mitchell), 1954.
Jazz Archives 158602: *Mildred Bailey—A Forgotten Lady*, 1996.
Mosaic MR6-109: *Edmond Hall's All-Star Quintet*, 1944.
RCA Victor LPM1729: *Red Plays the Blues*, 1957.
Savoy MG12088: *Move*, 1949–51.
Spotlite 127: *Red Norvo's Famous Jam*, 1945.

SELECTED VIDEOGRAPHY

Kultur Video: *Jazz at the Smithsonian—Red Norvo*, 1984.
Kultur Video: *Red Norvo* (with Tal Farlow), 1982.

SELECTED BIBLIOGRAPHY

Barrier, Gray. "Red Norvo's Xylophone Solo on 'Just a Mood.' " *PN* XXXVI, 1 (February 1998): 30–31.
Kastner, Kathleen. "The Xylophone in the United States between 1880 and 1930, Part I: The Artists." *Percussive Arts Society: Illinois Chapter Newsletter* (Winter 1986): 1–2.
Lylloff, Bent. "An Interview with Red Norvo." *PN* XXXI, 1 (October 1992): 42–51.
McCarthy, Albert. *Big Band Jazz*. New York: G. F. Putnam's Sons, 1974.
McCutchen, Thomas W. *An Examination of Selected Ragtime Solos by Zez Confrey, George Hamilton Green, Charles Johnson, and Red Norvo as Transcribed for Xylophone Solo with Marimba Ensemble Accompaniment*. DMA lecture-recital, North Texas State University, 1979.
Rogers, Lisa. "Red Norvo: The $100,000 Mallet Man." *PN* XXXV, 3 (June 1997): 70–72.
Rosen, Michael. "Red Norvo: 1908–1999." *PN* XXXVII, 3 (June 1999): 37–38.
Stewart, Rex. "Red Norvo: A Tale of A Pioneer." *DB* XXXIV, 18 (7 Sep 1967): 21–22.
Tynan, John. "Red Norvo: The Ageless One." *DB* XXV, 11 (29 May 1958): 14.
GEN. BIB.: Cahn, *XAR*; Strain, *XYLO*.

NUSSBAUM, ADAM (b. 29 Nov 1955, New York, New York). Drumset artist Adam Nussbaum studied with *Charli Persip, attended Emerson College (Boston) and the City College of New York, and has performed and/or recorded (60+ albums) with the American Jazz Orchestra, Köln Radio (WDR) Big Band, Stan Getz, *Gary Burton, Michael Brecker, John Scofield (1978–81), Hal Galper (1979), Dave Liebman (1980), Bill Evans (1983), Bobby Watson (1984), Art Farmer (1984), Gil Evans (1985), Toots Thielemans, Eddie Gomez, Steve Swallow, Jim McNeely, John Abercrombie, James Moody, Eliane Elias, and Jerry Bergonzi, among others. He has toured throughout Canada, Europe, Japan, Australia, New Zealand, the United States, and South America, and he has taught at the New School, Long Island and New York Universities, and Jamey Aebersold's Summer Jazz Camps.

SELECTED DISCOGRAPHY

A Records AL 73108: *Currents* (Charles Pillow), 1997.
Double Time DTRCD-142: *Jerry Bergonzi Trio*, 1998.
Enja 4004: *Shinola* (Steve Swallow), 1981.
Owl 046: *Homage to John Coltrane* (David Liebman), 1987/1993.
Timeless SJP151: *If They Only Knew* (David Liebman), 1981.

SELECTED BIBLIOGRAPHY

Woodard, Josef. "Adam Nussbaum: New York Dues." *MD* X, 6 (June 1986): 22–25.
GEN. BIB.: Kernfeld, *NGJ*; PASIC® program biographies, 1992.

O

O'DONNELL, RICHARD LEE "RICH" (b. 13 Feb 1937, St. Louis, Missouri). Rich O'Donnell started piano and percussion at age 7 and attended the St. Louis Institute of Music (1955–57) and North Texas State University (1957–59). At the latter he performed with the legendary "1 O'Clock Lab Band" (1957–59) and studied with Samuel Adler. Since 1959 he has served as principal percussionist with the St. Louis Symphony (1959–present), and several works have been written for him. Having appeared in Brazil (1966) and Mexico (1969), performed on television and in numerous recording studios, show and dance bands, and new music groups, he owns his own recording label, D'or Music, which specializes in contemporary music.

As a composer and performer of "new" music, O'Donnell has written television scores and received several commissions and grants (e.g., National Endowment for the Arts and the Mid-America Arts Alliance "Meet the Composer") involving electronic music, dance, and visual arts (multimedia). His "Microtimbre I" (1970) and "Polytimbre III" (1973) are published by Media Press, Inc., and he is director of the Electronic Music Studio, percussion instructor and founder-director of the percussion ensemble at Washington University (St. Louis, 1979–present), the St. Louis Percussion Quartet, and New Music Circle. Featured as a composer for a televised documentary, he has also designed and manufactured several percussion and electronic instruments for use in his works. O'Donnell can be heard on Somnath and Ecclesia record labels and with the St. Louis Symphony on Telarc, RCA Victor-Red Seal, EMI, and Nonesuch.

SELECTED DISCOGRAPHY

New Music Circle TS 71144145: *Microtimbre I*, 1969.
New World NW318-2: *Works by Colgrass and Druckman* (St. Louis Symphony), 1983.

SELECTED BIBLIOGRAPHY

O'Donnell, Rich. "Listening to a Different Drummer." *PN* XXVI, 3 (Spring 1988): 13–15.
Satterfield, Dave. "Rich O'Donnell." *PN* XXIII, 5 (July 1985): 30–31.
GEN. BIB.: Borland, *WWAMC.*

OLATUNJI, MICHAEL BABATUNDE (b. 1927, Ajido-Badagry, Nigeria). Influenced early on by the drummer Oyewe and the singer Denge, Babatunde Olatunji is a master African drummer of the Yoruba people. He studied at the Baptist Academy in Lagos, Nigeria and came to the United States in 1950, completing a bachelor's degree at Moorehouse College in Atlanta (1954); he then settled in New York City (1954) with dreams of graduate school. Short on funds, he started a dance troupe instead; the group performed in theaters, in concert halls, on television, at Radio City Music Hall (1958), and for the African Pavilion of the New York World's Fair (1964). With financial help from John Coltrane, Olatunji established a cultural center and performing arts school, the Olatunji Center for African Culture, in Harlem in the 1960s (also in Washington, D.C., in the 1990s) and toured widely with his dance-drumming troupe.

He has collaborated with many jazz and Latin musicians, including Clark Terry, Ray Barretto (*Zungo!*), Roger "Montego Joe" Sanders (*Flaming Drums!* and *High Life!*), John Coltrane, Yusef Lateef, Abbey Lincoln, and *Max Roach. In 1981 he gave a series of farewell concerts at Avery Fisher Hall (NY) and was preparing to retire to Nigeria, but civil strife there kept him in the United States. Following the successful recordings *Drums of Passion: The Beat* (1986), with *Mickey Hart, Carlos Santana, *Airto Moreira, and others, and *Drums of Passion: The Invocation* (1988), Olatunji performed and recorded with Hart in the percussion group, Planet Drum, during the 1990s.

SELECTED DISCOGRAPHY

Bear Family Records BCD 15747-1-DI: *Drums of Passion and More* (Columbia Recordings, 1959–1966), 1994 (includes the previous LPs: *Drums of Passion, Zungo!, High Life!*, and *More Drums of Passion*).
Blue Note LA853-H: *Horace Silver—Silver 'n Percussion*, 1977.
Ellipsis Arts CD3405: *The Big Bang—Global Percussion Masters*, 1994/1997.
Rykodisc RDC 10102: *The Invocation*, 1988.
Rykodisc RDC 10107: *The Beat*, 1986.
Rykodisc RDC 10206: *Planet Drum*, 1997.
Verve V6-8392: *Herbie Mann*, 1960.

SELECTED VIDEOGRAPHY

Interworld VH1081: *African Drumming—Babatunde Olatunji*, 1993.

SELECTED BIBLIOGRAPHY

"Afro Percussion and Olatunji." *LD* III, 1 (Spring 1963): 12.
Dietz, Betty, and Babatunde Olatunji. *Musical Instruments of Africa: Their Nature, Use and Place in the Life of a Deeply Musical People.* New York: John Day, 1965.
GEN. BIB.: Southern, *BDA-AAM.*

ORLANDO, ANTHONY C. (b. Reading, Pennsylvania). Attending Tanglewood Institute (1968) and earning a bachelor's degree from the Philadelphia Musical Academy (1969), Anthony Orlando studied with *Michael Bookspan and *Fred Hinger. He has been a member of the Philadelphia Orchestra since 1972, as well as principal percussionist and/or timpanist with the Lyric Opera Orchestra, Pennsylvania Ballet Orchestra, Penn Contemporary Players, Greater Trenton Symphony, Grand Teton Festival, Robin Hood Dell Summer series, and Rutgers Chamber Ensemble. An independent performing artist, he has premiered many works written for him. Orlando has taught at the Philadelphia College of the Performing Arts and the New School of Music in Philadelphia.

SELECTED DISCOGRAPHY

Capstone CPS-8631: *Evocations*, 1996.
CRI CD 681: *Tina Davidson—I Hear the Mermaids Singing*, 1996.

SELECTED BIBLIOGRAPHY

"Drumming Around." *PN* XVII, 3 (Spring/Summer 1979): 24.
Philadelphia Orchestra Percussion Personnel Biographies.

OTTE, ALLEN CARL (b. 17 Jan 1950, Sheyboygan, Wisconsin). Al Otte attended the University of Illinois (1972), earned a bachelor's degree from the Oberlin Conservatory (1972) and a master's degree from Northern Illinois University (1977), and studied with Herbert Brün, *Richard Weiner, and *Michael Rosen. Founder of the Oberlin Improvisation Group, he played with the Toledo Symphony and subbed with the Cleveland Symphony.

Otte chartered the Black Earth Percussion Group (1972–79), whose members were artists-in-residence at Northern Illinois University, where he taught from 1973 to 1977. Including *Garry and *Richard Kvistad, Chris Braun, and *Michael Udow, this group was a semiextension of the New Percussion Quartet of Buffalo, which had commissioned several works that were left unperformed. "In-residence" at the University of Illinois (1972), Blackearth toured the United States, Canada, and Europe and was reborn at the University of Cincinnati College Conservatory by Otte under a new name, The Percussion Group, as ensemble-in-residence (1979–present). The latter's configuration is essentially a trio and has included, at times, Otte, *Garry Kvistad, Bill Youhass, Stacey Bowers, Jack Brennan, James Culley, and Rusty Burge. Touring throughout North America and Europe, they have recorded for numerous independent labels and radio stations.

As a faculty member responsible for percussion, chamber music, eurhythmics, literature, composition, and world music, Otte occasionally leads a seminar in the music and philosophy of John Cage, whose personal association with, and compositions for, The Percussion Group dates from 1981, including touring with the ensemble in the United States and Europe. Their CD *What Mushroom? What Leaf?* features a 57-year retrospective of Cage's percussion music. Otte served on the Percussive Arts Society board of directors (1979–82), has been guest faculty at summer institutes in Portugal, Poland, and elsewhere, and received Special Merit awards for recordings reviewed in *Stereo Review* (1975/1982).

SELECTED DISCOGRAPHY

Non Sequitur Records 1–3: *Herbert Brün: Hit or Miss?* 1983.
Opus One 20: *Music of Rzewski* (Blackearth Percussion Group), 1973.
Opus One 22: *The Blackearth Percussion Group*, 1974.
Opus One 80/81: *Percussion Group—Cincinnati*, 1981.

SELECTED BIBLIOGRAPHY

Conway, Joan. "Blackearth—The Early Years." *New Performance II* (1981).
Otte, Allen. "Considerations for Compositions for Marimba." *Percussionist* XI, 4 (Summer 1974): 129–134.
Otte, Allen. "The Percussionist and For 1, 2, or 3 People." *PN Research Edition* XXII, 6 (September 1984): 56–58.
Otte, Allen. "Preferences in Percussion, 1973." *Percussionist* XI, 3 (Spring 1974): 89–97.
Otte, Allen. "Speaking to and through around and about for and against John Cage—A Musical Tribute." *PN* XXXI, 5 (June 1993): 50–51.
Reiss, Karl Leopold. *History of the Blackearth Percussion Group*. Doctoral thesis, University of Houston, 1986.
Salzman, Eric. "New Music: Percussion." *Stereo Review* (August 1982).
Smith, Stuart Saunders. *The Noble Snare*. Baltimore, MD: Smith Pub., 1988.
Information supplied by the subject, 1996.

OWEN, CHARLES E. "CHARLIE" (b. 1 Sep 1912, Kinsman, Ohio; d. 17 Apr 1985, Ann Arbor, Michigan). Raised in Youngstown, Ohio, where he studied bassoon and trombone, Charles Owen was inducted into the Percussive Arts Society Hall of Fame in 1981 and studied percussion with, among others, *George Hamilton Green, *Malcolm Gerlach (Pittsburgh Symphony), *Saul Goodman (New York Philharmonic), and *Bill Kieffer. He received a bachelor's degree from Catholic University in 1945; and after 20 years as percussionist, timpanist, and mallet soloist with the U.S. Marine Band (1934–54), he joined the Philadelphia Orchestra as principal percussionist for 18 years (1954–72). Owen taught at Temple University (1962–72), the University of Michigan (1972–82), the University of Oregon, Catholic University, the Saratoga School of Orchestra Studies, and Aspen Festival, among others. As part of the Philadelphia Orchestra's "First Chair Encores" series, he recorded the first movement of Paul Creston's popular *Concertino for Marimba*. A member of the Percussive Arts Society board of directors, Owen toured throughout Europe, Asia, and the Americas; he served as principal percussionist with the Casals Festival Orchestra in San Juan, Puerto Rico, and the Aspen Festival Orchestra (1978–83). He can also be heard on recordings with the Mormon Tabernacle Choir, Philadelphia Brass Quintet, and Philadelphia Woodwind Quintet.

SELECTED DISCOGRAPHY

CBS Records MYK-37217: *Carl Orff—Carmina Burana* (Philadelphia Orchestra), 1960/1981.
Columbia ML-5596: *Finlandia* (Philadelphia Orchestra), 1961.
Columbia ML-5617: *The Blue Danube—A Johann Strauss Festival* (Philadelphia Orchestra), 1961.
Columbia ML-5641: *Invitation to the Dance* (Philadelphia Orchestra), 1961.
Columbia MS-6977: *First Chair Encores,* vol. 2 (Philadelphia Orchestra), 1963.
University of Michigan SM 0016: *Re:percussions,* 1984.

SELECTED BIBLIOGRAPHY

Byrne, Frank (John R. Beck, ed.). "Charlie Owen: The Marine Band Years." *PN* XXV, 4 (Spring 1987): 45–50.
"Charles Owen: September 1, 1912—April 17, 1985." *PN* XXIII, 5 (July 1985): 24–25.
"In Memory." *The School Musician* (May 1985): 39.
Owen, Charles. "Military Band to Symphony Orchestra: A Personnel Survey." *PN* XXIII, 2 (January 1985): 28–31.
Udow, Michael W. "Charles Owen." *PN* XX, 2 (February 1982): 33.
GEN. BIB.: Cook, *LDT*, p. 391, 456 (photo); Larrick, *BET-CP*.

P

PAINE, FRED S. (b. Windsor, Ontario, Canada). Theater drummer and xylophone soloist ("Wizard of the Xylophone") with the Detroit Symphony for many years during the early twentieth century, Fred Paine played radio broadcasts on WWJ with the Detroit News Orchestra. He studied with F. R. Brown in Detroit and received rave reviews for his unique appearances as soloist—reportedly the first ever with a symphony—in both the *Detroit Free Press* and the *Evening Times*.
GEN. BIB.: Cook, *LDT*, p. 137.

PALIEV, DOBRI (b. 1928, Pernik, Bulgaria; d. Sep 1997, Sofia, Bulgaria). Professor of music (and formerly a student) at the State Academy of Music in Sofia until retiring in 1993, Dr. Dobri Paliev was an award-winning xylophone virtuoso and touring artist in his youth. He performed as principal percussionist and timpanist with the Bulgarian National Radio Symphony for several years and founded the Bulgarian State Percussion Ensemble, Polyrhythmia.

SELECTED BIBLIOGRAPHY

"Membership News." *Percussion News* (November 1997): 7.

PALMER, EARL C., SR. (b. 1924, New Orleans, Louisiana). A versatile studio drumset artist, Earl Palmer came from a vaudeville family background, got his first set at 6, and started lessons at 10. After serving in WWII he attended segregated Grunewald School of Music in New Orleans, where he studied theory and piano and took drum lessons from Bob Barbarin, brother of *Paul Barbarin. Starting his recording career with Little Richard and Fats Domino in the 1950s, Palmer was a rhythm and blues charter member, playing on such hits as "Blueberry Hill," "Tutti Frutti," and "Good Golly Miss Molly" and recording for Berry Gordy's Motown label. After moving to Los Angeles, where he made movie soundtracks in the 1960s–70s, he accompanied the likes of Ray Charles, the Temptations, Diana Ross, Sonny & Cher, Neil Young, and the Righteous Brothers, made recordings for rock-and-roll producer Phil Spector, and also worked with Red Callender, Buddy Collette, Benny Carter, and the Henry Mancini and Percy Faith Orchestras. Palmer served for 10 years as secretary-treasurer of the American Federation of Musicians, Local 47, in Los Angeles; he then returned to full-time performing.

SELECTED DISCOGRAPHY

Verve-Folkways FVS-9022/FTS-3013: *Lightnin' Hopkins*, 1965.

SELECTED VIDEOGRAPHY

DCI VH0171/CPP Media: *Earl Palmer and Herman Ernest: From R&B to Funk*, 1993.

SELECTED BIBLIOGRAPHY

Blaine, Hal (with David Goggin). *Hal Blaine and the Wrecking Crew, The Story of the World's Most Recorded Musician.* Emeryville, CA: Mix Books, 1990.
Cianci, Bob. *Great Rock Drummers of the Sixties.* Milwaukee, WI: Hal Leonard Publishing, 1989.
Claghorn, Charles Eugene. *Biographical Dictionary of American Music.* West Nyack, NY: Parker Publishing Co., Inc., 1973.
Thompson, Woody. "The Rhythm and Blues Drummers of New Orleans: Earl Palmer." *PN* XXXIV, 4 (August 1996): 28–29.

PANGBORN, ROBERT C. (b. 31 Dec 1934, Painesville, Ohio). An orchestral percussionist whose uncle founded the Hruby Conservatory of Music (Cleveland), Robert Pangborn was a student of *William Street, *Morris Goldenberg, and *Cloyd Duff. He attended the Eastman School (1952–53), the Juilliard School (1954–56), Case Western Reserve (1956–57), and Oakland University (Rochester, Michigan; 1975–76). A former member of the U.S. Military Academy Band (1953–56), he had varied professional performance experience, including positions as timpanist with the National Orchestra Association (New York), timpanist of the Indianapolis Symphony (1956–57), and percussionist-timpanist in the Minneapolis Symphony (1957). Staff percussionist for Motown Records (1968–73), Pangborn was a mallet specialist in the Cleveland Symphony (1957–63), with which he gave the premiere performance of Rolf Liebermann's *Concerto for Side Drum and Orchestra* in 1959; a percussionist and timpanist in the Metropolitan Opera Orchestra (1963–64); and since 1964 principal percussionist and assistant timpanist with the Detroit Symphony. The latter commissioned Donald Erb's *Concerto for Percussion and Orchestra*, which he premiered in 1966.

From 1968 to 1971, he performed on drumset and recorded two albums with an eclectic nine-piece group, Symphonic Metamorphosis, whose style was based on the fusion of classical, rock, and jazz genres. Founder and director of the percussion chamber groups Mostly Mallets, Detroit Percussion Trio, and Four for Percussion, he has held teaching posts at the Cleveland Institute (1958–63, where he initiated the first percussion ensemble) and at Oakland University (1975–89). Pangborn owned a vast personal collection of percussion instruments that he rented out through his own company, Professional Percussion Service. He can be heard with the Cleveland Symphony (1957–63) on the Epic and Columbia labels, and with the Detroit Symphony (since 1964) on the London recording label.

SELECTED BIBLIOGRAPHY

Shultis, Chris. "Robert Pangborn." *PN* XXIII, 4 (April 1985): 36–38.
GEN. BIB.: Larrick, *BET-CP.*

PARK, DONG-WOOK (b. 22 Jan 1935, Seoul, Korea). Earning a bachelor's degree from the Mannes School of Music (NY, 1970) and a master's degree from the University of Massachusetts at Lowell (1989), Dong-Wook Park was principal timpanist with the American Wind Symphony (1967–68), principal timpanist with the Bridgeport (CT) Symphony (1970–73), and principal timpanist for the Korean National Symphony (Seoul, 1973–81), with whom he debuted his own composition "Contrast" for percussion ensemble and winds (Carnegie Hall, 1979). Principal timpanist of the Korean Broadcasting System Orchestra (1981–82), Park conducted and served as soloist with the KNSO Chamber Ensemble (1973–81) and the "Pan-Music Festival" (Seoul, 1975–85); he also conducted both the Korean Percussion Ensemble (1973–86) and the Taipei Polyphony Ensemble (1976–77). He served many years as president of the Korean chapter of the Percussive Arts Society (from 1980), receiving the Korean "Musician of the Year" Award (1984) and the National Music Award from the Korean Association of Music Critics (1993). A faculty member at the Mannes School, he was founder and conductor of the Mannes Percussion Ensemble (1970–73) and established a percussion program at Seoul National University.

SELECTED BIBLIOGRAPHY

"New Board Members." *PN* XXIII, 2 (January 1985): 3.
Rugolo, John. "Dong Wook Park and the Music of Korea." *PN* XX, 3 (June 1982): 64–66.
Information supplied by the subject, 1996.

PARTCH, HARRY (b. 24 Jun 1901, Oakland, California; d. 3 Sep 1974, San Diego, California). Inducted into the Percussive Arts Society Hall of Fame in 1974, Harry Partch was surrounded early on with eclectic music from the previous far-flung stations of his missionary parents: Chinese lullabies, Yaqui Indian songs, Christian hymns, and others. After briefly attending the University of Southern California and working as a composer in the Western European tradition, he destroyed all his compositions at age 28. Experimenting with microtonality, Partch moved to England, returning destitute to the U.S. as a wandering "hobo" (1935–43, which ironically became an artistically fruitful period). He discovered jazz, Greek Philosophy, Congo puberty rites, and gamelan music, and these years yielded innovations which included supplanting equal temperament with a system based on just tuning and microtonality. For his unusual settings of texts borrowed from the Bible, Chinese poetry, and hobo graffiti, he conceived of a "corporeality" that demanded special sculpturelike instruments such as the Diamond Marimba (1946), Bass Marimba (1949–50), Marimba Eroica (1951), Cloud Chamber Bowls 1950–51), Spoils of War (1950–55), Boo (1955), Mazda Marimba (1959), and required percussionists to become actors-dancers-singers in dramatic musical theater settings. His major works include "The Wayward," "The Bewitched" (1955), "Oedipus," and "Daphne of the Dunes." Saved financially by a Guggenheim Fellowship (1943), he compiled his musical theories in the text *Genesis of a Music* (1949), and his works are sustained by performers (directed by Danlee Mitchell) who have access to the collected instruments and scores at San Diego State University. Many of his works have been staged (and films shown) at Percussive Arts Society International Conventions and at the Aspen, Berlin, and San Diego Jazz Festivals.

SELECTED DISCOGRAPHY

2 CBS MZ-30576: *Delusion of the Fury*, 1969.
Columbia MS7207: *The World of Harry Partch*, 1969/1972.
CRI S-213: *And on the 7th Day Petals Fell in Petaluma*, 1967.
Innova 401: *Enclosure II* (Several archival Partch recordings, 1930s–40s).
Innova 405: *Enclosure V* (*King Oedipus*, 1952; *The Bewitched*, 1980; *Ulysses at the Edge*, 1971).
New World 214: *Harry Partch/John Cage*, 1978.
Tomato R2 70390: *Revelation in the Courthouse Park*, 1989.

SELECTED VIDEOGRAPHY

Audio Visual Images/New Dimension Media: *The Dreamer That Remains: A Portrait of Harry Partch*, 1974 (produced by Betty Freeman and directed by Stephen Pouliot).
Film: *Revelation in the Courthouse Park*, 1961.
Innova 400/British Harry Partch Society: *Enclosure I* [includes *Rotate the Body in All Its Planes*, 1961; *Music Studio—Harry Partch*, 1958; *U.S. Highball*, 1968; *Windsong (Daphne of the Dunes)*, 1958].

Innova 404/British Harry Partch Society: *Enclosure IV* (includes *Delusion of the Fury*, 1969–72; *Daphne of the Dunes*, 1968).

SELECTED BIBLIOGRAPHY

Fierz, Stephen. "The Bewitched: Harry Partch's Corporealism." *PN* XXXV, 2 (October 1995): 66–70.

Fierz, Stephen D. "Lou Harrison and Harry Partch: A Brief Comparison." *PN* XXXV, 2 (April 1997): 74–75.

Gilmore, Bob. *Harry Partch: The Early Vocal Works, 1930–33.* Birmingham, England: British Harry Parch Society, 1996.

Partch, Harry. *Genesis of a Music.* New York: Da Capo Press, 1974.

"Percussive Arts Society Hall of Fame, 1974." *PN* XII, 3 (Spring 1974): 22.

Smith, J. B. "Instrument Innovations: The Harry Partch Instrument Collection and Ensemble." *PN* XXV, 4 (Spring 1987): 61–62.

Willis, Thomas. "The Ranks of the Unique Are Reduced by One." *Chicago Tribune* (3 Oct 1974): sec. 6, p. 6.

PASSERONE, FÉLIX (d. 1958). Timpanist with the Paris Orchestra and Paris Opera, Félix Passerone established the first percussion courses at the Paris Conservatory in 1947. He penned etudes, as well as a timpani method book, and compiled orchestral excerpts for timpani. Musicians from the Opera Orchestra of Paris honored him in 1959 with the recording *Hommage à Félix Passerone* (Véga C 30 S 244).

SELECTED BIBLIOGRAPHY

Dupin, François. "Dupin's Directory of French Percussionists." *PN* XXXII, 2 (April 1994): 29–31.

Passerone, Félix. *Exercises d'eprevure de technique pour quatre timbales.* Paris: Alphonse Leduc, 1955/1964.

PATTERSON, WILLIAM G. (b. 29 Aug 1949, Kingsville, Texas). A student of *Tony Ames, *Fred Begun, *Alan Abel, and *Elden "Buster" Bailey, William Patterson attended Del Mar College (TX, 1969), the University of Houston (bachelor's, 1971), and Catholic University (master's, 1974). He performed with the U.S. Marine Band (1971–75) and San Antonio Symphony (1978–) and also taught public school in Austin, Texas (1975–78), and at St. Mary's University (San Antonio, 1978–).
GEN. BIB.: Borland, *WWAMC.*

PATTON, DUNCAN. Principal timpanist with the Metropolitan Opera Orchestra since 1984, Duncan Patton earned a bachelor's degree from the Eastman School, where he received the *William Street Scholarship. Formerly with the

Colorado Philharmonic and Honolulu Symphonies, he has performed with the Manhattan Percussion Ensemble and the New Renaissance Chamber Artists, as well as for the Tongue of Wood Concert Series. Previously on the faculty of the State University of New York at Purchase, Patton has taught at the Manhattan School since 1989. He can be heard on the Deutsche Grammophon, Mercury, Philips, Decca, and Sony record labels.

SELECTED BIBLIOGRAPHY

Patton, Duncan. "Timpani: Basic Sound Production." *PN* XXXIV, 1 (February 1996): 54–56.
Manhattan School of Music Biographies, 1995; PASIC® program biographies, 1997.

PAULSON, WILLIAM "BILLY." Xylophone soloist for the last seasons of the John Philip Sousa Band (1930–32), Billy Paulson was a founding member of the Sousa Fraternal Society and also performed with Arthur Pryor (late 1920s–early 1930s), Don Voorhees, Leith Stevens, Victor Young, and Andre Kostelanetz. Later, as a studio musician in New York, Paulson could be heard on radio shows (e.g., *Telephone Hour* and Lucky Strike's *Hit Parade*), with *Harry Breuer, *Eddie Rubsam, and Irving Farberman on NBC radio (1927), and on early television.

SELECTED BIBLIOGRAPHY

Eyler, David P. "Development of the Marimba Ensemble in North America during the 1930s." *PN* XXXIV, 1 (February 1996): 66–71.
GEN. BIB.: Strain, *XYLO.*

PAYNE, SONNY PERCIVAL (b. 4 May 1926, New York, New York; d. 29 Jan 1979, Los Angeles, California). Son of pioneer drummer Chris Columbus (Louis Jordan's Tympany Five), drumset artist Sonny Payne took lessons from *Vic Berton (1936) and performed with Hot Lips Page (1944), Earl Bostic (1945–47), Tiny Grimes (1947/1949–50), and Erskine Hawkins (1950–53). After leading his own group (1953–55), he joined Count Basie (1955–65/1973–1974), Frank Sinatra (1965), and Harry James (1966–73) and fronted his own groups before touring with Milt Buckner, Don Cunningham, and Illinois Jacquet (Europe, 1976) near the end of his career. [Chris Columbus, b. Joseph Christopher Columbus Morris, Greenville, NC, 17 Jun 1902.]

SELECTED DISCOGRAPHY

Clef 678: *Count Basie Swings, Joe Williams Sings*, 1955.
Progressive PCD-7017: *Milt Buckner with Illinois Jacquet* et al., 1976.
Reprise 9 45946-2: *Count Basie Live at the Sands*, 1966/1998.

Roulette 7243 8 37241 2 3: *Count Basie and Sarah Vaughan*, 1961.
Roulette CDP 7 97969 2: *The Best of Count Basie*, 1991.
Roulette CDP 7243 8 28635 2 6: *The Complete Atomic Basie*, 1997.
Verve 840 815-2: *Count Basie at Newport*, 1957.
Verve MGVS6006: *Joe Williams with the Count Basie Orchestra*, 1956.
Verve V-8488: *Count Basie and His Orchestra*, 1955.
Verve V6-4061: *Ella Fitzgerald and Count Basie*, 1963.
Verve V6-8511: *Count Basie and His Orchestra*, 1962.
Verve V6-8659: *Count Basie and His Orchestra*, 1966.
WP 1261: *More Drums on Fire*, 1959.
WP 1264: *The Swingers* (Lambert, Hendricks, and Ross), 1959.

SELECTED BIBLIOGRAPHY

Tynan, John. "Sonny Payne: Count Basie's Swinger." *DB* XXIII, 13 (27 Jun 1956): 14.
GEN. BIB.: Kernfeld, *NGJ*, by Leroy Ostransky; Spagnardi, *GJD*.

PAYSON, ALBERT "AL" (b. 15 Jan 1934, Springfield, Illinois). Having studied snare, marimba, and timpani by the time he was in his teens, Al Payson earned a bachelor's degree from the University of Illinois in 1956 after a two-year hiatus performing in the U.S. Army's 44th Infantry Division Band (1951–53). His teachers include *Paul Price and Robert Kelly. Following a stint in the Louisville (KY) Orchestra (1956), Payson relocated to Chicago, where he worked with the Chicago Lyric Opera, the Royal Ballet of England, and others before securing the percussion position he has held since 1958 with the Chicago Symphony. As an educator, author-composer, and entrepreneur, he has taught at DePaul University, and written method books, percussion solos and ensembles, and percussion journal articles. He established the Payson Percussion Products Company, which markets percussion publications and accessories, and his invention, the "Roto-Tom," is manufactured and sold by the Remo, Inc., Drum Company.

SELECTED DISCOGRAPHY

Angel A CDC-47617: *Rimsky-Korsakov—Scheherazade* (Chicago Symphony, snare), 1969.
Deutsche Grammaphon-410895-2 GH: *Berlioz—Symphonie Fantastique* (Chicago Symphony, chimes), 1983.
Deutsche Grammaphon-419603-2 GH: *Prokofiev—Lt. Kije* (Chicago Symphony, snare), 1977.
London/Decca: *Ravel—Bolero* (Chicago Symphony, snare), 1974/1977.
London/Decca L-417704-2 LM: *Stravinsky—The Rite of Spring* (Chicago Symphony, bass drum), 1974.
London/Decca L-417754-2 LM: *Bartók—Concerto for Orchestra* (Chicago Symphony, snare), 1981.

RCA V RCD 1-5407: *Respighi—Pines of Rome* (Chicago Symphony, triangle/tambourine), 1959.

SELECTED BIBLIOGRAPHY

Payson, Al. *Elementary Marimba (and Xylophone) Method.* Northbrook, IL: Payson Percussion, 1973.
Payson, Al. *Progressive Studies in Double Stops for Mallet Instruments.* Ft. Lauderdale, FL: Music for Percussion, 1958/1967.
Payson, Al. *The Snare Drum in the Concert Hall.* Northbrook, IL: Payson Percussion, 1970/1985.
Payson, Al. *Techniques of Playing Bass Drum, Cymbals, and Accessories.* Northbrook, IL: Payson Percussion, 1971.
Payson, Al, and Jack McKenzie. *Music Educators' Guide to Percussion.* Rockville Centre, NY: Belwin, 1966.
GEN. BIB.: Larrick, *BET-CP.*

PEART, NEIL (b. 12 Nov 1952, Canada). Drumset artist with the musical group Rush, Neil Peart produced the *Burning for Buddy* series of videos and recordings and was elected to *Modern Drummer* magazine's Hall of Fame.

SELECTED DISCOGRAPHY

Atlantic 83010-2: *Burning for Buddy: A Tribute to the Music of Buddy Rich,* vol. 2, 1997.
Mercury 800 048-2: *Moving Pictures* (Rush), 1981/1997.

SELECTED VIDEOGRAPHY

DCI Music Video: *The Making of Burning for Buddy,* pts. 1–2, 1996.
DCI VH0293: *A Work in Progress,* 1997.

SELECTED BIBLIOGRAPHY

Fish, Scott K. "Neil Peart." *MD* (April 1984): 8–13.
Miller, William F. "Neil Peart: In Search of the Right Feel." *MD* XVIII, 2 (February 1994): 23–27.
Miller, William F. "The Reinvention of Neil Peart." *MD* XX, 11 (November 1996): 88–99.
Peart, Neil. "Starting Over." *MD* XIX, 11 (November 1995): 130–133.

PERAZA, ARMANDO (b. ca. 1924, Havana, Cuba). An orphan at the age of 7, conguero Armando Peraza started congas at 19 and, from 1943 to 1949, could be heard with Perez Prado, *Chano Pozo, and Celia Cruz. In 1950 he traveled to New York with *Mongo Santamaria, working 2 years with Slim Gaillard, 11 with George Shearing, 7 with *Cal Tjader, and 18 years with Carlos Santana.

His other collaborators included Jaco Pastorius, Jerry Garcia, Chick Corea, Sly and the Family Stone, Linda Ronstadt (movie soundtrack, *The Mambo Kings*), *Tito Puente, Art Tatum, Ray Charles, *Art Blakey, Chet Baker, Stan Kenton, Charlie Parker, Frank Foster, Dizzy Gillespie, among others.

SELECTED DISCOGRAPHY

Fantasy FCD-24712-2: *Los Ritmos Calientes* (Cal Tjader), 1954/1992.
Skye Records SK 50: *Wild Thing*, 1968.

SELECTED BIBLIOGRAPHY

Tolleson, Robin. "The Righteous Rhythm of Armando Peraza." *MD* XXIII, 1 (January 1999): 98–108.

PERSIP, CHARLI "SIP" (b. 26 Jul 1929, Morristown, New Jersey). Drummer, bandleader, and teacher who played and recorded with the Duke Ellington and Dizzy Gillespie Orchestras, as well as Harry James, Art Farmer, Tadd Dameron, Billy Eckstine, Hank Mobley, Gil Evans, Donald Byrd, Rahsaan Roland Kirk, and Cannonball Adderley, among others, Charli Persip led his own groups, "Superband" and "Persipitation."

SELECTED DISCOGRAPHY

Blue Note CDP 7 46816-2: *Lee Morgan*, 1957.
Blue Note (J) GXF-3064: *Two Bones* (Curtis Fuller), 1958.
Blue Note LA598-H2: *Little Niles* (Randy Weston), 1958.
Impulse GRD2-101: *Thirty Years of Jazz* (Gil Evans, et al.), 1960.
Roulette CDP 724382864127: *Gretsch Drum Night at Birdland*, 1960.
Specialty OJC CD-1762: *Dizzy Atmosphere* (Lee Morgan), 1957.
Verve 314 513 754-2: *Dizzy Gillespie at Newport*, 1957.
Verve 314 521 426: *Sonny Side Up* (Dizzy Gillespie, Sonny Rollins, Sonny Stitt), 1957.
Verve MGV8173: *Dizzy Gillespie Sextet*, 1954.
Verve MGV8166: *The Modern Jazz Sextet*, 1956.
Verve MGV8386: *Dizzy Gillespie and His Orchestra*, 1960.
Verve MGVS6016: *Harry Edison and Buck Clayton*, 1958.
Verve V-8411: *Dizzy Gillespie with Gunther Schuller Orchestra*, 1961.

SELECTED BIBLIOGRAPHY

Korall, Burt. "Charli Persip: His Own Man." *MD* XVIII, 12 (December 1994): 26–29.
Persip, Charli. *How Not to Play Drums: Not for Drummers Only*. New York: Second Floor Music, 1987.
Primack, Bret. "Charli Persip: The Art of Creative Accompaniment." *JazzTimes* XXI, 8 (November 1991): 56.
GEN. BIB.: Hunt, *52nd St.*

PETERS, GORDON BENES (b. 4 Jan 1931, Oak Park, Illinois). Before earning bachelor's and master's degrees from the Eastman School between 1953 and 1959, Gordon Peters attended Northwestern University (1949–50) and was enlisted as percussionist and assistant timpanist in the Military Academy Band at West Point (1950–53). While a student at Eastman, he created and arranged music for the mallet keyboard ensemble (plus string bass), the Marimba Masters (1955–59), whose expertise was featured with the Rochester (NY) and Buffalo (NY) Philharmonic Orchestras and on the *Ed Sullivan* and *Arthur Godfrey* television shows. During the Eastman years Peters also performed in the Rochester Philharmonic (NY, 1955–59) and Grant Park Symphony summer series (Chicago, 1955–58). Since 1959 he has held the principal percussionist and assistant timpanist chair in the Chicago Symphony in addition to fulfilling conducting duties with the Youth Symphony Orchestra of Greater Chicago (since 1959), the Chicago Civic Orchestra (1966–86+), and the Elmhurst (IL) Symphony (1968–73). He studied conducting with Pierre Monteux (summers, 1952–63), and his percussion teachers included *William Street, Otto Kristufek, *José Bethancourt, *Saul Goodman, *Clair Omar Musser, *Roy Knapp, and *Morris Goldenberg. During his tenure with Chicago, he was a featured percussion soloist and even sang (1960–63) with the Chicago Symphony Chorus. As a pedagogue, Peters was percussion editor of the *Instrumentalist* magazine and taught at Geneseo State (NY, 1957–58), the Eastman School (1958–59), and Northwestern University (1963–68/1991). His history-focused master's thesis was published in 1975 under the title *The Drummer: Man*, and he served as president of the Percussive Arts Society (1964–67).

SELECTED DISCOGRAPHY

Angel A S-37285: *Shostakovich—Symphony No. 5* (Chicago Symphony), 1977.
DG-415 136-1GH: *Orff—Carmina Burana* (Chicago Symphony), 1984.
Kendall Records LP 341: *The Marimba Masters*, 1956.
London/Decca 2L-410264-1 LJ2: *Mahler—Symphony No. 9* (Chicago Symphony), 1982.
London/Decca L-414192-2 LH: *Tchaikovsky—Symphony No. 4* (Chicago Symphony), 1984.
London/Decca L-417800-2 LH: *Beethoven—Symphony No. 9* (Chicago Symphony), 1986.
RCA V LSC-2893: *Ives—Variations on "America"* (Chicago Symphony), 1966.

SELECTED BIBLIOGRAPHY

Cook, Rob, ed. *Franks for the Memories.* Alma, MI: Rebeats Publications, 1993.
Furlong, William Barry. *Season with Solti: A Year in the Life of the Chicago Symphony.* New York: Macmillan Publishing, 1974.
Peters, Gordon. *The Drummer: Man.* Wilmette, IL: Kemper-Peters Publications, 1975.
Peters, Gordon. "Motivation for Saint Saens' use of the Xylophone in His *Dance Macabre*." *Percussionist* V, 3 (1968): 305–307.

Peters, Gordon. "Un-contestable Advice for Timpani and Marimba Players." *Instrumentalist* XXXIII (December 1978): 67–70.

Peters, Gordon, and T. Ames and F. A. Wickstrom. "Expert Advice for Percussion Students." *Instrumentalist* XXXIV, 10 (1980): 17–19.

GEN. BIB.: Borland, *WWAMC*; Larrick, *BET-CP*.

PETERS, MITCHELL T. (b. 17 Aug· 1935, Red Wing, Minnesota). Mitchell Peters studied with *William Street at the Eastman School, where he earned both the performer's certificate and a bachelor's degree in 1957, and the master's degree in 1958. He performed with the Rochester Philharmonic (1956–58) and the Marimba Masters (1953–58). Following a tour of duty with the Seventh U.S. Army Symphony in Germany (1958–60), Peters joined the Dallas Symphony as principal percussionist (1960–69). As percussionist and principal timpanist with the Los Angeles Philharmonic since 1969, he has recorded several film scores and is a member of the Philharmonic New Music Group. His teaching posts have included the University of California at Los Angeles, University of Southern California, California State University at Los Angeles, and Music Academy of the West (Santa Barbara). Peters has penned articles for the *Instrumentalist* and, as a composer, has contributed works to the percussion ensemble and solo repertoire that display both popular appeal and didactic utilization.

SELECTED DISCOGRAPHY

Cambria CD-1071: *The Music of William Kraft*, 1993.
Crystal Records CD-667: *Thomas Stevens*, 1989.
Crystal Records CD-801: *Hovhaness—Tzaikerk*, 1977.
Crystal Records CD-850: *Lou Harrison*, 1992.
Protone CSPR-163: *Kraft—Encounters III*, 1980s.

SELECTED BIBLIOGRAPHY

Cahn, Willam L. "Rochester's Classic Percussion: A Short History of the Percussion Section of the Rochester Philharmonic Orchestra." *PN* XXX, 5 (June 1992): 64–74.

Peters, Mitchell. "Concert Bass Drum Techniques." *LD* IV, 2 (Fall 1964): 30–31.

Peters, Mitchell. "Detached Rolls in Snare Drumming." *Instrumentalist* XVIII (December 1963): 68–70.

Peters, Mitchell. "Factors in Percussion Tone Quality." *Instrumentalist* XXI, (April 1967): 114–116.

Peters, Mitchell. *The Use of Mallet-Played Keyboard Percussion Instruments in Orchestral Literature.* Unpublished master's thesis, Eastman School of Music, University of Rochester, 1958.

GEN. BIB.: Borland, *WWAMC*; Larrick, *BET-CP*.

PETERSON, HOWARD MELVIN (b. 9 Jun 1904, Mooreton, North Dakota; d. 18 Jul 1991, Los Angeles, California). After moving to Seattle (1912), where he took piano lessons and experimented on drums, Howard Peterson became enthralled with the xylophone and continued to study that instrument after high school, working in banks and attending the University of Washington. He was playing for a local radio station when he signed with a talent agency that booked him on stations in Oakland (CA) during 1928–29. In 1932 he received a bachelor's degree from the University of Washington and then appeared with the group "Three Musical Keys" (xylophone, accordion, and saxophone), which was heard on radio in Seattle and Portland (OR).

Moving to Los Angeles late in 1933 and using the stage names Don Howard, Don Ricardo (1940s), and Juan Serrano, he played and recorded with orchestras led by Cecil Stewart (Swing Orchestra and Singing Symphonette, 1934–1960s), Ray Martinez (from 1949), Oreste Thomas (1942), José Gutierrez (1950s), and Eddie LeBaron (1940s–60s). He toured with the Charro Continental Marimba Orchestra and Rubio's Tipico Orchestra (1940s–60s) and performed with Mariscal's Marimba Band (from 1934, including a film appearance), the Vera Cruz Boys (1958–1960s, Reno and Las Vegas), Xavier Cugat (1940s–60s), and the Mexican Tipico Orchestra (1950s–70s, later known as the Los Angeles Civic Orchestra).

Peterson recorded motion picture soundtracks and was occasionally featured on camera, (e.g., MGM's *Holiday in Mexico* with Xavier Cugat and *Anchors Aweigh*, starring Frank Sinatra). He accompanied coloratura Yma Sumac, the "Peruvian Nightingale," on tour (1954–55, including Carnegie Hall), and his extensive road trips with Cugat's bands included the Hollywood Bowl, Las Vegas, and a recording session with Bing Crosby.

As a pedagogue, he taught in several Los Angeles area studios, wrote instruction manuals for both the xylophone and the marimba, and arranged several works published for the marimba. Peterson was the first American author of a marimba study to have his book published in Japan [*Elementary and Xylophone Etudes (sic)*, 1983]. He was made a Life Member of the American Federation of Musicians, Local 47, in 1964.

SELECTED BIBLIOGRAPHY

Peterson, Howard M. *Elementary Method for Xylophone or Marimba*. Chicago: Rubank, 1938.
Peterson, Howard M. *Fundamentals: Two-Four Hammer Playing*, Bks. 1–3. New York: Henry Adler, 1966.
Peterson, Howard M. *Keyboard Harmony for Marimba*. Chicago: Rubank, 1938.
Peterson, Howard M. *Marimba Solo Classics*. Boston: Boston Music Company, 1953.
Peterson, Howard M. *Peterson's Xylophone and Marimba Studies for Three and Four Hammer Playing*. Chicago: Rubank, 1937.

Peterson, Howard M. *A Tune a Day for Marimba,* Bks. 1–2. Boston: Boston Music Company.
Information supplied by Beatrice P. Hovig, 1996.

PFUNDT, ERNST GOTTHOLD BENJAMIN (b. 17 Jun 1806, Dommitzsch/Torgau, Germany; d. 7 Dec 1871, Leipzig, Germany). Timpanist in Leipzig's Gewandhaus Orchestra (1835–71) who played for Felix Mendelssohn (and was distantly related to Robert Schumann by marriage), Ernst Pfundt was a theology student and one of the first inventors of machine pedal timpani that were used in the Leipzig State Opera House. During the 1840s he played on three drums made by the Frankfurt inventor Johann Kaspar Einbigler. Pfundt solicited the technical expertise of a Herr Glanert in Leipzig who was manufacturing Einbigler's timpani, making design suggestions and improvements. At the same time, Friedrich Hentschel, timpanist of the Royal Opera in Berlin, improved on the Einbigler-Pfundt type with the help of engineer Carl Hoffmann thus giving birth to the Pfundt-Hoffman model, which could be found throughout all of Europe during the second half of the nineteenth century. Pfundt also penned one of the first German method books for timpani.

SELECTED BIBLIOGRAPHY

Beck, John H., ed. *Encyclopedia of Percussion.* New York: Garland Publishing, 1995. S.v. "The Kettledrum" by Edmund A. Bowles.
Cowden, Robert H., compiler. *Instrumental Virtuosi: A Bibliography of Biographical Materials.* Westport, CT: Greenwood Press, 1989.
Pfundt, Ernst. *Die Pauken/Paukenschule,* 3rd ed. Leipzig: Breitkopf & Haertel, 1849/1880 (revised by Hermann Schmidt, 1894).
Slonimsky, Nicholas, ed. *Baker's Biographical Dictionary of Musicians,* 7th ed. New York: Schirmer, 1984.

PHILIDOR, ANDRÉ (b. André Danican-Philidor, ca. 1647; d. 11 Aug 1730, Dreux, France). André Philidor was a librarian, copyist, composer, and wind musician in the service of the king of France. In 1685 he composed an unusual timpani duet ("Marches de timbales") for himself and his brother Jacques (b. 5 May 1657, Paris; d. 27 May 1708, Paris). The march was based on a first-inversion C-major chord and required two drums per player.

SELECTED BIBLIOGRAPHY

Sandman, Susan. "Indications of Snare-Drum Technique in Philidor Collection, MS 1163," *Galpin Society Journal* XXX (May 1977): 70–75.
Sandman, Susan. "The Wind Band at Louis XIV's Court," *Early Music* V (1977): 27–37.
Slonimsky, Nicholas, ed. *Baker's Biographical Dictionary of Musicians,* 7th ed. New York: Schirmer, 1984.

PICKING, ROBERT (b. 5 Jul 1879, Bucyrus, Ohio; d. 1983). Grandson of tinsmith and stove dealer Daniel Picking, who came to Bucyrus, Ohio, from Pennsylvania in 1837, Robert Picking guided the family business of hand-making copper kettles for timpani and other products for almost a century. After working in hardware around 1850, Daniel Picking started manufacturing copper kettles with a Mr. Geiger in 1878 under the firm name Picking and Geiger. He bought out Geiger and established a partnership with his sons, Charles and Wolford Picking, as D. Picking and Company. In 1880 the business branched out into other products, including copper kettles for timpani. Before WWII they made almost every timpani bowl in the United States and through the years have supplied handmade copper kettles to drum manufacturers Ludwig, Leedy, Slingerland, Conn, Gretsch, Nicoli, Hinger, American Drum [who now make their own], Wintrich, Goodman, Goodman-Lang, Stotz, and Clevelander. Daniel died around 1892, and the Picking building was selected by the U.S. Department of the Interior in the mid-1970s for inclusion on the National Register of Historic Places. Robert's daughter, Helen Picking Neff, began serving as president of the company in 1983.

SELECTED BIBLIOGRAPHY

Smith, D. Richard. "Mr. Robert Picking: Kettle Maker." *PN* XIII, 1 (Fall 1974): 22–24.
Stotz, Brian. "D. Picking & Company: A Century of Timpani Bowl Building." *PN* XXXI, 6 (August 1993): 68–72.

PIKE, DAVID SAMUEL "DAVE" (b. 1938, Detroit, Michigan) Vibraphonist and marimbist Dave Pike played with Herbie Mann, Paul Bley, and Babatunde Olatunji (marimba on *High Life!*, 1963), fronting his own groups.

SELECTED DISCOGRAPHY

Bear Family Records BCD 15747-1-DI: *Babatunde Olatunji—Drums of Passion and More* (Columbia Recordings, 1959–1966), 1994.

SELECTED BIBLIOGRAPHY

Claghorn, Charles Eugene. *Biographical Dictionary of American Music.* West Nyack, NY: Parker Publishing Co., Inc., 1973.
Coss, Bill. "Dave Pike: Vibist." *DB* XXX, 5 (28 Feb 1963): 22.

PILTZECKER, TED (b. 22 May 1950, Passaic, New Jersey). Composer, arranger, and jazz vibraphone artist Ted Piltzecker's background includes study with Ray Wright, Michael Gibbs, *David Samuels, and *Gary Burton, among others. He attended the Eastman School (bachelor's, 1972), Manhattan School (master's, 1985), and Ohio State University (1972–73). His performance and recording collaborations with groups both large and small include two years of worldwide tours with the George Shearing Quintet (reunited 1999), U.S. and Canadian performances with Pendulum (his duo with pianist, Jim Hodgkinson), and supporting roles with Wynton Marsalis, Slide Hampton, Jimmy Heath, Eddie Daniels, and Ernie Watts, among many others. An avid jazz pedagogue, Piltzecker taught at the University of Michigan (1985–87) and served as jazz coordinator of the Aspen Music Festival for eight years. He is a sought-after clinician who has been featured on various college campuses and at Percussive Arts Society and International Jazz Educators Conventions. He has been a featured soloist with the Billings (MT), Delaware, Tucson, and Regina (Saskatchewan) Symphonies and was guest conductor of the San Diego Symphony. The University of Nebraska, NEA, ASCAP, MacDowell Colony, and New York State Arts Council have all honored him for his creative contributions.

SELECTED DISCOGRAPHY

Canadian Broadcasting Company Enterprises: *Pendulum*, 1986.
Equilibrium, Ltd. EQ-7: *Unicycle Man*, 1997.
Sea Breeze SB-2027: *Destinations*, 1985.

SELECTED BIBLIOGRAPHY

Piltzecker, Ted. "The Art of Practicing." *PN* XXV, 2 (Winter 1987): 14–16.
GEN. BIB.: Larrick, *BET-CP*; PASIC® program biographies, 1992.

PIMENTEL, LINDA LORREN (b. 8 Sep 1940, Chattanooga, Tennessee). A graduate of San Jose (CA) State University (bachelor's, 1967, and master's, 1971), Linda Pimentel completed the Ph.D. at Ohio State University in 1983. She began the study of marimba and piano at an early age, and her teachers have included James Moore, *Anthony Cirone, and *Celso Hurtado. A guest artist with the San Francisco Symphony and throughout the United States, Pimentel taught junior high instrumental and vocal music in San Jose, served as an adjunct professor at Denison and Capital Universities (ca. 1977), and was on the faculty of Texas A & I University (1978–   ). For many years she was a contributing author to *Percussive Notes* ("The Marimba Bar" column).

SELECTED BIBLIOGRAPHY

Pimentel, Linda. "The Aristocracy of the Manufactured Marimbas." *PN* XXI, 1 (1982): 61–64.
Pimentel, Linda. *Bar Percussion Notebook*, vols. 1–2. Columbus, OH: Permus Publications, 1978/1980.
Pimentel, Linda. "Evolving Solo Technics for the Marimba." *Percussionist* X, 4 (Summer 1973): 107–110; and XI, 3 (Spring 1974): 97–101.

Pimentel, Linda. "Interval Study on Mallet Instruments." *Instrumentalist* XXXVI
        (November 1981): 83–86.
Pimentel, Linda. "Mallet Coordination and Flexibility Exercises." *PN* XIII, 1
        (1974): 33–34.
Pimentel, Linda. "Multiple Mallet Marimba Techniques." *Percussionist* XIV, 1
        (1976): 1–21.
Pimentel, Linda. "The Tonality-Based Problems of the Percussion Student." *Percussionist* XVI, 2 (1979): 73–93.
Pimentel, Linda, and James Moore. *The Solo Marimbist*, vols. 1–2. Columbus, OH:
        Permus Publications, 1976/1977.

PLASTER, THOMAS HAROLD (b. 1 Mar 1944, Joplin, Missouri). A student of Charmaine Asher-Wiley at the University of Missouri at Kansas City (1962–65), Tom Plaster performed at Starlight Theater (Kansas City, MO) from 1965 to 1980, and with the Kansas City Lyric Opera (1965–present), Kansas City Philharmonic (1965–80), and Kansas City Symphony (1980–present).
Information provided by the subject, 1996.

PLATT, WILLIAM H. Associated with the Cincinnati Symphony for 28 years, principal percussionist William Platt attended the Eastman School, where he studied with *William Street and did graduate work at the Cincinnati Conservatory. He also performed with the Rochester Philharmonic, Richmond (VA) Symphony, and the U.S. Army Band (Washington, D.C.).
PASIC® program biographies, 1999.

PODEMSKI, BENJAMIN "BENNY" (b. Riga, Latvia; d. ca. Jan 1956). Benjamin Podemski studied with Peter Lewin and began his professional career around 1905, serving as principal percussionist and cymbal specialist with the Philadelphia Orchestra (1921–1948/1951–54) [Kupferberg: *Those Fabulous Philadelphians*, states: 1923–54]. During the 1930s some of his Philadelphia percussion colleagues included *Oscar Schwar (timpanist), Emil Cressy [see *Kresse, Emil] (percussion and assistant timpanist), James Valerio, and *Cloyd Duff (Robin Hood Dell summer concert series). Podemski performed on radio broadcasts (e.g., *Chesterfield Hour*), in operas, for recordings on the Victor label, and under the world's greatest conductors, including Toscanini, Reiner, Herbert, R. Strauss, Stravinsky, Ormandy, and Stokowski.

SELECTED BIBLIOGRAPHY

Podemski, Benjamin. *Podemski's Standard Snare Drum Method.* New York: Mills
        Music, Inc., 1940.
"The Sounding Board." *Philadelphia Orchestra Program* (3–4 Feb 1956).
GEN. BIB.: Cook, *LDT*, p. 365 (photo).

POLLACK, BEN (b. 1903, Chicago, Illinois; d. 1971, Palm Springs, California). Drummer for the New Orleans Rhythm Kings (launched originally as the Friar's Society Orchestra in 1921), Ben Pollack started his own bands in 1924. His was one of the earliest white swing bands and employed later greats such as Benny Goodman (1925), Glenn Miller (1927), Jack Teagarden (trombone), and Jimmy McPartland (cornet). In the 1960s he owned Easy Street North, a club in Palm Springs (CA).

SELECTED BIBLIOGRAPHY

Brubaker, Robert L. *Making Music Chicago Style.* Chicago: Chicago Historical Society, 1985.
Claghorn, Charles Eugene. *Biographical Dictionary of American Music.* West Nyack, NY: Parker Publishing Co., Inc., 1973.

POLSTER, MAX [b. 1884, Reichenbach (sw of Chemnitz), Germany]. A drummer in the school band at the age of 5, Max Polster immigrated to the United States and joined the Boston Symphony as timpanist (1923–36+).

SELECTED BIBLIOGRAPHY

Brush, Gerome. *Boston Symphony Orchestra, 1936.* Boston: Merrymount Press, 1936.

PORCARO, JEFF (b. 1954; d. 5 Aug 1992, Hidden Hills, California). A member of the Grammy® Award–winning group Toto, Jeff Porcaro performed and/or recorded with John Fogerty, Steely Dan, and Bruce Springsteen, among others. Drummer for the *Sonny & Cher* television show, he was inducted into *Modern Drummer* magazine Reader's Poll Hall of Fame in 1993 and can be heard on the soundtracks of the movies *Glengary Glen Ross*, *Dune*, and *Dick Tracy*.

SELECTED DISCOGRAPHY

A&M SP 3038: *The Class of 1971* (Jack Daughterty), 1971.
A&M 75021 5297 2: *Apasionado* (Stan Getz), 1990.
Arista AL 9552: *Love All the Hurt Away* (Aretha Franklin), 1981.
Asylum 6E-107: *The Pretender* (Jackson Browne), 1976.
Atlantic SD 16037: *Songs of the Beatles* (Sarah Vaughan), 1981.
Blue Note LA711-G: *Willie Bobo—Tomorrow Is Here*, 1977.
Columbia CK 33920: *Silk Degrees* (Boz Scaggs), 1976.
Columbia CK 35317: *Toto*, 1977.
Columbia CK 37728: *Toto IV*, 1982 (Grammy® Award, 1982).
Columbia JC 36137: *Street Beat* (Tom Scott), 1979.
Columbia/Sony: *Kingdom of Desire*, 1991.

Creatchy SFB 1002: *Los Lobotomys*, 1989.
Denon CJ 74100: *Black Forest* (Luis Conte), 1989.
Epic PE 34426: *Captain Fingers* (Lee Ritenour), 1977.
MCA 2-8004: *Live in Las Vegas* (Sonny & Cher), 1973–74.
MCA MCAD-31194: *Katy Lied* (Steely Dan), 1975.
MCA MCAD-42245: *Larry Carlton*, 1988.
Warner Bros. 25166-1: *Behind the Sun* (Eric Clapton), 1985.

SELECTED VIDEOGRAPHY

Sony Video: *Toto Live in Paris*, 1990.
Star Licks Video/Music Video Distributors: *Jeff Porcaro—Drum Instruction*, 1990.

SELECTED BIBLIOGRAPHY

Flans, Robyn. "Jeff Porcaro: A Special Tribute." *MD* XVI, 12 (December 1992): 23–27.
Griffith, Mark. "Artist on Track: Jeff Porcaro." *MD* XXII, 7 (July 1998): 130–133.
"In Memoriam: Jeff Porcaro." *PN* XXXI, 1 (October 1992): 11.
Rule, Greg. "Goodbye, Jeff." *DRUM!* II, 2 (November/December 1992): 36–42.

PORCARO, JOSEPH THOMAS "JOE" (b. 29 Apr 1930, New Britain, Connecticut). Codirector of percussion curriculum at the Percussion Institute of Technology (PIT, 1981–95) and the Los Angeles Music Academy (LAMA, founded 1996), percussionist and drumset veteran Joe Porcaro studied with *Alexander Lepak at Hartt College, where he performed in the Hartford Symphony, eventually appearing with the Tommy Dorsey Orchestra, Bobby Hacket, Toshiko Akiyoshi, Chet Baker, and the Hindustani Jazz Sextet. Relocating to Los Angeles in the early 1960s, he is a first-call recording artist in Hollywood (e.g., *Mission Impossible* and *Men in Black*) and has played in the Don Ellis Big Band and with the Singers Unlimited, Toto, Gerry Mulligan, Barbra Streisand, the Rolling Stones, Roger Kellaway, Frank Sinatra, Sammy Davis, Jr., the Los Angeles Philharmonic, and his own group, Calamari. His manufacturing companies, JOPO and Porcaro Covers, respectively produce drumsticks with diamond-shaped tips and equipment bags.

SELECTED DISCOGRAPHY

Argo LPS-706: *Blues on the Other Side* (Mike Mainieri), 1962.
Impulse AS 9182: *Spirit of 1976*, 1976.
Uni 73008: *Stones* (Emil Richards), 1967.
Zebra ZD 44005-2: *Tribute to Jeff Porcaro* (Dave Garfield), 1997.

SELECTED VIDEOGRAPHY

Interworld VH0144: *Essence of Playing Mallets* (Emil Richards), 1991.
VDO Productions/Paiste America: *Joe Porcaro on Drums*, 1991.

SELECTED BIBLIOGRAPHY

Flans, Robyn. "Joe Porcaro and Ralph Humphrey: Partners in Education." *MD* XXI, 8 (August 1997): 134–140.
Flans, Robyn. "Joe Porcaro: Covering It All." *MD* XVIII, 11 (November 1994): 29–31.
Porcaro, Joe. *Joe Porcaro Drumset Method.* Hollywood, CA: JOPO Music Publications, 1983.
Porcaro, Joe. *Odd Times*: *A New Approach to Latin, Jazz, and Rock—Applied to Drumset.* Hollywood, CA: JOPO Music Publications, 1970.
Porcaro, Joe, and Dave Levine. "Reintroducing Odd Meters." *PN* XVI, 2 (Winter 1978): 48–50.
Information supplied by the subject, 1998.

POZNAN PERCUSSION ENSEMBLE (founded 1965). Founded by Jerzy Zgodzinski, a member of the Poznan Symphony and percussion instructor at the Conservatory of Music in Poznan, Poland, the Poznan Percussion Ensemble toured Europe and the Soviet Union and received the "Critics' Prize" at the 1973 Berlin Contemporary Music Festival.

SELECTED DISCOGRAPHY

Muza S-3 XW-1885: *Warsaw Autumn*, 1973.

POZO, LUCIANO POZO Y GONZALES "CHANO" (b. 1915, Havana, Cuba; d. Dec 1948). Conga and bongo artist Chano Pozo performed in New York with Tadd Dameron and Dizzy Gillespie's big band in the 1930s–40s and blended Cuban rhythms with the "bop" style of jazz.

SELECTED DISCOGRAPHY

Blue Note BLP5006: *James Moody and His Bop Men*, 1948.
Galaxy 204: *In the Beginning* (Milt Jackson), 1948.
RCA LPM2398: *The Greatest* (Dizzy Gillespie), 1947.
Verve MGV8065: *Illinois Jacquet and His Orchestra*, 1954.
Verve MGV8073: *Machito and His Orchestra*, 1950.

SELECTED BIBLIOGRAPHY

Goldberg, Norbert. "An Interview with Mongo Santamaria." *PN* XXII, 5 (July 1984): 55–58.
The National Music Awards. Chicago: American Music Conference, 1976.

PREISS, JAMES "JIM." Earning a bachelor's degree from the Eastman School and a master's degree from the Manhattan School, Jim Preiss studied with *William Street, *John Beck, *Fred Hinger, *Morris Lang, and *Paul Price. A member of the Manhattan School faculty (1970–83+), he served as timpanist and marimba soloist with the U.S. Marine Band and played in the Rochester Philharmonic, Brooklyn Philharmonia, Westchester Symphony, New York Opera Orchestra, Steve Reich and Musicians, among others.

SELECTED DISCOGRAPHY

Nonesuch 79430-2: *Steve Reich—Proverb Nagoya Marimbas/City Life*, 1996.
Opus One 72: *Frank Martin—Sonata da Chiesa*, 1981.
GEN. BIB.: Borland, *WWAMC.*

PRESS, ARTHUR CHARLES (b. 9 Jul 1930, Brooklyn, New York). A graduate of the Juilliard School (bachelor's and master's degrees) and a student of Sam Gershak, Al Howard, Roy Harte, *Saul Goodman, and *Morris Goldenberg, Arthur Press started his career with the Little Orchestra Society of New York (1950–51) and Radio City Music Hall (1950–56). He performed percussion and timpani with the Boston Symphony (1956–92) and the Boston Pops Orchestra. His pedagogical contributions include several journal articles (e.g., *Modern Percussionist*), a teaching post with the Boston Conservatory and Tanglewood School, and establishment of the Percussion Academy (1970).

SELECTED DISCOGRAPHY

Angel 4DS-49277: *Fireworks with Empire Brass*, 1988.
Angel CDC-49097: *Music of Christmas* (Empire Brass).
Capitol CDC-7 49277 2: *Fireworks—Empire Brass*, 1988.
Moss Music Group D-MMG 115: *The All-Star Percussion Ensemble*, 1983.
Music Minus One 5009: *Classical Percussion*, 1974.
Philips 6514-328: *Aisle Seat—Great Film Music* (Boston Pops), 1982.
Philips 9500-140: *Sibelius—Symphony No. 1 and Finlandia* (Boston Symphony), 1976.
Time-Life Records STLS-7001: *American Classics—Great Moments of Music* (Boston Pops), 1980.

SELECTED BIBLIOGRAPHY

Mattingly, Rick. "Arthur Press: Classical Wisdom." *MD* VIII, 9 (September 1984): 18–21.
Press, Arthur. "The Concert Snare Drum." *MP* I, 1 (December 1984–February 1985): 26–27.
Press, Arthur. *Mallet Repair.* Rockville Centre, NY: Belwin-Mills, 1971.
Smith, Dr. D. Richard. "A Most Televised Timpanist: Arthur Press of the Boston Pops." *PN* XIV, 2 (Winter 1976): 28–30.
Snyder, Louis. *Community of Sound: Boston Symphony and Its World of Players.* Boston: Beacon Press, 1979.
GEN. BIB.: Larrick, *BET-CP.*

PRICE, JESSE (b. 1 May 1909, Memphis, Tennessee; d. 19 Apr 1974, Los Angeles, California). Drumset artist Jesse Price toured with Sidney Desvignes, W. C. Handy, and Bessie Smith, among others, before relocating to Kansas City in the 1930s; there he collaborated with the Georgia Minstrels, Count Basie, Thamon Hayes, George E. Lee, Bill Martin, and led his own groups. In 1938 he toured with Ida Cox; by the 1940s he was backing Harlan Leonard, Louis Armstrong, Count Basie, Benny Carter, Ella Fitzgerald, Walter Fuller, Slim Gaillard, Jay McShann, and *Chick Webb. Also a blues singer, he was active on the West Coast during the late 1940s–60s, appearing at the Monterey Jazz Festival in 1971.

SELECTED DISCOGRAPHY

Mosaic MD12-170: *Classic Capitol Jazz Sessions*, vols. 1–4/9–12, 1942–44/1997.
GEN. BIB.: Southern, *BDA-AAM.*

PRICE, PAUL WILLIAM (b. 15 May 1921, Fitchburg, Massachusetts; d. 10 Jul 1986, Teaneck, New Jersey). Dubbed "Mr. Percussion" by Leopold Stokowski, Paul Price graduated from the New England Conservatory (1942) and was drafted into the U.S. Army, where he served four years as a medic (x-ray technician) in the South Pacific theater—including Okinawa. Surviving WWII, he performed as first percussionist and xylophone soloist with Frank Simon's ARMCO Band (1946–49), earned bachelor's (1948) and master's (1949) degrees from the Cincinnati Conservatory, and held the principal percussionist's chair in the Columbus (OH) Symphony during 1949. A former member of the American Symphony Orchestra, he studied with *Fred Noak and *George Carey and taught at the University of Illinois (1949–56), where he inaugurated the first accredited courses in the nation for percussion ensemble (1950) and percussion literature. Before teaching at Kean College (NJ) and the Manhattan School (1957–86), where his percussion ensemble toured Europe and the Middle East for the U.S. State Department (1968), Price performed, conducted, and taught at Boston University, Ithaca College, and Newark State College. He conducted the Paul Price Percussion Ensemble, owned Paul Price Publications, and was editor of Music for Percussion, Inc. Premiering over 300 new works for percussion ensemble, he made several recordings and appeared on television and radio. Price was cited by the National Association of American Composers and Conductors in 1967 for his "outstanding contribution to American music" and was inducted into the Percussive Arts Society Hall of Fame in 1975.

SELECTED DISCOGRAPHY

Avakian KO8P-1493 to 1498: *A 25-year Retrospective Concert of the Music of John Cage* (conductor, Manhattan Percussion Ensemble), 1958.
CRI 141: *Evocation for Violin, Piano, and Percussion* (Shapey), 1961.
CRI CD 742: *Music of Gardner Read*, 1959/1997.

CRI S-252: *Music of Harrison and Perry* (cond., Manhattan Perc. Ens.), 1970.
Golden Crest RE 7019: *Bassoon and Percussion Music*, 1967.
Music for Percussion MFP-513: *Paul Price Plays Snare Drum Solos*, 1950s/1970/1979.
Period Records SPL 743: *Music for Percussion* (cond., Manhattan Perc. Ens.), 1958.
Premier PRCD 1014: *Flagello—Divertimento/Electra* (Paul Price Perc. Ens.), 1991.
Time S-8000: *Concert Percussion for Orchestra* (cond., Manhattan Perc. Ens.), 1961.
University of Illinois CR53: *School of Music* (cond., University of Illinois Perc. Ens.).
Urania UR 5134: *Percussion* (cond., Manhattan Perc. Ens.), 1959.
Urania UX-5106: *Breaking the Sound Barrier*, vol. 1 (cond., American Percussion Society), 1956.
Vanguard 9230: *Noel* (Joan Baez), 1966.

SELECTED BIBLIOGRAPHY

"Mr. Percussion Plays." *Newsweek* (10 Aug 1959).
Price, Paul. *Beginning Snare Drum Method*. New York: Edwin H. Morris, 1955.
Price, Paul. "The Exciting World of Percussion!" *Hi-Fi/Stereo Review* (April 1961): 44–48.
Price, Paul. "A Percussion Progress Report." *PN* XVI, 2 (Winter 1978): 24–25.
Price, Paul. *Techniques and Exercises for Playing Triangle, Tambourine, and Castagnettes*. New York: Music for Percussion, 1967.
Salzman, Eric. "Disks: Percussive and Electronic." *New York Times* (Sunday, 2 Jul 1961).
Trueman, Peter. "Paul Price Wins Recognition." *Montreal Star* (Friday, 26 Jun 1959).
Wallace, Ed. "Concerto for 8 Rice Bowls to Beat Out at Caspany Hall." *New York World-Telegram and Sun* (Monday, 22 Feb 1960).
GEN. BIB.: Borland, *WWAMC*.

PTASZYNSKA, MARTA (b. 29 Jul 1943, Warsaw, Poland). After receiving a master's degree in theory and composition from the Warsaw Academy (1968), where she studied with Witold Rudzinski and others, percussionist-composer Marta Ptaszynska went to Paris under the tutelage of Nadia Boulanger (1970). In the United States she studied with *Richard Weiner, *Cloyd Duff, and Donald Erb at the Cleveland Institute, earning the artist diploma in 1974. Her Polish performance venues include the National Philharmonic, Warsaw Radio Symphony, and Poznan Percussion Ensemble. She has also collaborated with *Les Percussions de Strasbourg. As a teacher, Ptaszynska has filled faculty positions at the Warsaw Academy (1970–72), Bennington College (Vermont, 1974–77), University of California at Berkeley (1977–79), University of California at Santa Barbara (1980–82), San Francisco Conservatory, Eastman School, Manhattan School, and University of Chicago (1998–   ). Her extensive compositions for percussion have been honored by the American Society of Composers and Publishers (ASCAP) and the Polish government (Cross of Merit, 1995).

SELECTED DISCOGRAPHY

MUZA Polskie Nagrania SX 2709: *Concerto for Marimba*, 1990.
Pro Viva/Bestell Nv. ISPV-1987: *Space Model* (Performer/composer), 1988.

SELECTED BIBLIOGRAPHY

LePage, Jane Weiner. *Women Composers, Conductors and Musicians of the 20th Century*, vol. 2. Metuchen, NJ: Scarecrow Press, 1983.
Ptaszynska, Marta. "Fourth International Percussion Workshops, Bydgoszcz, Poland." *PN* XXIX, 4 (April 1991): 11–12.
GEN. BIB.: Borland, *WWAMC*; Larrick, *BET-CP*.

PUENTE, ERNEST ANTHONY, JR., "TITO" (b. 20 Apr 1923, New York, New York). Born in the Spanish Harlem neighborhood of New York to Puerto Rican parents, Tito Puente (from "Ernstito") is a four-time Grammy® Award recipient and has in excess of 120 record albums to his credit. At age 16 he played drums for the Noro Morales Orchestra and later studied at the Juilliard and New York Schools of Music. He was drafted into the U.S. Navy in 1942 and served aboard the *Santee* CVE29, a converted aircraft carrier. Early on, Puente fronted a Latin-jazz quintet on vibraphone, and his nine-piece group, the Piccadilly Boys, eventually became a full-size orchestra (1947–49). Admittedly influenced by *Gene Krupa and Stan Kenton, he blends Latin rhythms with big band jazz and has performed with Woody Herman, Count Basie, and Duke Ellington. Nicknamed "El Rey [the king] of the Mambo" (1950s), he has performed at the White House and is the composer of the often-recorded "Oye Como Va." The flambouyant *timbalero* was honored with a star on the Hollywood Walk of Fame for his many film appearances, including *The Mambo Kings* (1992), received an award from the National Endowment for the Arts, and was commemorated by the U.S. Postal Service with a stamp cancellation mark. In 1980 he returned to his earlier quintet format, and in 1995 he opened a restaurant sporting his moniker in New York. Host of the TV show *The World of Tito Puente* on Hispanic TV in 1968, Puente received the key to city from the mayor of New York (1969).

SELECTED DISCOGRAPHY

BMG/RCA 74321-46952-2: *Afro Cubano*, vols. 1–4 (1950), 1994–97.
Concord 295: *The Sound of Picante* (Monty Alexander), 1986.
Concord 4594: *Master Timbalero*, 1994.
Concord CJP-399-C: *Goza Mi Timbal* (Grammy® Award Winner), 1991.
Concord CJP-732-C: *Special Delivery*, 1996.
GNP 70: *Puente in Hollywood*, 1961.

Milan 7313835770–2: *Bending towards the Light...A Jazz Nativity*, 1995.
N2K 10023: *Hothouse* (Arturo Sandoval), 1998.
RCA LPM 3164: *Mambo on Broadway*, 1955.
RCA 2349-2-RL: *Cuban Carnival*, 1956/1990.
RCA CD 74749: *Puente Goes Jazz*, 1957/1995.
RCA 3264-2-RL: *Top Percussion*, 1957/1992.
RCA LPM 1447: *Night Beat*, 1957.
RCA 2467-2-RL: *Dance Mania*, vols. 1–2, 1958/1991–92.
RCA 74321-17448-2: *Revolving Bandstand*, 1960/1993.
RMD/RMC 81208: *Live at the Village Gate* (Tito Puente's Golden Latin Jazz All-Stars), 1992.
RMD/RMC 81208: *In Session* (Tito Puente's Golden Latin Jazz All-Stars), 1994.
RMD/RMC 81571: *Tito's Idea*, 1995.
RMD 82028: *Jazzin'*, 1996.
Tico JMTS-1422: *Puente in Percussion*, 1955/1978.

SELECTED VIDEOGRAPHY

Latin Percussion LPV100: *LPJE Live at Montreux*. 1980.
Sony 89312 VID: *The Mambo King, 100th LP*, 1991.

SELECTED BIBLIOGRAPHY

Bradley, Jeff. "Salsa King, Puente, Fiery at 71." *Denver Post* (Sunday, 21 Aug 1994).
Breton, Marcela. "Tito Puente: Championing the Latin Jazz Cause." *JazzTimes* XXI, 8 (November 1991): 29.
Mattingly, Rick. "They Keep Drumming, and Drumming, and...The Art of Percussive Longevity." *DB* LX, 11 (November 1993): 25–26.
"Puente, Tito," *Current Biography Yearbook*. New York: H. W. Wilson, 1977.
Roberts, John Storm. *The Latin Tinge: The Impact of Latin American Music on the United States*. New York: Oxford University Press, 1999.
GEN. BIB.: Hitchcock and Sadie, *NGA*, by John Storm Roberts.

PULK, BRUCE HARRY (b. 16 Dec 1950, Detroit, Michigan). Bruce Pulk studied privately with *Salvatore Rabbio (1965–73) and earned a bachelor's degree from the University of Michigan (1973), where he studied with *Charles Owen. He served as timpanist and section leader with the Flint (MI) Symphony (1969–74), timpanist with the Colorado Philharmonic (1974–75), and timpanist and artist-in-residence with the Grand Rapids Symphony (1974–82) until settling as principal timpanist with the Phoenix Symphony (1982–). With the latter he recorded an album of works by Aaron Copland, which was awarded "Best Classical Album of 1992" by the National Association of Independent Record Distributors (Koch label). From 1977 to 1982, Pulk taught at Grand Valley State College (MI) and Calvin College (MI).

SELECTED DISCOGRAPHY

Koch 2-7135-4:   Hermann—*Symphony No. 1*, Schuman—*New England Triptych* (Phoenix Symphony), 1992.
Koch 3-7222-2H1: *The Magnificent Seven* (Phoenix Symphony, soundtrack), 1994 (received European and NAID awards).
Koch: *Daniel Asia—Symphony Nos. 1 & 2* (Phoenix Symphony), 1993.
GEN. BIB.: Borland, *WWAMC.*

PURDIE, BERNARD. Studio drumset artist whose nickname is "Pretty," Bernard Purdie originated many of the rock and soul rhythmic "grooves" from the 1960s to the present, including the "Purdie Shuffle." A former music director for Aretha Franklin, he teaches in New York and has recorded and/or toured with several pioneers in the genres of rhythm and blues, soul, and funk, including Johnny "Hammond" Smith, Jimmy McGriff, Steely Dan, Quincy Jones, Herbie Hancock, Miles Davis, James Brown, Jimmy Smith, King Curtis, Herbie Mann, "Boogaloo" Joe Jones, Jeff Beck, Paul Simon, Ray Charles, Gato Barbieri, and Erroll Garner.

SELECTED DISCOGRAPHY

ACT 9253-2: *Soul to Jazz,* vols. 1–2, 1996–97.
Blue Note 84415: *Grant Green—The Final Comedown,* 1971.
Blue Note BLJ-48016: *Bireli Lagrene,* 1987.
Blue Note BT 85107: *Twilight Time* (Bennie Wallace), 1985.
Blue Note LA109-F: *Sassy Soul Strut* (Lou Donaldson), 1973.
Blue Note LA259-G: *Sweet Lou* (Lou Donaldson), 1974.
Blue Note LA406-G: *Silver 'n Brass* (Horace Silver), 1975.
Blue Note LA534-G: *Spoonful* (Jimmy Witherspoon), 1973.
MCA 1688: *Aja* (Steely Dan), 1977.
Rhino R2-71526: *Live at the Fillmore West* (Aretha Franklin), 1971.
Ubiquity URCD 010: *Bernard Purdie,* 1996.
Verve-Forecast FTS-3045: *Galt MacDermott,* 1968.
Zebra ZD 44005-2: *Tribute to Jeff Porcaro* (Dave Garfield), 1997.

SELECTED VIDEOGRAPHY

CPP Media VH 0185: *Bernard Purdie—Groove Master,* 1993.
DCI: *A History of R&B/Funk Drumming* by Yogi Horton, 1983.

SELECTED BIBLIOGRAPHY

Cianci, Bob. *Great Rock Drummers of the Sixties.* Milwaukee, WI: Hal Leonard Publishing, 1989.
Griffith, Mark. "Artist on Track: Bernard Purdie." *MD* XXII, 11 (November 1998): 158–160.
Griffith, Mark. "The Great Organ Trio Drummers." *MD* XXIII, 1 (January 1999): 118.
Iero, Cheech. "My First Gig." *MD* XX, 12 (December 1996): 148–151.

PUSTJENS, JAN (b. 31 Oct 1946, Sittard, Netherlands). A 1968 honors graduate of the Maastricht Conservatory, Jan Pustjens received a performer's degree and teaching certificate, studying with *Jan Labordus. His performance vitae includes principal percussionist and timpanist with the Enschede Opera (1966–68), principal percussionist with the Netherlands Philharmonic (aka Kunstmaand Orkest, 1968–74), and since 1974 principal percussionist and featured soloist with the Royal Concertgebouw Orchestra in Amsterdam. After performing and recording with the Dutch Wind Ensemble from 1970 to 1978, Pustjens established the New Amsterdam Percussion Group (1980), with which he has also recorded. He owns Pustjens Percussion Products and has taught at the Sweelinck Conservatory since 1969.

SELECTED DISCOGRAPHY

Philips 416378-2: *Bartók—Concerto for Two Pianos, Percussion, and Orchestra* (Royal Concertgebouw), 1985.
GEN. BIB.: Larrick, *BET-CP*. Information supplied by the subject, 1996.

R

RABBIO, SALVATORE "SAL" (b. 27 Jul 1934, Watertown, Massachusetts). Starting snare drum lessons in junior high school and establishing a reputation as a jazz drumset artist, Sal Rabbio attended Boston University (bachelor's, 1956) and studied with *Charles Smith. As a student he performed for the American premieres of Stravinsky's "The Rake's Progress" and Orff's "Carmina Burana." While on tour with the Boston Pops, he auditioned for and won the timpani chair in the Detroit Symphony and has been there since 1958. Rabbio has soloed with the Boston Pops, played in the Boston Percussion Ensemble, and premiered timpani concerti with Detroit. A popular clinician in the United States and Europe and at the Interlochen Music Camp, Percussive Arts Society International Conventions, and Oberlin Percussion Institute, he headed the percussion department at Wayne State University (Detroit) from 1962 to 1985. Rabbio designed a wooden timpani mallet specifically for use on plastic heads (Cooperman Drum Company) and has served as adjunct professor of timpani at the University of Michigan since 1988. His recordings with the Detroit Symphony since 1958 under the batons of Paray, Dorati, Freeman, and Järvi can be heard on Mercury, Columbia, RCA London, and Chandos labels.

SELECTED BIBLIOGRAPHY

Howard, Doug. "Interview with Salvatore Rabbio." *PN* XXIII, 4 (April 1985): 66–68.

Simco, Andrew P. "Salvatore Rabbio: The Detroit Symphony Years." *PN* XXXV, 4 (August 1997): 66–69.

RACKETT, ARTHUR HERBERT, JR. (b. 1864, Philadelphia, Pennsylvania; d. ca. Dec 1937, Chicago?, Illinois). American drummer, trumpeter, composer, saxophonist, and clarinetist who matured in Canada, Arthur Rackett began his playing career around 1874 as an apprentice in Kingston, Ontario, at the Royal School of Gunnery, where his father was bandmaster. After completing his tour of duty with the Royal Canadian Artillery Band as a trumpeter and drummer, he appeared independently as a drum soloist before relocating to the United States in 1881. There he toured with novelty shows, including the "Rackett Sextette Family Orchestra and Band," until settling in Chicago in 1889, securing work in theater orchestras as drummer and saxophonist. His many musical associations included the Innes, Kryl, and Pryor Bands, vaudeville in Europe and the United States (ca. 1898–1910), and service with Sousa's Naval Battalion Band (Great Lakes, Illinois) in WWI. After playing both snare and bass drum parts simultaneously with sticks for many years ("double drumming"), he was an early ardent advocate of the bass drum pedal.

SELECTED BIBLIOGRAPHY

Rackett, Arthur Herbert. *Arthur H. Rackett's 50 Years a Drummer*. Elkhorn, WI: By author, 1931.
Rackett, Arthur H. "Fifty Years a Drummer." *PN* XXXV, 4 (August 1997): 83–85 [reprinted from *Jacobs' Orchestra Monthly* (October 1925)].
Rackett, Arthur H. "The Talkies: Their Merits and Demerits." *IM* XXXVI, 4 (October 1928): 16.

RAMPTON, ROGER (b. 1935; d. 1995). At age 18 the first timpanist of the Utah Symphony, Roger Rampton appeared with the Nevada and Long Beach (CA) Symphonies and performed on the road twice with Elvis Presley. Inventor of the "Exactone" timpani-tuning gauge, he owned the Planet Percussion retail concern in Las Vegas, where he played shows for 35 years with such luminaries as Johnny Mathis, Nat King Cole, Louis Armstrong, and Andy Williams.

RANGANATHAN, TANJORE (b. 13 Mar 1925, Madras, India). Mrdangam artist Tanjore Ranganathan studied with Subramania Pillai and has recorded with Ramnad Krishnan and T. Viswanathan. He has performed in the United States, Europe, and England and at the Edinburgh Festival (1963). His teaching positions have included the American University (1967), California Institute of the Arts, and Wesleyan University (CT).
GEN. BIB.: Borland, *WWAMC.*

RANTA, MICHAEL (b. 1942, Minnesota). Percussionist and composer Michael Ranta attended the University of Illinois (bachelor's, 1966), taught at the Interlochen Arts Academy, and played with several U.S. orchestras, including the New Orleans Philharmonic and Chicago Little Symphony. He has freelanced in Western Europe (1968–   ), appearing in solo recitals and on German radio and television. Recording works by Takemitsu, Partch, Marirano, Kagel Lachenann, and Riedl, Ranta performed Karlheinz Stockhausen's compositions in the German pavilion at Expo '70 and constructed a multimedia environment for the 1972 Munich Olympics. In the mid-late 1970s, he lived in the Far East, recording and performing in Japan, Taiwan, and the Philippines, and created multimedia concerts in Karachi, Pakistan, and Kabul, Afganistan (1975).

SELECTED DISCOGRAPHY

Deutsche Grammophon 2740 105/Polydor: *Free Improvisation/Wired*, 1974.
Deutsche Grammophon MG 2331: *Toru Takemitsu—Seasons/Toward*, 1970.
Deutsche Grammophon MG 2476: *Toru Takemitsu—Miniatur*, 1970.
Wergo WER 60 122: *Helmut Lachenmann—Consolation I*, 1985.

SELECTED BIBLIOGRAPHY

Ranta, Michael. "Percussion in Japan—An Interview [with Sumire Yoshihara and Yasunori Yamaguchi]." *PN* XVI, 1 (Fall 1977): 36–39.

REED, TED (b. 1908; d. 20 Dec 1996, Clearwater, Florida). Ted Reed performed in society bands in New York but made his fame as a drum teacher who gave birth to some of the greats. He introduced his *Progressive Steps to Syncopation for the Modern Drummer* (Alfred Publishing) in the mid-1950s, and it is still considered one of the seminal method books in percussion pedagogy. Teaching upwards of 85 students a week in New York, Reed moved to Florida in 1970. He received a Lifetime Achievement Award at the Thoroughbred Florida Drum Expo and *Modern Drummer* magazine's Editors' Achievement Award (1994).

SELECTED BIBLIOGRAPHY

"In Memoriam." *MD* XXI, 5 (May 1997): 130.
Reed, Ted. *Drum Solos and Fill-ins for the Progressive Drummer*. Clearwater, FL: Ted Reed Publishing, 1959.
Reed, Ted. *Latin Rhythms for Drums and Timbales*. Clearwater, FL: Ted Reed Publishing, 1960.
Reed, Ted. *Progressive Steps to Bass Drum Technique*. Clearwater, FL: Ted Reed Publishing, 1986.
Reed, Ted. *Progressive Steps to Bongo and Conga Drum Technique*. Clearwater, FL: Ted Reed Publishing, 1961.

REITZ, WILLIAM H. (d. ca. April 1935, Philadelphia?, Pennsylvania). William Reitz was a xylophonist and drummer who worked for Victor Records (1914–19), recorded on bells, and later performed with the Victor Orchestra (1926), recording William R. Stobbe's compositions.

SELECTED DISCOGRAPHY

Victor 16934: "U.S.A. Patrol," 1911.
Victor 16969-A: *The Mocking Bird Fantasia*, 1911/1925.
Victor 17168: "Black Diamond Rag" (Henry Lodge) (Reitz on drums), 1912.
Victor 17308: "Florida Rag" (Van Eps Trio), 1912.
Victor 17337: "Little Flatterer Spoontime," 1911/1925.
Victor 17457: "Blood Lillies," 1913.

SELECTED BIBLIOGRAPHY

"Death Roll," *IM* (April 1935).
GEN. BIB.: Cahn, *XAR*.

REMSEN, ERIC SPENCER (b. Washington, D.C.).   Earning a bachelor's
degree from California State University at Los Angeles (1960) and a master's
degree from the University of Southern California (1983), Eric Remsen held positions as percussionist with the Milwaukee Symphony (1969–70), percussionist and timpanist with the San Antonio Symphony (1970–77) and Los Angeles
Chamber Orchestra (1978–81), and timpanist with the St. Paul Chamber Orchestra (1981–   ).   He authored *Timpani Tuning* (1977) and editions of eight-
eenth- and nineteenth-century timpani parts (1983).

SELECTED BIBLIOGRAPHY

Remsen, Eric. *Contemporary Timpani Studies*. Hollywood, CA: Try Publishing,
        1964.
Remsen, Eric. "Timpani Tuning: A Much Too Neglected and Misunderstood Sub-
        ject." *Percussionist* XVI, 2 (Winter 1977).
GEN. BIB.: Borland, *WWAMC*.

REMY, JACQUES (b. 25 Oct 1931, Saint-Cloud, France).   Performer, teacher,
and composer Jacques Remy studied with *Félix Passerone and graduated with
honors from the Paris Conservatory in 1950.   His professional performance associations have included the Cologne Orchestra (1950), the Festival d'Aix en
Provence (1953–56), the Orchestre du Domaine Musical (1954–60), the Radio-
France Symphony, the Paris Opera, the French National Orchestra, and the Paris
Orchestra, with which he has been principal timpanist since 1967.   From 1958
to 1964, he taught at the Parisian École Normale de Musique, a position his
teacher, Passerone, had previously held.   His published contribution to the or-
chestral percussion literature includes the edited timpani parts to Beethoven,
Schubert, and Schumann symphonies.   He can be heard on recordings with the
Paris Orchestra since 1967 on CBS, DGG, EMI, Erato, and Philips labels.

SELECTED BIBLIOGRAPHY

Dupin, François. "Dupin's Directory of French Percussionists." *PN* XXXII, 2 (April 1994): 29–31.

Remy, Jacques, ed. *Robert Schumann: Symphonies and Piano Concerto—Parties de Timbales*. Paris: Alphonse Leduc, 1989.

GEN. BIB.: Larrick, *BET-CP*.

RÉPERCUSSION (est. January 1974, Quebec City, Canada). The world music percussion ensemble Répercussion (now based in Montreal) has made more than 2,000 concert appearances, including Expo '86 and '92, and toured internationally throughout Europe, Asia and the Far East, and North, Central, and South America. The six original members who were advanced students at the Quebec Conservatoire de Musique had become a quartet by 1977. Among the ensemble's current members are two founding players, Chantal Simard and Robert Lépine, and two veteran performers, Aldo Mazza (since 1978) and Luc Langlois (since 1982). They have performed with Claude Bolling, Oliver Jones, and major Canadian symphonies and have recorded on numerous occasions for the Canadian Broadcasting Company's radio and television services.

Robert Lépine studied piano and/or percussion at the Quebec Conservatory, at McGill University, in England, and in New York; he now serves on the faculty of the University of Quebec. Chantal Simard attended the Quebec and Montreal Conservatories and teaches percussion in Trois-Rivières and Sherbrooke (Quebec). Aldo Mazza [b. 11 May 1952, Calabria, Italy] attended the University of Ottawa (bachelor's, 1972), McGill University (bachelor's, 1979), and the University of Montreal (graduate studies in ethnomusicology, 1993–94). He has had numerous collaborators as an independent artist (e.g., Celine Dion and Jon Bon Jovi), serves as artistic director of the KoSA International Percussion Workshop, and teaches at McGill Conservatory in Montreal. Luc Langlois earned a bachelor's degree in music from the University of Montreal and a degree in electrical engineering from l'École Polytechnique de Montreal.

SELECTED DISCOGRAPHY

ATM 2 9719: *Répercussion—Les Fantaisies Classiques*, 1994.
ATM CD 1009: *New Kong*, 1991.
Chandos Chan 9288: *Schedrin—Carmen Suite*, 1994.

SELECTED BIBLIOGRAPHY

Weiss, Lauren Vogel. "Répercussion: Percussive Ambassadors." *PN* XXXIV, 5 (October 1996): 57–60.

REYES, WALFREDO DE LOS, SR. (b. Havana, Cuba). Credited as the first to fuse jazz and Cuban rhythms utilizing the drumset and percussion simultaneously, Walfredo Reyes, Sr., matured in Puerto Rico; at 13 he moved with his family to Las Vegas. In demand for film and recording studio work since moving to Los Angeles in 1982, he has played and/or recorded with Santana, *Tito Puente, Sammy Davis, Jr., Josephine Baker, Wayne Newton, Tony Bennett, Larry Carlton, Linda Ronstadt, Irakere, Los Van Van, NG La Banda, El Medico De Salsa, Israel "Cachao" Lopez Descargo, and his own group, World of Percussion, among many others. His video, *All By Myself* (ca. 1997), demonstrates his ability to combine drumset and various percussion instruments simultaneously.

SELECTED DISCOGRAPHY

Pablo/OJC 5632: *Ecué: Ritmos Cubanos* (Louie Bellson), 1978/1991.
Rumba Records/Jasrac PCD-2364: *Sabor Cubano*.
Tumbao Cuban Classics TCD-054: *Fufuñando* (Orquesta Casino de la Playa), 1937/1995.
Tumbao Cuban Classics TCD-057: *Poco Loco* (Anselmo Sacasas), 1945/1995.

SELECTED VIDEOGRAPHY

DCI VHO 157/166: *Working It Out*, pts. 1–2 (with Dave Weckl), 1992/1993.
PASIC® program biographies, 1996.

RICH, BERNARD "BUDDY" (b. 30 Sep 1917, Albany, New York; d. 2 Apr 1987, Los Angeles, California). Dancer, singer, emcee, karate black-belt, and drumset artist, Buddy Rich started drums at 18 months of age, was billed as the "Biggest 'Little'Act in Vaudeville" (1921), and was the finale to his parents' act as "Traps, the Drum Wonder" at age 7. By 1925 he was touring internationally as a solo act; but as vaudeville's popularity waned, the 15-year-old Rich gave up show business to become a jazz drummer in the early 1930s. To that end, he cited the influence of *Jo Jones, *O'Neill Spencer, *Chick Webb, *Sid Catlett, *Gene Krupa, and Tony Briglia (Casa Loma Orchestra drummer). Although he didn't read music initially, he worked on a CBS radio show, the *Saturday Night Swing Club*, and fronted a band of his own in 1938. His first successes came with Bunny Berigan, Joe Marsala (1938), Artie Shaw (1939), and Tommy Dorsey (1939–45). The latter included an interim hiatus as a judo instructor at Camp Pendleton, California for the U.S. Marines (late 1942–44), where he received a medical discharge as a result of training injuries. Rich formed his first big band in 1945 with $50,000 backing from Frank Sinatra but disbanded it by 1949. During the 1950s he toured Europe with "Jazz at the Philharmonic" and performed and/or recorded with Dizzy Gillespie, Dexter Gordon, Thelonius Monk, Erroll Garner, Lester Young, Charlie Ventura, Frank Sinatra, Les Brown,

Benny Goodman, Bud Powell, Woody Herman, Benny Carter, Count Basie, *Lionel Hampton, Art Tatum, and Charlie Parker.

After a major heart attack in 1959, Rich went back to work with the Harry James Band (Las Vegas, early 1960s), eventually earning $1,500 per week, which secured him a spot in the *Guiness Book of World Records* as the "highest paid orchestral musician in the world" by 1966. That same year he retooled his 15-piece Buddy Rich Big Band for contemporary musical styles. A frequent television guest on Johnny Carson's *Tonight Show*, he owned a club in New York City in the 1970s called "Buddy's Place." He won *Down Beat* polls in 1941, 1942, and 1944, and as his health declined rapidly in the 1980s, he was inducted into the *Modern Drummer* Reader's Poll (1980) and the Percussive Arts Society Halls of Fame (1986).

SELECTED DISCOGRAPHY

Alto 721: *Drums Ablaze* (Art Blakey), 1960.
Black Lion 760137: *Anatomy of a Jam Session* (Nat Cole), 1945/1990.
Bluebird AXM2-5556: *The Complete Artie Shaw*, vols. 1–3 (1938–40), 1978.
Cafe Records CD 2-732: *Mr. Drums Live*, 1985.
Capitol T 926: *Hi-Fi Drums*, 1957.
Clef MGC-667: *The Lionel Hampton Quartet/Quintet*, 1954.
Clef MGC-684: *Krupa and Rich*, 1954.
Clef MGC-709: *The Hampton-Tatum-Rich Trio*, 1955.
Clef MGC-727: *Airmail Special* (Lionel Hampton), 1953-54.
French CBS: *The Orchestra and the Octet*, vol. 6, 1946/1950/1951 (Count Basie).
Groove Merchant GM 528/Beast Retro CD: *The Roar of '74*, 1974/1998.
Groove Merchant GM 3302: *Transition* (with Lionel Hampton), 1974.
Joyce 1007/1025/1045/1078/1153: *One Night Stand with Buddy Rich* (et al.), 1946/1953/1977/1979/1989.
Liberty LST-11006: *Keep the Customer Satisfied*, 1970.
Magic DAWE60: *Buddy Rich and His Orchestra, Europe '77*, 1977/1993.
Mercury 60133: *Roach versus Rich*, 1959.
Mercury-EmArcy MG 36071: *Giants of Jazz, vol. 8—The Jazz Greats, Drum Role*, 1959.
Mercury-EmArcy Jazz Series EMT 4-2-402: *Buddy Rich, Both Sides*, 1976.
Pablo/Musical Heritage Society MHS 7153T: *The Tatum Group Masterpieces* (Art Tatum), 1955/1976.
Pacific Jazz 20126: *The New One!* 1968.
Pacific Jazz CDP 7243 8 35232 2 1: *Buddy Rich—Swingin' New Big Band*, 1966/1995.
Pacific Jazz CDP 7243 8 54331 2 2: *Mercy, Mercy*, 1968/1997.
Pacific Jazz L4N 10090/Liberty ST 20117: *Big Swing Face*, 1967/1981.
RCA Victor LPM2078: *The Great Dance Bands of the '30s and '40s* (Bunny Berigan), 1959.
RCA Victor LPM6003: *That Sentimental Gentleman, Tommy Dorsey* (radio broadcasts, 1940–44), 1956.
RCA Victor LSP-4666: *Rich in London*, 1972.
RCA Victor VPS 6062/AXK2 5533: *This Is Artie Shaw*, vol. 2, 1977.

Sounds of Swing LP-106: *"Swing High"* (Tommy Dorsey), 1939/1971.
The Great American Gramophone Co. GADD-1030: *Class of '78,* 1977.
United Artists UXS 86 XD: *Superpak—Buddy Rich Big Band,* 1972.
Verve 8177882: *This One's for Basie,* 1956.
Verve 827 901-2: *The Genius of Bud Powell,* 1950.
Verve 8285: *Buddy Rich in Miami,* 1957.
Verve 831133-2: *Bird and Diz* (Charlie Parker and Dizzy Gillespie), 1950.
Verve 833 295-4: *Buddy Rich,* 1987.
Verve 835 3116-2: *Lester Young and Piano Giants* (Nat King Cole et al.), 1945.
Verve MG V-4003: *Ella Fitzgerald and Louis Armstrong,* 1956.
Verve MGV2009/2075: *Buddy Rich Just Sings,* 1956/1957.
Verve MGV2011: *Teddy Wilson Trio,* 1952.
Verve MGV8073: *Machito and His Orchestra,* 1950.
Verve MGV8083: *Charlie Ventura's Big Four,* 1951.
Verve MGV8090: *Count Basie Sextet,* 1952.
Verve MGV8105: *King of the Vibes* (Lionel Hampton), 1954.
Verve MGV8129: *Buddy and Sweets* (Harry "Sweets" Edison), 1955.
Verve MGV8162: *Pres* (Lester Young), 1950–52.
Verve MGV8223: *Lionel Hampton '58,* 1958.
Verve V/V6-8484: *Jazz at the Philharmonic: Gene Krupa and Buddy Rich, the Drum Battle,* 1952.
Verve V6-8425: *Blues Caravan,* 1961.
Verve V6-8471: *Burnin' Beat* (Krupa and Rich), 1962.
Verve/Polygram 840 033-4: *Jazz Club—Drums,* 1951–77.
World Pacific Jazz ST-20158: *Buddy and Soul.*
World Pacific WPS-21453: *Rich à la Rakha,* 1970/1982.

SELECTED VIDEOGRAPHY

Bogue-Reber Productions/Music Video Distributors: *Buddy Rich,* 1985.
DCI VH0196/0197: *Buddy Rich—Jazz Legend,* pts. 1–2 (1917–70/1970–87), 1994.
DCI VH0248: *Legends of Jazz Drumming,* pt. 1 (1920–50), 1996.
MGM Movie: *DuBarry Was A Lady* (Tommy Dorsey), 1944.
Music Video Distributors: *Buddy Rich—Mr. Drums Live,* 1990.
Vitaphone/Music Video Distributors: *Symphony of Swing* (1939–48), 1986.

SELECTED BIBLIOGRAPHY

Cook, Rob, ed. *Franks for the Memories: A History of the Legendary Chicago Drum Shop and the Story of Maurie and Jan Lishon.* Alma, MI: Rebeats Publications, 1993.
Cully, Dick. "Buddy Rich: The World's Greatest Teacher." *PN* XXXI, 8 (December 1993): 10–11.
Hoefer, George. "Buddy Rich: Portrait of a Man in Conflict, Pt. I–II." *DB* XXVII, 12 (9 Jun 1960): 17–19; XXVII, 13 (23 Jun 1960): 20–22.
Klauber, Dr. Bruce H. "Buddy Rich's Enduring Legacy." *Stick It* I, 1 (January 1998): 14–24.
Ludwig, William F., Jr. "Remembering Buddy Rich." *PN* XXVI, 1 (Fall 1987): 7–8.

Meriwether, Doug. *Mister, I Am the Band!* Milwaukee, WI: Hal Leonard, 1998 (formerly titled *We Don't Play Requests*).

Morgenstern, Dan. "Buddy Rich: Jazz Missionary." *DB* XXXVI, 6 (20 Mar 1969): 18–19.

Shaughnessy, Ed. "A Reminiscence of Buddy Rich with a Broken Arm." *PN* XXVI, 1 (Fall 1987): 11.

Siders, Harvey. "The Nouveau Rich."· *DB* XXXIV, 8 (20 Apr 1967): 19–21.

Torme, Mel. *Traps, the Drum Wonder: The Life of Buddy Rich.* New York: Oxford University Press, 1991.

"Traps, The Drum Wonder." *DB* XXVI, 21 (15 Oct 1959): 10.

Zildjian, Armand. "My Friend, Buddy Rich." *PN* XXVI, 1 (Fall 1987): 9–10.

GEN. BIB.: Hunt, *52nd St.*; Korall, *DM*; Spagnardi, *GJD*.

RICHARDS, EMIL (b. Emilio Joseph Radocchia, 2 Sep 1932, Hartford, Connecticut). Inducted into the Percussive Arts Society Hall of Fame in 1994 and dubbed "Mr. World of Percussion," Emil Richards began playing xylophone at the age of 6, and among his teachers were Lou Magnani (vibraphone) and *Alexander Lepak (timpani). He attended Hillard College and the Hartt School of Music (1949–52); performed in the Hartford (1949–52), Connecticut Pops, and New Britain Symphonies; played in the New England region with Chris Connor, Bobby Hackett, and Flip Phillips; and served as an assistant bandmaster in the First Cavalry Division Army Band in Japan (1952–53). Following his discharge, he relocated to New York in 1954, freelancing in collaboration with Charles Mingus, Ray Charles, Perry Como, among others, and toured on vibraphone with the George Shearing Quintet (1955–59). His Los Angeles move in 1959 eventually teamed him with Nelson Riddle, Sarah Vaughan, Doris Day, Judy Garland, the Paul Horn Quintet, and the Shorty Rogers Big Band, among others.

A film score recording artist since 1959, Richards is an established figure in all major Hollywood studios, averaging 20 film recordings per year (too numerous to list here!). Part of his success rests on a vast personal collection of, and performance ability on, percussion instruments from around the world. Film composers such as Michel Legrand, Jerry Goldsmith, Quincy Jones, Maurice Jarre, Lalo Schifrin, Dave Grusin, John Williams, and Henry Mancini, to name but a few, consult him first when looking for an unusual sound to aurally enhance screen imagery.

At the behest of President John F. Kennedy, Richards concertized around the world in 1962 with Frank Sinatra in an effort to bring attention to underprivileged children. During the 1960s he experimented with tonality and so-called odd meters, cofounding the Hindustani Jazz Sextet with Don Ellis and forming his own Microtonal Blues Band in 1965 with percussionist *Joe Porcaro and pianist Dave MacKay—both friends from Richards' childhood. He served as principal percussionist with Stan Kenton's Neophonic Orchestra in 1968 and performed with Roger Kellaway's Cello Quartet in 1969 (and sextet in 1993). From 1963-74, he was associated with the groundbreaking music and instruments of composer-innovator *Harry Partch. In 1974 Richards toured North America with former Beatle George Harrison and sitar artist Ravi Shankar; then he rejoined Sinatra for performances with the Count Basie Orchestra. Among the many other notables with whom he has recorded are Frank Zappa (member of Zappa's Electric Symphony, 1977), the Beach Boys, Bing Crosby, Jan & Dean, and Nat King Cole.

Richards donated his entire percussion library along with several of his instruments to the Percussive Arts Society in 1993–94. He was honored with the National Academy of Recording Arts and Sciences' Emeritus Award and, for six consecutive years, their Most Valuable Player Award.

SELECTED DISCOGRAPHY

A & M SP 3034/CD 3314: *Roger Kellaway 'Cello Quartet*, 1971/1989.
Angel CDC 7 54903 2 9: *Windows* (Roger Kellaway), 1994.
Blue Note LA462-G: *Carmen McRae—I Am Music*, 1975.
Blue Note LA584-G: *Alphonse Mouzon—The Man Incognito*, 1975.
Capitol T-1038: *Burnished Brass* (George Shearing), 1958/1962.
Impulse AS 9182: *Spirit of 1976*, 1976.
Interworld Music CD-914: *Emil Richards–The Wonderful World of Percussion*, 1994.
Interworld Music 923: *"Luntana" Afro-Cuban Jazz by Emil Richards*, 1996.
MGM SE-4825: *Sammy Davis with Count Basie and His Orchestra*, 1964.
Pablo 2310-851: *The Best of Louie Bellson*, 1980.
Signature-Mesa Bluemoon R2 79195: *Signature Series Presents...Steve Houghton*, 1994.
Uni 73008: *Stones*, 1967.
Warner Bros./Reprise FS 1008: *Sinatra and Basie*, 1962.
Zebra ZD 44005-2: *Tribute to Jeff Porcaro* (Dave Garfield), 1997.

SELECTED VIDEOGRAPHY

Interworld VH0144: *The Essence of Playing Mallets*, 1991.

SELECTED BIBLIOGRAPHY

Flans, Robyn. "Emil Richards." *MP* I, 2 (March 1985): 6.
Olmstead, Gary. "Interview with Emil Richards." *PN* XIX, 1 (Fall 1980): 46–50.
Richards, Emil. "Creating in the Studios." *MP* III, 2 (March 1987): 42.
Richards, Emil. *Emil Richard's World of Percussion*. Sherman Oaks, CA: Gwyn Pub. Co., 1972.
Tynan, John. "Emil Richards." *DB* XXVIII, 7 (30 Mar 1961): 17.
GEN. BIB.: Larrick, *BET-CP*. Information supplied by the subject, 1996.

RICHMOND, CHARLES DANIEL "DANNIE" (b. 15 Dec 1935, New York, New York; d. 16 Mar 1988). A rock-and-roll tenor saxophonist in his teens, drumset artist Dannie Richmond played with Bud Powell, Zoot Sims, and Chet

Baker, but he gained fame with Charles Mingus (1956–70/1974–79). Between Mingus collaborations, he led his own groups, toured with Elton John, and played for Joe Cocker, later working with Lew Tabackin, Don Pullen, and George Adams.

SELECTED DISCOGRAPHY

Affinity 778: *Live* (Charles Mingus), 1960.
Atlantic/Rhino: *Passions of a Man* (Charles Mingus), 1956–61.
Bethlehem BCP 6048: *The Book Cooks* (Booker Ervin), 1960.
Bluebird 4644-2-RB: *New Tijuana Moods* (Charles Mingus), 1957.
Blue Note BLJ-46907: *Song Everlasting* (Don Pullen-George Adams Quartet), 1987.
Blue Note BLP1573: *John Jenkins with Kenny Burrell*, 1957.
Blue Note CDP 7 46314-2: *Breakthrough* (Don Pullen-George Adams Quartet), 1986.
Blue Note S40034: *Charles Mingus—Town Hall Concert*, 1962.
Columbia CK-40648: *Mingus AH UM*, 1959.
Landmark LCD-1537-2: *The Last Mingus Band A.D.*, 1994.
Riverside 1120/OJC 303: *It Could Happen to You* (Chet Baker), 1958/1987.

SELECTED VIDEOGRAPHY

Music Video Distributors: *Charles Mingus—Live in Norway*, 1964.
Shanachie Entertainment: *Charles Mingus Sextet*, 1964.
GEN. BIB.: Hunt, *52nd St.*; Spagnardi, *GJD.*

RIFE, MARILYN N. (b. 12 Dec 1954, Chicago, Illinois).   Graduate of the Interlochen Arts Academy (1972), Marilyn Rife received a bachelor's degree from Oberlin College (1976) and attended Northwestern University.   She was principal timpanist and percussionist with the Chicago Civic Orchestra intermittently (1969–77); in 1977 she became assistant timpanist and percussionist with the San Antonio Symphony.   Rife has served as adjunct faculty at Trinity University (TX, 1978–   ), has coached the San Antonio Youth Orchestra since 1980, and has recorded with Alice Gomez in the duo Marimba Quest.

SELECTED DISCOGRAPHY

Talking Taco Music TT114D: *Incidents of Travel* (Marimba Quest), 1992.
Talking Taco Music TTCD115: *Christmas Carnaval* (Marimba Quest), 1992.
GEN. BIB.: Borland, *WWAMC.*

RIGOLI, CARL VINCENT (b. 29 Dec 1941, New York, New York).   A Hollywood studio percussionist, composer, and arranger who began playing drums at the age of 4, Carl Rigoli began his professional career at 14 in the Catskill

Mountains and New York City, and by 19 he was a xylophone soloist on Mackinac Island (MI). Freelancing while studying in New York in the 1960s, he received bachelor's (1964) and master's (1965) degrees from the Manhattan School before moving to the West Coast, where he attended California State University at Carson. His teachers have included *Morris Goldenberg, *Joe Porcaro, and *Earl Hatch, and he taught in the public schools. As a television recording studio artist (1970–90), he performed on the *Little Mermaid* cartoons, *Little House on the Prairie*, *Dallas*, *Bob Newhart Show*, *LaVerne & Shirley*, *Mork & Mindy*, and *Taxi*. His Hollywood film soundtrack credits include (1970–82) *Black Stallion*, *Star Trek*, *Rocky II*, *Players*, and *1941*. Between 1964 and 1990, Rigoli appeared at the New York World's Fair, the Waldrof Astoria, and the Copa Cabana; he also worked with Trini Lopez, the Los Angeles Pops Orchestra, Jim Nabors' Road Show, Civic Light Opera, Roger Wagner Chorale, and the Nelson Riddle, David Rose, and Les Brown Orchestras.

SELECTED BIBLIOGRAPHY

Rigoli, Carl. *Specialty Compositions and Arrangements for Vibraphone, Marimba, and Jazz Ensemble*. Los Angeles: Carl Rigoli Publications, 1990.
Young, Glenn. "An Interview with Carl Rigoli." *Drummers' Network* (Mission Viejo, CA) II, 3 (May/June 1986): 6–8.

RILEY, BEN (b. 17 Jul 1933, Savannah, Georgia). Drumset artist whose collaborators have included Billy Taylor, Stan Getz, Sonny Stitt, Kenny Burrell, Eddie "Lockjaw" Davis, Randy Weston, Ahmad Jamal, Andrew Hill, Sonny Stitt, Eric Dolphy, his own group, Sphere (with Kenny Barron and Charlie Rouse), among others, Ben Riley gained worldwide attention with Thelonius Monk (1964–67). He has also appeared with the New York Jazz Quartet (1971), Alice Coltrane, Ron Carter, Nina Simone, Kai Winding, Toots Thielemans, Woody Herman, Jim Hall, and Abdullah Ibrahim (1984).

SELECTED DISCOGRAPHY

Bluebird 07863-52572: *What's New?* (Sonny Rollins), 1962.
Blue Note CDP 7 92051 2: *Eternal Spirit* (Andrew Hill), 1989.
Candid 79053: *Ebony Rhapsody*, 1990.
Columbia/Sony 469183-2: *Live at the Jazz Workshop* (Thelonius Monk), 1964.
Concord 4740: *Yours and Mine* (Stan Getz), 1989.
Concord 4782-2: *Soul Eyes* (Stan Getz), 1997.
Concord CCD-42053-2: *Love Is the Answer* (Kenny Burrell), 1998.
Contemporary CCD-14044-2: *Red Hot and Blues* (Barney Kessel), 1988.
Verve 314 537 790-2: *A Little Sweeter* (Jeffrey Smith), 1998
VJ006: *Valery Ponomarev—Live at Vartan Jazz*, 1995.

SELECTED VIDEOGRAPHY

Rhapsody Films: *Monk in Oslo* (Thelonius Monk Quartet), 1966.

SELECTED BIBLIOGRAPHY

Davis, Steve. *Drummers: Masters of Time.* New Albany, IN: Aebersold Music, Inc., 1986.
Potter, Jeff. "Ben Riley: Making History." *MD* X, 9 (September 1986): 26–29.
GEN. BIB.: Hunt, *52nd St.*; Spagnardi, *GJD.*

RILEY, JOHN. A graduate of the University of North Texas (bachelor's) and the Manhattan School (master's), drumset artist John Riley has performed with the Vanguard Jazz Orchestra, Randy Brecker, John Patitucci, Woody Herman, Joe Lovano, Red Rodney, Miles Davis, John Scofield Quartet, Dizzy Gillespie, Stan Getz, *Milt Jackson, Michel LeGrand, Toots Thielemans, among others. He has penned articles for *Modern Drummer* magazine, performed at all major jazz festivals, played on over 30 recordings, and taught at the Manhattan School, the New School (Mannes College), William Patterson College, and New York University.

SELECTED DISCOGRAPHY

DMP 461: *Spectrum* (Bob Mintzer), 1988.
DMP 479: *Art of the Big Band* (Bob Mintzer), 1991.
DMP 501: *Only in New York* (Bob Mintzer), 1994.
New World 80534-2: *Lickety Split* (Vanguard Jazz Orchestra), 1997.

SELECTED VIDEOGRAPHY

Music Video Distributors: *Live Three Ways* (John Scofield), 1990.

SELECTED BIBLIOGRAPHY

Riley, John. *The Art of Bop Drumming.* Miami, FL: Manhattan Music/CPP Media, 1994 [with CD].
Riley, John. *Beyond Bop Drumming.* Miami, FL: Manhattan Music/Warner Bros., 1997 [with CD].
PASIC® program biographies, 1995.

RITTER, ALBERT (b. Germany). A prominent German timpanist who immigrated to the United States, Albert Ritter served as timpanist with the Philadelphia Orchestra (1902–03) and also with the Boston Symphony (1922–31+).

SELECTED BIBLIOGRAPHY

Howe, M. A. DeWolfe, and John N. Burk. *The Boston Symphony Orchestra, 1881–1931*. Boston: Houghton Mifflin Co., 1931.
Kupferberg, Herbert. *Those Fabulous Philadelphians*. New York: Charles Scribner's Sons, 1969.
GEN. BIB.: Cook, *LDT*, p. 16.

ROACH, MAXWELL LEMUEL "MAX" (10 Jan 1924/1925?, Elizabeth City/New Land, North Carolina). Called the "Dean of Modern Jazz Drumming," Max Roach debuted on drumset at the age of 10 in church, performed in the marching band, and was greatly influenced by listening to jazz on radio. He spent his formative years in Brooklyn and received a degree in composition from the Manhattan School. While still in his teens, Roach was one of the innovators of the "bop" drumming style at jazz fountainheads such as Minton's Playhouse and Clark Monroe's Uptown House in Harlem. Among his collaborators have been Coleman Hawkins (with whom he made his first recording in 1944), Dizzy Gillespie (his first quintet, 1944), Charlie Parker (1945–53), Miles Davis, Benny Carter (1944), Bud Powell, Clifford Brown (1954–56), J. J. Johnson, Sonny Rollins (1956–58), Howard Rumsey, Lester Young, and Thelonius Monk. Roach toured with "Jazz at the Philharmonic" during the mid-1950s and then led his own groups (1954–70s) until 1972, when he formed M'Boom RE: Percussion, an ensemble that employed African and Asian percussion instruments.

Known for his melodic, formally structured solos and compositional experimentation, he moved from bop through cool and free-jazz styles, and his creative talents have been recognized with commissions and awards from various sources, including the MacArthur Foundation and *Down Beat* magazine. His composition "Freedom Now Suite" was used in an award-winning film. Roach has taught on the faculty of the University of Massachusetts (1972–78) and the Lenox School of Jazz (summers, since 1957); he was bestowed with an honorary doctorate from the New England Conservatory in 1982, the same year that the Percussive Arts Society inducted him into their Hall of Fame. He was awarded an "American Jazz Masters" Fellowship from the National Endowment for the Arts in 1984, became of a member of the *Modern Drummer* Reader's Poll Hall of Fame in 1992, and in 1993 was voted into the International Association of Jazz Educators Hall of Fame.

SELECTED DISCOGRAPHY

Atlantic (J) CD AMCY-1043: *Drums Unlimited*, 1966.
Atlantic 1587: *Lift Every Voice and Sing*, 1971.
Bainbridge BCD1042: *Max Roach*, 1980.
Black Saint 0024: *Birth and Rebirth* (Anthony Braxton), 1978.
Blue Moon MRR 279182: *M'Boom Live at S.O.B.'s*, 1992.

Blue Note B21Y-81503: *The Amazing Bud Powell*, vol. 1, 1951.

Blue Note BLP1542: *Sonny Rollins*, 1956.

Blue Note BLP5010: *Max Roach Quintet*, 1949.

Blue Note BLP5020: *Gil Melle Sextet*, 1952.

Blue Note CDP 7-46398-2: *Money Jungle* (Duke Ellington), 1962.

Blue Note CDP 7-46536-2: *Introducing Johnny Griffin*, 1956.

Blue Note CDP 7-95636-2: *The Best of Thelonius Monk*, 1991.

Blue Note (F) BNP25107: *Milestones* (Booker Little), 1958.

Blue Note (J) K18P-9274: *Howard McGhee All-Stars*, 1950.

Blue Note 59352: *Herbie Nichols—The Complete Blue Note Recordings*, 1955–56.

Brunswick 58030: *Tenor Sax Stylings* (Coleman Hawkins), 1943.

Candid CD 9002: *Freedom Now Suite*, 1960.

Capitol 15404: *Move/Budo* (Miles Davis), 1949.

Columbia LP JLC 1030: *First Place* (J. J. Johnson), 1957.

Debut 107: *Drum Conversation*, 1953.

Debut OJC 646: *Speak, Brother, Speak!—At the Jazz Workshop*, 1962.

Debut OJC CD-044-2: *Jazz at Massey Hall* (Charlie Parker), 1953.

Decca CD MCAD 31371: *New York, New York* (George Russell), 1958.

Denon TX-7508-ND: *Tokyo Concert*, 1977.

EmArcy 838 306-2: *Brownie—The Complete Recordings of Clifford Brown*, 1954.

EmArcy 80010: *Max Roach Plus 4 at Newport*, 1958.

EmArcy CD 822673-2: *Max Roach + 4 (& More)*, 1957.

EmArcy MG-36108: *Jazz in 3/4 Time*, 1957.

EmArcy MG 36144/Mercury LP 80015: *Max Roach with the Boston Percussion Ensemble*, 1958.

EmArcy 814 646-2/EXPR-1008: *Study in Brown* (Clifford Brown), 1954.

EmArcy EXPR-1033: *Clifford Brown and Max Roach*, 1955/1981.

Hat Hut 6030: *One in Two—Two in One* (with Anthony Braxton), 1979.

Impulse (J) CDWMC5-121: *It's Time*, 1961.

Impulse CD GRP GRD122: *Percussion Bitter Sweet*, 1961.

Mercury 60133: *Roach versus Rich*, 1959.

Mercury 6877 001-6877-010: *Jazz* (Lionel Hampton), 1966.

Mercury EMS 2-403: *Clifford Brown—The Quintet*, 1954/1976.

Mercury LP MG36108: *Jazz in 3/4 Time*, 1957.

Mercury-EmArcy MG 36071: *Giants of Jazz*, vol. 8—The Jazz Greats, Drum Role, 1959.

Mosaic MR4-101: *Thelonious Monk Sextet*, 1952.

Mosaic MR5-116: *Bud Powell Trio*, 1951.

OJC 115/Debut DEB-198: *Autobiography in Jazz*, 1954/1984.

OJC CD 291-2: *Saxophone Colossus* (Sonny Rollins), 1956.

P-24024/OJC CD-044-2: *The Greatest Jazz Concert Ever* (Charlie Parker, Dizzy Gillespie et al.), 1953.

Pablo 5305/PACD 5305-2: *Jazz at the Philharmonic—Frankfurt*, 1952.

Prestige 702: *Maxology*, 1949.

Prestige OJC CD-009-2: *Sonny Stitt–Bud Powell–J. J. Johnson*, 1950.

Riverside OJC CD-026-2: *Brilliant Corners* (Thelonius Monk), 1956

Roulette B21Y 93902: *Roost Sessions* (Bud Powell), 1947.

Savoy 597: *Ko-Ko* (Charlie Parker), 1945.

Signature AK-40950: *The Big Three: Coleman Hawkins, Ben Webster, Lester Young,* 1943.
Sony/Columbia CL1303: *Blue Trombone* (J. J. Johnson), 1957/1958.
Soul Note (Italy) 121159-2: *Bright Moments,* 1987.
Soul Note CD 121093-2: *Survivors,* 1984.
Soul Note SN-1059CD: *M'Boom—Collage,* 1984.
Soul Note SN-1109: *Easy Winners,* 1985.
Soul Note 121053-2: *In the Light,* 1982.
Stash STCD 567/8/9/10: *Complete Bird on Dial* (Charlie Parker), 1947.
Time 2140: *Taste of Drums,* 1969.
Trip TLP-5574: *The Max Roach 4 Plays Charlie Parker,* 1957–58.
Verve 314 526 373-2: *Alone Together—The Best of the Mercury Years* (Clifford Brown), 1995.
Verve 833 288-2: *Charlie Parker,* 1948–53/1987.
Verve 845 148-2: *Jazz Club Mainstream: Drums,* 1951/1991.
Verve CD 825671-2: *Now's the Time—The Genius of Charlie Parker,* 1953.
Verve MGV8010: *Swedish Schnapps* (Charlie Parker), 1951.
Verve MGV8076: *Flip Phillips and His Orchestra,* 1952.
Verve MGV8141: *Dizzy Gillespie–Stan Getz Sextet,* 1953.
Verve MGV8153: *Bud Powell Trio,* 1949–50.

SELECTED VIDEOGRAPHY

Axis Video: *Max Roach—In Concert and in Session,* 1982.
DCI VH0248: *Legends of Jazz Drumming,* pt. 1 (1920–50), 1996.
Embassy Home Entertainment: *Jazz in America—Dizzy Gillespie,* 1981/1983.
Embassy Home Entertainment: *Jazz in America—Max Roach in Washington, D.C.,* 1981/1986.
Home Vision: *Sit Down and Listen—the Max Roach Story,* 1984.
Home Vision Cinema: *Repercussions: A Celebration of African-American Music,* vol. 2—*The Story of Max Roach,* 1984.
Music Video Distributors 45: *Max Roach—Jazz in America,* 1981.

SELECTED BIBLIOGRAPHY

"An Interview with Max Roach." *Black World* (November 1973): 62–71.
Bravos, Tony. "An Interview with Max Roach." *PN* XX, 3 (June 1982): 39–41.
Fish, Scott. "Max Roach." *MD* VI, 4 (1982): 8.
Gold, Don. "Max Roach." *DB* XXV, 6 (20 Mar 1958): 15.
Hentoff, Nat. "Roach and Brown, Inc., Dealers in Jazz." *DB* XXII, 9 (4 May 1955): 7.
Hoeffer, George. "Max Roach." *DB* XXXII, 7 (25 Mar 1965): 18.
Howland, Hal. "Max Roach: Back on the Bandstand." *MD* III, 1 (1979): 12.
Jones, James T. IV. "Max Roach: Avoiding the Musical Rerun." *JazzTimes* XXI, 8 (November 1991): 15–17.
Kettle, Rupert. "Roach vs. Rich." *DB* XXXIII, 6 (March 1966): 19–22.
"Max Roach." *Swing Journal* XXXI, 11 (1977): 288.
McElfresh, Suzanne. "Max Attack." *DB* LX, 11 (November 1993): 16–20.
Primack, Bret. "Max Roach: There's No Stoppin' the Professor from Boppin'." *DB* XLV, 18 (1978): 20.

Quinn, Bill. "Max Roach: Highlights." *DB* XXXV, 6 (21 Mar 1968): 19–21.
Richmond, N. "Max Roach: An Interview." *Coda* 172 (1980): 4.
Rusch, Bob. "Max Roach: Interview." *Cadence* V, 6 (June 1979): 3–8/24.
Shultz, Thomas. "A History of Jazz Drumming." *Percussionist* XVI, 3 (Spring/Summer 1979): 124.
Whitehead, Kevin. "Max Roach: Drum Architect." *DB* LII, 10 (1985): 16–18.
GEN. BIB.: Hunt, *52nd St.*; Kernfeld, *NGJ*, by Olly Wilson; Larrick, *BET-CP*; Southern, *BDA-AAM*; Spagnardi, *GJD*.

ROBERTS, WILLIAM L. (b. 31 Jan 1931, Denver, Colorado). William Roberts earned a bachelor's degree from the University of Denver (1959) and played with the U.S. Naval Academy Band (xylophone soloist), Denver Symphony (1958–), Central City Opera (CO), Ballet West, and San Francisco Ballet. Founder of the Denver Symphony Rock Ensemble and Denver Percussion Ensemble, he appeared with Harry Belafonte, Mel Torme, Tony Bennett, Della Reese, Burt Bacharch, and Bob Hope, among others. Roberts has served on the faculties of Metropolitan State College (CO, 1968–) and Indiana University (1985–).

SELECTED BIBLIOGRAPHY

Baldwin, Dr. John, ed. "On the Move." *PN* XXIII, 5 (July 1985): 14.
GEN. BIB.: Borland, *WWAMC*.

ROBINSON, GLENN (b. 1930, Ft. Thomas, Kentucky). Glenn Robinson began snare studies at 12 with J. B. McKenna, added keyboard instruments at 15, and by 16 was taking lessons from *George Carey, principal percussionist of the Cincinnati Symphony. He earned a bachelor's degree from the Cincinnati Conservatory (1952), where he studied with Carey and *Fred Noak, timpanist with the Cincinnati Symphony. While still a student, Robinson performed on radio with Frank Simon's ARMCO Band (1950) and as an "extra" with Cincinnati. He secured a full-time position in that orchestra (1952–72) and the Cincinnati Summer Opera, becoming principal percussionist in 1957. In 1972 Robinson relocated to Kansas City, where he subbed in the Kansas City Philharmonic until retiring from professional performing in 1980. In 1965 he began developing the "Septimbre Drum," which features three independent types of snares, and since 1990 he has marketed it through his company, Robinson Percussion. His many recordings with Cincinnati on the Remington and Decca labels reflect collaborations with Gerry Mulligan and Dave Brubeck, the music of Duke Ellington, and numerous works from the classical repertoire.

Information supplied by the subject, 1997.

ROBINSON, JOHN "J. R." (b. ca. 1955, Creston, Iowa). J. R. Robinson attended Berklee College (started 1973), studied with *Ed Soph, Gary Chaffee, and *Alan Dawson, and then joined the band Rufus/Chaka Khan in 1978, relocating with them to Los Angeles—a move that launched his studio recording career. He has recorded hundreds of albums and television and film soundtracks. He has also toured the world with Barbra Streisand, appearing and/or recording with Diana Ross, Crystal Gayle, Paul Anka, Peter Frampton, Madonna, Kenny Rogers, Larry Carlton, Quincy Jones, the Pointer Sisters, Placido Domingo, Whitney Houston, Lionel Richie, Wayne Newton, among others. Drummer on the cooperative smash single "We Are the World," Robinson serves on the faculty of the Los Angeles Music Academy.

SELECTED VIDEOGRAPHY

Star Licks Master Sessions: *John Robinson*, 1995.

SELECTED BIBLIOGRAPHY

Peterman, Tim. "John Robinson." *PN* XXIV, 1 (October 1985): 61–66.
PASIC® program biographies, 1995.

ROGERS, JOSEPH P., SR. (b. Dublin, Ireland). Settling in Farmingdale, New Jersey, Joseph Rogers founded a tannery in 1849 to make drum and banjo heads, and during the Civil War he was contracted by the government to make rope drums for the Union forces. In 1900 the family-owned company featured drum heads, and by the 1930s it produced poor-quality drums until Rogers' great-grandson, Cleveland Rogers, died without heirs in 1953 and the company was purchased by Henry Grossman (1960). Operations were moved to a new factory in Covington, Ohio, where calfskin heads gave way to plastic. With guidance from engineer George Thompson, innovations included the "Dyna-Sonic" snare drum, "Memriloc" hardware, and the "Accu-Sonic" pedal timpani; the timpani, patented in 1971 and made until 1983, featured acrylic hemispheric-shaped shallow bowls that emphasized fundamental rather than overtones. In 1966 Rogers was purchased by CBS Musical Instruments and moved to Fullerton, California, in 1969 as part of the conglomerate Fender, Rogers, Rhodes, and Squier.

SELECTED BIBLIOGRAPHY

Cangany, Harry. *The Great American Drums and the Companies That Made Them, 1920–1969*. Cedar Grove, NJ: Modern Drummer Publications, Inc., 1996.
Mulholland, Liam. "Death by Aluminum and Brass." *DRUM!* V, 7 (November-December 1996): 104–105.
Schmidt, Paul William. *History of the Ludwig Drum Company*. Fullerton, CA: Centerstream Publishing, 1991 (p. 59).
GEN. BIB.: Hitchcock and Sadie, *NGA*, by Edmund A. Bowles.

ROKER, MICKEY (b. 3 Sep 1932, Miami, Florida). Drumset artist Mickey Roker, initially a rhythm and blues drummer who moved to New York in the 1950s, performed and/or recorded with Gigi Gryce, Nancy Wilson (two years), Duke Pearson (two years), Lee Morgan (1969–71), *Milt Jackson, Dizzy Gillespie (nine years), Joe Williams, Nat Adderley, Ray Bryant, Jim Hall, Zoot Sims, Sonny Rollins, Ella Fitzgerald, Art Farmer, Herbie Hancock, Wes Montgomery, McCoy Tyner, Oscar Peterson, Horace Silver, among others. He was one of the favored drummers for Rudy Van Gelder's many Blue Note label jazz recordings and can be seen on the VIEW video production *40 Years of MJQ* (Modern Jazz Quartet).

SELECTED DISCOGRAPHY

Blue Note 7243 8 35228 2 8: *Live at the Lighthouse* (Lee Morgan), 1970.
Blue Note 84257: *Blue Mitchell—Boss Horn*, 1966.
Blue Note 84191: *Wahoo!* (Duke Pearson), 1964.
Blue Note 84240: *Rough 'n Tumble* (Stanley Turrentine), 1966.
Blue Note 84252: *Sweet Honey Bee* (Duke Pearson). 1966.
Blue Note 84256: *The Spoiler* (Stanley Turrentine), 1966.
Blue Note 84257: *Boss Horn* (Blue Mitchell), 1966.
Blue Note 84268: *Easy Walker* (Stanley Turrentine), 1966.
Blue Note 84276: *Introducing Duke Pearson's Big Band*, 1967.
Blue Note 84277: *Serenade to a Soul Sister* (Horace Silver), 1968.
Blue Note 84278: *Manhattan Fever* (Frank Foster), 1968.
Blue Note 84286: *The Look of Love* (Stanley Turrentine), 1968.
Blue Note 84293: *The Phantom* (Duke Pearson), 1967.
Blue Note 84298: *Always Something There* (Stanley Turrentine), 1968.
Blue Note 84308: *Now Hear This* (Duke Pearson), 1968.
Blue Note 84336: *Stanley Turrentine—Another Story*, 1969.
Blue Note 84344: *How Insensitive* (Duke Pearson), 1969.
Blue Note 84349: *Electric Byrd* (Donald Byrd), 1970.
Blue Note 84352: *That Healin' Feelin'* (Horace Silver Quintet), 1970.
Blue Note 84362: *San Francisco* (Bobby Hutcherson), 1970.
Blue Note 84368: *The United States of Mind Phase 2—Total Response* (Horace Silver), 1970.
Blue Note 84420: *The United States of Mind Phase 3—All* (Horace Silver), 1972
Blue Note B21Y 46136: *Speak like a Child* (Herbie Hancock), 1968.
Blue Note BLP 4303: *Now Hear This* (Duke Pearson), 1968.
Blue Note LA054-F: *Horace Silver—In Pursuit of the 27th Man*, 1972.
Blue Note LA317-G: *It Could Only Happen with You* (Duke Pearson), 1970.
Blue Note LA582-J2: *Lee Morgan*, 1969.
Blue Note LT-1096: *The Creeper* (Donald Byrd), 1967.
CBS ZK 44174: *Olinga* (Milt Jackson), 1988.
Double Time DTRCD-135: *To Each His Own* (Mike LeDonne), 1998.
Impluse MCAD 5655: *Sonny Rollins on Impulse*, 1965.
Pablo 2308-235: *Memories of Thelonius Sphere Monk* (Milt Jackson), 1982.
Pablo 2310-909/OJC 601: *It Don't Mean a Thing If You Can't Tap Your Foot to It* (Milt Jackson), 1976/1984.

Pablo OJC 498: *Quadrant* (Joe Pass), 1977.
Qwest 46607: *Milt Jackson—Sa Va Bella (For Lady Legends)*, 1997.
RCA R25J-1012: *The Standard Sonny Rollins*, 1962.
Verve V6-8761: *Milt Jackson and the Hip String Quartet*, 1968.
GEN. BIB.: Hunt, *52nd St.*; Spagnardi, *GJD.*

ROLLINI, ADRIAN (b. 28 Jun 1903, New York, New York; d. 15 May 1956, Homestead, Florida). Originally a pianist and xylophonist who recorded extensively with the California Ramblers and the Goofus Five in the early 1920s, Adrian Rollini played the unwieldy bass saxophone during the late 1920s and early 1930s to rave reviews. [The "Goofus" (couesnophone) was a mouthblown keyboard harmonica developed in France.] He took up vibraphone in the 1930s and rarely performed on sax again. His wife, Dixie, made mallets.

SELECTED DISCOGRAPHY

Columbia 2782D: "Jig Saw Puzzle Blues" (Joe Venuti), 1933.
Decca 787: "Tap Room Swing," 1936.
RCA Victor (Jp) RA-5325/LPM 10125: *Swing Sessions in the '30s/Adrian Rollini and His Orchestra* (1935–36), 1969.
Victor 25208: "Bouncin' in Rhythm," 1935.
World Records SH 391: *Jazz of the '30s*, 1976.

SELECTED BIBLIOGRAPHY

IM XL, 8 (February 1942): 18 (photo of Adrian Rollini Trio).
"Obituary." *DB* XXIII, 13 (1956): 9.
Rollini, Arthur. *Thirty Years with the Big Bands*. Chicago: University of Illinois Press, 1987.
Shoppee, T. "Adrian Rollini." *Jazz Journal* XXIII, 8 (1970): 20 [also XXIII, 10 (1970): 7].
Taylor, H. "Adrian Rollini." *Melody Maker* (6 Nov 1937): 10.
GEN. BIB.: Hitchcock and Sadie, *NGA*, by John Chilton.

ROPER, DALETH FERLE "DEL" (b. 10 Nov 1905, Lufkin, Texas). Mallet keyboard and carillon designer, tuner, and performer since 1930, Del Roper first played "pump" organ for church when only 7 years old and studied marimba with Walter E. Light of the Denver Symphony. A member of the AFM Local in 1932, he attended Pasadena City College three times between 1935 and 1974, and he played marimba with the Xavier Cougat, Don Ricardo [aka *Howard Peterson] (1932–35), Eddie LeBaron (1938–40, including New York's Rainbow Room), Ray Martinez, and Chuey Reyas Orchestras. A member of the Pasadena Symphony in 1932, Roper was a soloist with the NBC staff radio orchestra (KFI-Los Angeles, 1936), played in several motion pictures, and appeared at major venues, including New York's Rainbow Room and Waldorf-

Astoria Hotel (1937–40). As carillonneur, tuning consultant, and player of automatic rolls for Maas-Rowe Carillons of Los Angeles from 1950 to 1970, he created, and occasionally concertized on, carillons for the U.S. Coast Guard Academy, New York World's Fair (1964), New York Metropolitan Opera House, University of California at Los Angeles, University of Southern California, University of California at Santa Barbara, Disneyland (CA), University of Alaska, Honolulu and Hong Kong Methodist Churches, U.S. Air Force Base (Wiesbaden, Germany), Polytechnic Methodist Church (Ft. Worth, TX), and the world's largest and most complex carillon (in 1963) at the Los Angeles Music Center.

In 1946 Roper invented "The Monster" that was a combination three-octave chordal electric marimba (bars fitted with electric solenoids, struck from underneath and played by the right foot on the organ pedals), electric bass marimba (played by the left foot on the organ pedals), and vibraphone and marimba (played manually with mallets—the vibe dampener was operated by tilting the seat back and forth!). Controlling all this while seated at the instrument in the manner of an organist, Roper performed on the instrument in restaurants for four years; he then dismantled it when he discovered it was mechanically too noisy for recording. (He had used a pedalless version in 1945 with the Jimmie McKinzey Orchestra.) Roper followed this achievement by building the world's largest bass marimba (three octaves, nine feet long, 500 pounds!) in 1969. His long-time partner in instrument construction was Lowell Montz, who was coinventor of the "Equasonic" bars. He retired in 1970 to continue building custom mallet instruments, and in summer 1978 he supervised the construction of the first marimba (five octaves) for the Waunana Indian tribe of Panama.

SELECTED DISCOGRAPHY

Word W-3067-LP: *I Heard the Bells*, 1985.
Word W-3129-LP: *Del Roper's Swinging Percussions—Interpreting the Old Hymns*, 1958.

SELECTED BIBLIOGRAPHY

"Meet Del Roper, Innovator." *PN* XVII, 2 (Winter 1979): 39.
"People in Percussion." *PN* XVII, 1 (Fall 1978): 29.
Roper, Del. *How to Play the Symphonic Carillon*. Los Angeles: Maas-Rowe Carillons, 1950.
Information supplied by the subject, 1996.

ROSAURO, NEY GABRIEL (b. 24 Oct 1952, Rio de Janeiro, Brazil). Initially a guitarist and later a double bassist, Ney Rosauro studied composition and conducting at Universidade de Brasilia and then took percussion lessons privately with Luiz D'Anunciação, principal percussionist with the Orquestra Sinfonica Brasileira. He earned a master's degree from the Hochschule für Musik in Würzburg, Germany (1980–82/1985–87), where he studied with *Siegfried Fink, and a doctor of musical arts degree from the University of Miami (1992), where his major professor was *Fred Wickstrom. From 1975 to 1987, Rosauro taught percussion at the Escola de Musica de Brasilia and was principal timpanist and percussionist with the Orquestra do Teatro Nacional de Brasilia. Since 1987 he has served on the percussion faculty of the Universidade Federal de Santa Maria. Composer of numerous solo and chamber works and concerti for various percussion instruments, which have been recorded by artists around the world, he is an active performer who has concertized and given workshops and masterclasses throughout Europe, Brazil, Argentina, Cuba, England, the United States, and Japan.

SELECTED DISCOGRAPHY

Pró Percussão CD 11S-001: *Rapsódia*, 1993.
Pró Percussão 548.111: *Marimba Brasileira*, 1989.

SELECTED BIBLIOGRAPHY

Lambert, James. "An Interview with Brazilian Percussionist and Composer, Ney Rosauro." *PN* XXXV, 1 (February 1997): 41–43.
Rosauro, Ney. *Estudos para Percussão Múltipla* (Ten Easy Multi-percussion Studies). Santa Maria, RS, Brazil: Pró Percussão.
Rosauro, Ney. *Método Completo para Caixa Clara* (Complete Method for Snare Drum). Santa Maria, RS, Brazil: Pró Percussão.
Information supplied by the subject, 1996.

ROSEN, MICHAEL (b. 16 Jul 1942, Philadelphia, Pennsylvania). Having studied with *Charles Owen, *Fred Hinger, Jack McKenzie, and *Cloyd Duff, Michael Rosen earned a bachelor's degree (Temple University, 1964) and a master's degree (University of Illinois, 1966); he then served as principal percussionist with the Milwaukee Symphony (1966–72). He has performed with the Metropolitan Opera Orchestra (1974), as extra with the Cleveland Orchestra (since 1972), and with the Cleveland Contemporary Chamber Players (1985–87) and has also appeared throughout Europe, Asia, and the United States as a clinician and recitalist. Rosen's teaching positions have included the Wisconsin Conservatory (1967–71), Oberlin College Conservatory (since 1972), Kent State University (1975), and a "visiting professorship" at Beijing, China's Central Conservatory (1988). He has served on the board of directors for the Percussive Arts Society, been a panelist for the National Endowment for the Arts (1988), written the "Terms in Percussion" column for *Percussive Notes*, and recorded on Bayerische Rundfunk, CRI, and Lumina labels, among others.

SELECTED DISCOGRAPHY

Lumina L-002: *Soundscape for Percussion Ensemble* (conductor, Oberlin Percussion Group), 1981.
Opus One 80373: *Duo Exchanges*, 1979.
GEN. BIB.: Larrick, *BET-CP*.

ROSENBERGER, WALTER EMERSON, JR. (b. 2 Nov 1918, Rochester, Pennsylvania). Beginning drums and xylophone at the age of 8, Walter Rosenberger took private lessons with *George Hamilton Green (1937–40) and earned a bachelor's degree (1941) from the Juilliard School (Institute of Musical Art), where he studied with Edward H. Montray [d. ca. June 1941] and *Saul Goodman. He performed with the Pittsburgh Symphony (1941–43), freelanced in recording studios and radio (1943–44, e.g., NBC's *Firestone Radio Show* and *Salute to Youth*), and then served in the Special Services Division of the U.S. Army (1944–46). Joining the New York Philharmonic (1946–85), he became principal percussionist in 1972 and during the Philharmonic's off-season was an original member of the Sauter-Finnegan Orchestra (1952–53). Rosenberger premiered Michael Colgrass' "Déjà Vu" with the percussion section of the Philharmonic in 1977 and taught at the Mannes College of Music (1948–49), Manhattan School (1974–89), and Juilliard School (1981–87).

SELECTED DISCOGRAPHY

Columbia MS M34514/QLB 34511: *Bartók—The Wooden Prince* (New York Philharmonic, xylophone soloist), 1977.
Columbia MS-6956: *Bartók—Concerto for Two Pianos, Percussion, and Orchestra* (New York Philharmonic), 1966.
CRI S-186: *Hovhaness—Koke No Niwa*, 1964.
CRI S-263: *Lewis—Toccata for Solo Violin and Percussion*, 1970.
CRI SD-327: *Bazelon—Propulsions*, 1974.
Moss Music Group D-MMG 115: *The All-Star Percussion Ensemble*, 1983.
Opus One 9: *Thorne—Songs and Dances*, 1978.
RCA E2VB-6344(20-4866-A): *"Doodletown Fifers"* (Sauter-Finegan Orchestra, drum soloist), 1952.
Urania URLP 7144: *Chavez—Toccata*, 1954.

SELECTED BIBLIOGRAPHY

"Sauter-Finegan: Hit the Road." *Metronome* (July 1953).
"Sauter-Finegan at Meadowbrook." *Metronome* (August 1953).
Information supplied by the subject, 1996.

ROSENGARDEN, ROBERT MARSHALL "BOBBY" (b. 23 Apr 1924, Elgin, Illinois). Staff drummer for NBC television shows (1949–68), Bobby

Rosengarden practiced diligently from the age of 12, attended the University of Michigan, played in the U.S. Army Air Corps Band during WWII (1944–45), and then began a studio recording career in New York. He collaborated with Duke Ellington (1959), Miles Davis and Gil Evans (1961), Benny Goodman (1965, sporadically until the 1980s), the World's Greatest Jazz Band (1974–78), the New York Jazz Repertory Company (1974–   ), Gerry Mulligan (1976–   ), Soprano Summit (1975–78), and Blue Three (1981–83); he also fronted his own band on ABC-TV (*Dick Cavett Show*, 1969–74).

SELECTED DISCOGRAPHY

Atlantic 1671: *Satchmo Remembered* (Dick Hyman), 1974.
Chiaroscuro 188: *The Trio* (with Hank Jones/Milt Hinton), 1977.
Chiaroscuro 311: *Summit Reunion* (Bob Wilber), 1990.
Progressive PCD-7002: *Love for Sale* (Derek Smith Trio), 1976.
Progressive PRO-7007: *The Ray Turner Quartet-Star Dust*, 1988.
Solo Art SACD-104: *Eddie Higgins—By Request*, 1986.
Verve V6-8652: *Jimmy Smith*, 1966.
Verve V6-8657: *Kai Winding*, 1966.
Verve V6-8673: *Astrud Gilberto and Walter Wanderley*, 1966.
Verve V6-8707: *Stan Getz*, 1966.
Verve V/V6-8730: *Cal Tjader*, 1967.
World Jazz 5: *Soprano Summit* (Bob Wilber/Kenny Davern), 1973.
World Jazz 8: *The World's Greatest Jazz Band on Tour* (Yank Lawson/Bob Haggart), 1975.
GEN. BIB.: Kernfeld, *NGJ*, by Brian Peerless.

ROSS, JAMES JEROME "JIM" (b. James Jerome Rosenberg, 28 Feb 1901, Boston, Massachusetts; d. March 1981, Birmingham, Alabama). A graduate of the Faelton School of Music in Boston, Jim Ross began playing at the age of 18, studied at the New England Conservatory, and was taught by *George L. Stone (Boston) and *Karl Glassman (New York), among others. He appeared as xylophone soloist for one year at New York's Roxy Theater with a 110-piece orchestra (before the advent of "talkies") and with the original "Yerkes Flotilla Band." His first symphony position was with Cincinnati (1927–45) under Fritz Reiner; there he taught a children's xylophone band ("Woodpeckers"), performed with Frank Simon's ARMCO Band, and could be heard as solo xylophonist on WLW radio. Ross left the symphony and (with his future wife) created a double xylophone and marimba novelty act, which he continued for 25 years under the stage name "Jerry Jerome." He maintained this show full time for two years during WWII and later performed on the side to supplement his income. Their clever act included burning mallets, bubbles, spinning plates, and puppets. Joining Reiner and the Pittsburgh Symphony for 10 years after WWII, Ross moved again with Reiner to the Chicago Symphony (1953–67), where he served as principal percussionist until he "semiretired" to the Birmingham (Alabama) Symphony in 1967. During his career he played under Toscanini, Monteux,

Steinberg, Ozawa, and others, appeared with the San Francisco Symphony and on Chicago television, and taught at the Sherwood School of Music in Chicago.

SELECTED BIBLIOGRAPHY

Free, Van Tony. "An Interview with Jim Ross 'Jerry Jerome': Master Percussionist and Entertainer." *PN* XVII, 3 (Spring/Summer 1979): 38–39.
Ross, James. "The Marimba Act." *Percussionist* I, 4 (April 1964): 4–6.
GEN. BIB.: Cook, *LDT*, p. 191, 283, 438 (photos). Information supplied by James Ramsey Ross, 1996.

ROSS, JAMES RAMSEY (b. 8 Sep 1948, Cincinnati, Ohio). James Ross, son of the percussionist-entertainer, *James Jerome Ross, earned a bachelor's degree from the University of Northern Illinois (1971), where he studied with G. Allan O'Connor. A show and dance band drummer as well, he played with the Grant Park Symphony (1973–78/soloist, 1993) before joining the Chicago Symphony (1979–   ). With the latter, he toured Europe, Australia, the Soviet Union, and the Far East and was featured as soloist on Milhaud's *Concerto for Percussion* in 1986. He has traveled and recorded with Chicago Pro Musica, Chamber Music Chicago, and Summit Brass and is a founding member of the percussion quartet, Pulse Chicago. His composition *Piece for Commuting Trap Drummer, Jazz Timpanist, and Existential Tuba* (1971) has received several performances worldwide, and he has served as clinician for the Bands of America World Symposium, as percussion coach for the Chicago Civic Orchestra, and as faculty member of DePaul (1991–   ) and Northwestern Universities.

SELECTED DISCOGRAPHY

CRI-SD 355: *Praise* (Chicago Contemporary Chamber Players), 1976.
Newport Classic NPD 85537: *The Clarinet in My Mind* (Chicago Pro Musica), 1992.
Reference Recordings RR-29CD: *Three Penny Opera Suite* (Chicago Pro Musica), 1989.

SELECTED BIBLIOGRAPHY

Collier, David L. "Interview with Jim Ross, Percussionist with the Chicago Symphony." *PN* XXXVI, 3 (June 1998): 51–54.
O'Fallon, Dave. "Orchestral Cymbal Playing: An Interview with James Ross of the Chicago Symphony." *PN* XXVIII, 2 (Winter 1990): 10–17.
Information supplied by the subject, 1996.

ROTH, GEORG (fl. ca. 1798, Vienna, Austria). Georg Roth was a virtuoso timpanist who is immortalized in an illustration (28 Apr 1798) that depicts him performing upon 16 timpani using six mallets before the emperor and empress in Vienna.

SELECTED BIBLIOGRAPHY

CRD 3449: *Jonathan Haas—Virtuoso Timpanist*, 1988 (cover illustration from Dr. Edmund Bowles; liner notes by Dr. Harrison Powley].

ROY, "BADAL" [b. Amar Roy Chowdhury, ca. 1945, Comilla, India (later aka Bangladesh)]. Innovative Pakistani tabla artist Badal Roy was introduced to the instrument by his uncle at the age of 10, but he did not study in the traditional manner, although he did study briefly with Alla Rakha Khan. After completing a master's degree in statistics, he relocated to New York (1968), where he worked in restaurants until establishing his music career with Pharoah Sanders (1972), John McLaughlin, David Liebman (1973–76), *Airto Moreira, and others. He toured three years with Miles Davis (1972–75), performed with Pat Metheny in Canada, Herbie Hancock in Japan, and since 1987 with Ornette Coleman's group, Prime Time.

SELECTED DISCOGRAPHY

A&M Horizon 702: *Sweet Hands*, 1975.
Antilles 314 514 186-2: *Sanctified Shells* (Steve Turre), 1993.
Atlantic CS 19204: *Sun Belt* (Herbie Mann), 1978.
Columbia/Rykodisc RCD 10051: *My Goal's Beyond* (John McLaughlin), 1970/1987.
Columbia PGT 32866: *Big Fun* (Miles Davis), 1974.
Columbia CT 45154: *Dancing with the Lion* (Andreas Vollenweider), 1988.
Columbia 485256-2: *Get Up with It* (Miles Davis), 1974/1996.
Columbia KG 32092: *Miles Davis in Concert*, 1973.
Columbia CT53579: *On the Corner* (Miles Davis), 1993.
ECM 1046: *Drum Ode* (Dave Liebman), 1975.
ECM 1039: *Lookout Farm* (Dave Liebman), 1974.
Flying Dutchman FD 10163: *Astral Traveling* (Lonnie Liston Smith), 1973.
Impulse/ABC AS 9233: *Wisdom through Music* (Pharaoh Sanders), 1973.
Music of the World LAT 50610: *Yantra* (Steve Gorn), 1997.
Music of the World/Nomad: *Asian Journal* (Nana Vasconcelos), 1981/1996.
Nomad 50315: *One in the Pocket*, 1997.
Polydor CT-1-6364: *It's All Right* (Yoko Ono), 1982.
Verve 314 527 483-2: *Tone Dialing* (Ornette Coleman), 1995.

SELECTED BIBLIOGRAPHY

Brooks, Iris. "Badal Roy: Heart and Soul. Tale of a Tabla Nonconformist." *Drum!* VI, 7 (November/December 1997): 60–63.
Henschen, B. "Tabla Talk: Badal Roy." *MD* I, 4 (1977): 8.
GEN. BIB.: Kernfeld, *NGJ*.

RUBSAM, EDWARD F., SR., "EDDIE" (b. ca. 1875; d. 26 Apr 1946, Newark, New Jersey). A xylophonist who recorded for Columbia and National Phonograph Companies (1903–05), Eddie Rubsam performed with *Harry Breuer on NBC radio (1927), with the Raymond Paige Orchestra on CBS radio (1939), and in the Proctor, Paramount, and Blaney Theaters and the Waldman Opera House. He was *Billy Dorn's cousin and also played with the Yerkes Jazzarimba Orchestra, which included Breuer, Dorn, and *Joe Green. Rubsam held the rank of sargeant in the New Jersey National Guard and was a member of the Old Voss First Regiment Band. Active in the American Federation of Musicians, he served as director, vice-president, and president of Local 16 (Newark, New Jersey).

SELECTED DISCOGRAPHY

Columbia A139: "St. Louis Tickle," 1905.
Columbia A854: "Temptation Rag" (Henry Lodge), 1909.
Columbia A1038: "High Society March" (Porter Steele), 1911.
Columbia A2327: "Beale Street" (W. C. Handy), 1917.
Columbia A2524: "Going Up" (Louis Hirsch), 1918.
Turnabout TV 4159/Vox PLP 6010: *Bartók—Sonata for Two Pianos and Percussion*, 1969.

SELECTED BIBLIOGRAPHY

Eyler, David P. "Development of the Marimba Ensemble in North America during the 1930s." *PN* XXXIV, 1 (February 1996): 66–71.
"Obituary." *IM* XLI, 12 (June 1943): 6.
GEN. BIB.: Cahn, *XAR*; Cook, *LDT*, p. 438 (photo).

S

SALMON, JAMES DANIEL (b. 6 Nov 1914, Waukegan, Illinois; d. 26 Mar 1989). Inducted into the Percussive Arts Society Hall of Fame in 1974, James Salmon studied with *Roy Knapp, toured Europe with *Clair Omar Musser's Marimba Orchestra (1936), served as Musician First Class with the U.S. Navy for four and one-half years, and played with the Panama Symphony while in the Canal Zone. He earned bachelor's and master's degrees from the University of Michigan (1952) and enjoyed a long tenure as the first full-time percussion instructor there (1954–72). Also a veteran faculty member of *Roy Knapp's school, Salmon was one of the first contributing editors to the *Percussionist* journal and performed with the Chicago Businessmen's Symphony Orchestra.

SELECTED BIBLIOGRAPHY

Kastner, Kathleen. "In Memoriam: James D. Salmon." *PN* XXVII, 4 (Summer 1989): 54–55.
"Percussive Arts Society Hall of Fame, 1974." *PN* XII, 3 (Spring 1974): 23–24.
GEN. BIB.: Cook, *LDT*, p. 359 (photo).

SAMUELS, DAVID (b. 9 Oct 1948, Waukegan, Illinois). Vibraphone and marimba artist Dave Samuels studied percussion as a teen, received a bachelor's degree in psychology from Boston University, was a student of Gary Burton, and has managed to balance simultaneous musical bonds with several prominent groups of musicians. He freelanced in New York (1974–77), during which time his work with fellow keyboard percussionist *David Friedman led to the formation of Double Image in 1977. His involvement with the jazz-fusion group Spyro Gyra and with the Latin-jazz–based Caribbean Jazz Project has spawned several successful performance tours and recordings (late 1970s–90s). Among the many artists with whom Samuels has collaborated are Gerry Mulligan, Carla Bley, *Andy Narell, Frank Zappa, Chet Baker, Paul McCandless, Michael Pasqua, Art Lande, Gerry Niewood, Hubert Laws, Paquito d'Rivera, Harvie Swartz, Jackie and Roy Kral, and Bobby McFerrin. He has been active as a clinician and performer throughout Europe and the United States and has taught at the Manhattan School and the Berklee College of Music.

SELECTED DISCOGRAPHY

DMP CD-503: *Double Image—Open Hand*, 1994.
Enja 2096: *Double Image*, 1977.
FMCA-7010: *Keiko Abe and Dave Samuels—Live in Concert* , 1993.
Heads Up HUCD 3033: *The Caribbean Jazz Project*, 1995.
Infinity 9004: *Morning Dance* (Spyro Gyra), 1979.
Marimba Productions MP-002: *Dialogues* (Double Image), 1985.
MCA 2-6893: *Access All Areas* (Spyro Gyra), 1983.
MCA 37149: *Spyro Gyra*, 1977.
MCA D-42046: *Stories without Words* (Spyro Gyra), 1987.
Telarc 83377: *Gerry Mulligan—Dragonfly*, 1996.
Verve 314 557 086-2: *Tjaderized*, 1998.
Warner Bros./CPP Media EL96163CD: *Remembrances*, 1996.
Warner Bros. 9 46791: *Imaginary Day* (Pat Metheny), 1997.

SELECTED VIDEOGRAPHY

Video Artists International: *Time Groove* (Louis Bellson, Steve Gadd et al.), 1990.
Yamaha Video Series EV 28/CPP Media VH056/057: *Mallet Keyboard Musician-ship—Steps to Excellence,* vols. 1–2, 1993.

SELECTED BIBLIOGRAPHY

Matttingly, Rick. "Dave Samuels." *MP* III, 1 (December 1986): 8.
Nolan, H. "Dave Friedman and Dave Samuels: Two-Man Percussion Crusade." *DB* XLIII, 20 (1976): 12.
Peterscak, James. "Musically Speaking: A Candid Interview with David Samuels and David Friedman." *PN* XIV, 3 (Spring/Summer 1976): 18–19.
Samuels, Dave. *A Musical Approach to Four-Mallet Technique for Vibraphone*, vols. 1–2. Bryn Mawr, PA: Theodore Presser, 1982.
Samuels, Dave. "Choosing a Chord Voicing." *MP* I, 4 (September 1985): 50.
Samuels, Dave. *Contemporary Vibraphone Technique,* Books 1–2. Miami, FL: CPP Belwin, 1993 (with cassette tapes).
Samuels, Dave. "Relaxing Your Mind and Body through Warm-Ups." *Modern Per-cussionist* I, 1 (December, 1984–February, 1985): 40–42.
Samuels, Dave. "Using the New Technology." *MP* II, 3 (June 1986): 46.
Samuels, Dave. "Vibraphone Viewpoint: Triads for Voicings." *MP* III, 2 (March 1987): 52.
Schupp, Roger B. "Reunion: An Interview with David Samuels and David Fried-man." *PN* XXXII, 2 (April 1994): 37–41.

Via, David. "PASIC® '89: Dave Samuels Today." *PN* XXVII, 5 (September 1989): 19–23.
GEN. BIB.: Kernfeld, *NGJ*; Larrick, *BET-CP*.

SANKARAN, TRICHY (b. 1942, Trichy, India). A mrdangam and kanjira virtuoso who has earned the title "Mrdanga Kala Shironmani," Trichy Sankaran started mrdangam at age 7, studying with Sri P. A. Venkataraman and Sri Palani Subramania Pillai. He made his professional debut at 13; and in 1971 he was invited to join the faculty at York University (Toronto), where he is founding director of Indian music studies. Sankaran's varied collaborators have included Nexus, *Glen Velez, *Jamey Haddad, and *Abraham Adzenyah, among others. He has performed at venues such as the World Percussion Festival (Boston), the World Percussion Intensive, EXPO '86, the Commonwealth Drum Festival–1987 (Vancouver), and EXPO '88 (Australia). He was honored by the Percussive Arts Centre in Bangalore, India, with the Palghat Mani Award (1992); by the Ontario Confederation of University Faculty Association (1992); and by the University of Victoria (British Columbia) with an honorary doctorate (1998).

SELECTED DISCOGRAPHY

Music of the World CDT-141: *Lotus Signatures*, 1997.
Music of the World MOW-150: *The Language of Rhythm* (with Bikram Ghosh), 1997.
Music of the World T-120: *Laya Vinyas*, 1990.
Music of the World T-127: *Sunada*, 1992.

SELECTED VIDEOGRAPHY

Warner Bros./PASIC®: *Mrdangam and Kanjira Clinic*, 1995.

SELECTED BIBLIOGRAPHY

Lurie, Stephen M. "A Mrdangam Master in North America: An Interview with Trichy Sankaran." *PN* XXXVI, 1 (February 1998): 36–43.
Sankaran, Trichy. *Rhythmic Principles and Practice of South Indian Drumming.* Ontario, Canada: Lalith Publishing, 1994.
PASIC® program biographies, 1991, 1994, 1995, 1998.

SANTAMARIA, RAMON "MONGO" (b. 7 Apr 1922, Havana, Cuba). Conga master Mongo Santamaria, whose early style was influenced by his African grandfather, studied violin as a child, then embraced maracas and bongos as a teen. By age 17 he was playing professionally in Havana nightclubs while employed as a mechanic and mail carrier. After working in Mexico with a dance revue for about two years, he moved to the United States (1950), where he performed with Perez Prado, *Tito Puente (seven years), Dizzy Gillespie, Nat King Cole, Count Basie, and *Cal Tjader. After playing with Tjader for five years on the West Coast, Santamaria formed his own group (1961), which at times included Herbie Hancock, Chick Corea, and Hubert Laws. Instrumental in attracting other Latin percussion specialists to America (e.g., Carlos "Patato" Valdez), he made his first recording in 1955, appeared at the Montreux Jazz Festival in 1980, and has toured Scandinavia, Europe, and the United States.

SELECTED DISCOGRAPHY

Chesky JD/JR/JG 100: *Mongo Santamaria and Friends—Mambo Mongo*, 1992.
Columbia 9780: *Stone Soul*, 1969.
Columbia 9937: *Workin' on a Groovy Thing*, 1970s.
Fantasy 3267/OJC-276: *Yambu*, 1987.
Fantasy/OJC 643: *Latin Concert* (Cal Tjader), 1958.
Pablo/OJC 626: *Summertime* (Dizzy Gillespie and Toots Thielemans), 1980.
Prestige PCD-24018-2: *Afro-Roots*, 1958/1989.
Tico Records LP1149/Vaya VS 56: *Drums and Chants*, 1978.
Verve MGV8191: *Dizzy Gillespie and His Orchestra*, 1954.

SELECTED BIBLIOGRAPHY

Goldberg, Norbert. "An Interview with Mongo Santamaria." *PN* XXII, 5 (July 1984): 55–58.
GEN. BIB.: Southern, *BDA-AAM.*

SAUNDERS, THEODORE D. "RED" (b. 2 Mar 1912, Memphis, Tennessee; d. 4 Mar 1981, Chicago, Illinois). Drumset performer Red Saunders studied music in Milwaukee, Wisconsin, and then in the early 1930s moved to Chicago, where he played with various artists, including Tiny Parham. From 1937 to 1967, he fronted his own groups and worked occasionally with Louis Armstrong, Duke Ellington, Woody Herman, Art Hodes, and "Little Brother" Montgomery.

SELECTED DISCOGRAPHY

Chess CHV-415: *South-Side Jazz* (Eddie South), 1951/1971.
Columbia CK 64988: *Juke Joint Jump—A Boogie-Woogie Celebration* (1931–61), 1996.
Rhino R2 70291: *Bo Diddley Beats*, 1992.
GEN. BIB.: Southern, *BDA-AAM.*

SCHIMMEL, WILHELM (b. 2 Apr 1898, Steinau/Schlesien, Germany). Wilhelm Schimmel attended the Musikschule Ohlau (Schlesien), took private lessons, served in the military in WWI, and then moved to Switzerland, where

he was an active musician from 1922 to 1926. He performed with the Berlin Philharmonic (1926–62), was honored by them in 1956, retired in 1962, and in 1970 settled in Switzerland.
GEN. BIB.: Avgerinos, *KB*.

SCHINSTINE, WILLIAM JOSEPH (b. 16 Dec 1922, Easton, Pennsylvania; d. 3 Jan 1986, Allentown, Pennsylvania). A student of *George Hamilton Green, William Schinstine earned a bachelor's degree from the Eastman School (1945) and a master's degree from the University of Pennsylvania (1952). A prolific composer whose works addressed both didactic and performance genres, he was a percussionist with the National Symphony (1945–46) and Pittsburgh Symphony (1946–47), principal percussionist with the San Antonio Symphony (1947–51), and a teacher in the Pottstown, Pennsylvania, public schools (1952–79).
GEN. BIB.: Borland, *WWAMC*.

SCHLUTER, HENRY J. (b. 7 Apr 1889, Chicago, Illinois; d. 19 May 1971, Chicago, Illinois). International authority on pitch and tuning, Henry Schluter started sweeping floors at *J. C. Deagan, Inc., in 1905, retiring in 1969 as chief acoustical engineer after 64 years of sevice. Designer of the prototype vibraphone, Model 145 Deagan Vibra-Harp (1927), he was named honorary chair of the Deagan Board. [Leedy Drum Company engineers and designer–musical pitch authority, Herman Winterhoff, reportedly developed the vibrato technology in the early 1920s; see *Leedy, Ulysses Grant.] Schluter was blessed with perfect pitch and developed a harmonic tuning process in 1938 for carillon bells, which he installed from Pretoria, South Africa (1935), to the New York World's Fair (1939). He received a citation from the U.S. Navy in WWII for an acoustic detonator he helped develop to protect Allied ships from mines, and he built tuning devices for the U.S. Bureau of Standards to measure the exact pitch of musical instruments.

SELECTED BIBLIOGRAPHY

Culhane, John. "Bell Expert Rings Up 60 Years." *Chicago Daily News* (Saturday, 27 Mar 1965).
"In Memoriam." *PN* X, 1 (Fall 1971): 15.

SCHNEIDERMAN, WILLIAM (b. 10 Aug 1916, New York, New York). Earning diplomas from the Institute of Musical Arts (aka Juilliard School) in 1938, 1939, and 1940, William Schneiderman performed with the Ballet Russe de Basil (1940–41), with the Hurok Ballet Theater (1941–43), as solo timpanist in the Chautauqua Symphony and Opera (1943–58), and as solo timpanist

(1943–58) and percussionist (1958–82) with the Pittsburgh Symphony. He taught percussion at the Carnegie Institute of Technology (1945–58) and Duquesne University (1955–83+).
GEN. BIB.: Borland, *WWAMC.*

SCHNELLAR, HANS (fl. ca. 1851–1900s, Vienna, Austria). Timpanist of the Vienna Philharmonic and State Opera for nearly 40 years, Hans Schnellar is credited with improving the T-handle timpani-tuning mechanism of the Pfundt-Hoffman [German] type of drum at the turn of the century and with teaching at the Viennese Academy, where *Richard Hochrainer was one of his students. Hochrainer's improved version of Schnellar's deep-bowl timpani model is still produced in Vienna. Around 1903 he improvised a solo (ascending stepwise motion) in the last movement of Richard Strauss' "Sinfonia Domestica" (with the composer's blessing), which is still used today.

SELECTED BIBLIOGRAPHY

Beck, John H., ed. *Encyclopedia of Percussion.* New York: Garland Publishing, 1995. S.v. "The Kettledrum" by Edmund A. Bowles.
Ludwig, William F. *Ludwig Timpani Instructor.* Chicago: Ludwig Drum Co., 1957.

SCHORY, RICHARD L. "DICK" (b. 13 Dec 1931, Ames, Iowa). President and CEO of Ovation Records and Creative Music, Dick Schory matured in Chicago and attended Iowa State University before serving in the U.S. Air Force Command Band. He graduated from Northwestern University (bachelor's, 1957), was a featured soloist with Meredith Wilson, performed with the Chicago Symphony, and in the 1960s was vice-president in charge of marketing for the Ludwig Drum Company, where he was also editor of the *Ludwig Drummer.* Founder of and arranger, performer, and conductor for the Percussion Pops Orchestra, Schory toured for 13 years and made one of the first commercially available *stereo* LP recordings (*Re-Percussion*, 1957) with that group. Their second album (*Music for Bang, Baaroom, and Harp*, 1958) was the first stereo LP to sell a million copies. He received a Grammy® nomination as "Best Arranger" in 1960.

SELECTED DISCOGRAPHY

Everest 14-102/1232: *Re-Percussion* (Percussive Art Ensemble), 1957.
Ovation OV 14-10-2: *Dick Schory at Carnegie Hall*, 1970.
RCA LSA 2485: *Holiday for Percussion* (Percussion Pops Orchestra), 1962.
RCA LSA 2613: *Supercussion* (Percussion Pops Orchestra), 1963.
RCA LSA 2738: *Politely Percussive* (Percussion Pops Orchestra), 1963.
RCA LSA 2926: *Happy Hits* (Percussion Pops Orchestra), 1964.
RCA LSP 2806: *Dick Schory on Tour* (Percussion Pops Orchestra), 1964.
RCA LSP 3394: *Selections from "The Roar of the Greasepaint, The Smell of the Crowd,"* 1965.

RCA Victor 09026-68151-2: *Christmas Memories*, 1958/1996.

RCA Victor LSA 2306: *Runnin' Wild* (Percussion and Brass Ensemble), 1968.

RCA Victor LSA 2382: *Stereo Action Goes Broadway* (Percussion and Brass Ensemble), 1969.

RCA Victor LSP 1866: *Music for Bang, Baaroom, and Harp* (New Percussion Ensemble). 1958.

RCA Victor LSP 2125: *Music to Break Any Mood* (New Percussion Ensemble), 1960.

RCA Victor LSP 2289: *Wild Percussion and Horns A' Plenty* (New Percussion Ensemble), 1960.

SELECTED BIBLIOGRAPHY

"Dick Schory's Wild World of Percussion." *LD* I,1 (Fall 1961): 12–13.

Moore, Daniel. "The Impact of Richard L. "Dick" Schory on the Development of the Contemporary Percussion Ensemble." Doctoral dissertation, University of Kentucky (in progress), 1999.

Schory, Dick. "Age of Percussion." *LD* I, 1 (Fall 1961): 7.

Schory, Dick. "Arranging for Percussion, Part I—The Mallet Instruments: Xylophone." *LD* VI, 2 (Fall 1966): 21–23.

Schory, Dick. "Arranging for Percussion, Part II—The Marimba." *Ludwig Drummer* (Spring 1967): 21.

"Schory and Percussion Pops Orchestra Dazzles NAMM Audience!" *Ludwig Drummer* VII, 2 (Fall 1967): 27.

SCHUBERT, ERNST. Ernst Schubert performed as timpanist with the Berlin Symphony under Blüthner; after it disbanded in 1932, he became a substitute percussionist with the Berlin Philharmonic for one year before joining the Berlin Regional Orchestra (Landesorchester) as timpanist.

GEN. BIB.: Avgerinos, *KB.*

SCHWAR, WILLIAM OSCAR (b. 1875, Bautzen, Saxony, Germany; d. 27 Nov 1946, Philadelphia, Pennsylvania). Celebrated timpanist with the Philadelphia Orchestra (1903–46) for both regular seasons and their "Robin Hood Dell" summer concert series, Oscar Schwar started violin at the age of 10 and later studied timpani at the Royal Conservatory in Dresden with a Herr Heinemann, who was principal timpanist for the Dresden Royal Opera. Schwar performed with the St. Petersburg Royal Opera and in the cities of Karlsruhe, Koblenz, and Hanover, among others. He appeared as soloist with Philadelphia in 1923 and also taught at the Curtis Institute.

SELECTED BIBLIOGRAPHY

Kupferberg, Herbert. *Those Fabulous Philadelphians*. New York: Charles Scribner's Sons, 1969.

Simco, Andrew. "An Interview with Cloyd Duff." *PN* XXXI, 3 (February 1993): 55–60.

"The Closing Chord." *IM* XLV, 6 (December 1946): 15.

Wister, Frances Anne. *Twenty-five Years of the Philadelphia Orchestra, 1900–1925*. Philadelphia: Edward Stern & Co., 1925.

SEARCY, DAVID (b. 1946, Richmond, California). A student at the Tanglewood Institute and New England Conservatory (1964), where he studied with *Vic Firth, David Searcy also attended San Francisco State University, the Hamburg Musikhochschule, and the Vienna Academy of Music. His other teachers include Harry Bartlett, *Roland Kohloff, Robert Hinze, and *Richard Hochrainer, and he is solo timpanist and head of the percussion section for the La Scala Opera Orchestra and Philharmonic in Milan, Italy (1972–). Professor of percussion and timpani at Civica Scuola de Musica in Milan (1974–) and chair of the Italian Chapter of the Percussive Arts Society, Searcy has appeared with the Bayreuth Festival Orchestra (1974), the Canadian Opera Company, Musikselskabet (Norway), and the Bavarian State Opera Orchestra.

SELECTED BIBLIOGRAPHY

Searcy, David. "Behind the Looking Glass: An Excursion into Orchestral Percussion." *PN* XVII, 2 (Winter 1979): 40–41.
PASIC® program biographies, 1991.

SEELE, OTTO (fl. ca. 1880–1905). Timpanist with the Leipzig Symphony and Conservatory Orchestra (Germany) around 1880–1905, Otto Seele reportedly stated: "Tuning by pedals began in 1872 with Pittrich and Queisser, both of Dresden." Drummer and timpanist in theater and opera orchestras in Kassell, Halle, Berlin, Elberfeld, Frankfurt, Bad-Reichenhall, München, Bad Kissingen, Würzburg, Marienbad, Breslau, Hamburg, St. Petersburg (Russia), Nizza (France), and Lugano (Italy), Seele also conducted both the Leipzig Theater Orchestra and the Gewandhaus Orchestra.

SELECTED BIBLIOGRAPHY

Beck, John H., ed. *Encyclopedia of Percussion*. New York: Garland Publishing, 1995. S.v. "The Kettledrum" by Edmund A. Bowles.
Ludwig, William F. *Ludwig Timpani Instructor*. Chicago: Ludwig Drum Co., 1957.
Seele, Otto. *Schule für Pauke*. Frankfurt: Zimmerman, ca. 1910.
Seele, Otto. *Schule für Xylofon*, 15th revised ed. Frankfurt: Zimmerman, 1933.
Seele, Otto. "Self Instruction for the Kettle Drums—Leipzig, 1895." *Percussionist* V, 2 (December 1967): 253–259.

SEITZ, J. FREDERICK "FRED" [ALSO SIETZ] (d. ca. Feb 1941, Chicago, Illinois). Remembered in William F. Ludwig's memoirs as "'Pop' Zietz [*sic*]...because he was so generous to everyone seeking his help and advice," Frederick Seitz served as timpanist with the Chicago Grand Opera Company (ca. 1911–23) in a percussion section that included himself, Ruben Katz on bass drum, and Aldo Bartolotti on cymbals and accessories.

SELECTED BIBLIOGRAPHY

Seitz, J. Frederick. *Modern School of Timpani Playing.* Indianapolis: Leedy Mfg. Co., 1912.
GEN. BIB.: Cook, *LDT*, p. 13.

SHARPE, LEN "BOOGSIE" (b. 28 Oct 1953, Port of Spain, Trinidad, West Indies). Starting at 5 years of age, "Boogsie" Sharpe had mastered all pan styles by his teens and was supposedly the first pan artist to compose and arrange his own music for national competitions in calypso and classical genre. His recordings with soca and calypso singers include Lord Kitchener and the Mighty Sparrow, and his jazz collaborators include Monty Alexander, *Gary Burton, *Art Blakey, Wynton Marsalis, Eric Gale, Randy Weston, and Grover Washington. Touring Australia with the percussion group Nexus, Sharpe has performed in Europe, the United States, and Japan. His 50-member steelpan orchestra, Phase II, won the 1988 Trinidad Carnival Steel Band Competition. As a designated cultural ambassador, Sharpe has hosted dignitaries visiting Trinidad, including the queen of England.

SELECTED DISCOGRAPHY

Concord Picante CJP-359: *Monty Alexander's Ivory and Steel "Jamboree,"* 1988.
PASIC® program biographies, 1993.

SHAUGHNESSY, EDWIN T. "ED" (b. 29 Jan 1929, Jersey City, New Jersey). Initially influenced by *Sid Catlett, and equally at home with big band or combo, Ed Shaughnessy began drums at age 14, studying percussion with *Morris Goldenberg and Indian drumming with tabla master Alla Rakha Khan. His professional collaborations included Jack Teagarden, George Shearing (at age 19), two years with Charlie Ventura (including recording and experimenting with two bass drums), Tommy Dorsey (1950), Benny Goodman (European tour, 1950), and Lucky Millinder. He also performed with the New York Philharmonic (1954) and Pittsburgh, and NBC Symphonies. After a staff percussion job with the CBS Orchestra, he achieved widespread fame beginning in 1964, during his 29-year association with NBC's television orchestra for the *Tonight Show* with Johnny Carson.

A successful big band composer and columnist for *Down Beat* magazine (1968–69, "The Thinking Drummer"), he has recorded over 500 albums; worked with Booker Little, Duke Ellington, the Doc Severinsen Orchestra, Count Basie, *Gary McFarland, Charles Mingus, and *Teddy Charles; fronted his own bands ("Jazz In the Pocket" and "Energy Force"); and appeared with every major U.S. symphony. Shaughnessy was voted "Best Big Band Drummer" in *Modern Drummer* magazine's Readers' Poll five years in a row and was recipient of the Drum Master Award in New York City. He has given more than

600 clinics throughout the world and taught at New York University and Skidmore College (Saratoga, NY).

SELECTED DISCOGRAPHY

Amherst AMH 54406: *The Tonight Show Orchestra with Doc Severinsen*, 1991.
Atlantic 1274: *A Word from Bird* (Teddy Charles), 1956.
CMG CMD-8028: *Jazz in the Pocket*, 1991.
Command 905: *Broadway—Basie's Way* (Count Basie), 1966.
Command RS 912-SD: *Hollywood—Basie's Way* (Count Basie), 1967.
Decca MCAD 42330: *A Charlie Ventura Concert*, 1949.
Impulse 9132: *Happenings* (Oliver Nelson), 1966.
Prestige PRST 7225: *Afro-American Sketches* (Oliver Nelson), 1961.
RCA LPM 3360: *Groovy Sound of Music* (Gary Burton), 1964.
Riverside RLP 12-204: *Mundell Lowe Quartet*, 1991.
Savoy SV-0189: *The Jazz Guitarist* (Chuck Wayne), 1953.
Telarc CS-30177: *Big Band Hit Parade* (Cincinnati Pops Symphony), 1988.
Verve MGV8027: *Billie Holiday and Her Orchestra*, 1954.
Verve MGV8518: *The Gary McFarland Orchestra*, 1963.
Verve V6-8495: *Jack Teagarden*, 1962.
Verve V6-8507: *Cal Tjader*, 1963.
Verve V6-8687: *Count Basie and His Orchestra*, 1967.
Verve V/V6-8474: *Bashin'* (Jimmy Smith with Oliver Nelson's Orchestra), 1962.

SELECTED VIDEOGRAPHY

Video Conservatory: *Ed Shaughnessy's Drum Clinic*, 1989.
Warner Bros./DCI VH0270: *The Making of Burning for Buddy*, pt. 1, 1996.

SELECTED BIBLIOGRAPHY

Cook, Rob "Ed Shaughnessy: Swinger on Staff." *MD* II, 3 (1978): 6.
Flans, Robyn "Ed Shaughnessy." *MD* X, 4 (1986): 17.
Ogle, Katie. "Inside Ed Shaughnessy." *PN* XIX, 1 (Fall 1980): 38–40.
Shaughnessy, Ed. "Finger Control in Modern Drumming." *Percussionist* V, 3 (1968): 284–285.
Shaughnessy, Ed. *New Time Signatures in Jazz Drumming*. New York: Henry Adler, 1966.
Shaughnessy, Ed. "The Thinking Drummer." *DB* XXXVI (6 Feb 1969): 36.
Smith, T. "Driver's Seat: Ed Shaughnessy on the Road." *MD* VIII, 3 (1984): 60.
Tomkins, L. "Ed Shaughnessy Talks Drums." *Crescendo International* XVIII, 6 (1980): 6.
GEN. BIB.: Hunt, *52nd St.*; Kernfeld, *NGJ*, by Jeff Porter; Larrick, *BET-CP*; Spagnardi, *GJD*; PASIC® program biographies, 1991, 1994, 1997.

SHEPHERD, BERISFORD "SHEP" (b. 19 Jan 1917, Spanish Honduras, Central America). An infant immigrant to Philadelphia, where he eventually studied at the Mastbaum Conservatory, "Shep" Shepherd played for Jimmy

Gorham (1932–41), Benny Carter (1941–42), the U.S. Army Band (trombone and drums, 1943–46), Cab Calloway (1946), Buck Clayton (1947), Earl Bostic (1947–50), Bill Doggett (1952-59), and during the 1950s–1960s with Erskine Hawkins, Sy Oliver, and for off-Broadway musicals, touring with *Here's Love* (1963). In 1964 Shepherd relocated to San Francisco, where he remained musically active.

GEN. BIB.: Southern, *BDA-AAM.*

SHOEMAKE, CHARLES EDWARD "CHARLIE" (b. 27 Jul 1937, Houston, Texas). A vibist and bandleader who studied piano at Southern Methodist University for a year, Charlie Shoemake played in Los Angeles with Charles Lloyd, Art Pepper, and Howard Rumsey (1959–63). Taking up the vibraphone in 1965, he worked in recording studios and, from 1966 to 1973, played with the George Shearing Quintet. Shoemake taught jazz improvisation in his own studio (1973–90) and recorded as leader (1978–81/1984–85). He can be heard on the soundtrack of the movie *Bird.*

SELECTED DISCOGRAPHY

Discovery 856: *Away from the Crowd*, 1980–81.
GEN. BIB.: Kernfeld, *NGJ.*

SHOLLE, EMIL. Percussionist with the Cleveland Symphony (1924–ca. 1949?), Emil Sholle did staff radio orchestra work at WHK in Cleveland and taught in the public schools of Northfield, Ohio, and at the Hruby Conservatory of Music (Cleveland, 1922–?). Interestingly, he was a violinist who subbed occasionally in the percussion section and, without any percussive technical background, became a highly regarded cymbal specialist. Sholle also penned several percussion method books and etudes (reportedly with help from the Cleveland percussion section, which included his older brother, Frank).

SELECTED DISCOGRAPHY

Cleveland Institute of Music STV 20039: *Bartók—Sonata for Two Pianos and Percussion*, 1950s.

SELECTED BIBLIOGRAPHY

Sholle, Emil. *Here's to the Drum*, vol. 1. Cleveland Heights, OH: Brooks Publishing Co., 1959.

SINAI, JOSEPH "JOE" (b. ca. 1895, Russia; d. 15 Jan 1985, Santa Rosa, California). Immigrating to the San Francisco Bay area when he was 5 years old, Joe Sinai played triangle with the San Francisco Symphony (informally during a rehearsal) when he was 13, eventually appearing professionally with them for 65 years until his retirement in 1973. During the early 1920s Sinai performed in silent movie theaters in San Francisco with Paul Ashe's Synco Symphonists, earning a $20 gold piece "tip" from Charlie Chaplin after a premiere of one of his films. He was also a close friend of Arthur Fiedler, who always requested Sinai's presence when he conducted—an agreement that included tours and even the opening concert for the Kennedy Music Center, Washington, D.C.

SELECTED BIBLIOGRAPHY

Cirone, Anthony J., and Joe Sinai. *The Logic of It All.* Menloe Park, CA: Cirone Publications, 1977.
"In Memoriam: Joseph Sinai." *PN* XXIII, 4 (April 1985): 20.
GEN. BIB.: Cook, *LDT*, p. 17.

SINGLETON, ARTHUR JAMES "ZUTTY" (b. 14 May 1898, Bunkie, Louisiana; d. 14 Jul 1975, New York, New York). A student of Frank Cantrell and a veteran of Fate Marable's riverboat bands (1921–23), with whom he made his first recording (1924), Zutty Singleton started his professional career in New Orleans (1915). A WWI U.S. Army veteran, he played with New Orleans icons Papa Celestin, Luis Russell, and "Big Eye" Nelson, eschewing some of the fashionable accessory percussion instruments on the drumset of his time. After recording in St. Louis (1925), he moved to Chicago, where he performed with Doc Cooke, Jimmie Noone, Pee Wee Russell, Fats Waller, Clarence Jones, Louis Armstrong's "Hot Five," Jelly Roll Morton, Barney Bigard, Roy Eldridge, and Sidney Bechet, among others.

Following tours with Carroll Dickerson (1927–29), Singleton relocated to New York and worked with Fats Waller, Otto Hardwicke, and Bubber Miley, among others, before returning to Chicago (1933–37). Another move to New York paired him with Mezz Mezzrow and Sidney Bechet; he then settled in Los Angeles (1943–51) and worked on TV and films, including *Stormy Weather* (1943), *Love That Brute* (1950), and *New Orleans* (1947). Between 1951 and 1953, Singleton performed in France and traveled abroad until his resettlement in New York.

A pioneer in the use of wire brushes, hi-hat, ride cymbal patterns, rhythmic bass drum punctuations, and drum solos, Singleton was a transitional figure between New Orleans and swing drumming styles, freelancing with New York Dixieland bands later in his career and recording with Dizzy Gillespie and Charlie Parker. Incapacitated by a stroke in 1969, he received the Gene Krupa Award in 1974 and was inducted into the National Association of Recording Arts and Sciences (NARAS) Hall of Fame in 1975 for his 1928 recordings made with Louis Armstrong's Hot Five.

SELECTED DISCOGRAPHY

American Music AMCD-19: *Kid Ory—'44–'46.*
Beltone 753: "Dizzy Boogie" (Slim Gaillard), 1945.
Beltone 758: "Flat Foot Floogie" (Slim Gaillard), 1945.
Bluebird 10442: "Climax Rag" (Jelly Roll Morton), 1939.
Blue Note BLP7023: *Mezz Mezzrow and His Band,* 1951.
ESC Recording Corporation: *Drumface* (features previously unreleased material, including conversations), 1975.
Fat Cat's Jazz 100-101: *Zutty and the Clarinet Kings,* vols. 1–2, 1967.
Jazzology JCD-2/103: *Wild Bill Davison and His Jazzologists,* 1991.
Masters of Jazz, Media 7: *Anthology of Jazz Drumming,* vols. 1–2 (1904–35), 1997.
Mosaic MD 12-170: *Classical Capitol Jazz Sessions,* 1997.
Okeh 8703: "Muggles" (Louis Armstrong), 1928.
Okeh 8713: "Funny Feathers" (Victoria Spivey), 1929.
Okeh 40113: "Frankie and Johnny" (Fate Marable), 1924.
Victor 38601: "My Little Dixie Home/That's Like It Ought to Be" (Jelly Roll Morton), 1929.
Victor 404003: "Moppin' and Boppin' " (Fats Waller), 1943.

SELECTED VIDEOGRAPHY

Vintage Jazz Classics Video 2002: *Chicago and All That Jazz,* 1961.

SELECTED BIBLIOGRAPHY

Brown, Theodore D. *A History and Analysis of Jazz Drumming to 1942.* Ph.D. dissertation, University of Michigan, 1976.
"From the Past: Arthur 'Zutty' Singleton." *MD* XIX, 10 (October 1995): 102–103.
Shaughnessy, Ed. "About Face: Zutty Singleton." *DB* XXXVI, 11 (12 June 1969): 40.
Shultz, Thomas. "A History of Jazz Drumming." *Percussionist* XVI, 3 (Spring/Summer 1979): 111–112.
Williams, Martin. "Zutty Singleton, the Pioneer Jazz Forgot." *DB* XXX, 30 (21 Nov 1963): 18–20.
GEN. BIB.: Hitchcock and Sadie, *NGA,* by J. Bradford Robinson; Southern, *BDA-AAM;* Spagnardi, *GJD.*

SLINGERLAND, HENRY HEANON, SR. (b. 15 Mar 1875, Netherlands?; d. 13 Mar 1946, Chicago, Illinois). In 1921, entrepreneur (and nondrummer) H. H. Slingerland established the Slingerland Banjo and Drum Company in Chicago, where he maintained his own tannery to process natural skin hides. [Legend has it that he won the company in a card game.] Discontinuing the banjos, the company dropped the term from their title and produced drums exclusively (ca. 1933), specializing in timpani tuned by means of a cable mechanism between tension rods and pedal. After H. H., Sr.'s, passing, H. H., Jr. ("Bud," 16

Jul 1921–18 Jun 1980, also a nondrummer), moved the company to Niles, Illinois, where he purchased the *Leedy Manufacturing patents from C. G. Conn in 1955, producing Leedy drums for about three years. In 1970 Bud sold the entire company to CCM (Crowell, Collier, and MacMillan), which purchased several music-related concerns, including Conn. *J. C. Deagan Company, makers of keyboard percussion instruments, was added to this conglomerate in 1977. The combined subdivision of Slingerland-Leedy and Deagan was sold to Mardan Corporation (1980), then to the Sanlar Corporation (Sandra and Larry Rasp, 1984). The Rasps quickly sold Slingerland-Leedy to *Fred Gretsch III (Fred Gretsch Enterprises) in 1986, and Gretsch employed HSS (Hohner) as distributor. (The Deagan division had been purchased by the Yamaha Corporation in 1986.) Gretsch retained the Leedy trademark in 1994 when Slingerland was sold to the Gibson Guitar Company (aka Gibson Musical Instruments).

SELECTED BIBLIOGRAPHY

Cangany, Harry. *The Great American Drums and the Companies That Made Them,* Cedar Grove, NJ: Modern Drummer Publications, Inc., 1996.
Cook, Rob. *The Slingerland Book.* Alma, MI: Rebeats Publications, 1996.
Schmidt, Paul William. *History of the Ludwig Drum Company.* Fullerton, CA: Centerstream Publishing, 1991 (pp. 56–59).
GEN. BIB.: Hitchcock and Sadie, *NGA*, by Edmund A. Bowles.

SMALL, EDWARD PIERCE "TED" (b. 17 Jan 1942, Detroit, Michigan). A graduate of Michigan State University (bachelor's, 1965) and the Eastman School (master's, 1967), Ted Small studied with *Sal Rabbio, *William Street, *Charles Owen, and *John Beck. Following early performance experiences with the American Waterways Wind Orchestra, he was percussionist and featured marimba soloist with the U.S. Marine Band in Washington, D.C. (1967–71). Small has served as percussionist and assistant principal timpanist with the Colorado Symphony since 1972 and as timpanist for the Central City Opera (CO) since 1986. He has taught at the Lamont School of Music in Denver and presented clinics and performances throughout the Rocky Mountain region.

SELECTED DISCOGRAPHY

Pro Arte CDD-352: *George Gershwin—A Rhapsody in Blue* (Denver Pops), 1987.
Pro Arte CDD-361: *Bolero* (Denver Symphony), 1987.
Pro Arte CDD-410: *Vive la France* (Denver Symphony), 1988.
Pro Arte CDD-452: *A Touch of Fiedler* (Denver Pops), 1987.
Pro Arte CDD-453: *Mussorgsky—Pictures at an Exhibition* (Denver Symphony), 1989.

SELECTED BIBLIOGRAPHY

Small, Edward P. "An Index of Percussion Articles Appearing in *Down Beat.*" *Percussionist* VII, 2 (December 1969): 77–81.
Small, Edward P. "An Index of Percussion Articles Appearing in *Down Beat.*" *Percussionist* VII, 3 (March 1970): 104–107.
GEN. BIB.: Borland, *WWAMC*; Larrick, *BET-CP.*

SMITH, CHARLES (b. Newark, New Jersey). A student of *Alfred Friese, *Edward Rubsam, *Billy Dorn, *Saul Goodman, and *Gene Krupa, Charles Smith attended the Juilliard School, gave 600 performances of *Porgy and Bess* (1941–43) and secured a position with the Boston Symphony (1943–83), never missing a concert for 40 years. He taught at Boston University, gave prison lectures on percussion, composed *Background Music for Family Arguments*, and recorded William Kraft's *Concerto for Five Percussionists and Orchestra* with the Boston percussion section in 1967 for use on radio broadcasts.

SELECTED BIBLIOGRAPHY

"The Percussion Section of the Boston Symphony Orchestra." World Percussion Network (wpn.org/library/biography/), adapted from a Boston Symphony biography, 1983.
Smith, Charles. "Porgy and Me." *PN* XIX, 2 (Winter 1981): 65.

SMITH, CHARLES "CHARLIE" (b. 15 Apr 1927, New York, New York; d. 15 Jan 1966, New Haven, Connecticut). Drumset artist Charlie Smith was active in New York City from 1947, performing with Ella Fitzgerald (1948–), Duke Ellington (1951), Billy Taylor (1950s), Dizzy Gillespie, Charlie Parker, Oscar Peterson, Hot Lips Page, Artie Shaw, Erroll Garner, and Benny Goodman, among others. After relocating to Connecticut, he became active in teaching and composing.

SELECTED DISCOGRAPHY

Atlantic 109: *Piano Selections* (Erroll Garner), 1949.
Prestige 184: *Billy Taylor Trio*, 1954.
Riverside 234: *Sultry Serenade* (Herbie Mann), 1957.
Savoy SJL 1172: *Oscar Pettiford Discoveries*, 1952.
Verve MGV2013: *Slim Gaillard and His Orchestra*, 1951.
Vogue 655 005: *Milt Jackson and the All Stars*, 1954.

SELECTED VIDEOGRAPHY

Sony Video JO509: *Celebrating Bird*, 1952.

SELECTED BIBLIOGRAPHY

Korall, Burt. "A Blast from the Past: The Great Drummers of Duke Ellington." *MD*
    XXI, 12 (December 1997): 82–94.
GEN. BIB.: Hunt, *52nd St.*; Kernfeld, *NGJ*, by Rick Mattingly.

SMITH, STEVE (b. 21 Aug 1954, Brockton, Massachusetts). Starting drums
at age 9 with big band drummer Bill Blanagan, Steve Smith studied with Gary
Chaffee and *Alan Dawson at Berklee College of Music. He has toured and recorded with Jean-Luc Ponty (1976–77), the rock group Journey (1978–85), his
own group Vital Information (1983–   ), Steps Ahead (seven years), and artists
Mariah Carey, Stanley Clarke, Randy Brecker, and Allan Holdsworth, among
others. Smith's video garnered "Best Music Instructional Video" honors from
the American Video Conference (1987), and he was voted "Number One All-
Around Drummer" in *Modern Drummer* magazine's Readers' Poll for five
straight years (1987–91). During 1995–97 he toured with the resurrected Journey band and recorded the reunion album *Trial by Fire*.

SELECTED DISCOGRAPHY

CBS CK 67721: *Captured* (Journey), 1981/1996.
CBS CK 67723: *Frontiers* (Journey), 1983/1996.
CBS/Sony CK 67722: *Escape* (Journey), 1981/1996.
CBS/Sony CK 69139: *Greatest Hits Live/Best of Journey*, 1998.
CBS/Sony CT 67726: *Evolution* (Journey), 1979/1996.
Intuition 2161 2: *Ray of Hope* (Vital Information), 1996.
Intuition INT 3218 2: *Where We Came From* (Vital Information), 1998.
Tone Center 2624540002tc4002: *Vital Tech Tones*, 1998.
Tone Center TC 40012: *Show Me What You Can Do*, 1998.
Tone Center TC 40022: *Cause and Effect*, 1998.

SELECTED VIDEOGRAPHY

DCI VHO22/23: *Steve Smith,* pts. 1–2, 1987/1988.
Warner Bros./DCI VH0270: *The Making of Burning for Buddy*, No. 3, 1991.

SELECTED BIBLIOGRAPHY

Flans, Robyn. "Steve Smith: Journey Revisited." *MD* XXI, 4 (April 1997): 48–68.
Iero, Cheech. "My First Gig." *MD* XX, 12 (December 1996): 148–151.
Woodard, Josef. "Steve Smith and Vital Information: Blast Off." *JazzTimes* XXVIII, 9
    (November 1998): 34–37.
PASIC® program biographies, 1985/1993.

SMITH, TERRY JAMES (b. 5 Aug 1952, Tulsa, Oklahoma). Percussionist
with the Colorado Symphony since 1980, Terry Smith earned bachelor's (1973)

and doctorate (DMA, 1984) degrees from the University of Colorado, and a master's degree (1974) from the University of Michigan, studying respectively with John Galm and *Charles Owen. He has appeared as timpanist with the Minnesota Opera and the Canary Islands Opera Festival (1975), as substitute percussionist and timpanist with the St. Paul Chamber Orchestra (1978–80), as solo timpanist with the Central City (CO) Opera (1981–), and as principal percussionist with the Santa Fe (1980) and Metropolitan Operas. A former faculty member at the University of Wisconsin at River Falls (1975–80), Smith has also performed with Keith Jarrett, Roger Williams, and the American Ballet Theater.

SELECTED DISCOGRAPHY

CBS Masterworks IM-36662: *La Fiesta de la Posada* (St. Paul Chamber Orchestra), 1979.

Pro Arte CDD-352: *George Gershwin—Rhapsody in Blue* (Denver Symphony), 1987.

Pro Arte CDD-361: *Bolero* (Denver Symphony), 1987.

Pro Arte CDD-410: *Vive la France* (Denver Symphony), 1988.

Pro Arte CDD-452: *A Touch of Fiedler* (Denver Pops), 1989.

Pro Arte CDD-453: *Mussorgsky—Pictures at an Exhibition* (Denver Symphony), 1989.

GEN. BIB.: Borland, *WWAMC*; Larrick, *BET-CP*.

SMITH, WARREN I., JR. (b. 14 May 1934, Chicago, Illinois). Percussionist and drumset artist Warren Smith studied reed instruments with his father, harp with his mother, and drums with local teachers, beginning his professional career at age 15. A graduate of the University of Illinois, where he studied with *Paul Price (bachelor's, 1957), and the Manhattan School (master's, 1958), he also studied privately with Oliver Coleman, *Harold Farberman, and Coleridge Taylor Perkinson, among others. He performed on Broadway (e.g., *West Side Story*, 1968; *Lost in the Stars*, 1972; *Raisin*, 1973; the Negro Ensemble Company), and his numerous collaborators include George Russell, *Elvin Jones, Gil Evans, Nina Simone, Johnny Richards, *Tony Williams, Charles Mingus, Sam Rivers, and *Max Roach's M'Boom RE: Percussion. Smith was a 1964 charter member of the Symphony of the New World, performed in the American Symphony Orchestra, and toured Europe as music director for Janis Joplin (1969). He has appeared at major jazz festivals and as a lecturer and clinician. A published composer and author of didactic music manuals, he taught in the New York public schools (1958–68), at Third St. Settlement House (NY, 1960–67), and for the State University of New York at Purchase and at Old Westbury (1972–).

SELECTED DISCOGRAPHY

Blue Moon MRR 279182: *M'Boom Live at S.O.B.'s* (Max Roach), 1992.
Blue Note 84415: *Grant Green—The Final Comedown*, 1971.
Blue Note 84421: *Dig This* (Bobbi Humphrey), 1972.
Blue Note LA-506 H2: *The Prime Element* (Elvin Jones), 1973.
Columbia CK-48910: *Let My Children Hear Music* (Charles Mingus), 1971.
Polydor 24-4065: *Ego* (The Tony Williams Lifetime), 1971.
Sony 67397: *Miles Davis and Gil Evans—The Complete Columbia Studio Recordings*, 1996.
Soul Note SN-1059: *M'Boom—Collage* (Max Roach), 1984.
Strata-East SES 7422: *We've Been Around*, 1974.
Strata-East SES 19723: *Warren Smith—Composer's Workshop*, 1972.
Verve V6-8618: *Jimmy Smith*, 1965.
Verve V6-8691: *Kai Winding*, 1967.
GEN. BIB.: Hunt, *52nd St.*; Southern, *BDA-AAM.*

SNIDER, RONALD JOE (b. 4 Aug 1947, Rotan, Texas). Having attended North Texas State University and Mills College (CA), Ron Snider studied with Henk Badings, Pandit Mahapurush Misra, Pandit Ram Narayan, *Kalman Cherry, and *Anthony Cirone. He serves as percussionist with the Dallas Symphony and Dallas Civic Opera, appeared as soloist with the American Wind Symphony, toured the United States and South America, and has been a contributing author for *Percussive Notes*.
GEN. BIB.: Borland, *WWAMC.*

SNOW, FRANK A. (b. ca. 1866; d. ca. September 1950). Timpanist with the Sousa Band (1910–16), including the "World Tour," Frank Snow played 7 years with the Boston Municipal Band, with the Boston Symphony?, and 15 years with the Long Beach (CA) Municipal Band. Frequently mentioned in the *International Musician* (1940–50), he wrote a rudimental drum method that was published by the Leedy Drum Company. His percussive colleagues in the Long Beach Band for 23 years were O. F. Rominger and C. E. Seeley.

SNOW, WALLACE CARL "WALLY" (b. 10 Nov 1936, Maywood, California). A student of *Earl Hatch and *Murray Spivack, Hollywood percussionist Wally Snow studied drums early on with Ray Livingston and mallets with Sonny Anderson. He attended Los Angeles City College, receiving a bachelor's degree from the University of California at Los Angeles in 1959. As a member of the NBC staff orchestra (1967–73), Snow performed for various television shows, including *Dean Martin, Laugh-In, Captain & Tenille*; for the Emmy[c] and Golden Globe[c] Award shows; and for "specials" featuring the talents of Fred Astaire, Gene Kelly, Frank Sinatra, Ann-Margret, Bob Hope, and David Copperfield. He worked for Hanna-Barbera for 10 years, performed part time with the Los Angeles Philharmonic and with the Glendale and Pacific Symphonies, recorded on almost all of Ray Coniff's albums over a 30-year period, and can be heard on Frank Sinatra's *My Way* and Andy Williams' *Happy Heart* albums. Information supplied by the subject, 1996.

SOAMES, CYNTHIA ELIZABETH (b. 6 Oct 1946, Peru, Indiana). A graduate of the Cincinnati Conservatory (bachelor's, 1969) and the University of Miami (master's, 1973), Cynthia Soames served as percussionist with the Ft. Lauderdale (FL), North Carolina (1970–72), Nashville, Richmond (IN), and Indianapolis Symphonies and the Indianapolis Chamber Ensemble. She taught at Western Kentucky University (1969–70), St. Joseph's College (IN, 1970), the University of North Carolina at Chapel Hill (1971–72), and the University of Wisconsin at River Falls (1974–75). Soames also served as historian for the Percussive Arts Society (1977–81).
GEN. BIB.: Borland, *WWAMC.*

SOPH, EDWARD B. "ED" (b. 21 Mar 1945, Coronado, California). An alumnus of the legendary University of North Texas (UNT, 1963–68) "One O'Clock" Jazz Lab Band, Ed Soph matured in Houston, Texas, and worked early on with Arnett Cobb, Ray McKinley, Stan Kenton (1965), and Woody Herman (1968–71). He then relocated to New York in 1971, appearing with Dizzy Gillespie, Clark Terry (1972–80), Joe Henderson (1977), Bill Watrous (1974), David Liebman (1979), Randy Brecker, Bill Evans, Slide Hampton, and Lee Konitz. Soph teaches at Jamey Aebersold's Jazz Camps and heads the jazz percussion department at UNT (1987–   ), where he is recognized nationally as a performer, recording artist, journalist, and clinician.

SELECTED DISCOGRAPHY

Double-Time DTRCD 101: *Tribute to the Masters* (Bobby Shew), 1995.
Fantasy 9432: *Giant Steps* (Woody Herman) [Grammy® Award winner], 1973.
Heads Up HUCD 4006: *Vital Organ* (Eric Scortia), 1996.
Leaning House BB001: *Marchel's Mode* (Marchel Ivery), 1994.
Sea Breeze SB-3019: *Second Door on the Left* (Howie Smith), 1991/1995.
Wolf Tales 1001: *Looking Back on Tomorrow* (Fred Hamilton), 1994.

SELECTED VIDEOGRAPHY

Yamaha: *The Drumset: A Musical Approach*, 1984.

SELECTED BIBLIOGRAPHY

Soph, Ed. *Essential Techniques for Drum Set, Book 1.* Ft. Lauderdale, FL: Meredith Music, 1991.

GEN. BIB.: Kernfeld, *NGJ*; International Association of Jazz Educators Convention biographies; PASIC® program biographies, 1991.

SOROKA, JOHN G. (b. 22 Aug 1950, Philadelphia, Pennsylvania). A student at the Berkshire Music Center (1967–70), John Soroka received a performer's certificate from the Settlement Music School (Philadelphia) and a bachelor's degree from Temple University (1972); he also did graduate work at the Philadelphia Musical Academy (1972–73). His teachers included *Alan Abel, *Charles Owen, and *Michael Bookspan, and he was named a Tanglewood Fellow (1969–70). As a freelancer in Philadelphia (1968–73), he subbed in the Philadelphia Orchestra (1969–73) and played with the Philadelphia Lyric Opera, Grand Opera, Pennsylvania Ballet, Little Orchestra Society, and various community orchestras before securing employment as principal percussionist and associate principal timpanist with the Baltimore Symphony (1973–78). A founding member of Batterie Percussion Group (1969), Soroka has held the principal percussion and associate principal timpanist position in the Pittsburgh Symphony since 1978 and has appeared at the Grand Teton Festival (principal percussion, 1981–   ). He has taught at the Settlement Music School (1968–73), the University of Delaware (artist-lecturer, 1972–77), the Peabody Conservatory (percussion department head, 1973–78), and Carnegie-Mellon University (1978–   ). Soroka can be heard with the Pittsburgh and Baltimore Symphonies on Sony, EMI, Philips, New World, and other recording labels.

SELECTED DISCOGRAPHY

Moss Music Group D-MMG 115: *The All-Star Percussion Ensemble*, 1983.

SELECTED BIBLIOGRAPHY

Soroka, John. "John Soroka on the Cymbals, Pt. 1." *PN* XXVIII, 2 (Winter 1990): 58–60.
Soroka, John. "John Soroka on the Cymbals, Pt. 2." *PN* XXVIII, 3 (Spring 1990): 62–63.
GEN. BIB.: Borland, *WWAMC*.

SPENCER, JULIE ARLENE (b. 9 Jan 1962, Indianapolis, Indiana). A percussionist, marimbist, and composer, Julie Spencer studied early on with Jeff Nearpass in Indiana, earning a bachelor's degree (Eastman, 1985) and a master's degree in jazz and world music from the California Institute of the Arts (1990), where she was an adjunct faculty member from 1990 to 1994. She has appeared as a soloist and clinician throughout the United States, Canada, and Europe and was honored by the National Endowment for the Arts with a jazz composition fellowship in 1994. Commissioned by *Emil Richards to compose a large marimba work that utilizes his "rattle and slap" mallets, she premiered *Elim* at the 1994 Percussive Arts Society International Convention. Spencer has served as adjunct faculty since 1995 at the University of Michigan. With husband and multi-instrumentalist Gernot Blume, she has published numerous works for solo and multiple percussion, jazz combos, and big bands through Spencer-Blume Publishing. The Mike Balter Mallet Company manufactures her signature artist series "Tribeca" marimba mallets.

SELECTED DISCOGRAPHY

Capitol Records DPRO-79119: *Cal Arts Jazz Ensemble*, 1990.
Capitol Records DPRO-79263: *Cal Arts Jazz*, 1992.
Equilibrium EQ 3: *Imaginary Landscape*, 1996.
Etcetera Records KTC 1071: *Lou Harrison—Music for Guitar and Percussion*, 1990.
FGA.02.94: *Something Old, Something New* (Frank Glover), 1994.
Interworld CD 20002: *Ask*, 1992.
SBP CD001-29: *Changes Inside*, 1995.

SELECTED VIDEOGRAPHY

CPP Media/Warner Bros. PAS 9426: *The Common Ground Concert*, 1995
Interworld: *Essence of Playing Congas* (Jerry Steinholtz), 1991.

SELECTED BIBLIOGRAPHY

Spencer, Julie. "The Horizontal Concept of Marimba Technique." *PN* XXVI, 1 (Fall 1987): 38–39.
Spencer, Julie, and Gernot Blume. *The Unbook-Red*, 2nd ed./*The Unbook-Blue: 400 Original Jazz Compositions*. Ann Arbor, MI: Spencer-Blume Publishing, 1997.
Stout, Gordon. "Julie Spencer: A Brief Interview." *PN* XXIV, 4 (April 1986): 13–14.
Information supplied by the subject, 1997.

SPENCER, WILLIAM O'NEILL (b. 25 Nov 1909, Cedarville, Ohio; d. 24 Jul 1944, New York, New York). Drumset artist and singer O'Neill Spencer grew up in Springfield, Ohio, but started playing professionally in Buffalo, New York (1926). He worked with the Mills Blue Rhythm Band under Baron Lee (1931–36, later aka Lucky Millinder Orchestra), Red Allen (1935–36), and Mildred Bailey (1938–42). A brush expert with the John Kirby Band (1937–42), Spencer performed and/or recorded with Jimmie Noone (1937), Andy Kirk (1938), Nobel Sissle (1938), Johnny Dodds (1938, playing drums and washboard), Lil Armstrong, Sidney Bechet, and briefly with Louis Armstrong (1941) before dying from tuberculosis.

SELECTED DISCOGRAPHY

Circle CCD-14: *John Kirby and His Orchestra*, 1941–42.
Circle CCD-125: *Maxine Sullivan and John Kirby—The Biggest Little Band in the Land: More*, 1940–41.
Columbia CG 33557: *Boss of the Bass* (John Kirby), 1975.
Smithsonian Collection R013: *The Biggest Little Band* (John Kirby, 1937–41), 1978.
GEN. BIB.: Kernfeld, *NGJ*, by T. Dennis Brown; Korall, *DM*; Spagnardi, *GJD*.

SPERLING, JACK (b. 17 Aug 1922, Trenton, New Jersey). A drumset artist who flourished in New York and Los Angeles, Jack Sperling played with Bunny Berigan (1941–42), with a U.S. Navy band under Tex Beneke (1943–45), and in the Glenn Miller "ghost" band led by Beneke. An NBC-Hollywood staff drummer, he also worked with Les Brown (1949–53/1963/1974), Dave Pell (1953/1955/1957), Bob Crosby (1954–57/1960), Pete Fountain (1959–63, including the album *Pete Fountain Presents Jack Sperling and His Fascinatin' Rhythm*), Benny Goodman (1960), Charlie Barnet (1962/1966), and Bob Florence (1968).

SELECTED DISCOGRAPHY

Capitol T925: *I Had the Craziest Dream* (Dave Pell), 1955–57.
Coral 57170: *The Bob Cats in Hi-Fi* (Bob Crosby), 1957.

SELECTED BIBLIOGRAPHY

"Ludwig Parade of Stars." *LD*, 1961.
GEN. BIB.: Kernfeld, *NGJ*.

SPIVACK, MURRAY "MOE" (b. 6 Sep 1903, New York; d. 8 May 1994, Los Angeles, California). Inducted into the Percussive Arts Society Hall of Fame in 1991, Moe Spivack played in New York with the George Hall Orchestra and taught at *Karl Glassman's School of Drums and Timpani before moving to Los Angeles to work in early film sound at R.K.O. studios (ca. 1929) for movies that included *Rio Rita*. He employed and taught "finger technique" on snare drum and was over 90 years old when he gave *Louie Bellson the video lesson listed below.

SELECTED VIDEOGRAPHY

CPP Media VH0256: *Murray Spivack—A Lesson with Louie Bellson*, 1995.
GEN. BIB.: Cook, *LDT*, p. 169, 226.

STEELE, GLENN A. Professor of percussion at Temple University, Glenn Steele studied with *Alan Abel, *Fred Hinger, and *Charles Owen. He has performed with the Philadelphia Orchestra and Philly Pops, the Chicago Contemporary Players, the Oklahoma Symphony, and the West Point Band. Composer of *Sonata for Timpani* (Penn Oak, 1998), Steele authored the snare drum method *Percussion Learning Sequence* (1996) and created the exercise video *Musician's Body Warm-Up Program* (1990).

SELECTED DISCOGRAPHY

CRS 8219: *American Composers*, 1982.
North/South NS r 1012: *Postcards* (Kryzwicki—*Nocturne 2*), 1997.
GEN. BIB.: Larrick, *BET-CP.* Information supplied by the subject, 1999.

STERNBURG, SIMON (fl. ca. 1906–36+). Percussionist Simon Sternberg was a member of the Boston Symphony (1922–36+). He authored percussion method books, spoke German and French, and also read Latin.

SELECTED BIBLIOGRAPHY

"Big Time Ludwig Users." *LD*, 1936.
Brush, Gerome. *Boston Symphony Orchestra, 1936.* Boston: Merrymount, 1936.
Sternburg, Simon. *Drumming Made Easy.* New York: Charles Colin, 1977.
Sternburg, Simon. *Modern Drum Studies.* New York: Alfred Music Co., 1950/1988 (first printed in 1933 by Revelation Publishing).

STEVENS, LEIGH HOWARD (b. 9 Mar 1953, Orange, New Jersey). A 1975 graduate of the Eastman School with a bachelor's degree and performer's certificate, Leigh Stevens studied with *Billy Dorn, *Joe Morello, *Vida Chenoweth, and *John Beck. Having established himself as a marimba virtuoso, he gave his Town Hall (NYC) debut in 1979 and has appeared throughout the United States, Europe, and China to critical acclaim as both a soloist and a clinician. A consistent contributor as author and column editor for percussion journals, Stevens has been featured on the National Public Radio program *All Things Considered* and the Voice of America's/Arlene Francis' international broadcast *New York, New York.* He coordinated and judged the first Leigh Howard Stevens International Marimba Competition and Festival held in Asbury Park, New Jersey, in 1995. Stevens, who has been awarded three U.S. patents for marimba design, oversees mallet and keyboard percussion manufacturing and mallet music publishing, respectively, at Malletech (an independent subsidiary of the Avedis Zildjian Company) and Marimba Productions.

SELECTED DISCOGRAPHY

CRI SD-367: *Four Preludes for Marimba—William Penn*, 1976.
Delos DE 3142: *Marimba When...*, 1993.
Musical Heritage Society MHS 419489T: *Bach on Marimba*, 1987.

SELECTED BIBLIOGRAPHY

Burritt, Michael. "An Interview with Leigh Howard Stevens." *PN* XXXI, 2 (December 1992): 10–14.
Stevens, Leigh Howard. "Marimba Perspectives: Four-Mallet Grip Needed." *Modern Percussionist* I, 3 (June 1985): 30.
Stevens, Leigh Howard. *Method of Movement for Marimba*. Asbury Park, NJ: Marimba Productions, 1979.
Vogel, Lauren. "An Interview with Leigh Howard Stevens." *PN* XXI, 1 (October 1982): 66–70.
GEN. BIB.: Larrick, *BET-CP*.

STOBBE, WILLIAM R. (fl. 1886–1903). A composer of xylophone solos ("Fantasia on Irish and Scotch Melodies," Carl Fischer, 1908) and method books, William Stobbe served as timpanist for the first season of the Philadelphia Orchestra (1900–01), during which his brother, Walter H. Stobbe, performed as percussionist. Early xylophone artists Charles Daab and William Reitz both recorded Stobbe's "The Mockingbird: Fantasia for Xylophone Solo" (Carl Fischer, 1903).

SELECTED DISCOGRAPHY

Edison Blue Amberol 1514: *The Mocking Bird—Fantasia* (Charles Daab, xylophone soloist), 1912. [Also recorded by William H. Reitz on Victor: 16969-A, 1911/1925.]
Edison Blue Amberol 2052: *Irish and Scotch Melodies—Fantasia* (Charles Daab, xylophone soloist), 1913.
GEN. BIB.: Strain, *XYLO*.

STOLLER, ALVIN (b. 7 Oct 1925, New York, New York; d. 19 Oct 1992, Los Angeles, California). A drumset artist who also recorded as a singer, Alvin Stoller played on *Buddy Rich's "vocal" album and worked in New York and Hollywood, recording for television, film, and radio. His many collaborators on stage and in the studio over several decades included Erroll Garner, Ray Brown, Oscar Peterson, Billie Holiday, Ella Fitzgerald, Ben Webster, Buddy DeFranco, Art Tatum, Benny Goodman (1942), Charlie Spivak (1943–45), Tommy Dorsey (1945–47), Claude Thornhill, Harry James (1950–51), Billy May (1951–57), Coleman Hawkins (1957), and Benny Carter (1966), among many others.

SELECTED DISCOGRAPHY

Capitol T 926: *Hi-Fi Drums*, 1957.
EmArcy 36076: *Around the Horn with Maynard Ferguson*, 1955–56.
Impulse 9116: *Additions to Further Definitions* (Benny Carter), 1966.

Mercury 830 922-2: *Early Bebop* (Neal Hefti), 1946.
Pacific Jazz 4: *Sweets at the Haig* (Harry Edison), 1953.
Time 2140: *Taste of Drums*, 1969.
Verve 833 296-2: *Coleman Hawkins and Ben Webster*, 1957.
Verve MGV2009: *Buddy Rich* (vocal), 1956.
Verve MGV2027: *Charlie Barnet and His Orchestra*, 1954.
Verve MGV2096: *Woody Herman*, 1957.
Verve MGV4001-2: *Ella Fitzgerald Sings the Cole Porter Songbook*, 1956.
Verve MGV8022: *Ray Brown Big Band*, 1956.
Verve MGV8076: *Flip Phillips Sextet*, 1952.
Verve MGV8064: *Tatum-Eldridge-Stoller-Simmons Quartet*, 1955.
Verve MGV8089: *Roy Eldridge Quintet*, 1953.
Verve MGV8097: *Harry Edison*, 1956.
Verve MGV8127: *Oscar Peterson Quartet*, 1951.
Verve MGV8171: *Herb Ellis (Ellis in Wonderland?)*, 1955.
Verve MGV8206: *Stuff Smith*, 1957.
Verve MGV8261: *The Genius of Coleman Hawkins*, 1957.
Verve MGV8329: *Billie Holiday*, 1956.
Verve MGVS6165: *Buddy DeFranco*, 1957.

SELECTED BIBLIOGRAPHY

"Obituary." *Cadence* XVIII (December 1992): 109.
GEN. BIB.: Hunt, *52nd St.*; Kernfeld, *NGJ*, by Scott Yanow; Korall, *DM*.

STONE, GEORGE BURT (b. 1856; d. 1912, Boston, Massachusetts). Drum major, rudimental drummer, band director, teacher, and violinist George B. Stone founded the George B. Stone & Son, Inc., drum-manufacturing company (Everett, MA; fl. 1890–early 1930s), School of Drumming, and full-service music store, which included catalog sales. The factory's machinery had been in storage for almost 20 years when it was purchased in 1950 by Ralph G. Eames, who produced rope-tensioned drums until Joseph McSweeney bought it in 1978. Stone edited "The Drummer" column in *Jacobs' Orchestra and Band Journals*, and his original drums are now considered collector's items.

SELECTED BIBLIOGRAPHY

Cangany, Harry. "The Stone Master Model." *MD* XXI, 7 (July 1997): 154.
Obituary. *Jacobs' Orchestra Monthly* III, 3 (March 1912).
GEN. BIB.: Strain, *XYLO*.

STONE, GEORGE LAWRENCE "LARRY" "STONY" (b. 1886, Boston, Massachusetts; d. 19 Nov 1967, Boston, Massachusetts). Introduced to violin and drumming by his father, *George B. Stone, George L. Stone studied at the New England Conservatory and with *Oscar Schwar of the Philadelphia Symphony and *Harry Bower of the Boston Symphony. He joined the musicians' union in 1902 and performed as "The Wizard of the Xylophone" for the Keith Vaudeville Circuit (1910), appearing as timpanist or percussionist at the Boston Colonial Theater and with Stewart's Boston Band, the Walter Smith Broadcasting Band, the Boston Symphony (five years), and the Boston Festival and Opera Orchestras. [His colleagues in the Boston Opera Orchestra included Frankie Dodge, James N. "Jimmie" Harrington, and Tommy Hawkins.] From his father he inherited Stone & Son School of Drumming, as well as, editorship of "The Drummer" column in *Jacobs' Orchestra and Band Journal*, later writing the "Technique of Percussion" column in the *International Musician*. A charter member (and president for 15 years) of the National Association of Rudimental Drummers (NARD), Stone instructed the Marlboro, Massachusetts, Drum & Bugle Corps, which won American Legion National Championships in 1933, 1934, and 1938. Prolific author of percussion method books, he established the Stone Drum and Xylophone School of Boston, and among his students were legendary drumset artists *Joe Morello, *Sid Catlett, *Lionel Hampton, *George Wettling, and *Gene Krupa. Stone retired in 1950, selling the business to his former student Ralph G. Eames; it was subsequently purchased by Joseph McSweeney in 1978.

SELECTED BIBLIOGRAPHY

Hannum, Susan, and Rick Mattingly. "George Lawrence Stone: Dedication to Drumming." *MD* IX, 9 (September 1985): 18–21.

"In Memorium [sic]: George Lawrence Stone, 1886–1967." *LD* VIII, 1 (Spring 1968): 44.

Mattingly, Rick. "1997 PAS® Hall of Fame: George Lawrence Stone." *PN* XXXV, 6 (December 1997): 10–11.

Stone, George Lawrence. *Accents and Rebounds for the Practicing Drummer*. Boston: George B. Stone and Son, Inc., 1961.

Stone, George Lawrence. *Mallet Control*. Boston: George B. Stone and Son, Inc., 1949.

Stone, George Lawrence. *Military Drum Beats*. Boston: George B. Stone and Son, Inc., 1931.

Stone, George Lawrence. *Stick Control for the Snare Dummer*. Boston: George B. Stone and Son, Inc., 1935/1963.

GEN. BIB.: Strain, *XYLO.*

STOUT, GORDON B. (b. 5 Oct 1952, Wichita, Kansas). Marimbist, xylophonist, and composer, Gordon Stout received bachelor's (1974) and master's (1976) degrees from the Eastman School. His teachers have included *Warren Benson, Samuel Adler, *John Beck, *James Salmon, *Keiko Abe, and *Vida Chenoweth. A 1986 National Endowment for the Arts grant recipient, Stout has been a contributing author and editor for the *Percussive Notes* journal and *Sticks & Mallets* magazine and an elected member of the Percussive Arts Society board of directors. He has served as assistant music director of the Tidewater Music Festival, appeared as a lecture-recitalist at several national percussion conventions, and taught on the faculties of St. Mary's College (MD, 1976–79) and Ithaca College (NY, 1980–   ). Many of his etudes and solo compositions have secured a permanent niche in the marimba repertoire.

SELECTED DISCOGRAPHY

Crystal Records S-393: *Brian Bowman, Euphonium*, 1979.
Crystal Records S-858: *Organist David Craighead*, 1977.
Golden Crest Records CRS-4190: *Alec Wilder's. Music for Marimba and Other Instruments*, 1979.
Mercury Golden Imports SRI-75108: *Nola—Eastman Marimba Band*, 1976.
Neuma Records 450-72: *New Music Series*, vol. 2, 1989.
Peppermint Artist Productions PA7001-CD: *Perpetual—Michael Burritt*, 1991.
Soundspells Productions CD 103: *Images of Chagall—Meyer Kupferman*, 1989.
Studio 4 Productions S4P-R100: *Gordon Stout—Music for Solo Marimba*, 1977.
Studio 4 Productions S4P-R102: *Gordon Stout II*, 1979.

SELECTED BIBLIOGRAPHY

Stewart, William R., and Donald Bick. "An Interview with Gordon Stout." *PN* XVI, 1 (Fall 1978): 27–28.
Stout, Gordon. *Etudes for Marimba, Book III.* Van Nuys, CA: Alfred, 1990.
Stout, Gordon. *Five Etudes for Marimba, Book I.* Fort Lauderdale, FL: Paul Price Publications, 1975.
GEN. BIB.: Larrick, *BET-CP.*

STRAIGHT, EDWARD B. "ED" "EDDIE" (b. ca. 1872; d. ca. March 1949, Chicago, Illinois). Charter member of the National Association of Rudimental Drummers (NARD, 1933), Ed Straight played on vaudeville for a youthful George M. Cohan in the family act "The Four Cohans" (dad, mom, son, daughter); for Williams and Walker, George Primrose, and Barney Fagin; and for W. C. Fields' tramp juggler act (ca. 1890). During the early 1900s in Chicago he managed the drum department at the Dixie Music House (est. 1902, later aka Frank's Drum Shop; see *Lishon, Maurice).

SELECTED DISCOGRAPHY

Ludwig Drum Co. 14-100/WFL-301: *The 13 Essential Drum Rudiments*, 1948/1960 (includes J. Burns Moore, Edward B. Straight, William F. Ludwig, Sr. and Jr.).

SELECTED BIBLIOGRAPHY

Rogers, Lisa. "The Straight Way." *PN* XXXV, 3 (June 1997): 84–85.
Stone, George Lawrence. "Technique of Percussion." *IM* (July 1949): 19.

Straight, Edward B. *The Straight System of Modern Drumming*, Books 1–4, Chicago: Edward B. Straight, 1909/1923 [reprinted later by Frank's Drum Shop in Chicago].

STREET, WILLIAM G. "BILL" (b. 30 Mar 1895, Hamilton, Ontario, Canada; d. 2 Aug 1973, Rochester, New York). William Street began his professional career at the age of 15 performing after school for theaters in the Rochester, New York, area and in later years at the famous Hippodrome and Piccadilly Theaters. In 1922 he became a charter member of a core group of musicians that would thereafter be known by various names, including the Eastman Theater Orchestra, the Rochester Philharmonic, the Rochester Civic Orchestra, and the Rochester Pops. First as principal percussionist, then as principal timpanist in 1932 (at the behest of Fritz Reiner), Street performed with the "Philharmonic" until 1956; he retired from the "Civic" in 1958. During his long tenure he and his brother, Stanley (both students of *George Hamilton Green), were featured artists on solos, in duets, and in chamber settings that had very popular audience appeal. Recruited by Howard Hanson as professor of percussion at the Eastman School, he taught there for four decades (1927–67) and influenced generations of percussionists who have filled chairs in many major American orchestras, bands, and university teaching positions. Street was inducted into the Percussive Arts Society Hall of Fame in 1976.

SELECTED BIBLIOGRAPHY

Cahn, Willam L. "Rochester's Classic Percussion: A Short History of the Percussion Section of the Rochester Philharmonic Orchestra." *PN* XXX, 5 (June 1992): 64–74.
"In Memoriam." *PN* XII, 1 (Fall 1973): 11.
"William G. Street Inducted into P.A.S. Hall of Fame." *PN* XV, 2 (Winter 1977): 17.
GEN. BIB.: Larrick, *BET-CP*; Strain, *XYLO.*

STRESLIN, WILLIAM. William Streslin appeared as solo xylophonist with Arthur Pryor's Band, performed with the New York Philharmonic and New York Symphony, and penned a xylophone method book.
GEN. BIB.: Strain, *XYLO.*

STUBBS, THOMAS "TOM" (b. Hutchinson, Kansas?). Cymbal specialist and assistant timpanist with the St. Louis Symphony since 1970, Tom Stubbs graduated from the Juilliard School (1970), where he studied with *Saul Goodman. A private student of *Elden "Buster" Bailey, he also attended the Aspen School (1968–70), where his teachers included *Roland Kohloff, *George Gaber, *Richard Holmes, and Gary Werdesheim. He has appeared with the New Music Circle and Discovery Series in St. Louis, been featured on the premiere recording of Michael Colgrass' "Déjà Vu," and performed as principal timpanist for the St. Louis Symphony's 1985 European tour. Stubbs has taught at the St. Louis Conservatory, St. Louis University, University of Missouri at St. Louis, University of Missouri at Columbia, Aspen Music Festival, and Indiana University (1994–96). He can be heard on RCA, Angel Telarc, Vox, New World, and Nonesuch recording labels.

SELECTED DISCOGRAPHY

New Music Circle NMC-1985: *Reflections*, 1982/1985.
New World NW318-2: *Works by Colgrass and Druckman* (St. Louis Symphony), 1983.
Aaspen Music Festival faculty biographies, 1998; PASIC® program biographies, 1987.

STUMPFF, JOHANN C. N. (fl. ca. 1815–21, Amsterdam, Netherlands). In 1815 Johann Stumpff developed timpani (patented 1821) that changed pitch by rotating the entire bowl.

SELECTED BIBLIOGRAPHY

Beck, John H., ed. *Encyclopedia of Percussion.* New York: Garland Publishing, 1995. S.v. "The Kettledrum" by Edmund A. Bowles.
Ludwig, William F. *Ludwig Timpani Instructor.* Chicago: Ludwig Drum Co., 1957.

SUMARSAM (b. 27 Jul 1944, Bojonegoro, East Java, Indonesia). A gamelan performing artist, composer, and puppeteer since 1952 who earned a teaching diploma (1964) and bachelor's degree (1968) from the Indonesian National Music Conservatory (Surakarta), Sumarsam came to the United States in 1972. He received a master's degree (1976) from Wesleyan University (CT) and a Ph.D. (1992) from Cornell University. He has taught gamelan music at the Indonesian National Conservatory (1966–71), at Williams College (MA), at the University of Wisconsin at Madison, in Australia, and at Wesleyan University (CT, 1972–present). A veteran of concert tours in Indonesia, Australia, Japan, and the United States, he has contributed articles to professional journals.

SELECTED BIBLIOGRAPHY

Sumarsam. *Gamelan: Cultural Interaction and Musical Development in Central Java.* Chicago: University of Chicago Press, 1995.

SZULC, ROMAN JOSEF (b. 21 May 1894, Warsaw, Poland). A former faculty member at the New England Conservatory, Roman Szulc came to the

United States around 1935, serving as timpanist with the Boston Symphony until 1952.

SELECTED BIBLIOGRAPHY

Brush, Gerome. *Boston Symphony Orchestra, 1936.* Boston: Merrymount Press, 1936.
"Percussion in Our Orchestras." *IM* (June 1949):' 24–25 (photo).

T

TACHOIR, JERRY (b. 7 Aug 1955, McKeesport, Pennsylvania). Grammy®-nominated mallet artist (vibes, marimba, and mallet synthesizer) Jerry Tachoir graduated from the Berklee College (bachelor's degree), has appeared with the American Wind Symphony, Pittsburgh Symphony, and International Symphony (Switzerland), and has been a clinician since 1972. His group, Tachoir, released its fifth recording (*Beyond Stereotype*), and his music can be heard on National Public Radio's *Morning Edition*, CBS sports broadcasts, and many North American radio stations. A journalist and method book author, Tachoir has performed in the United States, Canada, and Europe and at the Ottawa, Montreal, North Sea, Montreux, and Mellon (Pittsburgh, PA) Jazz Festivals. He has taught at Berklee and Belmont College (Nashville, TN).

SELECTED DISCOGRAPHY

Avita 1006: *Tachoir Vision (Tash-wah)*, ca. 1990.
Avita 1-1002/I.T.I. Records JL-012: *Canvas* (Grammy® Award nominee), 1981/1984.
Klavier KD 77017: *La Bamba* (O-Zone Percussion Group), 1996.
Trutone 520462: *Forces*, 1978.

SELECTED VIDEOGRAPHY

DCI: *Percussion Mallet Techniques*, 1988.

SELECTED BIBLIOGRAPHY

Tachoir, Jerry. *Contemporary Mallet Method—An Approach to the Vibraphone and Marimba*. Hendersonville, TN: Riohcat Music.
PASIC® program biographies, 1998.

TATE, GRADY (b. 14 Jan 1932, Durham, North Carolina). A drumset artist who has also recorded as a singer and worked as an actor, Grady Tate began drums at 5, studying jazz drumset styles during military service (U.S. Air Force, 1951–55). He attended North Carolina College and has played with Wild Bill Davis, Quincy Jones (New York, ca. 1963), Oliver Nelson, Donald Byrd, Duke Ellington, Stan Getz, Count Basie, Lena Horne, Miles Davis, Peggy Lee, Kenny Burrell, Sarah Vaughan, Monty Alexander (1985), and Jimmy Smith, among many others.

SELECTED DISCOGRAPHY

A&M/Horizon 3023: *Walking in Space* (Quincy Jones), 1969.
Arbors ARCD 19152: *Jane Jarvis Jams*, 1995.
Audiophile ACD-254: *Barbara Carroll—Old Friends*, 1989.
Audiophile ACD-258: *Jane Jarvis Trio—Cut Glass*, 1990.
Blue Note 57729: *Bob Dorough—Right On My Way Home*, 1997.
Blue Note 84188: *I'm Tryin' to Get Home* (Donald Byrd), 1964.
Blue Note 84286: *The Look of Love* (Stanley Turrentine), 1968.
Blue Note 84415: *Grant Green—The Final Comedown*, 1971.
Blue Note BT 85125: *Go For Whatcha Know* (Jimmy Smith), 1986.
Blue Note BTDK 85117: *One Night with Blue Note Preserved*, 1985.
Blue Note CDP 7 46100-2: *Joyride* (Stanley Turrentine), 1965.
Blue Note LA024-F: *Sophisticated Lou* (Lou Donaldson), 1972.
Blue Note LA143-F: *From the Depths of My Soul* (Marlena Shaw), 1973.
Concord 293: *Don't Forget the Blues* (Ray Brown), 1985.
Enja 3025: *Blues for Sarka* (New York Jazz Quartet), 1978.
Impulse 75/A (S)9101: *More Blues and Abstract Truth* (Oliver Nelson), 1964.
Jazz Club 2M056-64824: *Blackout 1977* (Lionel Hampton), 1977.
Muse 5290: *The 3 R's* (Red Rodney), 1979.
Musical Heritage Society MHS 7514A: *Ain't But A Few Of Us Left* (Milt Jackson), 1987.
Pablo 2312103: *Silent Partner* (Oscar Peterson), 1979.
Pablo OJC CD-444-2: *Zoot Sims and the Gershwin Brothers*, 1975.
Telarc CD-83308: *Lionel Hampton and the Golden Men of Jazz*, 1991.
Telarc CD-83313: *Just Jazz—Live at the Blue Note (Lionel Hampton and the Golden Men of Jazz)*, 1992.
Verve V6-8610: *Wes Montgomery*, 1964.
Verve V6-8612: *Kenny Burrell*, 1965.
Verve V6-8637: *Cal Tjader*, 1966.
Verve V6-8643: *Astrud Gilberto*, 1965.
Verve V6-8657: *Kai Winding*, 1966.
Verve V6-8678/821577-2: *The Dynamic Duo* (Jimmy Smith), 1966.
Verve V6-8680: *Johnny Hodges*, 1966.
Verve V6-8693/815054-2: *Sweet Rain* (Stan Getz), 1967.
Verve V6-8709: *Now Please Don't You Cry, Beautiful Edith* (Rahsaan Roland Kirk), 1967.
Verve V6-8791: *Phil Woods*, 1969.

Who's Who In Jazz WWLP 21004: *Lionel Hampton Presents Earl "Fatha" Hines*, 1977.

SELECTED BIBLIOGRAPHY

Davis, Steve. *Drummers: Masters of Time*. New Albany, IN: Aebersold Music, Inc., 1986.
GEN. BIB.: Hunt, *52nd St.*; Kernfeld, *NGJ*, by J. Kent Williams.

TAYLOR, ARTHUR S. "ART" (b. 6 Apr 1929, New York, New York; d. 6 Feb 1995). Drummer and author Art Taylor was leader of Taylor's Wailers (1950s/1980s). In 1963 he moved to Paris, where he worked with Johnny Griffin, Don Byas, Dexter Gordon, Coleman Hawkins, Bud Powell, Miles Davis, Thelonius Monk, Art Farmer, Charlie Parker, and the Red Garland Trio with John Coltrane. While in Paris he taught at *Kenny Clarke's drum school, then moved back to New York in 1981, recording with his own group and hosting a radio talk show (1984).

SELECTED DISCOGRAPHY

Atlantic 1311-2: *Giant Steps* (John Coltrane), 1959.
Blue Note 56586: *Orgy in Rhythm,* vosl. 1–2, 1957.
Blue Note 57302: *The Squirrel* (Dexter Gordon), 1967.
Blue Note 81575: *City Lights* (Lee Morgan), 1957.
Blue Note 84004/84005: *A Message from Blakey—Holiday for Skins*, 1958.
Blue Note 84006: *Blues in Trinity* (Dizzy Reece), 1958.
Blue Note 84007: *Off to the Races* (Donald Byrd), 1958.
Blue Note 84018: *Davis Cup* (Walter Davis, Jr.), 1959.
Blue Note 84019: *Byrd in Hand* (Donald Byrd), 1959.
Blue Note 84023: *Star Bright* (Dizzy Reece), 1959.
Blue Note 84024: *Swing, Swang, Swingin'!* (Jackie McLean), 1959.
Blue Note 84033: *Soundin' Off* (Dizzy Reece), 1960.
Blue Note 84038: *Capuchin Swing* (Jackie McLean), 1960.
Blue Note 84047: *A. T.'s Delight*, 1960.
Blue Note 84176: *One Flight Up* (Dexter Gordon), 1964.
Blue Note 84424: *Z. T.'s Blues* (Stanley Turrentine), 1961.
Blue Note B21Y 81504: *The Amazing Bud Powell,* vol. 2 (1949–53), 1958.
Blue Note BLP1545: *Wailing with Lou* (Lou Donaldson), 1957.
Blue Note BLP1565: *Cliff Jordan*, 1957.
Blue Note BLP1567: *The Opener* (Curtis Fuller), 1957.
Blue Note BLP1568: *Hank Mobley*, 1957.
Blue Note BLP1572: *Bone & Bari* (Curtis Fuller), 1957.
Blue Note BLP1591: *Lou Takes Off* (Lou Donaldson), 1957.
Blue Note CDP 7 46142-2: *Jackie's Bag/Street Singer* (Jackie McLean), 1960.
Blue Note CDP 7 46508-2: *Candy* (Lee Morgan), 1957.
Blue Note CDP 7 46533-2: *Bass on Top* (Paul Chambers), 1957.
Blue Note CDP 7 46819-2: *Sonny's Crib* (Sonny Clark), 1957.

Blue Note CDP 7 46824-2: *Flight to Jordan* (Duke Jordan), 1960.

Blue Note (J) BNJ61006: *Hank Mobley Quintet*, 1957.

Blue Note (J) GFX-3062: *Tippin' the Scales* (Jackie McLean), 1962.

Columbia CK 40784: *Miles Ahead* (Miles Davis), 1957.

DCC Compact Classics GZS-1046: *Soultrane* (John Coltrane), 1958/1993.

Enja 7017 2: *Mr. A. T.*, 1992.

Jazz Life 2673212: *Bud Powell in Europe*, 1988.

Mosiac MD6-174: *The Complete Atlantic Recordings of Lennie Tristano, Lee Konitz, and Warne Marsh*, 1997.

Mosaic MR4-106: *True Blue* (Tina Brooks), 1960.

Mosaic MR5-116: *Bud Powell Trio*, 1953.

Mosaic MR5-118: *Herb Nichols Trio*, 1955.

New Jazz 8279: *4, 5 and 6* (Jackie McLean), 1983.

OJC 013 2: *The Happy Blues* (Gene Ammons), 1956/1969.

OJC 129: *Jammin' in Hi-Fi* (Gene Ammons), 1992.

OJC 211: *Jammin' with Gene* (Gene Ammons), 1991.

OJC 6005: *The 60s*, vol. 1 (Gene Ammons), 1960/1988.

Prestige OJC 651: *The Big Sound* (Gene Ammons), 1958.

Prestige OJC CD-012-2: *Miles Davis Quintet/Sextet*, 1955.

Prestige OJC CD-1852-2: *Taylor's Tenors*, 1959.

Prestige PCD-24097-2: *Four Trombones—The Debut Recordings* (J. J. Johnson et al.), 1953/1990.

Prestige PRLP7123/GZS-1098: *Traneing In* (John Coltrane), 1957/1996.

Progressive PRO-7001: *The George Wallington Quintet at the Cafe Bohemia*, 1955.

Riverside RLP-1138: *Thelonius Monk Orchestra at Town Hall*, 1959.

Riverside RLP12-305: *Five by Monk by Five* (Thelonious Monk), 1959.

Roulette 7243 8 37137: *Bud Plays Bird* (Bud Powell), 1957-58/1996.

Sony 67397: *Miles Davis and Gil Evans—The Complete Columbia Studio Recordings*, 1996.

Verve 314 519 677: *Wailin' at the Vanguard*, 1993.

Verve 314 527 631: *Damn!* (Jimmy Smith), 1995.

Verve MGV8007: *Charlie Parker Plays Cole Porter*, 1954.

SELECTED BIBLIOGRAPHY

Gitler, Ira. "Art Taylor: A Look at Mr. Cool." *DB* XXVII, 21 (13 Oct 1960): 23.

Mattingly, Rick. "Arthur Taylor: Jazz Elder Statesman Lives On." *MD* XVIII, 5 (May 1994): 20–25.

Primack, Bret. "Arthur Taylor: Still Wailing after All These Years." *JazzTimes* XXIII, 9 (November 1993): 40–41.

Taylor, Arthur. *Note and Tones: Musician to Musician Interviews*. New York: Da Capo, 1993.

Van Horn, Rick. "In Memoriam: Art Taylor." *MD* XIX, 6 (June 1995): 126.

GEN. BIB.: Hunt, *52nd St.*

THAMM, DUANE (b. 11 Jul 1927, Oak Park, Illinois). A student of *Bobby Christian, *Ed Straight, *José Bethancourt, *Marjorie Hyams, *Roy Knapp,

Walter Dellers, and *Ed Metzenger, Duane Thamm was a featured member of *Dick Schory's Percussion Pops Orchestra and has appeared on stage and television with Barbra Streisand, Henry Mancini, Roger Williams, and Andy Williams, among others. He taught percussion at Elmhurst College (ca. 1978); his percussion solos and ensembles are published by Creative Music.

SELECTED BIBLIOGRAPHY

Thamm, Duane. *The Complete Xylophone and Marimba Method.* Chicago: Creative Music, 1966.
Ludwig Drum Company clinician biographies, 1968.

THÄRICHEN, WERNER (b. 18 Aug 1921, Neuhardenberg, Germany). A timpanist of the Berlin Philharmonic, Werner Thärichen studied piano, improvisation, and in 1936 composition, conducting, and timpani (with Franz Krüger) at the Berlin Hochschule für Musik. From 1939 to 1940, he performed with the Berlin Folk Opera; and despite being drafted into the military in 1940, he served as organist and choir director in Metz in 1942. Following his discharge, he performed with the Hamburg City Opera (1945–48) before securing a position with the Berlin Philharmonic in 1948. From 1954 to 1957, and 1966 to 1969, he belonged to the orchestra's advisory council (Fünferrat), serving as manager from 1957 to 1966. In this leadership capacity he helped rebuild the orchestra by leading many labor negotiations with the Senate in Berlin, securing wage contract agreements. Thärichen composed many works for various instruments, including his *Timpani Concerto*, Op. 34 (Bote and Bock, 1954), which he has performed in Germany and abroad. In 1960 he was honored by the city of Berlin for his work with and devotion to the Berlin Philharmonic, and in 1964 he received the Robert Schumann Prize from the city of Düsseldorf. He has appeared as conductor with various well-known orchestras in Germany and Japan and presented timpani and percussion lectures in 1966 at the Musashino Music School and Tokyo University, where he was appointed an honorary professor in 1970.
GEN. BIB.: Avgerinos, *KB.*

THIGPEN, EDMUND "ED" (b. 28 Dec 1930, Chicago, Illinois). Son of veteran drummer Ben Thigpen, drumset artist, educator, and author Ed Thigpen matured in Los Angeles and was initially a pianist who started drums around age 10, studying with Ralph Collier. After early professional engagements with Buddy Collette (1948) and service in the Eighth U.S. Army Band (Korea), he performed with Bud Powell, Billy Taylor (1956–58), and Oscar Peterson (until 1965). Thigpen, Ray Brown, Oscar Peterson, and Phil Nimmons founded the Advanced School of Contemporary Music in Toronto, Canada, in 1959—the same year Thigpen received *Down Beat* magazine's Critics' New Star Award. Between two separate stints with Ella Fitzgerald (second time, 1968), he moved to Los Angeles (1967), where he was associated with Johnny Mathis, Peggy

Lee, and Oliver Nelson and did freelance studio work. In 1972 Thigpen relocated to Copenhagen, where he has taught at the Denmark Music Conservatory since 1974 and led his own groups throughout Europe. A master of brush technique who appeared on the television show *The Subject Is Jazz* and at numerous jazz festivals worldwide, he has collaborated with a bevy of jazz greats, including Dorothy Donegan, Kenny Drew, Teddy Wilson, Ernie Wilkins, Hank Jones, Art Farmer, Johnny Hodges, Lennie Tristano, Sonny Stitt, among others. Thigpen has given clinics and masterclasses throughout the United States, Europe, and Asia and has authored numerous books and articles, including the rhythm primer *Rhythm Brought to Life*.

SELECTED DISCOGRAPHY

Blue Note BLP1517: *Patterns in Jazz* (Gil Melle), 1956.
BR-5030/BCP-6066: *Winner's Circle* (John Coltrane), 1957.
Concord Jazz CJ 422: *The River* (Monty Alexander), 1990.
Just A Memory 9507: *Oscar Peterson Trio Live at CBC Studios*, 1960.
Limetree 24: *Saturday Night* (Monty Alexander), 1988.
Mercury MG-20975: *Oscar Peterson Trio Plus One*, 1964.
Milestone 8264: *Dream Session—The All-Stars Play Miles Davis Classics*, 1996.
Soul Note 121026-2: *Manhattan* (Art Farmer), 1981.
Verve 821 987-2: *Oscar Peterson Plays the Cole Porter Book*, 1959.
Verve 849 396-2: *Sonny Stitt Sits In with Oscar Peterson*, 1959.
Verve V/V6-8663: *Out of the Storm*, 1966.
Verve 810 047-2: *We Get Requests* (Oscar Peterson), 1997.
Verve MGVS6020: *Blossom Dearie*, 1958.
Verve MGVS6116 et al.: *The Trio—Live from Chicago* (Oscar Peterson), 1959–62.
Verve V6-8454: *West Side Story* (Oscar Peterson), 1962.
Verve V6-8606: *Oscar Peterson Trio*, 1964.

SELECTED VIDEOGRAPHY

DCI Music Video, Inc: *Ed Thigpen "On Jazz Drumming,"* 1985.
Interworld VH0147: *Ed Thigpen—The Essence of Brushes*, 1991.

SELECTED BIBLIOGRAPHY

Bassler, Moss. "The Creative Ed Thigpen." *LD* I, 2 Spring 1962): 3–4.
DeMichael, Don. "Edmund Thigpen: Gentleman and Jazzman." *DB* XXVIII, 18 (31 Aug 1961): 17.
Mattingly, Rick. "They Keep Drumming, and Drumming, and...The Art of Percussive Longevity." *DB* LX, 11 (November 1993): 25–26.
McNamara, Helen. "Ed Thigpen: On the Move." *DB* XXXIV, 6 (23 Mar 1967): 18–19.
Soph, Ed. "Ed Thigpen." *PN* XXIII, 2 (January 1985): 22–25.
Thigpen, Ed, and Ray Brown. "The Rhythm Section." *LD* IV, 1 (Spring 1964): 6–8.
Thigpen, Ed. *The Sound of Brushes*. Miami, FL: CPP/Belwin, 1992.
GEN. BIB.: Spagnardi, *GJD*.

THOMPSON, HAROLD J. "TOMMY" (b. Akron, Ohio; d. 5 Feb 1968, Massachusetts Turnpike). Tommy Thompson embraced drums at the age of 12, studying with *Charles Wilcoxon. He later attended the Cincinnati Conservatory and performed eight years with the Cincinnati Symphony before joining the Boston Symphony (1953–1968) as a cymbal specialist.

SELECTED BIBLIOGRAPHY

"Boston Symphony Cymbalist Killed in Auto Accident." *School Musician* XXXIX (April 1968): 88.
"Closing Chord—Harold (Tommy) Thompson." *IM* LXVI, 10 (April 1968): 14.
"In Memoriam." *PN* VI, 3 (nd): 17.
"Obituary." *Instrumentalist* XXII (June 1968): 82.

TILLES, ROBERT "BOB" (b. 14 Mar 1920, Chicago, Illinois; d. 7 May 1976, Chicago, Illinois). A student of *José Bethancourt, *Henry Adler, *Otto Kristufek, *Marjorie Hyams, and *John P. Noonan, Bob Tilles served with the 346th Army Service Force Band for three and one-half years during WWII, studying at Midwestern Conservatory of Music after the war and graduating from the *Roy Knapp School. For 13 years he worked as a staff percussionist for WBBM-CBS (Chicago) and played on NBC, Mutual Broadcasting, television (*Ed Sullivan*, *Arthur Godfrey*, *In Town Tonight*) and radio shows in addition to recording for many major labels. His various collaborators on stage or in the studio included Sammy Davis, Jr., Nat "King" Cole, Sarah Vaughan, Tony Bennett, Ella Fitzgerald, Duke Ellington, Errol Garner, Edie Gorme, Steve Lawrence, Louis Armstrong, Jack Benny, Bing Crosby, Phil Harris, and Bob Hope, among many others.

Tilles was percussion department head at De Paul University, where he also conducted the percussion ensemble. He taught at the Knapp School of Music for 11 years before joining De Paul's faculty. A former member of the board of directors for the Percussive Arts Society, he was a regular columnist for *Percussionist*, *Percussive Notes*, and the *Ludwig Drummer*. *Down Beat* magazine cited him as "One of America's Foremost College Percussion Instructors and Clinicians."

SELECTED BIBLIOGRAPHY

"Bob Tilles: A Memorial Tribute." *PN* XV, 1 (Fall 1976): 16.
"Percussion Personalities." *Percussionist* IV, 3 (March 1967): 151–152.
Tilles, Bob. *Practical Improvisation*. Rockville Centre, NY: Belwin, 1967.
Tilles, Bob. *Practical Percussion Studies*. New York: Adler/Belwin, 1962.
Tilles, Bob. "The Show Drummer." *LD* II, 1 (Fall 1962): 6–8.
Information supplied by Jacqueline Tilles, 1999.

TJADER, CALLEN RADCLIFFE, JR., "CAL" (b. 16 Jul 1925, St. Louis, Missouri; d. 5 May 1982, Manila, Philippines). Drummer for Dave Brubeck

(1949–51) who switched to vibraphone in George Shearing's group (1953), Cal Tjader attended San Francisco State University and led his own groups, which musically bridged jazz and Latin styles. He won a Grammy® Award (1980) for "Best Latin Album" [*La Onda Va Bien*, Concord 113 (1979)] and was nominated for a Grammy® in 1981 for *Gozamel Pero Ya*.

SELECTED DISCOGRAPHY

Concord 159: *The Shining Sea*, 1981.
Concord 176: *A Fuego Vivo*, 1981.
Concord 295: *The Sound of Picante* (Monty Alexander), 1986.
Fantasy 3-17: *Cal Tjader Plays Afro-Cuban*, 1954.
Fantasy 3211: *Cal Tjader Plays Tjazz*, 1955.
Fantasy 3239: *The Octet* (Dave Brubeck), 1946/1991.
Fantasy 3262: *Más Ritmo Caliente*, 1957.
Fantasy 3266: *Cal Tjader—Stan Getz Sextet*, 1958.
Fantasy 8038: *Concert by the Sea*, 1959.
Fantasy 8054: *West Side Story*, 1960.
Fantasy/OJC 271: *Mambo with Tjader*, 1973.
Fantasy/OJC 274: *Tjader Plays Mambo*, 1954/1996
Fantasy/OJC 642: *Latin Kick*, 1959/1991.
Fantasy/OJC 643: *Latin Concert*, 1958/1991.
Galaxy 5107: *Breathe Easy*, 1977.
Savoy 9036: *Vibist*, 1953.
Verve (E) VSP35/36: *George Shearing*, 1949–53.
Verve V6-8419: *Cal Tjader*, 1961.
Verve V6-8459: *Cal Tjader Quartet*, 1962.
Verve V6-8470: *Cal Tjader*, 1962.
Verve V6-8472: *Anita O'Day and Cal Tjader*, 1962.
Verve V6-8507: *Cal Tjader with Lalo Schifrin's Orchestra*, 1963.
Verve V6-8531/8575: *Cal Tjader*, 1963.
Verve V6-8585: *Warm Wave*, 1964.
Verve V6-8614: *Soul Sauce*, 1964.
Verve V6-8626: *Cal Tjader*, 1965.
Verve V6-8637: *Cal Tjader*, 1966.
Verve V6-8651: *Cal Tjader and Eddie Palmieri*, 1966.
Verve V6-8671/8730/8769: *Cal Tjader*, 1967.

SELECTED BIBLIOGRAPHY

"Closing Chord—Callen 'Cal' Tjader." *IM* LXXXI, 1 (July 1982): 12.
Siders, Harvey. "The Latinization of Cal Tjader." *DB* XXXIII, 18 (8 Sep 1966): 21–23.
GEN. BIB.: Kernfeld, *NGJ*, by John Storm Roberts.

TORO, EFRAIN (b. Puerto Rico). At age 21, Latin percussionist and drumset artist Efrain Toro moved to Boston, where he attended the New England Conservatory and studied with *Alan Dawson. After relocating to Los Angeles in 1979, he recorded television scores, film soundtracks, and albums with such artists as Bette Midler, Placido Domingo, Chicago, Heart, Stan Getz, and Los Lobos. Toro has taught at Hollywood's Musician Institute subsidiary, Percussion Institute of Technology (PIT), for more than 16 years.

SELECTED DISCOGRAPHY

Contemporary S-14005: *Peaceful Heart, Gentle Spirit* (Chico Freeman), 1980.
PASIC® program biographies, 1995.

TORREBRUNO, LUIGI. First timpanist for 21 years with the orchestra of La Scala (Milan, Italy), Luigi Torrebruno taught for 17 years at the Verdi Conservatory in Milan and 4 years at the Paganini Conservatory in Genoa. In 1977 he designed a new model of timpani in which four drums were joined by one resonating chamber.

SELECTED BIBLIOGRAPHY

"Percussion Around the World." *PN* XVI, 1 (Fall 1977): 25.
Torrebruno, Luigi. "The Composite Timpano: The New Family of Timpani in the Modern Orchestra," ed. by Kristen Shiner. *PN* XXII, 5 (July 1984): 68–69.
Torrebruno, Luigi. *Il Timpano.* Italy: G. Ricordi, 1954.

TOUGH, DAVID "DAVE" "DAVEY" (b. 26 Apr 1908, Oak Park, Illinois; d. 9 Dec 1948, Newark, New Jersey). A drumset performer with Bud Freeman, Jimmy McPartland, Frank Teschemacher, Husk O'Hare's Wolverines (c. 1926), and the Austin High Gang in Chicago, Dave Tough started playing drums as a Boy Scout, was influenced by watching *Baby Dodds on Chicago's South Side, and by age 15 was playing professionally. From 1927 to 1929, he played in Belgium and France, becoming acquainted with F. Scott Fitzgerald, the Prince of Wales, and others from the artistic circles of 1920s Paris. He recorded in Germany and performed on the return cruise to the United States.

Supposedly a student of *Ed Straight and *Roy Knapp, Tough could read music. He moved to New York, where he played with, among others, Tommy Dorsey (1936–39+), *Red Norvo, Bunny Berigan, Benny Goodman (1938/1940–41) and Red Nichols, Joe Marsala, Artie Shaw (1941–44, including Shaw's U.S. Navy service band in the South Pacific), Woody Herman's "First Herd" (1944–45), Charlie Spivak, Charlie Ventura, and Jack Teagarden. His cymbal-focused style influenced other drummers; he reportedly never took solos, was not a "showman," and had very little technique. The author of *Paradiddle Studies*, Tough won *Down Beat* and *Metronome* polls, was cited in *Esquire* for his drumming, and traveled with Jazz at the Philharmonic near the end of his career.

Highly intelligent, he was tormented by the lack of familial support and validation for his jazz lifestyle, which included his interracial relationship with Casey Major. He held no interest in percussion performance beyond the drumset and was also a frustrated writer who suffered from poor health exacerbated by epilepsy and alcoholism. Tough spelled *Gene Krupa briefly at *Metronome* magazine, writing drum columns [e.g., "The Effects of Chewing Gum on Swing Drumming" (August 1937)] and an article for the *Esquire 1947 Jazz Book* ("Three Ways to Smoke a Pipe").

SELECTED DISCOGRAPHY

Bluebird AXM2-5549: *The Complete Tommy Dorsey*, vols. 2–6 (1936–38), 1977–81.
Columbia: "Prince of Wails" (Bud Freeman), 1940.
Columbia CK40846: *Genius of the Electric Guitar* (Charlie Christian), 1939.
Columbia CK44108: *The Thundering Herds* (Woody Herman), 1945.
Harmony HL 7046: *Bud Freeman All-Star Jazz*, 1961.
Jazz Information CAH 3000: *Bunny Berigan, the 1936 Sessions,* vol. 1, 1986.
Masters of Jazz, Media 7: *Anthology of Jazz Drumming,* vols. 1–3, 1904–38.
Mercury 830-968-2: *Small Herd* (Chubby Jackson), 1945.
RCA/Bluebird AXK2-5567: *The Complete Benny Goodman*, vols. 5–8 (1937–39), 1978–88.
RCA/Bluebird AXK2-5576: *The Complete Artie Shaw*, vols. 5–6 (1941–45), 1981.
RCA Victor LPT-1020: *My Concerto* (Artie Shaw), 1955.
RCA Victor VPS 6062: *This Is Artie Shaw,* vol. 2, 1972.
Sunbeam SB 137: *Red Nichols featuring Benny Goodman*, 1973.
Verve MGV8132: *Charlie Ventura*, 1947.

SELECTED VIDEOGRAPHY

DCI VH0248: *Legends of Jazz Drumming,* pt. 1 (1920–50), 1996.

SELECTED BIBLIOGRAPHY

Brubaker, Robert L. *Making Music Chicago Style.* Chicago: Chicago Historical Society, 1985.
Feather, Leonard. "The Dave Tough Story." *DB* XX, 13 (1 July 1953): 21.
Fish, Scott Kevin. "Profile of a Legend: Dave Tough." *MD* (January/February 1979): 51.
"From the Past: Dave Tough." *MD* XIX, 7 (July 1995): 116–117.
Shultz, Thomas. "A History of Jazz Drumming." *Percussionist* XVI, 3 (Spring/Summer 1979): 114–115.
GEN. BIB.: Hunt, *52nd St.*; Korall, *DM*; Spagnardi, *GJD*.

TUNDO, SAMUEL A. "SYMPHONY SAM" (b. 25 Apr 1937, Detroit, Michigan). After attending Wayne State University (1955–59) and studying with Jack Ledingham and Arthur Cooper [principal percussionist with Detroit who retired in 1964], percussionist Sam Tundo joined the Florida Symphony (1959–61). He toured with the North Carolina Symphony in 1961 and performed with the Santa Fe Opera (principal timpanist and percussionist, 1962–68). Following employment with the New Orleans Symphony (1961–68), he joined the Detroit Symphony—a position he has held since 1968. During 1969–71 Tundo performed (and recorded on the London label) with the rock group Symphonic Metamorphosis, which consisted of musicians from the Detroit Symphony. Previously co-owner of the percussion shop Percussion World, Inc. (1976–85), he has served on the faculty of Wayne State University since 1988. Tundo can be heard with the Detroit Symphony conducted by Neemi Jarvi and Antal Dorati on both Chandos and London Decca labels.

GEN. BIB.: Borland, *WWAMC.* Information supplied by the subject, 1996.

TWEEDY, ROBERT "BOB" (b. Kansas). Robert Tweedy studied cello with Raymond Stuhl, earning a performance degree in cello from the Eastman School; he then secured a position as a cellist with the Minneapolis Symphony. While Tweedy was there, Henry Denecke, Jr., gave up the timpani position to become a conductor, and Tweedy replaced him (1952–72). Antal Dorati, conductor of Minneapolis, appreciated Tweedy's timpani talents and invited him to perform for his European summer orchestras.

SELECTED BIBLIOGRAPHY

Kogan, Peter. "Henry Denecke, Jr." *PN* XXXIII, 3 (June 1995): 62.
Information supplied by George Boberg, 1997.

U

UDELL, BENJAMIN W. (b. Benjamin W. Yudelowitz, ca. 1920, New York, New York; d. 15 Nov 1978, Prairie Village, Kansas). Principal timpanist with the Kansas City Philharmonic, Lyric Theater, and Starlight Theater Orchestras, Ben Udell claimed fame as *Saul Goodman's first student (supported by a scholarship from the New York Philharmonic). He attended the Juilliard School, played drumset in New York during the orchestra's off-season, and was an artist and playwright.

SELECTED BIBLIOGRAPHY

"Obituary." *Variety* CCLXLIII (22 Nov 1978): 135.
"Percussion in Our Orchestras." *IM* (June 1949): 24–25 (photo).

UDOW, MICHAEL WILLIAM (b. 10 Mar 1949, Detroit, Michigan). A graduate of the University of Illinois with bachelor's (1971), master's (1975), and doctorate (1978) degrees, Michael Udow attended the Interlochen Arts Academy and National Music Camp. His teachers have included Tom Siwe, *Alan Abel, Frederick Fairchild, *Warren Benson, Jack McKenzie, *Michael Ranta, and *Russell Hartenberger, among others. Udow has served as principal percussionist for the Santa Fe Opera since 1968; he performed with Blackearth Percussion group (1973), was percussionist in the New Orleans Philharmonic (1971–72), toured with the Barton Workshop (England, 1974–75), held a "Creative Performing Arts" Fellowship at the University of Illinois (1976–77), and performed and toured with the Summit Brass (1990s). His many performance venues include Lincoln Center, National Public Radio, Percussive Arts Society conventions, the Santa Fe Chamber Music Festival, and tours of Europe and Japan with such collaborators as Keiko Abe—including radio and television performances. He premiered the stage role of "Drummer/Madman" in the Santa

Fe Opera production of Hans Werner Henze's *We Come to the River* and the solo percussion part for David Felder's *Between* with the Buffalo Philharmonic.

Internationally known as a composer, Udow has had several of his works recorded, and he performs his own works in a percussion and dance duo with his wife in their group Equilibrium. He has taught on the faculties of the University of Missouri at Kansas City (1978–81), Penn State (1980–81), Dartington College in Devon, England (1977/1979), Northern Illinois University (1973), and the University of Michigan (since 1982), where he performs with the Michigan Chamber Players. Recipient of a Fulbright Scholarship to Poland in 1972, Udow has also served on the board of directors for the Percussive Arts Society. Labels for which he has recorded and/or on which several of his works have been recorded include Columbia, CRI, Opus One, Orion, Columbia/Denon, Gemini, New World, Non-Sequitor, and Advance.

SELECTED DISCOGRAPHY

Columbia/Denon CD CD-4219: *Marimba Spiritual* (Keiko Abe), 1989.

EQ/University of Michigan SM0019: *Four Chamber Percussion Works*, 1986.

New World NW 288-2: *Virgil Thomson—The Mother of Us All* (Santa Fe Opera), 1977/1990.

NEXUS CD 10339: *The Solo Percussionist* (Music of William Cahn), (soloist on "Won't You Join the Dance?"), 1997.

Opus One 22: *The Blackearth Percussion Group*, 1974.

Orion OC-686: *Michael Colgrass—The Earth's a Baked Apple* (New Orleans Philharmonic), 1972.

Xebec (Japan) XECC-1003: *Conversation* (Keiko Abe/Michigan Chamber Players), 1997.

SELECTED BIBLIOGRAPHY

Udow, Michael. "From Hearing and Reading to Listening and Understanding: An Attempt to Bridge the Gap." *PN Research Edition* XXI, 6 (September 1983): 72–75.

Udow, Michael. "An Interview with Karlheinz Stockhausen." *PN Research Edition* XXIII, 6 (September 1985): 4–47.

Udow, Michael. "Visual Correspondence between Notation Systems and Instrument Configurations." *Percussionist* (*PN Research Edition*) XVIII, 2 (Winter 1981): 15–29.

GEN. BIB.: Larrick, *BET-CP.*

ULRICH, KURT (d. 24 Mar 1944, Berlin, Germany). A student of Franz Krüger at Berlin's Hochschule für Musik, Kurt Ulrich performed with the German Broadcasting Orchestra of Berlin before joining the Berlin Philharmonic as timpanist in 1937. He died during an Allied bomb attack on Berlin during WWII.

GEN. BIB.: Avgerinos, *KB.*

UMBARGER, GAYLON RAY (b. 5 Jan 1943, Topeka, Kansas). Gaylon Umbarger attended Grinnell College (IA, 1961–64) and the University of Missouri at Kansas City (UMKC, 1964–67), where he received a bachelor's degree. He studied with Charmaine Asher-Wiley at UMKC, *Vince Bilardo of the Kansas City Philharmonic, and *Alan Abel of the Philadelphia Orchestra. Umbarger performed with the Kansas City Philharmonic (1971–82) and has remained with its successor, the Kansas City Symphony, since 1982. He has also appeared with the Kansas City Lyric Opera (1974–95), the Kansas City Piano-Percussion Quartet (1968–71), and various local jazz combos and dance bands (1965–85).

SELECTED DISCOGRAPHY

Kansas City Symphony CDP 943 S4912D: *American Voices*, 1994.
Newport Classic NDP 85585: *The Devil and Daniel Webster*, 1995.
Information supplied by the subject, 1996.

V

VAN GEEM, JACK WILLIAM, JR. (b. 3 Apr 1952, Oakland, California). Initially a wind instrumentalist, Jack Van Geem earned bachelor's (1973) and master's (1974) degrees from Hayward State University (CSU-Hayward) and studied with *Anthony Cirone and Jerome Neff in the United States and Cristoph Caskel in Köln, Germany (1974). Percussionist with the San Francisco Ballet from 1975 to 1980, he has served as principal percussionist and assistant timpanist with the San Francisco Symphony since 1981, taught at Hayward State (1976–83) and the San Francisco Conservatory, and recorded with the San Francisco percussion quartet Xylo. His publications include *Four Mallet Democracy* and *Rags and Hot Choruses*.

SELECTED DISCOGRAPHY

New Albion NA079CD: *Where the Heart Is Pure* (Peter Scott Lewis), 1994/1996.
Orion ORS 85479: *Duo-Piano Concert* (Alfred Kanwischer), 1985.
Sonic Arts: *76 Sounds of Explosive Percussion*, 1979.
GEN. BIB.: Borland, *WWAMC*; PASIC® program biographies, 1991, 1997.

VAN HYNING, HOWARD. Howard Van Hyning earned bachelor's and master's degrees from the Juilliard School, where he studied with *Morris Goldenberg and *Saul Goodman. Percussionist with the Baltimore Symphony, Brooklyn Philharmonic, American Ballet Theater, New York Opera Orchestra (ca. 1983), he has freelanced with the Royal Ballet, American Symphony, Stuttgart Ballet, and toured Europe with New York's Contemporary Chamber Ensemble (1973). Van Hyning teaches at the Mannes College of Music (1975–   ) and has conducted recording sessions for the New World and Newport Classic recording labels.
GEN. BIB.: Borland, *WWAMC*.

VAN SICE, ROBERT (b. 1961). Debuting at age 15 in Albuquerque, New Mexico, marimbist Robert Van Sice studied with *Keiko Abe, *Leigh Howard Stevens, and *Michael Rosen. He earned a bachelor's degree from the Cleveland Institute of Music, where he studied with *Cloyd Duff, and at the age of 17 was the youngest winner of the Cleveland Institute Music Competition. Soloist with the London Sinfonietta and heard on BBC, NHK, and Radio France, he presented the first full-length marimba recital at the Concertgebouw in Amsterdam (1989), has performed in Japan, North and South America, Africa, and Scandinavia and has given 40 world premieres of concerti, chamber works, and unaccompanied works. Director of the percussion department at Yale (1997–   ), Van Sice served on the faculty of the Peabody Conservatory (1996), the Royal Conservatory in Brussels, was director of Europe's first diploma program for marimba soloists at the Rotterdam Conservatory (1988–97), and has been a visiting lecturer at the Sweelinck Conservatory in Amsterdam and Royal Conservatory in Madrid.

SELECTED DISCOGRAPHY

Claremont GSE 606: *Robert van Sice*, 1985.
Etcetera KTC 1085: *Robert van Sice—Marimba Concertos*, 1990.
Etcetera KTC 1113: *Crystals of the Zodiac*, 1991.
Etcetera KTC 1143: *Japanese Music for Marimba*, 1992.
Mode 51: *Village Burial with Fire/Spirit Festival with Lamentations*, 1995.

SELECTED BIBLIOGRAPHY

Burritt, Michael. "Interview with Marimbist, Robert Van Sice." *PN* XXX, 4 (April 1992): 15–20.

VAN WINKLE, A. T. A xylophone recording artist for Edison Records (1889) and Thomas Edison's North American Phonograph Company (1889/1890), A. T. Van Winkle may have made the first xylophone recording (1889) for the latter as part of the first series used in coin-operated machines. His recordings included "Selections from The Owls Overture," "My Treasure Polka," and "Galop Brilliant."

SELECTED BIBLIOGRAPHY

Kastner, Kathleen. "The Xylophone in the United States between 1880 and 1930, Part I: The Artists." *Percussive Arts Society: Illinois Chapter Newsletter* (Winter 1986): 1–2.
GEN. BIB.: Cahn, *XAR*.

VASCONCELOS, NANA (b. ca. 1945, Recife, Brazil). Percussionist Nana Vasconcelos performed as a youth with his guitarist father, then with Milton

Nascimento, eventually touring Europe, Argentina, and the United States (1971) with Gato Barbieri. He appeared with Pat Metheny (1980–83), with Don Cherry and Collin Walcott in the eclectic group Codona (1978–84), and in Cherry's band Mu (1984).

SELECTED DISCOGRAPHY

ECM 1089: *Danca des cabecas* (Egberto Gismonti), 1976.
ECM 1132: *Codona*, 1978.
ECM 1147: *Saudades*, 1979.
ECM 1177: *Codona*, 1980.
ECM 1216: *Offramp* (Pat Metheny), 1981.
ECM 1243: *Codona*, 1982.
Elektra 9 61272-2: *Upfront* (David Sanborn), 1992.
Lovely Music LCD 1021: *Vernal Equinox* (Jon Hassell), 1990.
Nomad NMD 50303: *Asian Journal*, 1996.
GEN. BIB.: Kernfeld, *NGJ*, by Barry Kernfeld.

VELEZ, GLEN (b. Dallas, Texas). Virtuoso hand drummer, ethnomusicologist, and composer Glen Velez began frame drum lessons around 1975, studying with Ramnad Raghavan, Hanna Birhigehas, Zevulon Avshalomov. He has performed with the Paul Winter Consort (since 1983), Marc Cohen, Suzanne Vega, NEXUS, Steve Reich (for 17 years), the Stuttgart and New York City Ballets, and Trio Globo, among others, and currently serves on the faculty of the Mannes College of Music. Recipient of a Rockefeller Commission for composition, he has written for National Public Radio's *All Things Considered* and John Schaefer's *New Sounds*. Leader of the Handance Frame Drum Ensemble, Velez has recorded with Eddie Gomez, Lyle Mays, Suzanne Vega, Richard Stoltzman, Eddie Daniels, and others, on CMP, RCA, ECM, CBS, Vanguard, Deutsche Gramophon, Opus One, and New World labels. Remo Inc., manufactures his signature line of frame drums.

SELECTED DISCOGRAPHY

Audioquest AQCD1024: *Afrique* (Mokave), 1994.
Audioquest AQ 1006/1007: *Mokave*, vols. 1–2, 1992.
CMP 30CS: *Seven Heaven*, 1987.
CMP CD 42: *Assyrian Rose*, 1989.
CMP CD 54: *Doctrine of Signatures*, 1991.
CMP CD 23: *Internal Combustion*, 1985.
Ellipsis Arts CD 4140: *Rhythmcolor Exotica* (Handance), 1996.
Ellipsis Arts CD3405: *The Big Bang—Global Percussion Masters*, 1994/1997.
Interworld Music CD-21907: *Border States*, 1993.
Music Masters 01612-67058-4/Oolitic Music OM 1111: *Hymnody of Earth*
      (Malcolm Dalglish), 1991/1997.
Nomad NMD 50301: *Handdance*, 1996.

Nomad NMD 50307: *Ramana*, 1991/1997.
Nomad 50315: *One in the Pocket* (Amit Chatterjee and Badal Roy), 1997.
Opus One 69: *Ritual Sounds* (Nancy Chance), 1981.
Silver Wave SD806: *Trio Globo*, 1994.
Sounds True Records M006S: *Rhythms of the Chakras*, 1998.
Warner Bros. 9 46791: *Imaginary Day* (Pat Metheny), 1997.

SELECTED VIDEOGRAPHY

Interworld 076: *The Art and Joy of Hand Drumming* (John Bergamo), 1990.
Interworld VH0284/0285: *Handance Method, Steps 1 & 2*, 1997.
Interworld VH077: *The Fantastic World of Frame Drums*, 1990.

SELECTED BIBLIOGRAPHY

Dorsey, Ed. "Ethnic Percussion: An Interview with Glen Velez." *PN* XXV, 4
     (Spring 1987): 56–60.
PASIC® program biographies, 1994, 1997, 1998.

VIG, TOMMY (b. 14 Jul 1938, Budapest, Hungary). A jazz vibist, drummer, composer, and conductor who left his native Hungary in 1956, Tommy Vig studied at the Juilliard School and played in Las Vegas during the 1960s, relocating to Los Angeles in 1969. He has performed with *Terry Gibbs, Don Ellis, Red Rodney, Cat Anderson, and Joe Pass, among others; conducted his own big band; and composed film scores. Vig won *Down Beat* magazine's Critics' Poll in the vibraphone category in 1967.

SELECTED DISCOGRAPHY

Discovery DS-780: *Encounter with Time*, 1977.
Discovery DSCD-925: *Space Race*, 1986.
Dobre Records DR1005: *The Vigs—Somebody Loves Me*, 1978.
Dobre 1015: *Tommy Vig 1978*.
Milestone MSP 9007: *The Sound of the Seventies* (Tommy Vig Orchestra), 1967.
Mortney Records: *Tommy Vig in Budapest*.

SELECTED BIBLIOGRAPHY

Coss, Bill. "Focus on Tommy Vig." *DB* XXVIII, 25 (7 Dec 1961): 18.
Feather, Leonard, and Ira Gitler. *The Encyclopedia of Jazz in the Seventies*. New
     York: Horizon Press, 1976.

VOGLER, OSWALD (b. 28 Nov 1930, Hamm/Westfalia, Germany). After six years of lessons with his father, Oswald Vogler studied with Professor Rebhan at the Dortmund Conservatory (1945–49). He served as substitute timpanist with the Hagen Orchestra (1949–52), as principal timpanist (and manager,

1955–57) with the Bochum Symphony (1952), and then as timpanist with the Berlin Philharmonic, which he joined in 1970. Vogler was also featured occasionally as timpani soloist.

GEN. BIB.: Avgerinos, *KB.*

VON MOISY, HEINRICH G. "HEINZ" (b. 11 May 1935, Kolberg, Germany). Heinz von Moisy attended Berklee College of Music, where he studied with *Alan Dawson. Since 1980 he has performed at the Landestheater Tübingen; drummed (1995–   ) for Melting Pot, which includes mallet artist *Bill Molenhof; and appeared in concert with Carmell Jones, Leo Wright, Barney Kessel, Elie "Lucky" Thompson, and Werner Heider. He has given concerts, masterclasses, and clinics throughout Europe, Russia, Great Britain, Brazil, Mexico, Canada, and the United States. Percussion chair (1979–   ) of the Tübinger Musikschule in Tübingen, Germany, where he organized the "Days of Percussion" for 15 years, von Moisy taught at the Musikhochschule Detmold and Pädagogische Hochschule Berlin. He has served on the Percussive Arts Society board of directors for eight years and is a member of the International Committee.

SELECTED DISCOGRAPHY

MTS-118L: *Heinz von Moisy & Manfred Burzlaff—On Tour*, 1985.
Thorofon ATH 174: *Heinz von Moisy Irisation—Las Plantas*, 1977.
Thorofon MTH 253: *Ars Nova Ensemble Nürnberg*, 1977.

SELECTED BIBLIOGRAPHY

Lambert, James. "Interviews with Two German Percussionists: Heinz von Moisy and Nebojsa Zivkovic, Tübingen, Germany, November, 1990." *PN* XXIX, 4 (April 1991): 15–22.
von Moisy, Heinz. "The Drummer/Musician." *PN* XXXII, 2 (April 1994): 17–20.
von Moisy, Heinz. *Advanced Technique for the Drumset*. London: Simrock, 1971.
von Moisy, Heinz. *The Drumset in Practise*. Frankfurt: Zimmerman, 1991.
Information supplied by the subject, 1996.

VON OHLEN, JOHN "BARON" (b. 13 May 1941, Indianapolis, Indiana). A drumset artist who worked with Woody Herman (Monterey Jazz Festival, 1967), Billy Maxted (1967–68), and Stan Kenton (1970–72), John Von Ohlen led his own big band in the 1970s and teaches at the Cincinnati Conservatory.

SELECTED DISCOGRAPHY

CW 3001: *The Baron*, 1973.
Verve V6-8764: *Woody Herman and His Orchestra*, 1967.

SELECTED BIBLIOGRAPHY

Fish, Scott K.: "John Von Ohlen: Natural Style." *MD* IX (March 1985): 16–19.
GEN. BIB.: Kernfeld, *NGJ.*

WAITS, FREDERICK DOUGLAS "FREDDIE" "DAHOUD" (b. 27 Apr 1943, Jackson, Mississippi; d. 18 Nov 1989). Drumset artist and percussionist who began by playing blues with John Lee Hooker, Freddie Waits toured with soul groups in the 1960s, then relocated to New York, where he collaborated with Andrew Hill (1968–69/1980), McCoy Tyner (1968–70), Ella Fitzgerald (1973), Hank Mobley, Freddie Hubbard, and Cecil Taylor (1987), among others. He was a member of *Max Roach's M'Boom RE: Percussion (1971–) and of Colloquium III (1979, with *Billy Hart and *Horacee Arnold).

SELECTED DISCOGRAPHY

Atlantic LP 1501: *High Blues Pressure* (Freddie Hubbard), 1967.
Blue Note 84238: *Mustang* (Donald Byrd), 1966.
Blue Note 84303: *Grass Roots* (Andrew Hill), 1968.
Blue Note 84307: *Time for Tyner* (McCoy Tyner), 1986.
Blue Note 84330: *Lift Every Voice* (Andrew Hill), 1969.
Blue Note 84338: *Expansions* (McCoy Tyner), 1968.
Blue Note 84423: *Gene Harris of the Three Sounds*, 1972.
Blue Note 84901: *Lee Morgan*, 1971.
Blue Note LA460-H2: *McCoy Tyner*, 1969.
Muse 5002: *Epistrophy and Now's the Time* (Richard Davis), 1972.
Muse MCD 5384: *Capitol Hill* (Buck Hill), 1991.
Soul Note 1059: *M'Boom—Collage* (Max Roach), 1984.
Verve V6-8751: *Kenny Burrell*, 1969.
Verve V6-8753: *Johnny Hodges*, 1968.
GEN. BIB.: Hunt, *52nd St.*; Kernfeld, *NGJ*, by Barry Kernfeld.

WALCOTT, COLLIN (b. 24 Apr 1945, New York, New York; d. 8 Nov 1984, Magdeburg, Germany). Percussionist, tablist, and sitarist who studied with Alla Rakha and Ravi Shankar, Collin Walcott graduated from Indiana University (bachelor's, 1966) and studied ethnomusicology at the University of California at Los Angeles. He performed and/or recorded in the Columbus, Detroit, Kalamazoo, and Toronto Symphonies, with Miles Davis (1972) and Tony Scott (1967–69), and with the musically eclectic groups Paul Winter Consort (1970–71), Oregon (fourteen albums, 1980–84), and Codona (three albums, 1978–84).

SELECTED DISCOGRAPHY

Columbia KC31906: *On the Corner* (Miles Davis), 1972.
CRI SD 327: *Bazelon—Propulsions*, 1974.
ECM 1062: *Cloud Dance*, 1975.
ECM 1096: *Grazing Dreams*, 1977.
ECM 1132: *Codona*, 1978.
Epic 31643: *Icarus* (Paul Winter Consort), 1972.
Verve 68742: *Music for Yoga Meditation and Other Joys* (Tony Scott), 1967.

SELECTED BIBLIOGRAPHY

"Closing Chord: Collin Walcott." *IM* (February 1985): 11.
GEN. BIB.: Kernfeld, *NGJ*, by Barry Kernfeld.

WANSER, WILLIAM M. "BILL" (b. 9 Oct 1949, Seattle, Washington). Earning a bachelor's degree (1972) from the University of Washington and a master's degree (1974) from the Manhattan School, William Wanser studied with *Fred Hinger and has been principal percussionist (assistant timpanist, 1992–93) with the Phoenix Symphony since 1975. He has performed with the Florida Symphony (1974–75), the Grand Teton Festival (1979), the Summit Brass (1993–94), and the Marrowstone Music Festival (Seattle), and has taught at Phoenix College (1978–82) and Arizona State University (1997–   ).
PASIC® program biographies, 1995. Information supplied by the subject, 1999.

WASHINGTON, KENNY (b. 29 May 1958, Brooklyn, New York). Drumset artist Kenny Washington cites the influence of *Philly Joe Jones, *Mel Lewis, and *Louis Hayes. He made his first major appearance with Lee Konitz (1977–78). Among his many collaborators are Betty Carter (1978–79), Johnny Griffin (1980–   ), *Milt Jackson, Clark Terry, the Carnegie Hall Jazz Band, Cedar Walton, and Tommy Flanagan. Washington hosts the *Big Band Dance Party* on Newark, New Jersey's, WBGO radio station.

SELECTED DISCOGRAPHY

Criss Cross 1022: *Presenting Michael Weiss*, 1986.
Galaxy 5146: *Call It Whachawana*, 1983.
Muse 5420: *May I Come In?* (Lorez Alexandria), 1991.

SELECTED BIBLIOGRAPHY

Porter, Bob. "Before and After: Kenny Washington—The Ears Have It, Again and
    Again." *JazzTimes* XXVIII, 9 (November 1998): 55–58.
GEN. BIB.: Kernfeld, *NGJ*, by Chuck Braman.

WASITODININGRAT, K.R.T. [KANJENG RADEN TUMENGGUNG]
(b. 1909, Java, Indonesia). Director for several years of National Radio in
Jogyakarta, Indonesia, and the gamelans in Paku Alaman in central Java,
K.R.T. Wasitodiningrat toured Asia, the former U.S.S.R., and Europe. He
taught throughout Indonesia and the United States and held a faculty position at
the California Institute of the Arts.

SELECTED DISCOGRAPHY

CMP 3007: *The Music of K.R.T. Wasitodiningrat*, 1990/1992.
PASIC® program biographies, 1985.

WATSON, KENNETH EDWARD "KEN" (b. 8 Aug 1937, Canton, Ohio).
A student of *Cloyd Duff and *William Kraft, Ken Watson attended Michigan
State University (bachelor's, 1961) and the University of Southern California
(master's, 1962) and has performed with the San Francisco (cimbalom) and Seattle Symphonies (cimbalom), Los Angeles Chamber Orchestra (timpani and
percussion), Hollywood Bowl Orchestra, Los Angeles Music Center Opera
(timpani), Pasadena Symphony (timpani), and Los Angeles Philharmonic (percussion and cimbalom). He has worked in all the major Los Angeles film and
television studios, recording for composers such as Jerry Goldsmith, Franz
Waxman, John Williams, Bruce Boughton, Lalo Schifrin, John Corigliano,
David Raksin, John Barry, Michel Legrand, and George Delerue. Examples of
his studio work from 1963 to the present include *Jaws*, *ET*, *Star Trek* (movie
and TV), and *Mission Impossible* (TV).

   Premiering Pierre Boulez's *Eclat* (cimbalom), *William Kraft's *Double Trio*
(1966), Karl Kohn's *Rhapsodies for Marimba, Vibraphone, and Percussion*
(written for Watson, 1968), and Dorrance Stalvey's *Points-Lines-Circles* (1968),
he played for Igor Stravinsky, Boulez, Kraft, and Luciano Berio on the *Monday
Evening Concerts* (1965–82) and at the Ojai Music Festival (1965–84). As a
pedagogue, he taught at the Stan Kenton Stage Band clinics, directed the Percussion Collective (1978), and served as adjunct associate professor and head of
the percussion department at the University of Southern California (1965–91).

He is currently percussion instructor at California Polytechnic University-San
Luis Obipso (Cal Poly, 1994–). Personnel manager for the Hollywood Bowl
Orchestra since 1991, Watson also contracts musicians for films and television
in the Los Angeles area.

SELECTED DISCOGRAPHY

Ars Nova AN-1008: *Metamorphosis* (Stalvey), 1970.
Candide CE-31072: *Cadence III for Violin and Two Percussion* (Lazarof), 1973.
Cinema Maestro (AUS)/Label X LXCD 11: *Continuum Journeys* (Lalo Schifrin,
    commissioned by Ken Watson), 1973.
CRI SD 269: *Tree Music* (Paul Chihara), 1971.
Crystal S-532: *Cleveland Composer's Guild,* vol. 2 (Walter Watson's *Recital Suite
    for Marimba,* commissioned by Ken Watson), 1978.
Nonesuch H-71223: *Music for Instruments and Electronic Sounds* (Donald Erb),
    1977.
RCA Victor LSP 3414: *Jazz Suite on the Mass Texts* (Paul Horn/Lalo Schifrin),
    1965.
Warner Bros. BS2912: *In the Pocket* (James Taylor), 1976.

SELECTED BIBLIOGRAPHY

Crawford, Dorothy. *Evenings On and Off the Roof: Pioneering Concerts in Los
    Angeles, 1939–1971.* Berkeley, CA: University of California Press, 1995.
GEN. BIB.: Borland, *WWAMC.* Information supplied by the subject, 1996.

WAY, GEORGE HARRISON (b. George Harrison Bassett, 8 Jan 1891, San
Francisco, California; d. 21 Feb 1969, Elkhart, Indiana). Employed by *George
B. Stone's drum store in Boston, George Way studied percussion with Stone
during the early 1900s, taking his stepfather's name at the age of 13. He played
professionally for fifteen years (touring for nine) on riverboats, with minstrel
shows, Buffalo Bill's *Wild West Show* ("Cowboy Band"), the Ringling Brothers
Circus, and for George M. Cohan and Al Jolson. In Alberta, Canada, where he
performed at the Pantages Theater, he opened his own drum manufacturing plant
(Advance Drum Company, 1915). Way joined the Leedy Drum Company in
Indianapolis, where he was sales manager and editor of the newsletter *Leedy
Drum Topics.* Credited with inventing the "floating head concept" and parallel
snare strainers, he remained at Leedy from 1921 to 1955, except for interludes
with the American Rawhide Company (Amrawco, 1942–47), the Slingerland
Drum Company, and a drum shop venture in Hollywood during WWII. Late in
his career he founded the predecessor of the Camco Drum Company and worked
for the Rogers Drum Company.

SELECTED BIBLIOGRAPHY

Cangany, Harry. "George Way Prototype." *MD* XX, 9 (September 1996): 150–152.

"Closing Chord—George H. Way." *IM* LXVII, 10 (April 1969): 29.

Cook, Rob. *Complete History of the Leedy Drum Company.* Fullerton, CA: Centerstream Publishing, 1993.

Cook, Rob, compiler. *George Way's Little Black Book.* Alma, MI: Rebeats Publications, 1992.

"In Memoriam." *PN* VII, 3 (1969): 6.

GEN. BIB.: Cook, *LDT.*

WEBB, WILLIAM HENRY "CHICK" (b. 10 Feb 1902, Baltimore, Maryland; d. 16 Jun 1939, Baltimore, Maryland). Suffering chronic pain and physio-
logical challenges caused by crushed vertebrae from being dropped in childhood,
William Henry Webb was dubbed "Chick" due to his diminutive stature. He
sold newspapers to earn enough money to purchase a used drumset and soon
played on Chesapeake Bay excursion boats. Webb moved to New York in
1924, playing with Edgar Dowell in 1925, leading his own band in 1926 at the
Roseland Ballroom and the Cotton Club, touring with the Hot Chocolates Revue (1930), and fronting the house band at Harlem's famed Savoy Ballroom
(from 1931). At the latter he "battled" other drummers, who always testified to
his amazing speed and musicality. On one such occasion, 11 May 1937, *Gene
Krupa, playing with the Benny Goodman Band, surrendered to Webb's drumming and showmanship. In 1934 he "discovered" and became legal guardian to
the orphan chanteuse Ella Fitzgerald, who generated immense popularity for the
band and managed his group for three years after his untimely death from tuberculosis. Their 1938 recording of "A Tisket, A Tasket" was placed into the
Record Hall of Fame by the Music Academy in 1986. Webb was the first jazz
musician to receive an honorary doctorate from Yale University (*Chicago Defender*, 1937) and was inducted into the Percussive Arts Society Hall of Fame in
1985.

SELECTED DISCOGRAPHY

Circle CCD-72: *Chick Webb and His Orchestra*, 1936.

Classics 502: *Chick Webb, 1929–1934.*

Columbia CL2639/Jazz Archive Series: *The Immortal Chick Webb-Stompin' at the
Savoy* (1933–36), 1967.

Decca DL 9223: *Chick Webb—King of the Savoy*, vol. 2 (1937–39), 1967.

Decca/Jazz Heritage Series DL 79222: *Chick Webb—A Legend*, vol. 1 (1929–36),
1967.

Jazz Archives JA-33: *Bronzeville Stomp*, 1967.

Masters of Jazz MJCD 804/Media 7: *Anthology of Jazz Drumming*, vols. 1–3
(1904–38), 1997.

Smithsonian Folkways 02818: *Chick Webb and His Orchestra Featuring Ella
Fitzgerald*, 1992.

SELECTED VIDEOGRAPHY

DCI VH0248: *Legends of Jazz Drumming,* pt. 1 (1920–50), 1996.

SELECTED BIBLIOGRAPHY

Chilton, John. *Who's Who of Jazz: Storyville to Swing Street,* 4th ed. New York:
    Da Capo, 1985, pp. 348–349.
"From the Past: William 'Chick' Webb." *MD* XIX (March 1995): 120–121.
Hillary, Robert. "The Legendary Chick Webb: A Profile in Courage." *MD* (July
    1977): 22–23.
Robbins, James. "Hall of Fame Awards: Chick Webb." *PN* XXIV, 2 (January 1986):
    5–6.
Shultz, Thomas. "A History of Jazz Drumming." *Percussionist* XVI, 3
    (Spring/Summer 1979): 116–118.
Simon, George T. *Simon Says: The Sights and Sounds of the Swing Era,
    1935–1955.* New Rochelle, NY: Arlington House, 1971.
"The Secrets of Chick Webb's Drumming Technique." *DB* V, 9 (September 1938): 23.
GEN. BIB.: Kernfeld, *NGJ*, by J. Bradford Robinson; Korall, *DM*; Southern, *BDA-AAM*; Spag-
    nardi, *GJD*.

WECHTER, JULIUS L. (b. 10 May 1935, Chicago, Illinois). A Hollywood
studio artist who earned an associate's degree in music (Los Angeles City College, 1956) and a master's degree in clinical psychology (Antioch University,
1994), Julius Wechter played and recorded with Herb Alpert and the Tijuana
Brass (17 albums, A&M label), the Baja Marimba Band (12 albums, A&M
label), and the Martin Denny Group (Hawaii, 1957–61; 13 albums, Liberty label). He performed on *Bob Hope* shows, played on Phil Spector recordings
(e.g., Righteous Brothers: "You've Lost That Loving Feeling"), and published
the hit song "Spanish Flea" (Almo).

SELECTED BIBLIOGRAPHY

Wechter, Julius. *Play Vibes!* New York: Henry Adler/Belwin Mills, 1962.
Information supplied by the subject, 1996.

WECKL, DAVID "DAVE" (b. 8 Jan 1960, St. Louis, Missouri). Starting
drums at age 8, Dave Weckl studied in high school with Bob Matheny and Joe
Buerger, then began his professional career locally at 16. After attending the
University of Bridgeport (CT, 1979), he established his reputation in New York
City with the groups Nite Sprite and French Toast (piano trio with Michel
Camillo and Anthony Jackson) and with the Simon and Garfunkel Reunion
Tour (1983). Since then, Weckl has recorded several radio and television jin-
gles and collaborated live and in the studio with the Brecker Brothers, Peabo
Bryson, Diana Ross, Robert Plant, Chick Corea's Akoustic and Elektric Bands

(1985–92, including three videos, nine recordings, and a Grammy® Award for the Akoustic band's first release), Elaine Elias, George Benson, and the GRP All-Star Big Band. Current information concerning his varied projects can be accessed on the Internet.

SELECTED DISCOGRAPHY

Atlantic 82835-4: *Between the Lines* (Mike Stern), 1996.
Blue Note BLJ-48016: *Bireli Lagrene—Inferno*, 1987.
Concord 9016-2: *Rhythm of the Soul*, 1998.
GRD 9627: *Chick Corea Akoustic Band—Alive*, 1991.
GRP/GRC-9619: *Master Plan* (with Steve Gadd), 1990.
GRP/GRC-9673: *Heads Up*, 1992.
N2K Encoded Music: *Dave Grusin Presents "West Side Story,"* 1997.
Zebra ZD 44005-2: *Tribute to Jeff* (Dave Garfield), 1997.

SELECTED VIDEOGRAPHY

DCI VHO 157/166: *Working It Out,* pts. 1–2 (with Walfredo Reyes, Sr.), 1992/1993.
DCI/Warner Bros. VHO39: *Back to Basics*, 1988.
DCI/Warner Bros. VH050: *The Next Step*, 1989.
PASIC® program biographies, 1992, 1997.

WEFLIN, EMIL T. (d. ca. February 1947). Percussionist, timpanist, and drumset artist with the Detroit Symphony who also played on radio (KSTP) in St. Paul (MN), Emil Weflin reportedly was a reformed alcoholic, the right side of his face was paralyzed, and he slept with one eye open.

SELECTED BIBLIOGRAPHY

Lylloff, Bent. "An Interview with Red Norvo." *PN* XXXI, 1 (October 1992): 42–51.

WEINER, RICHARD "DICK" (b. 8 Mar 1940, Philadelphia, Pennsylvania). Embracing music at age 8 and later performing with the Philadelphia Youth Orchestra and All-Philadelphia High School Symphony and Jazz Band, Richard Weiner studied with *George Gaber in 1962 at the Aspen School; while there, he played xylophone for the world premieres of Olivier Messiaen's *Oiseaux Exotiques* and *Reveil des Oiseaux*. He attended Temple University (bachelor's degree, 1962), where he studied with *Charles Owen, and earned a master's degree and performer's certificate—the first percussionist to receive the latter—from Indiana University (1963), where he continued studies with Gaber. Appointed percussionist with the Cleveland Orchestra in 1963 (principal percussionist, 1968), Weiner toured with them in the Far East, Soviet Union, Australia, New Zealand, Europe, South and Central America, and the United States. He performed the American premiere of Messiaen's *Chronochromie* (1967) and appeared as soloist with Cleveland for Donald Erb's *Percussion Concerto*. His recording credits include several compositions by Erb, three collaborations with the Cleveland Symphonic Winds on the Telarc label, and works by Messiaen (Cleveland Orchestra, 1993).

While a student at Temple, he taught at the Settlement Music School, the Philadelphia Musical Academy, and Combs College of Music. A former faculty member at Oberlin College (1968–71), he has taught at the Cleveland Institute since 1963 (co-chair of the percussion and timpani department and director of the percussion ensemble), and his former students fill orchestral positions in Cleveland, Los Angeles, San Francisco, Pittsburgh, Minnesota, Cincinnati, Atlanta, the National Symphony, the Metropolitan Opera Orchestra, the St. Paul Chamber Orchestra, and Hollywood studios, among others. He has been a contributing editor to the *Percussive Notes* magazine and has served as a clinician for Percussive Arts Society International Conventions. Weiner earned the J.D. degree from Cleveland State University in 1976, was admitted to Ohio Bar in 1977, and has applied his legal expertise in matters concerning the Cleveland Orchestra.

SELECTED BIBLIOGRAPHY

Snider, Larry. "An Interview with Richard Weiner." *PN* XVIII, 1 (Fall 1979): 42–45. Information supplied by the subject, 1996.

WEISS, HERMAN J. (b. Germany; d. 19 Aug 1938, Schulenberg, Texas). Original timpanist with the Houston Symphony, 1913–38, Herman Weiss immigrated to San Antonio, Texas, with his parents when he was six years old. He was timpanist with the San Antonio Symphony, drummer for Houston's Interstate Vaudeville Theater, president and secretary of the American Federation of Musicians (AFM) Local 65 (Houston), and appeared as a delegate to AFM conventions during the 1920s.

SELECTED BIBLIOGRAPHY

"Here, There and Everywhere: Herman Weiss." *IM* XXXVI, 6 (September 1938): 4.
Roussel, Hubert. *The Houston Symphony Orchestra, 1913–1971*. Austin: University of Texas Press, 1972.

WETTLING, GEORGE GODFREY (b. 1907, Topeka, Kansas; d. 6 Jun 1968, New York, New York). Moving to Chicago with his family in 1921, George Wettling was most influenced by *Baby Dodds and first played professionally in 1924, going on to perform drumset with the Wolverines (replacing *Dave Tough, 1926), Red Nichols' Five Pennies, *Red Norvo, Artie Shaw, Bunny Berigan, Woody Herman, Charlie Barnet, Eddie Condon, Louis Panico, Paul Whiteman (1938–40), and Muggsy Spanier (1940). His first recording was with the Jungle Kings (Paramount, 1927), which also included Spanier and Frank Teschemacher. Moving to New York in 1935, Wettling was an excellent timpanist and sight-reader who served as staff percussionist for ABC radio (1943–52) and led his own bands during the 1950s before succumbing to lung cancer. Active as a painter, photographer, and journalist, he wrote column articles for *Down Beat* ("Wettling on Drums," "Diggin' the Drums," "Tips for Tubmen") and *Playboy* magazines.

SELECTED DISCOGRAPHY

Audiophile ACD-1: *Lee Wiley Sings Ira and George Gershwin and Cole Porter*, 1938/1940.
Audiophile ACD-10: *Lee Wiley Sings the Songs of Richard Rodgers* et al., 1940/1943.
Audiophile AP-1: *Lee Wiley Sings Ira and George Gershwin*, 1939–40.
Circle CCD-3: *Red Norvo and His Orchestra—Red and Mildred*, 1938.
Commodore XLF 14941: *Three's No Crowd* (Bud Freeman Trio), 1979.
Jazzology JCD-22: *Wild Bill Davison—After Hours*, 1960/1980.
Jazzology JCD-103: *Wild Bill Davison and His Jazz Band*, 1943/1982.
RCA Victor VPS 6062: *This Is Artie Shaw*, vol. 2, 1971.
Solo Art SACD-10: *Lucky Roberts & Ralph Sutton*, 1952.
Verve (E) 2683051: *Eddie Condon and His Boys*, 1958.
Verve V6-8495: *Jack Teagarden*, 1962.

SELECTED BIBLIOGRAPHY

"Closing Chord—George Wettling." *IM* LXVII, 2 (August 1968): 23.
Gehman, Richard. "George, the Legendary Wettling." *Jazz* (October 1965): 19.
Jones, Max. "George Wettling." *Melody Maker* (16 Feb 1957).
Lee, Amy. "Wettling's Solid Tubbing Kicks with Any Size Ork." *DB* XI, 4 (15 Feb 1944): 12.
Shultz, Thomas. "A History of Jazz Drumming." *Percussionist* XVI, 3 (Spring/Summer 1979): 114.
Wettling, George, and Brad Spinney. *Professional Drum Studies*. New York: Capitol Songs, Inc., 1946.
Wettling, George. *America's Greatest Drum Stylists*. New York: Capitol Songs, Inc., 1945.
GEN. BIB.: Korall, *DM*; Spagnardi, *GJD*.

WHITE, CHARLES LAFAYETTE (b. ca. 1893, Marshfield, Oregon; d. 1974, Los Angeles, California). Beginning drums at age 12 with the Coos Bay Band (Oregon), Charles White moved to San Diego, where he performed on vaudeville, in tent shows, and with the San Diego Popular Symphony Orchestra. Relocating to Los Angeles to play in theaters, he became a charter member of the Los Angeles Philharmonic as timpanist (1919–62), composed percussion ensemble works, and manufactured tuning gauges for timpani.

SELECTED BIBLIOGRAPHY

"In Memoriam." *PN* XIII, 1 (Fall 1974): 18.

White, Charles L. *Drums through the Ages.* Los Angeles: Sterling Press, 1960.

White, Charles L. "The 'Rite' Timpani Player." *Percussionist* VIII, 4 (Summer 1971): 130–134.

White, Charles L. *Timpani Instructions for Playing Igor Stravinsky's "Rite of Spring."* Los
Angeles, Charles L. White, 1965.

White, Charles L. *Timpani Instructions for Playing Stravinsky's "Sacre du Printemps."* New York: McGinnis and Marx, ca. 1965.

White, Charles L. "Tympani or Timpani?" *Percussionist* IX, 3 (Spring 1972): 67–70.

GEN. BIB.: Cook, *LDT*, p. 19.

WHITE, LAWRENCE R. "LARRY" (b. 1907, Salmon, Idaho). A self-taught mallet specialist who performed marimba for Paderewski and was with the Boston Symphony for 18 years (1928–46?), Lawrence White earned bachelor's and master's degrees from the New England Conservatory (graduated in 1928) and served in the Pacific theater in WWII as a Special Services music officer. Former faculty of the New England Conservatory and Boston University, he was staff percussionist for Mutual Broadcasting System radio (WGN) in Chicago (1951), headed the percussion department at DePaul University, was a guest orchestra conductor and composer, and in his later years performed in the Ft. Lauderdale, Florida, area.

SELECTED BIBLIOGRAPHY

Brush, Gerome. *Boston Symphony Orchestra, 1936.* Boston: Merrymount Press, 1936.

Stone, George L. "Technique of Percussion." *IM* (July 1951): 21.

White, Lawrence R. "Some Precautions for Percussion." *Educational Music Magazine* (ca. 1950).

GEN. BIB.: Cook, *LDT*, p. 425, 467 (photo).

WHITE, LEONARD, III, "LENNY" (b. 19 Dec 1949, New York, New York). Self-taught jazz drumset artist who began at the age of 14 and plays left-handed/right-footed, Lenny White was one of the seminal "fusion" innovators. He performed and/or recorded with Nancy Wilson, Jackie McLean (1968), George Russell, Stan Getz (in Latin-rock influenced Azteca), Gil Evans, Miles Davis (1969), Chaka Khan, Woody Shaw and Freddie Hubbard (1970), Joe Henderson (1970–71), Gil Evans and Gato Barbieri (1971), and Chick Corea's group, Return to Forever (1973–76).

SELECTED DISCOGRAPHY

Atlantic Jazz 82591-2: *Acoustic Masters II* (Bobby Hutcherson et al.), 1994.
Blue Note BLJ-46994: *Eliane Elias—Illusions*, 1986.
Columbia GP26/G2K-40577: *Bitches Brew* (Miles Davis), 1969.
Creed Taylor CTI 6007: *Red Clay* (Freddie Hubbard), 1970.
Elektra 60021: *Echoes of An Era* (Chick Corea, Freddie Hubbard et al.), 1981
Milestone MSP9034: *In Pursuit of Blackness* (Joe Henderson), 1971.
Polydor 6512: *No Mystery* (Chick Corea), 1975.
TCB Music 97602: *Buster Williams Quintet—Somewhere Along the Way*, 1998.

SELECTED VIDEOGRAPHY

DCI Music Video: *Lenny White—In Clinic*, 1985.

SELECTED BIBLIOGRAPHY

Iero, Cheech. "My First Gig." *MD* XX, 12 (December 1996): 148–151.
Nolan, H. "Blindfold Test." *DB* LXI (14 Mar 1974): 29.
Wald, Aran. "Beyond Forever: *MD* Talks with Lenny White." *MD* I, 4 (October 1977): 4–5.
Wittet, T. Bruce. "Lenny White: A New Brew." *MD* XXI, 6 (June 1997): 64–80.
GEN. BIB.: Hunt, *52nd St.*; Kernfeld, *NGJ*, by Barry Kernfeld.

WHITLOW, KENNETH WILBOURN (b. 30 Dec 1944, Little Rock, Arkansas). Ken Whitlow earned a bachelor's degree from Centenary College of Louisiana (1967) and did graduate work at Southern Illinois University in 1972. His teachers included *Eddy Kozak (1962–67) and, from 1970 to 1975, *Richard Holmes, *Rich O'Donnell, *John Kasica, and *Tom Stubbs. He was essentially a drumset artist (1960–68) and a public school band director (1967–68) while performing with the Shreveport (LA) Symphony (1962–68). Whitlow also served in the U.S. Air Force Military Airlift Command Band at Scott Air Force Base, Illinois (1968–72). An extra with the St. Louis Symphony (including orchestral recordings, 1976–77) and timpanist with the St. Louis Philharmonic, he performed in the Young Audience's percussion quartet until securing a position as assistant principal percussionist in the North Carolina Symphony, where he has been since 1975.
Information supplied by the subject, 1996.

WICKSTROM, FREDERICK A., JR., "FRED" (b. Chicago, Illinois). A student of Alla Rakha Khan (1977), J.H.K. Nketia, and Kobla Ladzekpo, among others, Fred Wickstrom earned a bachelor's degree (1953) from Northwestern University and a master's degree (1960) from the University of Illinois; he also studied at the University of California at Los Angeles (1977). From 1953 to 1959, he pursued an active freelance career in Chicago in jazz clubs, recording studios, and performances with the Chicago Symphony. A faculty member of the University of Miami at Coral Gables since 1960, he was timpanist and principal percussionist with the Florida Philharmonic and Miami Symphony, played on NBC and CBS television, and performed throughout the United States, Latin America, and the Caribbean.

SELECTED BIBLIOGRAPHY

Wickstrom, Fred. "One for the Show." *LD* III, 2 (Fall 1963): 8–9.
Wickstrom, Fred. *Latin Percussion Techniques* (with play-along LP). Park Ridge, IL: Payson Percussion, 1974.
Wickstrom, Fred. *Keyboard Mastery for Mallet Percussion,* vols. 1–2. Miami: University of Miami Press, 1971/72.
Information supplied by the subject, 1996.

WIGGINS, WILLIAM "BILL" (b. 1 Apr 1946, Nashville, Tennessee). Principal timpanist of the Nashville Symphony since 1969, Bill Wiggins earned a bachelor's degree from George Peabody College and a master's degree from Northwestern University. He performs in the Blair Chamber Players at the Blair School of Music (Vanderbilt University), where he is adjunct professor of timpani and percussion and coordinator of the precollege program. A two-time host of the Percussive Arts Society International Convention, Wiggins has served on the faculties of George Peabody College, Belmont College, Sewanee Summer Music Center, Tennessee Governor's School for the Arts, Nashville Institute for the Arts, and the National High School Music Institute at Northwestern University.
PASIC® program biographies, 1996. Information supplied by the subject, 1998.

WILCOXON, CHARLES "CHARLEY" (b. 26 Nov 1894, Newark, Ohio; d. 1978, Rocky River/Cleveland, Ohio). Relocating with his family to Coshocton, Ohio, Charles Wilcoxon studied piano with his mother and was essentially a self-taught drummer. He began playing in local movie houses in Coshocton as a child; by his midteens he was touring with minstrel groups as far west as Denver. Some of these troupes included The Spring Maid Company (1912–13, with whom he acquired the nickname "Coshoc") and the A. G. Fields Minstrels (1913–14). Leaving home with only a snare drum, Wilcoxon returned with timpani, bells, xylophone, bass drum, and snare, then toured for almost three years with the theater orchestra for D. W. Griffith's movie *Intolerance*, and spent seven years at the B. F. Keith Hippodrome in Youngstown, Ohio, before playing eleven years at the Palace Theater in Cleveland (1922–33) until vaudeville bowed to the "talkies." Circus band legend Merle Evans remarked that he was the finest left-handed drummer in the country, and in his later years Wilcoxon occasionally "sat in" with circus bands.

Now regarded primarily as a teacher and publisher of method books, he taught his first students when he was 12 and opened the Wilcoxon Drum Shop and Studio in Cleveland (ca. 1934). Beginning with dowel sticks in his youth, he eventually lathed his own custom "Super Balance" hickory drum sticks that many professional drummers of his era endorsed. Wilcoxon was inducted into the Percussive Arts Society Hall of Fame in 1981.

SELECTED BIBLIOGRAPHY

"The Arcade." *Cleveland Plain Dealer Sunday Magazine* (Sunday, 21 May 1967).

Gresmer, Olive. "Drummer Boy at 10, Still Drumming at 68." *Cleveland Plain Dealer*, ca. 1962–63.

Wilcoxon, Charles. *The All-American Drummer*. Cleveland, OH: Ludwig Music Publishing Co., 1979.

Wilcoxon, Charles. *Drum Method*. Cleveland, OH: Ludwig Music Publishing Co., 1981.

Wilcoxon, Charles. *Drumming plus Hummin' a Tune*. Cleveland, OH: Ludwig Music Publishing Co., 1979.

Wilcoxon, Charles. *Modern Rudimental Swing Solos for the Advanced Drummer*. Cleveland, OH: Ludwig Music Publishing Co., 1941.

Wilcoxon, Charles. *Wrist and Finger Control for the Advanced Drummer*. Cleveland, OH: Ludwig Music Publishing Co., 1979.

GEN. BIB.: Cook, *LDT*, p. 270 (photo).

WILLIAMS, ANTHONY "TONY" (b. 12 Dec 1945, Chicago, Illinois; d. 23 Feb 1997, Daly City, California). Moving to Boston as a toddler, the 10-year-old Tony Williams subsequently studied with *Alan Dawson, starting his professional career by 15 with Sam Rivers. In 1962 he relocated to New York, where he recorded and toured with Jackie McLean, joined the Miles Davis Quintet at age 17 (1963–69, recording thirteen albums), then formed his own group, Lifetime (four albums, 1969–73), which originally included guitarist, John McLaughlin and organist, Larry Young. [The 1975 reincarnation featured Allan Holdsworth and Alan Pasqua.] Williams worked with Weather Report, Herbie Hancock, Sonny Rollins, Paul Chambers, Eric Dolphy, Hank Jones (The Great Jazz Trio), John Coltrane, and Cecil Taylor; he performed and recorded with Freddie Hubbard's "VSOP" (late 1970s), was voted into *Modern Drummer* magazine's Reader's Poll Hall of Fame in 1986, and received a Grammy® Award (1995) for the tour recording *The Tribute to Miles Davis*. In 1990 several of his compositions were premiered at the San Francisco Jazz Festival, including one work that featured him, Herbie Hancock, and the Kronos String Quartet.

SELECTED DISCOGRAPHY

ARK 21-724385457128: *Wilderness* (as composer and drummer), 1996.

Blue Note B2 93170: *Native Heart*, 1989.

Blue Note B21K 46757/BT 85138: *Civilization*, 1986.

Blue Note CDP 7 484942: *Angel Street*, 1988.

Blue Note B214-93170: *The Story of Neptune*, 1991.
Blue Note 84163/CDP 746524: *Out to Lunch* (Eric Dolphy), 1964.
Blue Note B21K 46289/BT-85119: *Foreign Intrigue*, 1985.
Blue Note BTDK 85117: *One Night with Blue Note Preserved*, 1985.
Blue Note CDP 7243 8 30028: *Twenty One* (Geri Allen), 1994.
Blue Note CDP 7 46135/84216: *Spring*, 1965.
Blue Note CDP 7 91785 2: *New Beginnings* (Don Pullen), 1989.
Blue Note CDP 7 46515-2: *Una Más* (Kenny Dorham), 1963.
Blue Note 84195: *Maiden Voyage* (Herbie Hancock), 1965.
Blue Note 84153: *Evolution* (Grachan Moncur III), 1963/1985.
Blue Note 84184: *Fuchsia Swing Song* (Sam Rivers), 1964.
Blue Note 84126: *My Point of View* (Herbie Hancock), 1963.
Blue Note CDP 0777 7 99031 2 2: *Tokyo Live*, 1992.
Blue Note CDP 7 46821 2: *One Step Beyond* (Jackie McLean and Bobby Hutcherson), 1963/1987.
Blue Note CDP 7 84167: *Point of Departure* (Andrew Hill), 1964.
Blue Note CDP 7 84175 2: *Empyrean Isles* (Herbie Hancock), 1964.
Blue Note CDP 7 84180 2: *Life Time*, 1964/1987.
Blue Note LT-1085: *Vertigo* (Jackie McLean), 1963.
Blue Note TOCJ4177: *Some Other Stuff* (Grachan Moncur III), 1964.
Columbia/Sony JC 35705: *Joy of Flying*, 1979/1997.
Columbia PC 34263: *Million Dollar Legs* (Tony Williams Lifetime), 1976.
Columbia 34688: *VSOP*, 1988.
Columbia COL 471063 2: *Live Under the Sky* (VSOP), 1979.
Columbia CK 47484: *The Collection*, 1992.
Columbia C12453: *Four and More* (Miles Davis), 1964.
Columbia C2 38266/CK 66955: *Miles Davis—Live at the Plugged Nickel*, 1965.
Columbia C2K-48821-2: *The Complete Concert, 1964* (Miles Davis).
Columbia CD CK-40580: *In a Silent Way* (Miles Davis), 1969.
Columbia CD CK-46863: *E.S.P.* (Miles Davis), 1998.
Columbia CD CK-48849: *Miles Smiles* (Miles Davis), 1966.
Columbia CK-44113: *Nefertiti* (Miles Davis), 1967.
Columbia CK-48827/PC-8851: *Seven Steps to Heaven* (Miles Davis), 1963.
Columbia CK-48954: *Miles in the Sky* (Miles Davis), 1968.
Columbia CL 2732: *The Sorcerer* (Miles Davis), 1993.
Columbia Legacy 67398: *Miles Davis Quintet, 1965–68: The Complete Columbia Studio Recordings*.
Columbia PC 33836: *The New Tony Williams Lifetime—Believe It*, 1975.
Columbia PCT-9106: *My Funny Valentine* (Miles Davis), 1964.
Inner City IC 6029: *New Wine in Old Bottles* (Jackie McLean), 1978.
Jazz Heritage 524808T: *Silver City* (Sonny Rollins), 1997.
Milestone M 9091: *Passion Dance* (McCoy Tyner), 1979.
Polydor 24-4065: *Turn It Over*, 1970.
Polydor 849 068-2: *Emergency!* (Tony Williams Lifetime), 1969.
Sony 32DP 529: *Miles Davis in Tokyo*, 1964.
Sony 67397: *Miles Davis and Gil Evans—The Complete Columbia Studio Recordings*, 1996.
Sony CSCS 5147: *Miles Davis in Berlin*, 1964.

Sony/Columbia CTDP-096353: *Young at Heart*, 1996.
Verve 314537075-2: *The Tony Williams Lifetime—Spectrum: The Anthology*, 1997.

SELECTED VIDEOGRAPHY

Blue Note Video B5-40009: *New York Live*, 1989.
Blue Note Video BTDK 85117: *One Night with Blue Note Preserved*, 1985.
DCI VH0249: *Legends of Jazz Drumming*, pt. 2 (1950–70), 1996.

SELECTED BIBLIOGRAPHY

DeMichael, Don. "Tony Williams." *DB* XXXII, 7 (25 Mar 1965): 19.
Griffith, Mark. "Artist on Track: Tony Williams, Part 1." *MD* XX, 2 (February 1996): 140–143.
Griffith, Mark. "Artist on Track: Tony Williams, Part 2." *MD* XX, 3 (March 1996): 126–128.
Griffith, Mark. "A Lifetime on Track: The Recorded Legacy of Tony Williams." *MD* XXI, 8 (August 1997): 104–106.
Mahoney, Mark. "Great Rhythm Sections in Jazz." *MD* XXII, 12 (December 1998): 158–161.
Mattingly, Rick. "1997 PAS® Hall of Fame: Tony Williams." *PN* XXXV, 6 (December 1997): 12–13.
Milkowski, Bill. "A Tribute to Tony Williams." *MD* XXI, 8 (August 1997): 50–64.
Milkowski, Bill. "Tony Williams: A Master's Perspective." *MD* XVI (July 1992): 20–25.
Milkowski, Bill. "Tony Williams: The Final *MD* Interview." *MD* XXI, 8 (August 1997): 68–80.
Point, Michael. "Tony Williams: The Final Interview." *DB* (April 1997): 22–24.
Riley, John. "Style and Analysis: Tony Williams." *MD* XXI, 8 (August 1997): 100–103.
Shultz, Thomas. "A History of Jazz Drumming." *Percussionist* XVI, 3 (Spring/Summer 1979): 127.
"Tony Remembered." *MD* XXI, 8 (August 1997): 84–98.
Wichterman, K. Paul. "Drum Set Forum: An Interview with Tony Williams." *PN* XXVI, 2 (Winter 1988): 23–27.
GEN. BIB.: Hunt, *52nd St.*; Spagnardi, *GJD*.

WILSON, ROSSIERE "SHADOW" (b. 25 Sep 1919, Yonkers, New York; d. 11 Jul 1959, New York, New York). Drumset artist Shadow Wilson's early associations included Frank Fairfax, Lucky Millinder (1939), Benny Carter (1940), *Lionel Hampton (1940–41), and Earl Hines (1941–43). Replacing *Jo Jones for Count Basie in 1944 (during Jones' military obligations), he received *Esquire* magazine's "New Star" Award (1947). Wilson appeared with Woody Herman (1949), Illinois Jacquet (sporadically in the 1940s and 1950s), Erroll Garner, and Ella Fitzgerald (1954–55); he also played and/or recorded with Louis Jordan and the Tympany Five (early "jump blues" and rock-and-roll), Sonny Stitt, Tadd Dameron, Lee Konitz, and Thelonius Monk (1957–58).

SELECTED DISCOGRAPHY

Black Lion 760171: *Sunset Swing*, 1945/1992.
Blue Note BLP1513: *Detroit—New York Junction* (Thad Jones), 1956.
Blue Note BLP1531/1532: *The Fabulous Fats Navarro*, vols. 1–2 (1948), 1983–84.
Blue Note CDP 7-95636-2: *The Best of Thelonius Monk*, 1991.
Blue Note LA507-H2: *Tadd Dameron Sextet*, 1947.
Circle CCD-53: *Louis Jordan and His Tympany Five*, 1944–45.
Circle CCD-60: *Count Basie and His Orchestra*, 1944.
Circle CCD-130: *Count Basie and His Orchestra*, 1944/1945.
Columbia CK 47035: *Body and Soul* (Erroll Garner), 1951–52.
Fresh Sounds CD 92: *Sonny Stitt Plays*, 1956.
Jazzland OJC CD-039-2: *Thelonious Monk with John Coltrane*, 1957.
Mosaic MR4-101: *Thelonious Monk Quartet*, 1948.
Prestige OJC 654: *Early Stan* (Stan Getz/Terry Gibbs), 1962.
Savoy SV-0151: *Johnson's Jazz Quintets* (J. J. Johnson), 1947.
Sony 258P 5121: *One O'Clock Jump* (Count Basie), 1946.
Verve MGV8084: *Illinois Jacquet and His Orchestra*, 1952.
GEN. BIB.: Hunt, *52nd St.*; Kernfeld, *NGJ*, by Mark Gardner; Spagnardi, *GJD*.

WINTRICH, MAX A. A road show veteran, Max Wintrich played snare and timpani with the Chicago Symphony (ca. 1898–1932), replacing *Joseph Zettleman. Also an entrepreneur, he manufactured percussion equipment at his company in Chicago (e.g., snares, pedals, traps, and timpani made from copper bowls purchased from *D. Picking and Co. in Ohio).

SELECTED BIBLIOGRAPHY

Cook, Rob. *Complete History of the Leedy Drum Company.* Fullerton, CA: Centerstream Publishing, 1993.
GEN. BIB.: Cook, *LDT*, p. 42, 287.

WOODYARD, SAMUEL "SAM" (b. 7 Jan 1925, Elizabeth, New Jersey; d. 20 Sep 1988). Self-taught drumset artist Sam Woodyard worked locally before collaborating with Roy Eldridge (1952), Milt Buckner (1953–55), Duke Ellington (1955–71, with hiatuses in 1959, 1965, 1971), Ella Fitzgerald, John Coltrane, Claude Bolling (1970s), and Teddy Wilson (1983), among others. He relocated to France in 1975, contracting cancer in 1985.

SELECTED DISCOGRAPHY

Bethlehem BCP-60: *Historically Speaking* (Duke Ellington), 1956.
Blue Note CD1523: *Duke Ellington—Live at the Blue Note*, 1992.
Columbia C2K 53584: *Live at Newport, 1958* (Duke Ellington).
Columbia CL 934/CK-40587: *Ellington at Newport* (Duke Ellington), 1956.

MCAD 39103: *Coltrane and Ellington* (John Coltrane), 1962.
Reprise FS 1024: *Francis A. & Edward K.* (Sinatra and Ellington), 1967.
Saja 7 91042-2/91231-2: *Duke Ellington,* vols. 2/7, 1957–58.
Timeless 185-6: *Swingin' the Forties with the Great Eight,* 1983.
Verve MGV4010-4: *Ella Fitzgerald with Duke Ellington and His Orchestra,* 1957.
Verve MGV8145: *Johnny Hodges and His Orchestra,* 1956.
Verve V6-8452: *Johnny Hodges with Billy Strayhorn and the Orchestra,* 1961.
Verve V6-8701: *Duke Ellington and His Orchestra,* 1966.
Verve V6-8732: *Johnny Hodges and Earl Hines,* 1967.

SELECTED VIDEOGRAPHY

Goodyear/Nostalgia Family Video: *Jazz Concert No. 1—Louis Armstrong and Duke Ellington,* 1961.

SELECTED BIBLIOGRAPHY

Dance, Stanley. "Putting on the Pots and Pans: An Interview with Duke Ellington Drummer, Sam Woodyard." *DB* XXXII, 7 (25 Mar 1965): 20–21.
Korall, Burt. "A Blast from the Past: The Great Drummers of Duke Ellington." *MD* XXI, 12 (December 1997): 82–94.
GEN. BIB.: Hunt, *52nd St.*; Kernfeld, *NGJ*, by Eddie Lambert.

WUEBOLD, EDWARD B., JR. (b. 13 Jun 1927, Cincinnati, Ohio). Percussionist Ed Wuebold played with the U.S. Coast Guard Band (Curtis Bay, MD) for one year, was a teacher and composer (*Fantasy for Timpani and Piano,* 1949), and was honored in 1978 after 25 years of performance with the Cincinnati Symphony.

SELECTED BIBLIOGRAPHY

"Drumming Around." *PN* XVII, 1 (Fall 1978): 17.

WULIGER, DAVID (b. ca. 1922, Cleveland, Ohio; d. 2 Jul 1998, Houston, Texas). Timpanist with the Houston Symphony (1946–86), David Wuliger studied with *Saul Goodman and taught at the University of Houston for 30 years.

SELECTED BIBLIOGRAPHY

"In Remembrance." *Percussion News* (September 1998): 18.

WYRE, JOHN (b. 17 May 1941, Philadelphia, Pennsylvania). A graduate of the Eastman School (bachelor's degree, 1964), John Wyre studied with *Fred

Hinger and *William Street. He has filled the timpanist's chair for the Canadian Opera Company, Milwaukee Symphony, Oklahoma City Symphony, and Toronto Symphony (1966–80), as well as at the Marlboro Festival. He has also performed with the Rochester Philharmonic, San Francisco Symphony, Japan Philharmonic, and Boston Symphony. A charter member of the world percussion group NEXUS (Percussive Arts Society Hall of Fame, 1999), he has worked as artistic director for several World Drum Festivals in Canada and Australia since 1984. Wyre has taught at the University of Toronto, Central State University, Queen's University, the Banff Summer School of the Performing Arts, and the Wisconsin Conservatory of Music. He is a commissioned composer whose works have been performed by NEXUS and the New York Philharmonic, among others.

SELECTED DISCOGRAPHY

Black Sun CD 15002-2: *The Altitude of the Sun* (NEXUS and Paul Horn), 1989.
CBC Musica Viva 2-1037: *Dance of the Octopus* (NEXUS et al.), 1989.
CBC SMCD 5154: *Music for Heaven and Earth* (NEXUS with Esprit Orchestra), 1995.
CP2 11: *Jo Kondo* (NEXUS performs "Under the Umbrella"), 1981.
Epic KE 33561: *Paul Horn and NEXUS*, 1975.
Heron Pond 1001/Interworld: *Vagabond Dream*, 1991.
InRespect IRJ 009302 H: *The Mother of the Book* (NEXUS et al.), 1994.
NEXUS 10251: *The Best of NEXUS* (1976–86), 1989.
NEXUS 10262: *NEXUS Now*, 1990.
NEXUS 10273: *NEXUS Plays the Novelty Music of George Hamilton Green*, 1990.
NEXUS 10284: *NEXUS Ragtime Concert*, 1992.
NEXUS 10295: *NEXUS—Origins*, 1992.
NEXUS 10306: *The Story of Percussion in the Orchestra* (NEXUS/Rochester Philharmonic), 1992.
NEXUS 10317: *Voices* (NEXUS and Rochester Philharmonic), 1994.
NEXUS 10328: *There Is a Time* (Becker), 1995.
NEXUS 10410: *Toccata*, 1997
NEXUS NE-01: *Music of NEXUS*, 1981.
NEXUS NE-02/03/04: *NEXUS and Earle Birney* (Albums 1–3), 1982.
NEXUS NE-05: *Changes* (NEXUS), 1982.
Papa Bear Records G01: *World Diary—Tony Levin* (NEXUS et al.), 1995.
Point Records 454 126-2: *Farewell to Philosophy* (Gavin Bryars), 1996.
RCA SX 2022: *Seiji Ozawa Conducts Toru Takemitsu* (Toronto Symphony), 1969.
Sony Classical SK 63044: *Takemitsu—From Me Flows What You Call Time* (Pacific Symphony), 1998.

SELECTED VIDEOGRAPHY

Bullfrog Films, Inc.: *World Drums* (Vancouver Expo), 1989.
Necavenue A88V-3: *Supercussion* (Tokyo Music Joy Festival), 1988.

SELECTED BIBLIOGRAPHY

Brooks, Iris. "The World Drum Festival." *MP* III, 1 (December 1986): 14.

Bump, Michael. "A Conversation with NEXUS." *PN* XXXI, 5 (June 1993): 30–36.

Cherry, Kalman. "John Wyre." *PN* XXXIV, 4 (August 1996): 18–20.

Ford, Mark. "Nexus Now." *PN* XXIX, 3 (February 1991): 64.

Larrick, Geary. *Analytical and Biographical Writings in Percussion Music.* New York: Peter Lang Publishing, 1989.

Mattingly, Rick. "Nexus." *MP* I, 3 (June–August 1985): 8–13/36–41.

GEN. BIB.: Larrick, *BET-CP;* PASIC® program biographies, 1997.

Y

YANCICH, MARK (b. 7 February 1956, Rochester, New York). Beginning percussion studies at 14 with *Bill and Ruth Cahn and Vincent Ruggiero, Mark Yancich attended the Cleveland Institute (bachelor's, 1978), where he studied with *Cloyd Duff and *Richard Weiner, and independently with *Saul Goodman. He performed with the Maracaibo (co-principal and assistant timpanist, 1978–79) and Caracas (timpanist and principal percussionist, 1979–81) Orchestras of Venezuela and with the Lake Placid (NY) Sinfonietta (timpanist and percussionist, 1976–79) before becoming principal timpanist with the Atlanta Symphony (since 1981). Yancich serves on the faculty of Emory University, where he hosts the Atlanta Percussion Seminar each summer, and in 1998 initiated the first Mark Yancich Timpani Class. He is president of Timpani and Percussion (TAP) Products and Collected Editions, Ltd., music publisher.

SELECTED DISCOGRAPHY

Pro Arte CDS 3430: *Beethoven—Symphony No. 9* (Atlanta Symphony and Chorus), 1992.
Telarc CD 80078: *Copland—Fanfare for the Common Man* et al. (Atlanta Symphony), 1982.
Telarc CD 80085: *Respighi—Pines of Rome* et al. (Atlanta Symphony), 1985.
Telarc CD 80109: *Berlioz—Requiem* et al. (Atlanta Symphony and Chorus), 1997.
Telarc CD 80195: *Hindemith—Mathis der Maler* et al. (Atlanta Symphony), 1989.
Telarc CD 80215: *Shostakovich—Symphony Nos. 5 & 9* (Atlanta Symphony), 1990.
Telarc CD 80250: *Music of Samuel Barber* (Atlanta Symphony), 1992.
Telarc CD 80266: *Stravinsky—The Rite of Spring* et al. (Atlanta Symphony), 1992.
Telarc CD 80296: *Mussorgsky—A Night on Bald Mountain* et al. (Atlanta Symphony), 1991.
Telarc CD 80358: *Beethoven Overtures—Egmont, Fidelio,* et al. (Atlanta Symphony), 1997.

SELECTED VIDEOGRAPHY

TAP Productions: *The Art of Timpani Video Series* (with Mark Yancich):
  Changing and Tuning Plastic Timpani Heads, 1994.
  Oliverio—Timpani Concerto No. 1, 1994.
  Tucking Calfskin Timpani Heads with Cloyd Duff, 1995.
  Sewing Felt Timpani Sticks, 1998.

SELECTED BIBLIOGRAPHY

"Membership News." *Percussion News* (July 1997): 7.
Information supplied by the subject, 1998.

YANCICH, PAUL (b. 23 Jun 1953, East Lansing, Michigan).   Raised in Rochester, New York, Paul Yancich studied with *William Street, Norman Fickett, William Platt, Jack Moore, Harrison Powley, *William Cahn, and *Saul Goodman. He attended the Cleveland Institute (bachelor's, 1978), where he studied with *Cloyd Duff and *Richard Weiner. Timpanist with the Atlanta Symphony for six years, he has served in the same capacity with the Cleveland Orchestra since 1981. Yancich is co-chair of the percussion department at Cleveland Institute and previously taught at Georgia State University. Founder and owner of Clevelander Drum Company, he has given masterclasses in the United States, Europe, Japan, Korea, and New Zealand. In 1990 he gave the world premiere of James Oliverio's *Timpani Concerto No. 1* with the Cleveland Orchestra.

PASIC® program biographies, 1995.

YERKES, HARRY A. Harry Yerkes led the Yerkes Jazzarimba Orchestra, a Columbia Records dance and recording band that featured *George Hamilton Green, *Joseph Green, *Harry Breuer, *Billy Dorn, and *Eddie Rubsam.   Its augmented instrumentation included, variously, strings, three saxes, piano, trumpet, tuba, drums, and banjo. The same group became the "Flotilla Orchestra" when playing at the Flotilla Restaurant in New York City.

SELECTED BIBLIOGRAPHY

Eyler, David P. "Development of the Marimba Ensemble in North America during the 1930s." *PN* XXXIV, 1 (February 1996): 66–71.
GEN. BIB.: Cahn, *XAR*.

Z

ZELTSMAN, NANCY (b. 9 Jun 1958, Morristown, New Jersey). Studying piano from age 5 and then switching to percussion at 13, marimbist Nancy Zeltsman received a bachelor's degree in percussion performance from the New England Conservatory (1982), where she was a student of *Vic Firth. She is a two-time National Endowment for the Arts (NEA) Solo Recitalist grant recipient who also studied percussion with Robert Ayers, keyboard percussion with *Ian Finkel, jazz improvisation with *Dave Samuels, and composition with William Thomas McKinley.

Her collaborative duo Marimolin (co-founded with violinist Sharan Leventhal in 1985) has premiered more than 75 new works through the auspices of their annual composition contest, various grants, and commissions. A clinician and recitalist throughout the United States and Europe, Zeltsman teaches at Berklee College and the Boston Conservatory and was co-founder of the marimba duo Madam Rubio, with Janis Potter.

SELECTED DISCOGRAPHY

Catalyst/BMG 09026-62667-2 CD: *Combo Platter* (Marimolin), 1995.
GM 2023CD: *Marimolin* (duo with Sharan Leventhal), 1988.
GM 2041CD: *Godfrey, Schwartz, Frank—Music for Strings and Percussion*, 1993.
GM 2043CD: *Woodcuts*, 1993.
GM 2048CD: *Phantasmata* (Marimolin), 1996.

SELECTED BIBLIOGRAPHY

Holly, Rich. "An Interview with Nancy Zeltsman." *PN* XXXI, 2 (December 1992): 15–18.
Zeltsman, Nancy. "Establishing the Standard Range of the Marimba." *PN* XXXI, 4 (April 1993): 29–33.

Zeltsman, Nancy. "Musings on the Marimba and Its Study, 1997, Part 1." *PN* XXXV, 5 (October 1997): 51–55.

Zeltsman, Nancy. "Traditional Four-Mallet Grip." *PN* XXXIII, 4 (August 1995): 50–54.

Information supplied by the subject, 1996.

ZETTLEMAN, JOSEPH [ALSO JOSEF ZETTELMAN] (d. ca. June 1930, Chicago?, Illinois).

Timpanist with the Theodore Thomas Symphony [aka, the Chicago Symphony, 1916], Joseph Zettleman played in well-known European orchestras, for two seasons was the snare drummer for Liberati's Band (ca. 1890), performed in the Innes Band (ca. 1920s), and retired from the timpani chair in the Chicago Symphony at the beginning of its fortieth season.

SELECTED BIBLIOGRAPHY

Kristufek, Otto. *The Ludwig & Ludwig Tympani Instructor.* Elkhart, IN: Ludwig & Ludwig, rev. 1945.

Ludwig, William F., Sr. *My Life at the Drums: Eighty Years a Drummer.* Chicago: Ludwig Industries, 1972.

Schmidt, Paul William. *History of the Ludwig Drum Company.* Fullerton, CA: Centerstream Publishing, 1991 (photo, p. 119).

ZILDJIAN, AVEDIS, III (b. 6 Dec 1888, Istanbul, Turkey; d. 8 Feb 1979, Boston, Massachusetts).

Inducted into the Percussive Arts Society Hall of Fame in 1979, world-reknowned cymbal maker Avedis Zildjian ("Zildjian" is Turkish for "son of the cymbalsmith.") apprenticed in his family's cymbal business (est. 1623) in Turkey before immigrating to Boston (1908), where he worked in a candy factory, eventually starting his own candy business. He was named for his grandfather, Avedis II, who introduced the cymbals to Europe in 1851 under his own name (from 1623 to 1851, they were simply called "Turkish Cymbals"), winning first prize and medals at various expositions. Avedis II died in 1865 and was succeeded by his brother, Kerope Zildjian, who passed away in 1909. When his uncle, Aram, who headed the Turkish concern, informed him in 1927 that as the oldest surviving male he would inherit the cymbal business and the "secret metallic formulas," Avedis III convinced his uncle to relocate the company to the United States. In 1929 the Avedis Zildjian Cymbal Company commenced in Quincy, Massachusetts (supported initially by the candy business), and survived the Great Depression, destruction by fire in 1939, and WWII (thanks to U.S. and British government military band contracts).

Befriending working drummers through the years, Zildjian developed various new models to satisfy increasing musical demands and sophisticated musical tastes of each generation of percussionists. Some of these variations included the "sizzle," "splash," and thinner versions of the crash, ride, and hi-hat cymbals.

Drummers such as *Chick Webb, *Gene Krupa, and *Louie Bellson endorsed his products, giving technical and musical advice, and the company became the largest in the world, moving into more ample facilities in Norwell, Massachusetts, in 1971. A U.S. Army veteran of WWI, Zildjian was cited by the Armenian Bicentennial Committee in 1976 for his excellence in the musical arts.

Avedis' sons, Armand Arthur (b. 1921; Percussive Arts Society Hall of Fame, 1994) and Robert (Percussive Arts Society Industry Award, 1996), parted ways after Armand, the eldest, inherited control of the company. Robert established a new company on 4 December 1982 from Zildjian's Canadian operations and named it after the first two letters in each of his children's names: Sally, Bill, and Andy (SABIAN). Armand, who received a Fiftieth Anniversary Commemorative Medallion at the 1996 commencement of the Berklee College of Music, where he is a trustee emeritus, has groomed his daughter, Craigie, to assume eventual leadership of the Zildjian Company. Television's Cable News Network (CNN) aired a segment around 1997 on its *Pinnacle* program, which honors industry leaders, profiling the Zildjian family and their company.

SELECTED BIBLIOGRAPHY

"Avedis Zildjian: 1888–1979." *The Music Trades* (March 1979): 50.

The Avedis Zildjian Story. Accord, MA: Avedis Zildjian Company.

DiMuzio, Lennie. "The Avedis Zildjian Story." *PN* XXVIII, 2 (Winter, 1990): 18–23.

"In Memoriam: Avedis Zildjian." *PN* XVII, 3 (Spring/Summer 1979): 27.

Kearns, Kevin. "Mr Sabian: Robert Zildjian." *MD* XXI, 7 (July 1997): 150–153.

Navin, Thomas. "World's Leading Cymbal Maker: Avedis Zildjian Company." *PN* IV, 1 (September 1965): 3–5.

Plazonja, Jonathan. "Avedis Zildjian: The Father of Cymbals." *MD* XIX, 11 (November 1995): 134–135.

Roberts, Jonnie L. "Ting, Bong, Clang! The Zildjian Clan Symbolizes Cymbals." *Wall Street Journal* (Monday, 6 Jun 1983).

Schmidt, Paul William. *History of the Ludwig Drum Company.* Fullerton, CA: Centerstream Publishing, 1991.

Shayt, David H. "Manufacturing Secrecy: The Dueling Cymbalmakers of North America." *PN* XXX, 1 (October 1991): 78–87.

Van Horn, Rick. "Zildjian at 370." *MD* XVII (December 1993): 30–33.

ZINSMEISTER, OLIVER "OLLIE" (b. 22 Jul 1911, Rochester, New York). Percussionist with the U.S. Marine Band (Washington, D.C., ca. 1935–55), Oliver Zinsmeister attended the Eastman School of Music, where he was the first percussion student, studying with *William Street and performing in the Rochester Philharmonic. [Some of his colleagues in the U.S. Marine Band (ca. 1936) included *Charles Owen, Charles Viner, and John Auer.] He later worked in studios, featuring his xylophone talents on radio broadcasts (WHAM, Rochester). In 1991 Zinsmeister donated his 60-year collection of musicians' photographs to the Sibley Music Library at the Eastman School.

SELECTED BIBLIOGRAPHY

Barbaro, Cosmo. "Interpretations of Sousa Marches: An Interview with Ollie Zinsmeister." *PN* XXXV, 4 (August 1997): 29–36.

Byrne, Frank (John R. Beck, ed.). "Charlie Owen: The Marine Band Years." *PN*
XXV, 4 (Spring 1987): 45–50.

Eyles, Randall. "Zinsmeister's Photo Collection." *PN* XXX, 1 (October 1991):
54–61.

GEN. BIB.: Cook, *LDT* (photo, p. 391).

APPENDIX

Information for the following musicians was insufficient to include them in the main body of the text. As an aid to researchers, partial biographical material is provided where available. Sources from the General Bibliography are credited in brackets.

Alias, Don. Latin percussionist who has played and/or recorded with Nina Simone, Compost, and a host of others.

Allen, Peter. Principal timpanist of the London Philharmonic, ca. 1950s–60s.

Baker, Harry J. Percussionist with the Philadelphia Orchestra, 1923–24.

Bambridge, John. Timpanist with the St. Louis Symphony, ca. 1916.

Barth, W. Percussionist with the Boston Symphony, 1900–1901.

Bernstein, S. Timpanist with the New York Philharmonic Society, ca. 1892.

Bradshaw, James "Jimmy." Principal timpanist of the London Philharmonia, ca. 1950s.

Brosche, C. Bell player with the New York Philharmonic Society, ca. 1892.

Burkhardt, H. Violinist (1891–92) and percussionist (1905–21) with the Boston Symphony.

Byrne, John H. Vaudeville xylophonist who appeared at J. S. Berry's theater, 1881. [Strain]

Chapman, Chris. Xylophone artist who recorded "St. Louis Rag" (1906) and "Dill Pickles" (1908). [Cahn]

Charbonneau, Louis. Percussionist in the Montreal Symphony, 1970s.

Clark, William. Percussionist with the St. Louis Symphony, ca. 1960s–70s(?).

Cleather, G. Gordon. English timpanist who flourished ca. late nineteenth–early twentieth century and composed a work for 13 timpani. Author of "The Timpani, with Special Reference to Their Use with the Organ" (lecture given to the Royal College of Organists, 1908.) [Blades]

Cooper, Arthur "Art." Principal percussionist with the Detroit Symphony who retired ca. 1964.

Cooper, Charles F. Percussionist with the Detroit Symphony, ca. 1949.

DeMont, Addie. Boston piano teacher who also concertized on zither and xylophone, ca. 1880s. [Strain]

de Pontigny, Victor. English timpanist, ca. 1875. [Beck]

Des Roches, Raymond. Contemporary percussion recording artist who was director of the New Jersey Percussion Ensemble at William Paterson College.

Donaldson, Charles. Principal percussionist of the London Symphony, ca. 1950s–60s.

Eder, Anton. Timpanist and percussionist of the Vienna Orchestra who was active ca. 1820s.

Escher, Charles E., Jr. Philadelphia publisher and composer of xylophone solos who manufactured "Escher's Improved Wood & Straw Instrument." [Strain]

Fineberg, Fraya. Percussionist with the Houston Symphony, 1970–71. [Roussel]

Fulgham, Henry. Percussionist with the Houston Symphony, 1970–71. [Roussel]

Geldard, Samuel W. "Sammy." Timpanist with the Halle Orchestra who studied under William Gezink. [Blades]

Gentile, Ettore. Bass drummer for the Roxy Theater Orchestra, ca. 1927.

Gezink, Willem [William] (d. 1928). Timpanist with Covent Garden and the Halle Orchestra. [Blades]

Goedicke, Kurt Hans. Principal timpanist of the London Symphony, ca. 1963–(?).

Goodwin, Walter. Percussionist with the Los Angeles Philharmonic who served in the U.S. Army–Air Force Band.

Greinert, H. Bass drummer with the New York Philharmonic Society, ca. 1892.

Grupp, David "Dave." New York radio soloist (ca. 1928), percussionist with the Ipana Troubador Orchestra (ca. 1928) and NBC Symphony (1940s), as well as timpanist with the Philadelphia Orchestra (1946–51), Grupp also offered a percussion correspondence course (ca. 1928).

Henderson, Charles. Timpanist(?) of the London Symphony, ca. 1899. [Beck]

Hoffman, Jacob. Percussionist with the Philadelphia Orchestra, 1950–52.

Holbrook, Billy. Xylophone soloist with the Sousa Band (ca. pre–1911). [Strain]

Horowitz, Richard "Dick." Former timpanist with the New York Metropolitan Opera Orchestra (ca. 1930s) who studied with *Saul Goodman.

Howe, Walter G. Timpanist with the National Symphony (ca. 1938) who began playing percussion ca. 1922.

Jabukovksy, Sankson (fl. 1860s–80s, Paris, France). Solo xylophonist who was mistaken for *Michael Guzikov by a Parisian magazine and may have influenced Camille Saint Saens' use of xylophone in his *Danse Macabre*. [Peters]

Jordan, E. Timpanist with the New York Philharmonic Society, ca. 1892.

Kandler, F. Timpanist with the Boston Symphony, 1907–18/1920–23.

King, Ed, Jr. Xylophone soloist in Ned Harrigan's touring company, ca. 1910s–20s(?). [Strain]

King, Ed, Sr. Recording xylophone soloist in New York (ca. 1890s–1920s?) who played for Dave Braham's pit orchestra heard in Ned Harrigan's Broadway productions. [Strain, Cahn]

Kresse, Emil. Timpanist, percussionist, and violinist with the Philadelphia Orchestra, 1901–45 [possibly 1901–02/1904–25].

Kristufek, Otto. Timpanist and percussionist who performed in the St. Louis Symphony (ca. 1910–1916), played with the Chicago Symphony in the 1920s, and penned the *Leedy & Ludwig Tympani Instructor*. [*IM* XII, 10 (April 1913): 11 features a photo of him behind five Leedy timpani.]

Lambert, Basil Garwood (aka Professor Lamberti; d. 13 Mar 1950, Hollywood, California). Comedy xylophonist and stage comedian.

Leavitt, Joseph "Joe." Bostonian who performed with the Baltimore Symphony, and on snare and xylophone in the National Symphony (ca. 1950) [*IM* (March 1950): 19].

Lewin, Peter. Xylophone soloist with the U.S. Marine Band, ca. 1902–14. [Strain, Cahn]

Libonati, Jess. Xylophonist who was active ca. 1900–20. [Cahn]

Ludwig, C. F. Percussionist with the Boston Symphony, 1905–07/1918–30.

Ludwig, C. Richard. Timpanist with the Boston Symphony, 1890–1910.

Martin, William H. (d. 18 Aug 1943, Kansas City, Missouri). Vaudeville drummer who performed in Arthur Pryor's Band and the Kansas City Philharmonic for several years. He also served as vice-president of AFM Local 34 (Kansas City).

Mayer, Gustav. Percussionist with the Philadelphia Orchestra, 1916–23.

Mayer, Henry, Jr. Percussionist with the Philadelphia Orchestra, 1907–23 (d. ca. December 1939, Philadelphia?).

Naseman, Henry. Timpanist for the Roxy Theater Orchestra, ca. 1927.

Neumann, S. Timpanist with the Boston Symphony, 1910–22.

Peinkofer, Karl. Timpanist with the Munich Staatsoper Orchestra.

Poussard, M. (fl. ca. 1845, Paris, France). Timpanist of the Paris Opera to whom Jean-George Kastner dedicated his method book.

Pratt, John S. (b. 19 Jan 1931). Composer of numerous snare drum solos.

Rago, James. Timpanist with the Louisville Orchestra.

Rettberg, A. Percussionist with the Boston Symphony, 1898–1912/1920–22.

Rich, Al. Percussionist in the New York Philharmonic, ca. 1940s.

Robbins, Harry C. English xylophonist who wrote the *Modern Tutor for Xylophone*, ca. 1920s. [Cook]

Roth, Manuel. Percussionist-violinist with the Philadelphia Orchestra, 1924–69+(?).

Rubel, A. Triangle player with the New York Philharmonic Society, ca. 1892.

Schneitzhoeffer, Jean. French timpanist, ca. 1820s. [Beck]

Schulman, Leonard. Timpanist with the Philadelphia Orchestra, 1945–53.

Senia, T. B. Percussionist with the Boston Symphony, 1904–15.

Simon, James. Principal percussionist with the Houston Symphony, 1970–71. [Roussel]

Simpson, H. D. Timpanist with the Boston Symphony, 1881–98.

Sinatra, Frank. Timpanist and percussionist with the Philadelphia Orchestra, 1945–46.

Smith, J. A. Celebrated English timpanist for whom Julius Tausch may have written his *March and Polonaise* (ca. 1878) for six timpani and orchestra (transcribed as *A Concert Piece for Timpani and Piano* by Percival Kirby and published by Hinrichsen, 1959.) [Blades]

Smith, Viola. Drummer for the All-Girl's Swing Band, the Coquettes (ca. 1940), and Phil Spitalny's All-Girl Orchestra. She studied with *Ted Reed and purchased a snare drum from *Billy Gladstone ca. 1950 [cover photo and article, *IM* (April 1951)].

Starita, Rudy. English xylophonist, ca. 1920s. [Cook]

Stillman, Harry. Snare drummer for the Roxy Theater Orchestra, ca. 1927.

Stockton, Doris. A student of *Clair Omar Musser's who concertized on marimba in the 1940s and early 1950s. There may be RCA Victor 78 rpm recordings of her playing light, classical transcriptions on the marimba. A Deagan publicity photo of her with marimba and vibes, holding four mallets, appears in *IM* XLII, 12 (June 1944): 11.

Stokes, E. E. "Joe." Original percussionist with the Houston Symphony (1913–49+?) and secretary of AFM Local 65, he served as emcee at the AFM convention of 1938 in Houston. [Roussel]

Taylor, Henry W. English timpanist and author who improved upon *Saul Goodman's chain-and-sprocket hand tuning mechanism.

Tiedge, Hans. Percussionist and violinist with the Philadelphia Orchestra, 1902–17.

Valerio, James. Percussionist with the Philadelphia Orchestra, 1924–59.

Valverde, Mariano (b. Quezaltenango, Guatemala). Marimba virtuoso and composer. [Peters]

Van Sciver, Israel S. Percussionist with the Philadelphia Orchestra, 1900–1901.

Vito, Ben. Timpanist with the St. Louis Symphony, 1920s.

Webster, Gilbert. Former principal percussionist in the BBC Symphony.

Williams, Emma. May have been the first woman to record on xylophone for the American Graphophone Company (Columbia cylinders), ca. 1893. [Cahn]

Wood, ?. Original percussionist with the New York Philharmonic Society, ca. 1842.

Zahn, F. Percussionist and violinist-violist with the Boston Symphony, 1891–1926.

GENERAL BIBLIOGRAPHY

ASCAP Biographical Dictionary, 4th ed. New York: Jacques Cattell Press/R. R. Bowker Co., 1980.

Avgerinos, Gerassimos. *Künstler-Biographien: Die Mitglieder im Berliner Philharmonischen Orchester von 1882–1972*. Gerassimos Avgerinos, 1972.

Bajzek, Dieter. *Percussion: An Annotated Bibliography*. Metuchen, NJ: Scarecrow Press, Inc., 1988.

Beck, John H., ed. *Encyclopedia of Percussion*. New York: Garland Publishing, 1995.

Blades, James. *Percussion Instruments and Their History*. London: Faber and Faber, 1984.

Borland, Carol, ed. *Who's Who in American Music: Classical*. New York: Jaques Cattell Press/R. R. Bowker Co., 1983.

Brown, Theodore Dennis. *A History and Analysis of Jazz Drumming to 1942*. Ph.D. dissertation, University of Michigan, 1976.

Bruynincx, Walter. *Sixty Years of Recorded Jazz, 1917–1977*. 16 vols. Mechelen, Belgium: Bruynincx, 1980.

Cahn, William L. *The Xylophone in Acoustic Recordings (1877–1929)*. Bloomfield, NY: William L. Cahn Publishing, 1996.

Claghorn, Charles Eugene. *Biographical Dictionary of American Music*. West Nyack, NY: Parker Publishing Co., Inc., 1973.

Claghorn, Charles E. *Biographical Dictionary of Jazz*. Englewood Cliffs, NJ: Prentice-Hall, 1982.

Cook, Rob, compiler. *Leedy Drum Topics (1923–1941)*. Anaheim Hills, CA: Cedarcreek Publishing, 1993.

Cuscuna, Michael, and Michel Ruppli, compilers. *The Blue Note Label: A Discography*. Westport, CT: Greenwood Press, 1988.

Hitchcock, H. Wiley, and Stanley Sadie, eds. *The New Grove Dictionary of American Music*. 4 vols. London: Macmillan, 1986.

Hunt, Joe. *52nd Street Beat*. New Albany, IN: Aebersold Music, Inc., 1994.

Jepsen, J. G. *Jazz Records A–Z, 1942–1969: A Discography.* 8 vols. Holte, Denmark: Knudsen, 1963–70.

Kernfeld, Barry, ed. *The New Grove Dictionary of Jazz*, vols. 1–2. New York: Grove Dictionaries of Music Inc., 1988.

Korall, Burt. *Drummin' Men.* New York: Schirmer Books, 1990.

Larrick, Geary. *Biographical Essays on Twentieth-Century Percussionists.* Lewiston, NY: Edwin Mellen Press, 1992.

Lord, Tom. *The Jazz Discography.* Redwood, NY: North Country Distributors (covers 1898–present; multiple volumes, in progress).

McCarthy, Albert, Alun Morgan, Paul Oliver, and Max Harrison. *Jazz on Record: A Critical Guide to the First 50 Years, 1917–67.* New York: Oak Publications, 1968.

Meza, Fernando A. *Percussion Discography: An International Compilation of Solo and Chamber Percussion Music.* Westport, CT: Greenwood Press, 1990.

Percussion Anthology. Evanston, IL: The Instrumentalist Co., 1977.

Peters, Gordon. *The Drummer: Man.* Wilmette, Illinois: Kemper-Peters Publications, 1975.

Recordings, 1916–88. Chicago: Chicago Symphony Orchestra, 1989.

Roussel, Hubert. *The Houston Symphony Orchestra, 1913–1971.* Austin: University of Texas Press, 1972.

Ruppli, Michel, compiler. *The Clef/Verve Labels: A Discography*, vols. 1–2. Westport, CT: Greenwood Press, 1986.

Rust, Brian A. L. *American Dance Band Discography, 1917–42.* New Rochelle, NY: Arlington House, 1975.

Rust, Brian A. L., and Allen G. Debus. *The Complete Entertainment Discography from 1897–1942*, 2nd ed. New York: Da Capo Press, 1989.

Rust, Brian A. L., compiler. *Brian Rust's Guide to Discography.* Westport, CT: Greenwood Press, 1980.

Rust, Brian A. L., compiler. *Discography of Historical Records on Cylinders and 78s.* Westport, CT: Greenwood Press, 1979.

Sadie, Stanley, ed. *The New Grove Dictionary of Music and Musicians.* London: Macmillan Press, 1980.

Schmidt, Paul William. *History of the Ludwig Drum Company.* Fullerton, CA: Centerstream Publishing, 1991.

Siwe, Thomas, ed. *Percussion Ensemble and Solo Literature.* Champaign, IL: Media Press, Inc., 1995.

Slonimsky, Nicholas, ed. *Baker's Biographical Dictionary of Musicians*, 8th ed. New York: Schirmer Books, 1992.

Southern, Eileen. *Biographical Dictionary of Afro-American and African Musicians.* Westport, CT: Greenwood Press, 1982.

Spagnardi, Ronald. *The Great Jazz Drummers.* Cedar Grove, NJ: Modern Drummer Publications, 1992.

Strain, James Allen. *The Xylophone, ca. 1878–1930: Its Published Literature, Development as a Concert Instrument, and Use in Musical Ensembles.* DMA dissertation, University of Rochester, Eastman School of Music, 1995.

INDEX

Numbers in **boldface** indicate a main entry.

About the Author

STEPHEN L. BARNHART is Associate Professor of Music at the University of Wyoming. He has played for music festivals in Europe and Taiwan and performs varieties of music from popular to classical.

ISBN 0-313-29627-8

90000>

EAN

9 780313 296277

HARDCOVER BAR CODE